Portraits of New Zealand Native Birds
with excerpts from the Proceedings of the Royal Society of New Zealand 1868–1961
Third Edition

John Elmer Lee

Essential Press

104 Meander Drive • Welcome Bay • Tauranga, 3112 • New Zealand

+64 22 121 3211

Web: johnelmerlee.com

Email: john@johnelmerlee.com

Third Edition Published 2018

Copyright © 2015, 2018 text and photographs John Elmer Lee

with excerpts from the Proceedings of the Royal Society of New Zealand 1868–1961

The rights of John Elmer Lee to be identified as author of this work in terms of

section 96 of the Copyright Act 1996

All rights reserved

Without limiting the rights under copyright reserved above, no part of this publication may be reproduced, stored in or introduced into a retrieval system, or transmitted in any form or by any means (electronic, mechanical, photocopying, recording or otherwise), without the prior written permission of both the copyright owner and the above publisher of the book

ISBN 978 1 8875550 3 6

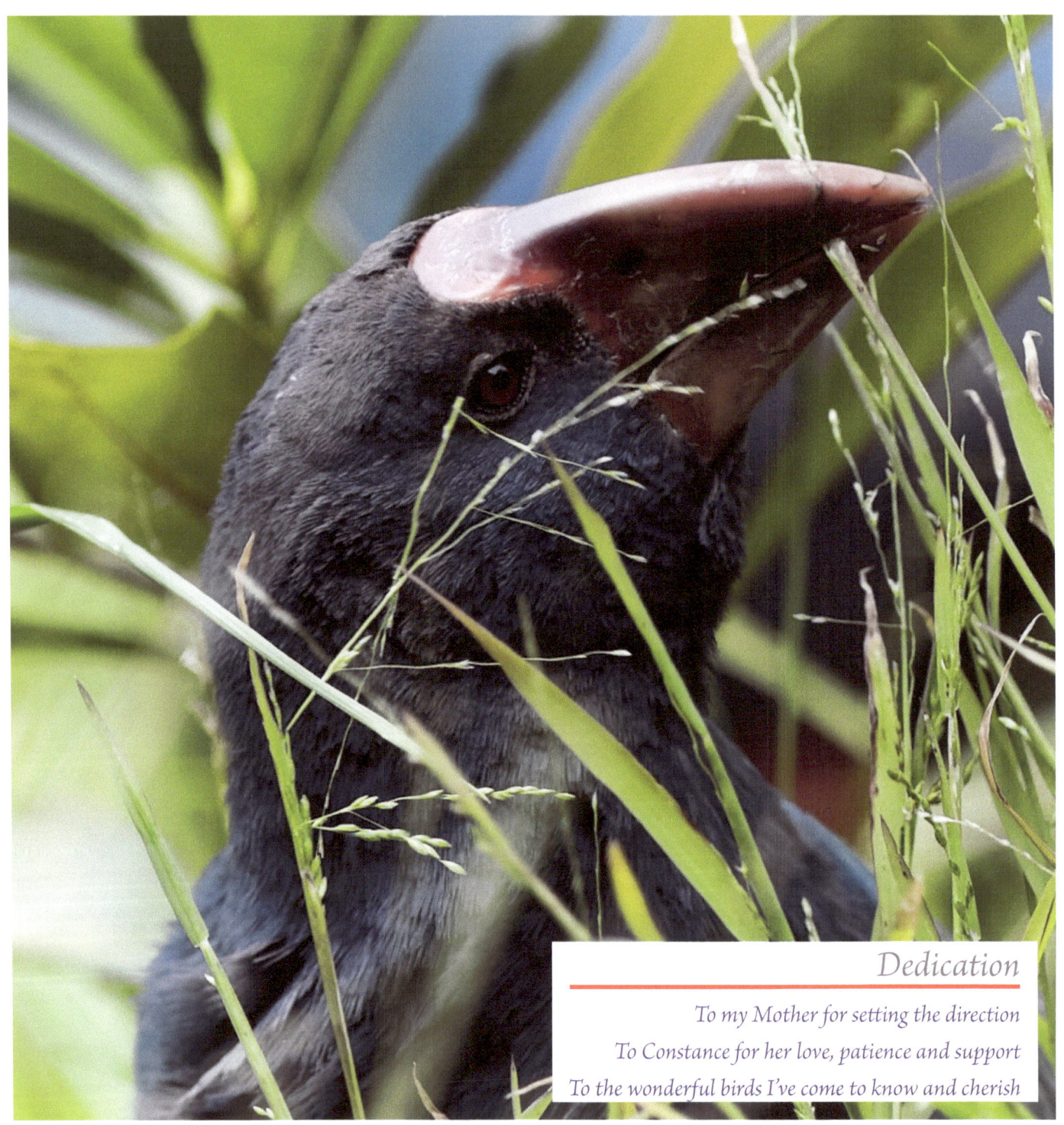

Dedication

To my Mother for setting the direction
To Constance for her love, patience and support
To the wonderful birds I've come to know and cherish

Table of Contents

Preface	5
Prologue	7

Birds of the Bush — 9

Tui or Parson Bird *Prosthemadera novaeseelandiae*	10
Korimako or Bellbird *Anthornis melanura*	18
Hihi or Stitchbird *Notiomystis cinta*	23
North Island Kokako or Crow *Callaeas cinerea wilsoni*	29
Tieke or Saddleback *Philesturnus carunculatus refusater*	36
Toutouwai or North Island Robin *Petroica australis longipes*	40
Miromiro or Tomtit *Petroica macrocephala toitoi*	46
Popokotea or Whitehead *Mohoua albicilla*	48
Riroriro or Grey Warbler *Gerygone igata*	51
Piwakawaka or North Island Fantail *Rhipidura fuliginosa placabilis*	53
Tauhou or Silvereye *Zosterops lateralis lateralis*	57
Kaka or Bush Parrot *Nestor meridionalis septentrionalis*	60
Kea or Mountain Parrot *Nestor notabilis*	69
Kakariki or Red-fronted Parakeet *Cyanoramphus novazelandiae*	73
Kereru or New Zealand Pigeon *Hemiphaga novaeseelandiae*	77
Ruru or Morepork *Ninox novaeseelandiae*	84

Field of Dreams — 89

Takahe or Notornis *Porphyrio mantelli hochstetteri*	90
Pukeko or Purple Swamphen *Porphyrio porphyrio melanotus*	100
Weka or Woodhen *Gallirallus australis greyi*	102
Moho-pereru or Banded Rail *Raillus philippensis*	108
Kahu or Australasian Harrier *Circus approximans*	110
Karearea or New Zealand Falcon *Falco novaeselandiai*	111
Pihoihoi or New Zealand Pipit *Anthus novaeseelandiae*	120
Warou or Welcome Swallow *Hirundo tahitica neoxena*	124

Water Fowl — 127

Tete or Grey Teal *Anas gracilis*	128
Pateke or Brown Teal *Anas aucklandica*	130
Papango or New Zealand Scaup *Aythya novaeseelandiae*	131
Kuruwhengi or New Zealand Shoveler *Anas rhynchotis variegata*	133
Putangitangi or Paradise Shelduck *Tadorna variegata*	135
Chestnut Breasted Shelduck *Tadorna tadornoides*	138
Parera or Grey Duck *Anas superciliosa superciliosa*	141
Parera or Australian Coot *Fulica atra*	145

Wading in Deep Water — 147

Kotuku or White Heron *Egretta alba modesta*	148
White-faced Heron *Ardea novaehollandiae*	159
Kotuku-ngutupapa or Royal Spoonbill *Platalea regia*	162
Spur-Winged Plover *Vanellus miles*	166
Poaka or Pied Stilt *Himantopus himantopus leucocephalus*	169

By the Sea — 173

Tuturuatu or Shore Plover *Thinornis noveeseelandiae*	174
Wrybill *Anarhynchus frontalis*	179
Kuaka or Bar-Tailed Godwit *Limosa lapponica*	181
Kotare or Kingfisher *Halcyon sancta*	186
Torea or Variable Oystercatcher *Haematopus unicolor*	189
Karoro or Black-backed Gull *Larus dominicanus dominicanus*	192
Tarapunga or Red-billed Gull *Larus novaehollandiae*	196
Kawau or Black Shag *Phalacrocorax carbo novaehollandiae*	199
Kawaupaka or Little Shag *Phalacrocorax melanoleucos brevirostris*	200
Karuhiruhi or Pied Shag *Phalacrocorax varius*	201
Taranui or Caspian Tern *Sterna Caspia*	203
Tara or White-fronted Tern *Sterna striata*	206

Out at Sea	211	Epilogue	251
Takapu or Australasian Gannet *Morus serrator*	212	Acknowledgements	253
Toroa or Royal Albatross *Diomedea epomophora*	220	Appendix One Author's Influences	254
Toroa or Wandering Albatross *Diomedea exulans*	224	Appendix Two Field Notes	256
New Zealand White Capped Mollymawk *Diomedea cauta steadi*	232	Appendix Three Camera Setup	260
Salvin's Mollymawk *Diomedea cauta salvini*	237	Appendix Four Meditation in the Bush	262
Flesh-footed Shearwater *Puffinus carneipes*	243	Appendix Five Quotation Reference	264
Panguranguru or Northern Giant Petrel *Macronectes giganteus*	243	Appendix Six Further Reading	267
Titore or Cape Pigeon *Daption capense*	248	Index	268
Korora or White–flippered Penguin *Eudyptula minor*	250		

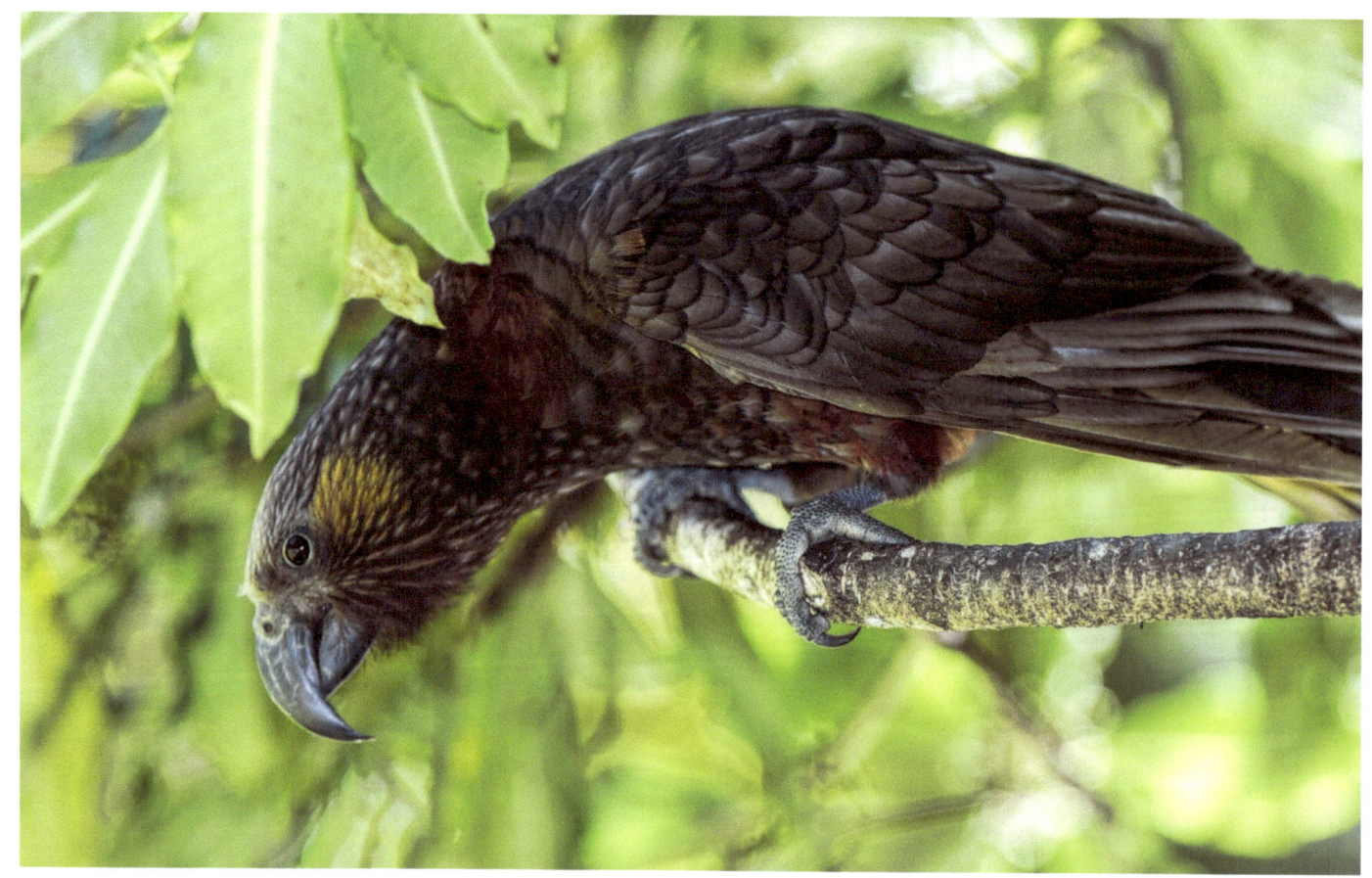

Preface

About the Author

In 2006, at the age of sixty-one, I arrived in New Zealand. As a wildlife photographer, I was charmed by the unique birds here and decided to make photographic portraits of as many of our native, endemic and migratory birds as possible. As the years passed, the project took on a life of its own. I added more birds each year until, in 2015, I published the first version of this book with images of fifty different bird species in the Apple bookstore. In 2017, I completed the Amazon Kindle Fire bookstore version. In this, the third edition and the first version in paperback format, I've added an additional twenty more pages and eight more species. Also, I have updated many of the portraits in the book with higher resolution images.

I am now seventy-three years old, and I recognise that my dream of capturing a photographic record of all of the native birds is probably not going to be realised. This book presents what I have seen and photographed so far. As my years and good health allow, I will continue to add more birds to this book in future revisions.

Voices from the Past

As you view the photographs herein, you will find scattered amongst them quotes from some of New Zealand's greatest naturalists of the 19th and early 20th centuries. These quotes provide a glimpse into New Zealand's past, as seen through the naturalist's eyes. Their voices also remind us of a past when protecting species was in its infancy. We've come a long way since then, but we still have a long way to go if we wish to adequately protect our native species.

Extinctions Past and Present

Around seven hundred years ago the last Moa died. At the same time the last Haast's Eagle joined the Moa. A hundred years ago the last Huia died. As did the last Piopio and the last Auckland Island Merganser. Eighty-five years ago the last Laughing Owl died. Thirty-five years ago the last Bush Wren was sighted. All these birds are gone forever. Extinct. Since humans arrived in New Zealand, a total of fifty-seven bird species have been driven to extinction.

Many of the birds represented in "Portraits of New Zealand Native Birds" are threatened or endangered. Encroachment on their habitats by humans, and the pests they brought with them into New Zealand, are the principal reason for many of our native birds' precipitous decline, and only human intervention can save them. Of the birds in this new edition, four species are nationally critically endangered. One species is endangered. Four species are nationally vulnerable. Seven species are considered at risk. Of all of New Zealand's four hundred twenty-six bird species, seventy-one are considered Threatened, and one hundred and seven are considered At Risk.[1]

The Cause of New Zealand's Species Extinctions

When we examine New Zealand's species extinctions, we begin to see why so many of our species have become extinct. Causes include New Zealand's historical land use practices, native habitat conversion to farming and land development, archaic attitudes towards wildlife, predator and invasive species importations, and the widespread killing of native species by farmers, food and trophy hunters, naturalists, and early indigenous populations. New Zealand's extinct species didn't just die off. It is an incontrovertible fact that human interventions were the primary cause of virtually all species extinctions in New Zealand for the last thousand years.

We Must Act Now

New Zealand's native birds are truly our "canaries in the mine" and they are pleading for us to wake up. The same unenlightened choices that were made in the past are still being made today by many of us through inaction, indifference, or callous disregard of our role in the demise of our native species. We are not winning the battle. If we are to preserve our wildlife and wild places, and respect nature and our dependence on it, we must take action now. A country that calls itself clean and green must do more than lip service to this ideal.

Current measures are having limited success in reversing this trend. Greater protection of the native, endemic and migrant birds of New Zealand is vitally needed. We need increased funding of the New Zealand Department of Conservation. We need to expand and protect native bush, create protected mainland and off shore havens, restore our rivers, steams, wetlands, and foreshore, and eradicate or greatly reduce imported predators and invasive species. We need to hold fully accountable those humans whose actions are responsible for the degradation of our soil and watersheds, for native species habitat loss, and for the killing of vulnerable native species. In addition, each of us must examine what we, as individuals, can do that positively impacts the survival of our native species. And we must start now.

For better or worse, we humans have become the stewards of the earth. This is our watch. Let us not tolerate the shame of inaction, indifference and hand-wringing, or continue on a path that leaves our children and grandchildren a world worse that we found it.

In 1854, Chief Seattle is attributed to have said, "The air is precious to man. For all things share the same breath – the beasts, the trees, man, they all share the same breath…

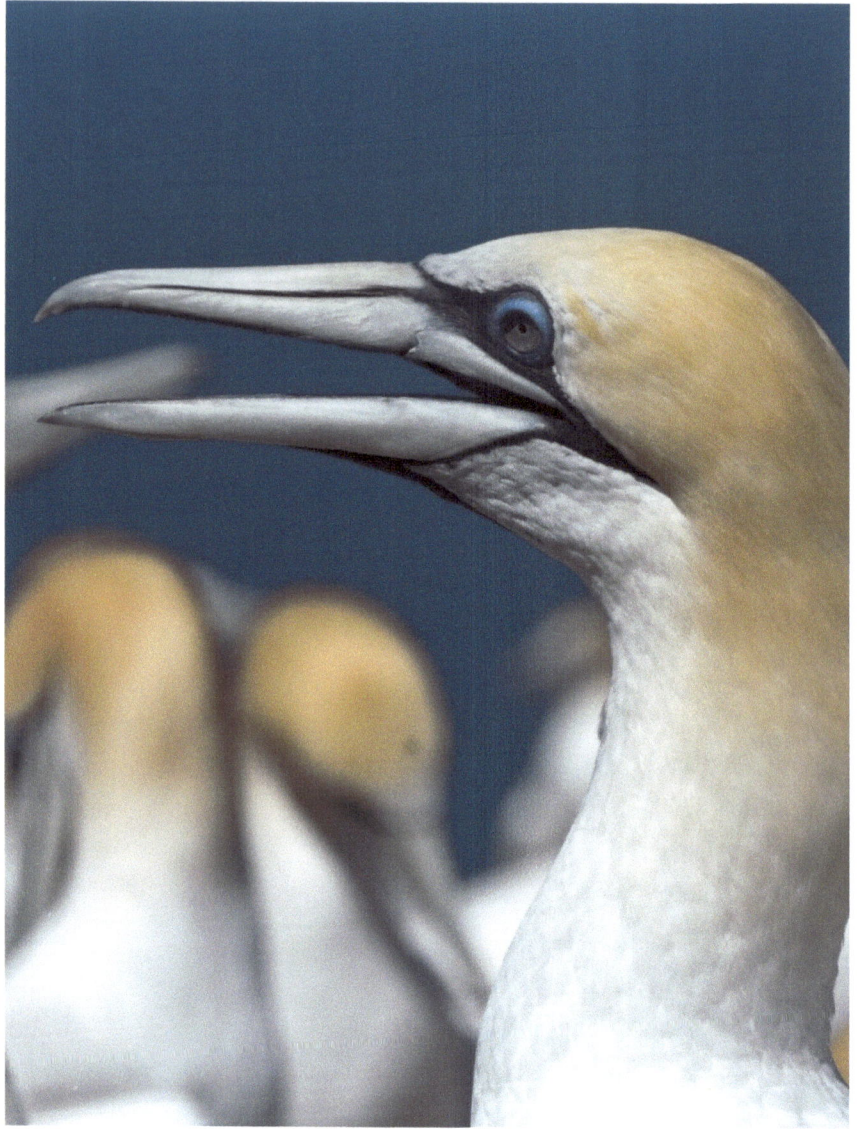

What is man without the beasts? If all the beasts were gone, men would die from a great loneliness of spirit. For whatever happens to the beasts, soon happens to man. All things are connected. Whatever befalls the earth befalls the sons of the earth."

[1] http://www.doc.govt.nz/Documents/science-and-technical/nztcs19entire.pdf

Prologue

First shoot in my new home...

The day is clearing as I pull out of my drive and head down to Kandallah Road and the suburb of Ngaio. The road through Ngaio is a narrow two lanes as it crosses the hills above Wellington City to Crofton Downs, and Wadestown, and Kelburn, and eventually to Karori. I pass the turn to Karori Wildlife Sanctuary with its massive predator–proof fence and, instead, go right as the road leads down and then up higher into the hills. The tarmac makes a sweeping right turn up and around a hill and dramatically opens out onto farm land. It then dives and narrows as it winds its way down into the Makara Valley. Wellington has vanished, and I have suddenly been transported back to the Thirties or Forties. Everything is green, as I pass the sheep pastures and scattered homes and farms. Three massive trees loom on the left, with scarred knobs marking where heavy branches once hung over the road. The bustle of the city fades from my mind as I enter the small hamlet of Makara. Not much to be seen – low buildings, farm implements, a few houses. I leave the village and the road follows a constricted stream wedged between high green grass hills dotted with ten to twenty metre tall trees.

Thoughts jangle in my head as I perseverate over lists of tasks not yet done. Finally, at a divide, I peel off to the left and head toward Makara Beach. I was here a few weeks ago and was intrigued by the hills along the south coast. I had walked along the beach collecting paua shells, but the hour was late and I headed back before I could discover more. Today, I am here for a landscape shoot.

The road curves up over a rise and down into a river valley that reminds me of areas on the South Island's west coast. As I near the beach, the river widens. I see flocks of birds along the far bank – Paradise Shelducks, Canada Geese, White–Faced Herons, Shags. I drive through the village of Makara Beach out onto the rocky shore. I park and get my equipment out of the boot, stopping for a moment to admire the view. Then, I head south along the track just above the beach. My mind is filled with anticipation, with a lot of chit–chat swirling around. Would the weather hold? Did I remember to lock the car? Did I take extra memory cards? I should have brought a hat...

I carry a tripod, camera, lenses and equipment, so I'm mindful where I step. After about half a kilometre the track divides. The track I seek follows a steep sheep path near the edge of a bank falling steeply to the Tasman Sea below. After a few hundred metres I turn around and take a few shots back to the village. Deep in thought about the shots I just took, I step back, trip and fall onto my backpack. I remind myself to not do that again, especially this close to the drop-off to the sea below.

As I climb, a fence on the left curves in and forces the track to follow the cliff even more closely. With care, I continue up the incline. A pair of sheep slowly walk ahead of me. Further up, a flock grazes sleepily. I think of shooting a few images of them, stop to get a few close-up shots of a ewe with a lock of wool swept down covering her left eye. The track narrows again and follows the cliff, sometimes right to the edge. The bank falls down to the beach at a sixty to seventy degree angle. The grass is long, letting me know that it is too steep for the sheep, and too steep for me.

When I can, I veer away from the cliff. The wind is whipping now, swirling and buffeting me as I climb. It catches the tripod case and pushes it, and me, to the side. I stop to catch my breath, and as I pause, my mind chatters away: I wish I hadn't brought the tripod. It looks steep ahead. I'm glad I brought the tripod. I hope I don't fall again. If I do, I hope I don't land on the camera...

In the distance I can see the quarry of this journey, an old battery from World War II at the top of the rise. To see and feel what war brought to this lonely place. I slowly make my way up the hill and then turn inland a bit so that I can come up behind and above the abandoned fortress. At the top, I set up my tripod and camera and take a couple of panoramic shots and a few bracketed exposures. As I am breaking down the equipment, I notice that my chattering has quieted.

I am standing on top of the world, one hundred-eighty degrees of lush green at my back and one hundred-eighty degrees of aquamarine and the South Island in the distance before me. Above me is blue sky, and beneath my feet is dark earth, ripe and verdant. I am alone, and I am at peace. There are no other humans within a few kilometres, only sheep, soaring gulls, nature and me. No thoughts of the distant rumblings of past wars, or new ones on the horizon. No threats to fear. No thoughts of tasks or things undone. Only this moment.

I drift aimlessly around the hilltop and down to the abandoned batteries where, over seventy years before, this hill had been alive with activity in preparation for invasions. Here were men and women both afraid of, and anticipating, the approach of war. And now, the place I stand has been transformed by time into something entirely different. A monument to patriotism, yes, but also a crumbled ruin, that said war had not, indeed, come to this shore. The earth, the sea and sky, the cracked, and broken concrete are all that remain of that time. Only now, with no wars looming on these shores, it is a poignant reminder that all wars do end, that peace does come.

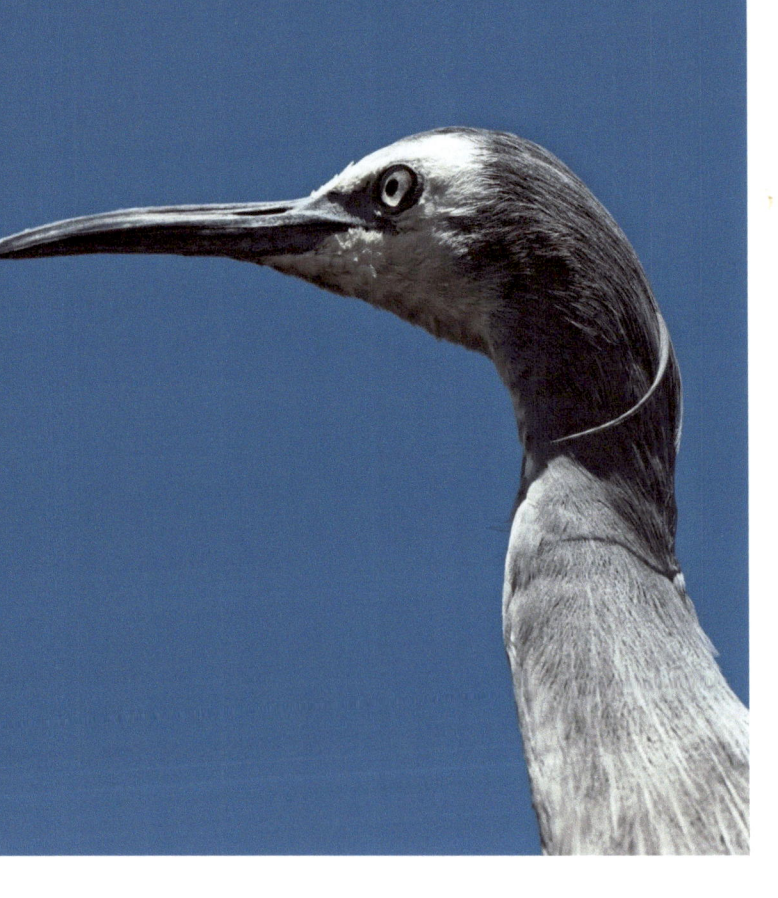

As new wars and conflicts rage across the globe, it is good to be reminded that it is not all bad. That fear and worries don't always define me. That peace and tranquility are there as well, waiting to be found. And I am reminded, by this journey up a hill, that there is more to me than the puny thoughts I conjure up to fill the space between my ears.

I gather myself and make my way down the hill. The sun is low in the west and the way is clear. What looked like obstacles on the way up seem to have vanished. Time to head home.

~John Elmer Lee, July, 2006

Chapter One
Birds of the Bush

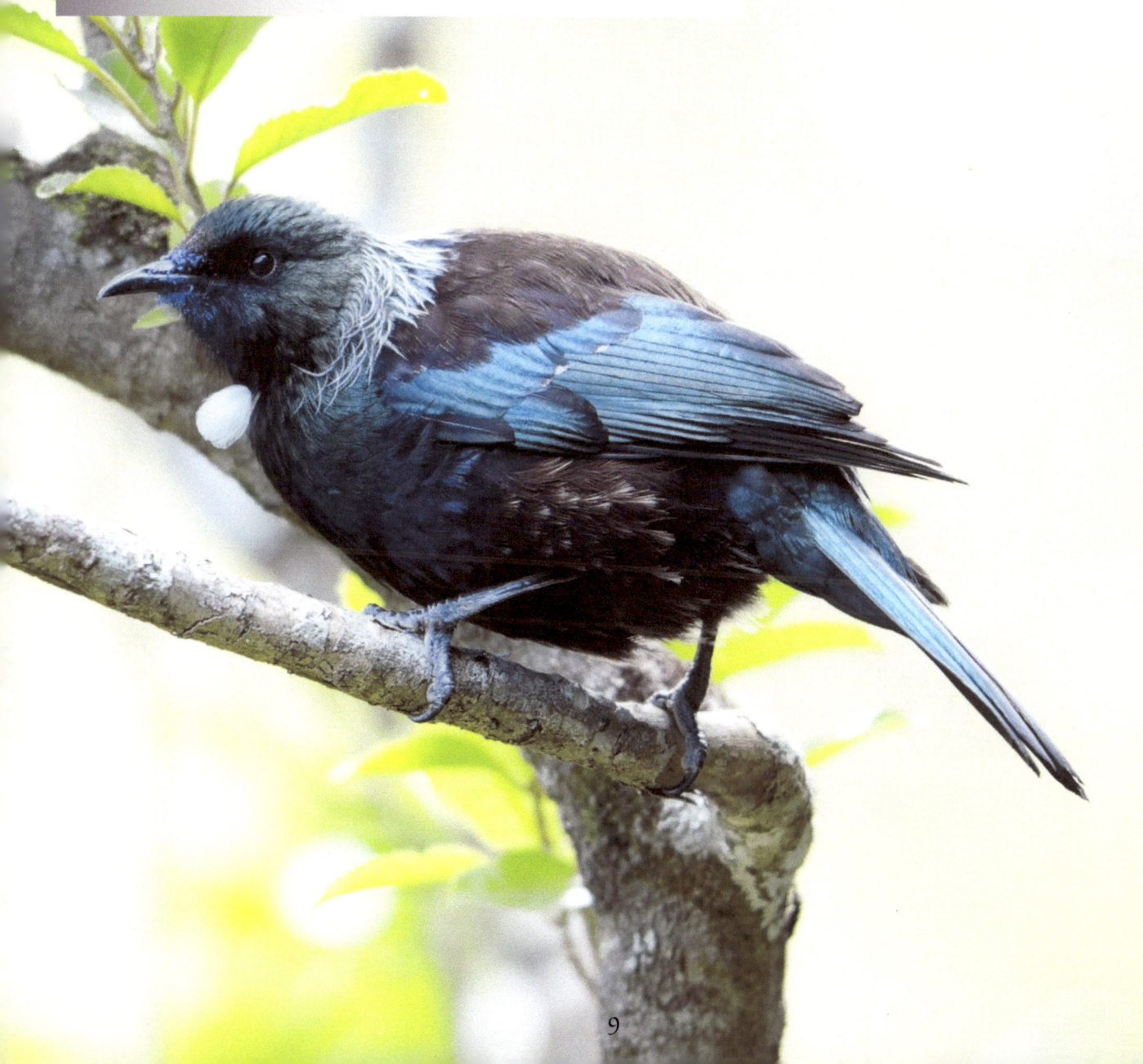

Tui or Parson Bird
Prosthemadera novaeseelandiae

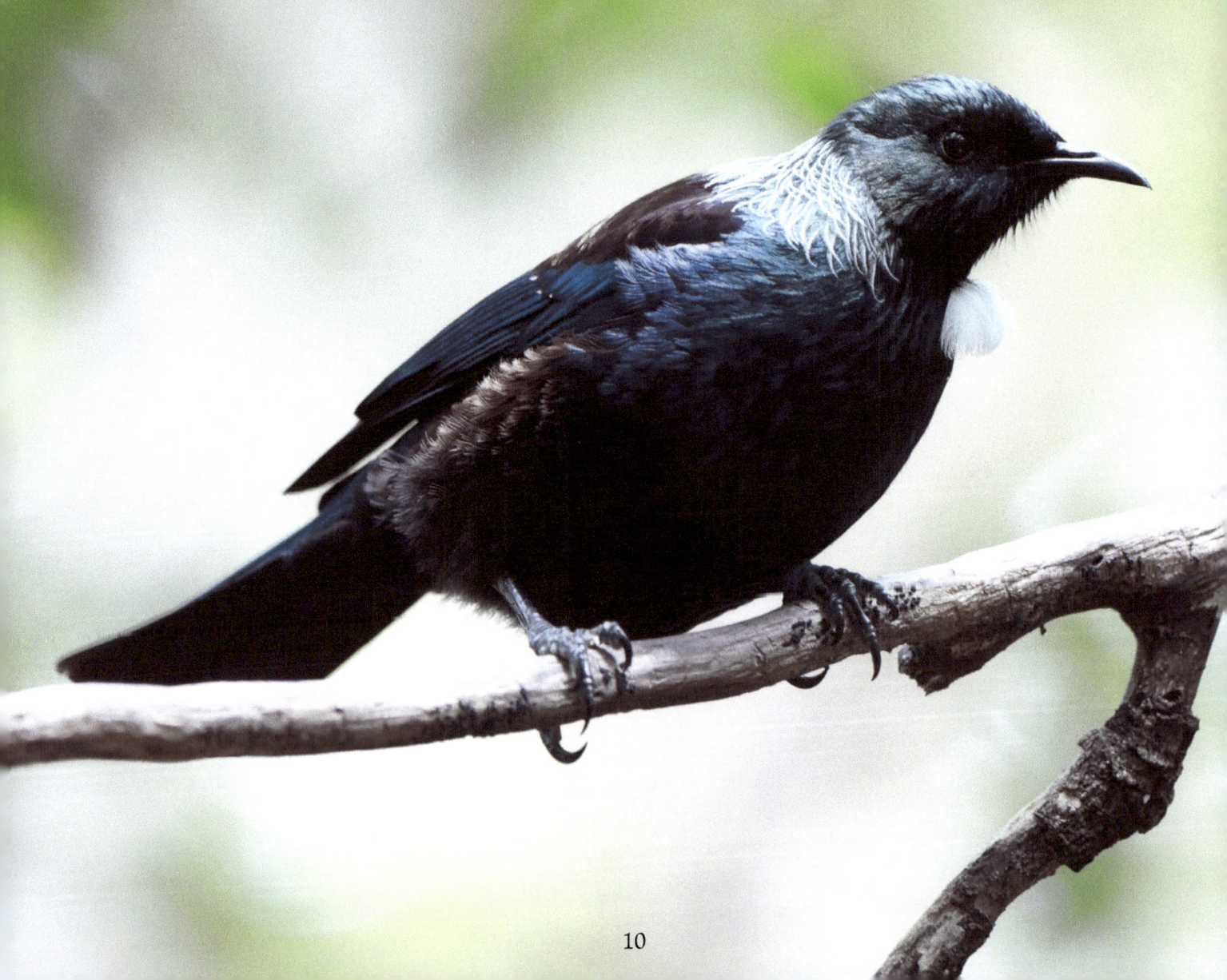

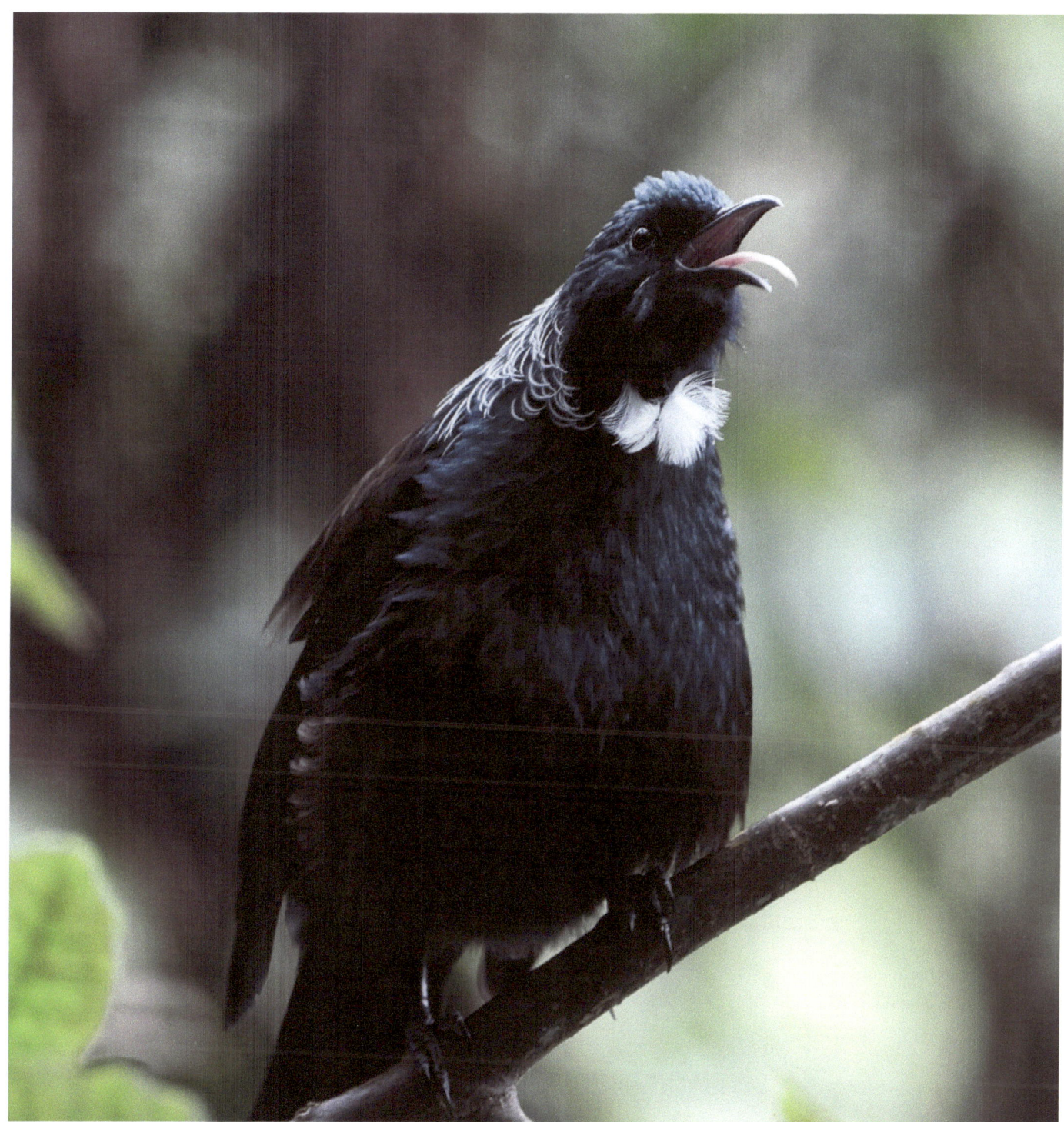

Of the honey-eaters we have two—the tui and the wax-eye or blight-bird. To those who have been once only in our New Zealand woods it is unnecessary to dilate on the tui. Throughout the years, almost at any hour, even through the warm, light summer nights, his pleasing notes blend with the unceasing rustle and stir of leaves and the sound of the wind in the tree-tops. In its wild state even the tui is an accomplished mimic, taking off the squeal of the wild pigs particularly well. Mr. Brandon tells me that not infrequently his collies have mistaken its imitation of a shepherd's whistle for the genuine article. One nest I examined was built of small branches of manuka, lacebark, lichen and mosses woven together, while the delicate, white, rather long eggs lay in a thick bed of the brown glaucous hair of the tree-fern's crown; a second was built entirely of the little jagged branches of the lawyer, and lined with bush-grass and a few feathers.

~H. Guthrie-Smith, 1895

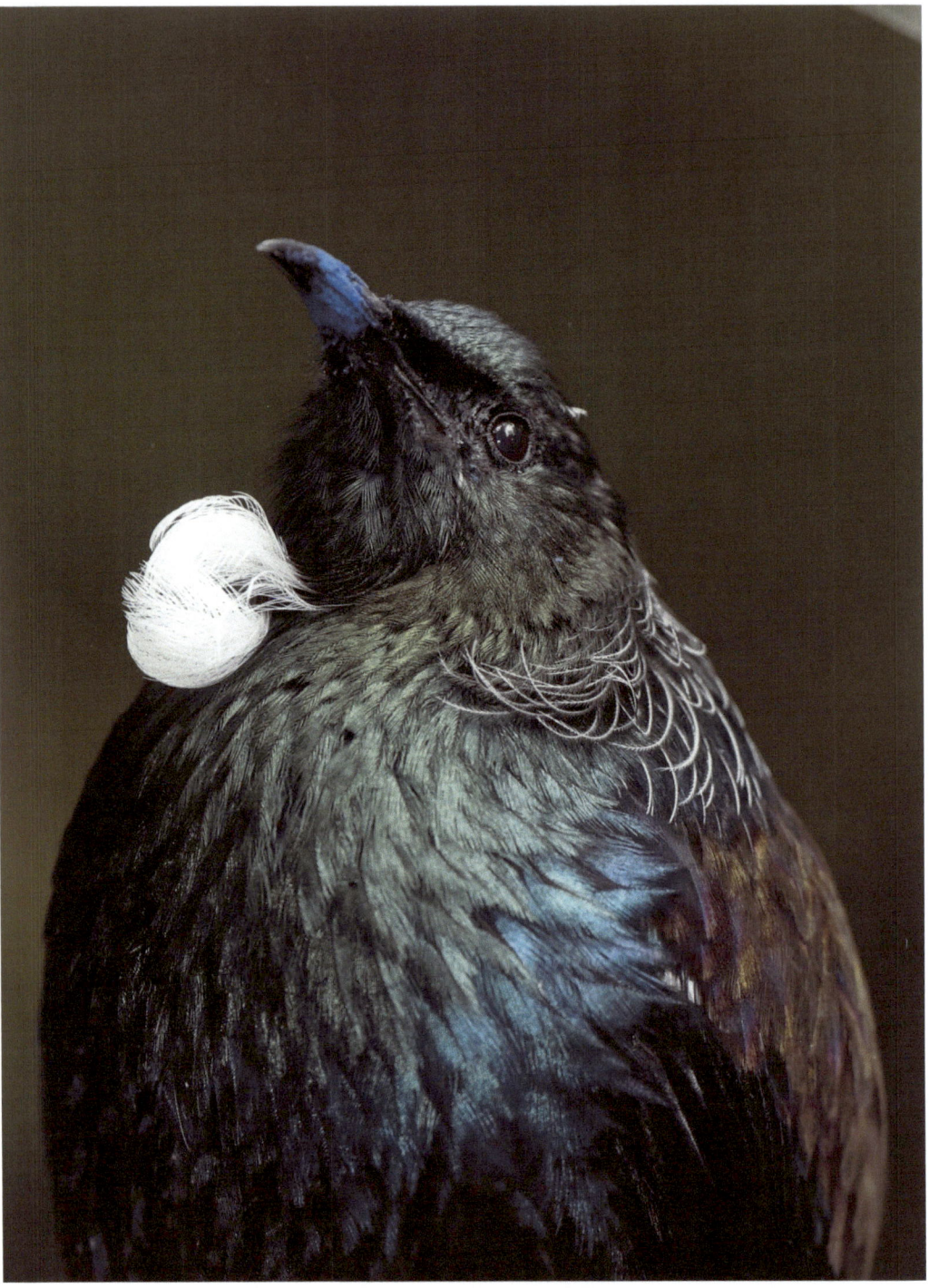

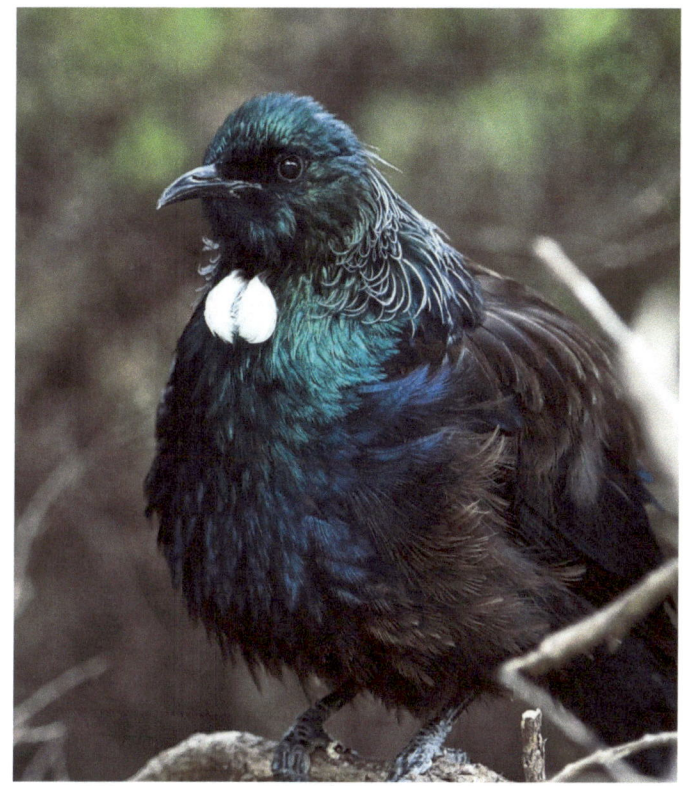 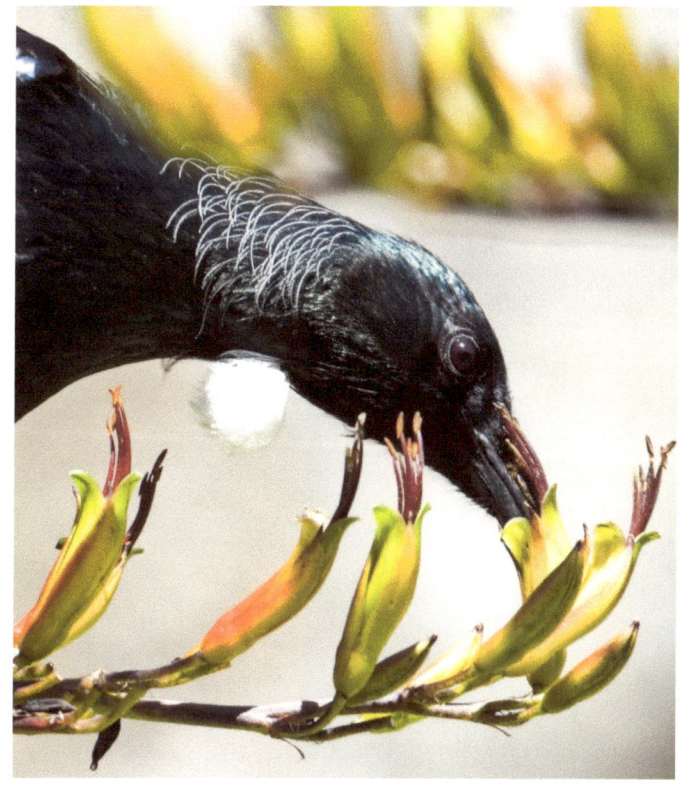

"The Tui poses as a songster, and shows off to the greatest perfection. Whilst the hen-bird is sitting the male is accustomed to perch himself on the high limb of a tree not far distant from his mate, using this as a post of outlook; and then, throughout the whole day, he pours out his soul in song. Puffing out his body-feathers and gesticulating freely, so as to give greater emphasis to his song, he produces quite a medley of musical notes, interspersed at intervals with that peculiar cough, and a sound not unlike the breaking of a pane of glass, followed by a series of gentle sobs. Then, quick as thought, he dashes upwards and makes a wide circuit in the air, or silently dives into the bush to exchange courtesies with his mate, snaps at a fly on the way, and then returns to his post of observation and song. After sunset, and as the shadows of evening begin to darken the forest, he alters his song, and utters a succession of notes like the tolling of a distant bell. Many of the passages in the Tui's ordinary song are of surpassing sweetness, and so rapid is the change from one set of notes to another that one never tires of listening to the wild melody. Both sexes sing, but in the breeding season the female confines her efforts to a produced note like the low chirping of a turkey-hen. As already mentioned, the male has an evening song quite distinct from that of the bright morning. To many ears it has a resemblance to the tolling of a highly pitched silver bell, but to me it is more suggestive of the distant tapping on a metal anvil. Of course, these resemblances are merely fanciful, but the musical cadence of the note is exquisite, as all who are familiar with it will readily admit… On a quiet summer evening the Tui may sometimes be heard long after dusk. On the wooded shores of the Papaitonga Lake I have heard them tolling up to 9 o'clock at night, the notes having a very sweet effect on the water."

~Sir Walter L. Buller, 1898

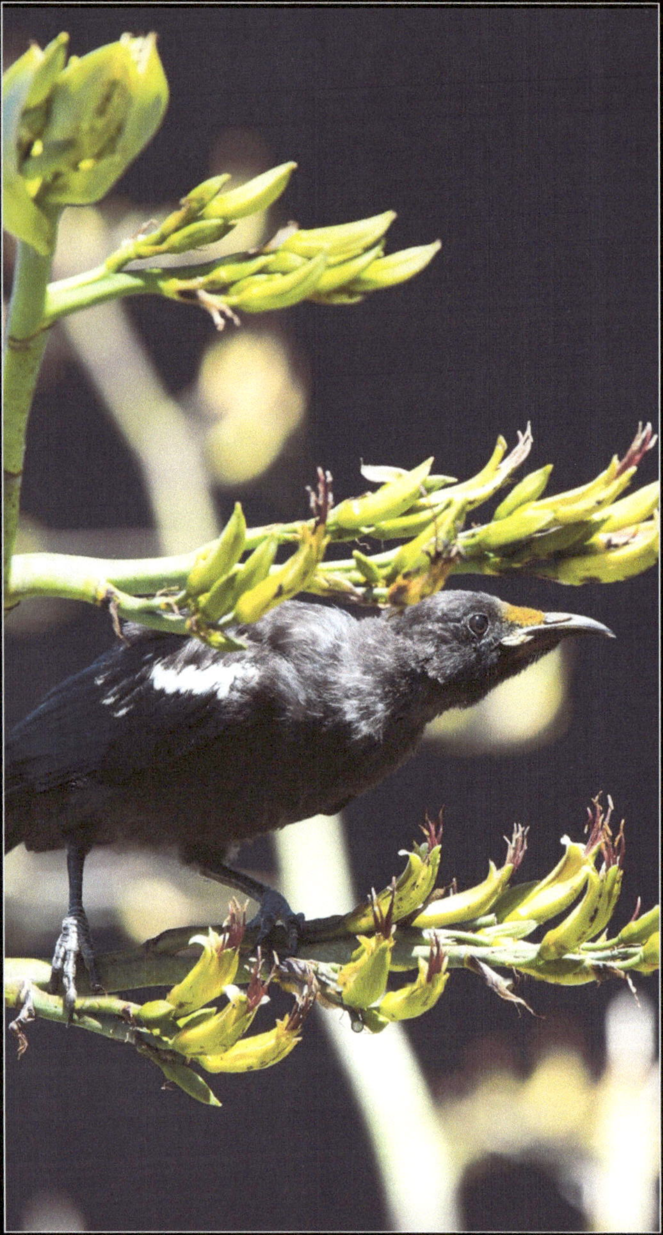

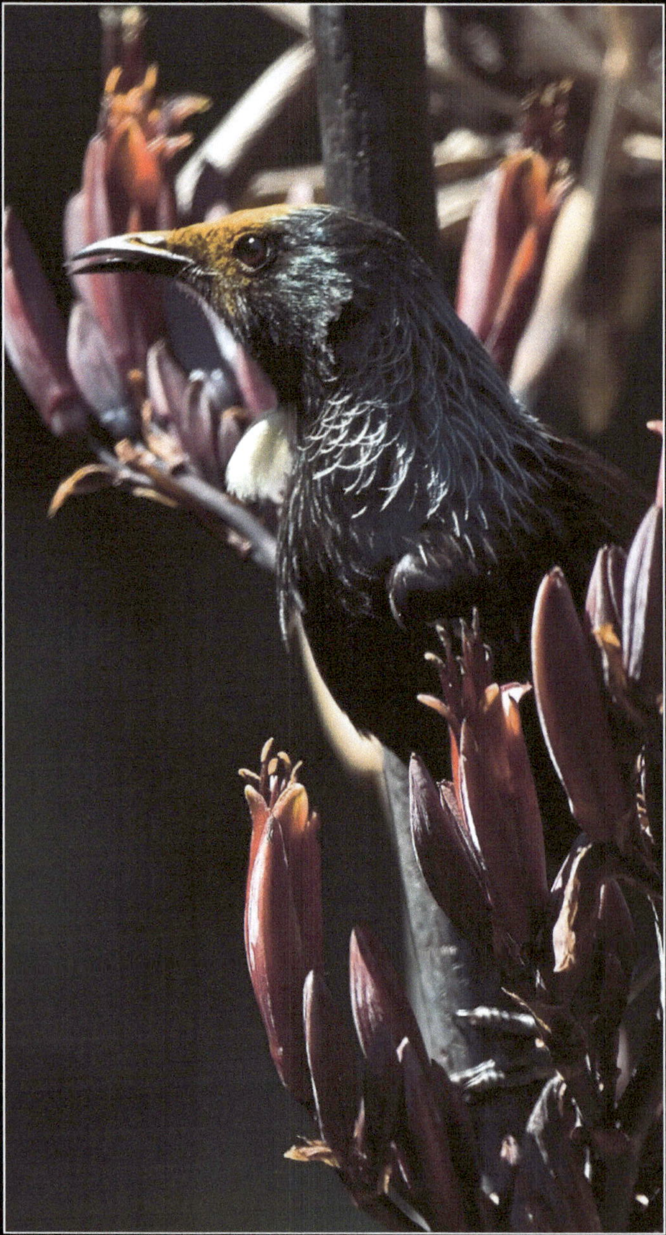

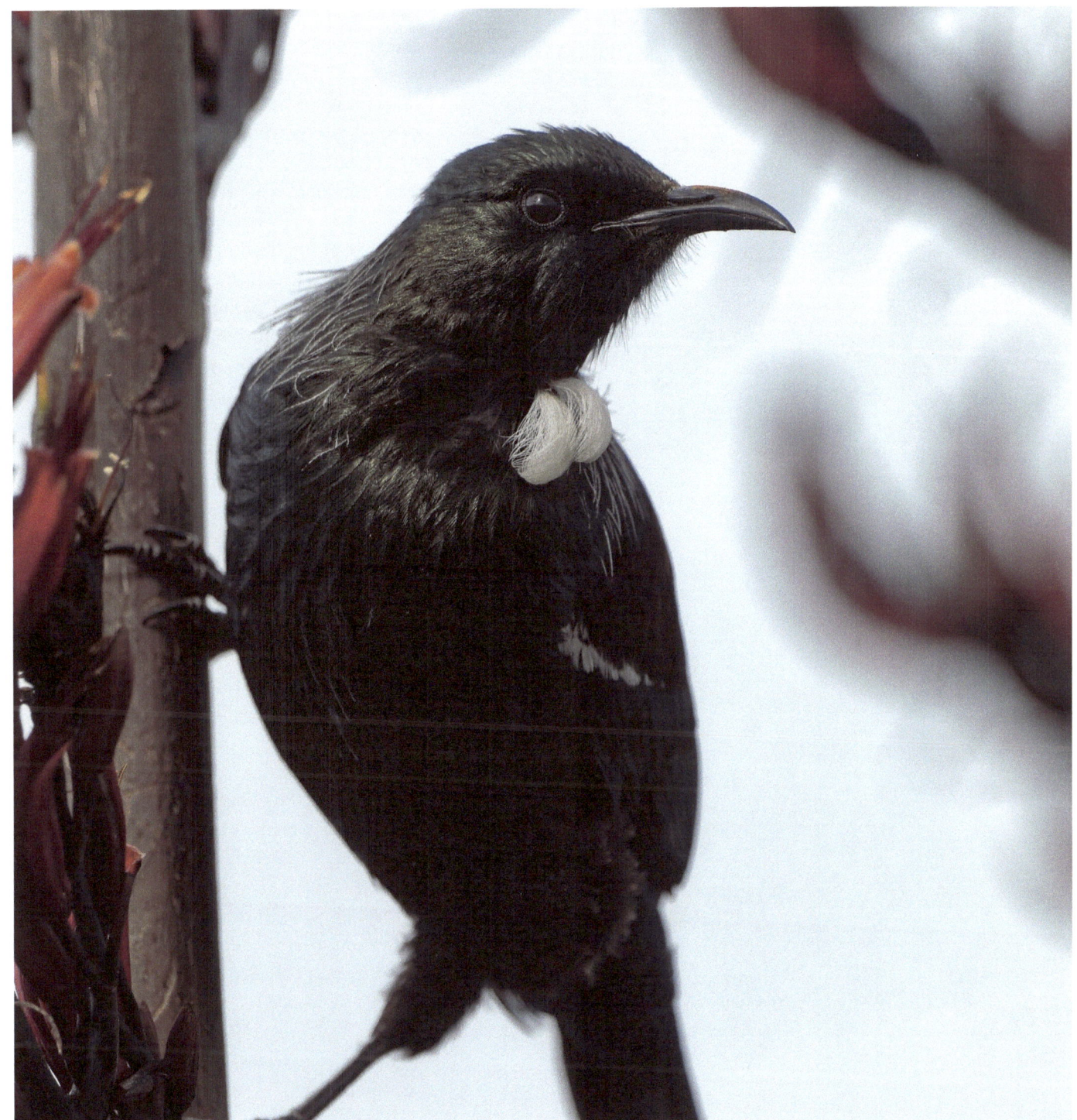

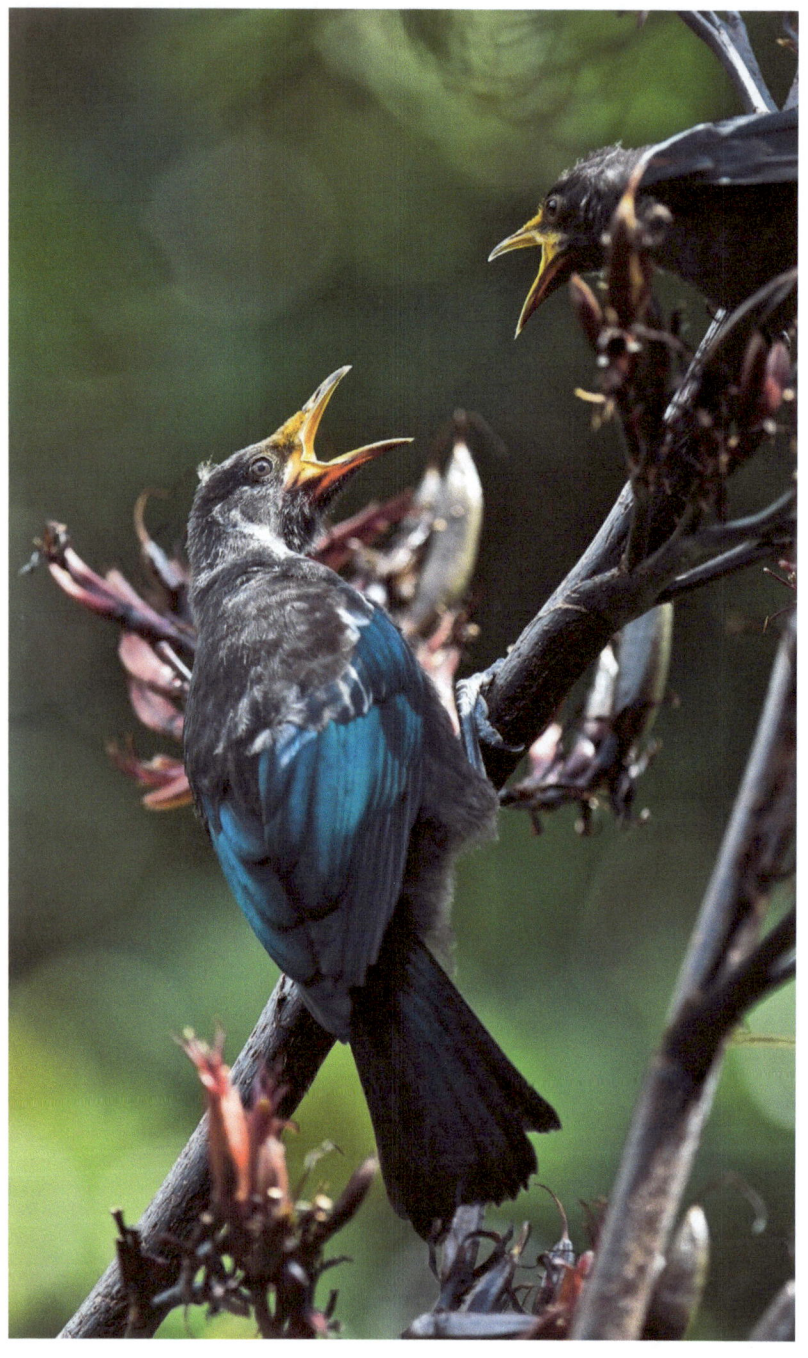

"Mr. C. Howard Tripp, of Timaru, has been good enough to send the following note on tuis singing in harmony: 'Though I was brought up close to native bush, and amongst native birds, particularly the tui, or parsonbird, I have only twice heard them singing in harmony, and have only met one other person who had also heard them. The first time was many years ago when camping in the bush up the gorge of the Orari River, when, shortly after sunrise in the summer holidays, about fifty or more tuis in the trees over and adjacent to our tent commenced to sing in most perfect harmony, and continued to do so for fully half an hour, and without leaving their perches. The second occasion was at the Orari Gorge homestead, a few years later, again on a bright sunny early summer morning; but then the harmony lasted for only about five minutes. As the bush near the Orari used to be favourite places for tuis, I have, of course, many times heard large numbers of tuis singing together, and have listened attentively for this harmony, but failed to hear it. Captain Cook, in his 'First Voyage', describing Queen Charlotte Sound, writes as follows: 'The ship lay at the distance of somewhat less than a quarter of a mile from the shore; and in the morning we were awakened by the singing of the birds; the number was incredible, and they seemed to strain their throats in emulation of each other. This wild melody was infinitely superior to any that we had ever heard of the same kind. It seemed to be like small bells most exquisitely tuned, and perhaps the distance and the water between might be no small advantage to the sound.'"

~Johannes C. Andersen, 1914

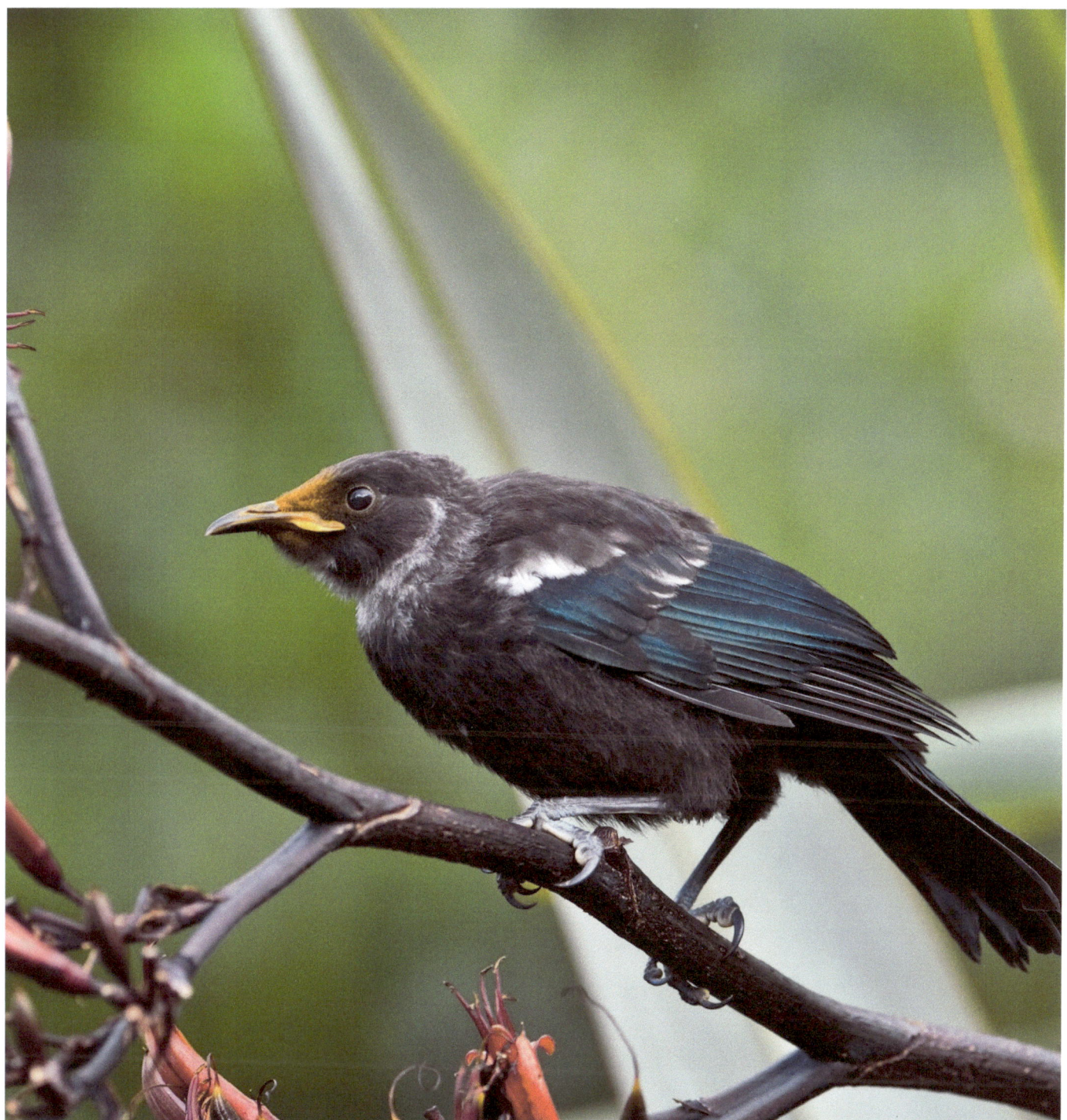

Korimako or Bellbird
Anthornis melanura

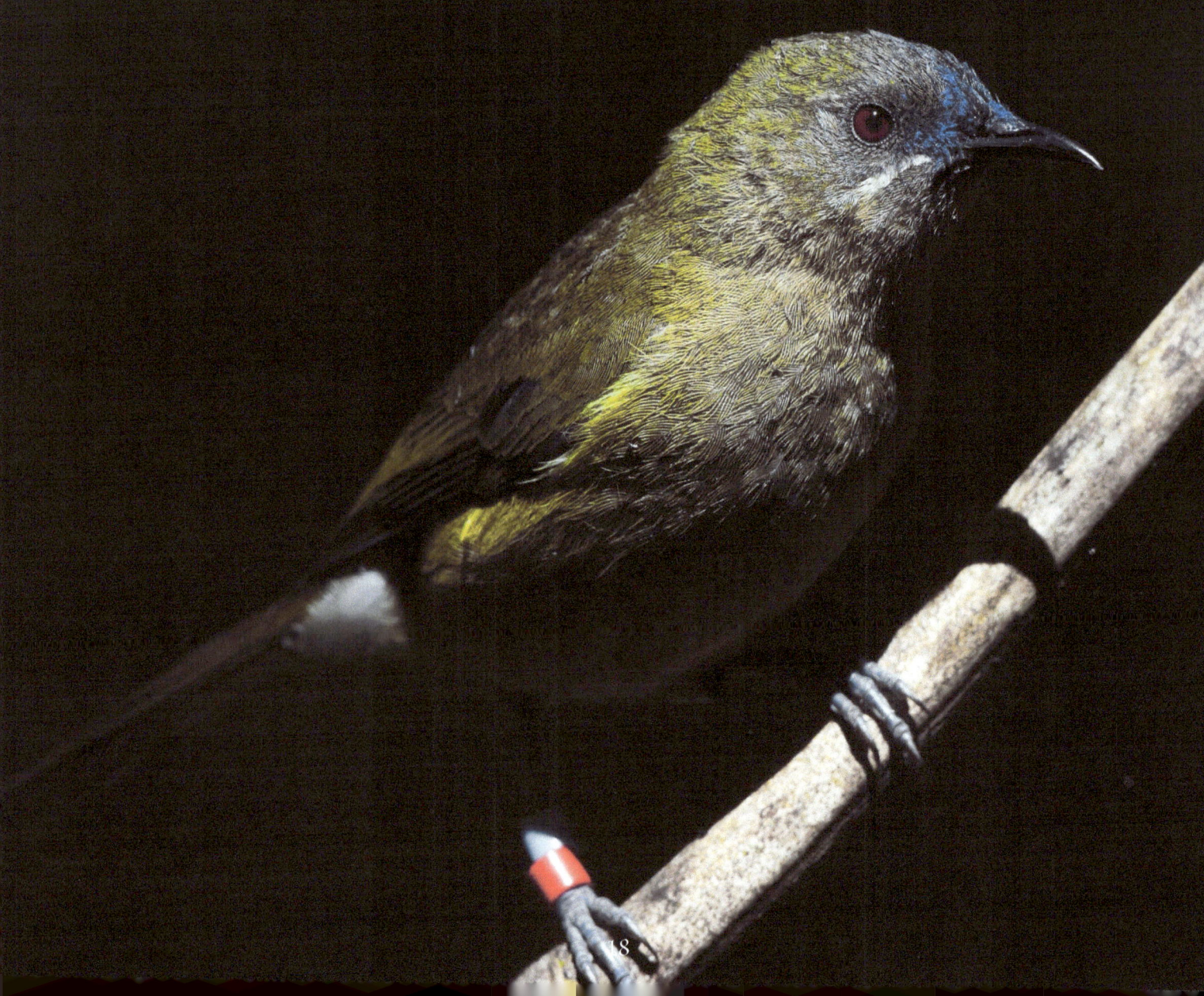

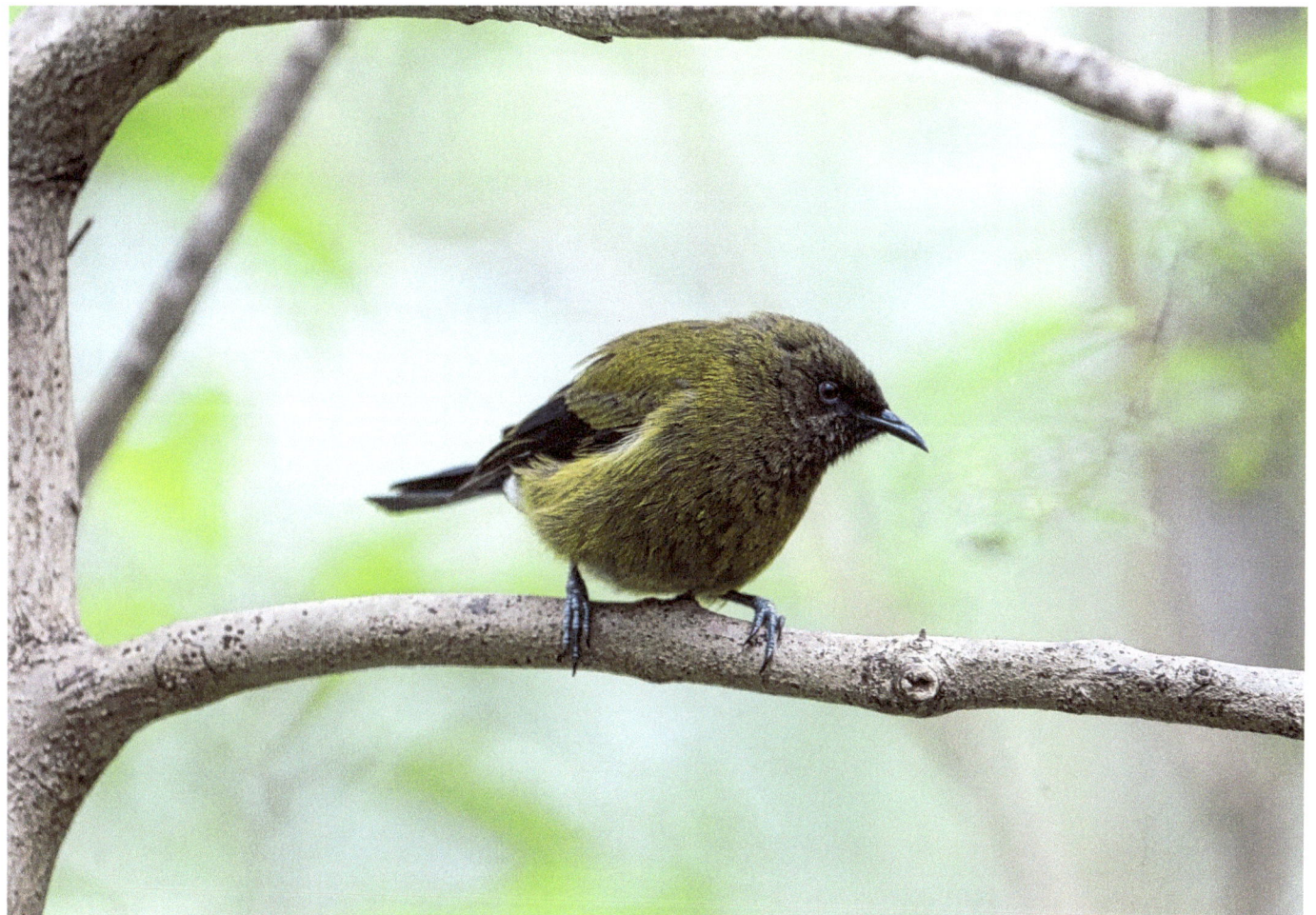

"Guided by my observations, I should say that the bell-bird... is the most plentiful. It is found in all parts of the island, and seems to be present in countless numbers. The best feature of its presence is the fact that it is increasing at a fairly rapid rate. Its nest is often found in thick manuka and bush within fifty yards of Mr. Shakespear's house. Mr. Shakespear told me that in the previous season a pair safely hatched out their brood in a clump of manuka overshadowing the meat-safe, ten yards from the back door. Twenty years ago Sir Walter Buller said that 'it is only a question of a few years and the sweet notes of this native songster will cease to be heard in the grove, and naturalists, when compelled to admit the fact, will be left to speculate and argue as to the causes of its extinction.' A visit to the Little Barrier sanctuary shows that there are no grounds for adopting such a pessimistic tone. If the bellbird was chased entirely off the mainland—which is a remote probability according to reports received lately—there is every likelihood that it will live on the Little Barrier as long as the forest there is preserved and the sacred character of the island is maintained."

~James Drummond, 1907

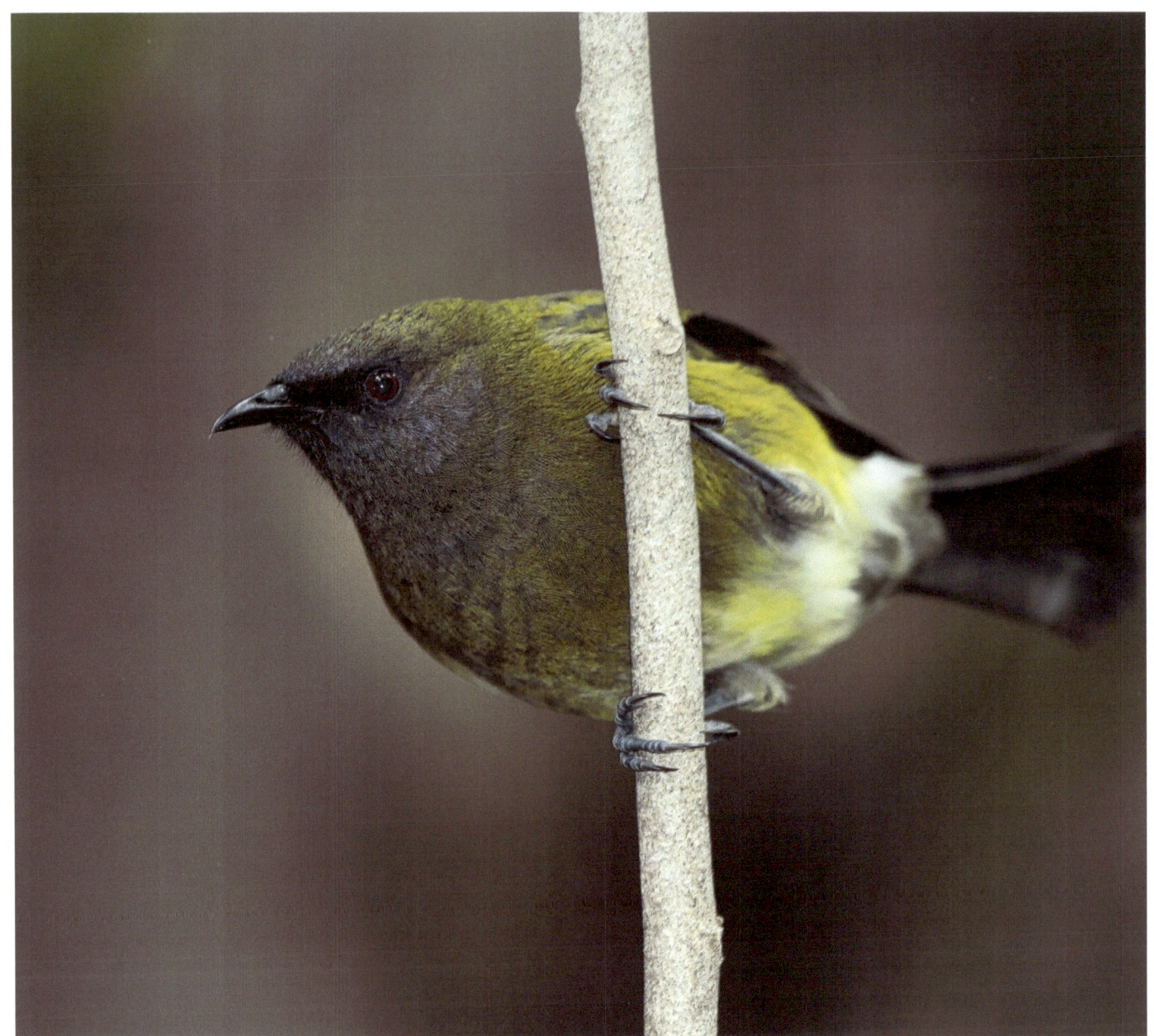

"The only sound worth noticing was the beautiful melody, towards morning, of the bellbirds. Thousands of these were singing together, and, probably by some auricular delusion, the sound seemed to arrange itself into scales, like peals of bells running down octaves. As the sun rose this music ceased altogether."

~*Major Charles Heaphy, 1879*

"Everyone who has rambled through the bush, or even strayed amongst the shrubby thickets that fringe our numerous gullies, must have become familiar with the clear metallic ring of the Bellbird's note. It may be said to sing matins and vespers for the warblers of the bush, as it is at the grey break of dawn, and the still hour that closes in the day, that its chime strikes clearest on the ear. It is comparatively silent during the noontide heat, unless some few individuals meet on a tree or shrub, that offers a tempting show of honey-bearing blossoms, a note or two is briefly sounded, the numbers rapidly increase; after much noisy fluttering of wings, a gush of clanging melody bursts forth from a score of quivering throats, forming a concert of inharmonious, yet most pleasing sounds. Probably Cook indicated the Bellbird, then in a comparatively unmolested state, when he wrote, 'the ship lay at the distance of somewhat less than a quarter of a mile from the shore, and in the morning we were awakened by the singing of the birds; the number was incredible, and they seemed to strain their throats in emulation of each other. This wild melody was infinitely superior to any that we had ever heard of the same kind; it seemed to be like small bells, most exquisitely tuned, and perhaps the distance and the water between, might be of no small advantage to the sound.'... 'Placed at no great elevation from the ground, the nest may be found in a variety of positions, but we certainly have noticed it most frequently beneath a sheltering canopy of 'Bush-lawyer' (Rubus australis.) It is rather flat, and loosely constructed of sprays, grass, moss, etc., well lined with feathers. On examining the foundation of a nest, we found green sprays of Manuka amongst the interlaced materials... We fancy that the lining feathers are selected in such a manner as to afford some evidence of harmony of colour in their arrangement; as, for instance, we have noted specimens, with the inner lining entirely composed of the red feathers of the Kaka, another adorned with the green feathers of the Parroquet; near the farm, where many kinds of poultry are kept, we have had instances of lining, white, black, speckled, buff, etc., but uniformity of colour has been displayed."

~T. H. Potts, 1869

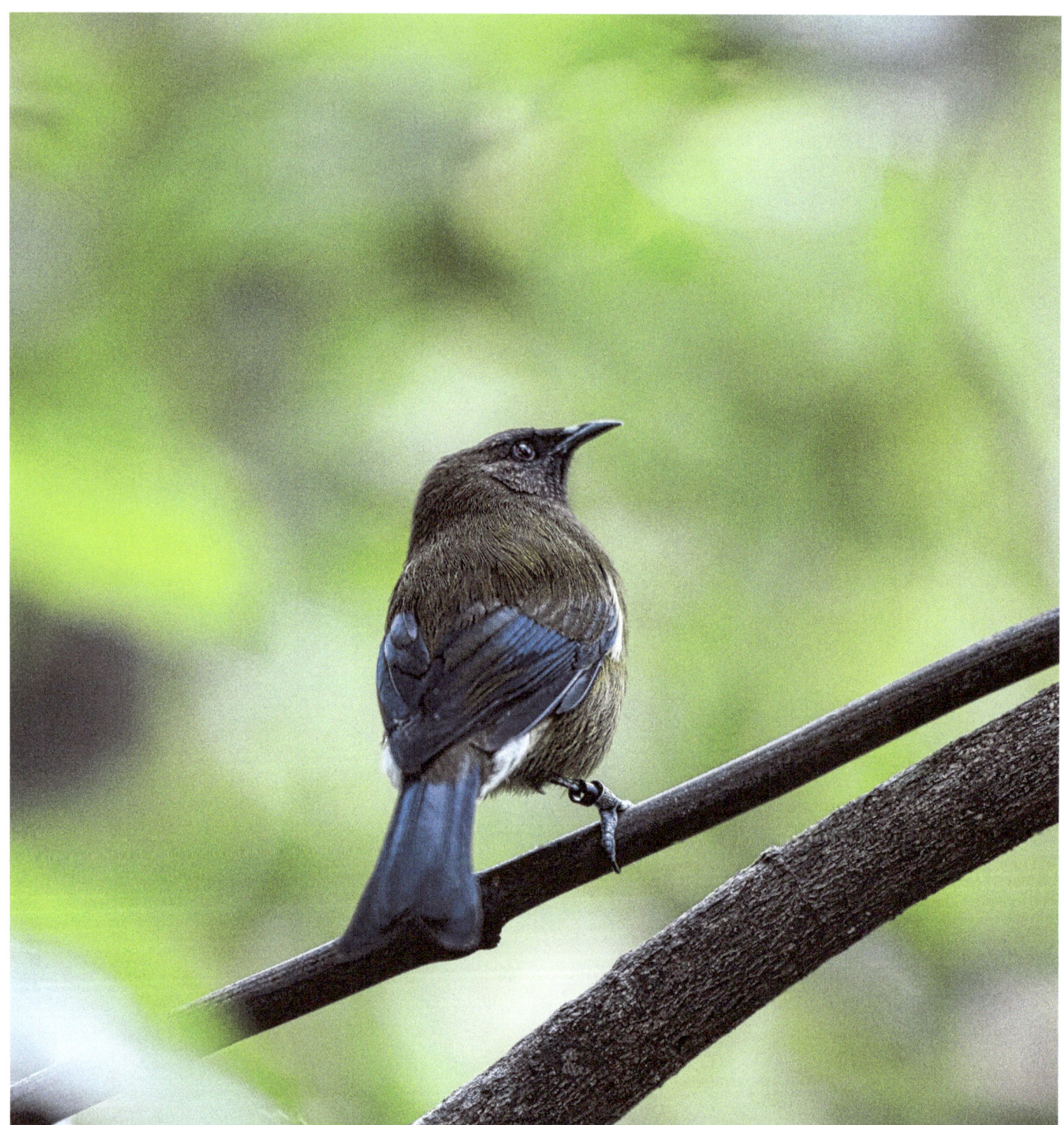

Hihi or Stitchbird
Notiomystis cinta

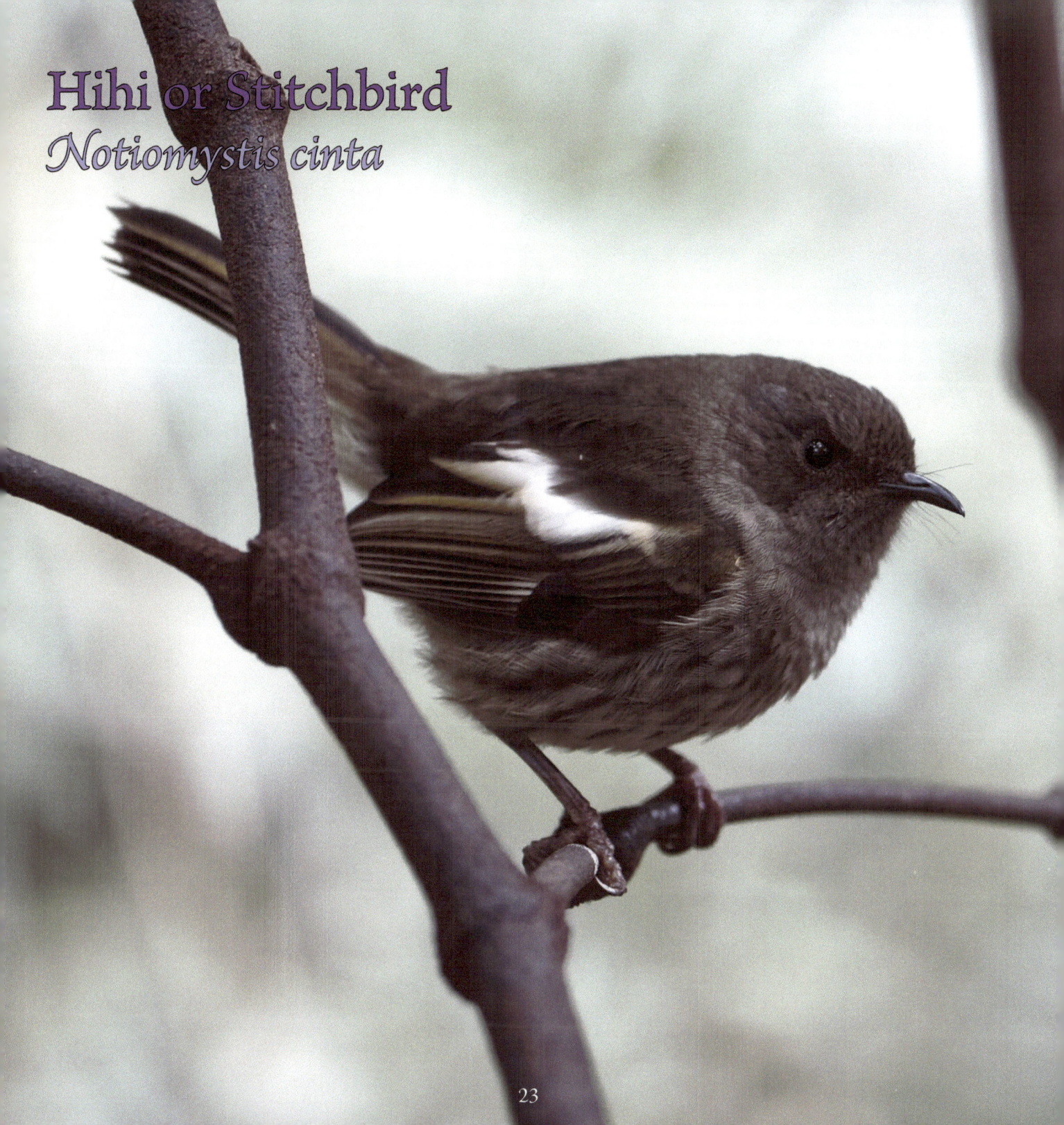

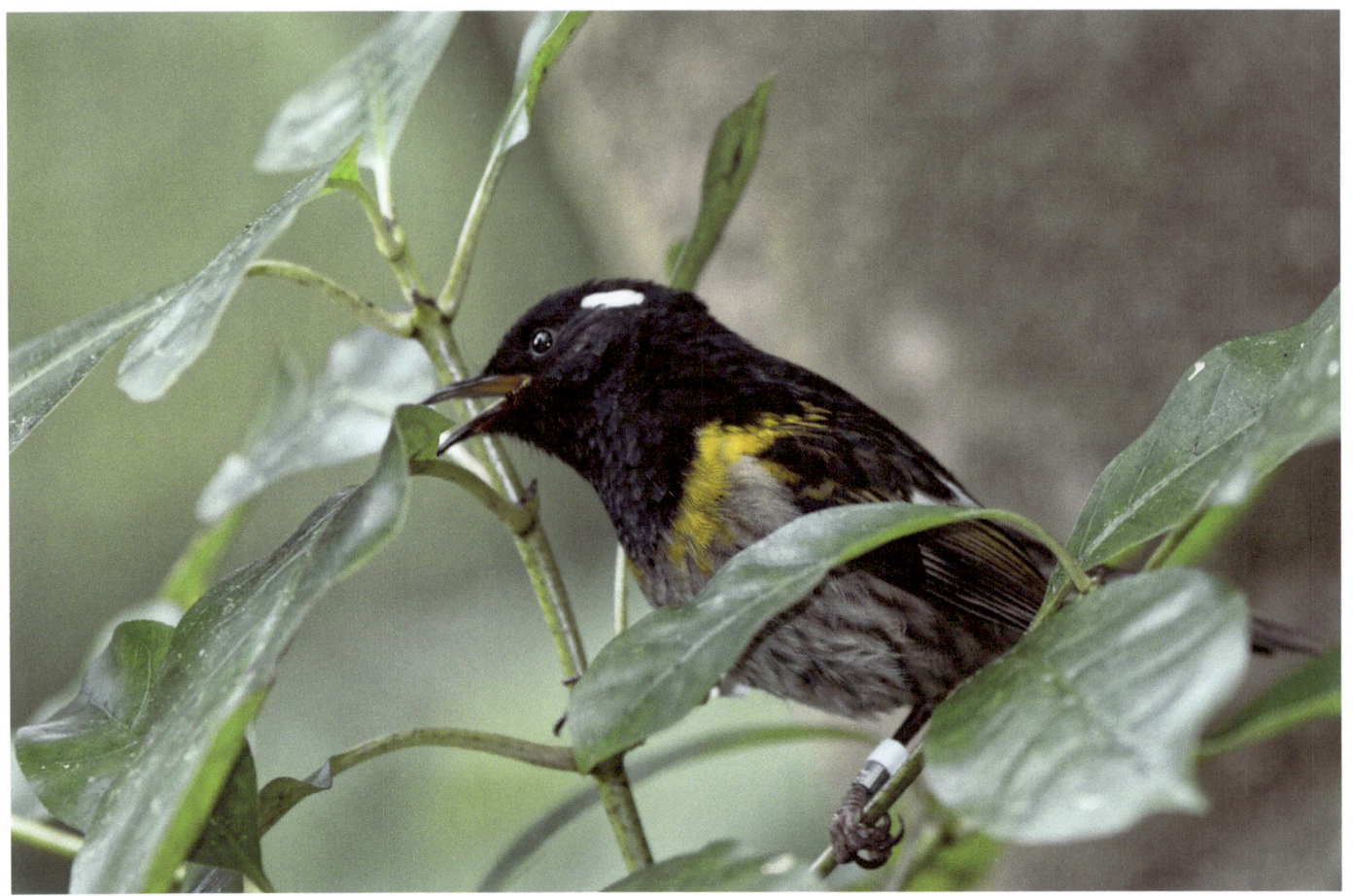

"The time at my disposal on the island was drawing to a close before I saw a stitchbird (Pogonornis cincta, Maori hihi)… We were on our way to the Heri–Kohu Peak, and at noon, when we were walking along a bushy track, a stitch–bird, which had come down from the heights, flitted about in an excited manner on the boughs above our heads. When its cry was imitated it came closer, and flew among some saplings, uttering a cry which might be written 'steech, steech,' repeated quickly several times. The bird was a female. She ran along the boughs, carrying her tail erect, at almost a right angle with her body, and her wings drooping. She turned round several times, and was the very embodiment of motion. Her cry hardly ceased, and there were very few moments when she took her black eyes off us. We saw seven stitch–birds on that occasion. They were all females. This is rather strange, as the female is described by several naturalists as being specially shy and retiring. The stitchbirds I saw on the Little Barrier were very tame. They had no fear, and even when a stone was thrown into the trees on which they alighted, they only flitted off to another bough. The locality which they favour with their presence most is in the north of the island. The haunt can be visited only with great difficulty and inconvenience. There these birds are numerous, and as many as fifteen have been counted at one time."

~*James Drummond, 1907*

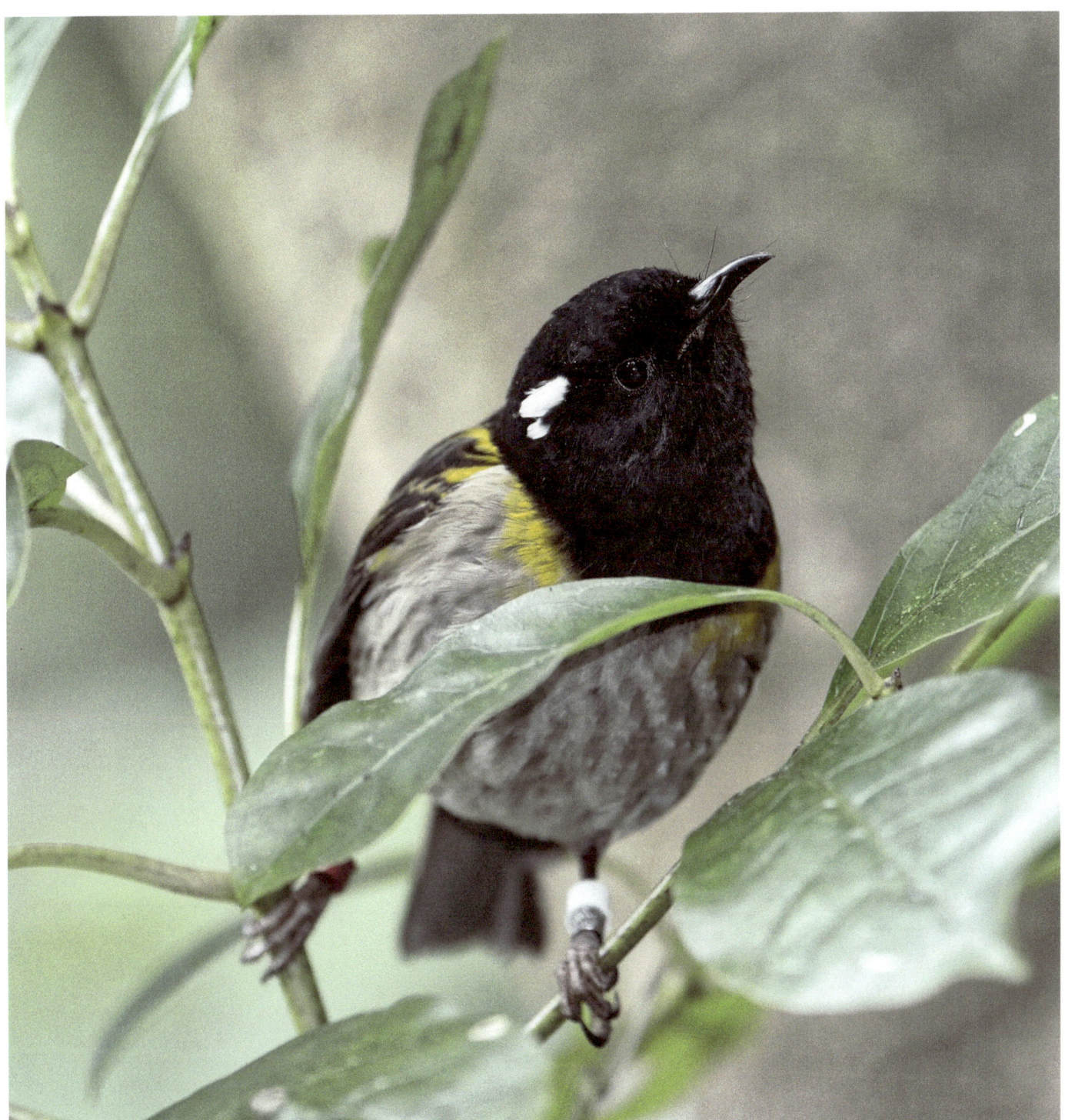

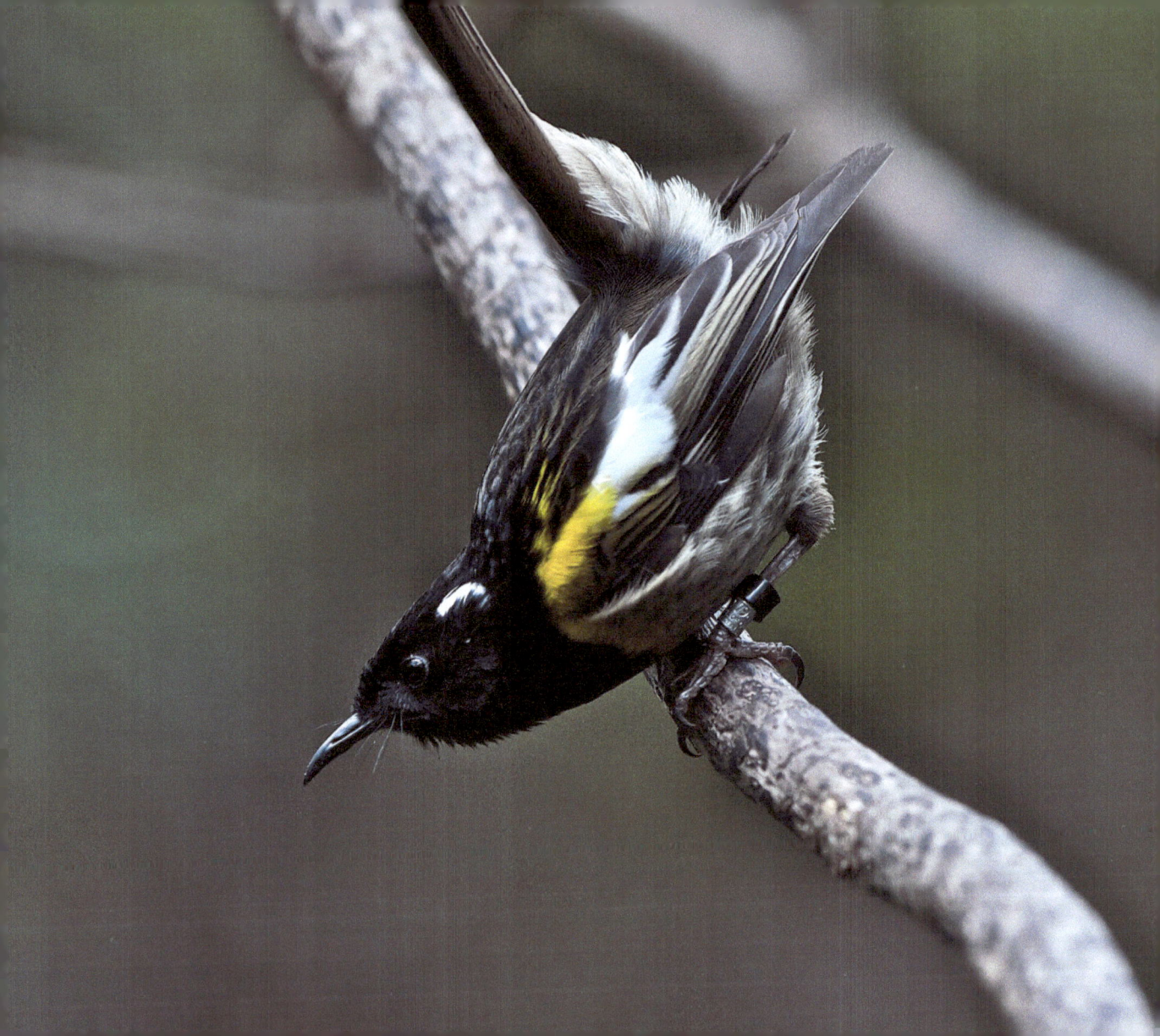

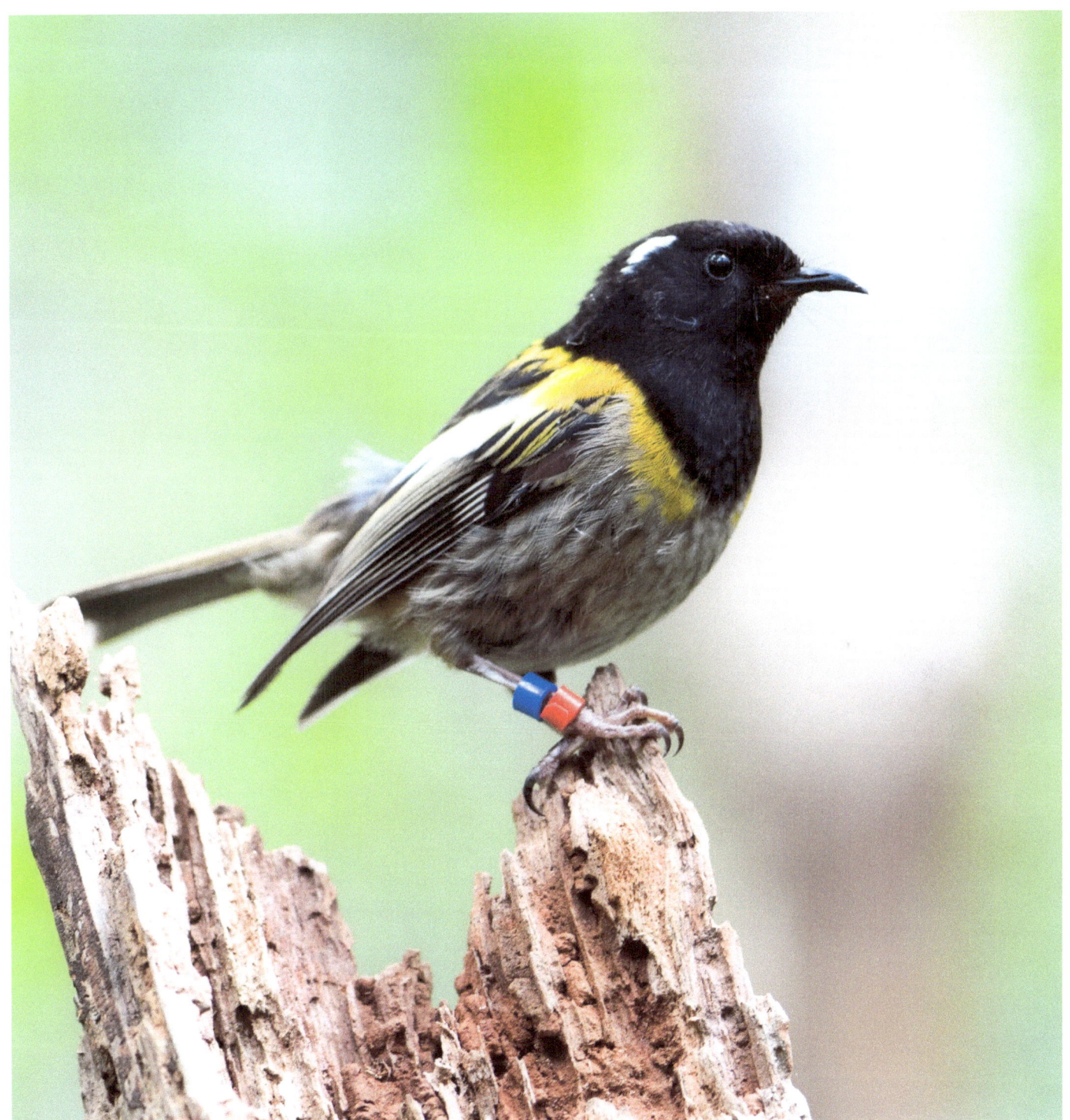

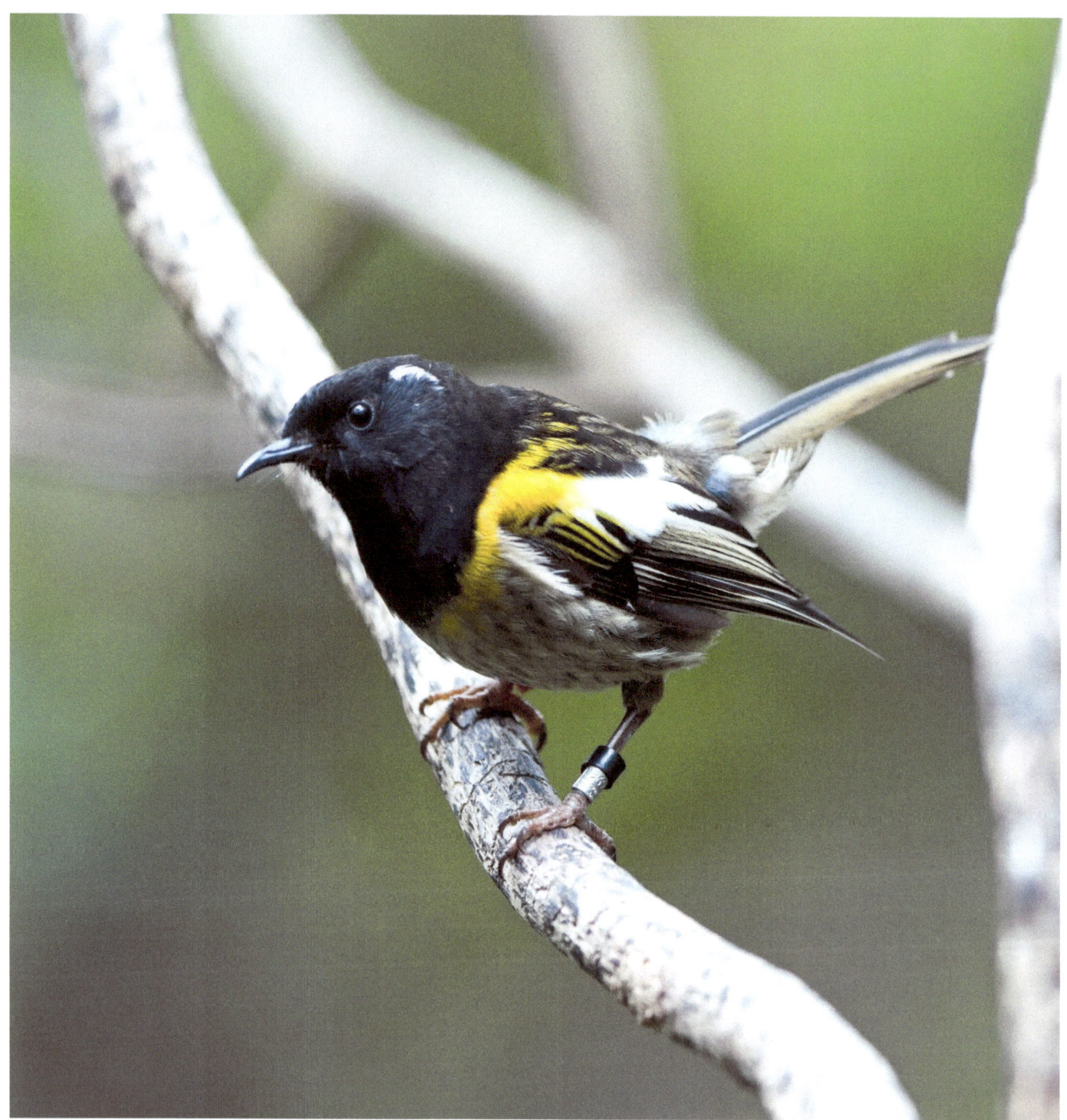

North Island Kokako
Callaeas cinerea wilsoni

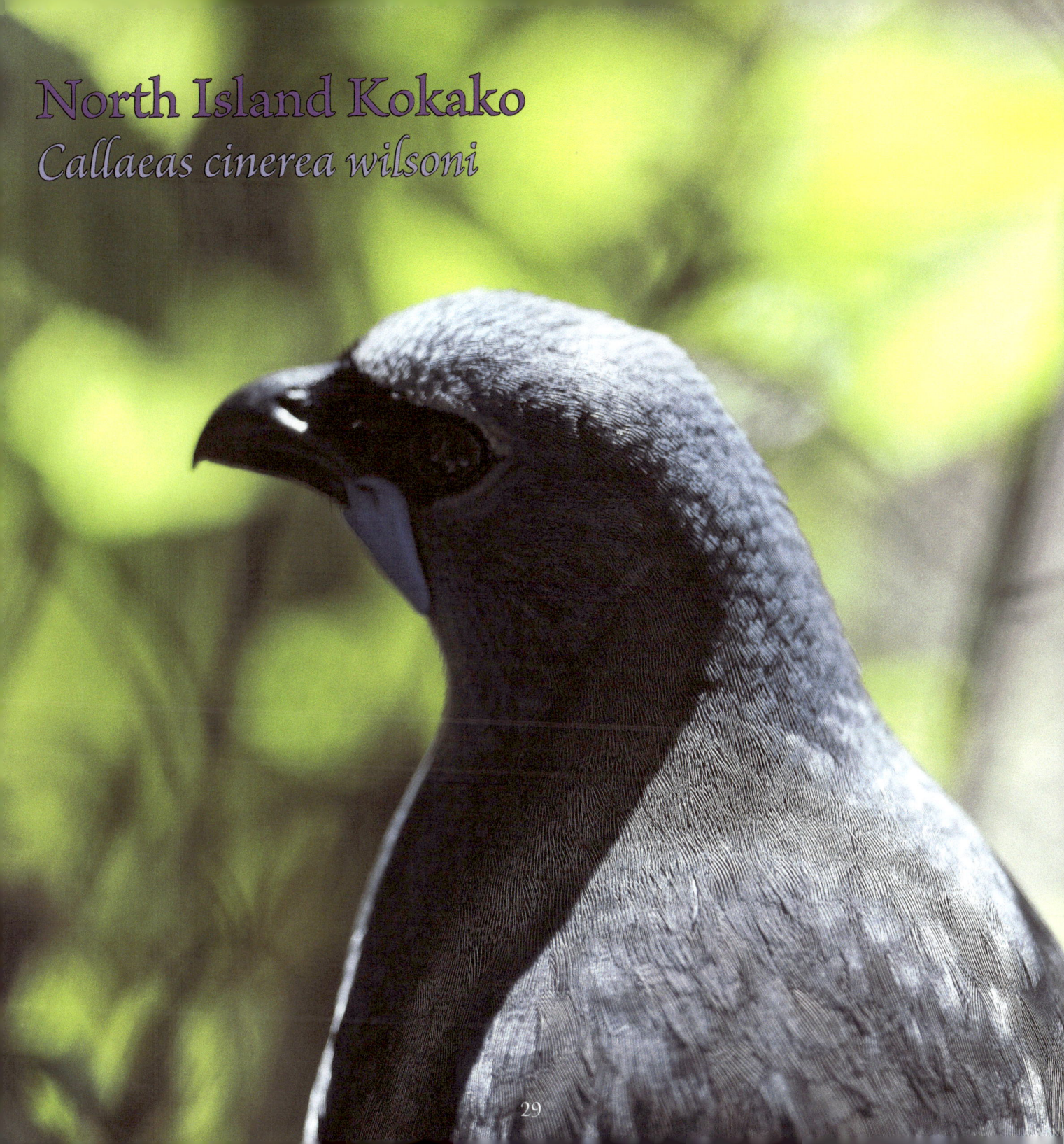

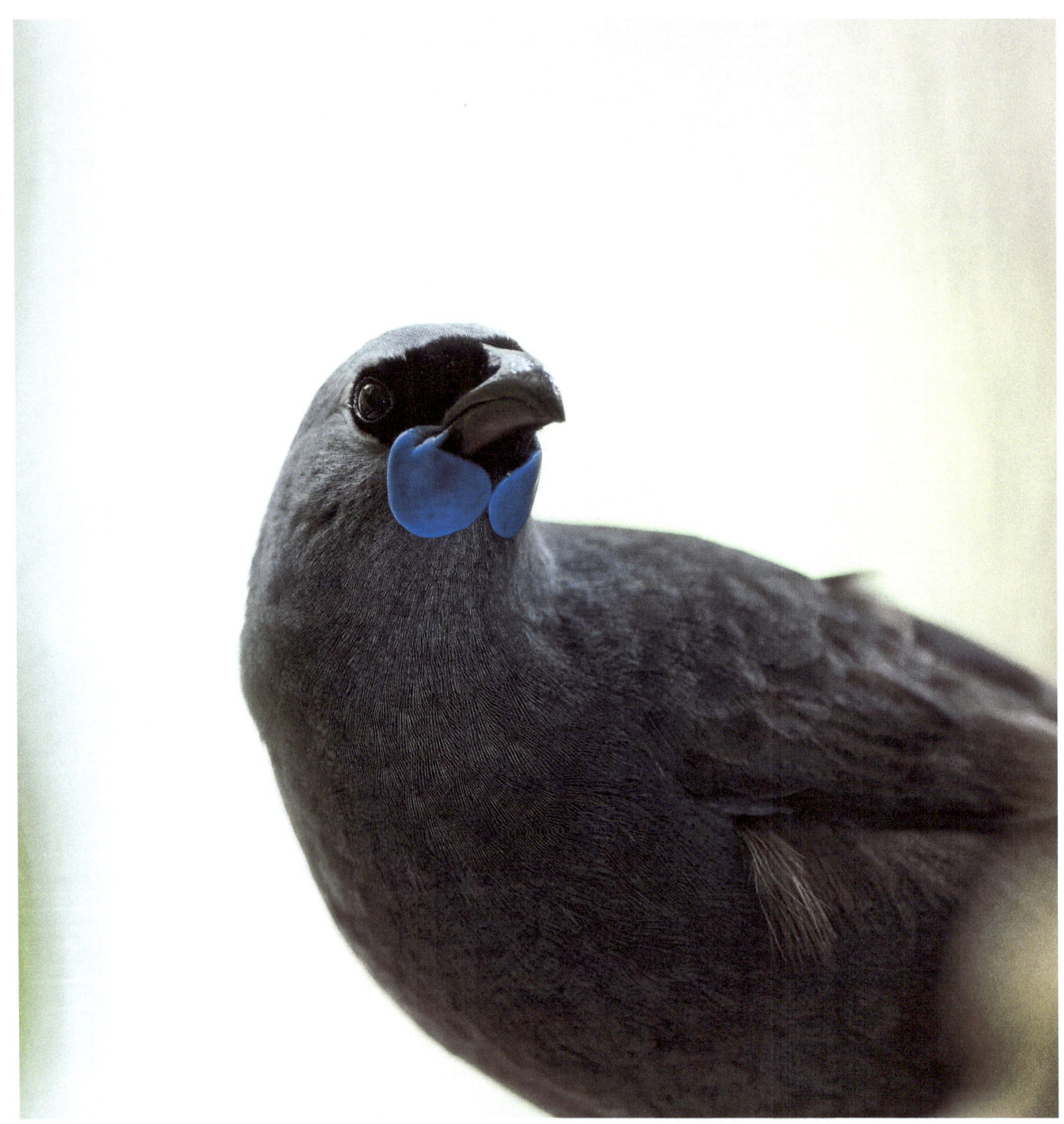

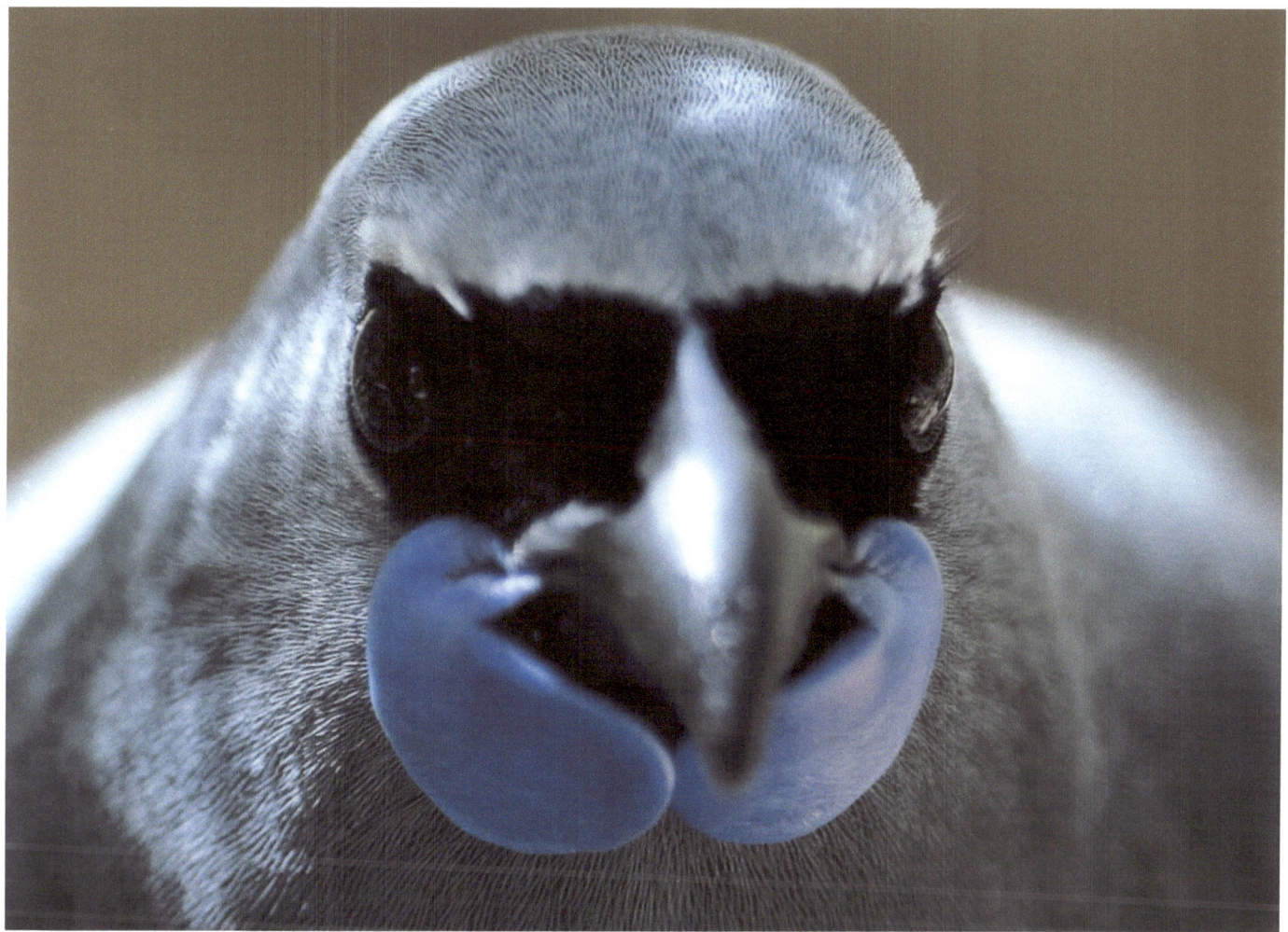

"The Glaucopis cinerea, (Kokako), of the Middle Island, is rarely found below an altitude of two or three thousand feet, and, indeed, is found in greatest numbers at and above the higher of these altitudes, in the glens of the Fagus forest. I am inclined to think that these birds pair for life, as they are almost invariably found in couples at all seasons of the year. They are extremely active, hopping with long strides along the ground, and from branch to branch, in their search for insects. Their chief food, however, consists of sow-thistle and other succulent herbs, and it is remarkable that, in eating such substances, they hold them with the fist precisely as a parrot holds his food, tearing off and swallowing large fragments... The note of this bird is wonderfully sweet and plaintive, and, during the breeding season, its song is one of the most varied and beautiful of all the New Zealand birds. It appears, however, always to be pitched in a minor key. The male birds are very pugnacious, fighting, whenever they meet, with the greatest determination. They are still numerous in the forests adjoining my station, but I fear the wild cats are likely to clear them out within a few years."

~W. T. L. Travers, 1871

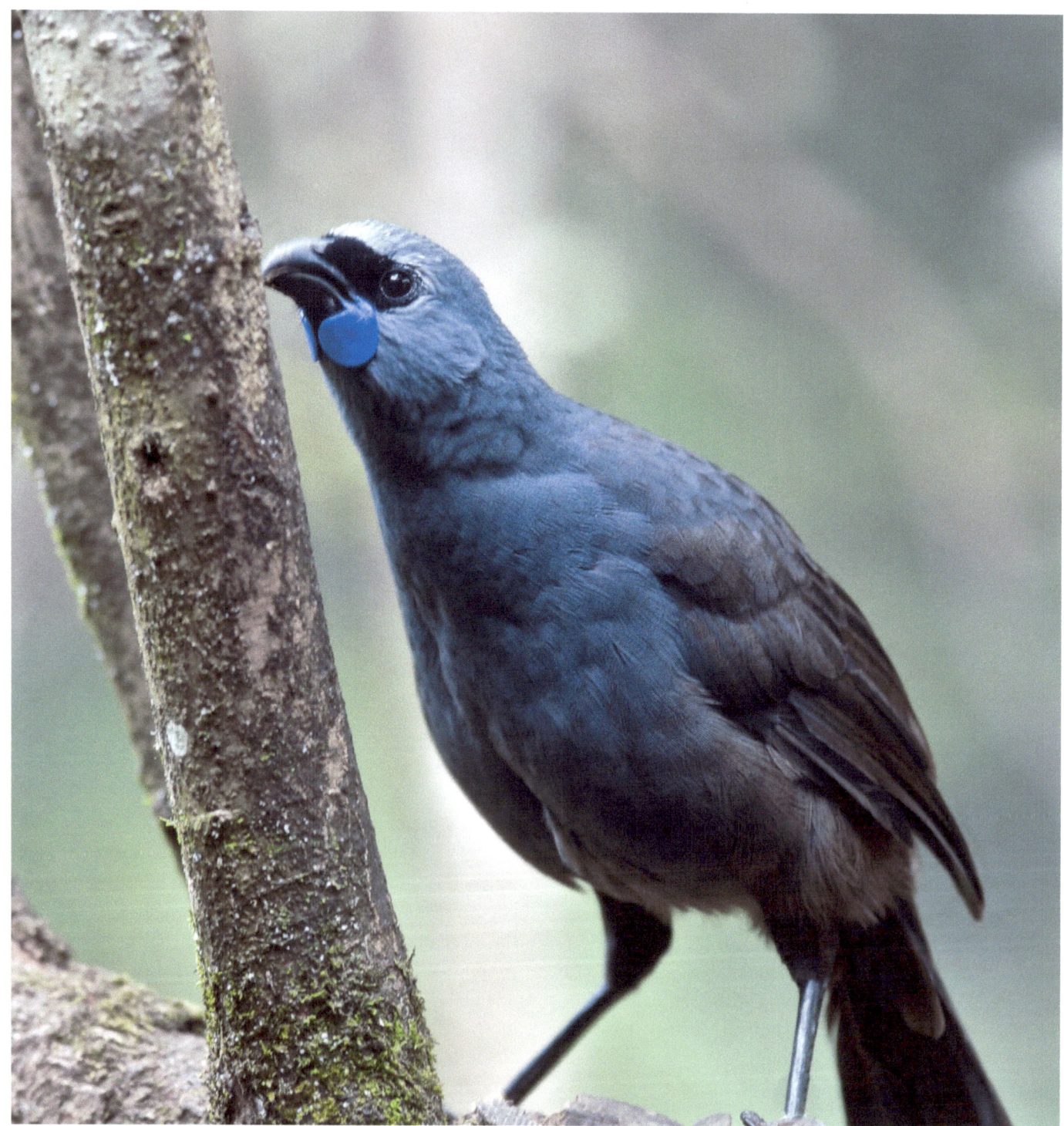

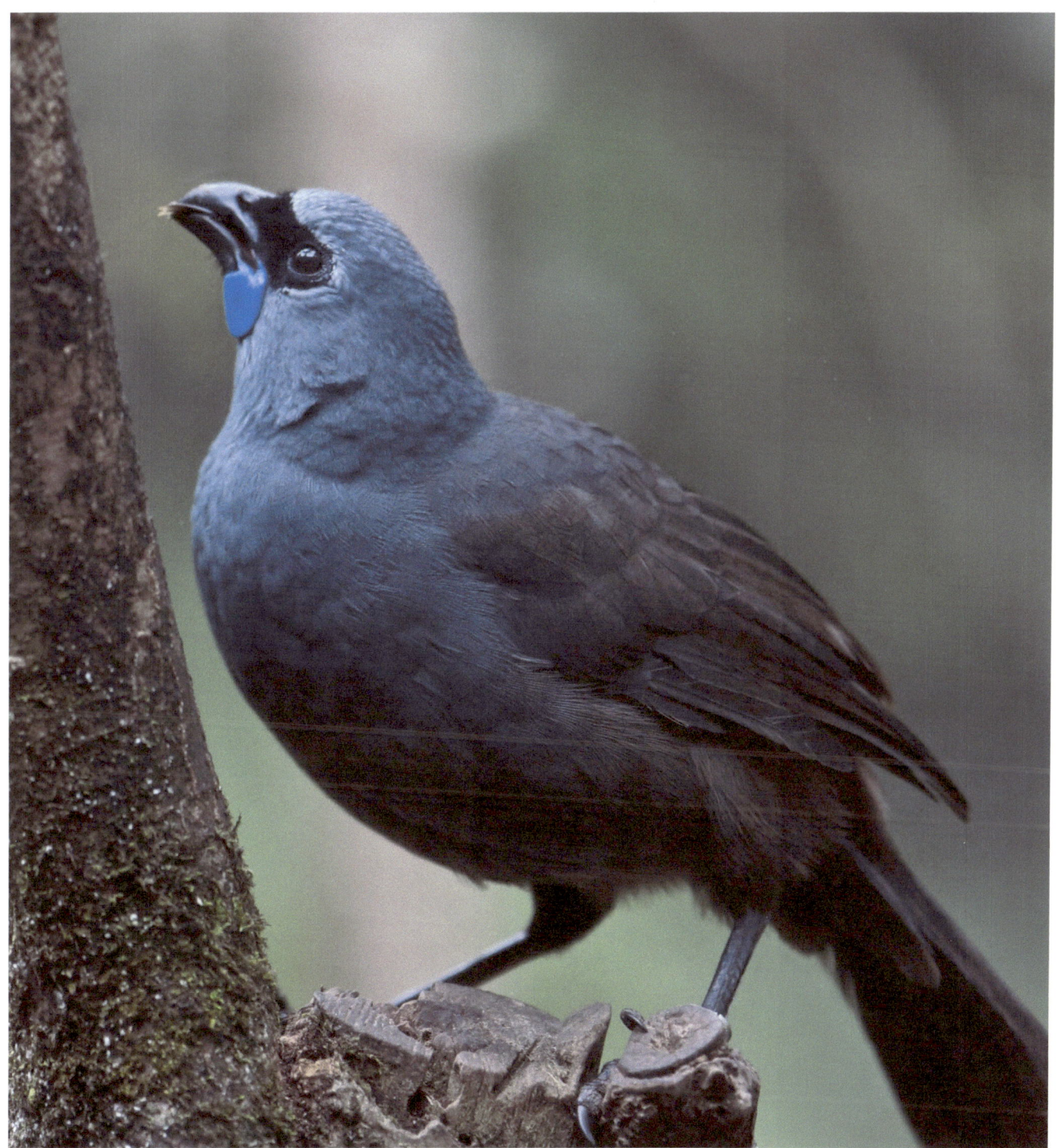

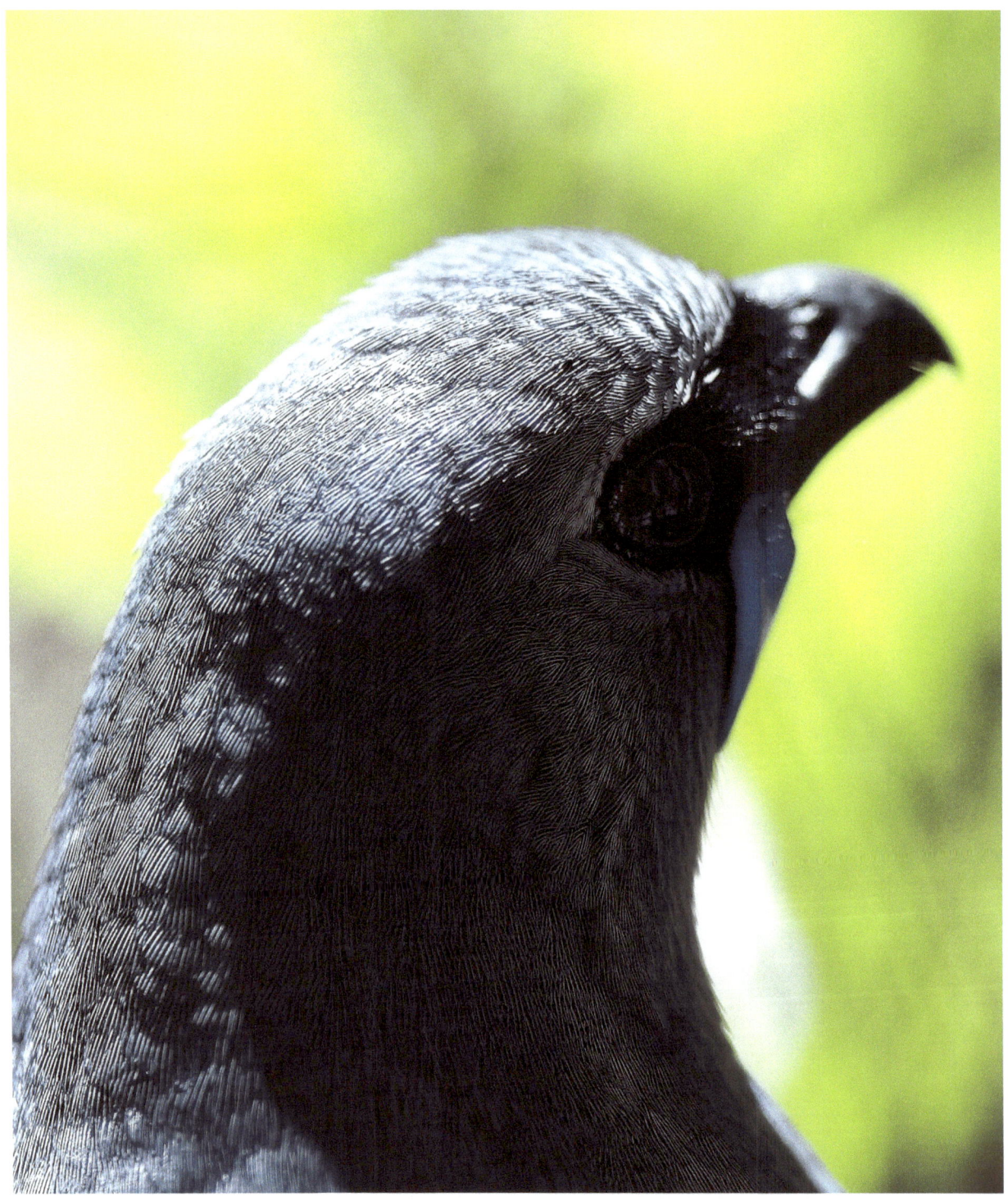

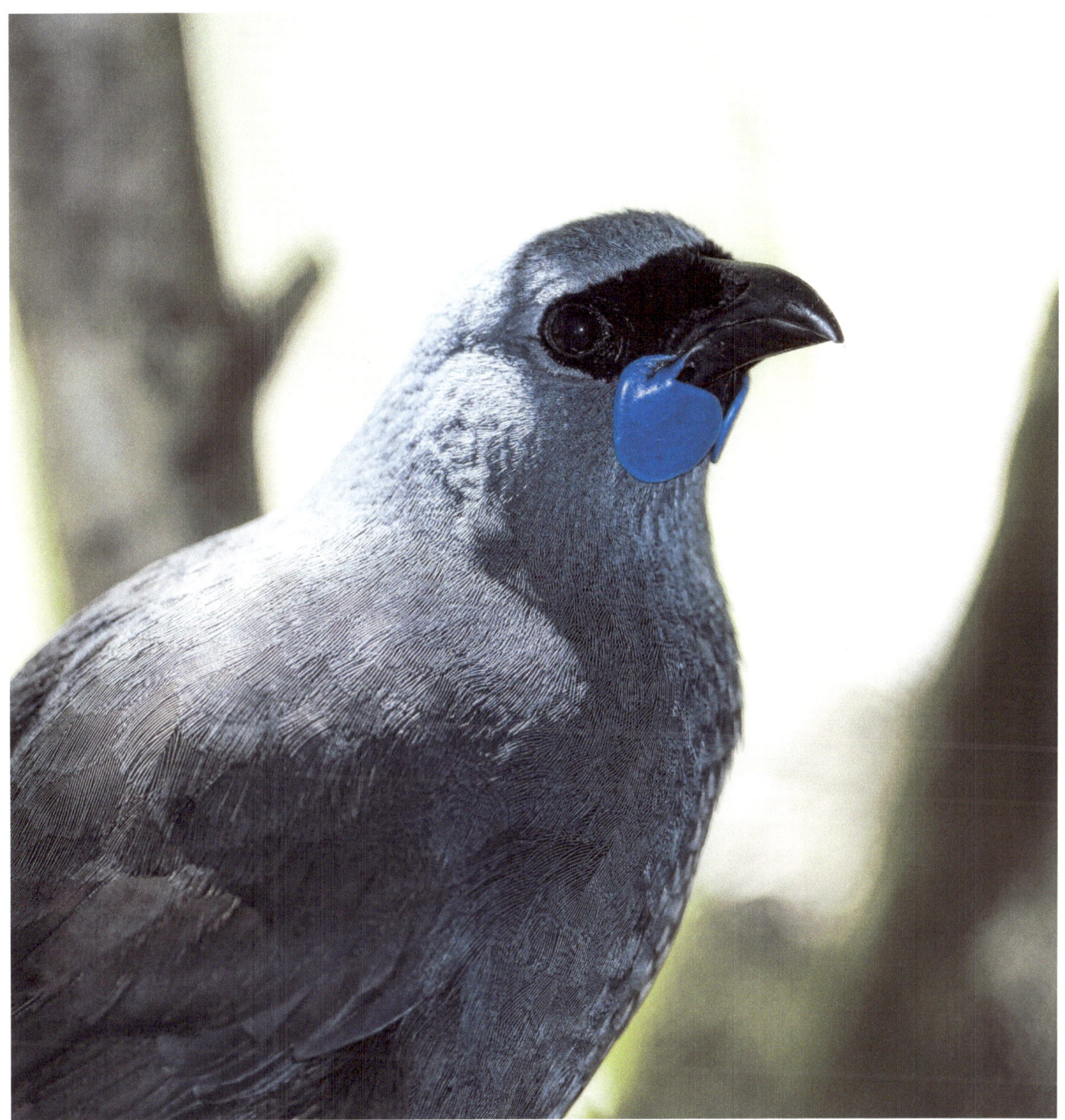

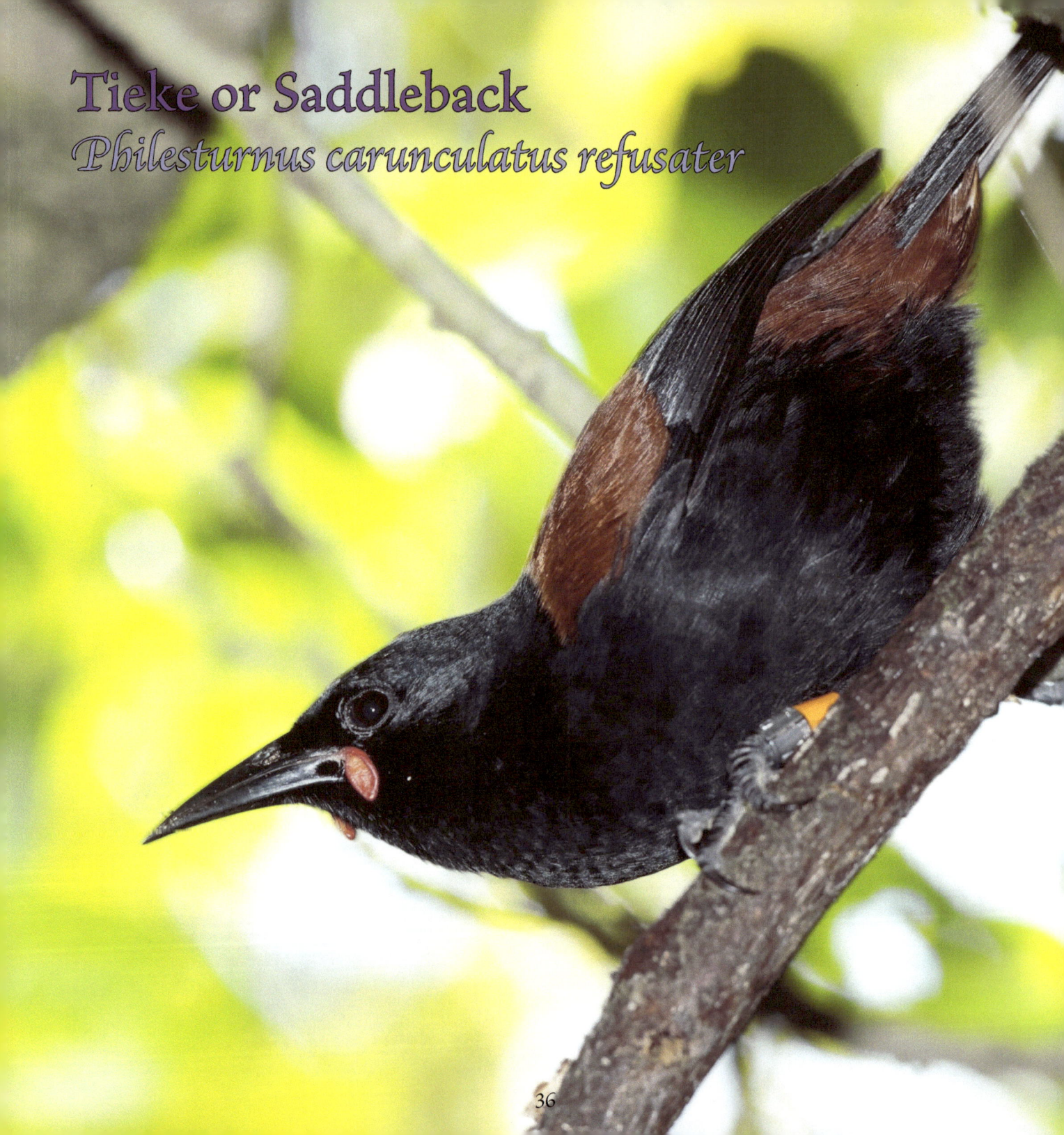

Tieke or Saddleback
Philesturnus carunculatus refusater

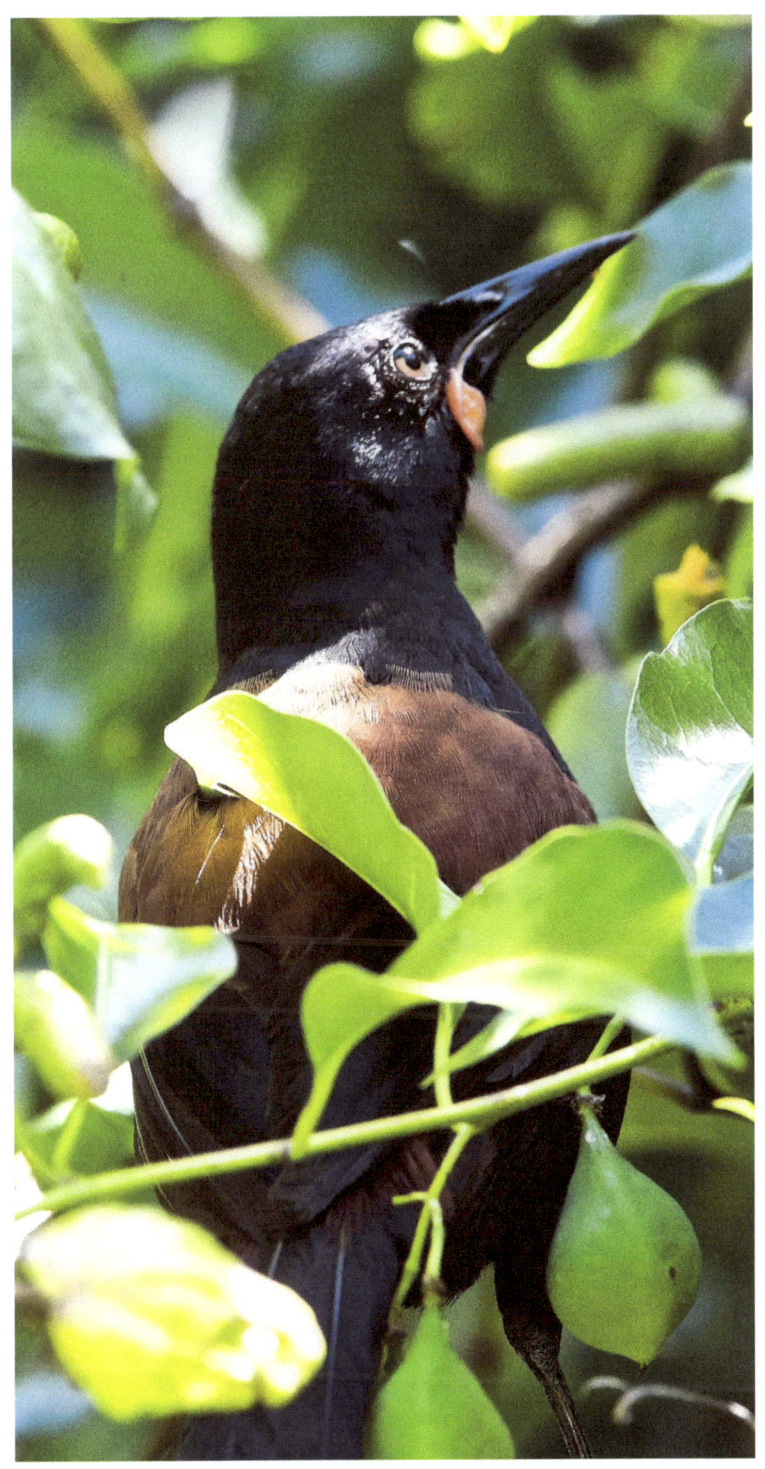

"This species is very irregular in its distribution. I have endeavoured to describe its range in my 'Birds of New Zealand.' I omitted, however, to mention that in one locality north of Auckland–a small wood at Kaitaia called Mauteringi, some three or four miles in extent–this bird is comparatively plentiful, although rarely ever met with in other parts of that district. Although never seen in the Bay of Plenty woods, it is numerous enough in the Ngatiporou country, where the natives regard it as a bird of omen. A war party hearing the cry of the tieke to the right of their path will count it an omen of victory, but to the left a signal of evil. It is also the mythical bird that is supposed to guard the ancient treasures of the Maoris. The relics of the Whanauapanui tribe–mere pounamus and other heir–looms of great antiquity and value–are hidden away in the hollow of a tree at Cape Runaway, and it is popularly believed that the tieke keeps guard over these lost treasures. According to Maori tradition, among these hidden things is a stone atua, which possessed at one time the faculty of moving from place to place of its own accord, but has since become inactive. The natives state that this species usually places its nest in the hollow of a tree, and they point to holes in well–known trees where the tieke has reared its young for many years in succession. A pair is said to be still breeding in the hollow of the famous tree at Omaruteangi, known all over the country as 'Putatieke.' The bird is accordingly regarded with some degree of superstitious reverence by the Arawa, who will not allow it to be wilfully destroyed. Those who have read Maori history will be familiar with the story of Ngatoroirangi and his sacred tiekes of Cuvier Island. Hence the proverb, 'Manu mohio kei Reponga,' commonly applied to a man wise in council, and used in the sense of our own proverbial saying 'Old birds are not to be caught with chaff.'"

~Walter L. Buller, 1877

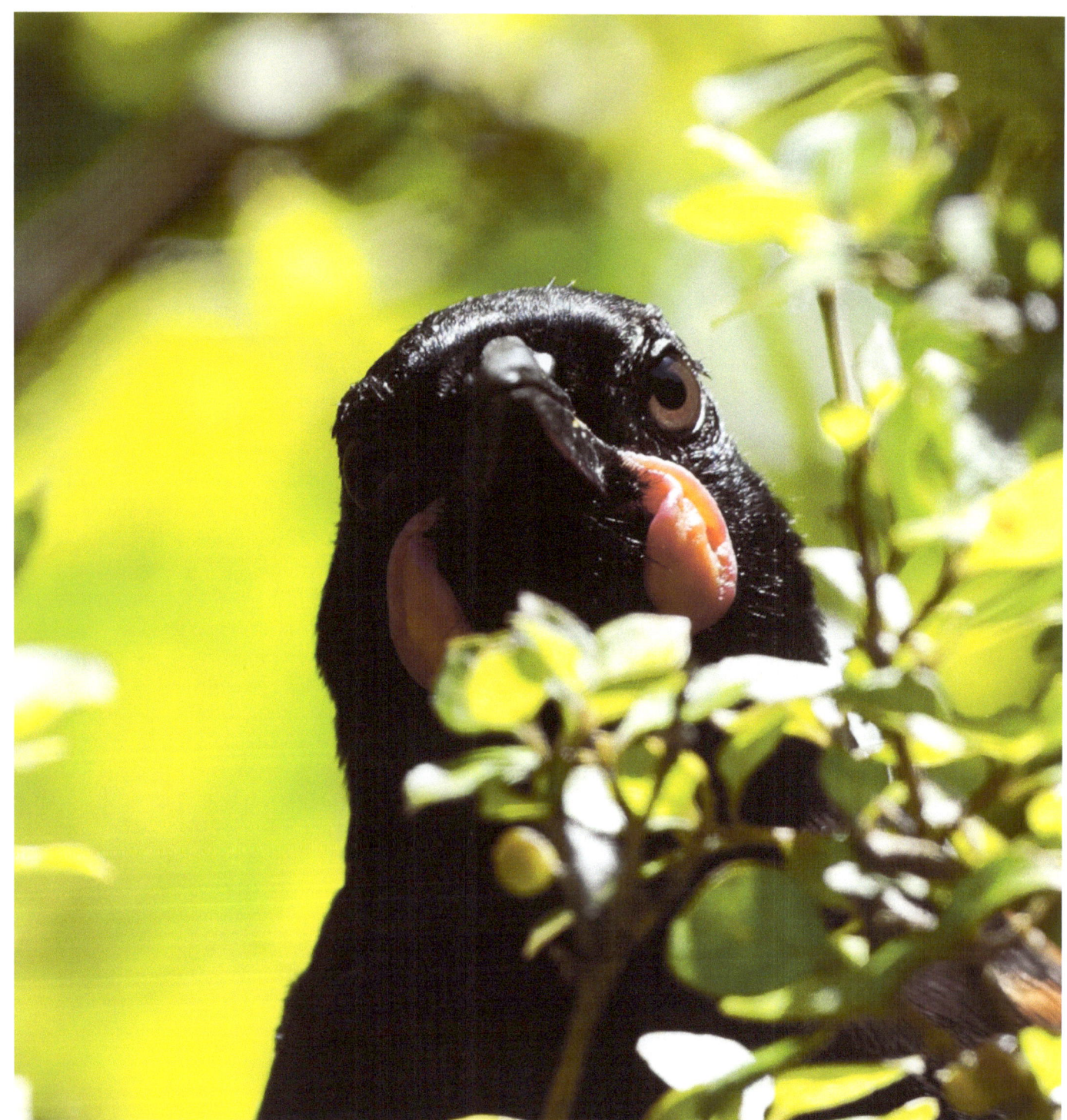

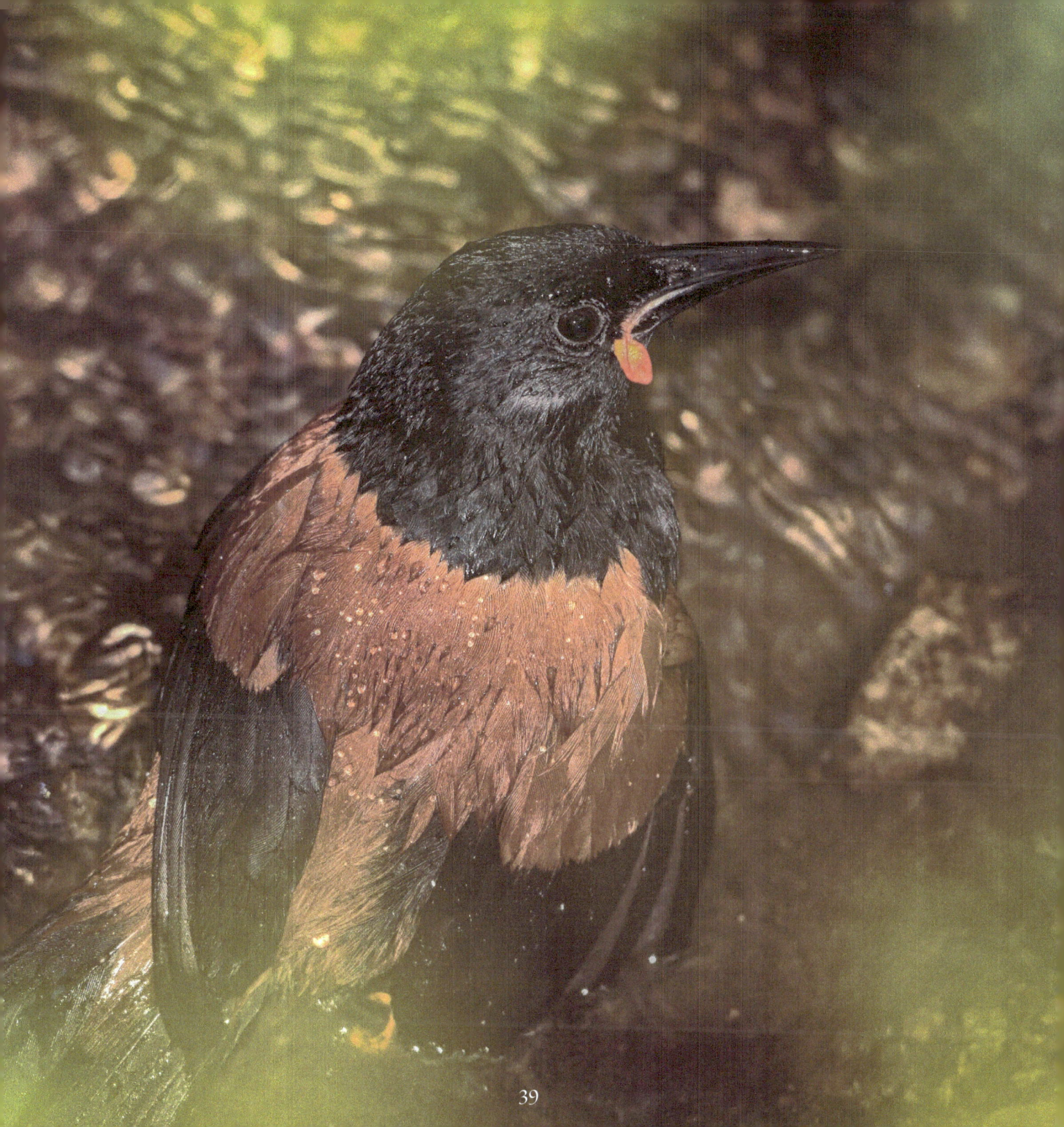

Toutouwai or North Island Robin
Petroica australis longipes

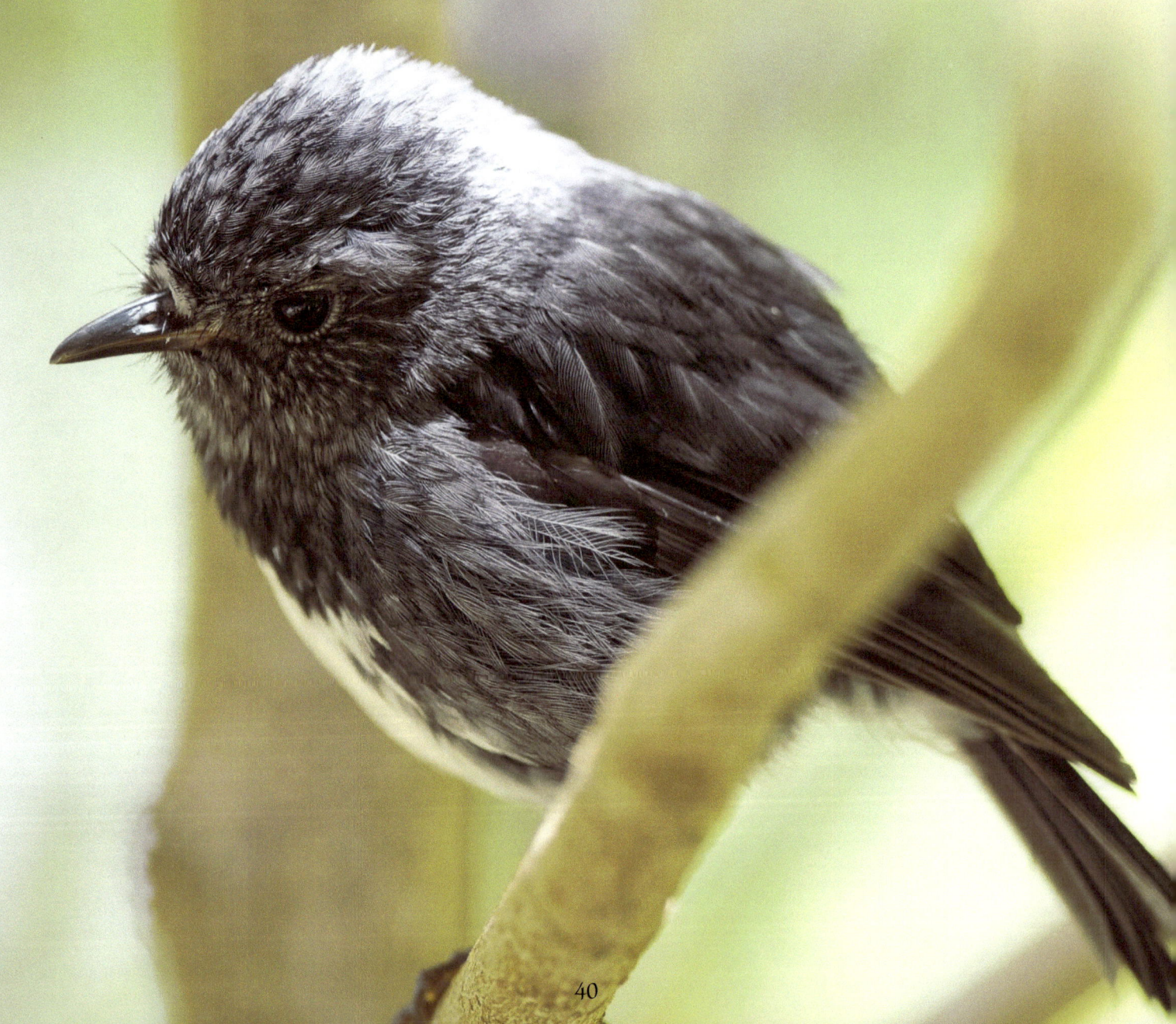

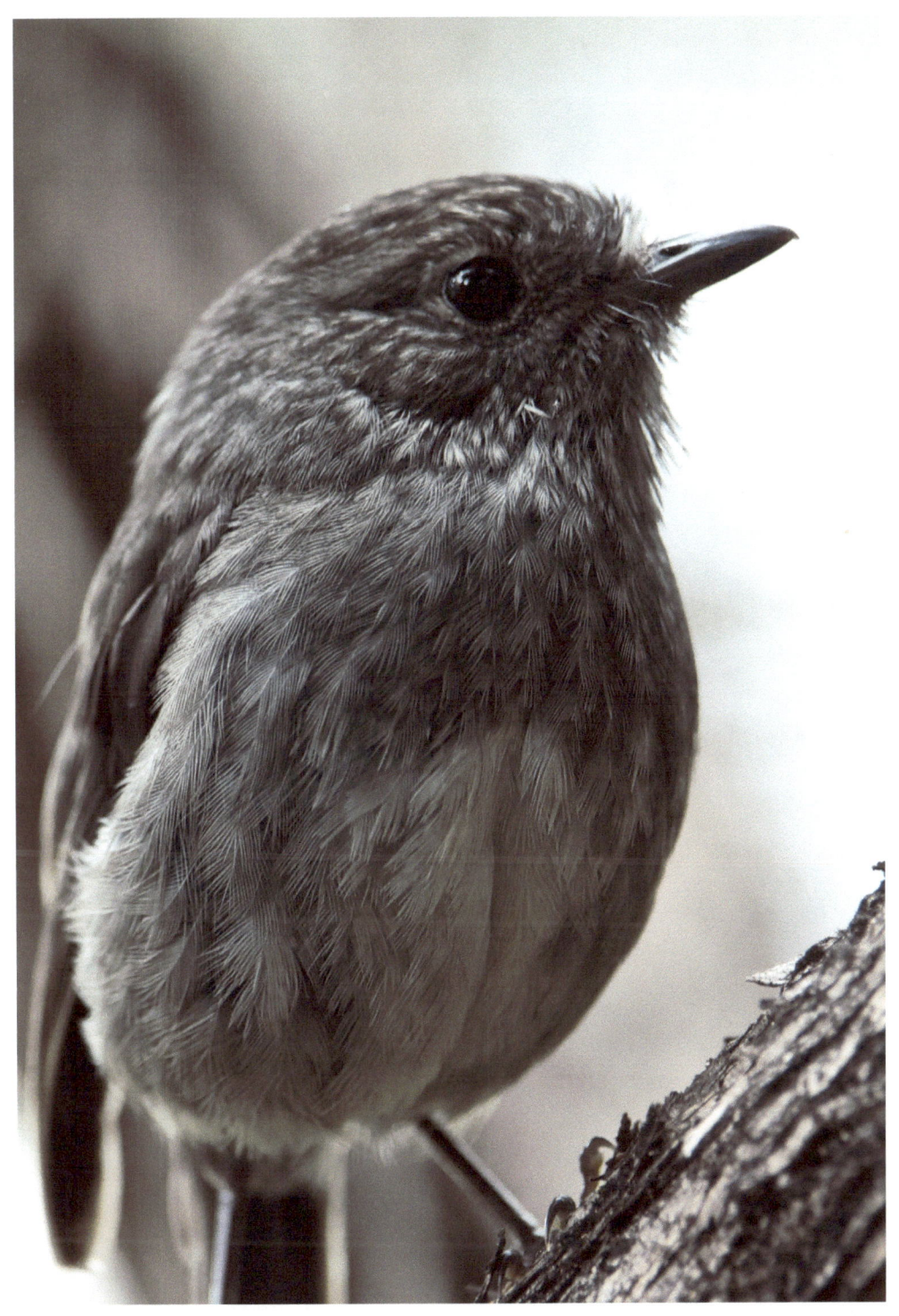

"The Robin... is a very bold bird, its tameness evidently springing not merely from a sense of security, but also from an absence of fear. It is to be found in every part of the forest, and the traveller rarely rests for a few minutes before one of them is to be seen seeking for insects on the ground disturbed by his footsteps, or upon the site of some piece of decayed wood which he may have moved. I have had these birds more than once sitting on my head as I lay on the ground, and hopping about me pecking at my watch chain, or at anything else which took their fancy. On one occasion I fed one with crumbs of bread, which it ate readily. After satisfying its hunger, it proceeded to hide what it could not eat under the edges of foliaceous lichens upon a gnarled old tree close to where I was sitting, no doubt resorting to this store when it next felt hungry. As Mr. Potts has observed, the song of this bird is sweet, but, as I think, wanting in continuity. However, it is an amusing little fellow, and its familiarity diminishes that sense of loneliness which is always more or less inspired by the stillness and monotony of the great Beech forests."

~W. T. L. Travers, 1871

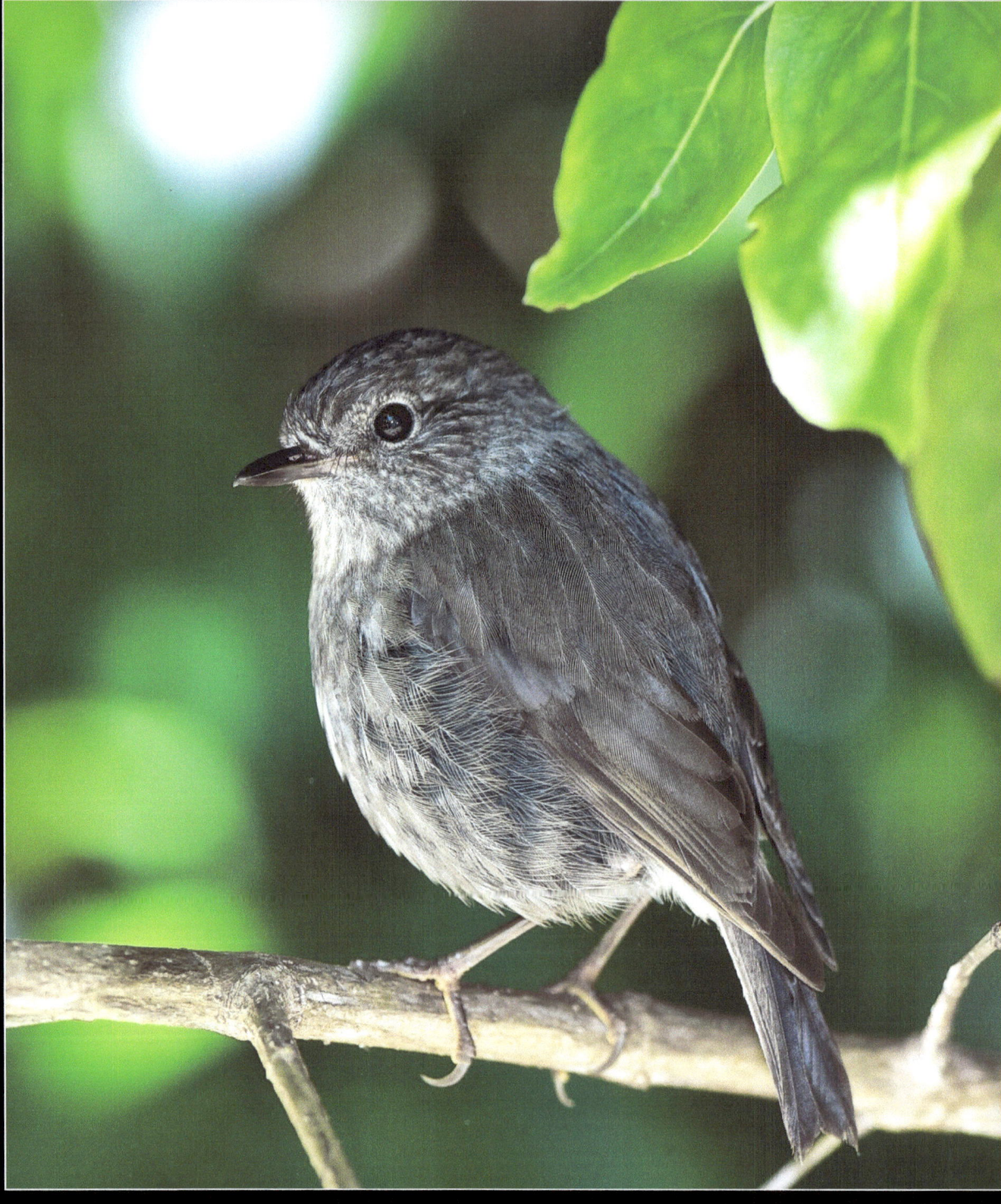

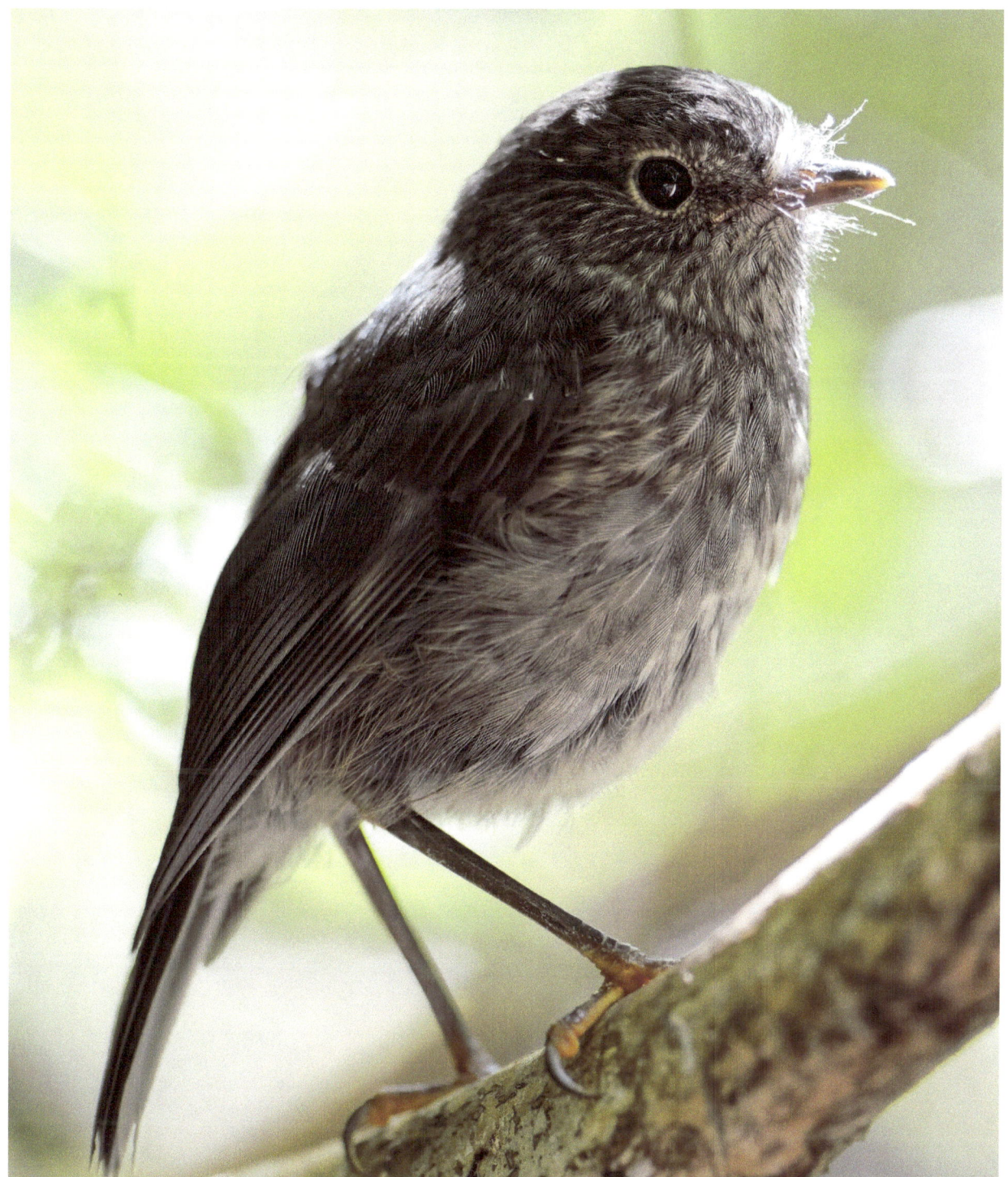

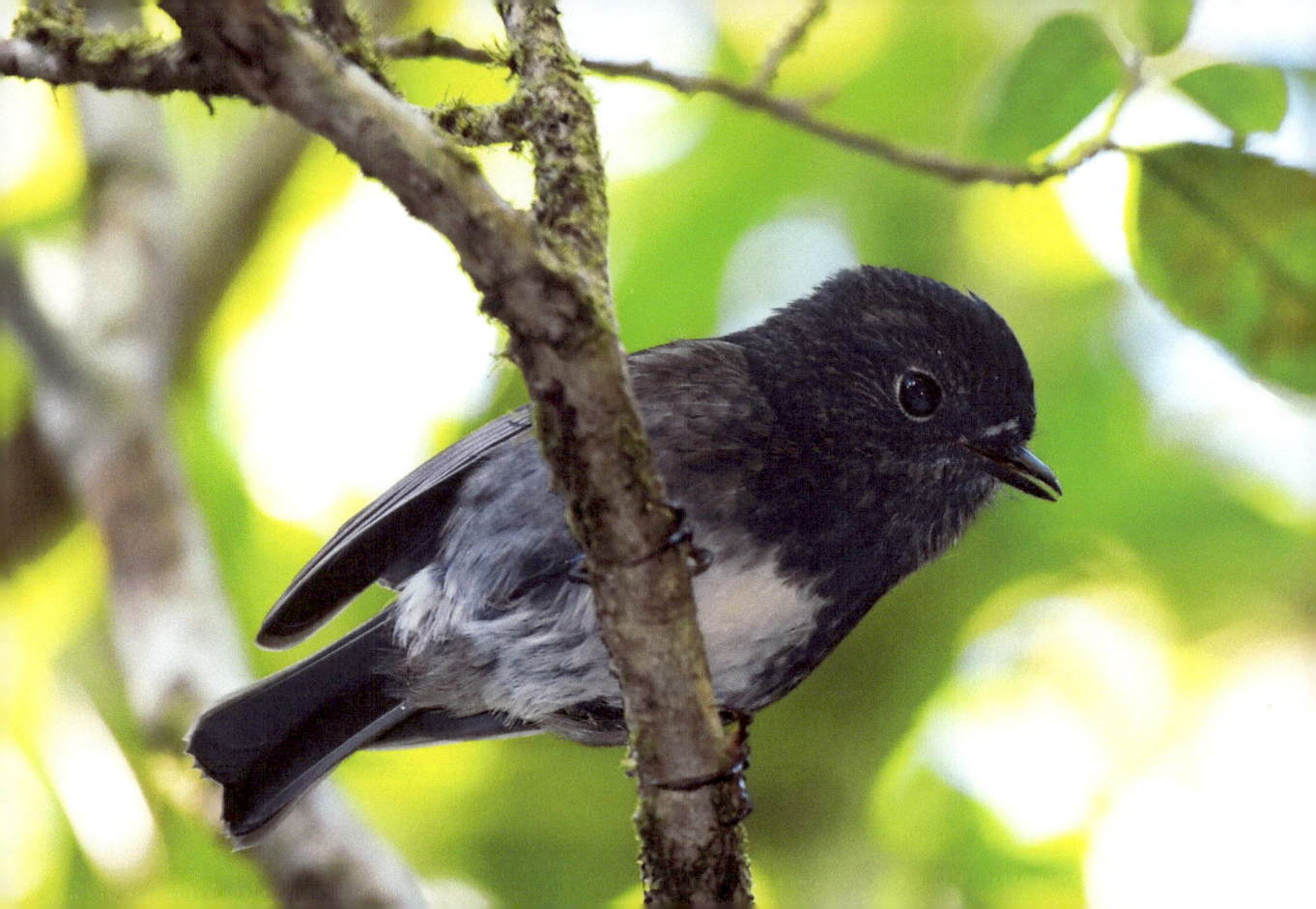

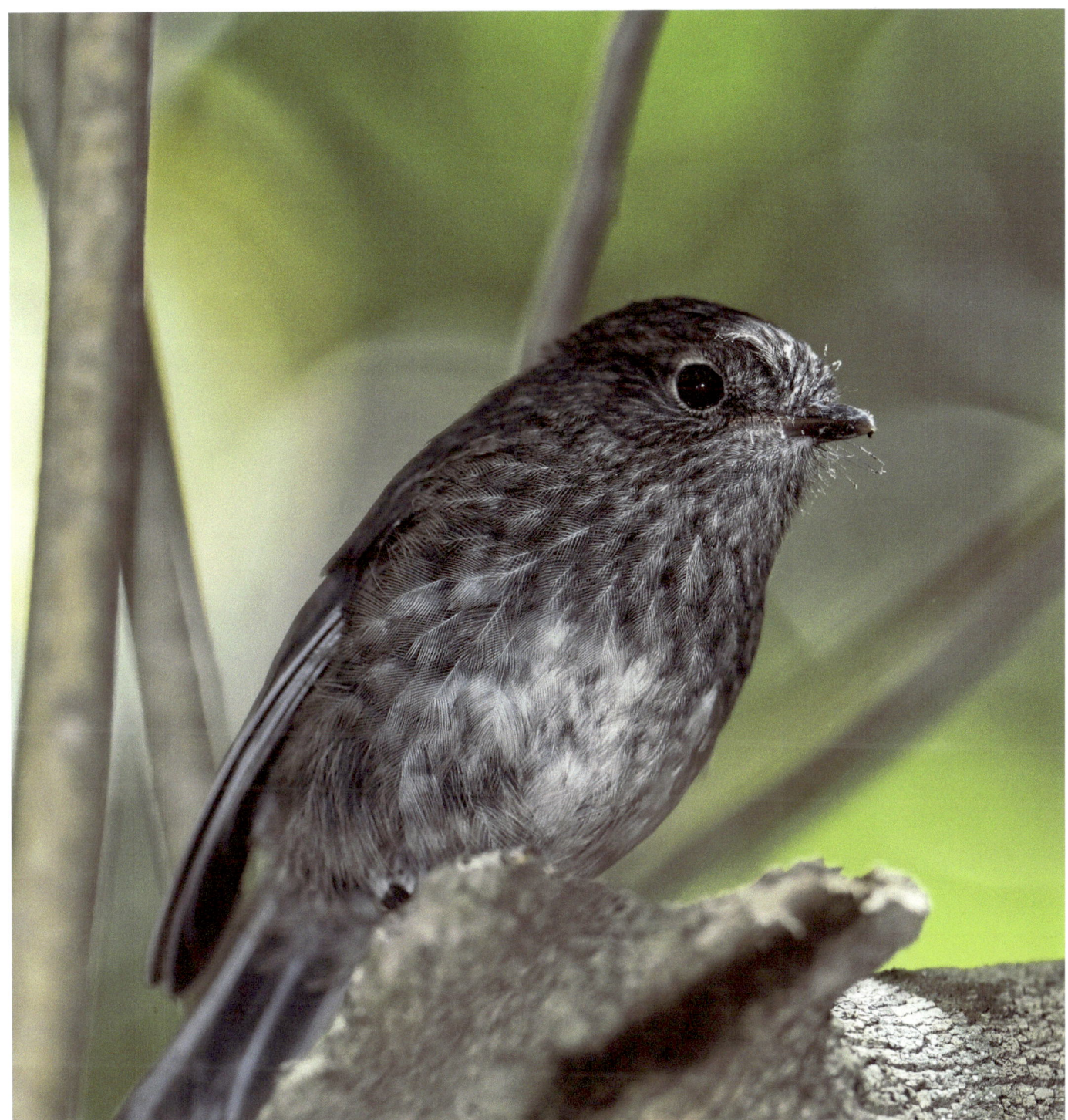

Miromiro or Tomtit
Petroica macrocephala toitoi

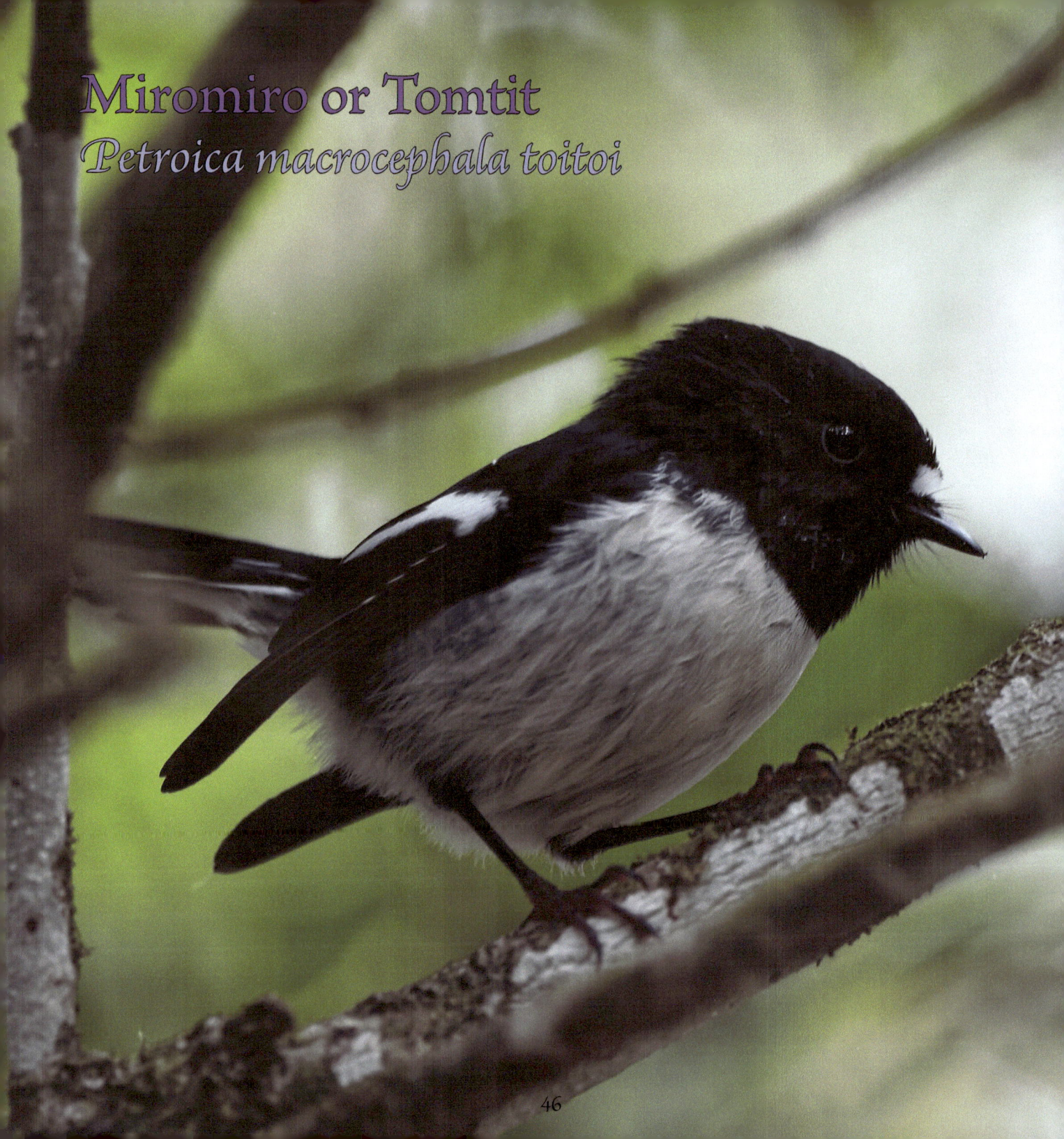

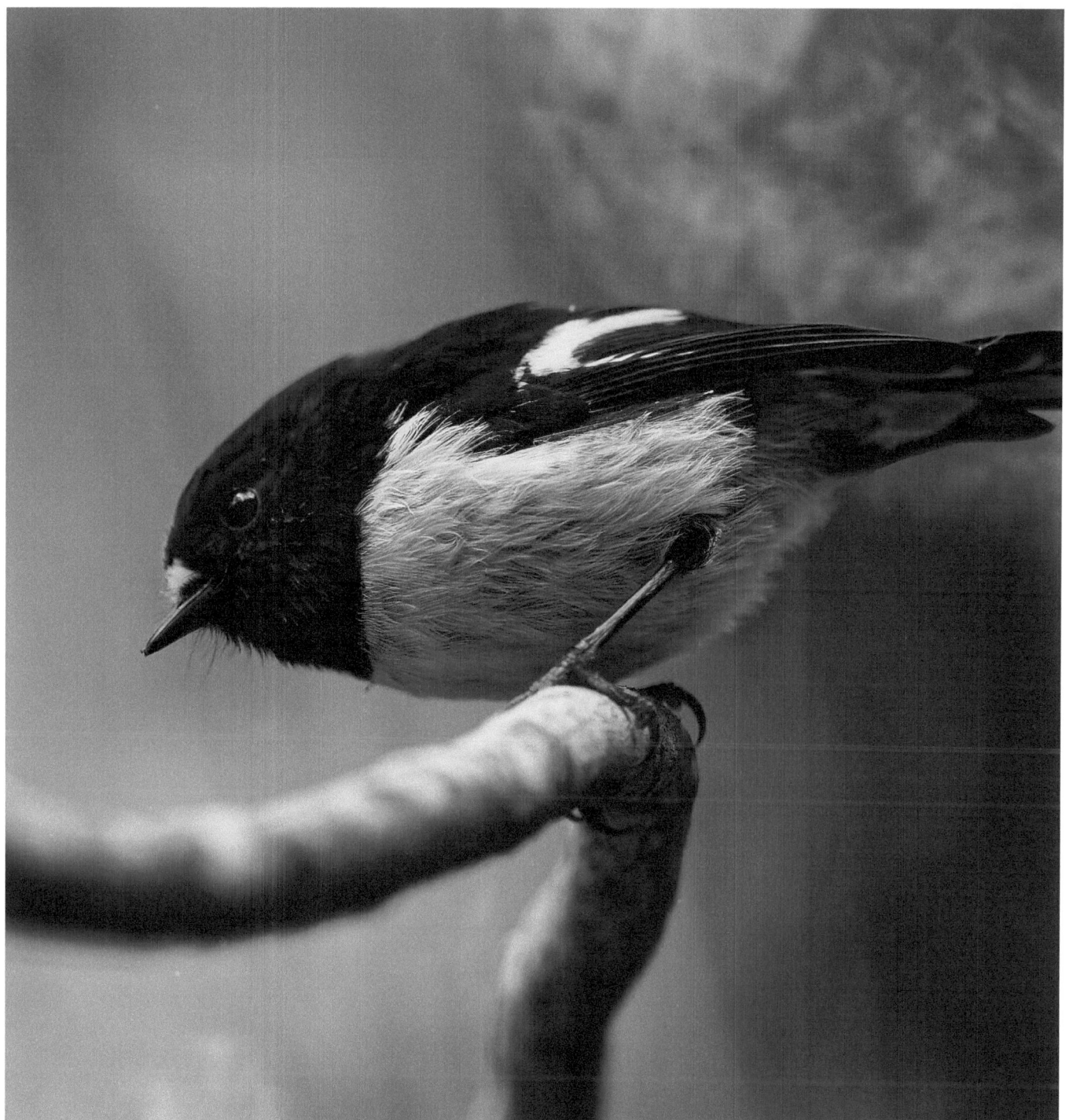

Popokotea or Whitehead
Mohoua albicilla

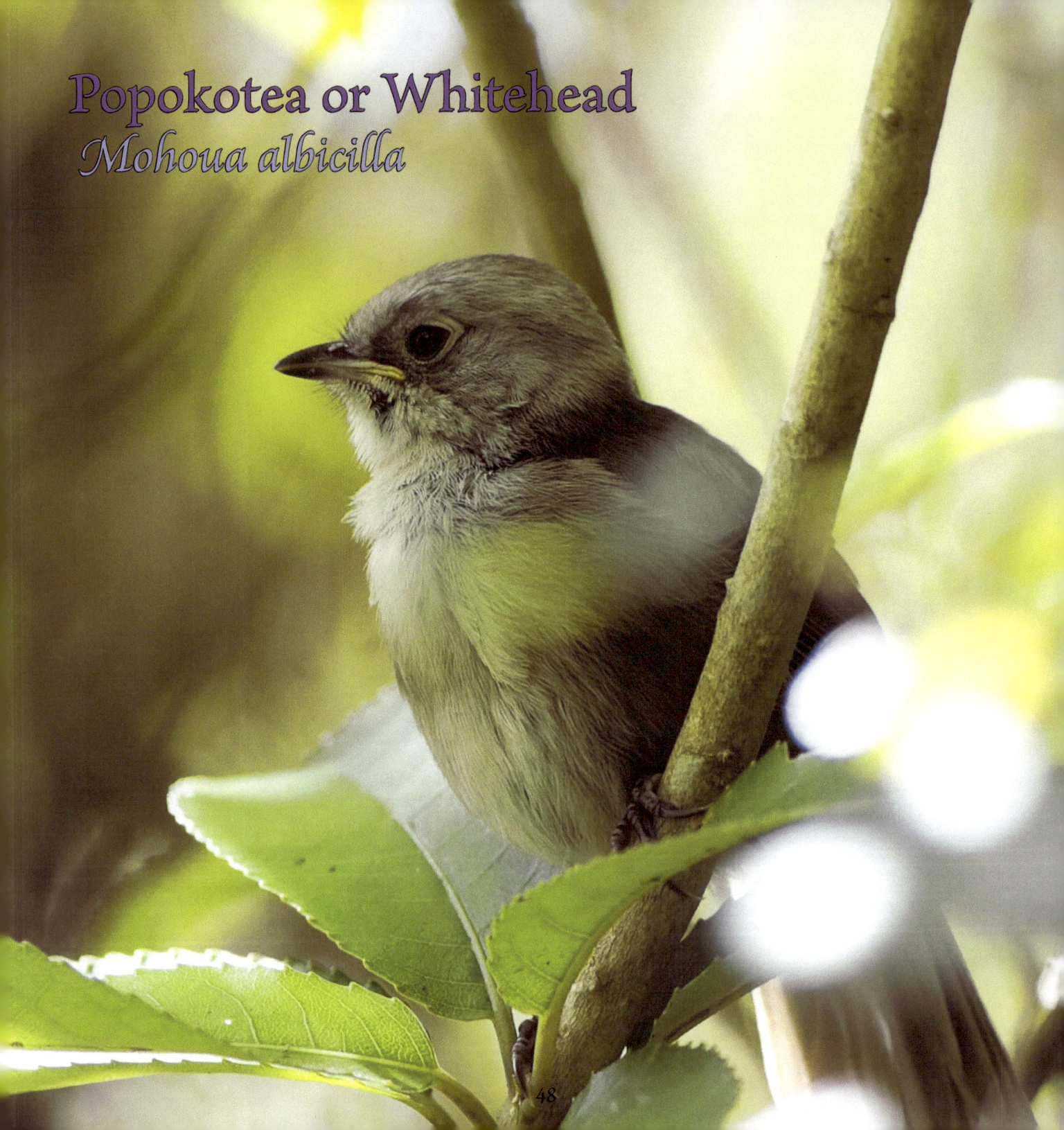

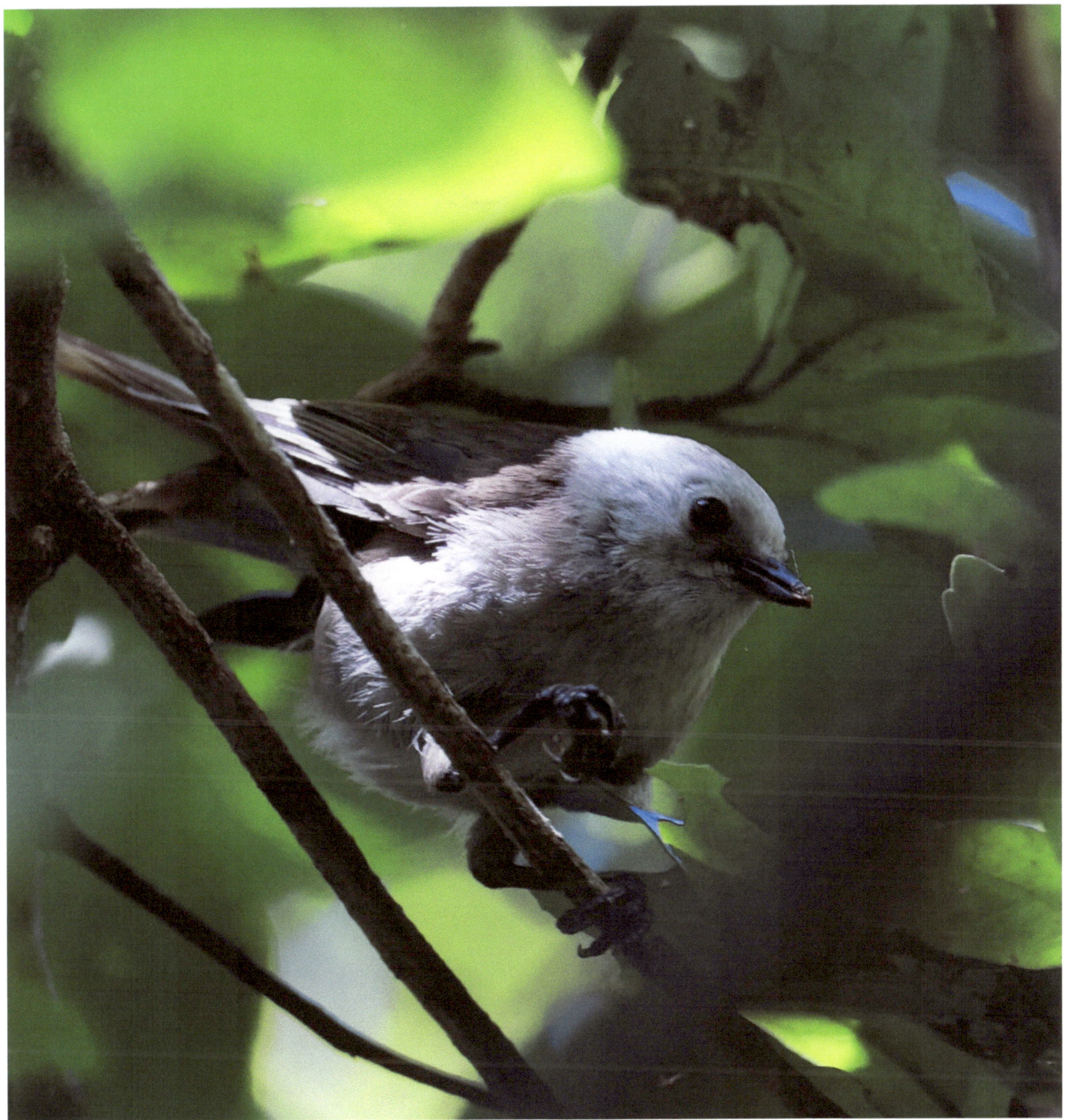

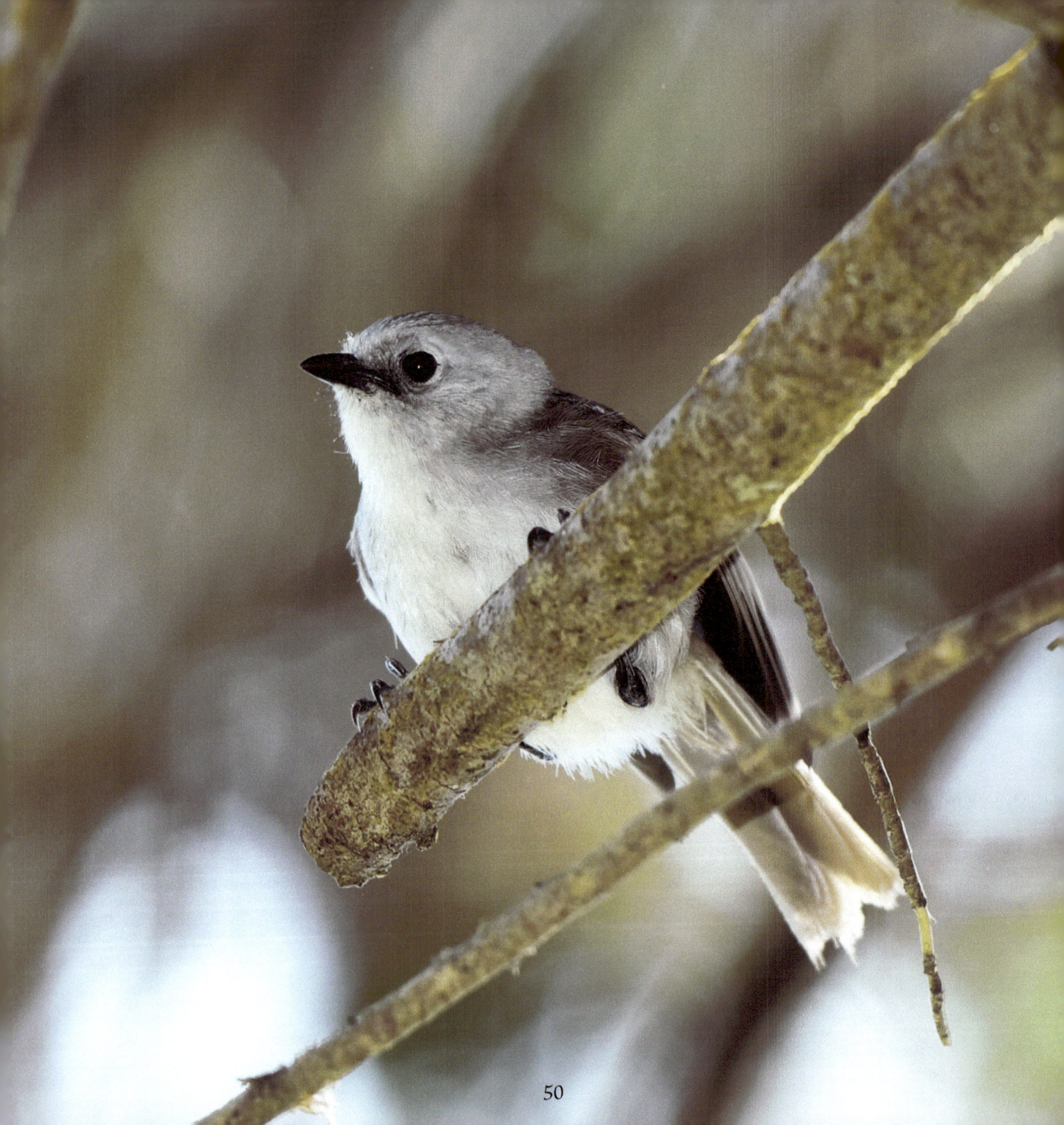

Riroriro or Grey Warbler
Gerygone igata

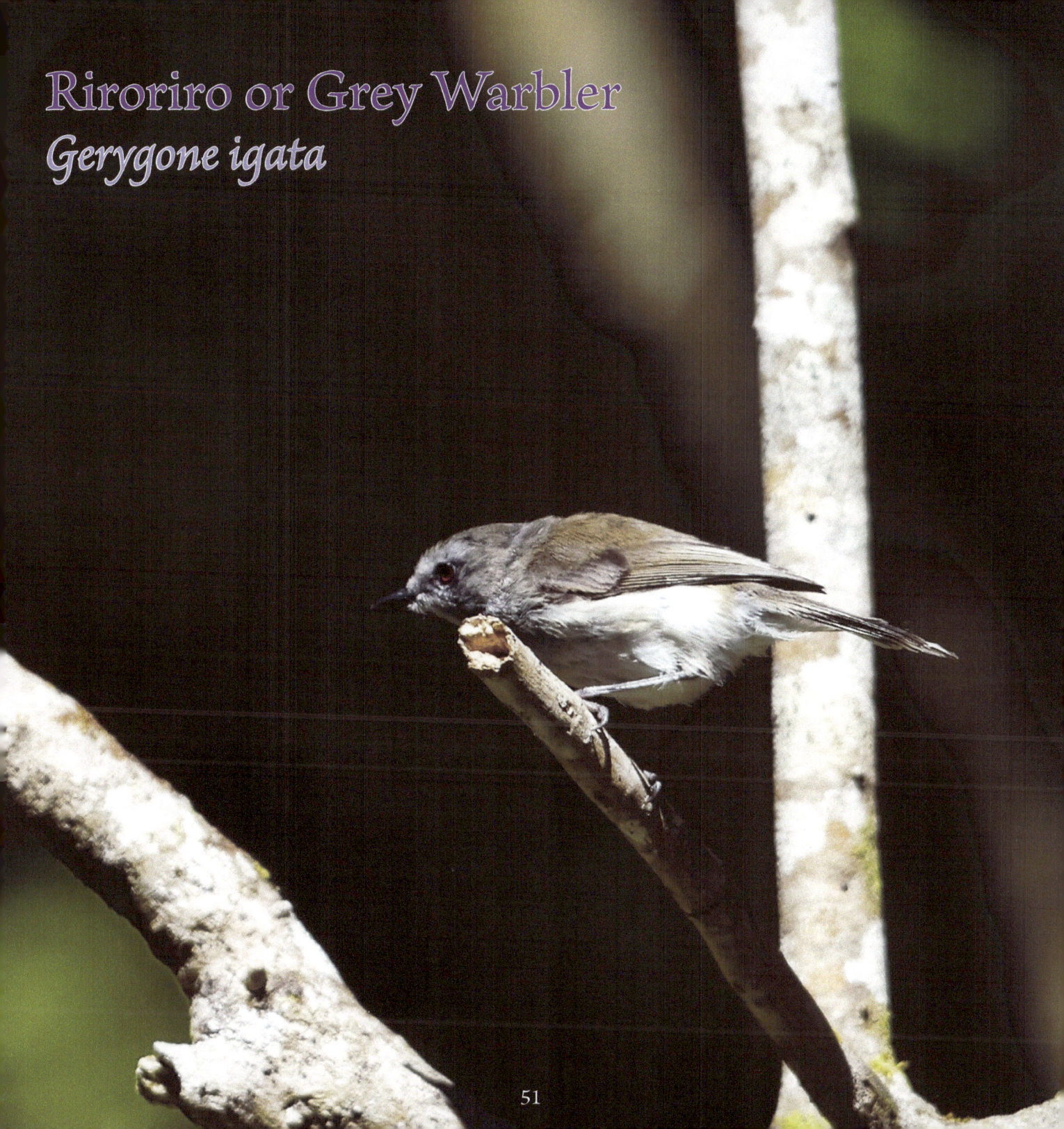

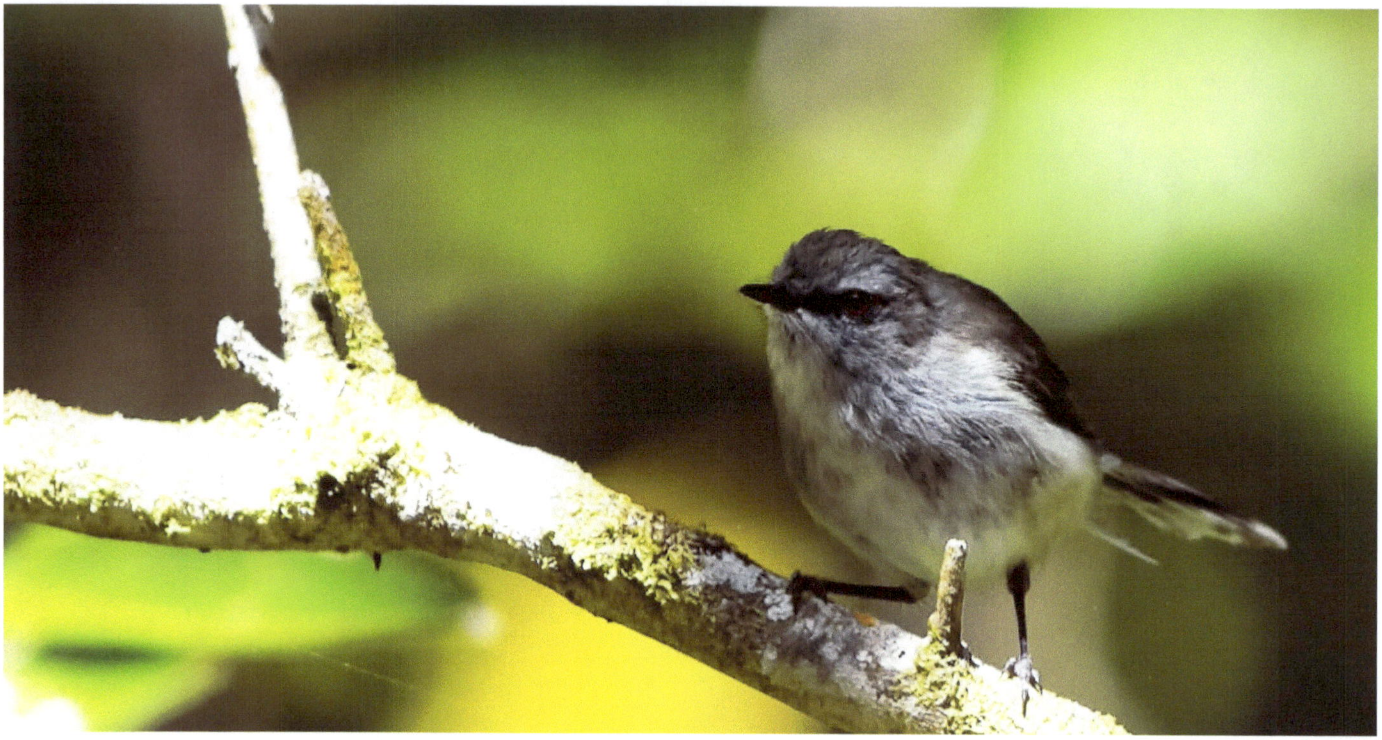

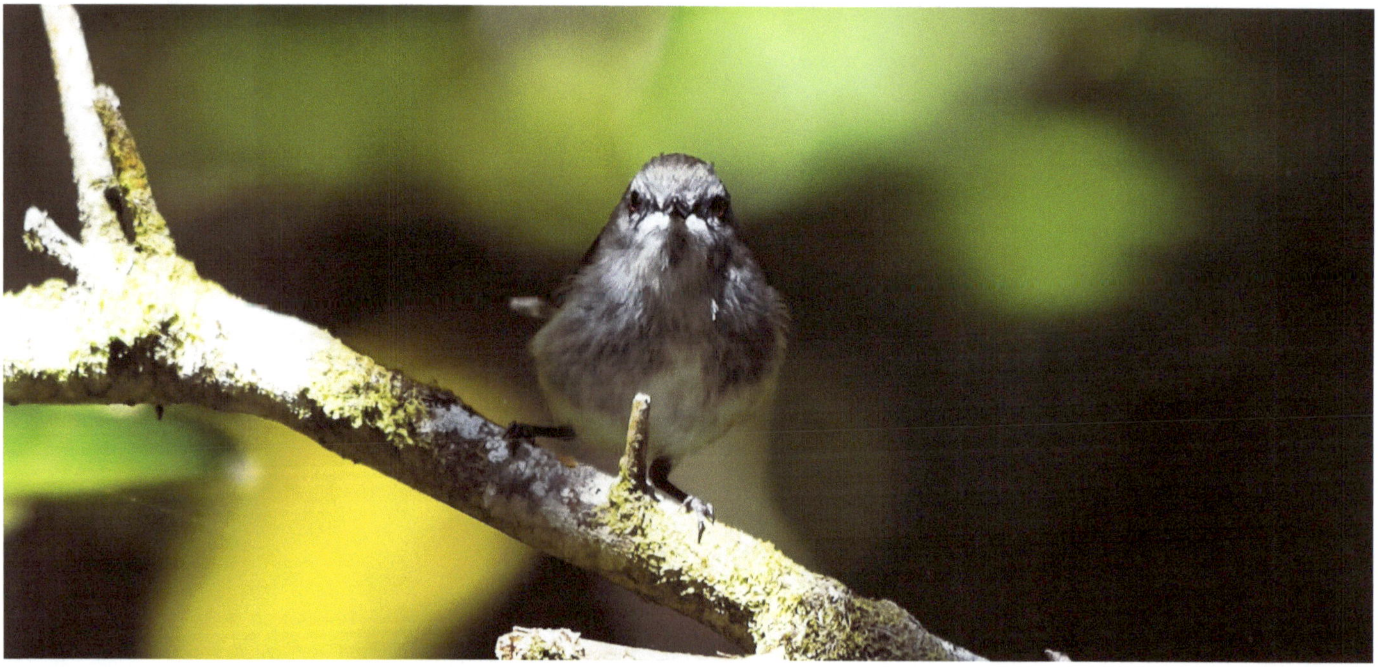

52

Piwakawaka or North Island Fantail
Rhipidura fuliginosa placabilis

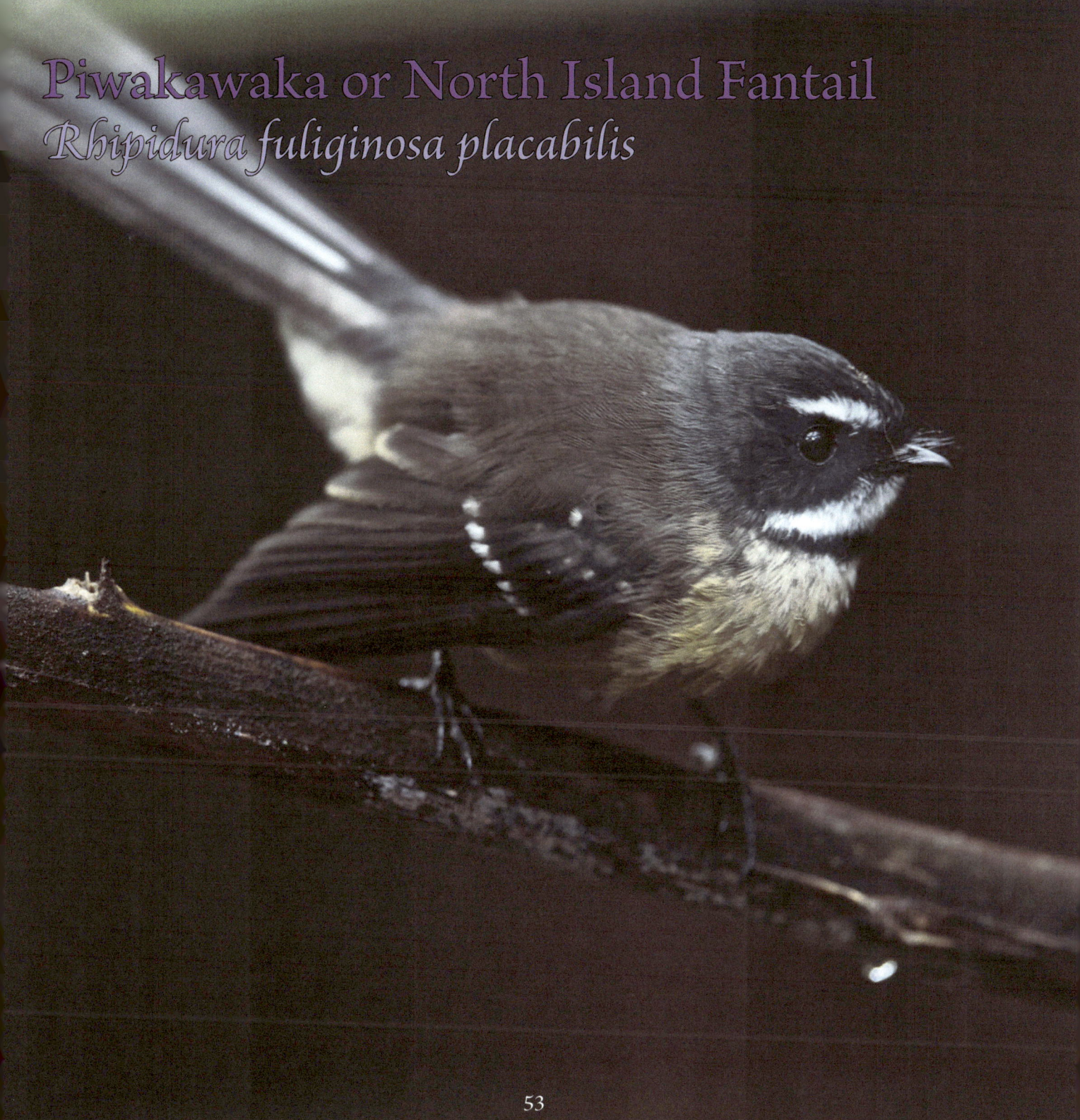

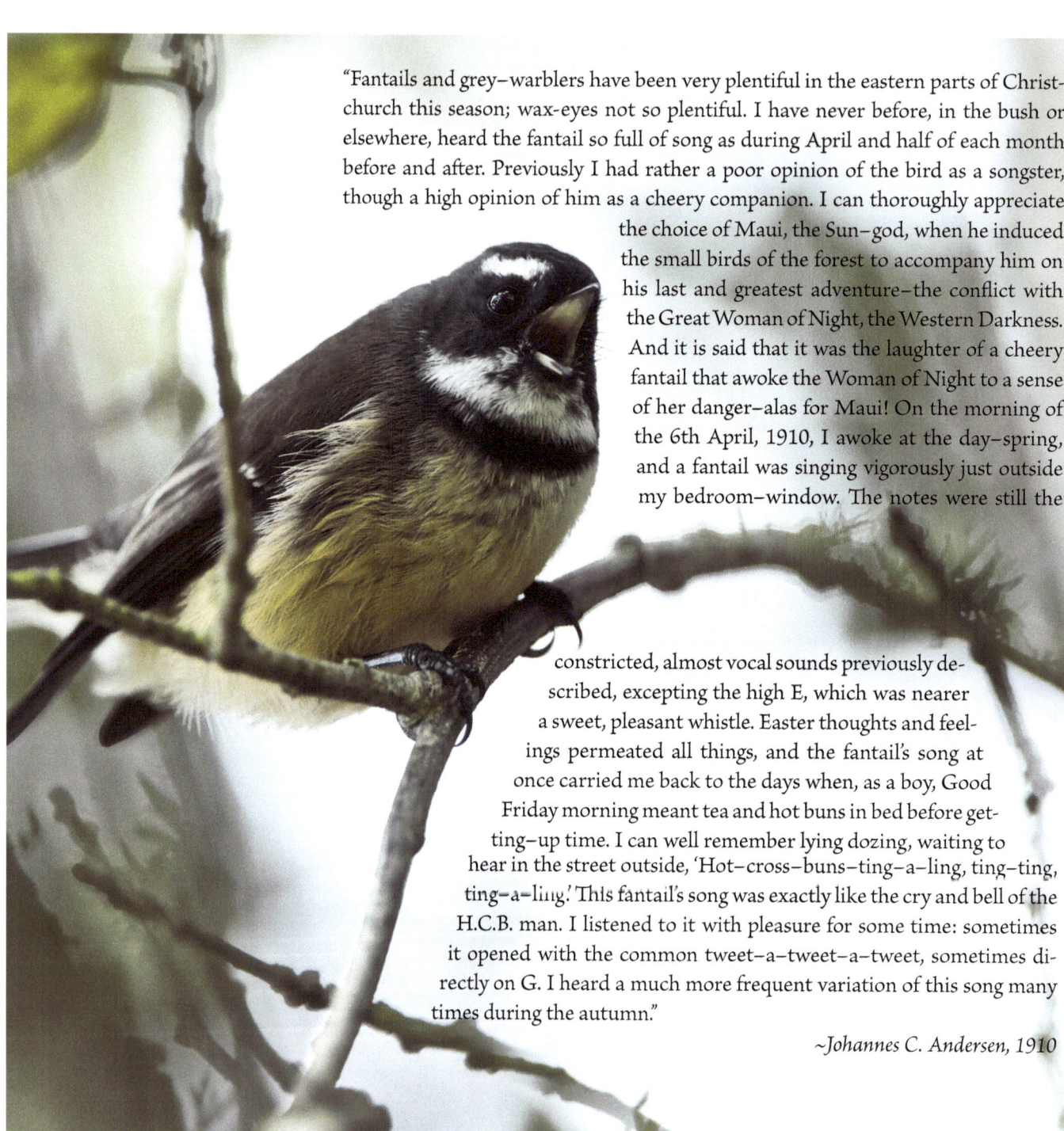

"Fantails and grey-warblers have been very plentiful in the eastern parts of Christchurch this season; wax-eyes not so plentiful. I have never before, in the bush or elsewhere, heard the fantail so full of song as during April and half of each month before and after. Previously I had rather a poor opinion of the bird as a songster, though a high opinion of him as a cheery companion. I can thoroughly appreciate the choice of Maui, the Sun-god, when he induced the small birds of the forest to accompany him on his last and greatest adventure—the conflict with the Great Woman of Night, the Western Darkness. And it is said that it was the laughter of a cheery fantail that awoke the Woman of Night to a sense of her danger—alas for Maui! On the morning of the 6th April, 1910, I awoke at the day-spring, and a fantail was singing vigorously just outside my bedroom-window. The notes were still the constricted, almost vocal sounds previously described, excepting the high E, which was nearer a sweet, pleasant whistle. Easter thoughts and feelings permeated all things, and the fantail's song at once carried me back to the days when, as a boy, Good Friday morning meant tea and hot buns in bed before getting-up time. I can well remember lying dozing, waiting to hear in the street outside, 'Hot-cross-buns-ting-a-ling, ting-ting, ting-a-ling.' This fantail's song was exactly like the cry and bell of the H.C.B. man. I listened to it with pleasure for some time: sometimes it opened with the common tweet-a-tweet-a-tweet, sometimes directly on G. I heard a much more frequent variation of this song many times during the autumn."

~Johannes C. Andersen, 1910

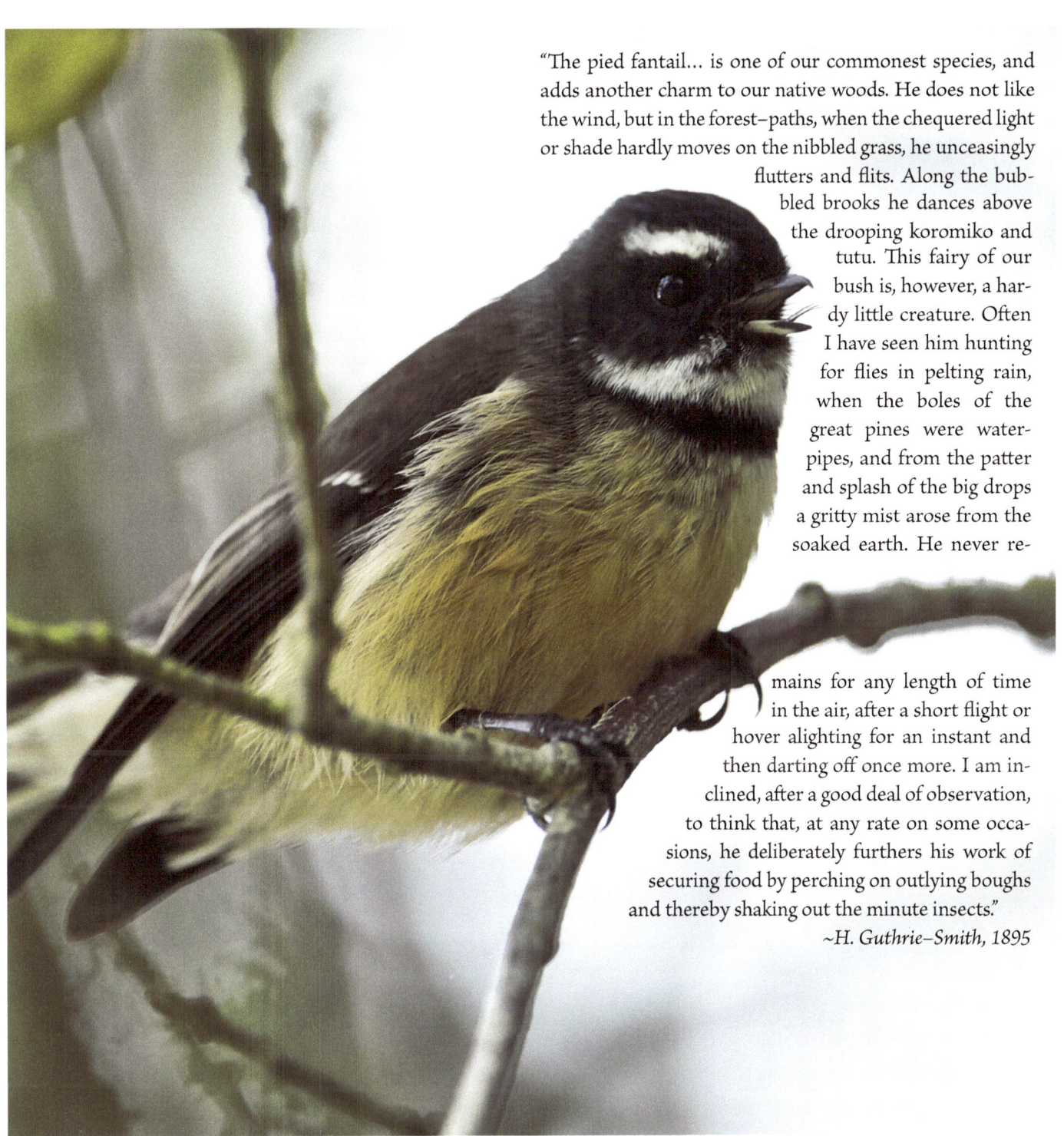

"The pied fantail... is one of our commonest species, and adds another charm to our native woods. He does not like the wind, but in the forest–paths, when the chequered light or shade hardly moves on the nibbled grass, he unceasingly flutters and flits. Along the bubbled brooks he dances above the drooping koromiko and tutu. This fairy of our bush is, however, a hardy little creature. Often I have seen him hunting for flies in pelting rain, when the boles of the great pines were waterpipes, and from the patter and splash of the big drops a gritty mist arose from the soaked earth. He never remains for any length of time in the air, after a short flight or hover alighting for an instant and then darting off once more. I am inclined, after a good deal of observation, to think that, at any rate on some occasions, he deliberately furthers his work of securing food by perching on outlying boughs and thereby shaking out the minute insects."
~H. Guthrie-Smith, 1895

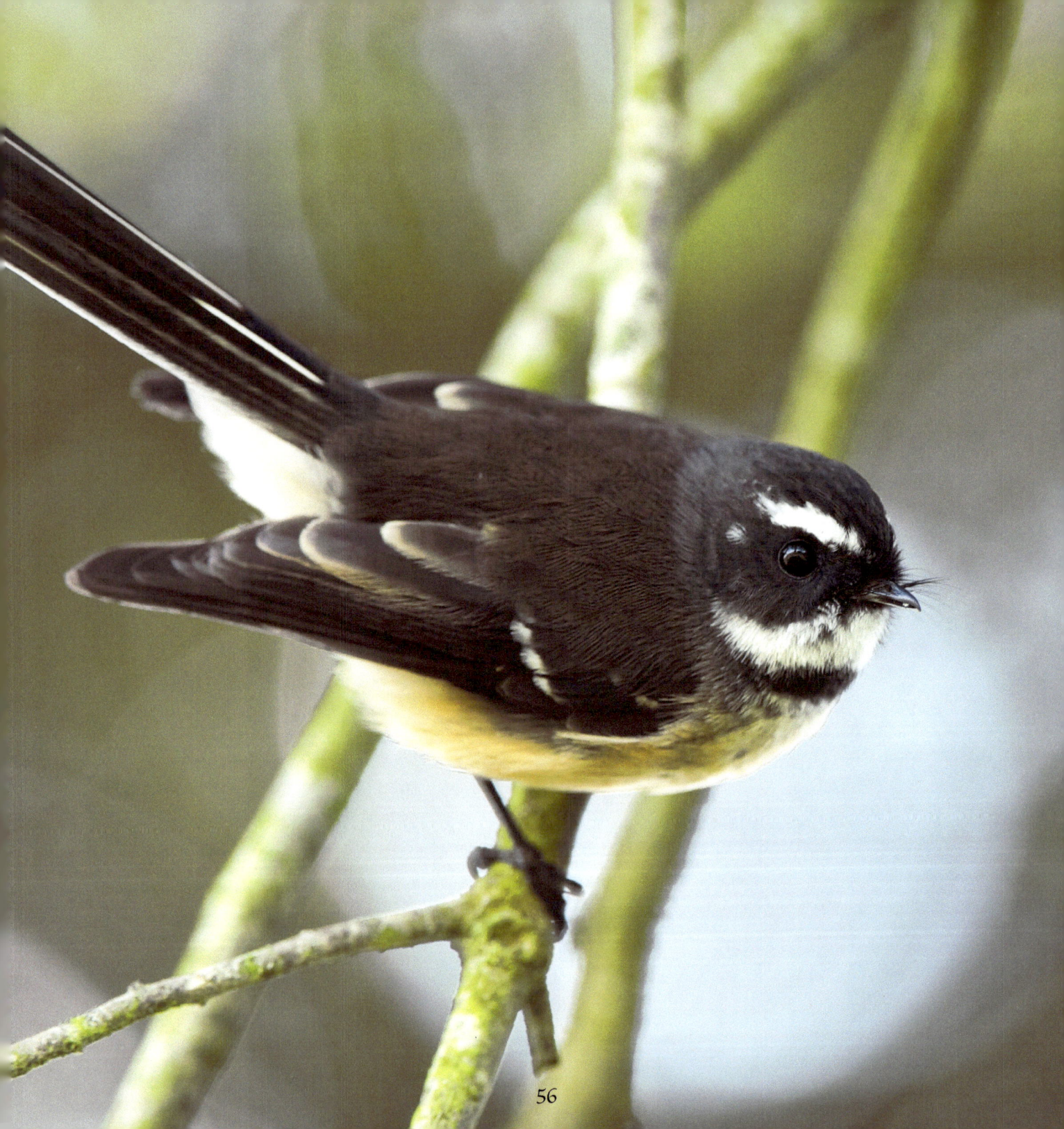

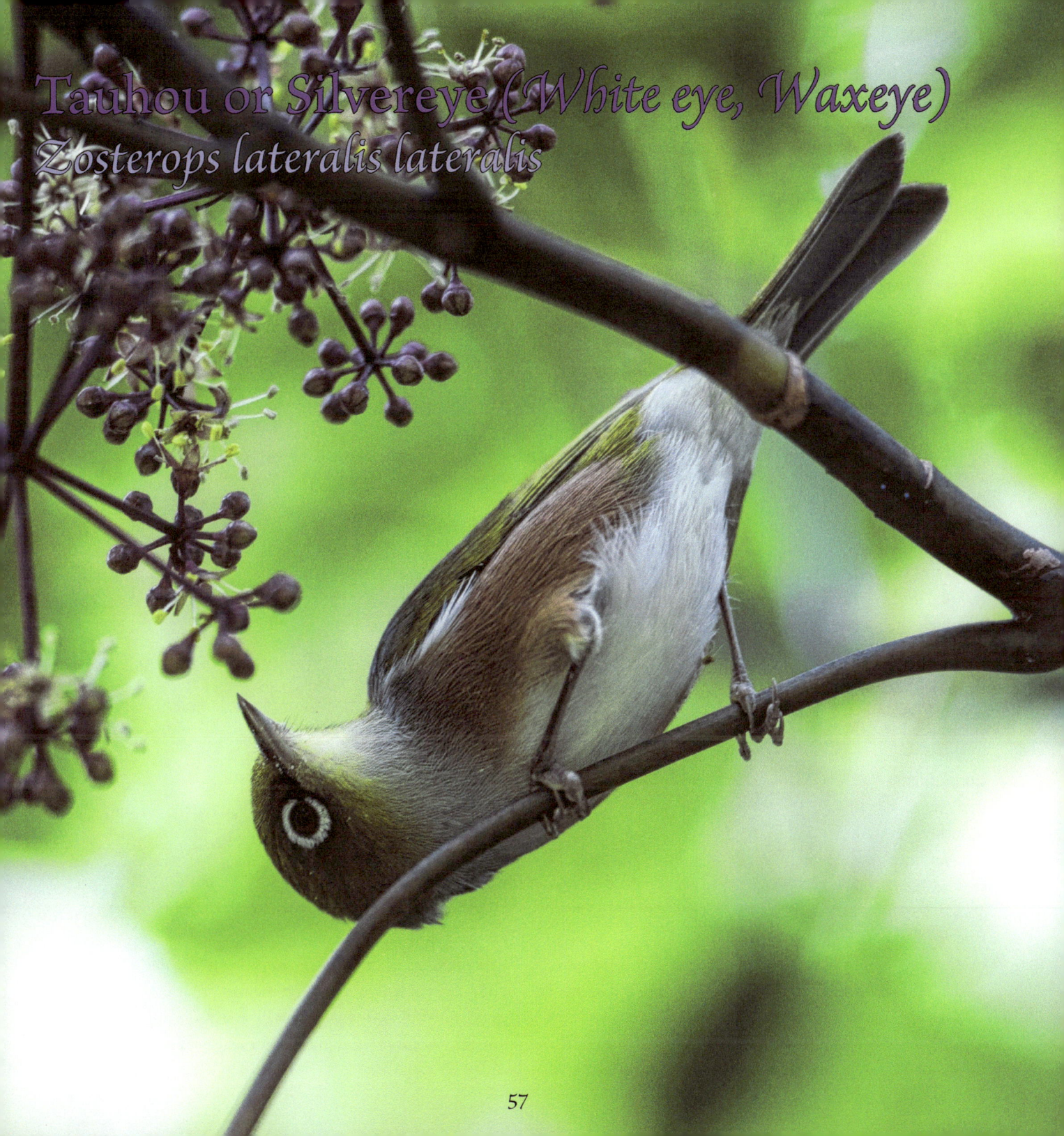

Tauhou or Silvereye (White eye, Waxeye)
Zosterops lateralis lateralis

"We first noticed this bird on some Fagus trees in the Rockwood Valley, Malvern Hills, July 28th, 1856, Its numbers, since then, have increased with great rapidity. It very soon obtained the name of the Blight-bird, in recognition of its services to gardens and orchards, from its habit of feeding on the American blight, with which apple trees in this colony are so generally infested; but, although the gardener noticed with satisfaction its labours in this direction, during the winter months, yet as summer returned and fruits ripened, its incessant depredations on cherries and plums were witnessed with anything but pleasure… The nest and eggs form as pleasing an object as those of the Hedge-sparrow at home. The gift of song does not appear to be equally shared by these birds; in addition to the quick, sharp note or chirrup, which all seem to have in common, now and then an individual bird is heard pouring forth a low, well-sustained, melodious song; possibly the power may exist in all adult males, only to be indulged in at pairing time. One of the pensile nest-builders, which seem to be almost equally rare in our temperate clime as they are in the old country…Now, as pensile nests are peculiarly adapted for ensuring the safety of their contents against the predatory attacks of various egg-robbers, does not the suspension of the habitation of the Zosterops,–the instinctive precaution of a foreign land afford an indication that it is a recent colonist, not yet so thoroughly acclimatized as to be fully aware of the immunity it enjoys from ravages of snakes, etc.?"

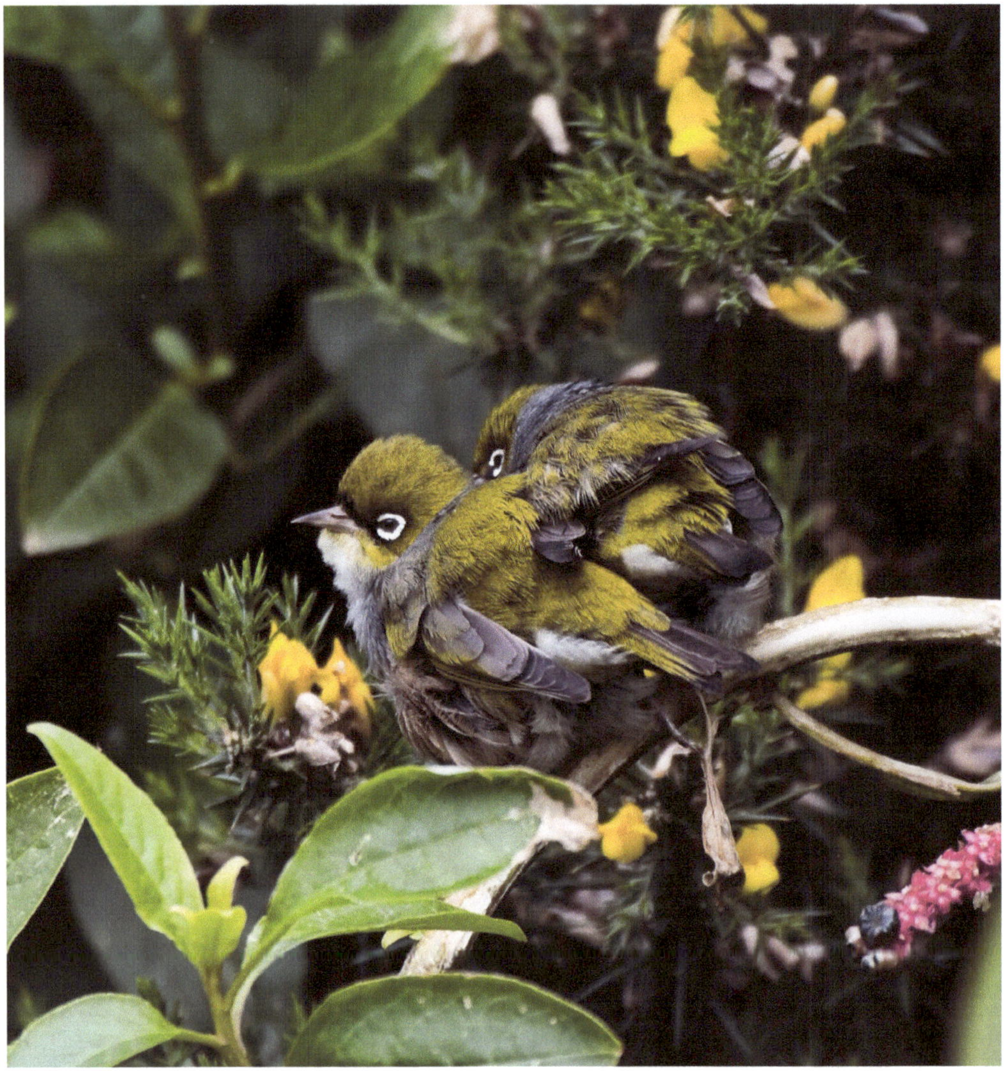

~T. H. Potts, 1869

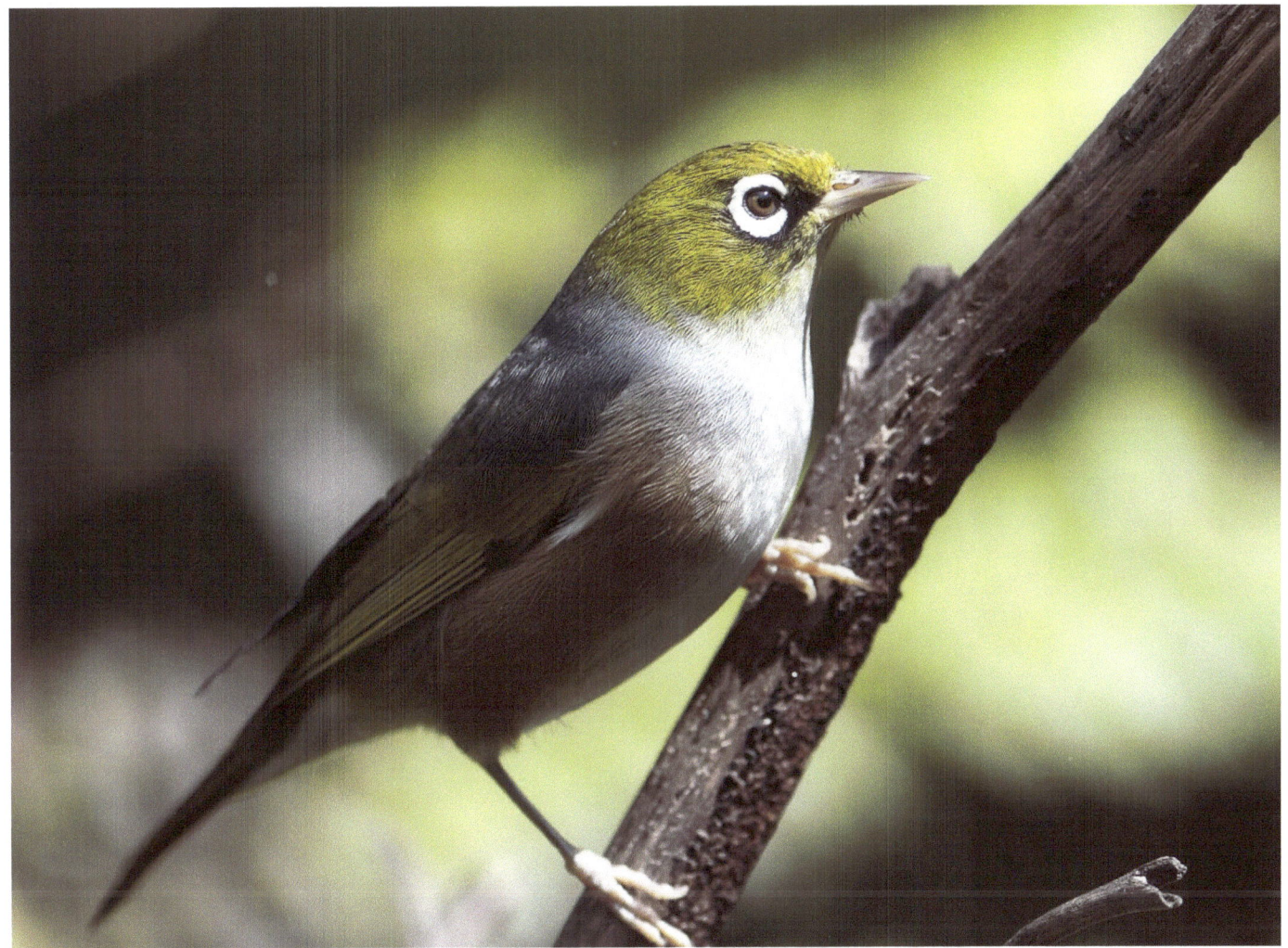

"The date of its first occurrence in Otago is doubtful, but in 1856 it appeared on both sides of Cook Strait in considerable numbers. Before then it was unknown, both to the Europeans and the Maoris, the latter calling it 'tauhau,' which means "a stranger." In 1860–61 it had spread all over the South Island and the southern parts of the North Island, but it did not reach Auckland until 1865. It has also spread to the Chatham Islands, Snares, Auckland Islands, and Campbell Island. Evidently it is a new arrival, for the restless habits of the bird forbid us from thinking that it had remained for many years in Otago without spreading northwards. I should call the white-eye a wanderer, and not a straggler, for, unlike the others, it crossed the ocean in sufficiently large numbers to establish itself both in New Zealand and afterwards in the outlying islands…These facts show us that the passage across the Tasman Sea is possible, even for some small land–birds. The distance as the crow flies is about a thousand miles, and it would take a bird twenty–four to thirty–six hours to accomplish the distance, flying at its ordinary speed."

~*Captain F. W. Hutton, 1900*

Kaka or Bush Parrot
Nestor meridionalis septentrionalis

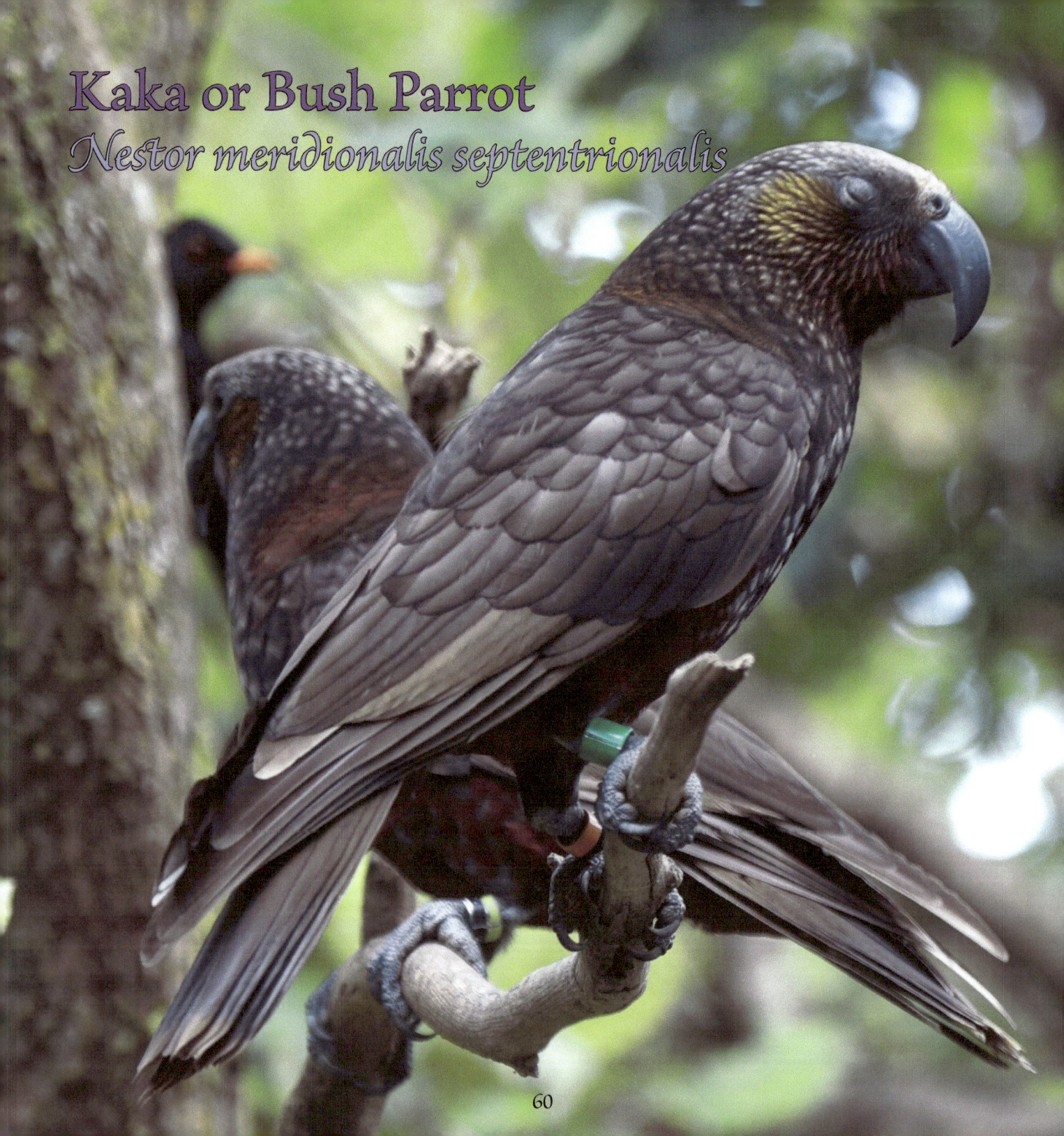

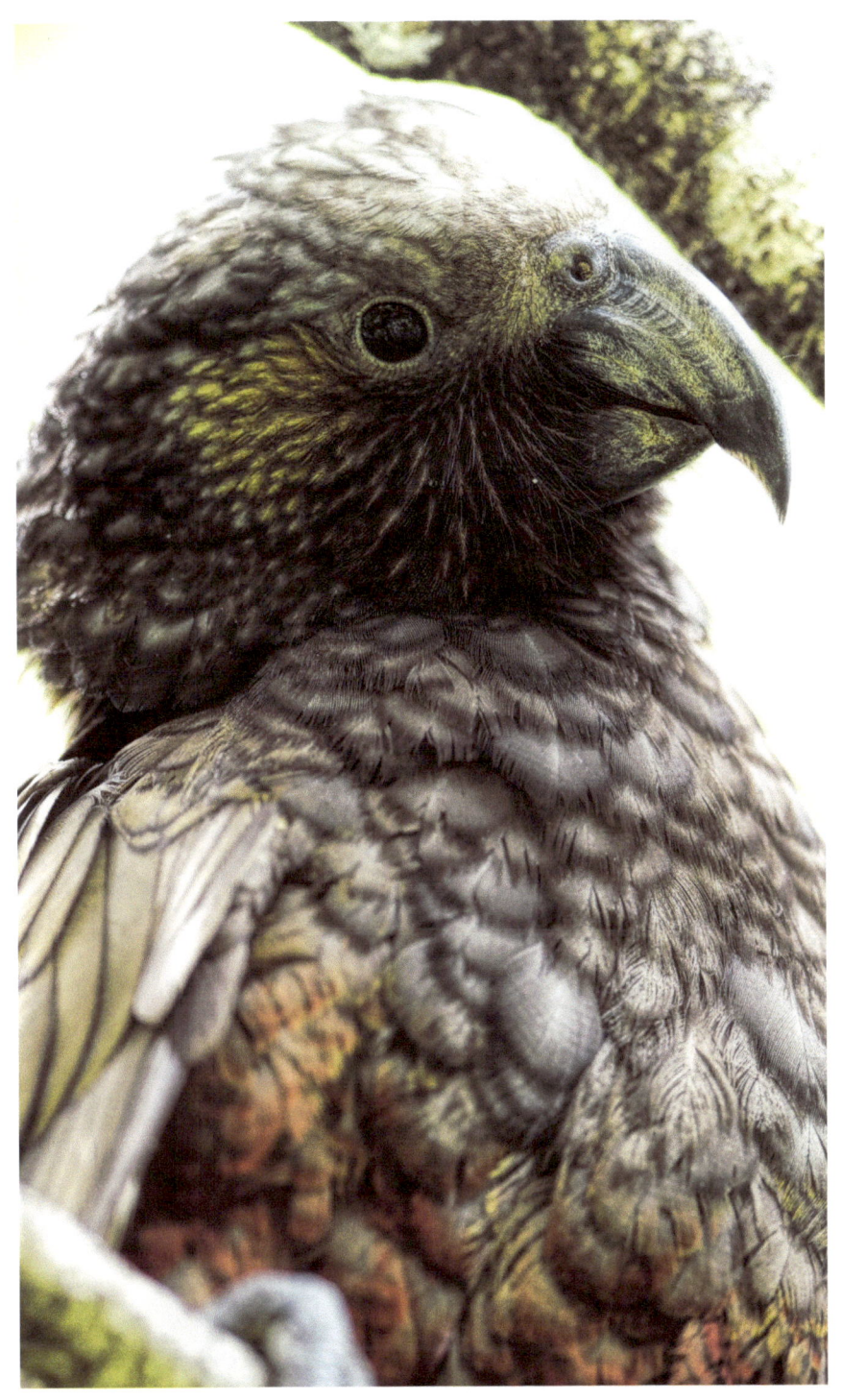

"The habits of the Kaka are in many respects remarkable. In its absolutely wild state it is fearless and inquisitive. I have often, whilst resting on the banks of a stream which falls into the lake and runs through forest frequented by these birds, seen several of them gravely take post upon some tree close to me, eying me with the utmost apparent curiosity, and chattering to themselves, as if discussing the character and intentions of the intruder. After the lapse of a few minutes they have darted away, uttering loud cries, as if proclaiming to the rest of the forest the presence of a stranger, who was either to be avoided or not, as the case might be. During the winter season the wild birds often unhesitatingly enter the house for food, making themselves thoroughly at home, and even roosting on the cross–beams in the kitchen on specially inclement nights. Two of these in particular soon learnt how to open the door of the dairy, which they were fond of getting into, in order to regale themselves on cream and butter, both of which they appeared to like excessively. I have had several of these wild birds billing on the eaves of the house in the evening, waiting to be fed, and coming readily to receive from the hand pieces of bread spread thickly with butter and strewed with sugar. But they rarely eat any of the bread itself, dropping it as soon as they had cleared off the butter and sugar. If one bird happened to have finished his portion before the others, he unhesitatingly helped himself to a share of some neighbour's goods, which was always yielded without the slightest demur."
~*W. T. L. Travers, 1871*

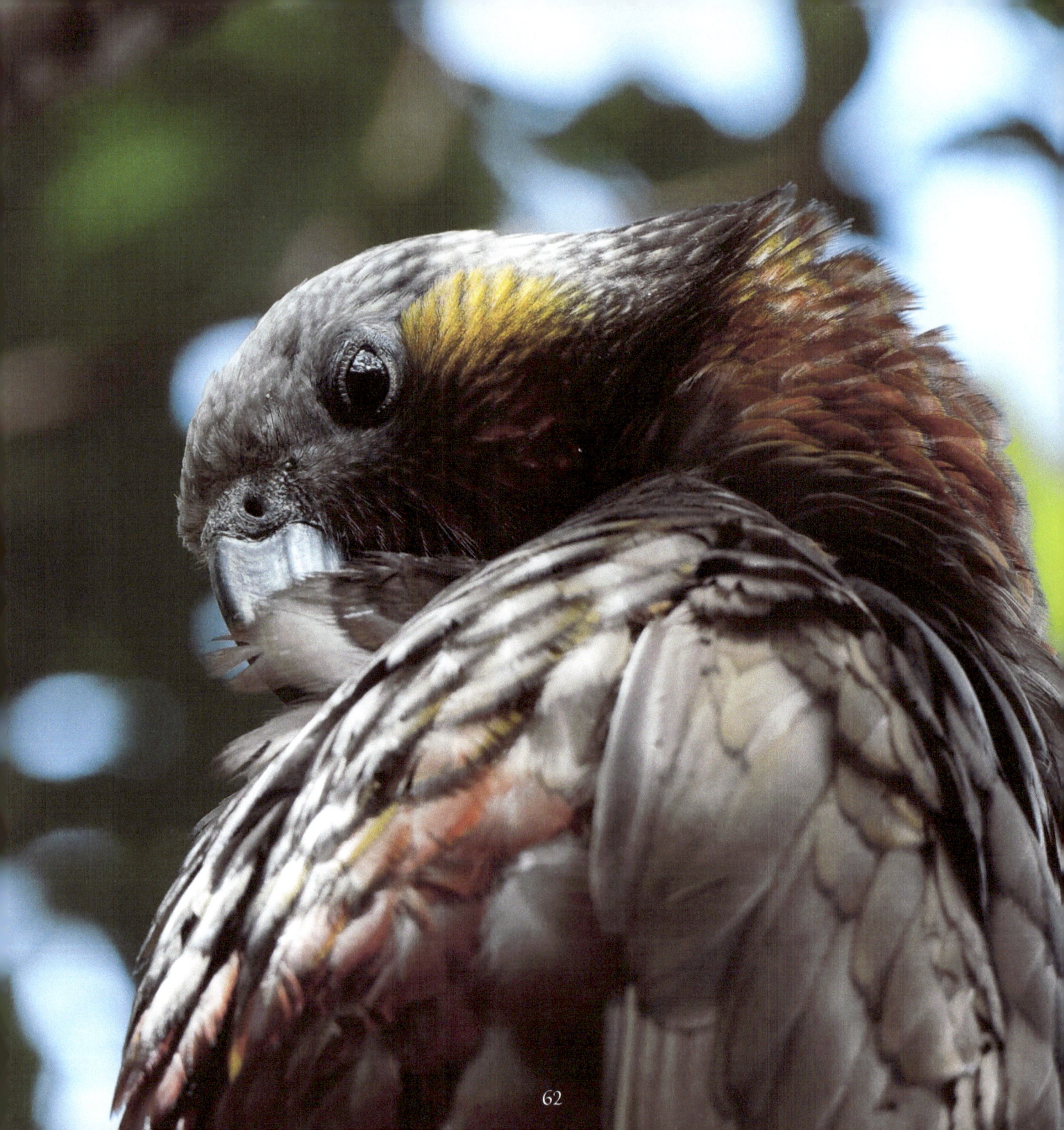

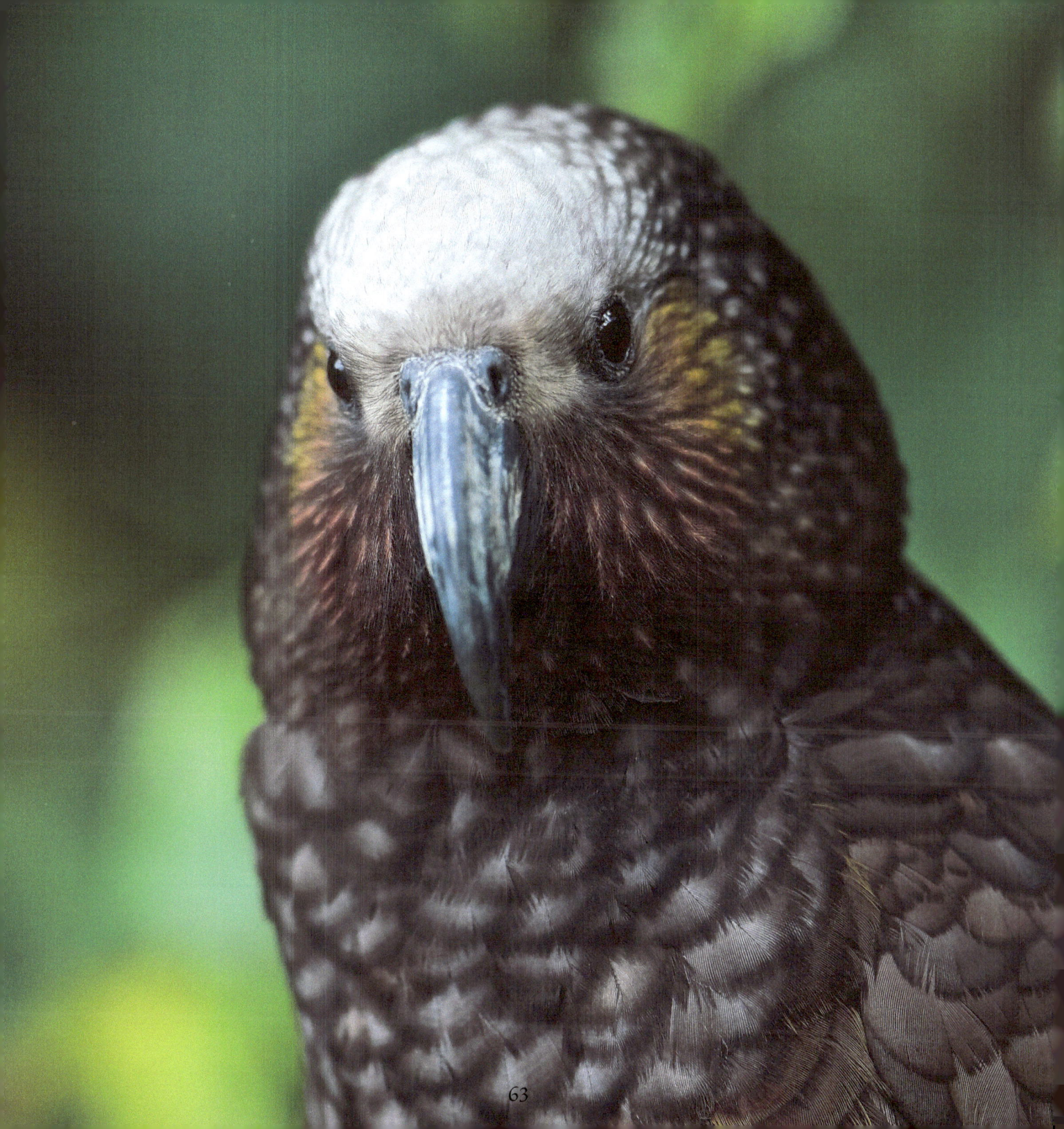

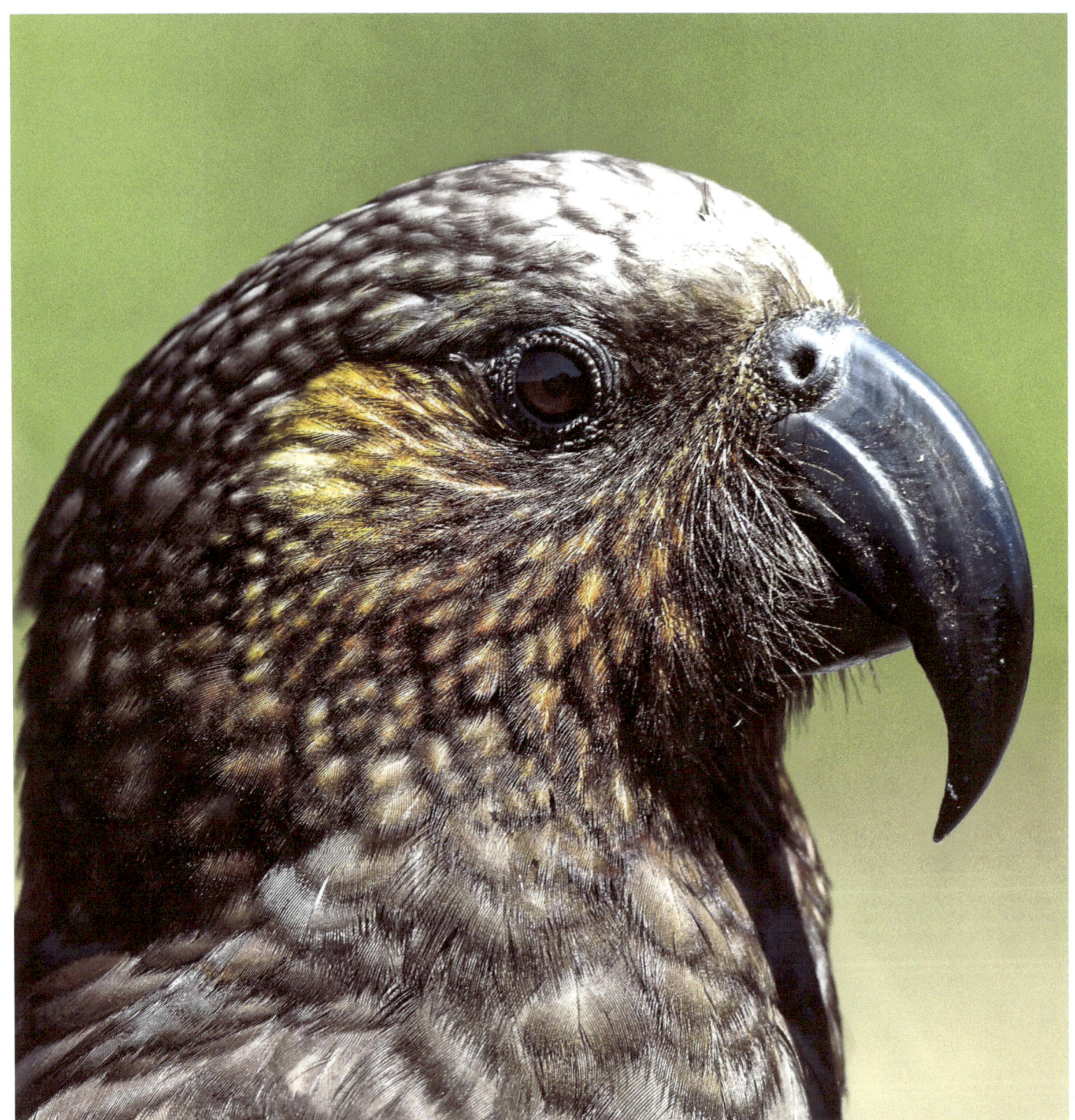

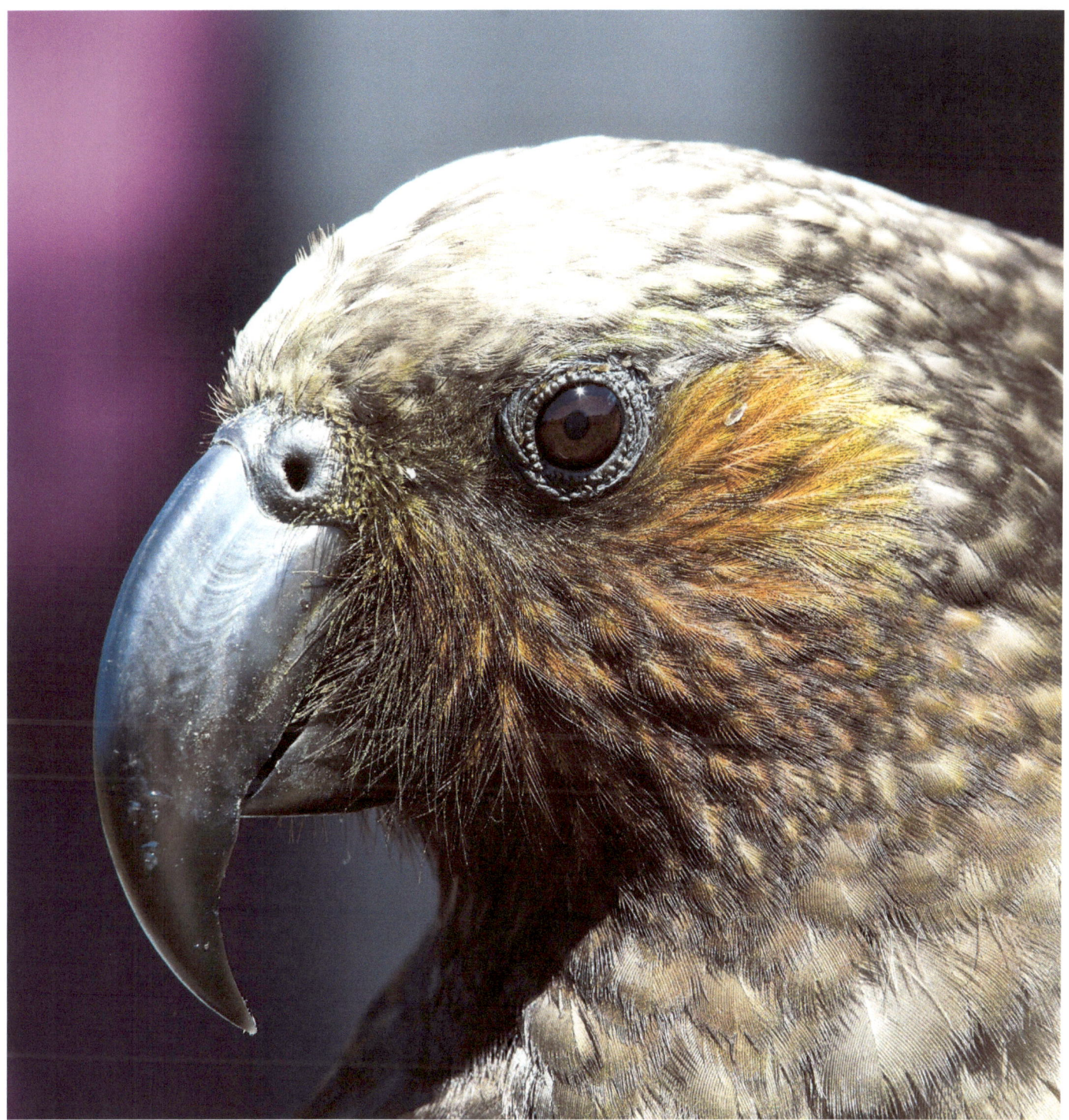

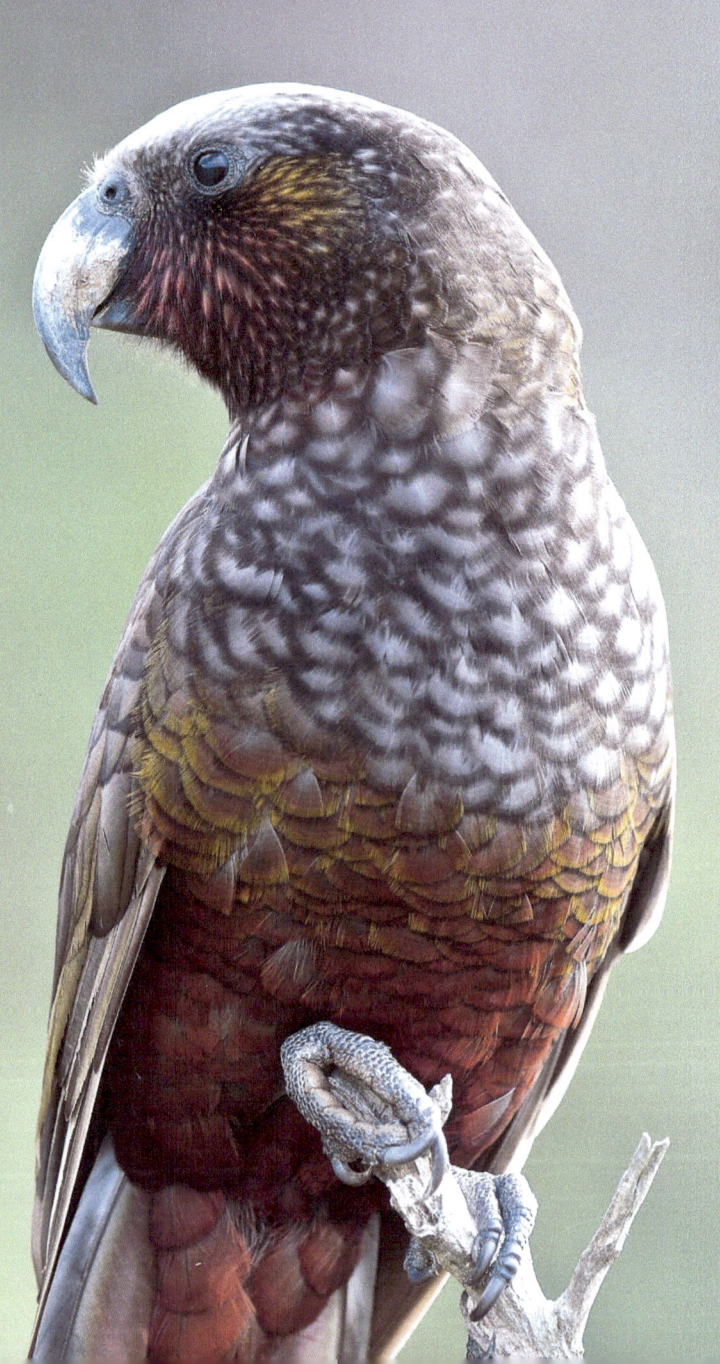

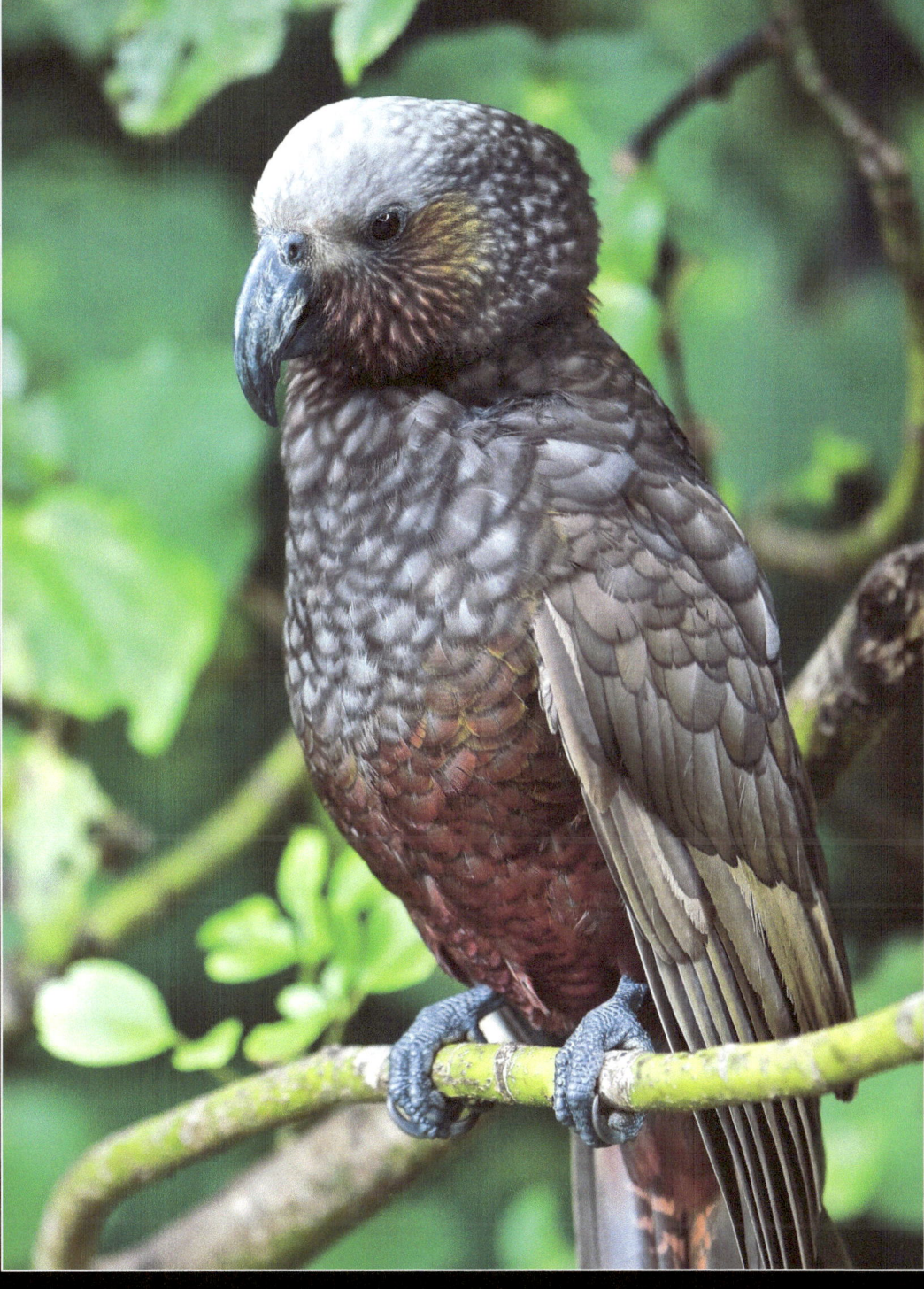

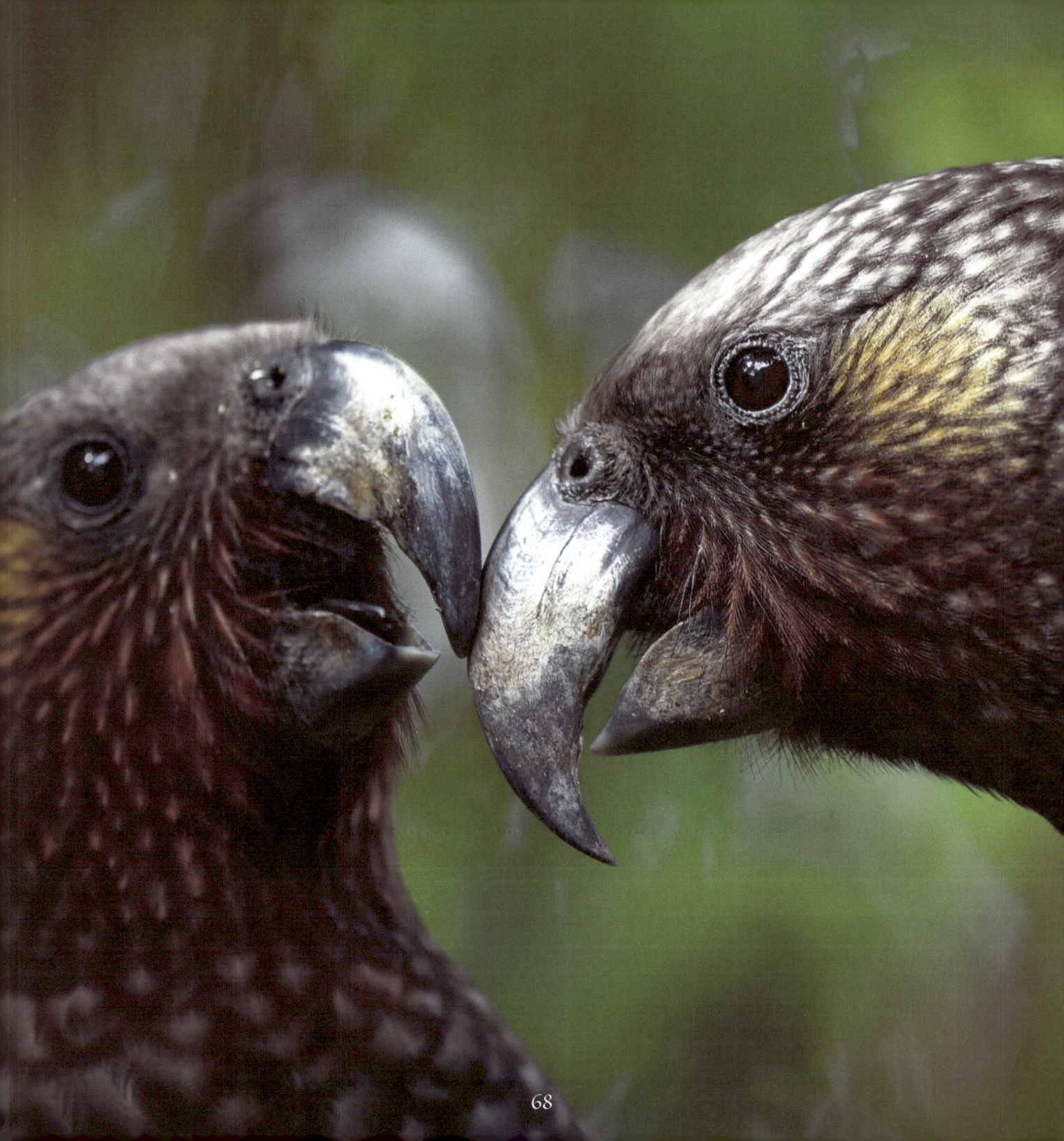

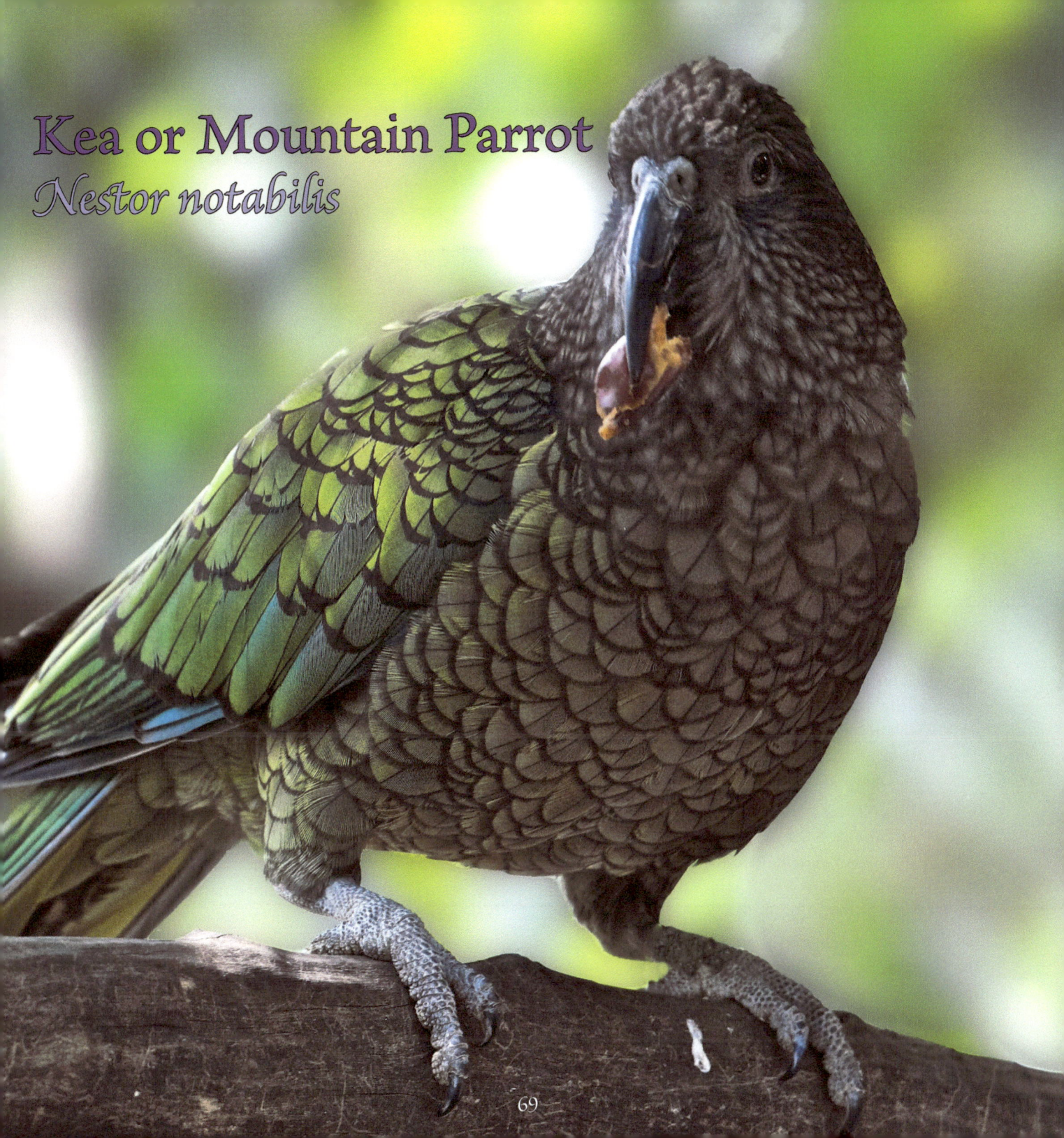

Kea or Mountain Parrot
Nestor notabilis

"The kea always lived high up the mountains a long distance above the forest-line, for you must understand that on a mountain-side each variety of tree has its limit of elevation. The mixed bush grows on the plain; and a short distance above, where these trees, as rimu, white-pine, black-pine, &c., are at their highest, and cease to grow, come the different kinds of Fayus, of which the so-called black-birch attains the highest elevation. On glancing along the alpine hills, such as, for instance, those on either shore of Lake Wakatipu, you will see with surprise that the dark-green of the trees reaches so far up the mountain-side, and is then cut off level and clean as far as the eye-sight can extend into the far distance. Above this level line of dark forest comes the brown straw-colour of the mountain-grass, which in turn gives way to the slate-grey or yellow-grey of the rocky summits and their débris of broken stones. On this same forest limit grew also the tall bracken fern, so the dark-green of the forest would be at places for a considerable extent varied by the brighter green of the fern. But both forest and fern attained the same elevations, and so the long line of green was only changed in shade of colour, and did not encroach upon the area of the yellow grasses.

The kea lived above this forest limit, and was mostly seen moving about the rocks and boulders on the ridge of the mountain-tops. The name 'kea' would seem to be an imitation of a frequent call of this bird. But it also makes a number of other sounds. About the first I can remember of this bird was at a time when I resided near the head-waters of the Oreti or New River. One hot day – it probably was in the summer-time – when walking across the valley between the mountains, my attention was attracted by a remarkable sound or series of cries. These I mistook for the noise of several small puppies of the wild dog, crying from hunger in the nest. I at once set to work to climb up the steep mountain-side to capture these creatures; but the result was not as was expected, but a dull-green-coloured bird was found seated on a projecting piece of rock. These birds are coloured green, shaded with black, and have bright oranged-red feathers of small size on the underside of their wings.

They are about the size of a kaka, rather narrower across the back, and have the hooked point of the upper mandible somewhat longer... On first becoming acquainted with man they showed little sign of fear. In fact, I have, when on the mountain-top, remained standing perfectly still, with keas hopping round me, but would have ultimately to drive them away, for one would come to inspect the brass eyelets in my boots, and try to pick them out, when, seeing that the boot-laces would quickly be cut through, I would require a stop to this performance."

~Taylor White, 1894

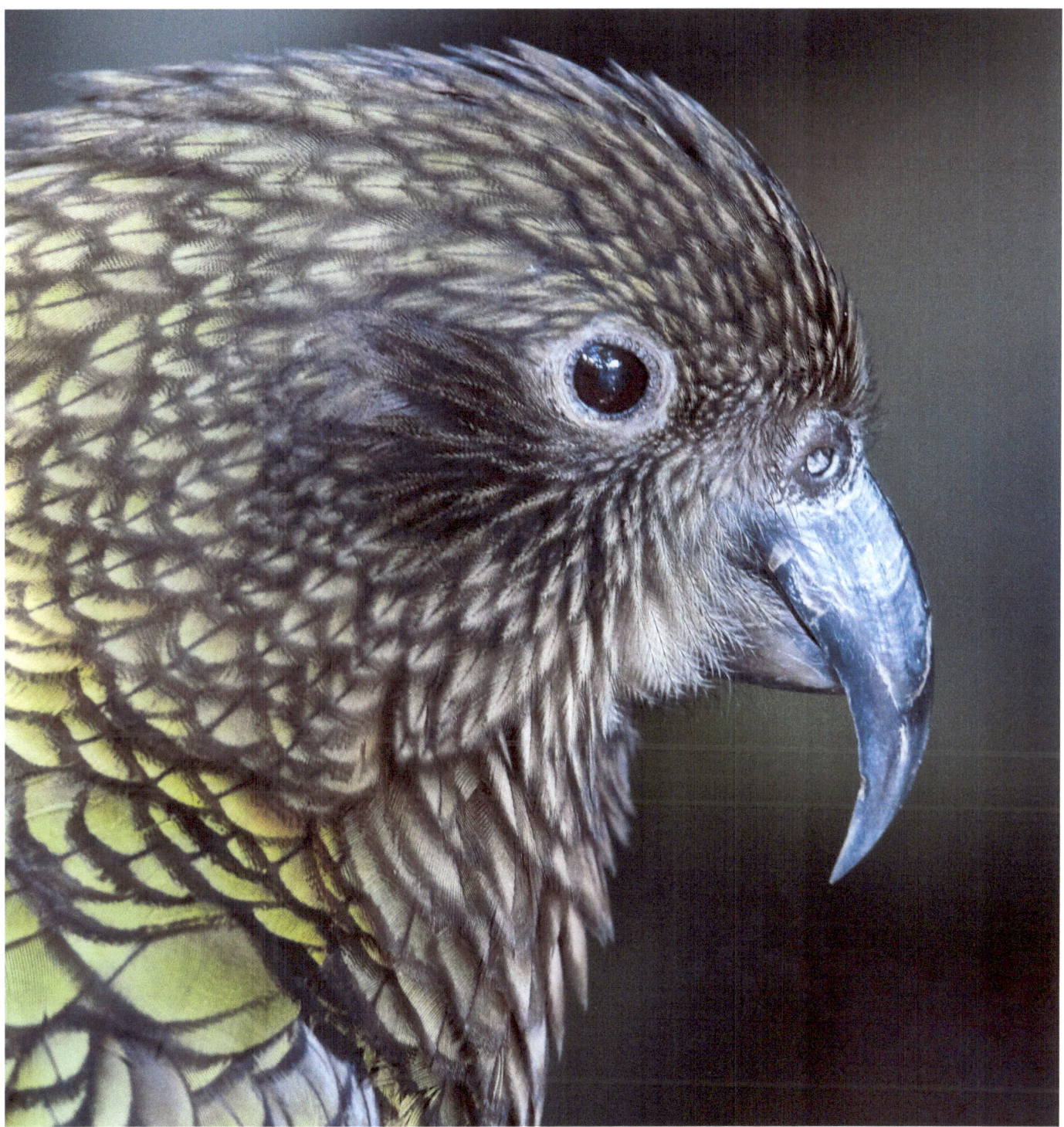

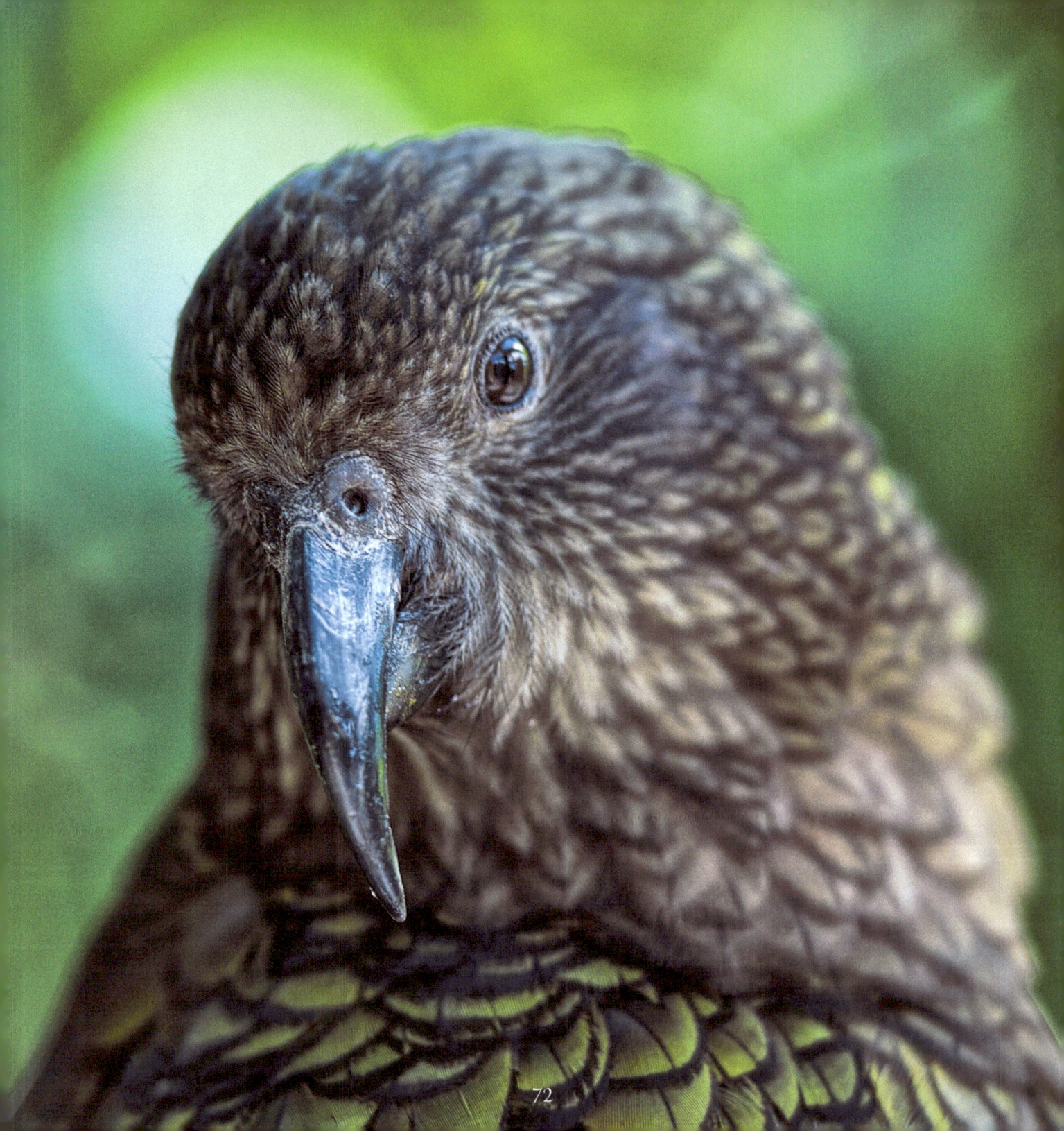

Kakariki or Red-fronted Parakeet
Cyanoramphus novazelandiae

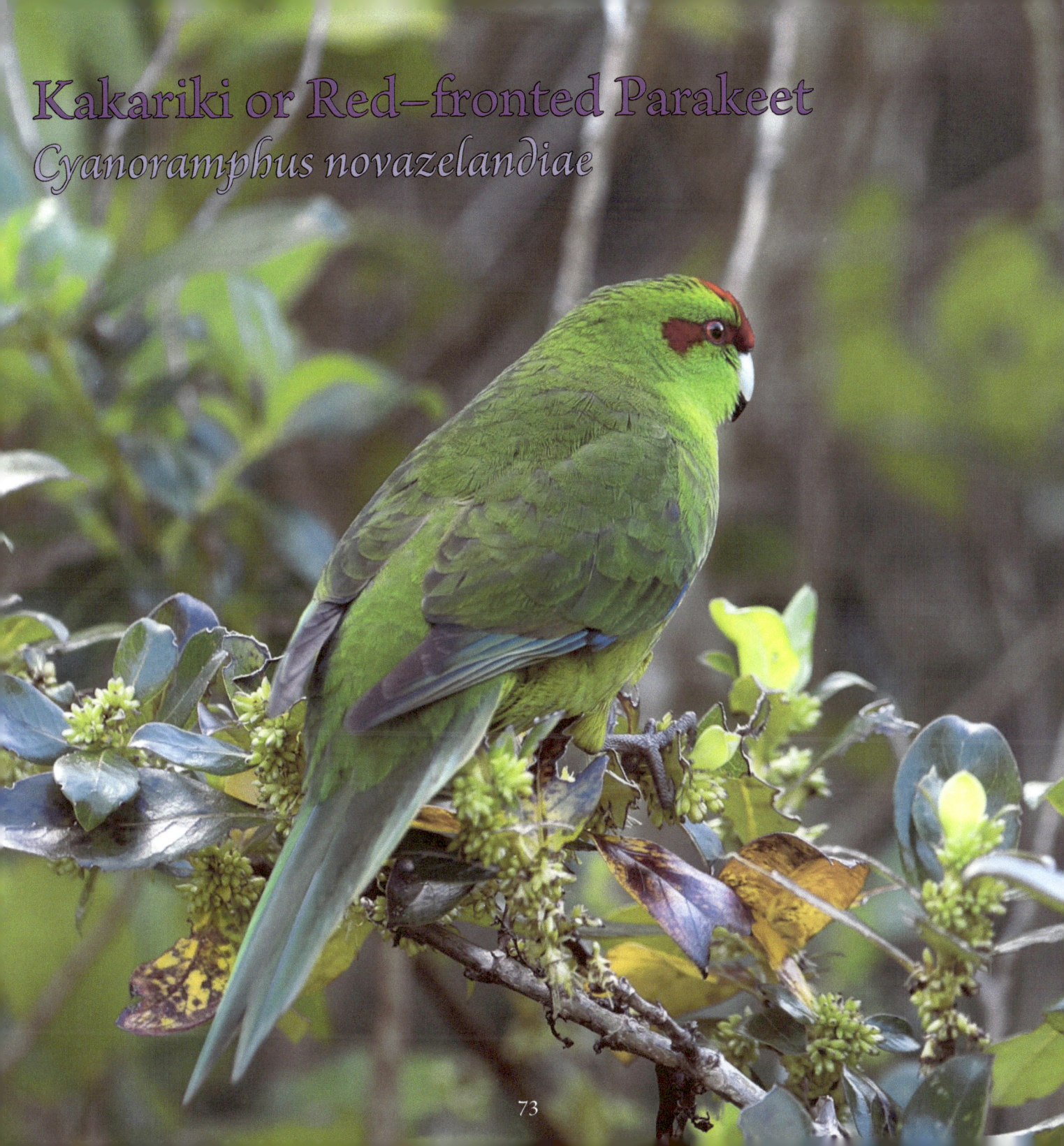

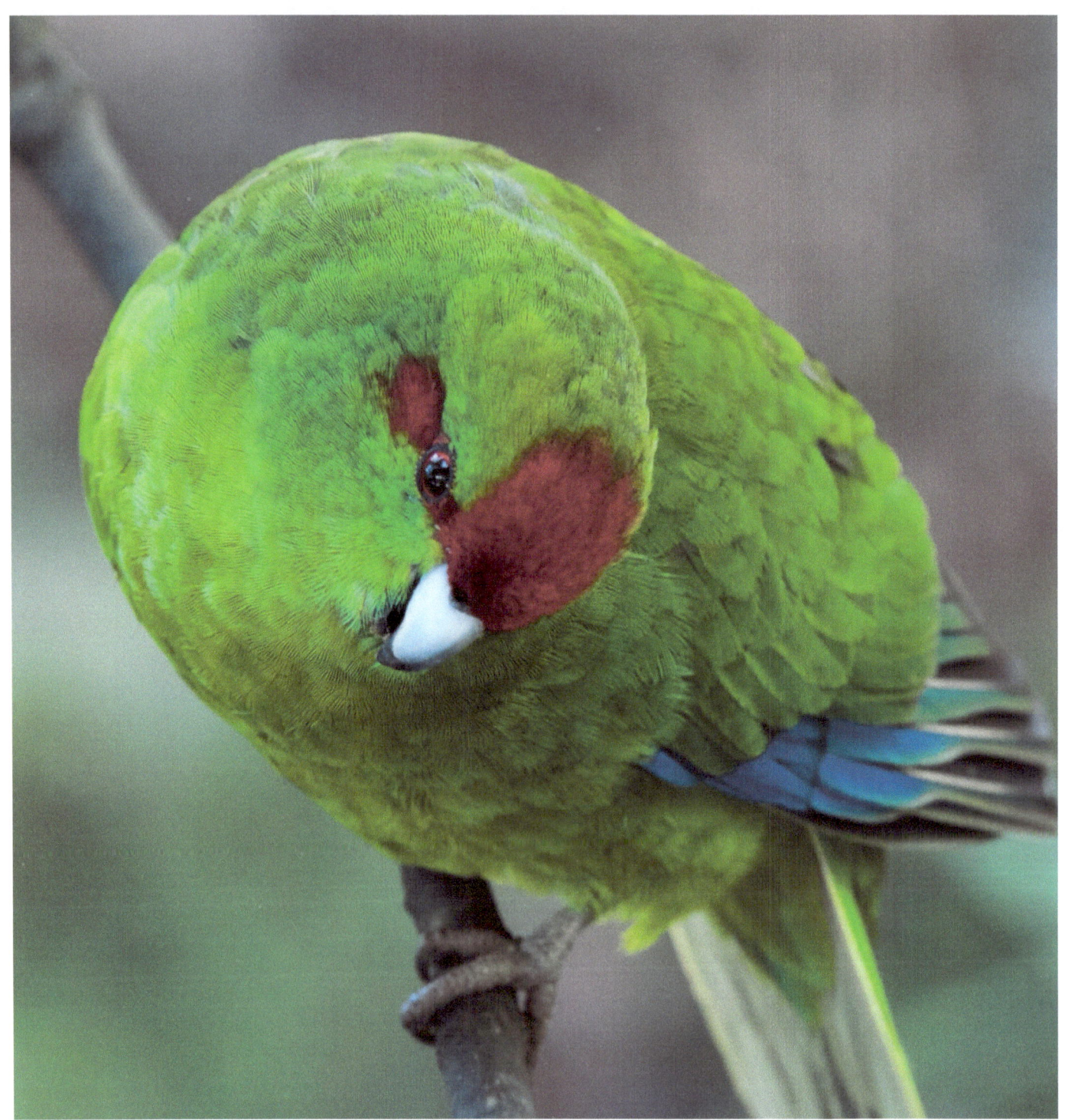

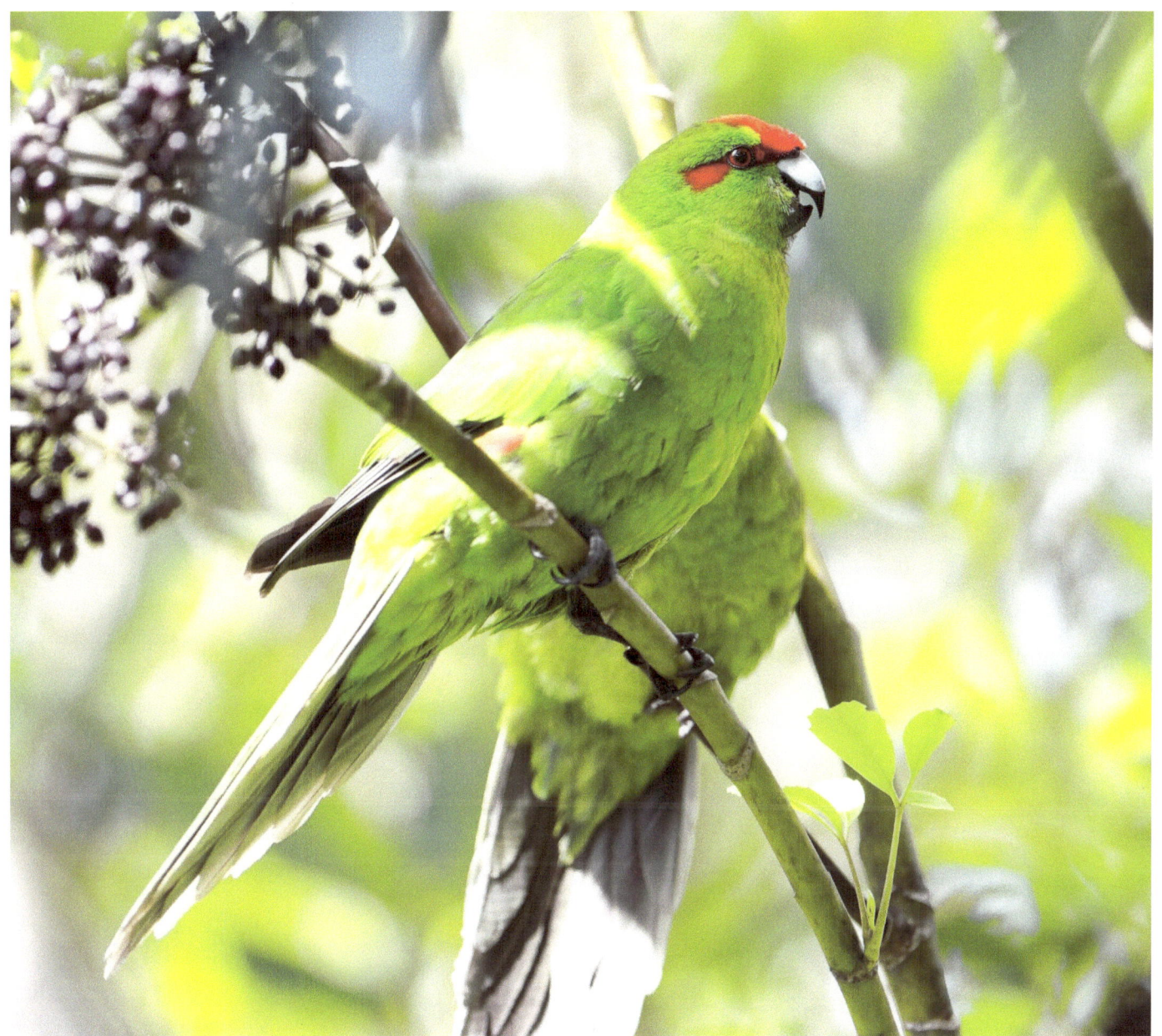

"The Hon. W. Fox, who has just returned from a trip through the Canterbury district, informs me that the farmers have suffered this season a visitation, tens of thousands of these birds having descended on their ripening crops of corn and proved almost as destructive as an army of locusts. It is difficult to account for these occasional irruptions in such numbers, in the case of a bird not otherwise plentiful."

~*Walter L. Buller, 1877*

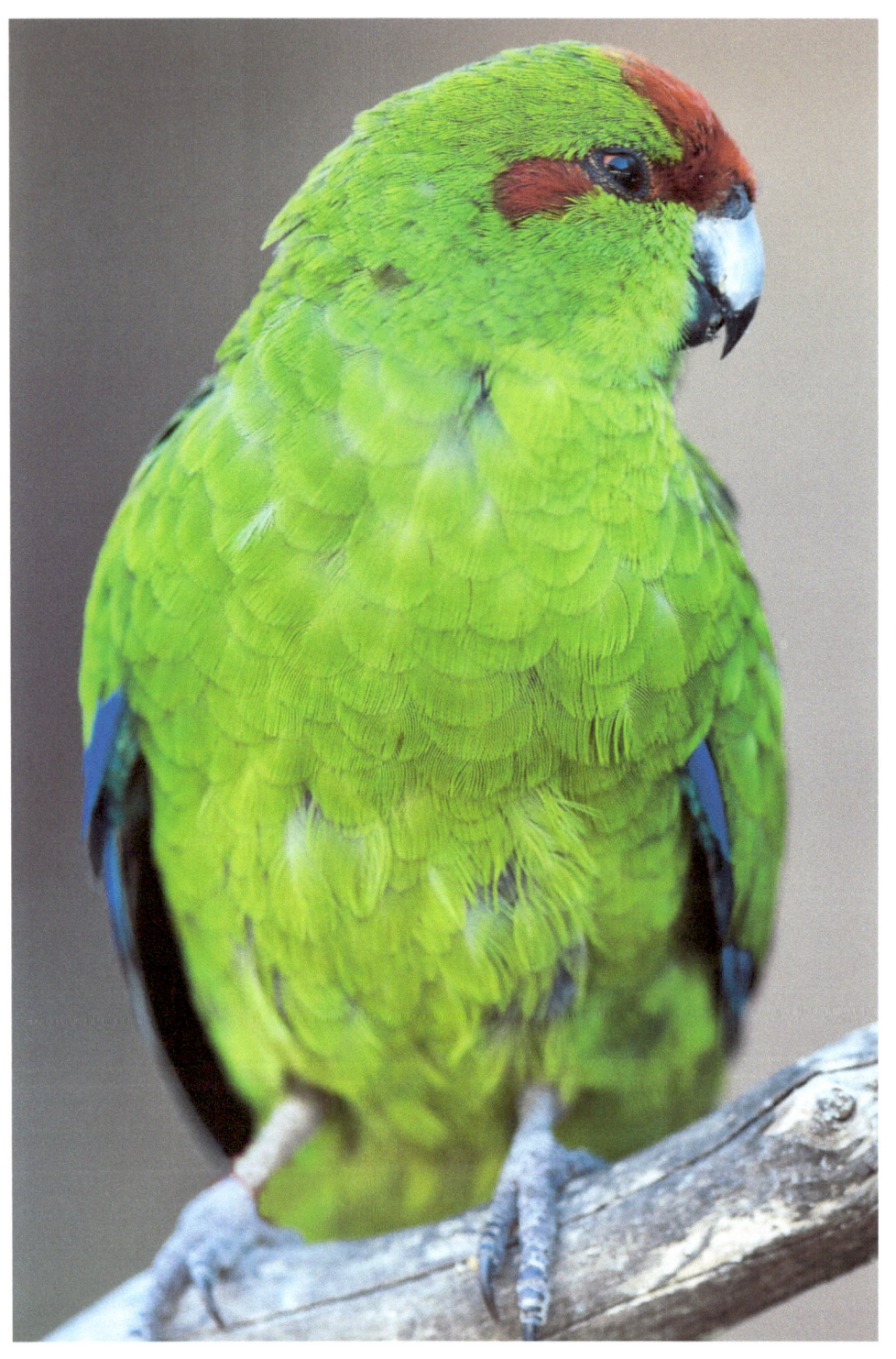

"Mr. Alexander MacDonald, of the Awahuri, mentioned to me a curious incident which had come under his own observation. His young people had obtained a nest of young Parrakeets, and succeeded in rearing them. When adult, two of the birds mated and became quite inseparable, always occupying the same perch, and cuddling up to each other in the most affectionate manner. One day the male bird made his escape from the cage, and in being recaptured had his tail pulled out. Thus dismantled, the fugitive went back to his cage in a very sorry plight. The female bird immediately discarded her disfigured mate, rejected all his advances, and before long paired with one of the other birds, whose caudal appendage was the very pink of perfection. But the curious part of the story has yet to come. In course of time the divorced lover had renewed his tail, and then the inconstant lady forsook her second mate and restored to favour her 'first love' in all the glory of his long, new tail. Not a bad proof, I think, that even birds are not insensible to the charms of personal appearance. It may be added that the last–deserted mate forthwith moped, refused to eat food, and died of a broken heart."

~*Sir Walter L. Buller, 1895*

Kereru or New Zealand Pigeon
Hemiphaga novaeseelandiae

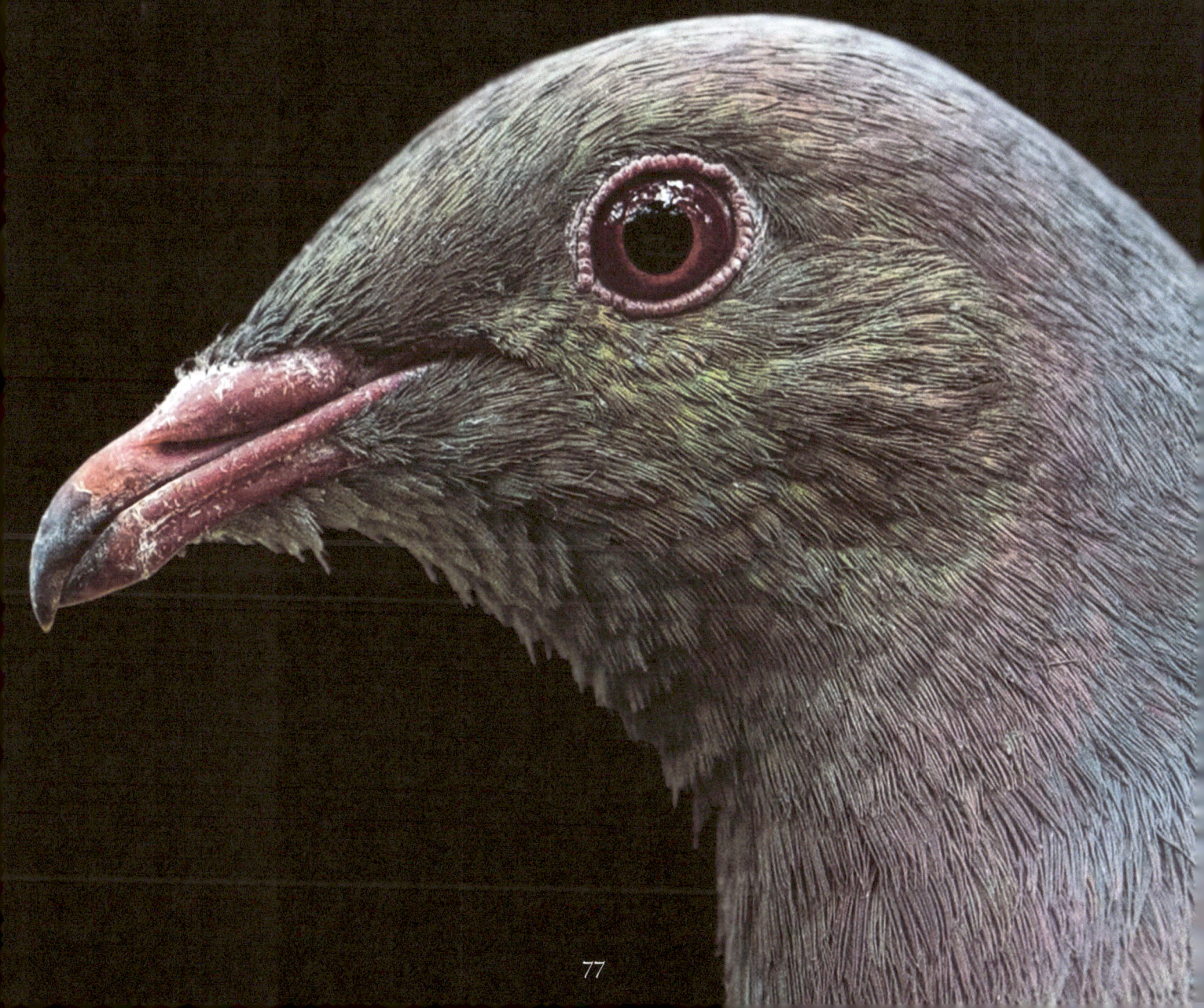

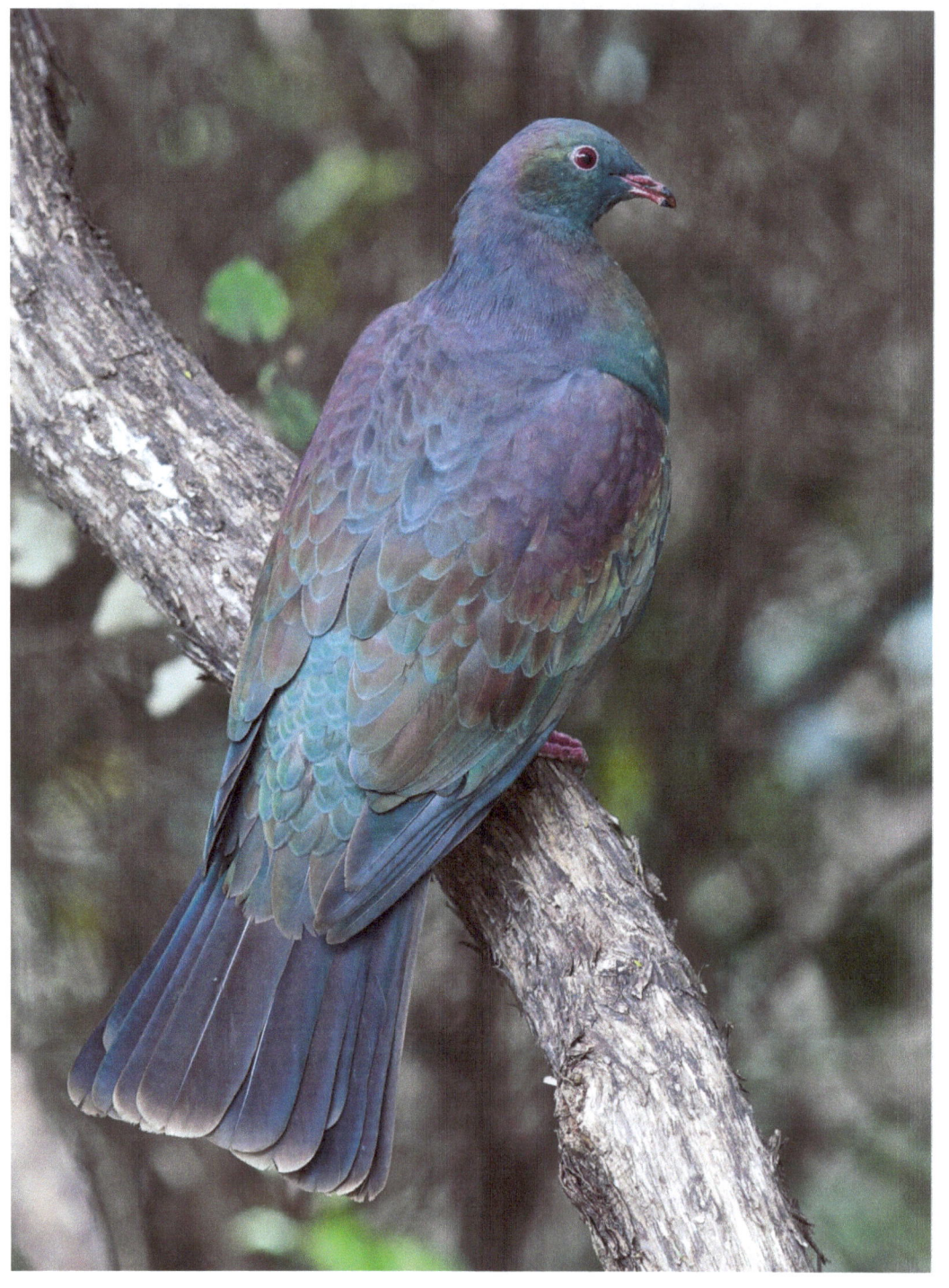

"The native pigeon is a celebrated bird in southern estimation. My Maori friends laid great stress on its connection with the story of Maui. It is commonly called kereru, but is also known as kukupa. When Maui was a boy he went down into the underworld to find his father, and he painted his mouth and legs red and put on a white maro, or kilt, and transformed himself into a pigeon. One of my informants said, 'The white on the breast of the kereru is the napkin, or maro, Maui was wrapped in as a babe.' Maui in the shape of a pigeon flew on to the handle of the ko (spade) of his father, who spoke to the bird; but all it could do was to nod its head and answer, 'Ku, ku.' Any one familiar with the bird knows the way it wags and nods its head–this is in memory of Maui– and all it can say is what Maui answered his father, 'Ku, ku.'"

~H. Beatty, 1920
Communicated by
H. D. Skinner

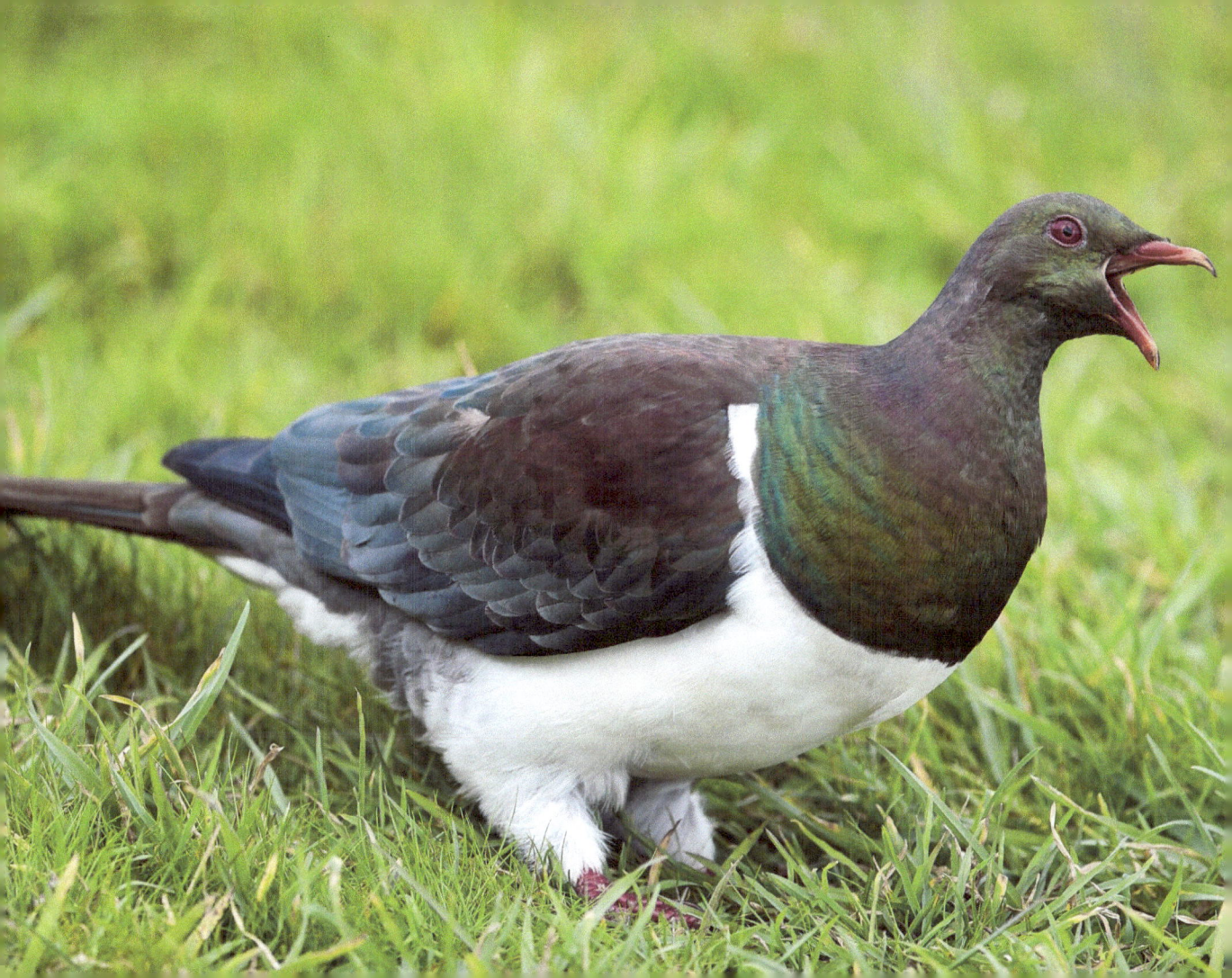

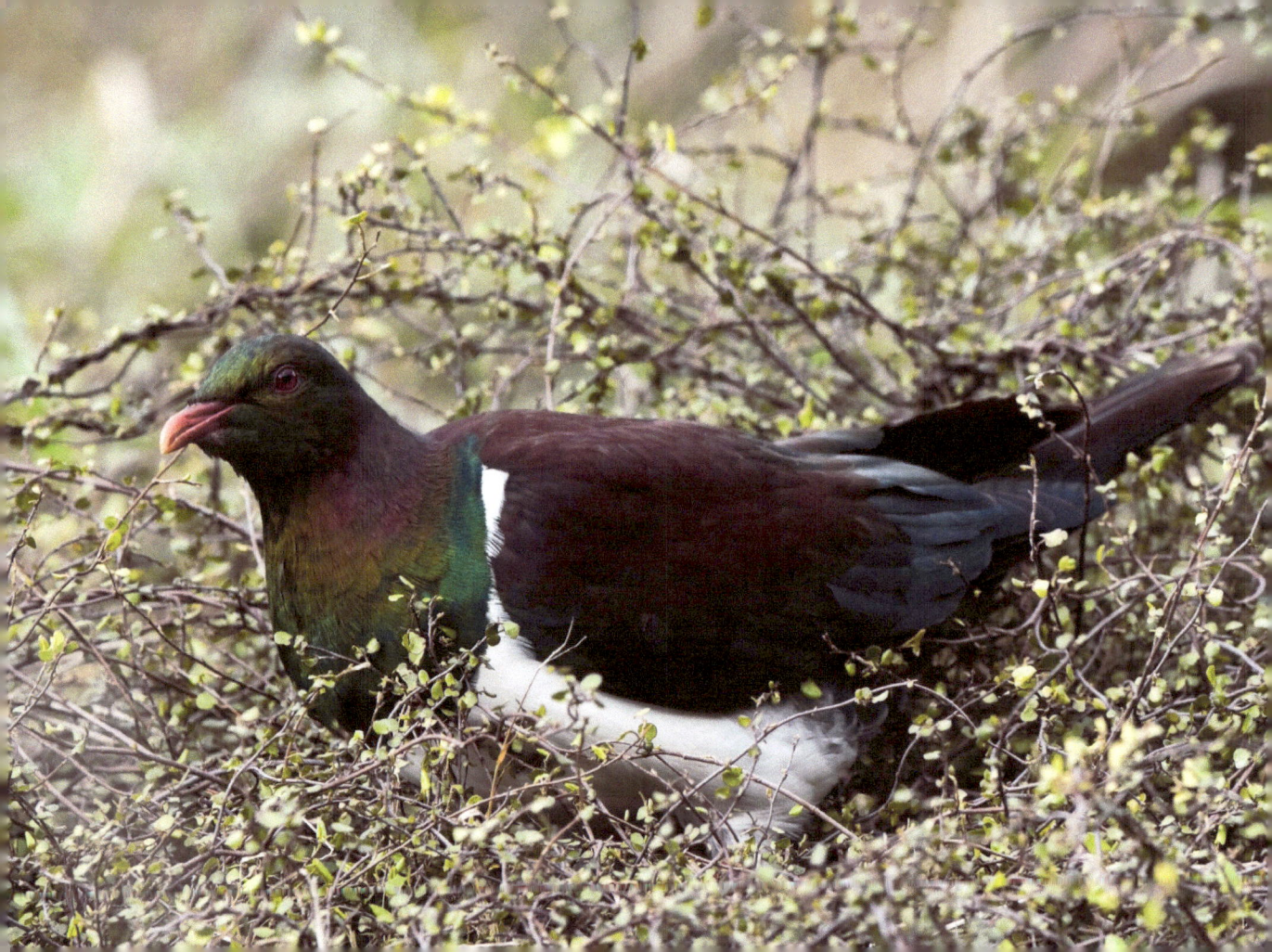

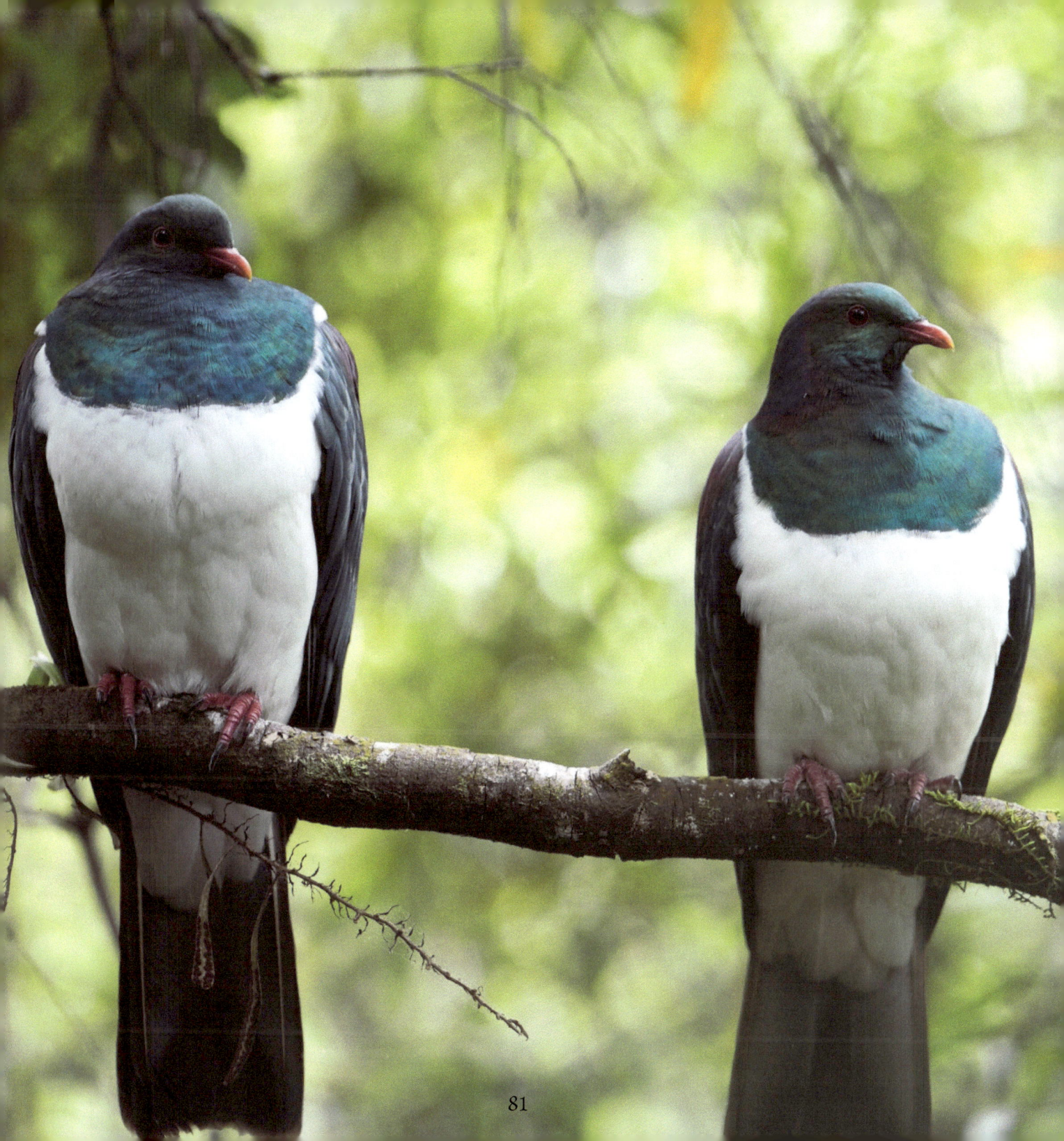

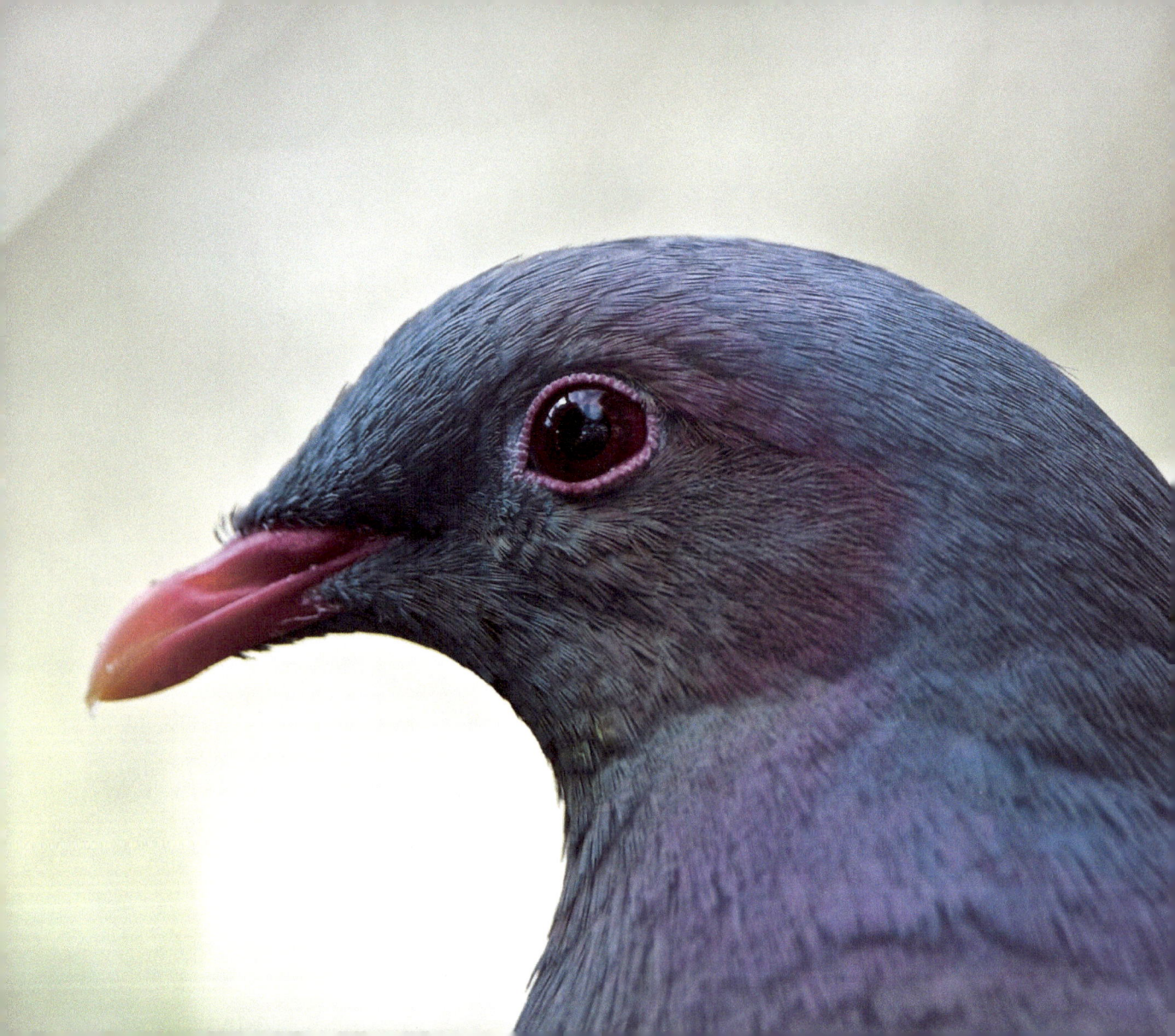

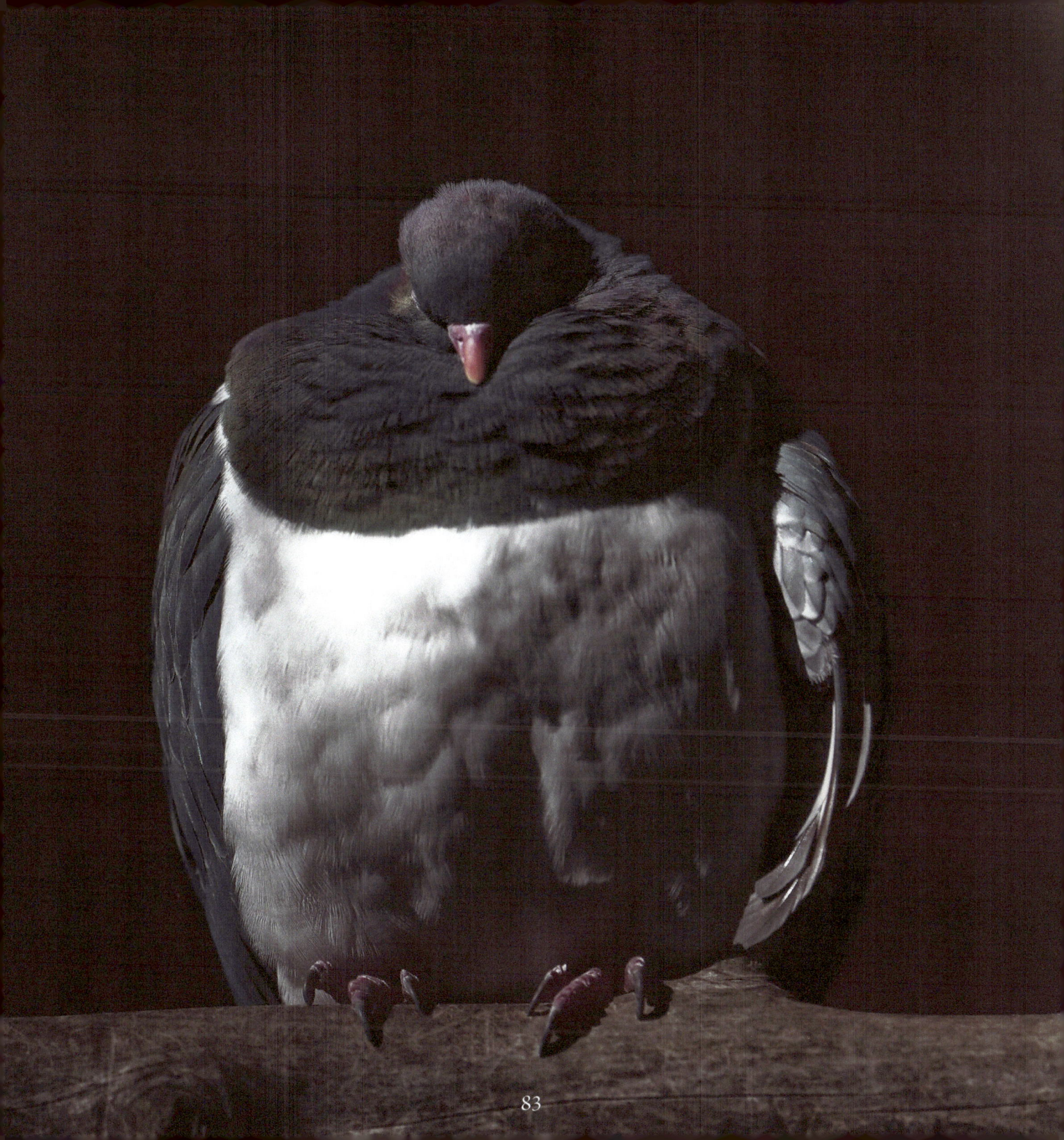

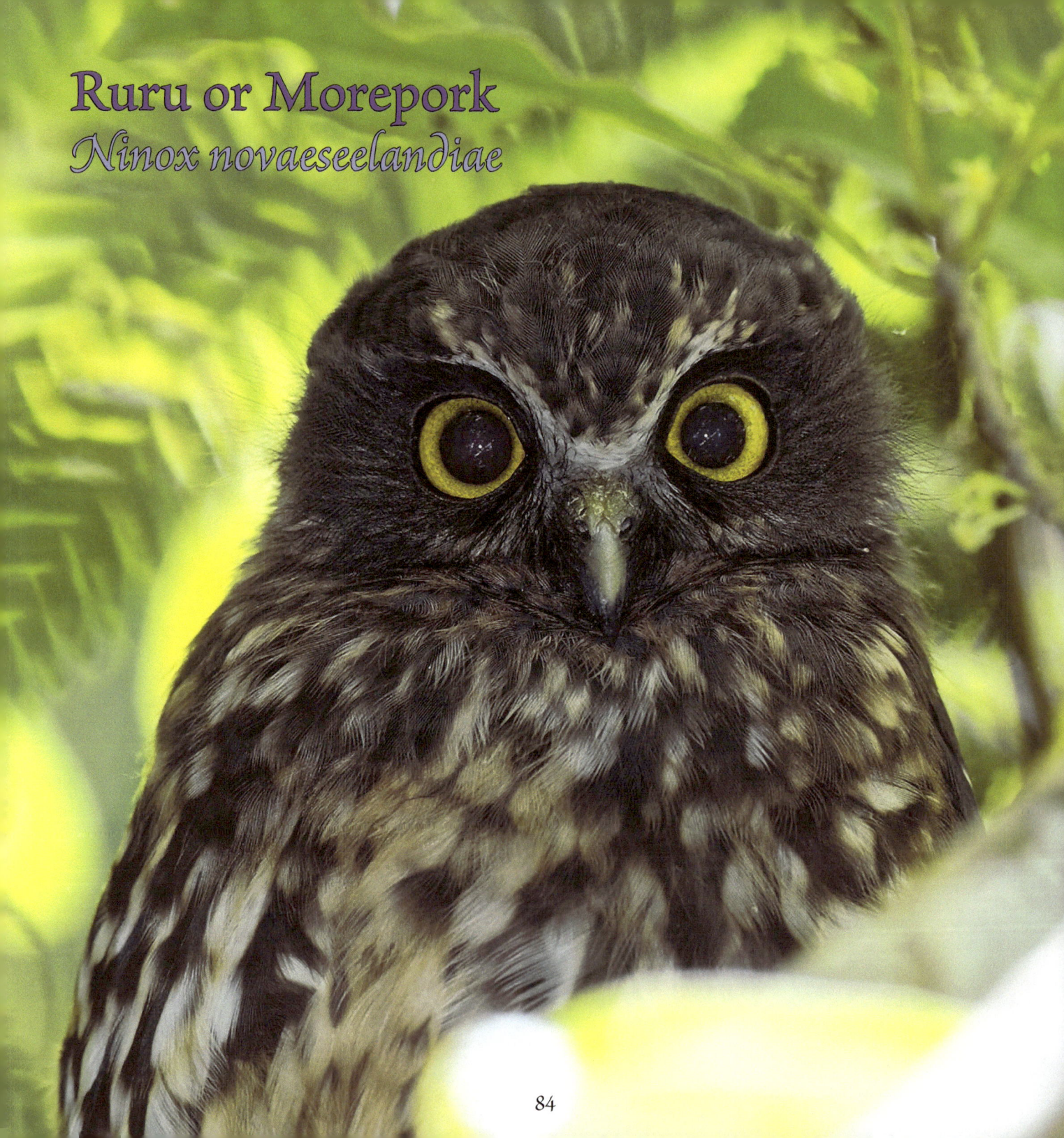

Ruru or Morepork
Ninox novaeseelandiae

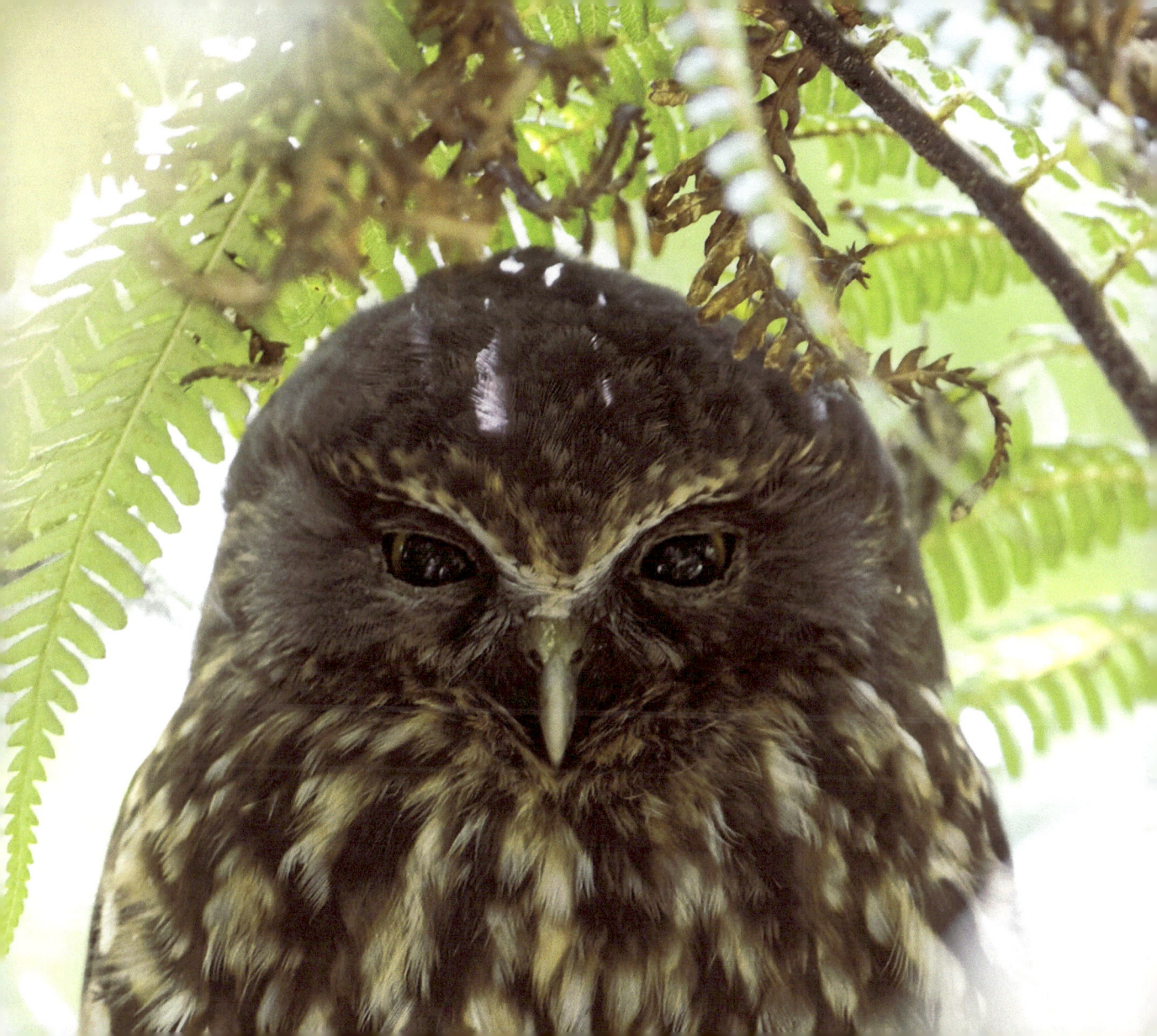

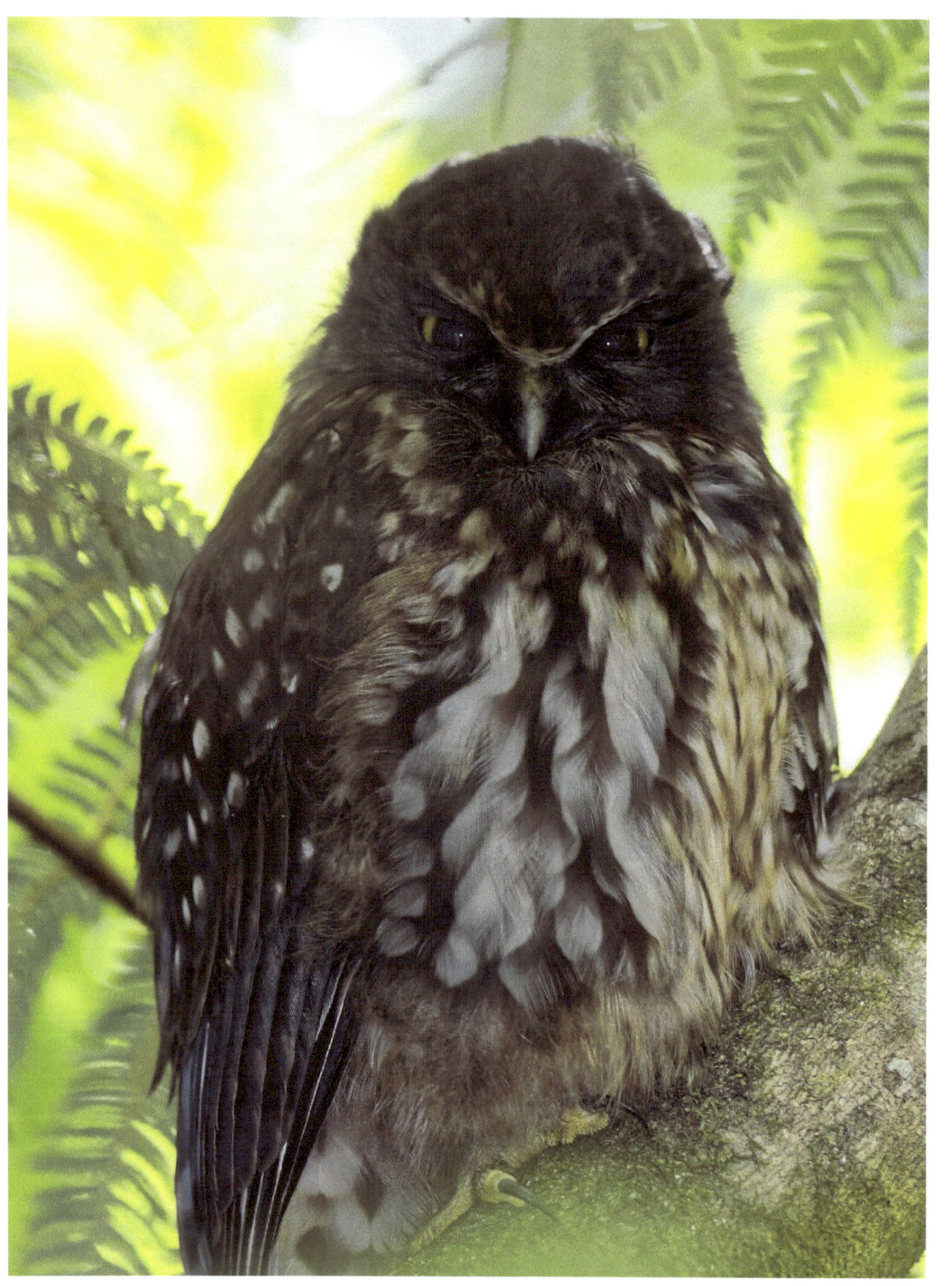

"This little owl is common everywhere. In the forests it prefers deep, dark gullies, hiding during the day in hollow trees, or between the thick foliage, and in caves; but in the evening, when it comes out to seek its food, its melancholy call, 'more–pork,' or 'ruru,' is heard. We can forgive it for catching a bird now and then, on account of the great number of rats, mice, and insects it destroys. On returning to the house of Mr. Wilson, Northern Wairoa, one bright moonlight night in 1879, I saw a Morepork swooping down; then heard a squeak; when suddenly it flew upwards, and let something drop, repeating this action several times, ultimately remaining on the ground for a time, and then flying away. On examining the spot, I found the skin, head, legs, and tail of a rat."
~A. Reischek, 1895

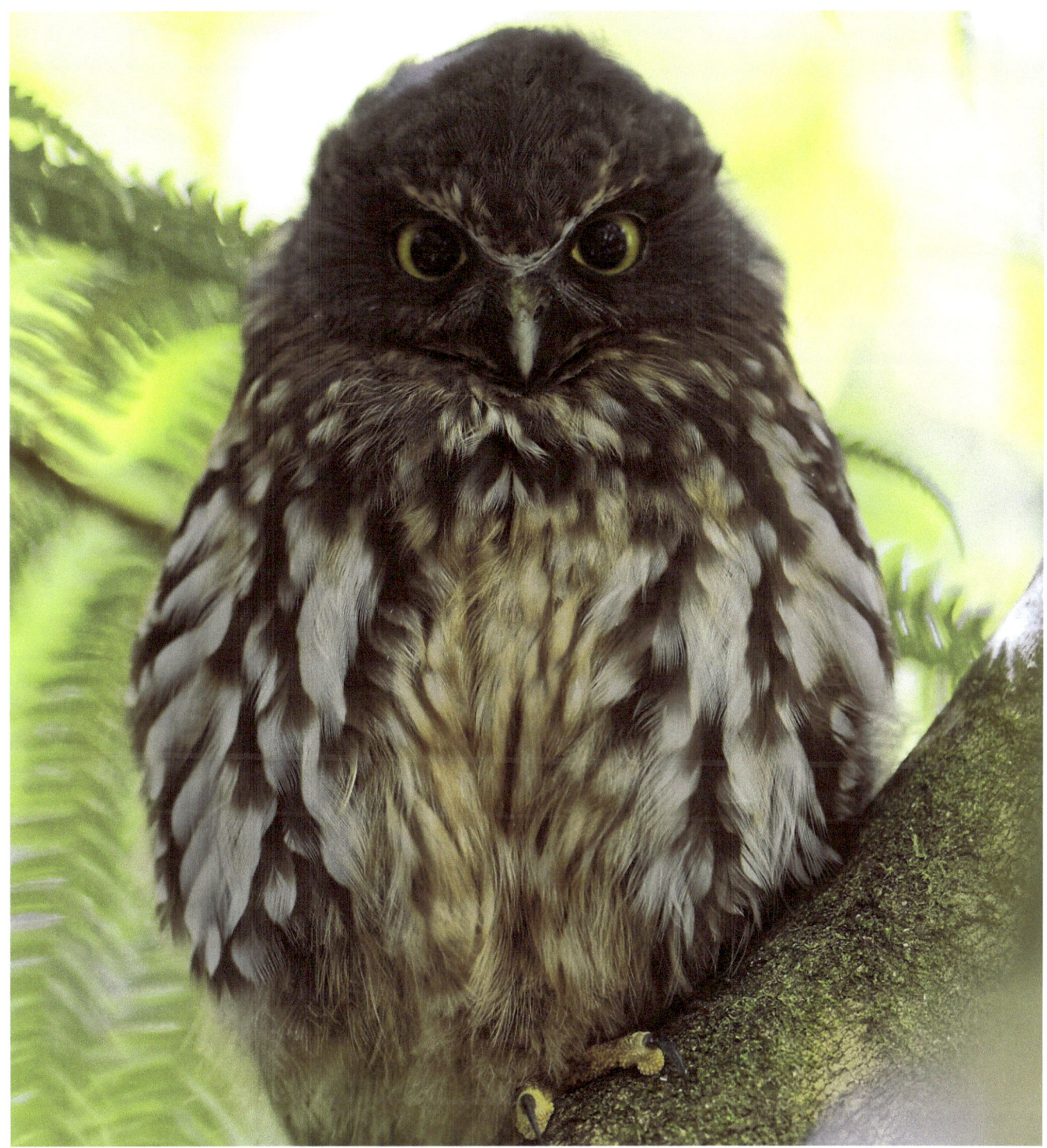

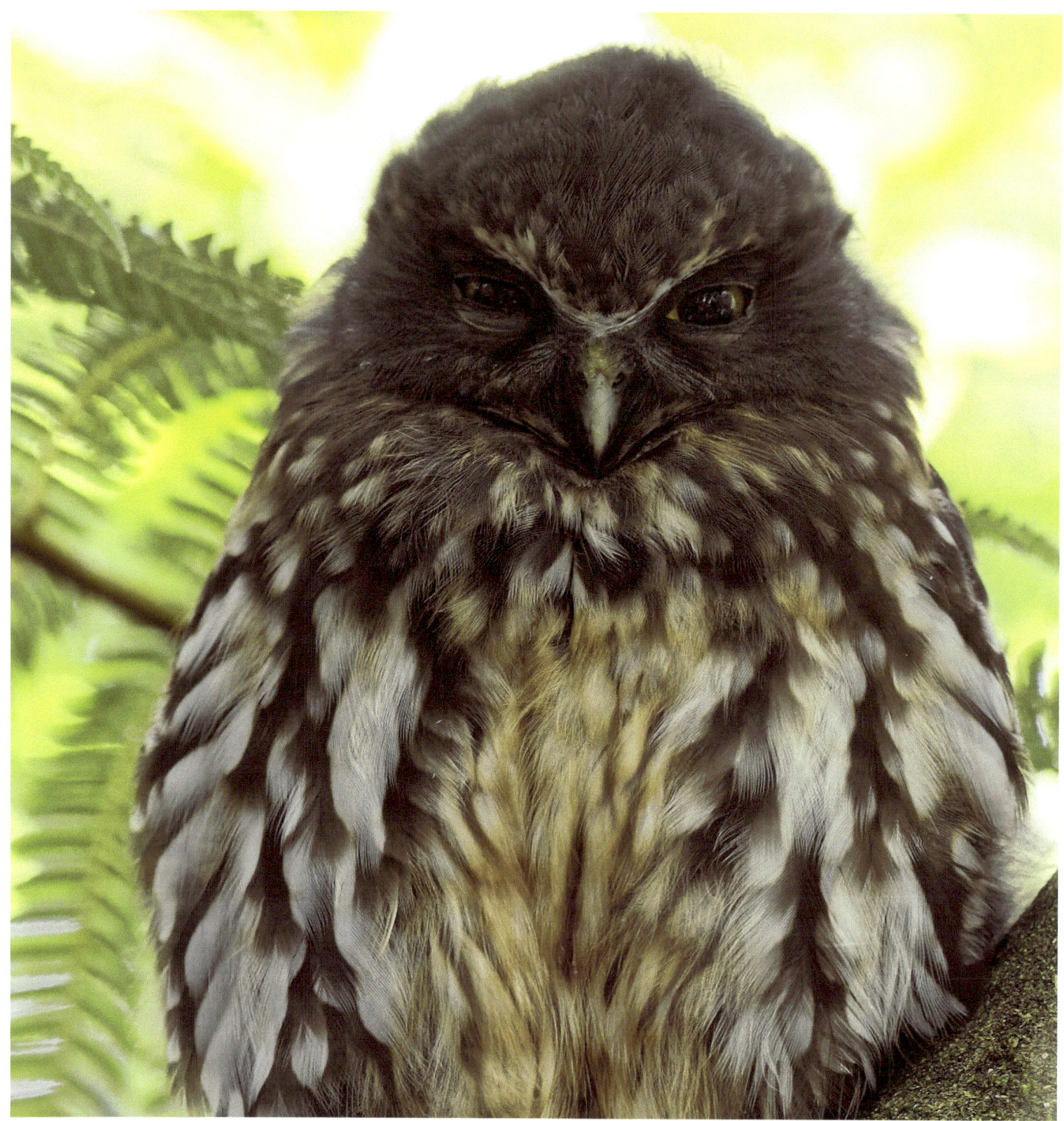

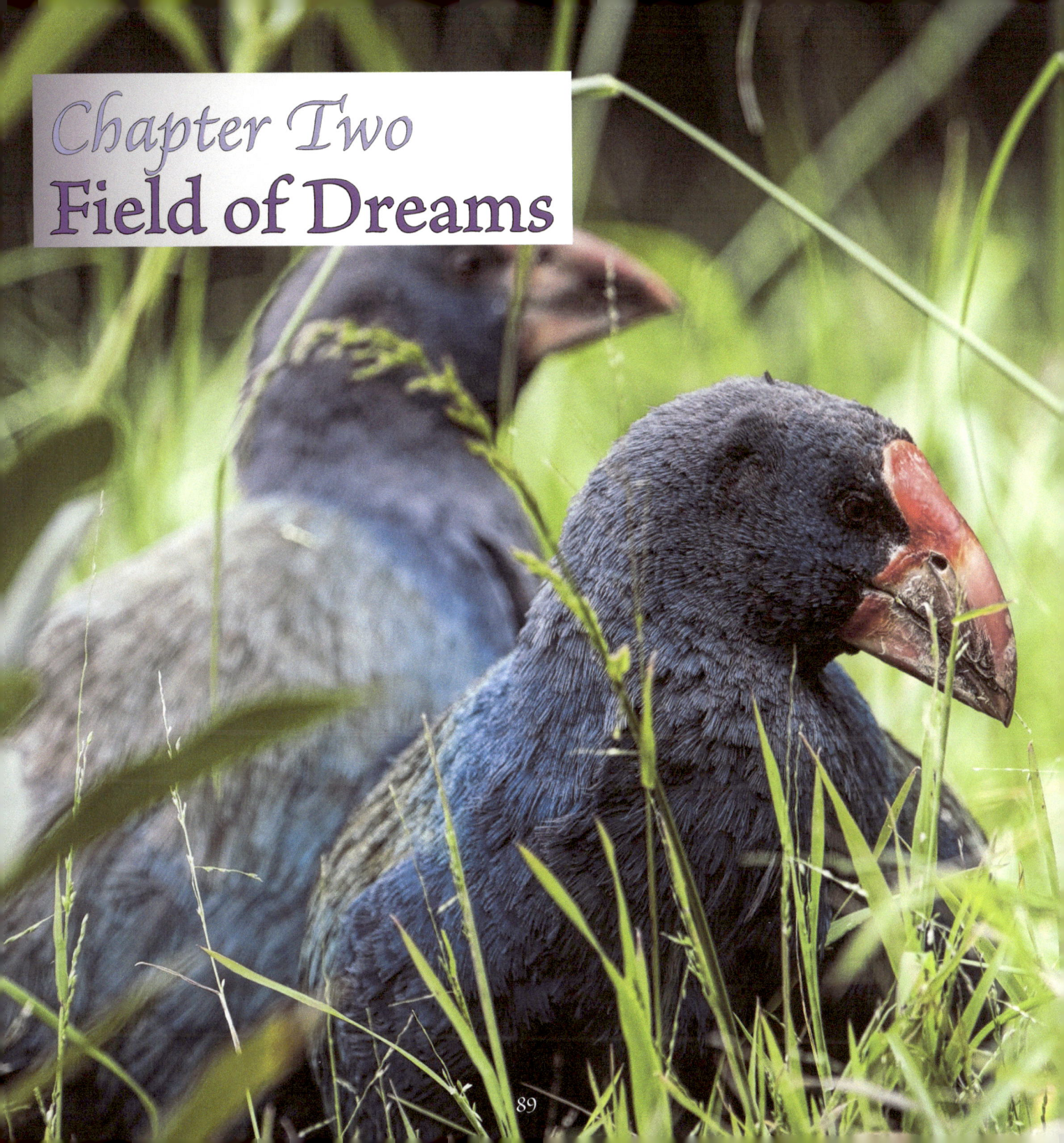

Chapter Two
Field of Dreams

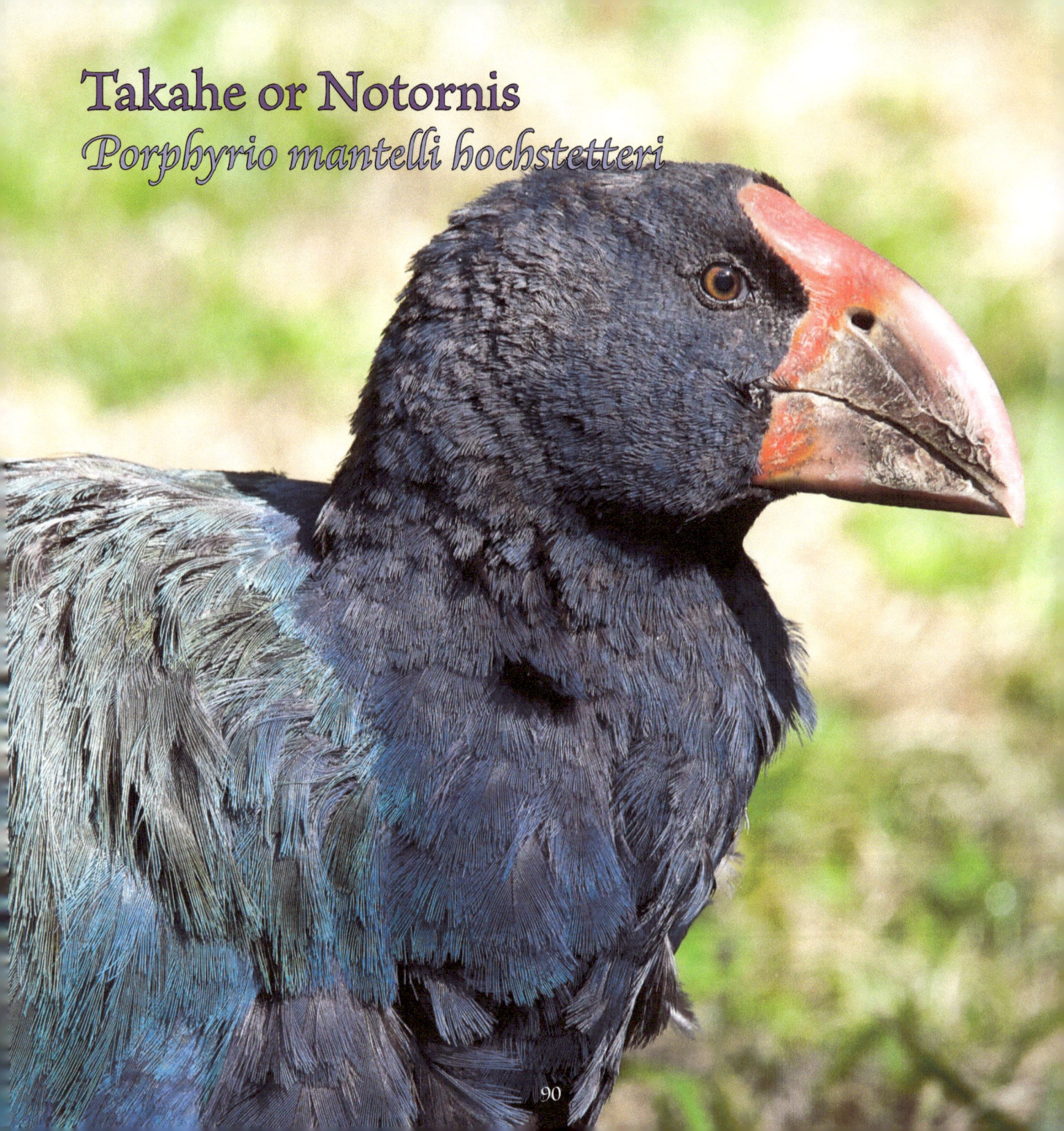

Takahe or Notornis
Porphyrio mantelli hochstetteri

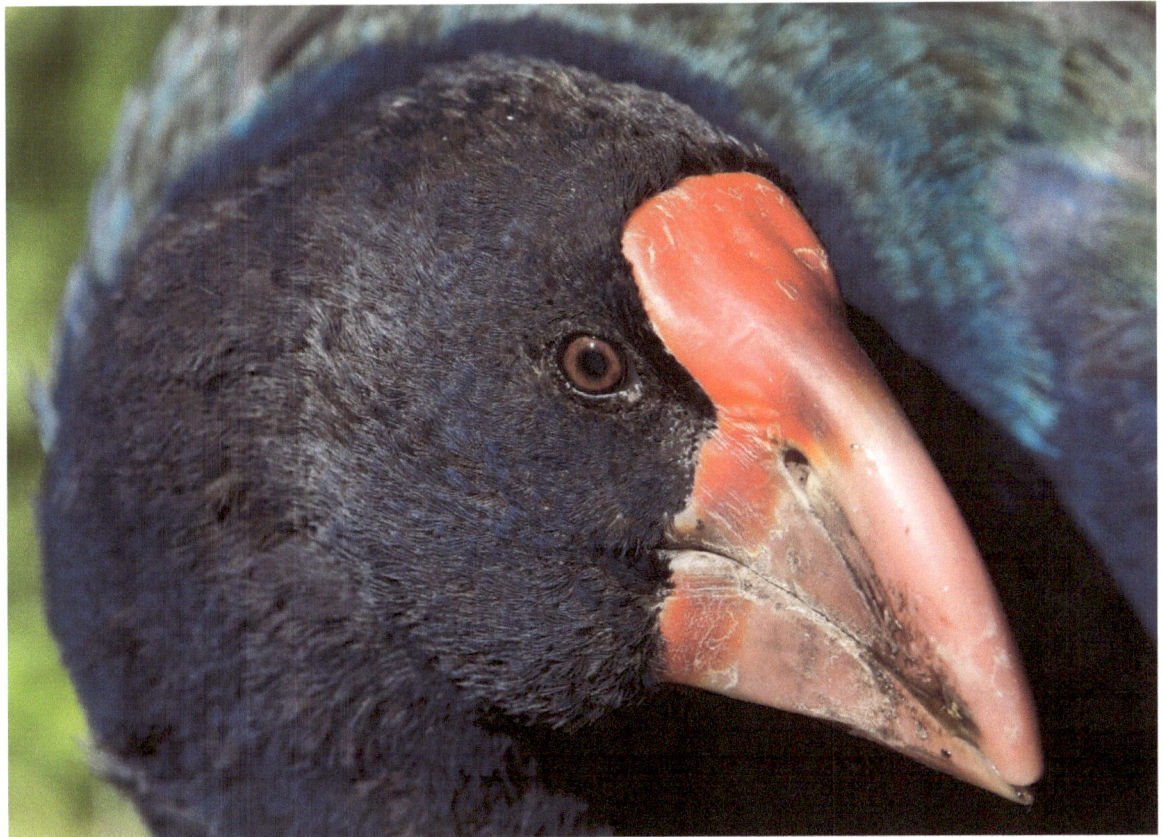

"The rediscovery of a colony of this large, flightless rail in 1948, on the western side of Lake Te Anau, in the South Island, caused interest throughout the world; and the flavour of the excitement of that time appears strongly in the discoverer's account (Orbell, 1949). The find was a most unexpected one for, in the century before, only five recent specimens had come to light and, as 50 years had passed since the last, the species was regarded as extinct. Takahe feed by holding down the shoots with a claw, as does a parrot, and then nipping through low down with the powerful beak. Sometimes a bird may even grub below the ground or pull shoots up bodily if the clump is not too big. Then, still grasping the shoots parrot-fashion, the dead material is stripped off before the chosen portion is eaten and the rest discarded. The foot is not used for picking up material directly–this is done by bill and the material then transferred... In a place where birds have been feeding actively the rejected tussock shoots lie in swathes almost as though they had been scythed. When feeding on the seed–heads of the Danthonias takahe sweep the partly–open bill smoothly along the stalks and strip the seeds from them. As the bird moves its head from stalk to stalk and runs its bill upwards turning its head at the same time, the observer obtains the impression of graceful weaving action."

~*G. R. Williams, 1960-1961*

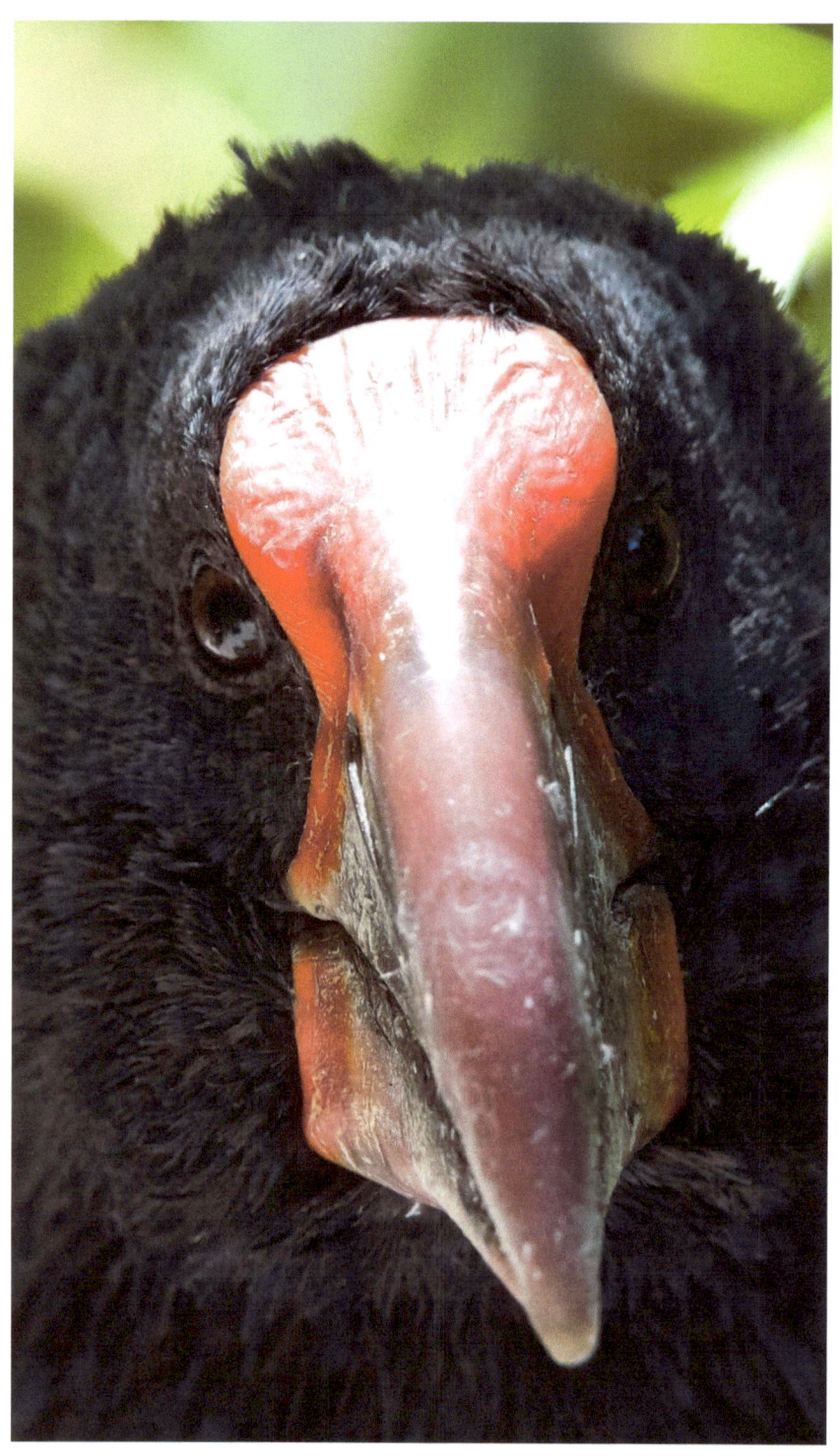

"In size the bird is like a goose, but in colouration it resembles the Pukeko; its breast is a beautiful rich dark-blue, becoming duller on the neck, head, abdomen, and legs. These last are clothed with feathers for a greater distance than in the native turkey, but they are relatively shorter and much thicker than in the latter bird. The legs in both birds have the scaly part, technically termed 'tarso-metatarsus,' as well as the toes, coloured salmon-red. The feathers of the back, wings, and tail are olive-green, with an almost metallic lustre in certain lights; below the short tail the feathers are pure white. When the bird is seen from in front these colours are at their brightest and best; seen from behind… the brightness is lost: the blue becomes dull and nearly black, the green becomes greenish-grey, so that if it were not for the white tail the bird, when retreating, would be very inconspicuous in the feeble light of the bush. This white tail-piece occurs in the Pukeko, as well as in some mammals, such as the rabbit and deer, but its meaning is not always obvious; although the general inconspicuousness to foes is diminished, yet its recognition by friends appears to be attained thereby. The eyes are red-brown. But perhaps one of the most noticeable features of the bird is its beak—a great equilateral triangle of hard pink horn, with one angle directed forwards. At the upper side of the base of the beak is a bright-red band of soft tissue like an attempt at a 'comb,' such as we get in cocks, only transversely placed. The whole is a handsome bird of heavy gait, absolutely unable to use its wings for their natural purpose of flying. Indeed, one of the interests, zoologically, is that, like several of our native birds, it is flightless, while its congeners in other countries are endued with powers of flight."

~Sir Walter L. Buller, 1898

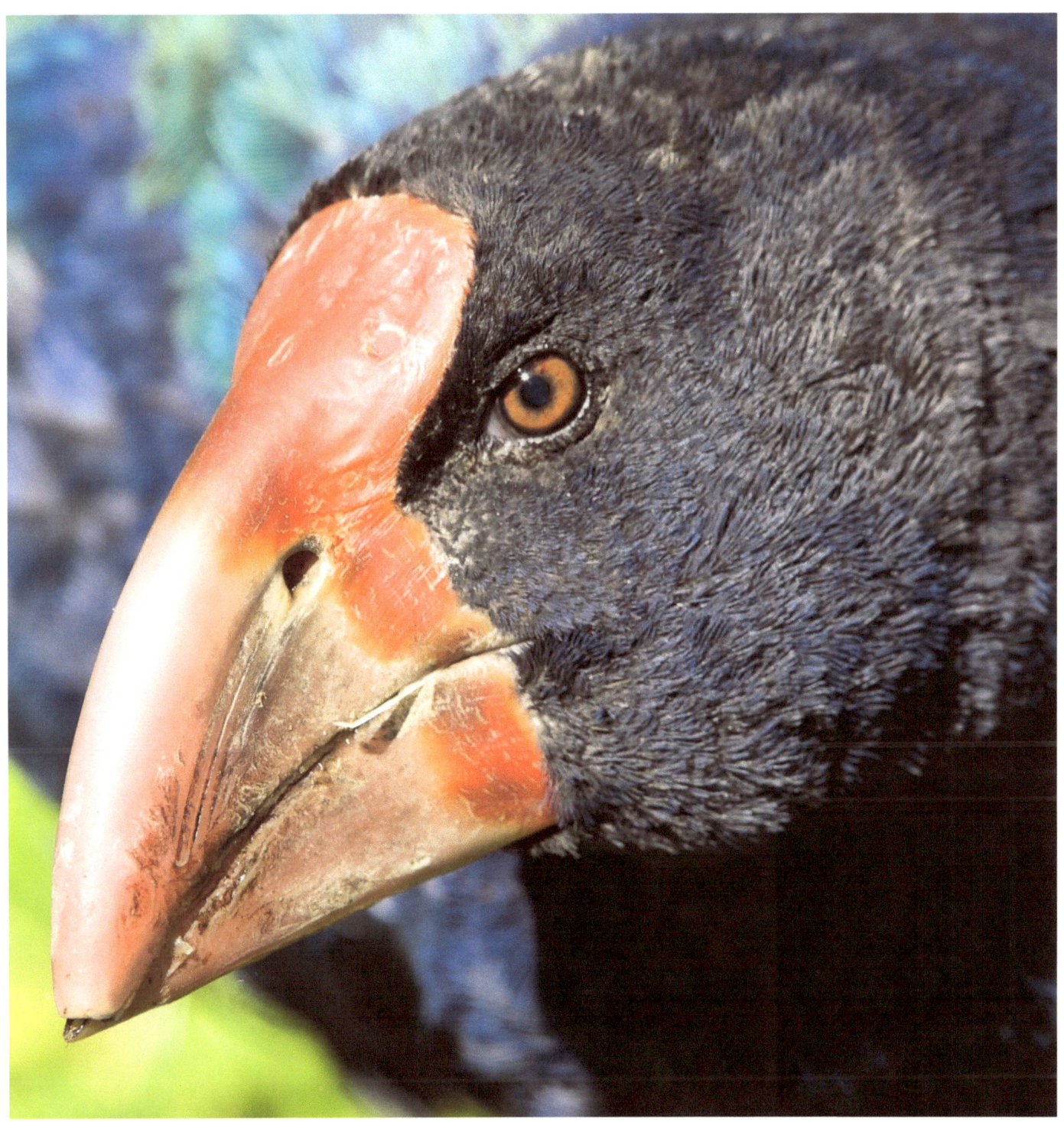

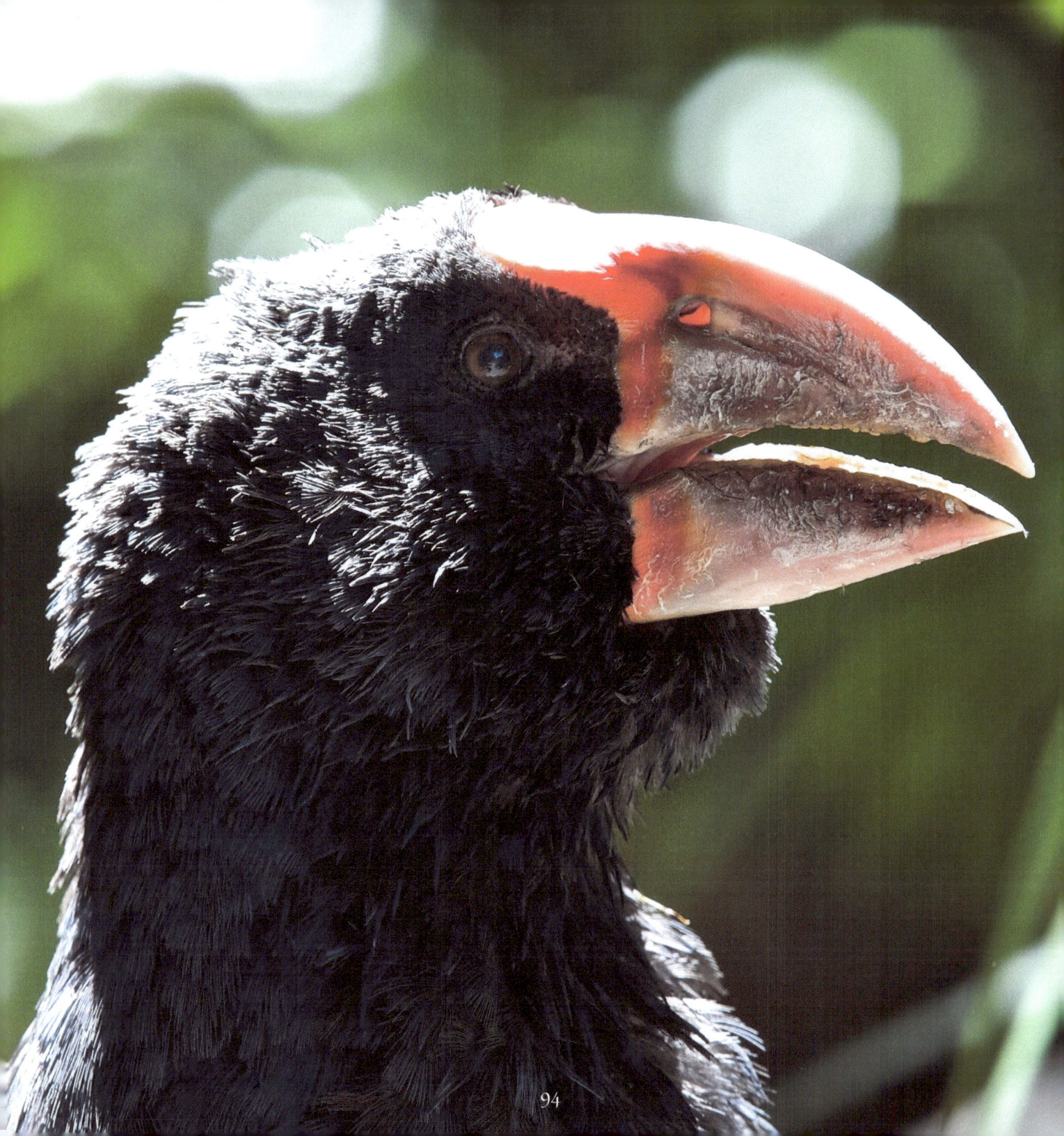

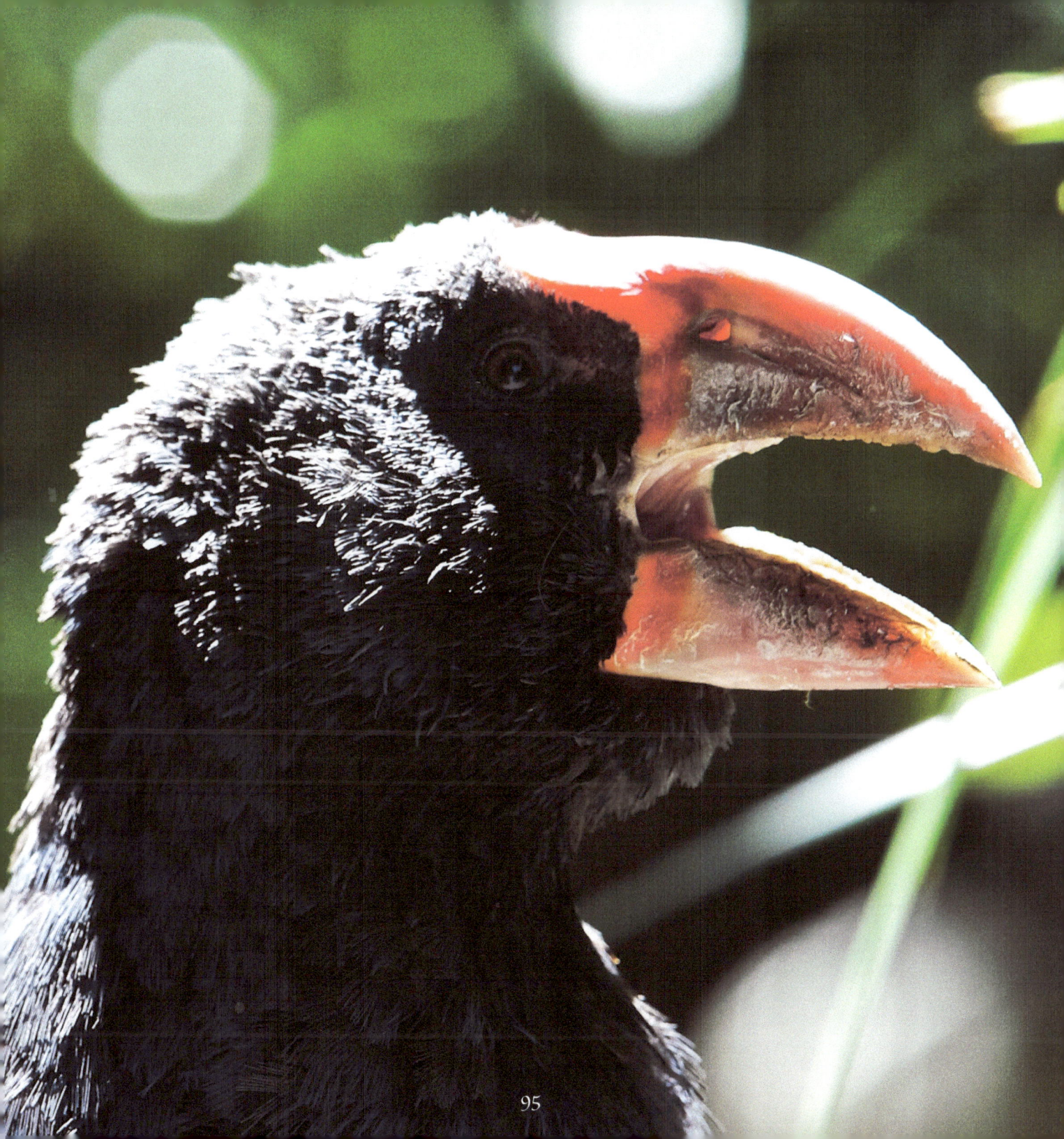

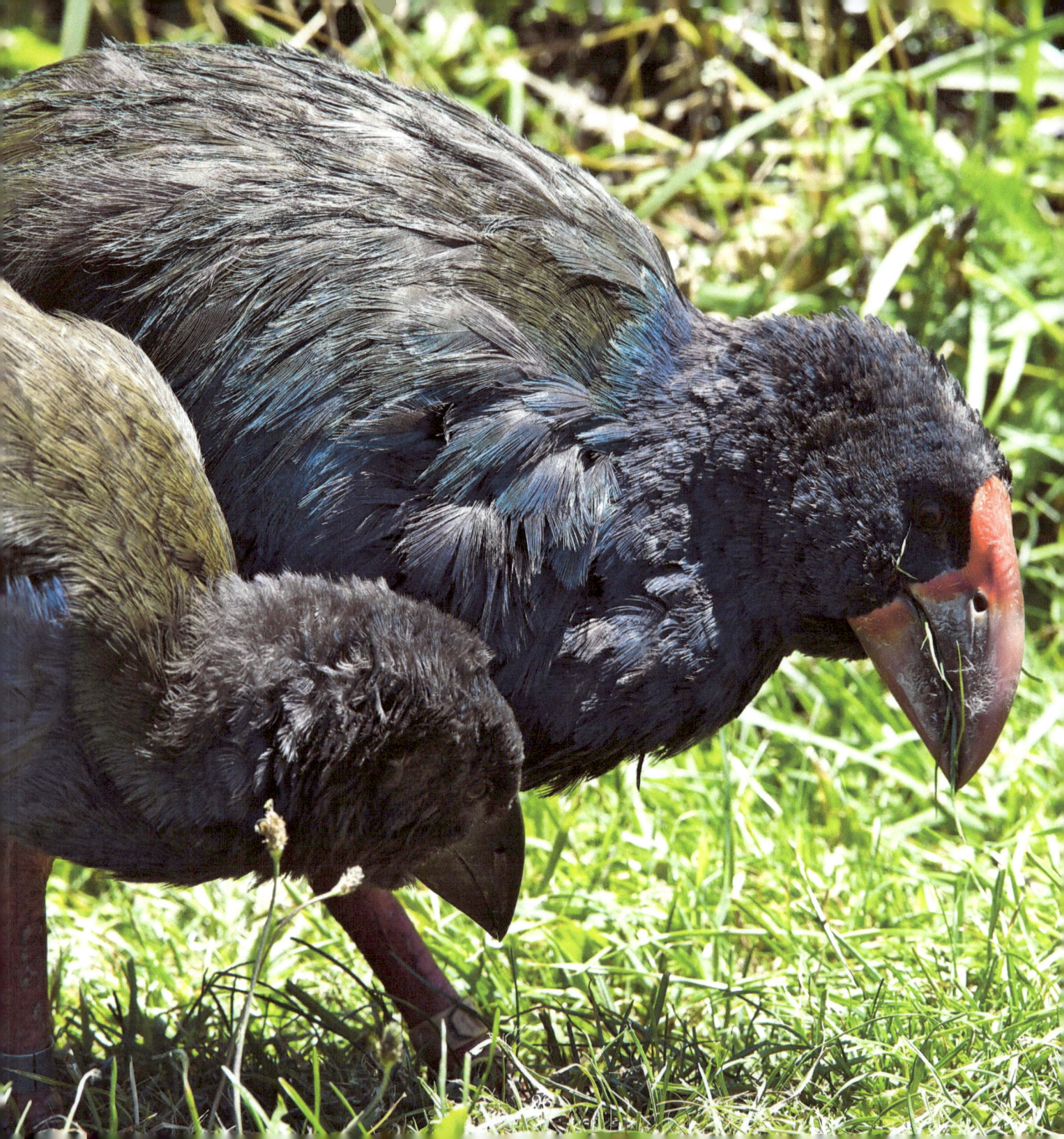

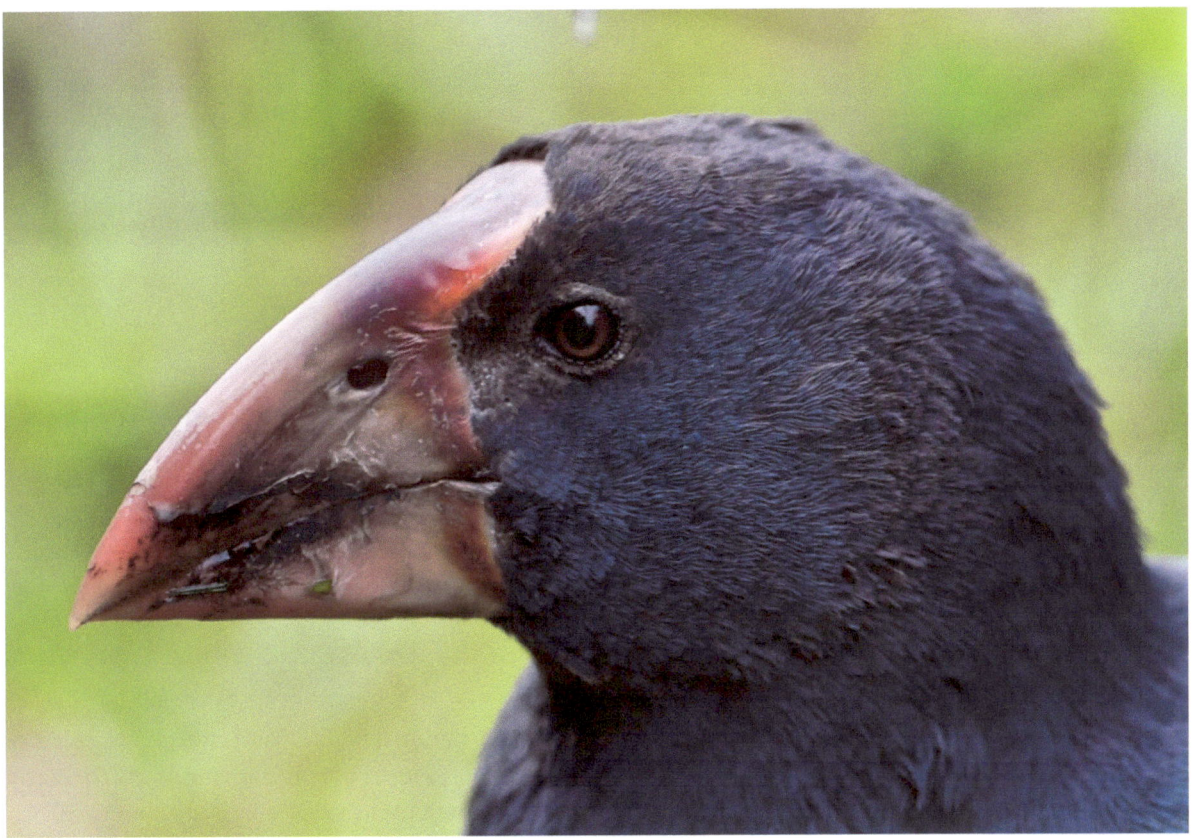

"During the summer of 1880-81 I was engaged under Mr. A. McKay, F.G.S. Assistant Geologist, who was making a geological exploration of the Wanaka country. Mr. John Buchanan, F.L.S., also accompanied the party as botanist. On the 20th January, 1881, we proceeded up the south branch of the Matukituki River, and camped at Cascade Creek, behind Mount Aspiring. That evening we were startled by the loud booming note of a strange bird, uttered at short intervals throughout the greater part of the night. Next evening a decoy-fire was lit in the bush near the camp to attract the bird, in the hope of being able to effect its capture; but in this we were unsuccessful, although on several occasions it approached quite close to the fire. We learnt, however, that it was of a curious nature, like many of our New Zealand birds; that its height was certainly less than 20in., judging from the free manner in which it moved below the dense matted scrub; and that its note was so deep and intense as to make the ground vibrate distinctly for a distance of several yards around. On the 29th January we shifted camp to the forks of Matukituki, opposite Mount Aspiring, and while camped there we again heard the same strange booming note; but, as before, all efforts to capture its mysterious author were futile.

However on one occasion I caught a passing glimpse of it and on examining the same place next day I found that it had been scratching in the sand. I also examined its footprints in the soft mud near the

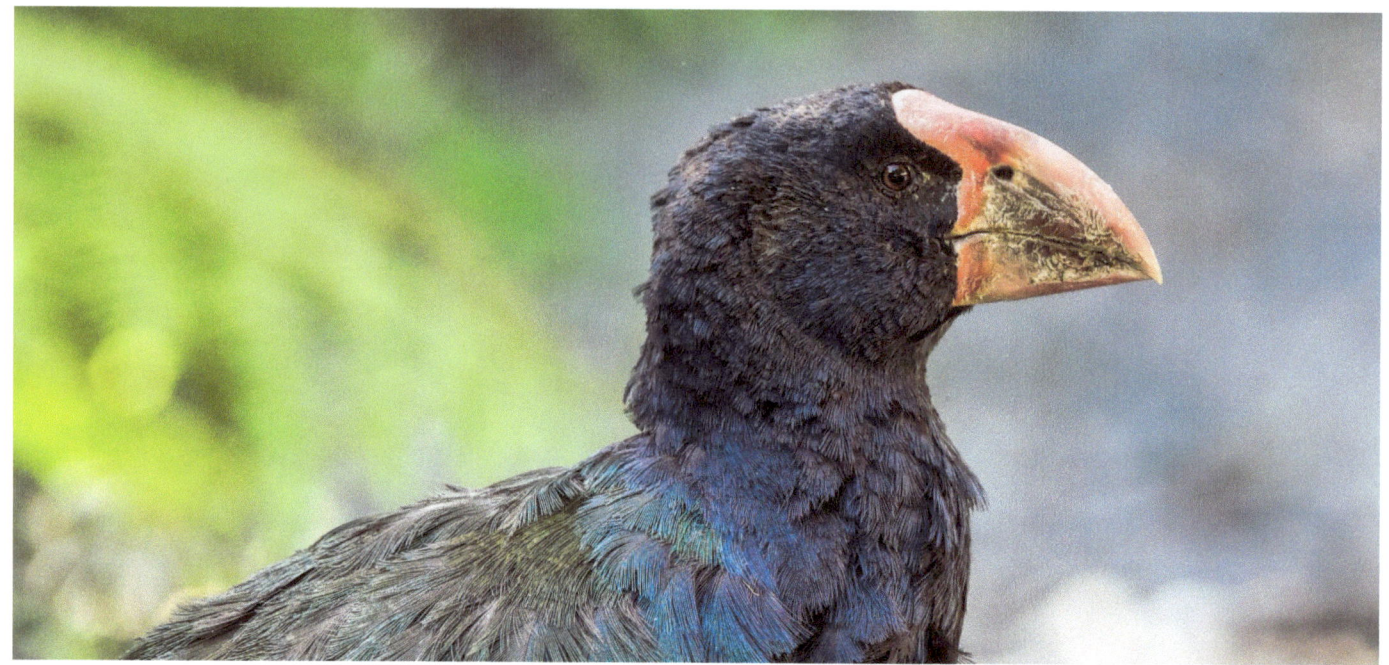

bank of the river, and at the time made a sketch of them on a loose slip of paper. I did not mention this latter circumstance in my paper on the takahe because I was unable to lay my hand on the sketch, but I remember quite distinctly that the footprints had a general resemblance to those of the weka. They certainly had no resemblance to the shuffling track of the kakapo. After a lapse of seven years I again met our booming visitant of the Matukituki Valley. In the beginning of January, 1888, I visited Dusky Sound, and the day after my arrival, while accompanying Mr. Docherty to his pyrrhotine lode on the slopes of Mount Hodge, I heard the old, familiar, but almost forgotten, booming note of 1881. On returning to the hut in the evening my field-hand informed me that while fishing off the point he had heard the boom of the takahe in the direction of Mount Hodge. He said he had been rabbiting on the Mararoa Flat, and had seen and heard the takahe... Previous to this occasion I had never heard the Notornis referred to as the takahe. I considered this circumstantial evidence, and my own previous experience, sufficient to justify me in arriving at the conclusion that the takahe was the author of this mysterious note. Mr. Melland's case is, I understand, as follows: He has heard, he says, the booming note described by me. He admits its unusual and startling character, and speaks of it as a 'powerful and alarming sound,' which, he says, he has 'heard across the still waters of Lake Te Anau, a distance of five or six miles.' As to the author of this unusual note he professes to have no doubt whatever, the mystery having been solved some years ago by Mr. R. Henry, of Lake Te Anau. It is strange that a 'powerful and alarming sound' like this should remain unsolved until the arrival of Mr. Henry, a few years ago, and stranger still that, when solved, it was not thought worth recording. Mr. Melland says the booming is warlike, Mr. Henry that it is amatory. On this question I am unable to express an opinion, but would in passing remark that the bird continued its deep booming note as it manœuvred around the decoy-fire."

~James Park, 1890

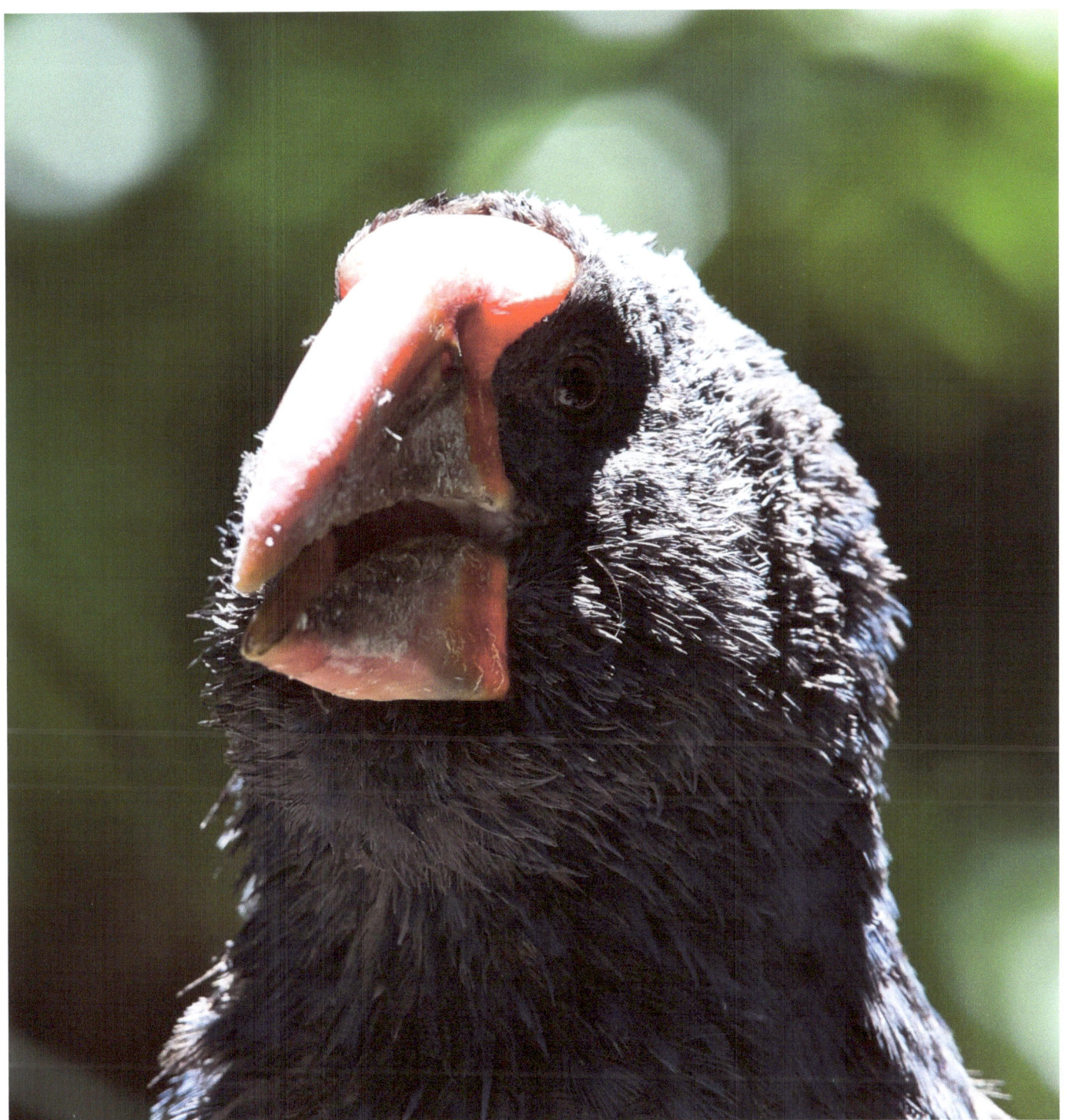

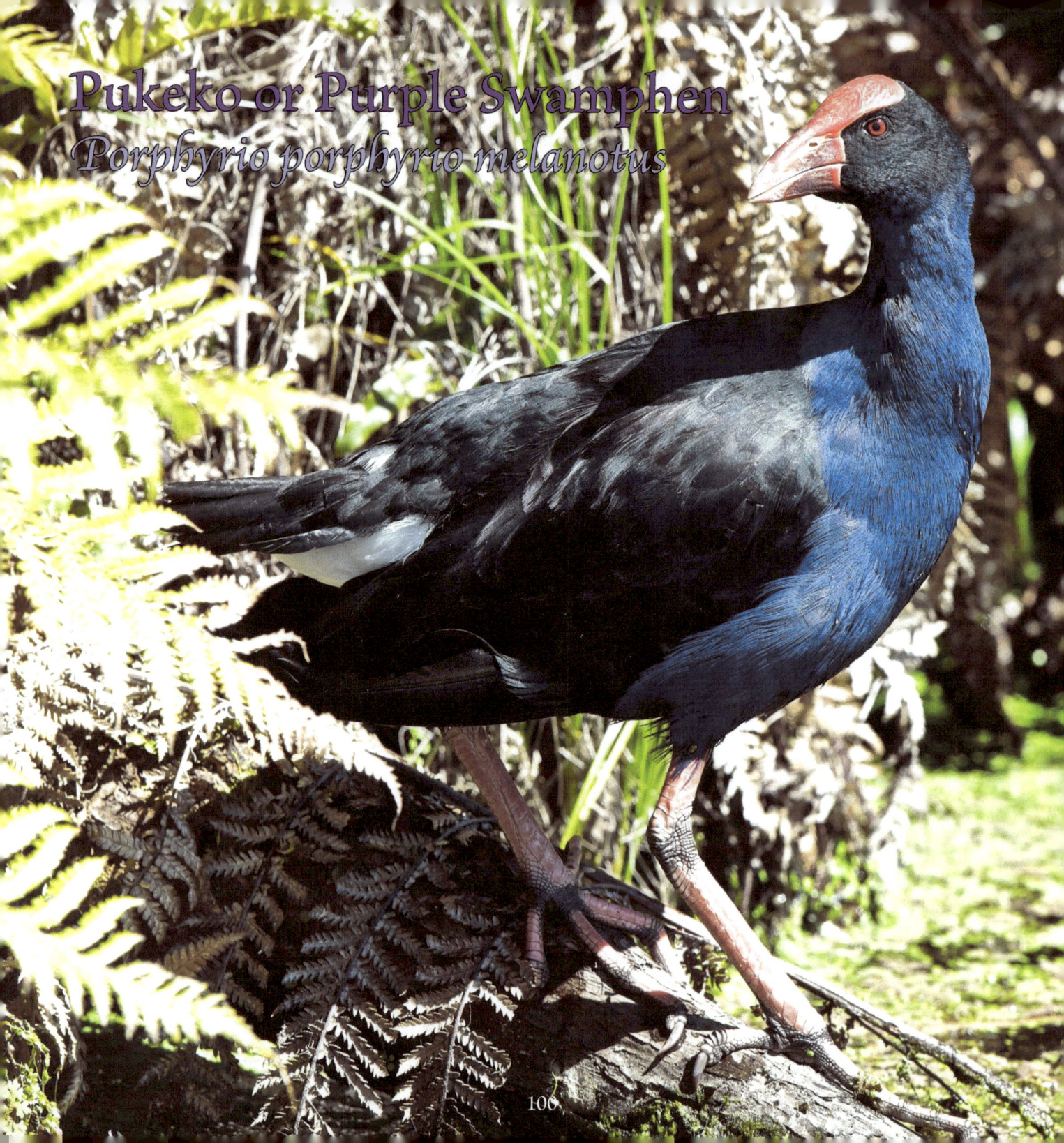

Pukeko or Purple Swamphen
Porphyrio porphyrio melanotus

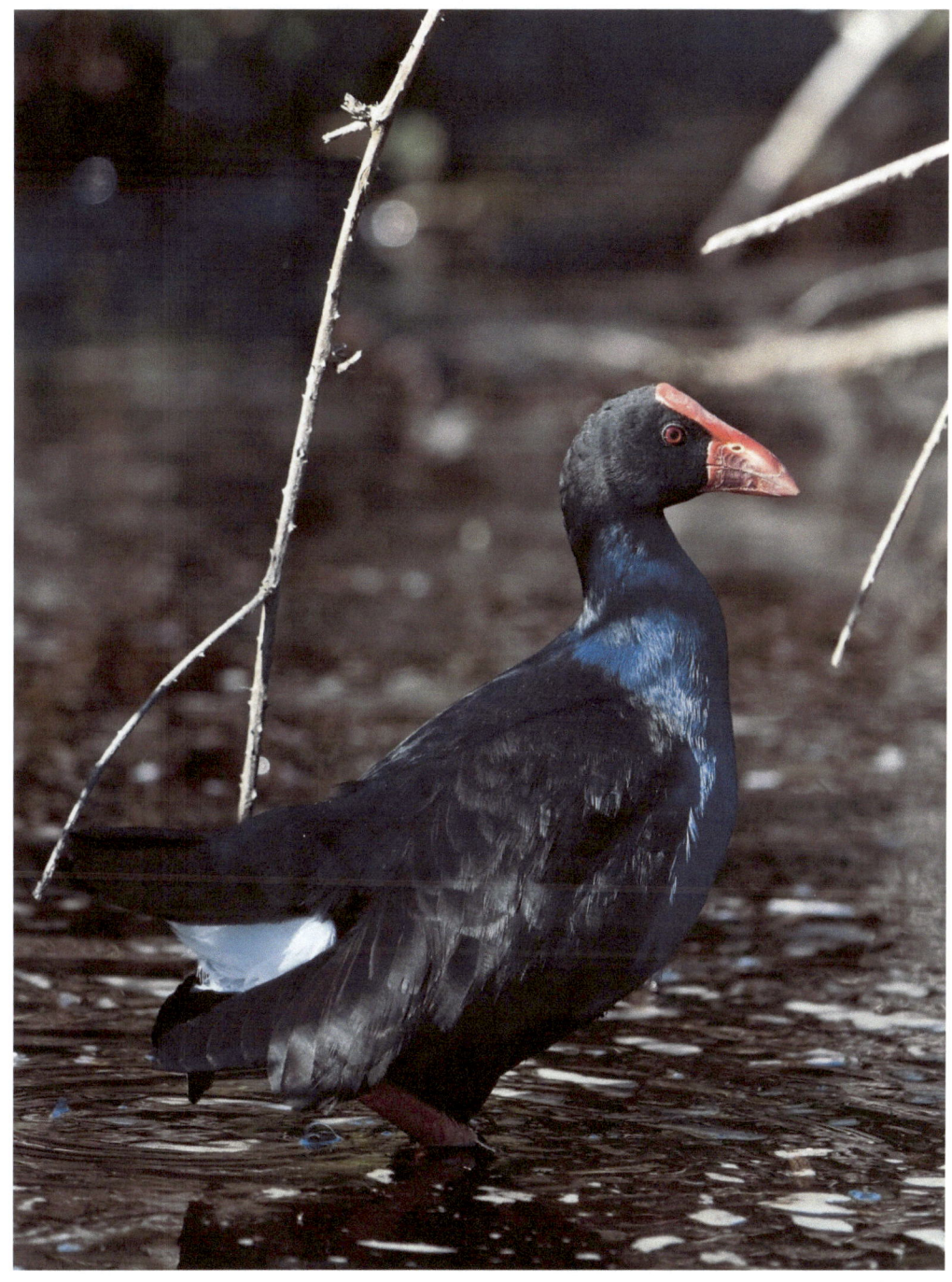

"This beautiful rail delights in swamps, where its nest is also to be found, built of grass; the top is sometimes more than a foot above the ground, and not unfrequently it may be observed surrounded by water. The number of eggs to a nest varies considerably, as we have found from two to seven, five may be considered the usual complement, in shape ovoiconical, greyish–brown, with dots and blotches of reddish–brown, measuring through the axis 2 inches 2 lines, with a diameter of 1 inch 6 lines. These dimensions appear very small for so large a bird, more especially when compared with those of the egg of Apteryx Mantelli. The young run about as soon as they are hatched, and on being disturbed conceal themselves with great art. They are thickly clothed with black velvety down, interspersed with fine hair–like points of silver–grey; legs dullish–red, beak has a yellowish ivory look, which contrasts pleasingly with the rest of the body.

~T. H. Potts, 1869

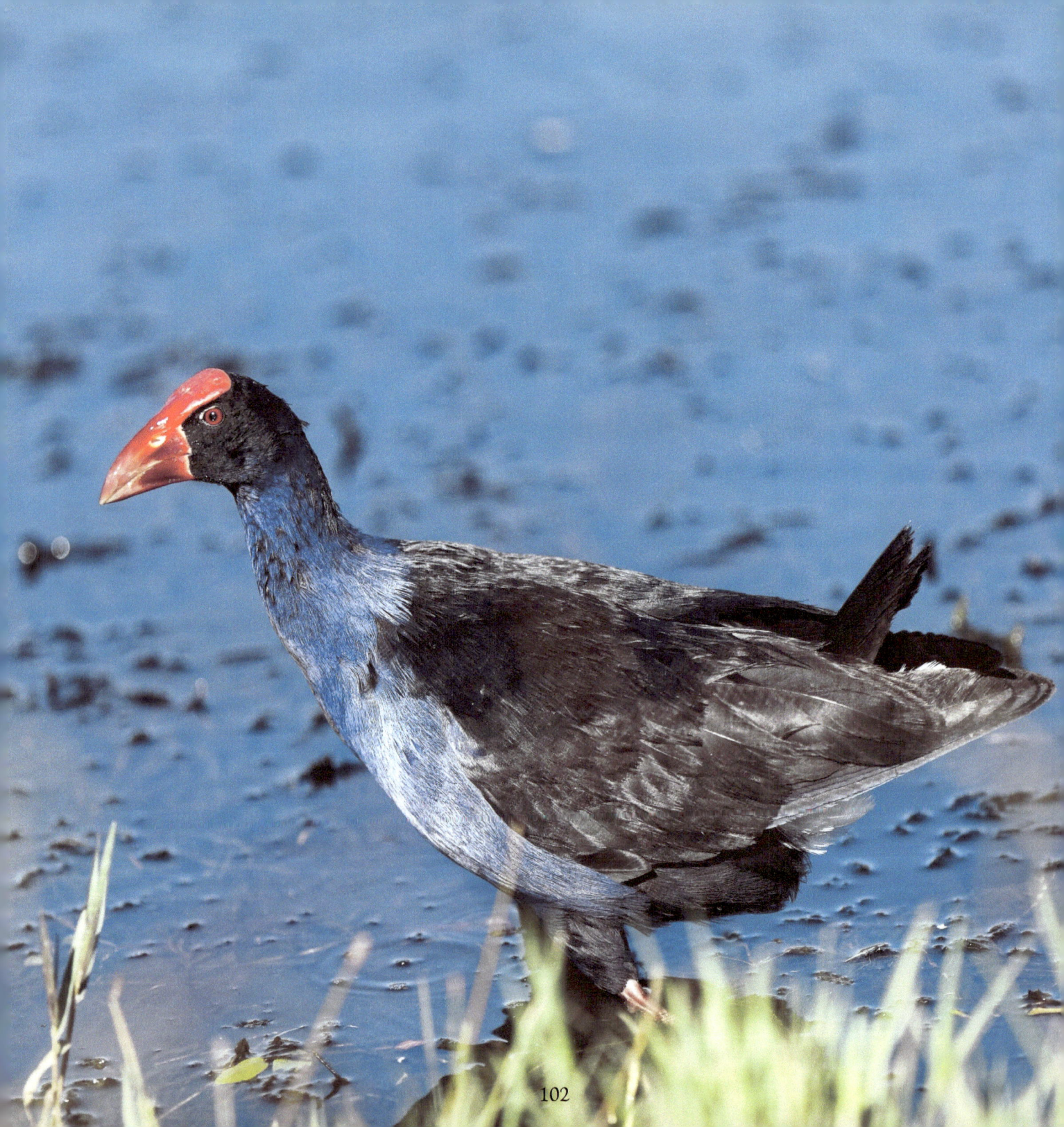

Weka or Woodhen
Gallirallus australis greyi

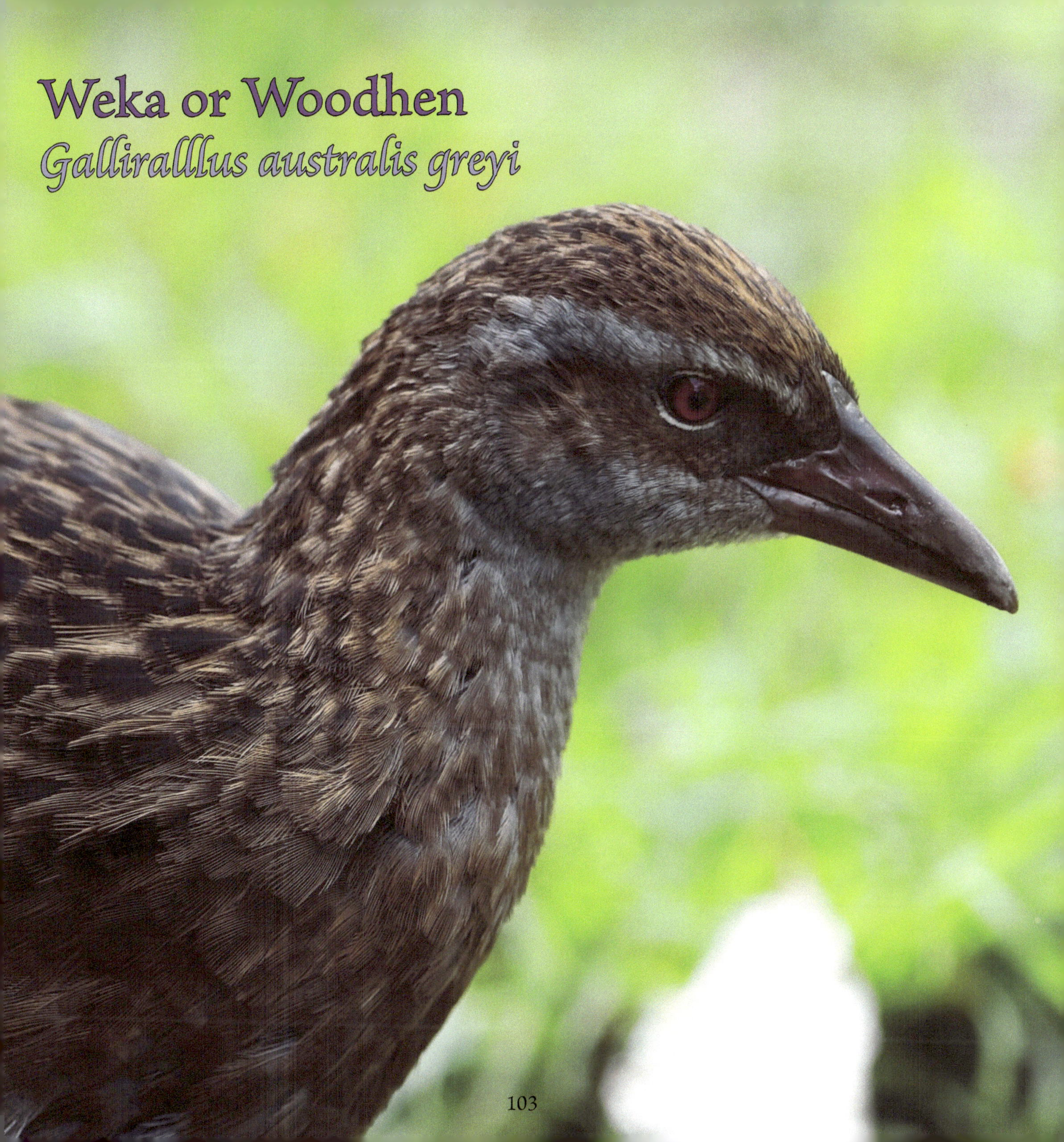

"We have cleared most of the little peninsula on which our house stands, and now it is a favourite place for the wood-hens, but they do not like each other's company, and there are seldom more than two to be seen at once, though there are half a dozen occasional visitors. They often treat us to some spirited races across the open, and are no mean runners when assisted by their wings, but all seem to be so well matched that they generally run dead heats. If there happens to be one a little slow it is sure to be minus its tail, which is not of much account anyway; yet they seem to think a great deal of it, for the pulling of a feather is sure to bring on a fight, very fierce at first, but quickly dying away into threatening attitudes and various grunts which may represent bad language. The championship appears to be awarded more for courage than muscle, because the smallest hen, when she was thinking of nesting, would hunt away all the others, both males and females, except her mate, with whom she was generally friendly, but not always so. Those were the only pair here mated throughout the winter, and the only pair that would sing in concert… I saw her on a new nest, but fearing she might forsake that also I came away and left them. A day or two later… I went away to see the eggs; but the nest was empty–no eggs and no young ones. 'All a hoax,' said I, 'or else the rats have eaten them.' But next day, when coming home, we met them near the beach, and they scolded and threatened the dogs, so that I knew they had chickens; but I had to wait a long time before the old ones got confidence enough to call out of their hiding three tiny little black chickens, which were just able

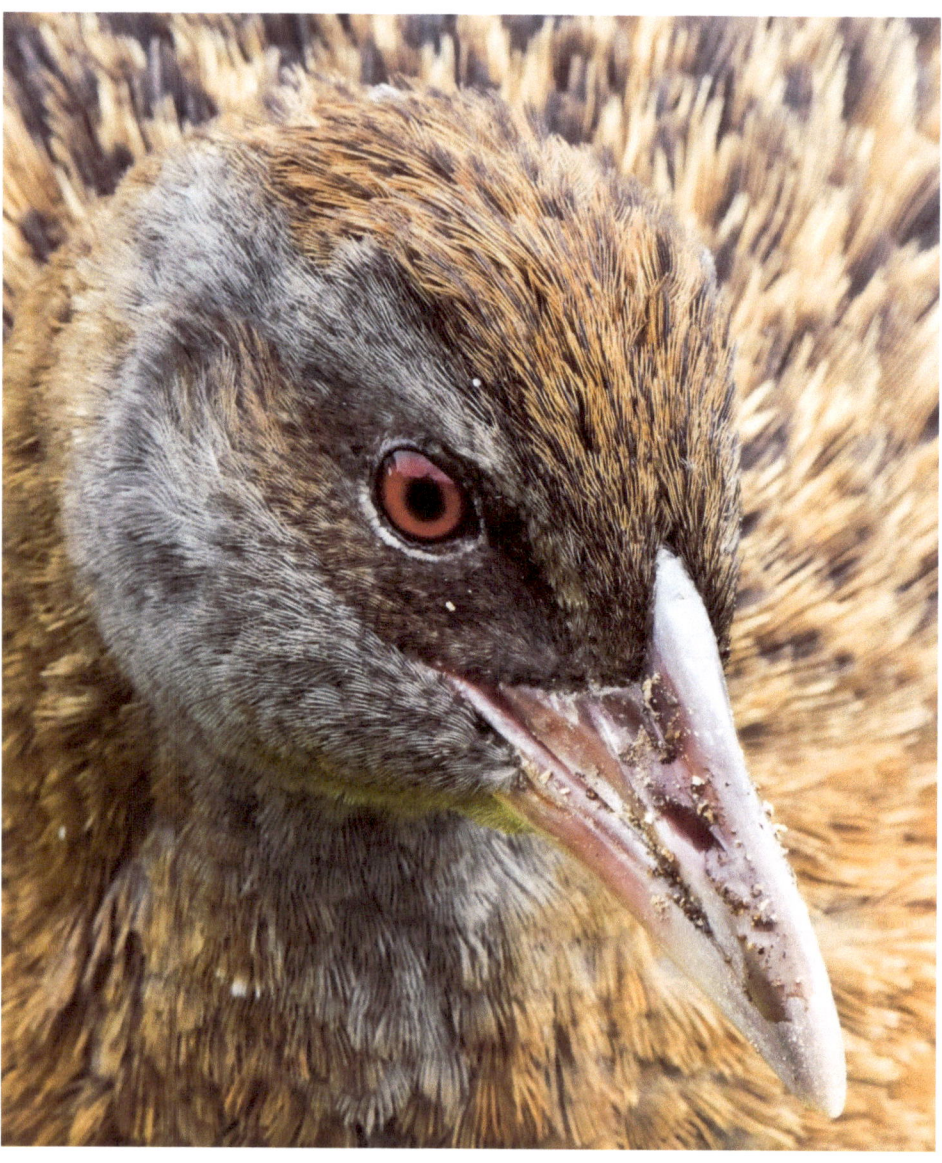

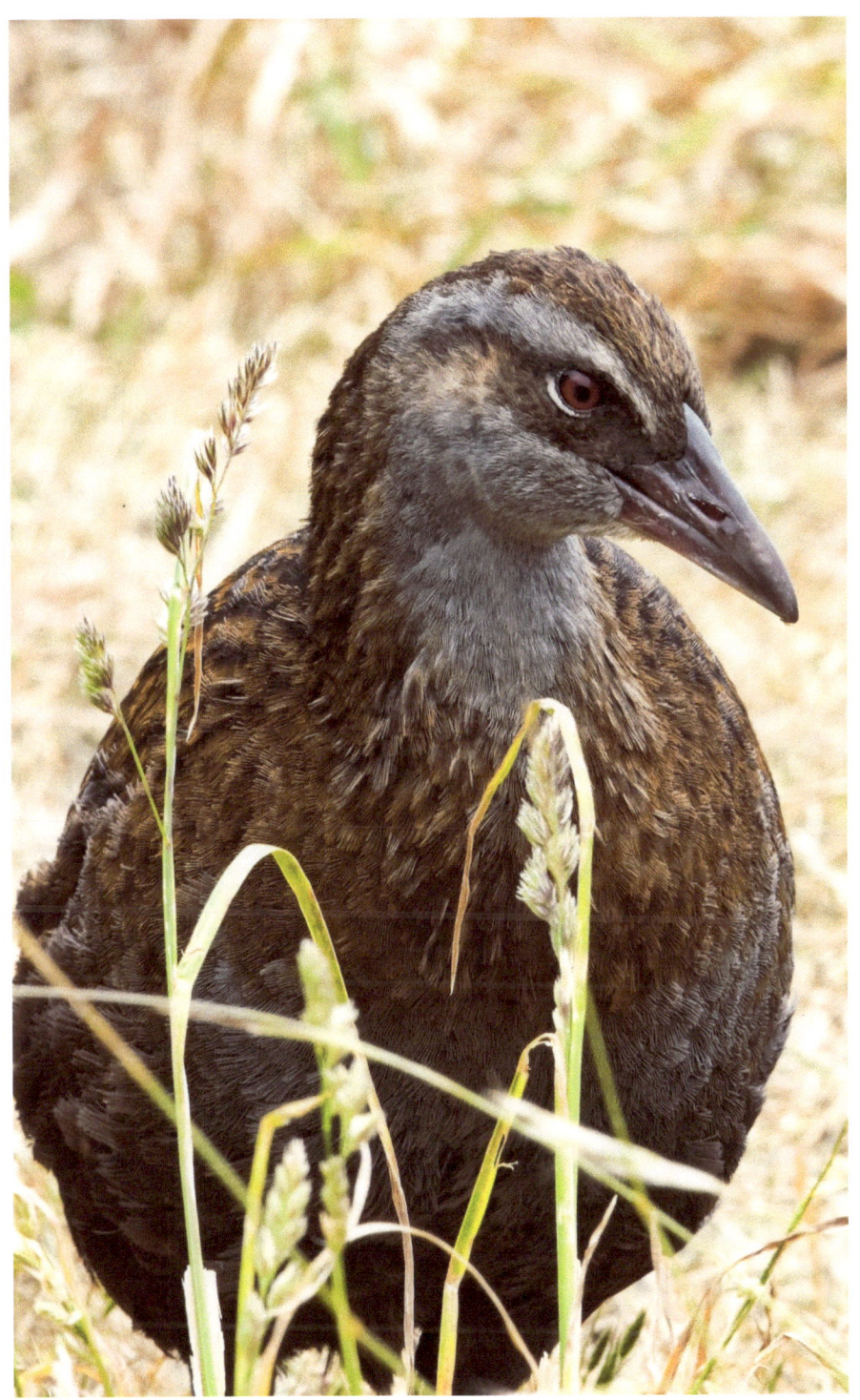

to stagger about, yet with sense enough to scramble under cover when the old ones told them to do so. They gradually brought them nearer the house until they occupied a sheltered corner, where the little ones remained while the parents went away for food. They are the very best of nurses. The male in particular is never tired of running here and there and bringing home something.

They seldom succeed in getting more than enough, because when we give them too much they cram the little ones until they cannot eat–another scrap, and then the old ones become solicitous, and hold up food to them with a crooning, pitiful note, as if they feared the little gluttons were going to die because they could not eat… The staple food of the wekas appears to be sand–fleas, which are here in plenty, not only on the beaches, but all through the bush, under the dead leaves and rubbish; and they are never tired raking over this and pulling about the seaweed in search of them. They also pull about the dead grass and turn over every chip in search of other things, but it is all done with the beak–they are not such fools as to go kicking things all over the place like common fowls. The sand–fleas are lively, and can make long jumps, so that whilst a rooster would be turning round to look for them they would have all jumped away. Of course, there are hosts of other insects, including cockroaches in plenty and monster earthworms, which they may catch at night, for they are often out on mild nights, and always active late in the evening… There is a little plant with

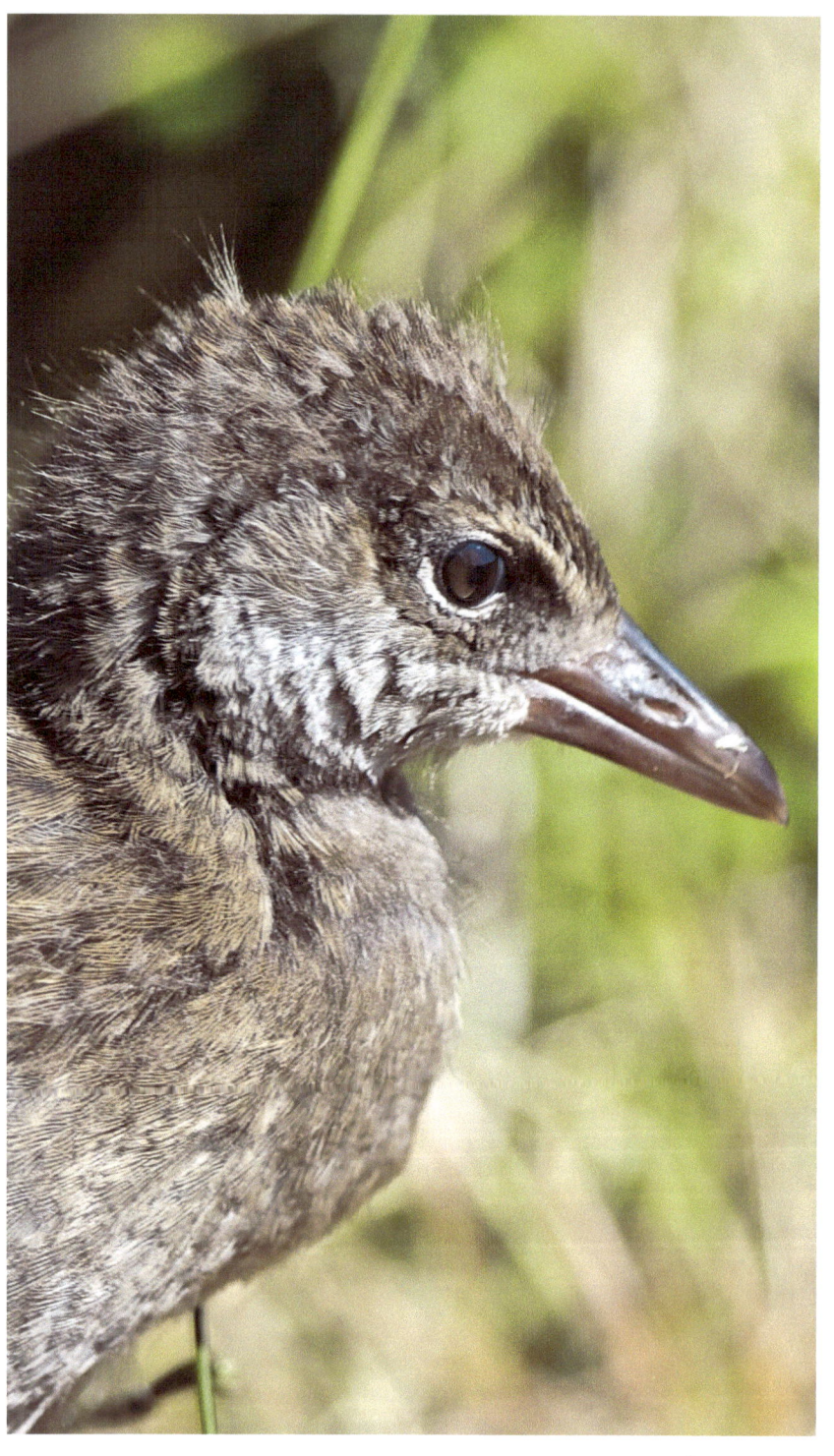

a white bulb like a marble which they know well, and like to eat, but it is watery and quite tasteless… In July, when out at the clearing, I heard a woodhen screaming in distress down in a gully, and as it continued I called to Burt, who was nearer the spot, to see what was the matter. Guided by the sound, he went down quickly and found a sparrow-hawk holding on to a woodhen under a log. He caught the hawk, and the hen ran away. When I went over I saw that the hawk's beak was full of the inner down of the hen, so that she had a narrow escape that time, and by calling for help exchanged places with her enemy. They have a special note to indicate the presence of a sparrow-hawk, and generally let us know when there is one about. The tuis, mokos, and robins can also sing out 'Sparrow-hawk!' in their own language, and all the others understand; so that he is proclaimed everywhere he goes, which is just what he does not want, and he must have a very vexatious time of it trying to get a living. On another occasion I hung a fishing-net on the clothes-lines to dry, and when we came home a little male sparrow-hawk was caught in the net about 1 ft. from the ground. Our tame weka was in a great state of agitation, yet bold enough to come up and peck at the hawk in defence of her chickens, who was probably stooping for one of them when the net caught him… When the tide is low and the wekas are tempted away out on the beaches I think the hawks take 90 per cent of the young ones, which may be quite desirable, because from recent developments the wekas appear to be the worst enemies of the ducks."

~Richard Henry, 1897

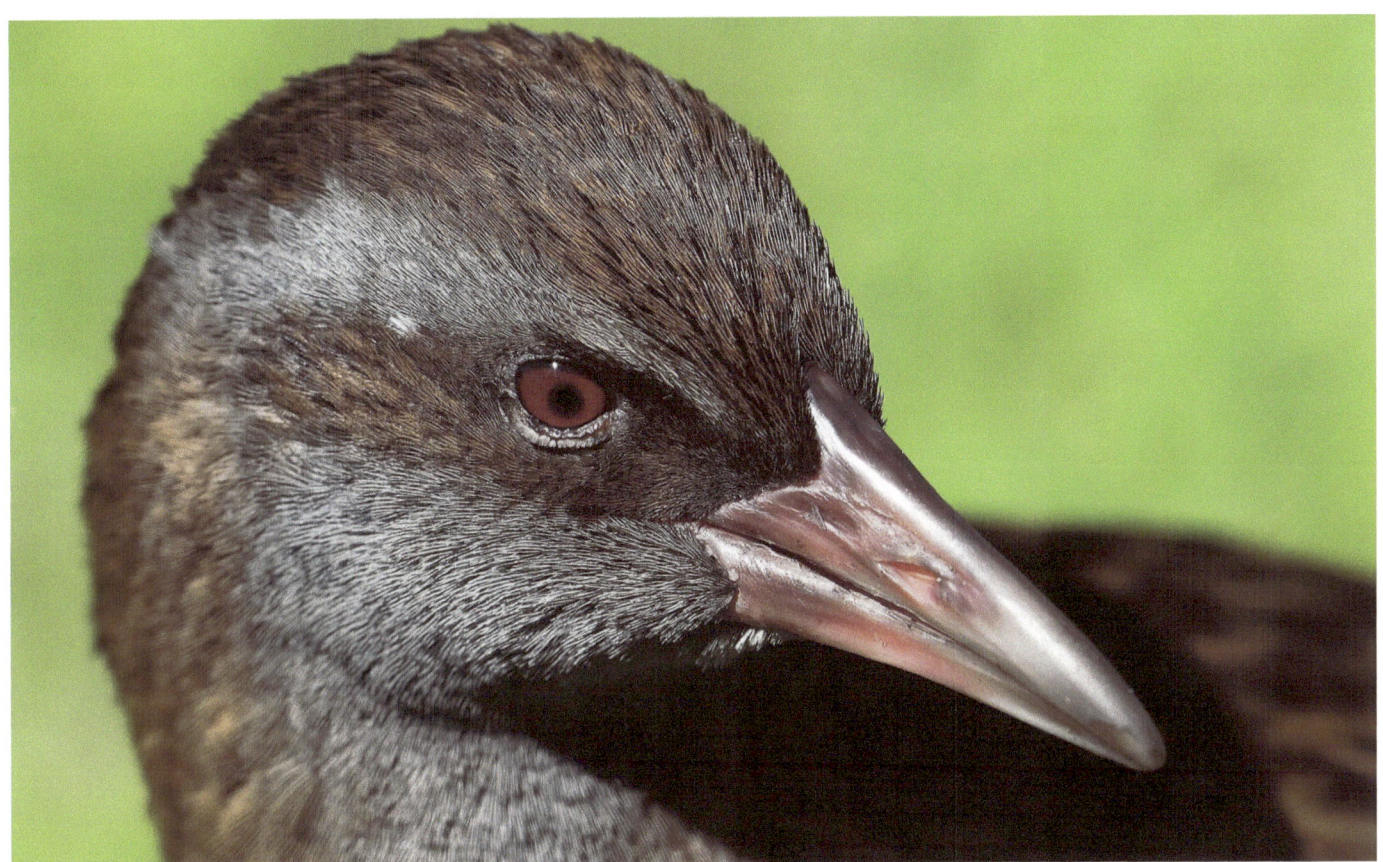

"The habits of the Weka have been noticed in Mr. Potts' interesting papers published in the second and third RSNZ Volumes of the Transactions of the New Zealand Institute, but a few points which he has not mentioned may probably be acceptable. It will have been observed by those who have examined the structure of this bird, that the metacarpal and phalangial bones are represented by a single sharp spur about with the backs turned forward, and it th half an inch in length. When irritated it extends its wings en uses this spur as a weapon of offence. It delights in prowling about the low bushes at the edge of the forest, and on the banks of rivers, creeping along with a stealthy cat–like tread, and preying on any small bird which may come within its reach. It is specially destructive to eggs and young poultry. I have seen a Weka drive its beak into an egg, and then, raising its head to a nearly upright position, run away into the bush with the egg impaled upon it… They pair for the breeding season, the male bird assisting in the work of incubation, and accompanying the female and her young ones until the latter are weaned. I have seen seven and eight young ones in a single brood. I may add that many persons, some of whom must be considered of high authority, have stated that this bird breeds with the common domestic fowl. The statement, if correct, is so extraordinary, that all the facts in support of it ought to be made known. As the case has never come under my own observation I merely mention this statement, in the hope that those who possess any knowledge on the subject will publish the facts."

~*W. T. L. Travers, 1871*

Moho-pereru or Banded Rail
Raillus philippensis

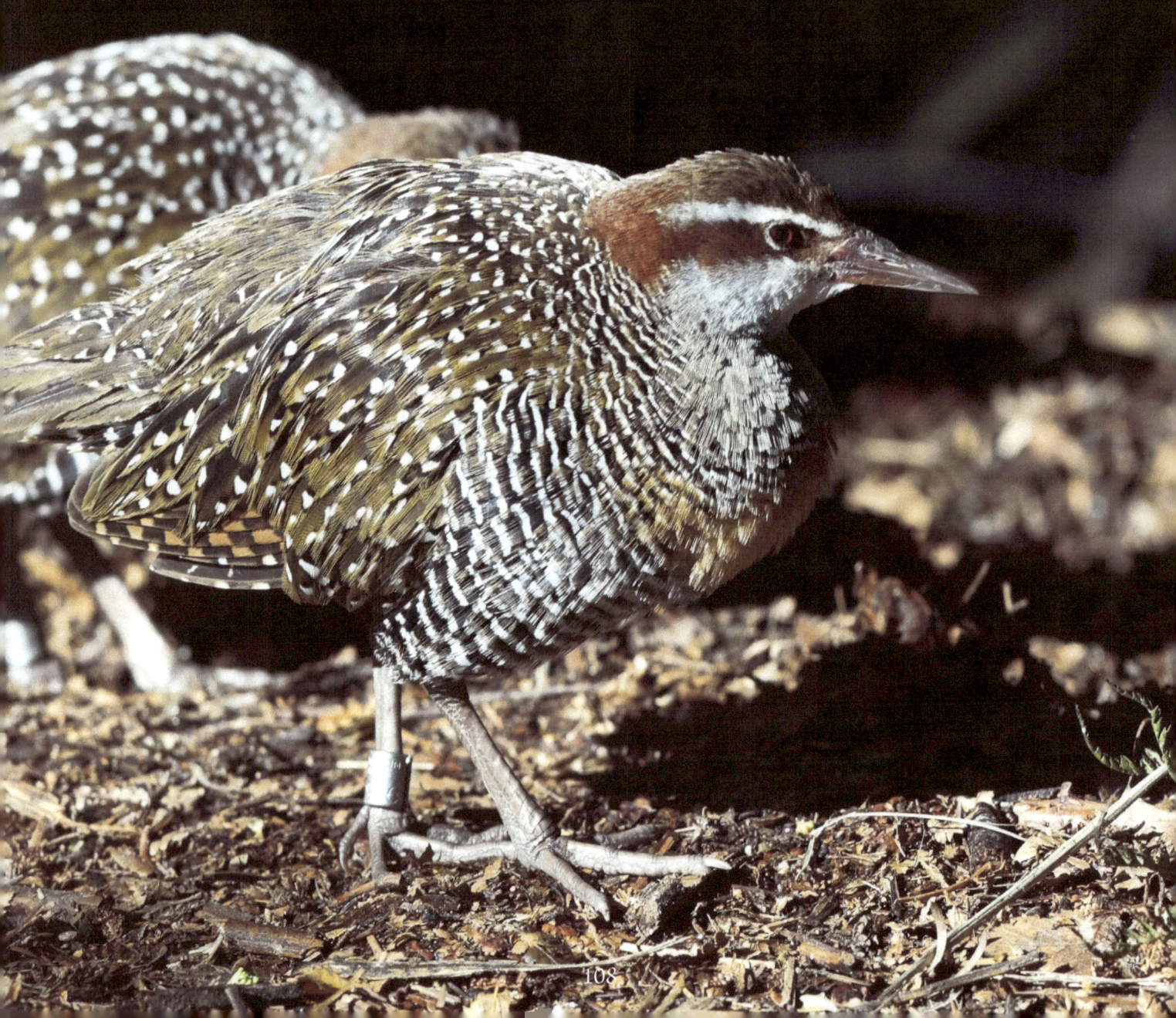

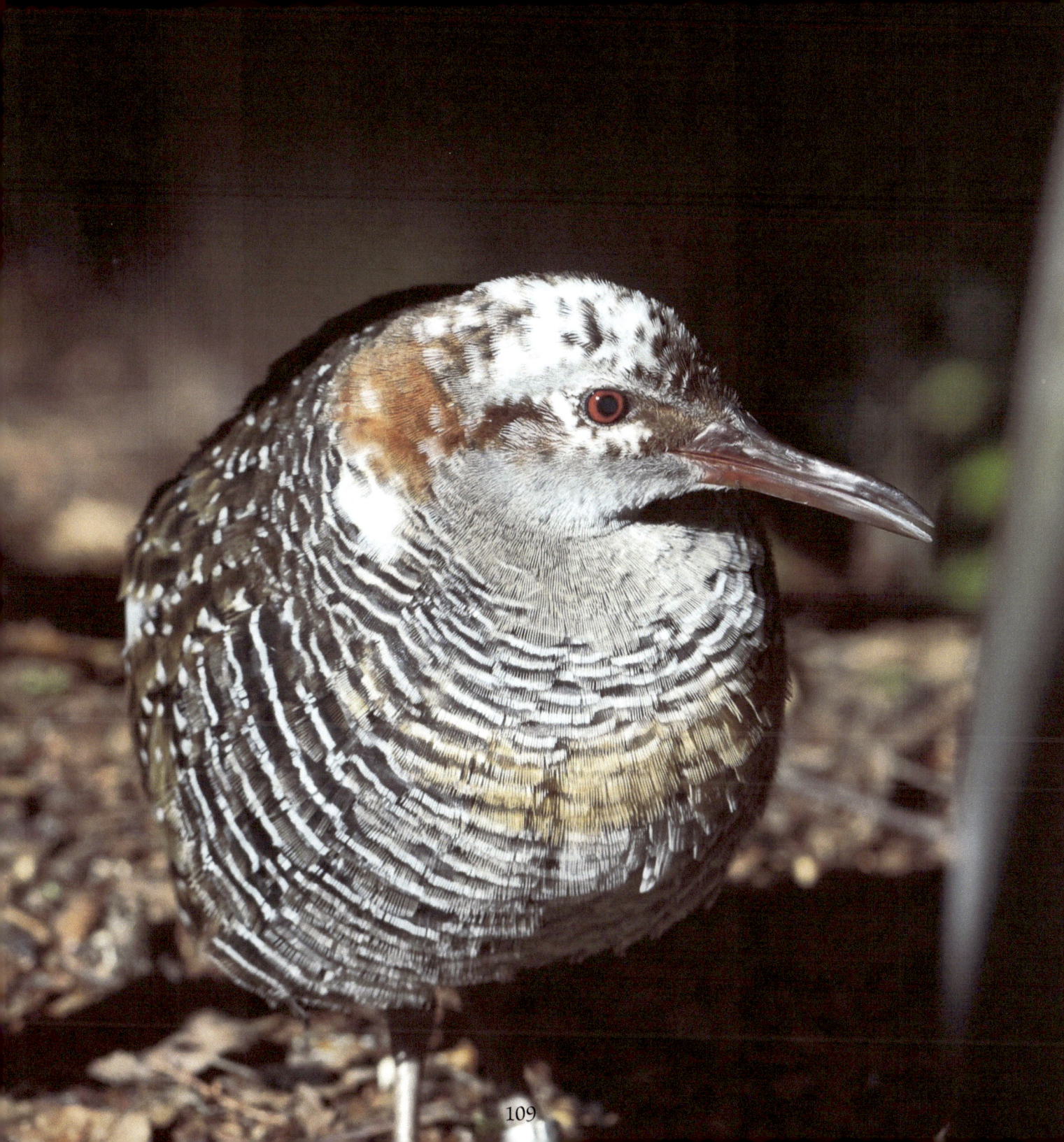

Kahu or Australasian Harrier
Circus approximans

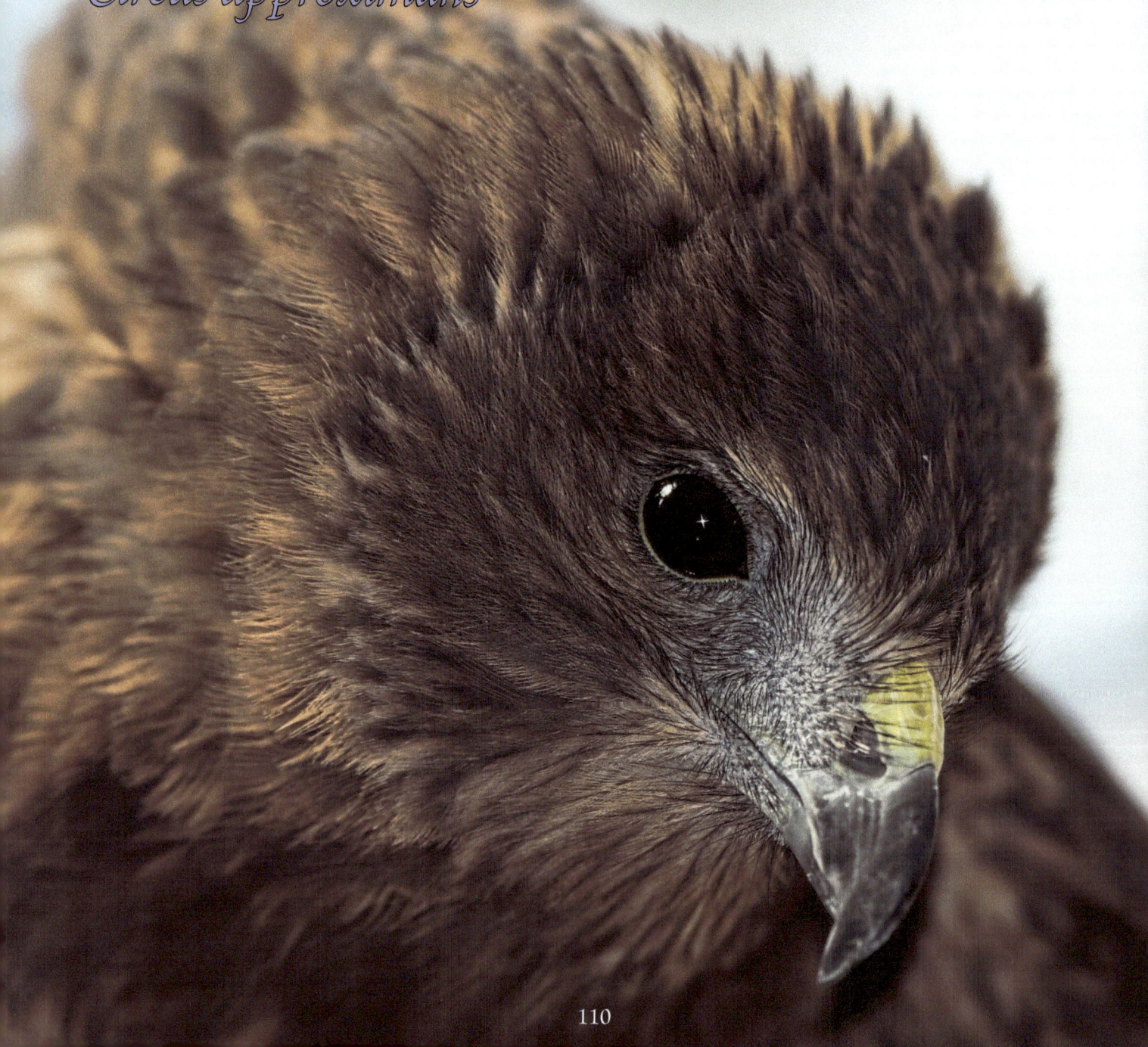

Karearea or New Zealand Falcon
Falco novaeseelandiae

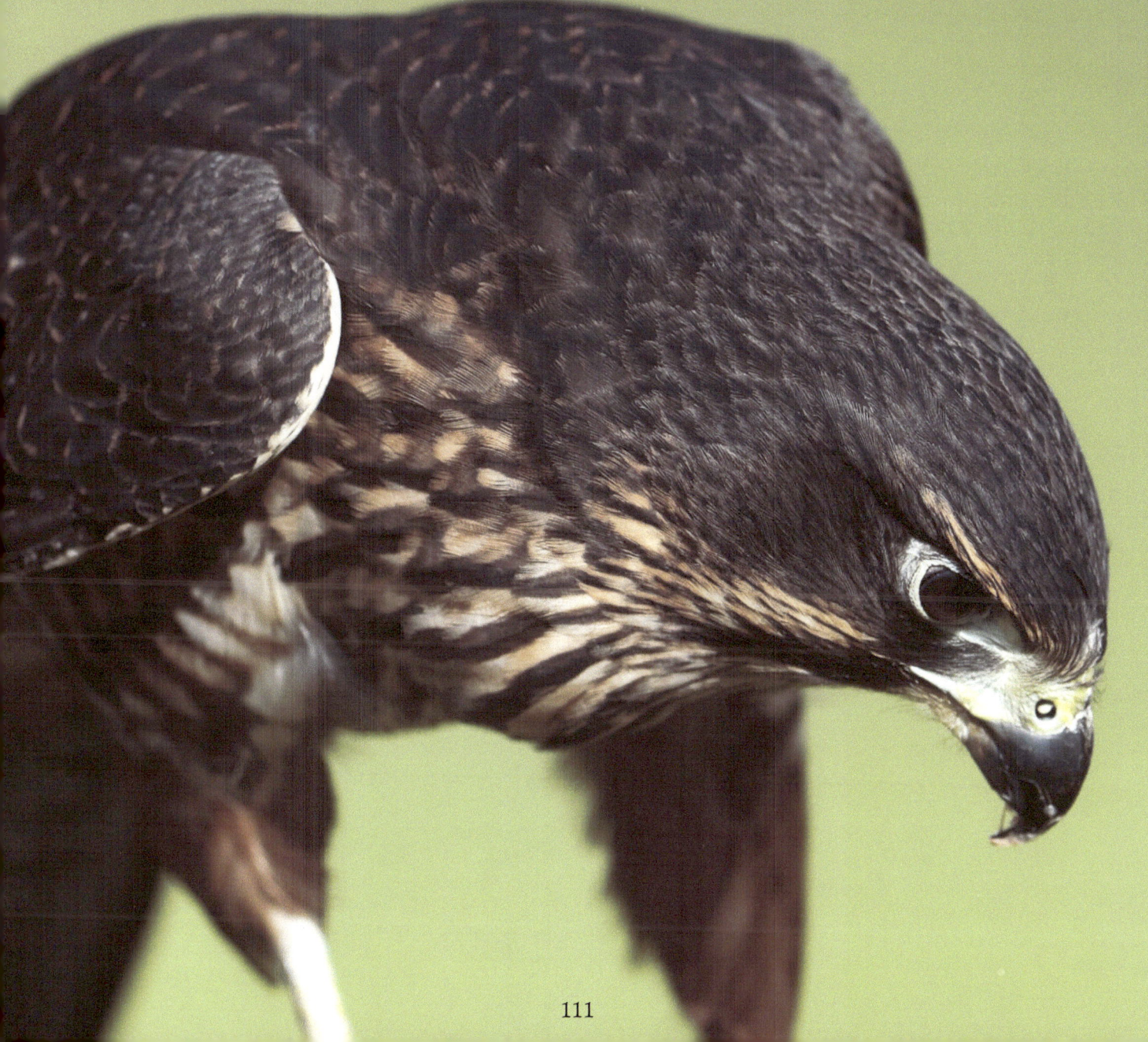

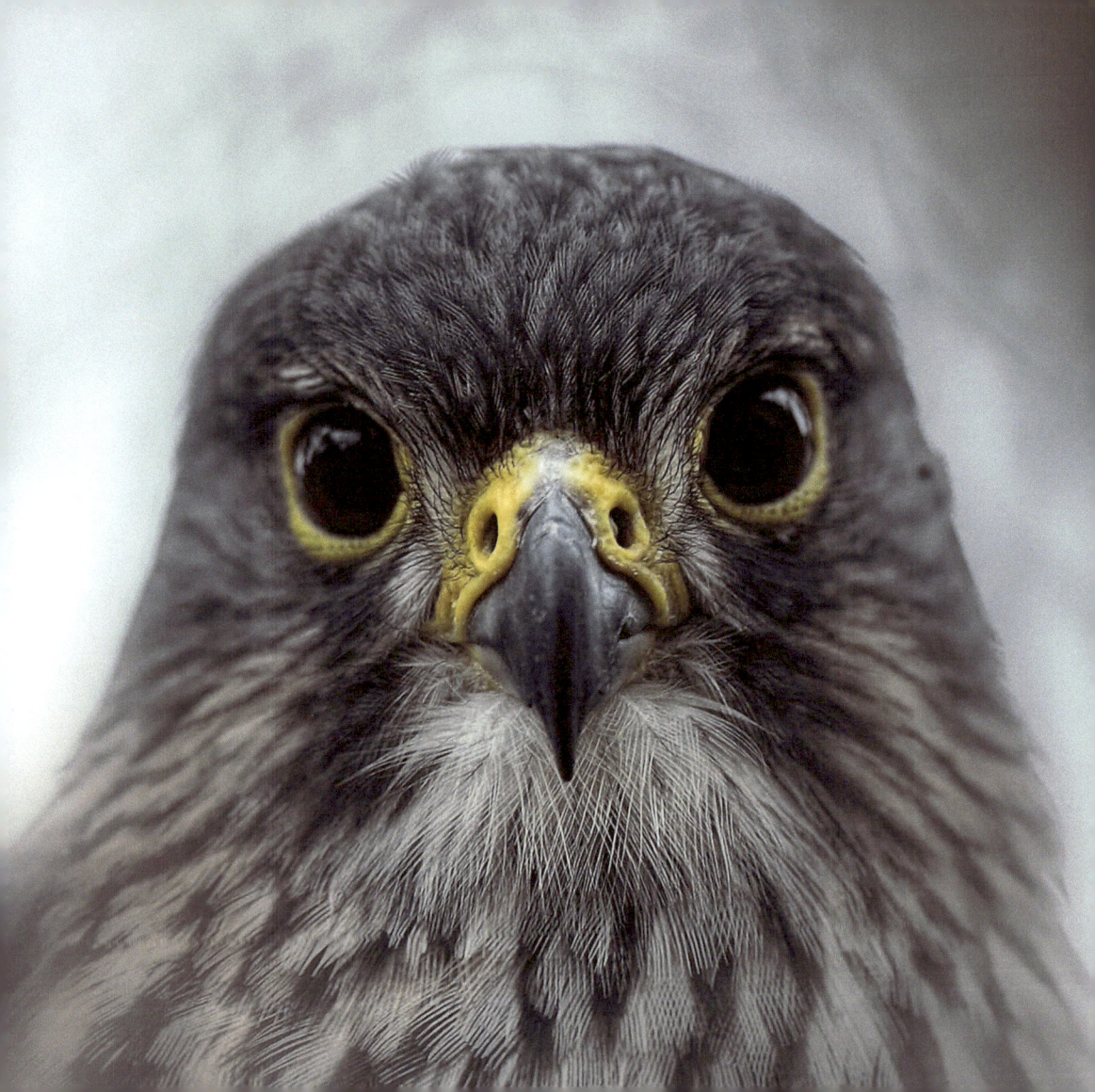

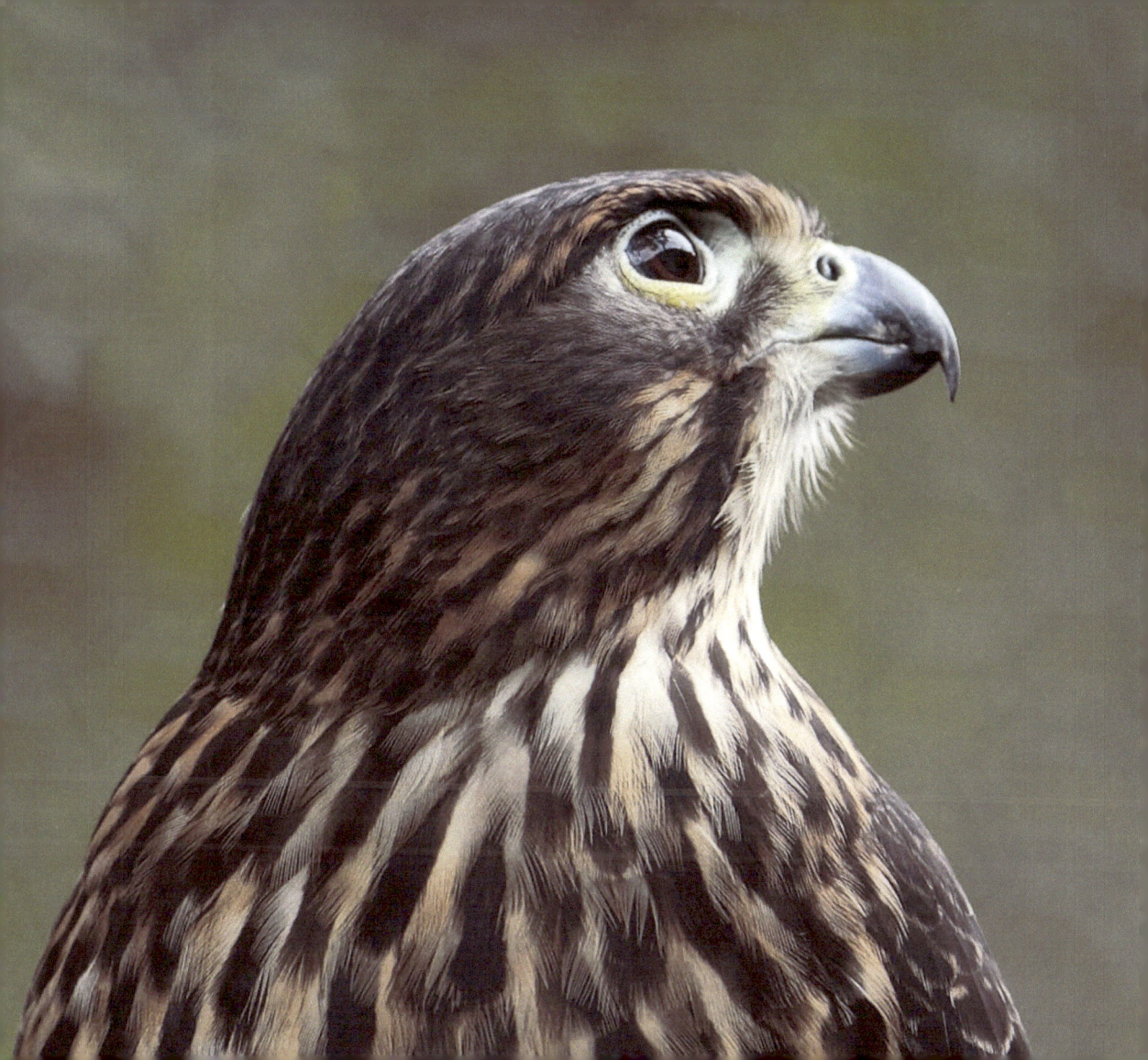

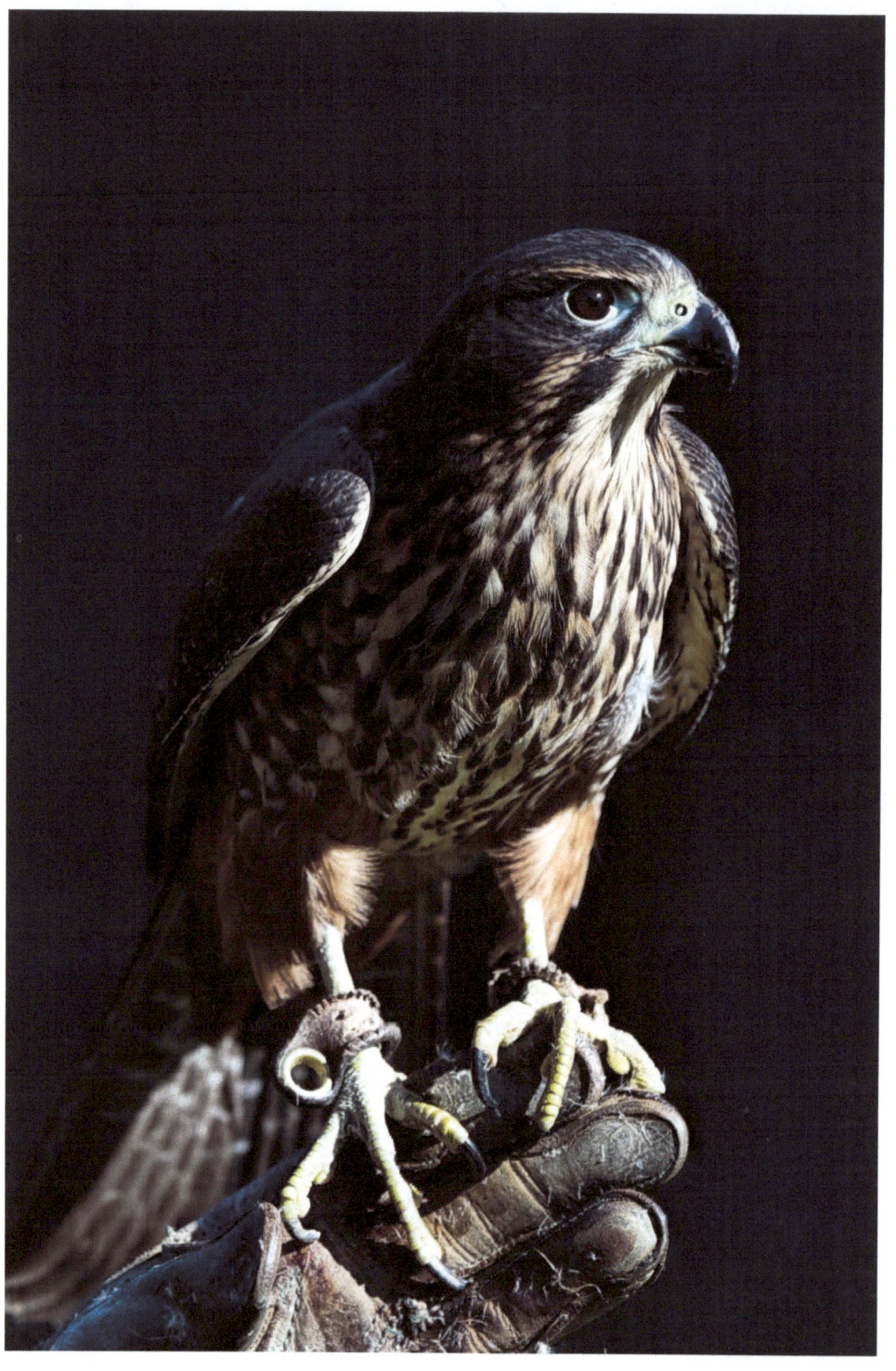

"In New Zealand, the courageous family of the Raptores is very feebly represented, the honourable post, of head of the family must fairly be assigned to this bird, which is commonly known by the name of the Quail or Sparrowhawk; 'the hardy Sperhauke eke the Quales foe,' as Chaucer has it. This bold little Falcon, which, a few years since, was so frequently seen, is now of comparatively rare occurrence. How seldom do we now hear that wild chattering scream, which gave notice of its approach, and spread alarm amongst the denizens of the poultry yard…

At present it is in the 'back country' only, that we can hope to find its breeding-place, which is usually on a ledge of rock commanding a prospect over some extent of country. Such an out-look gives an advantage of no little value, of which the Falcon is not slow to avail itself, should such a bird as a Tui or Pigeon appear in sight.

Several of the breeding-places, which we have had opportunities of examining, have presented, in a remarkable degree, very similar conditions as regards situation. Amongst bold rocks on the mountain side, somewhat sheltered by a projecting or overhanging mass, appears to be the favourite site for rearing its young…"

~T. H. Potts, 1873

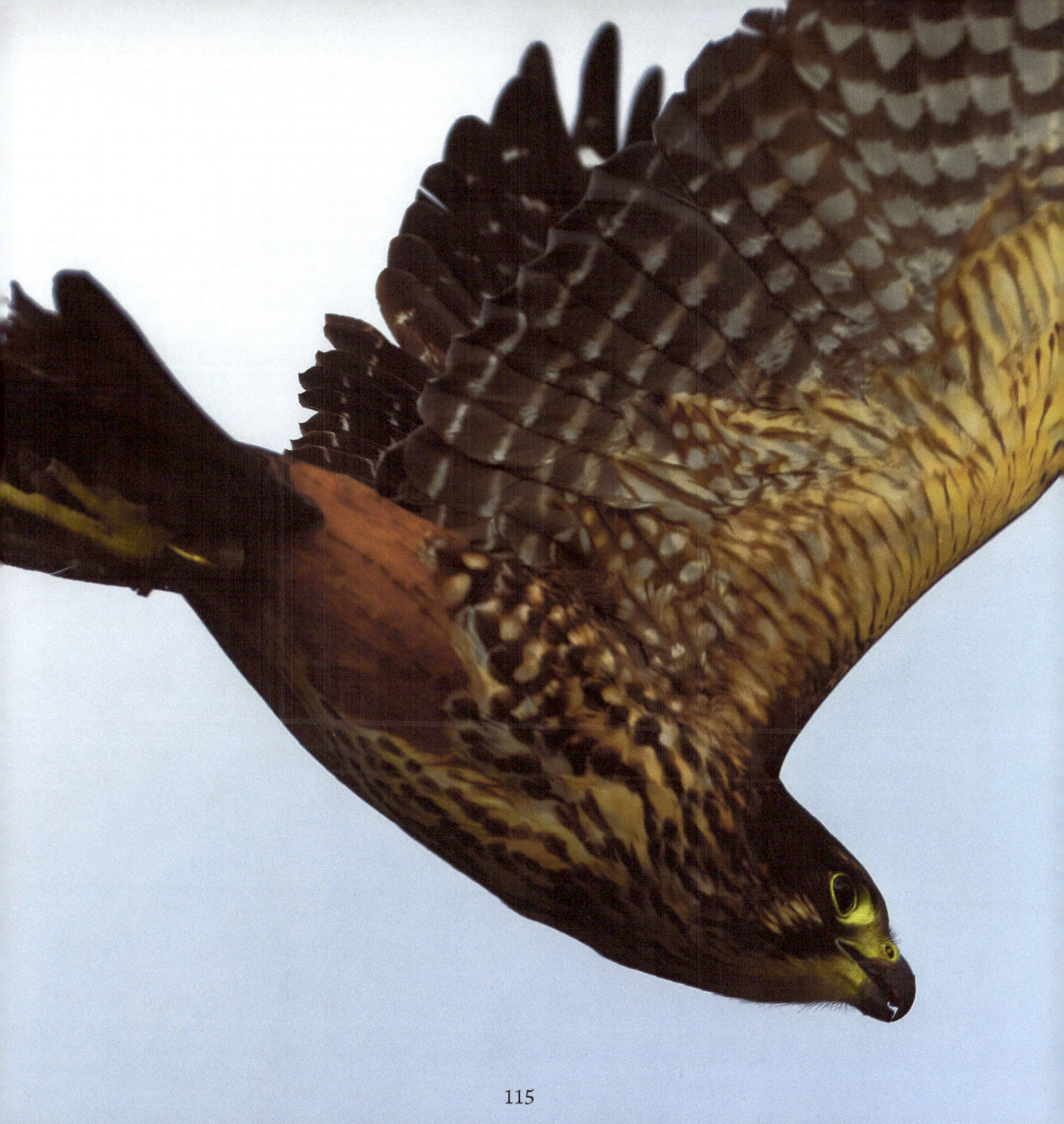

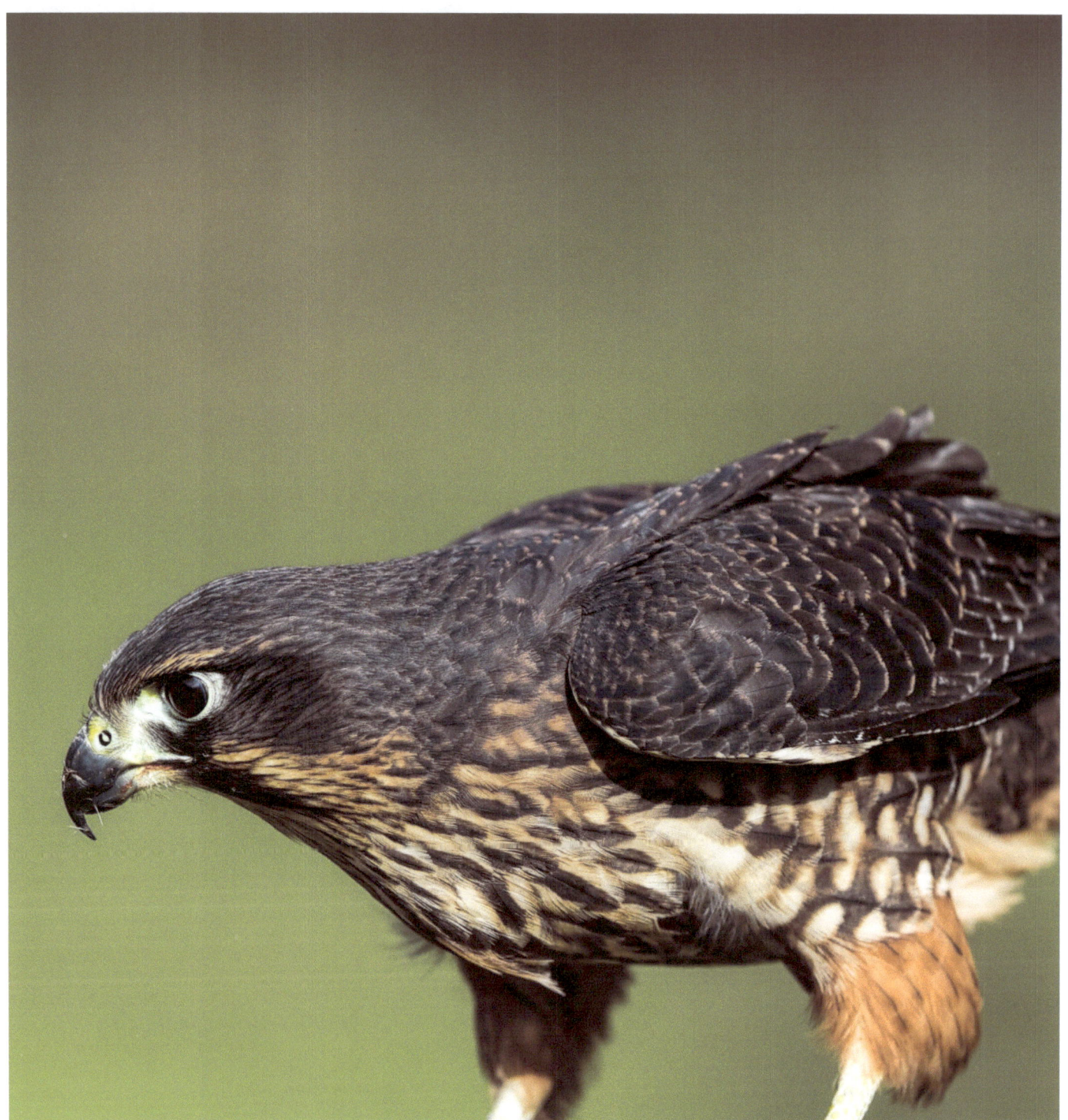

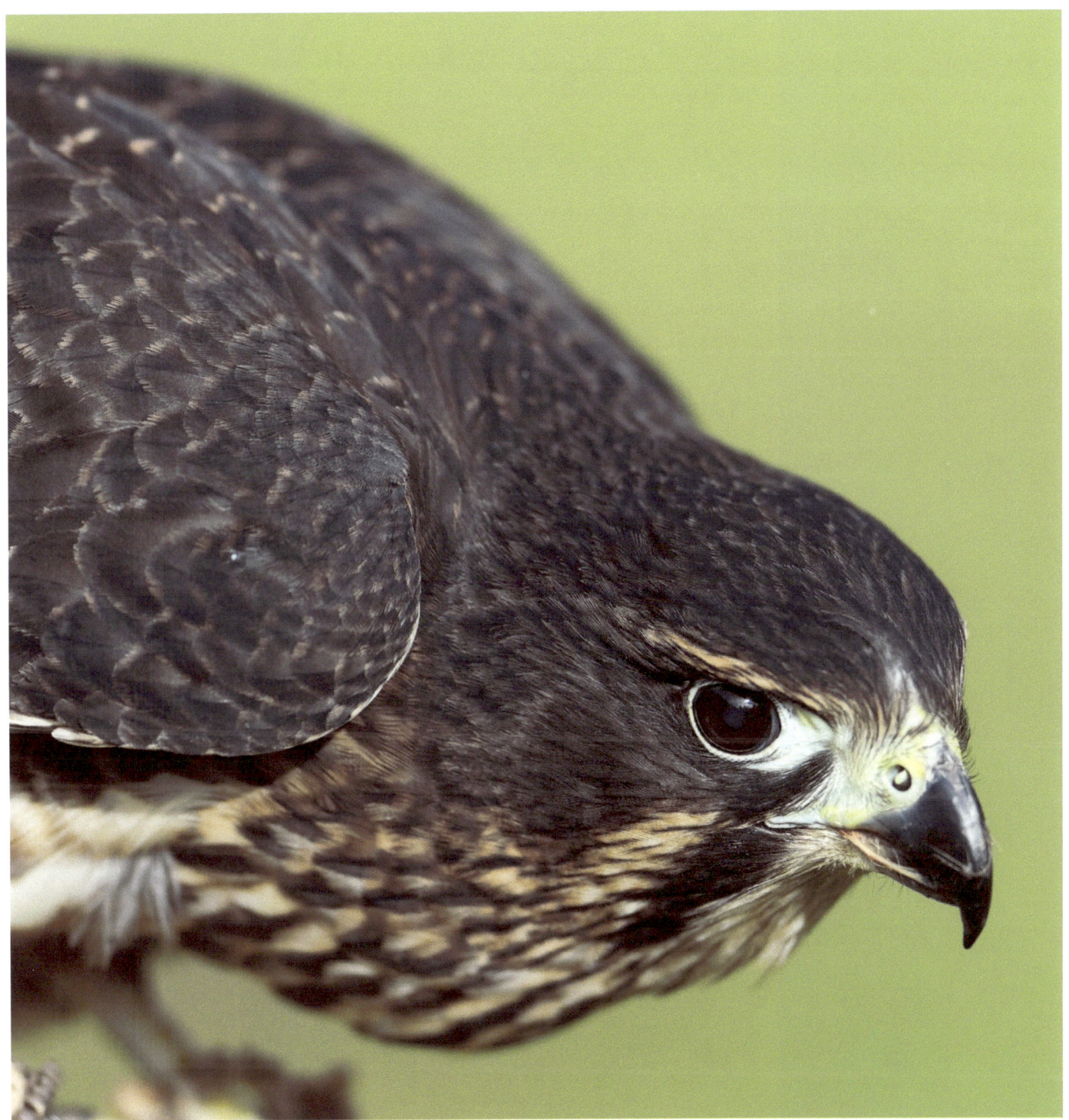

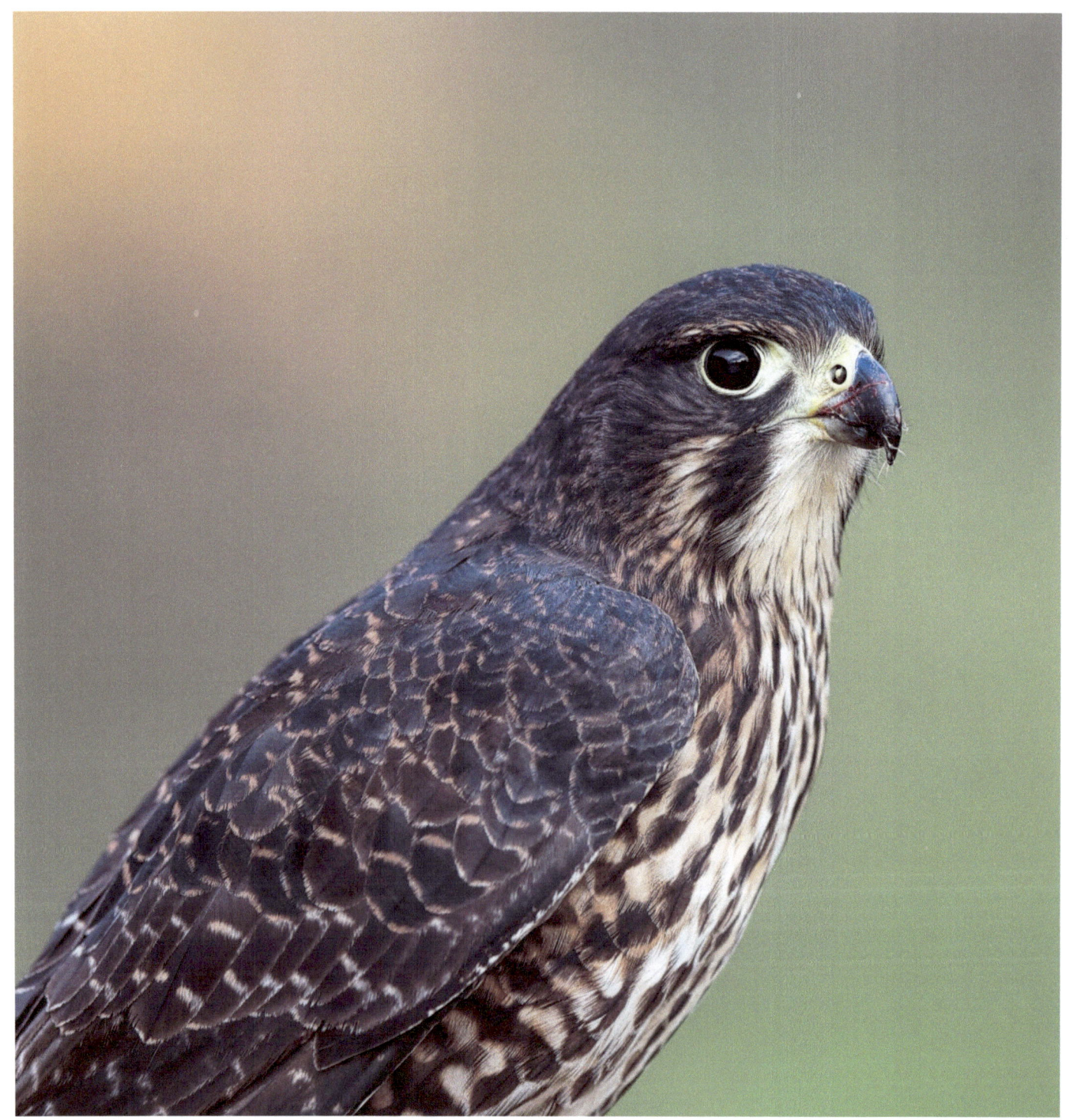

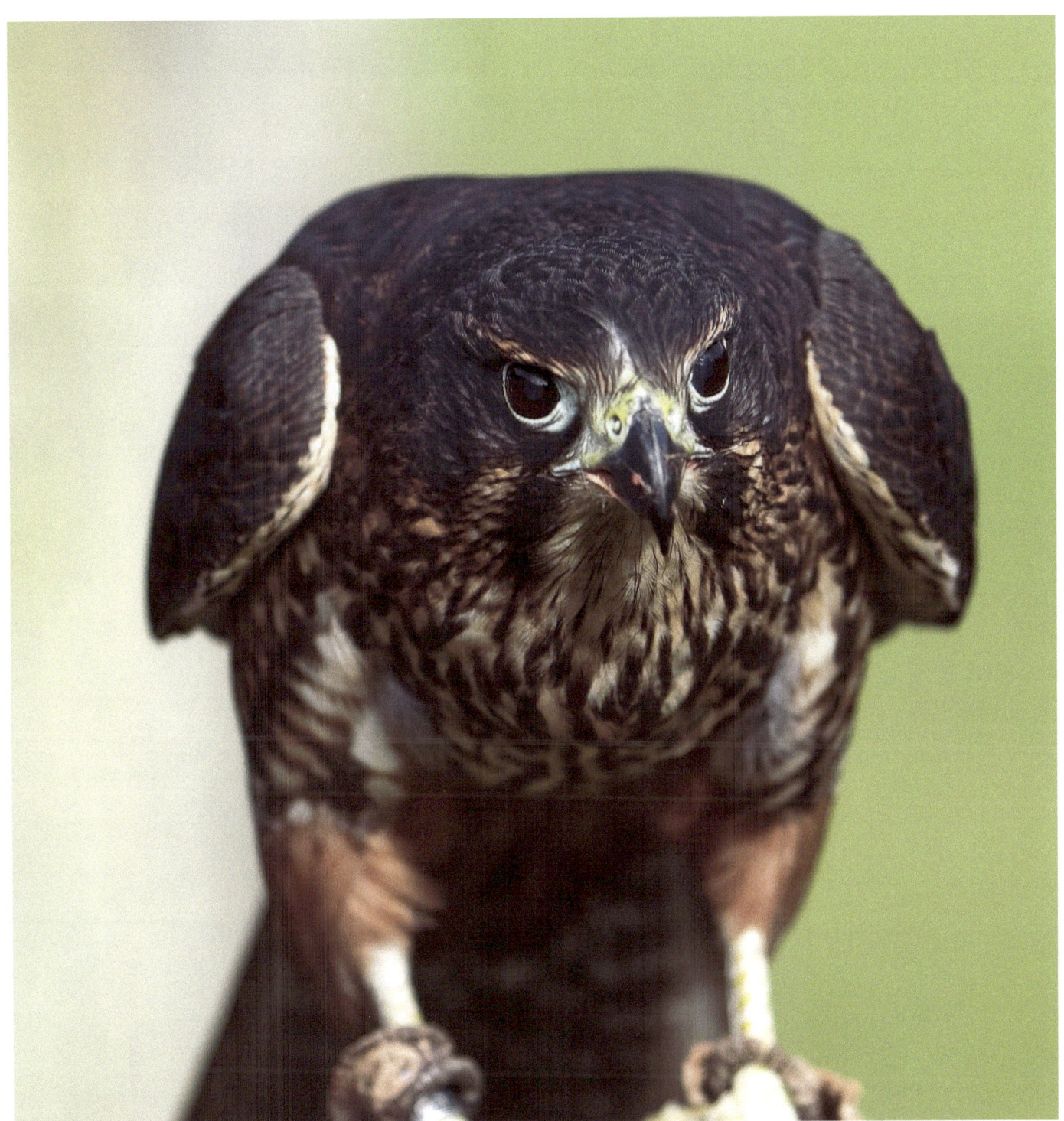

Pihoihoi or New Zealand Pipit
Anthus novaeseelandiae

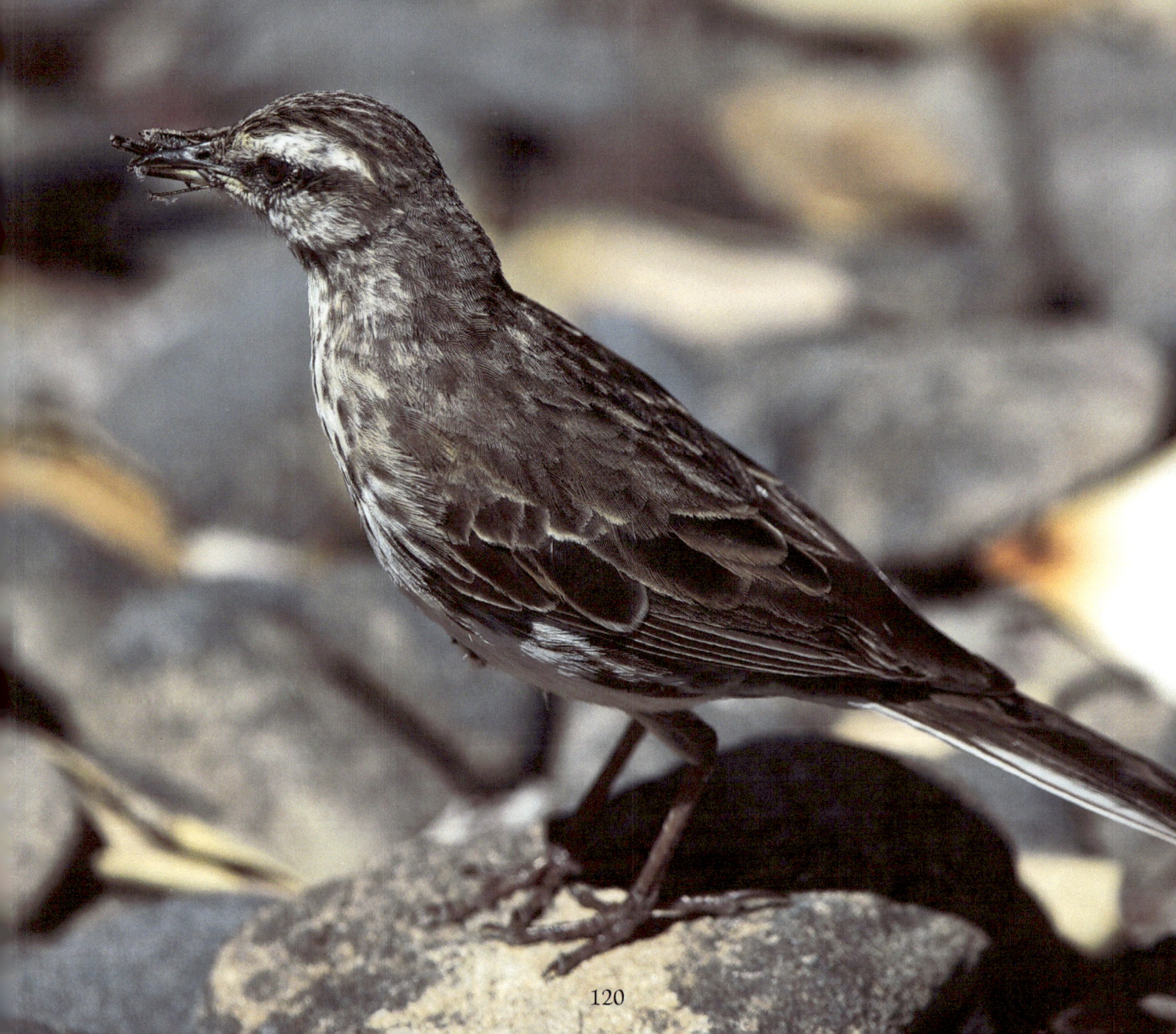

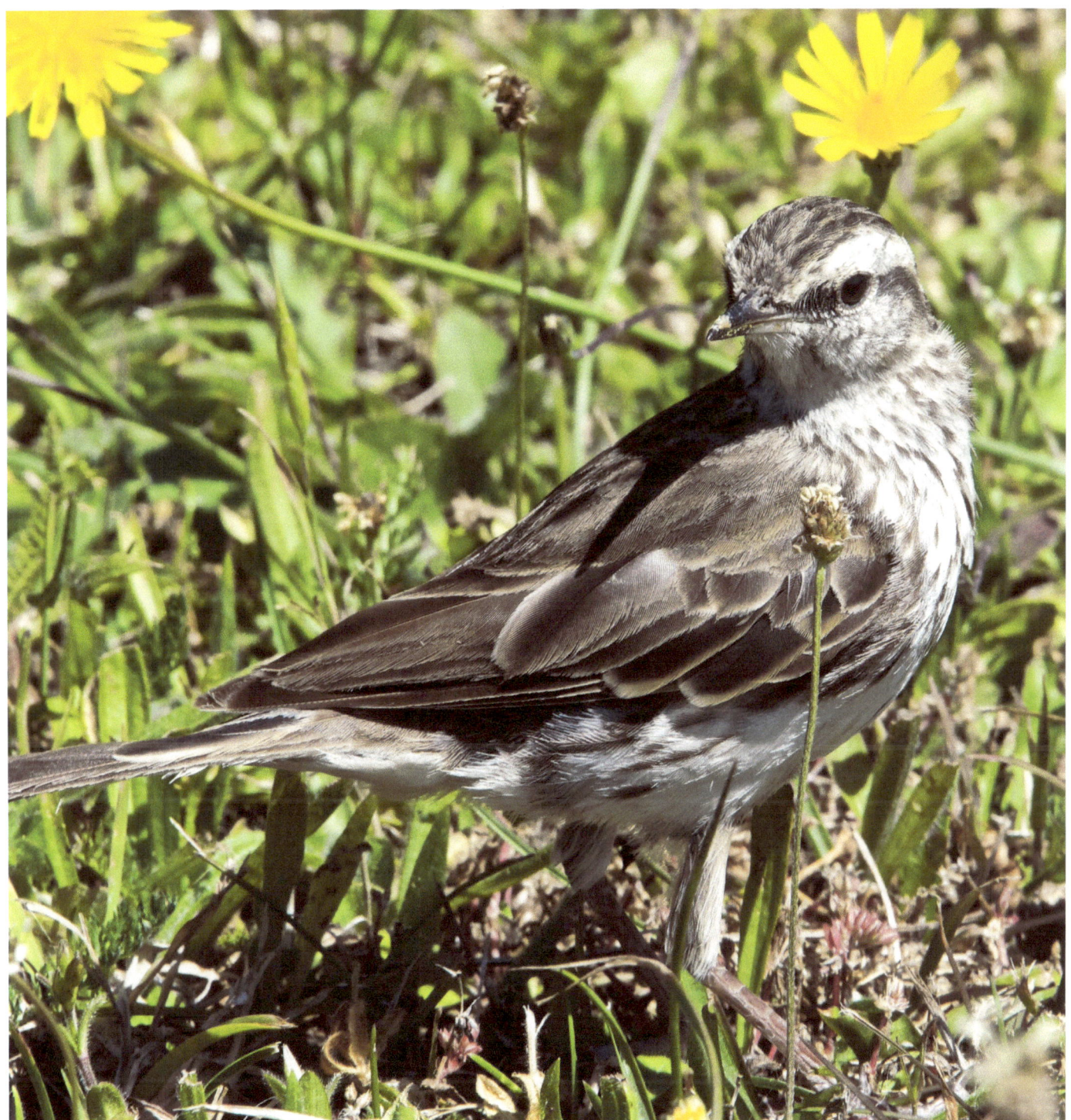

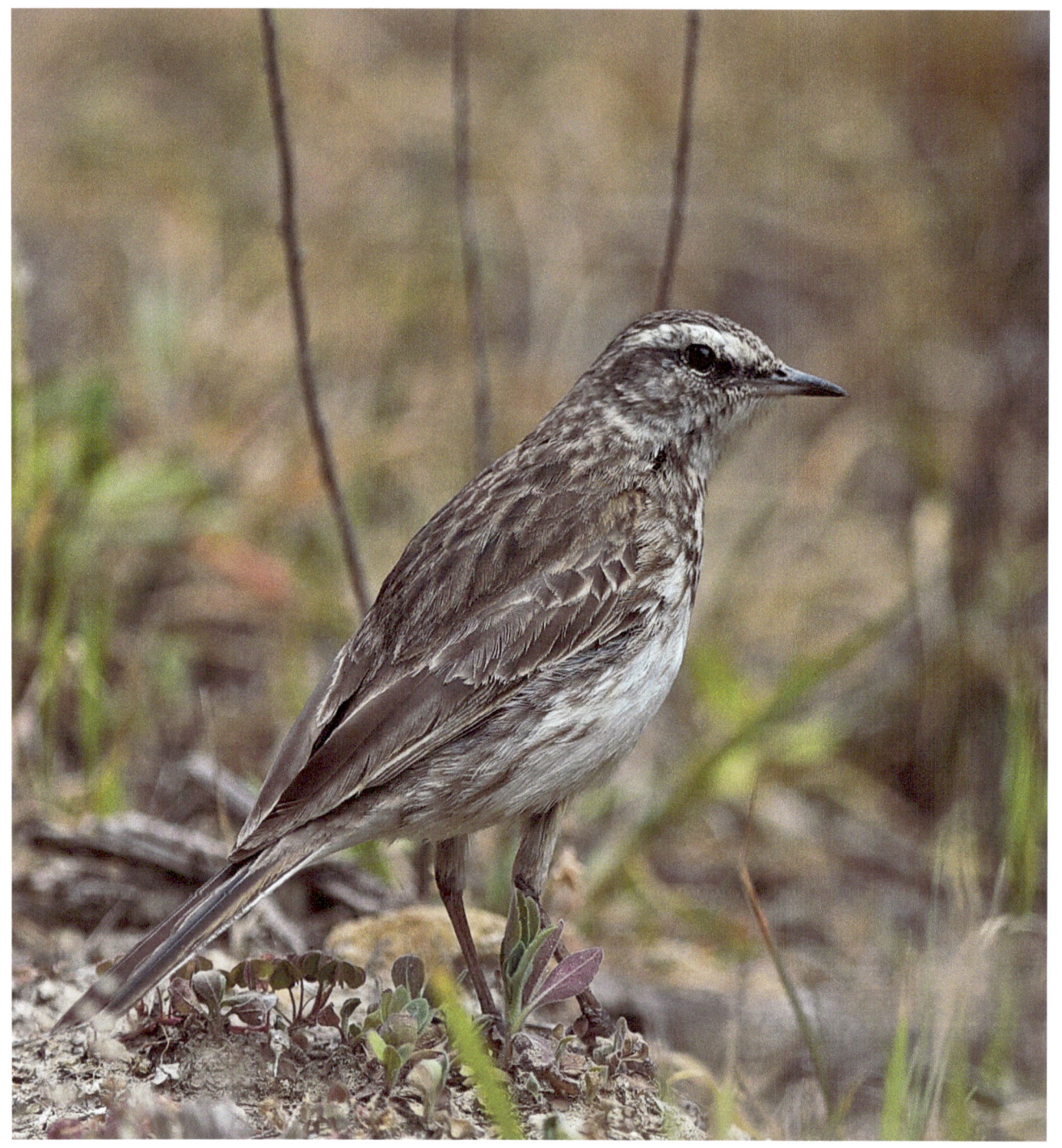

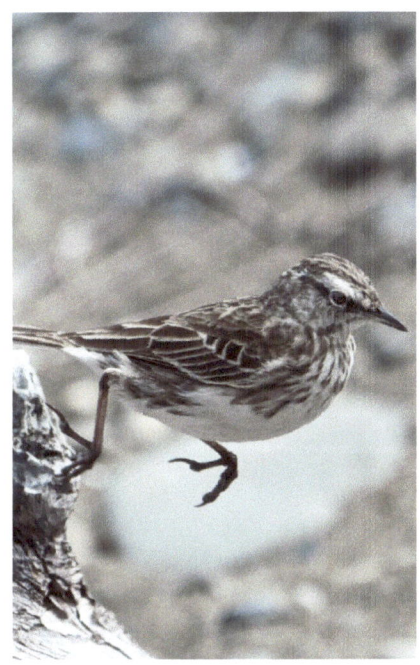

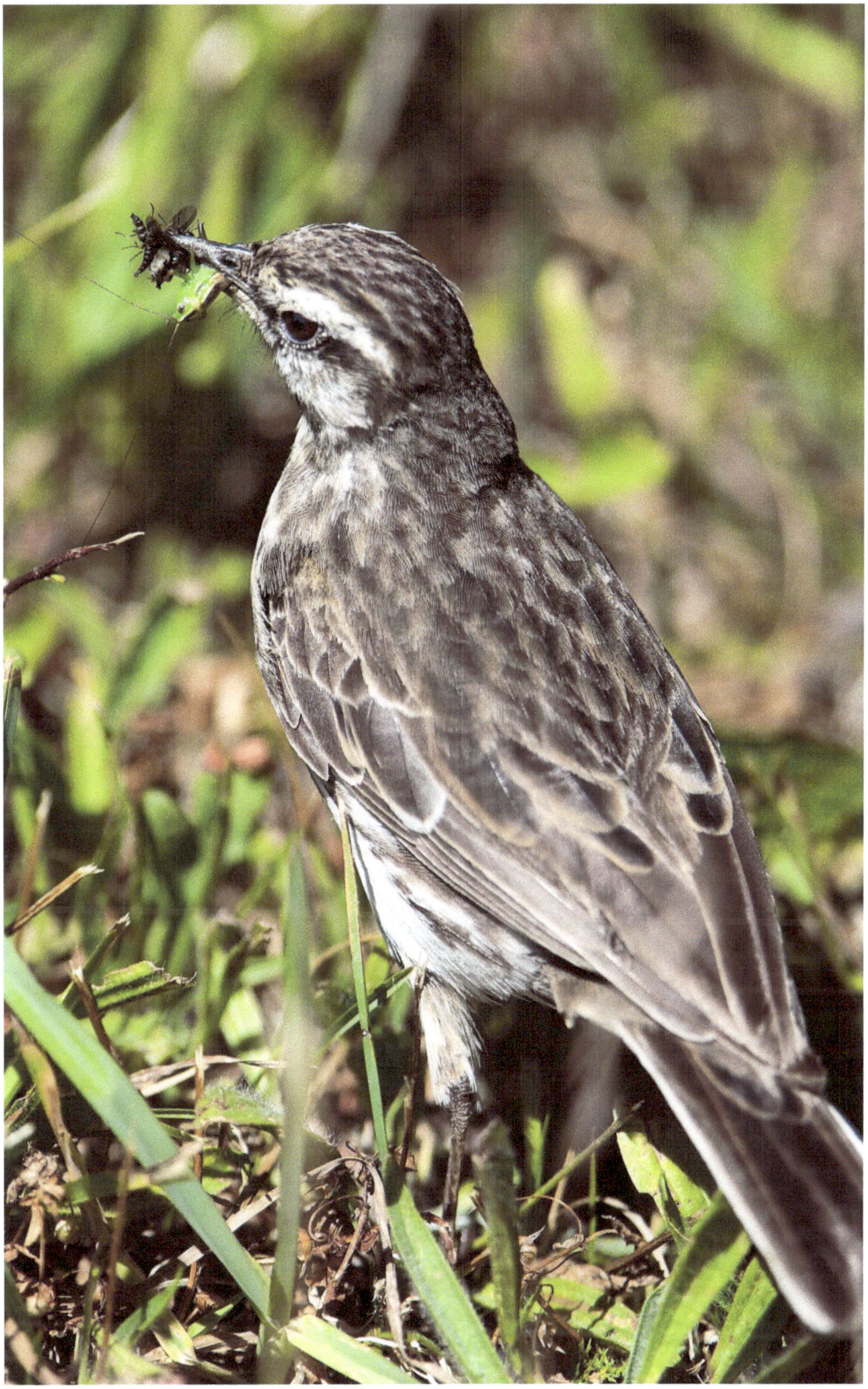

"It is very clear that these birds congregate in autumn. During a ride to and from Owhaoko... I met with numerous flocks, numbering from twenty to fifty at a time. I hardly saw a single bird detached from the flocks. I have already noticed the inquisitive disposition of this Pipit, and mentioned the circumstance of a flock keeping pace with a train for some miles. There is another evidence of it: as you ride along the road they keep before you, almost allowing your horse to tread on them, then rising with a shrill 'cheep,' flying a few yards further, and so on again till their curiosity is satisfied, when they wheel upwards and fall to the rear."

~*Sir Walter L. Buller, 1895*

Warou or Welcome Swallow
Hirundo tahitica neoxena

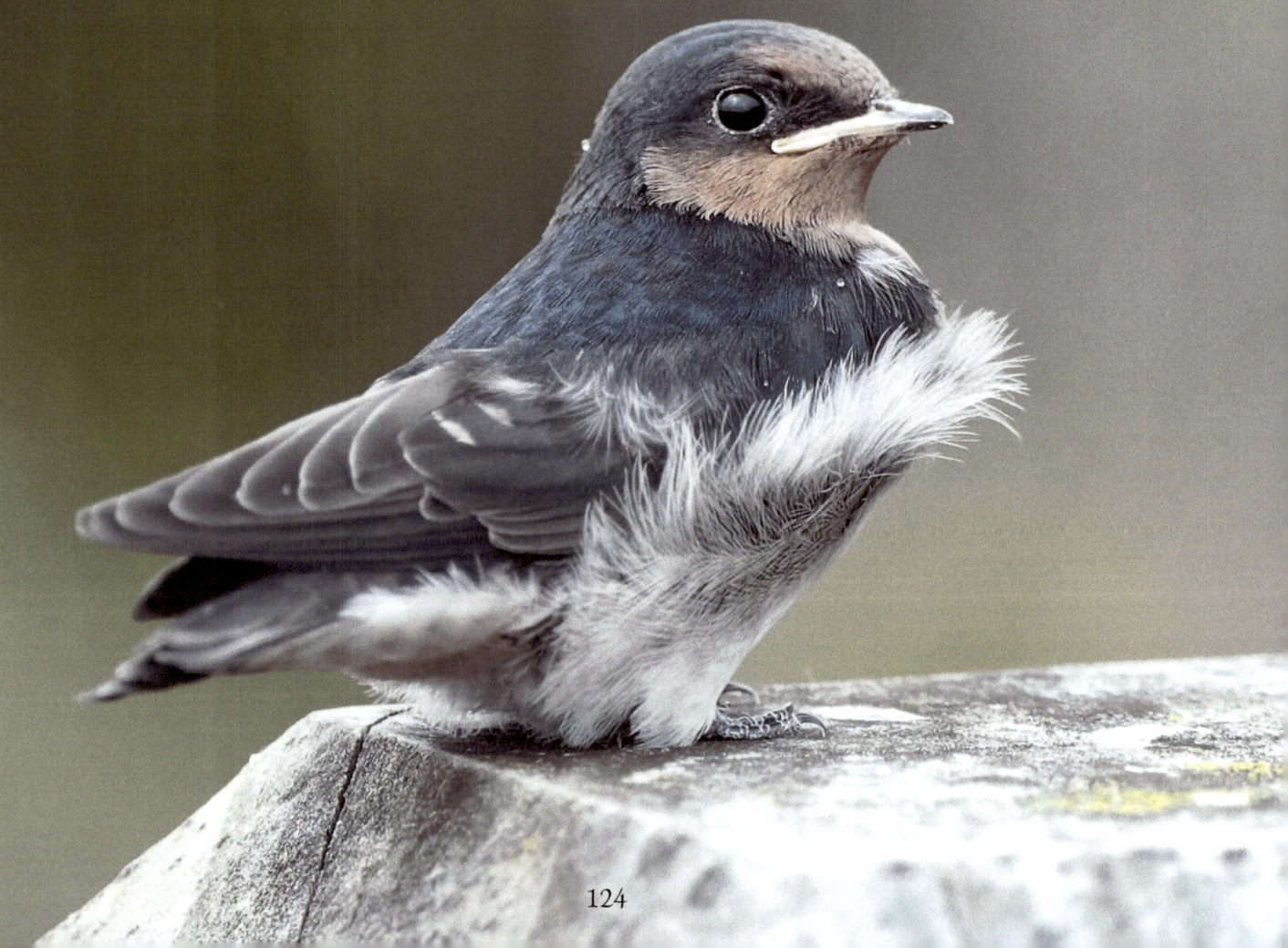

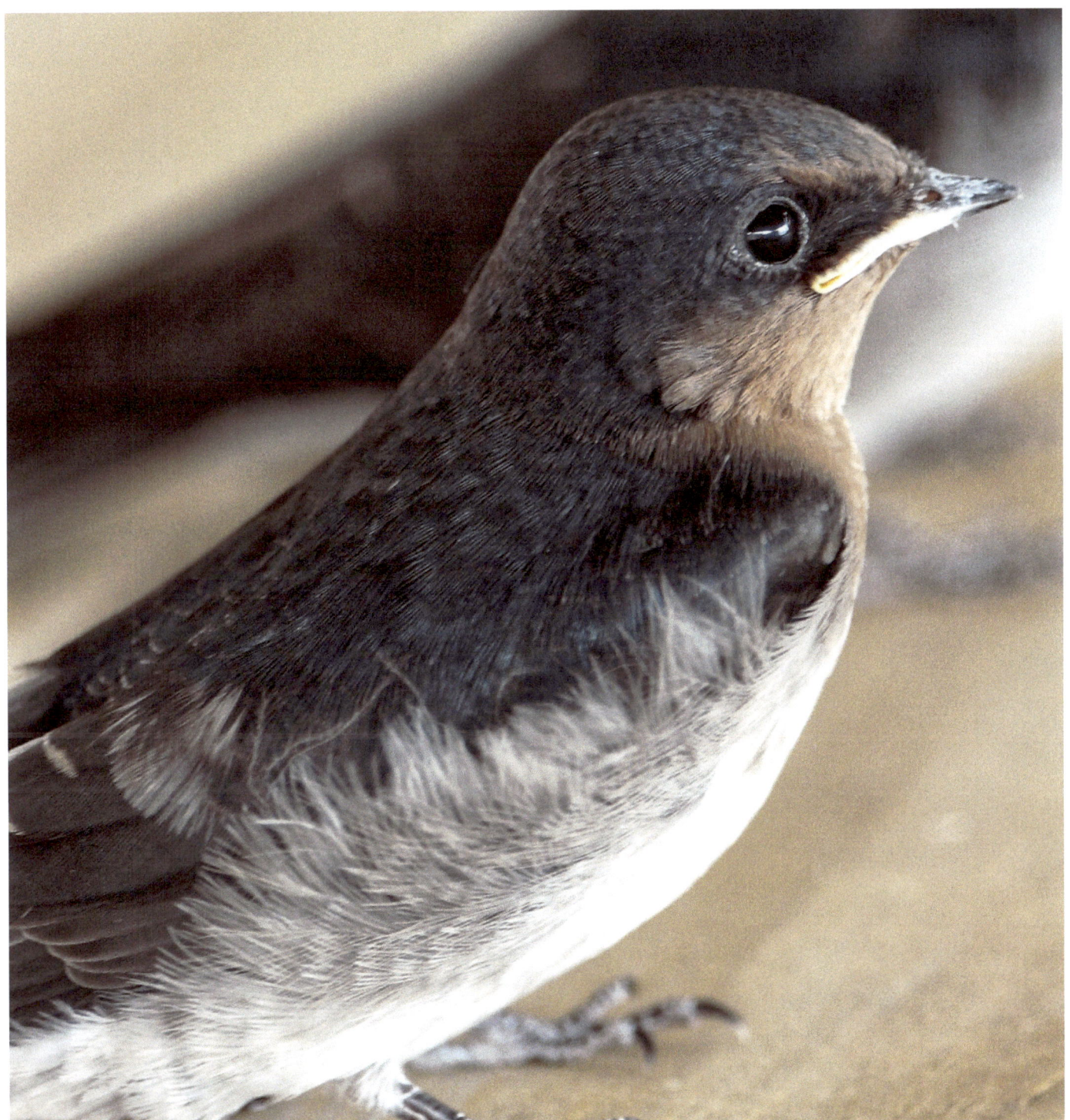

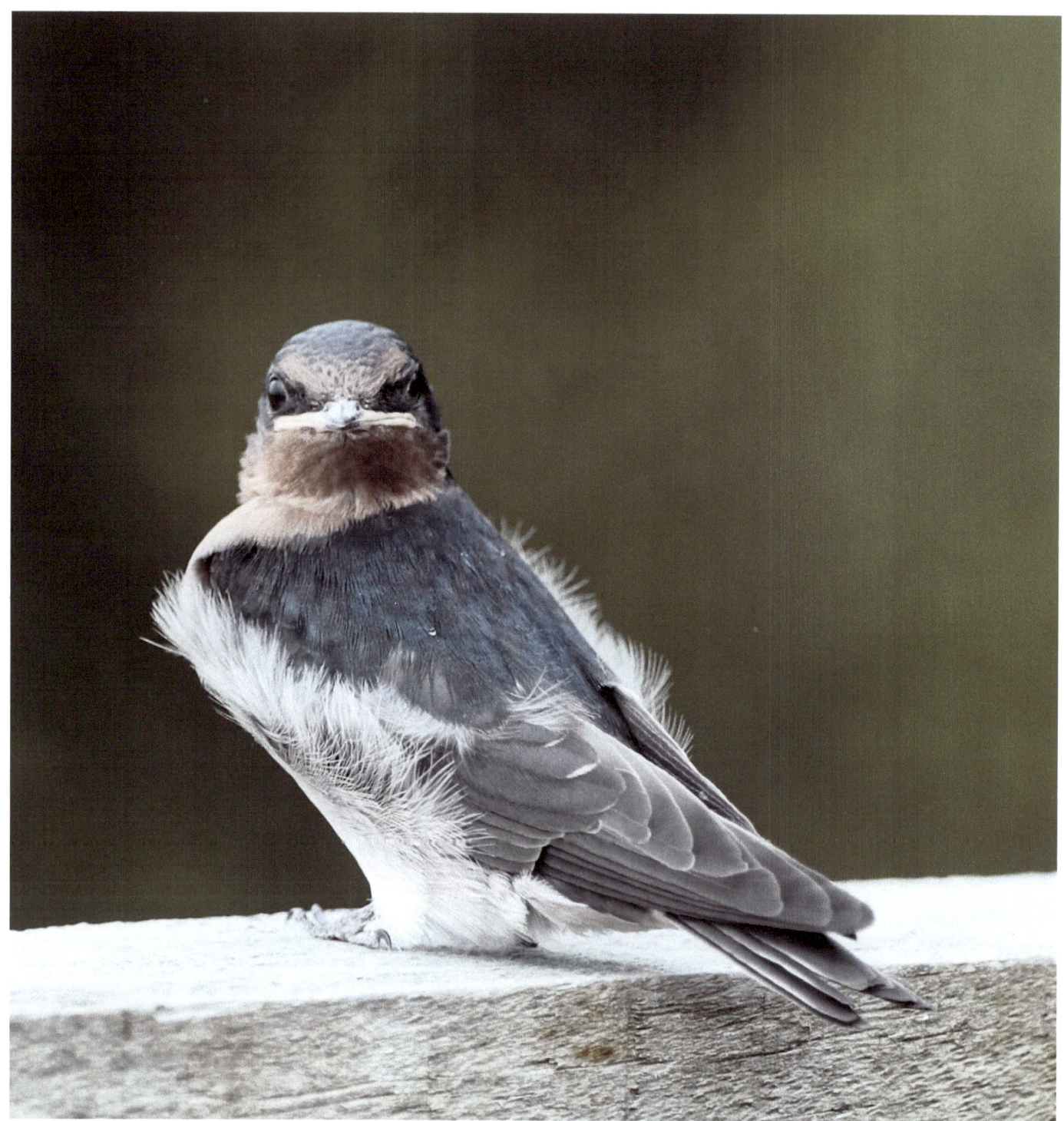

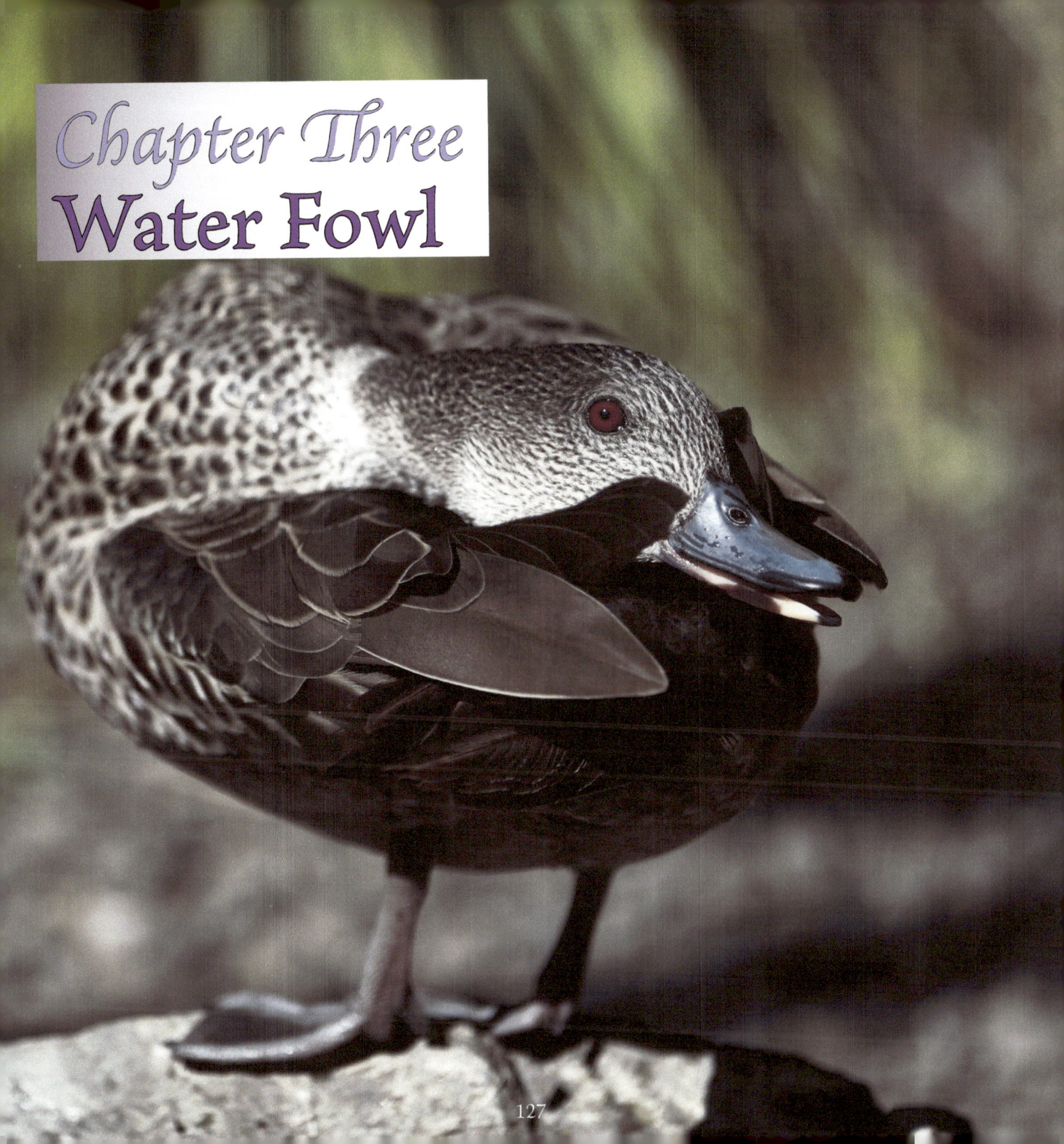

Chapter Three
Water Fowl

Tete or Gray Teal
Anas gracilis

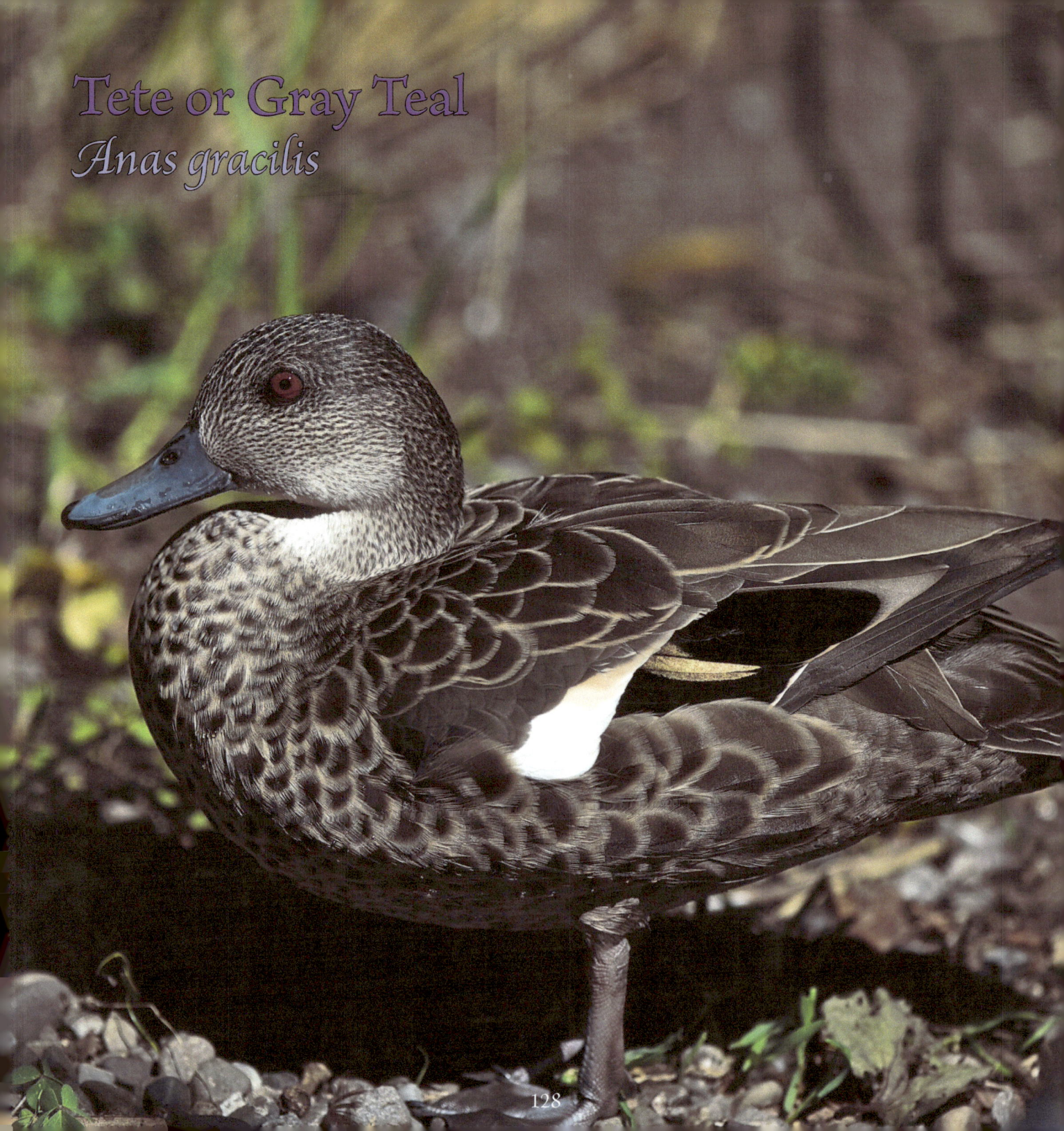

128

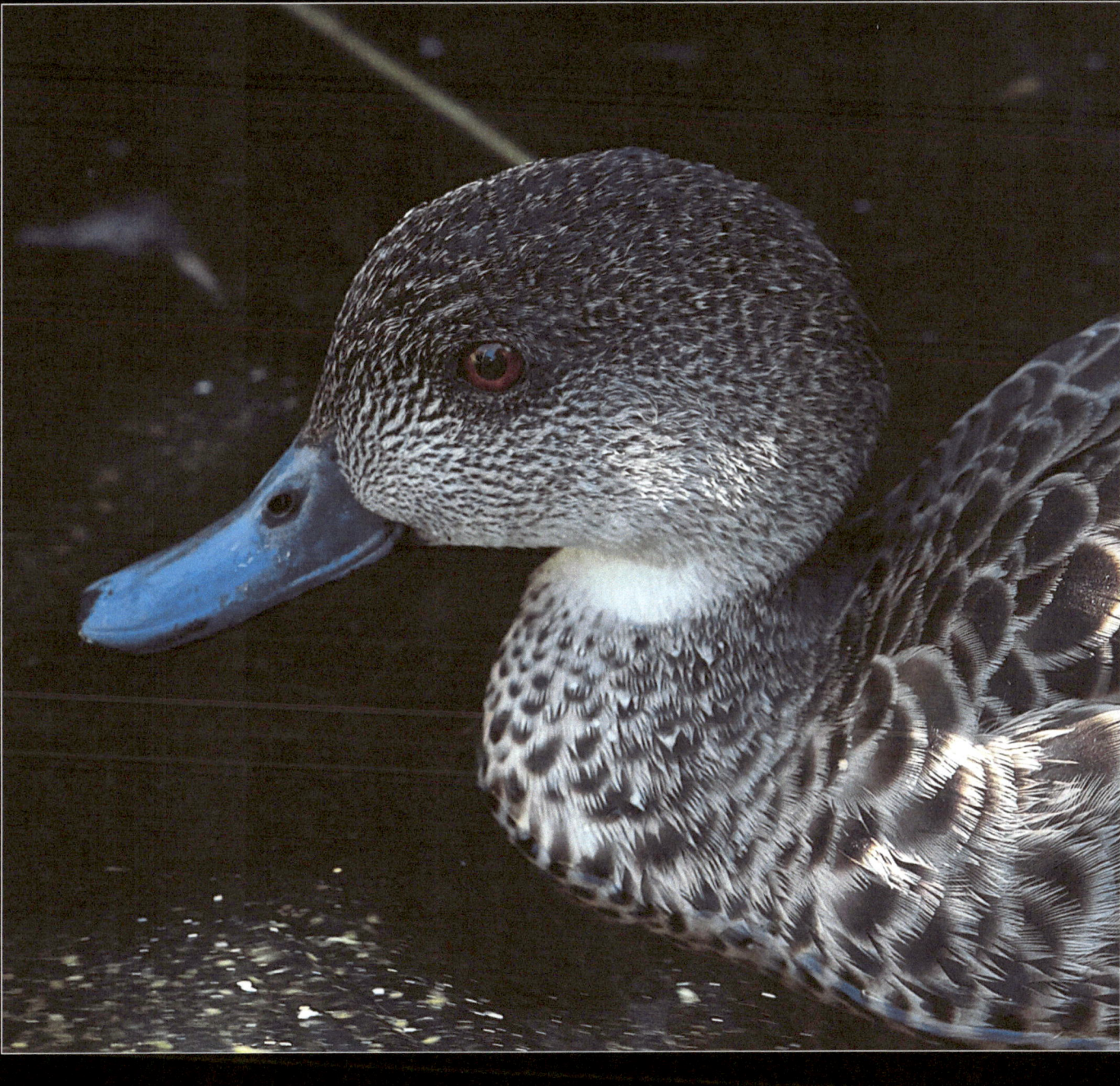

Pateke or Brown Teal
Anas aucklandica

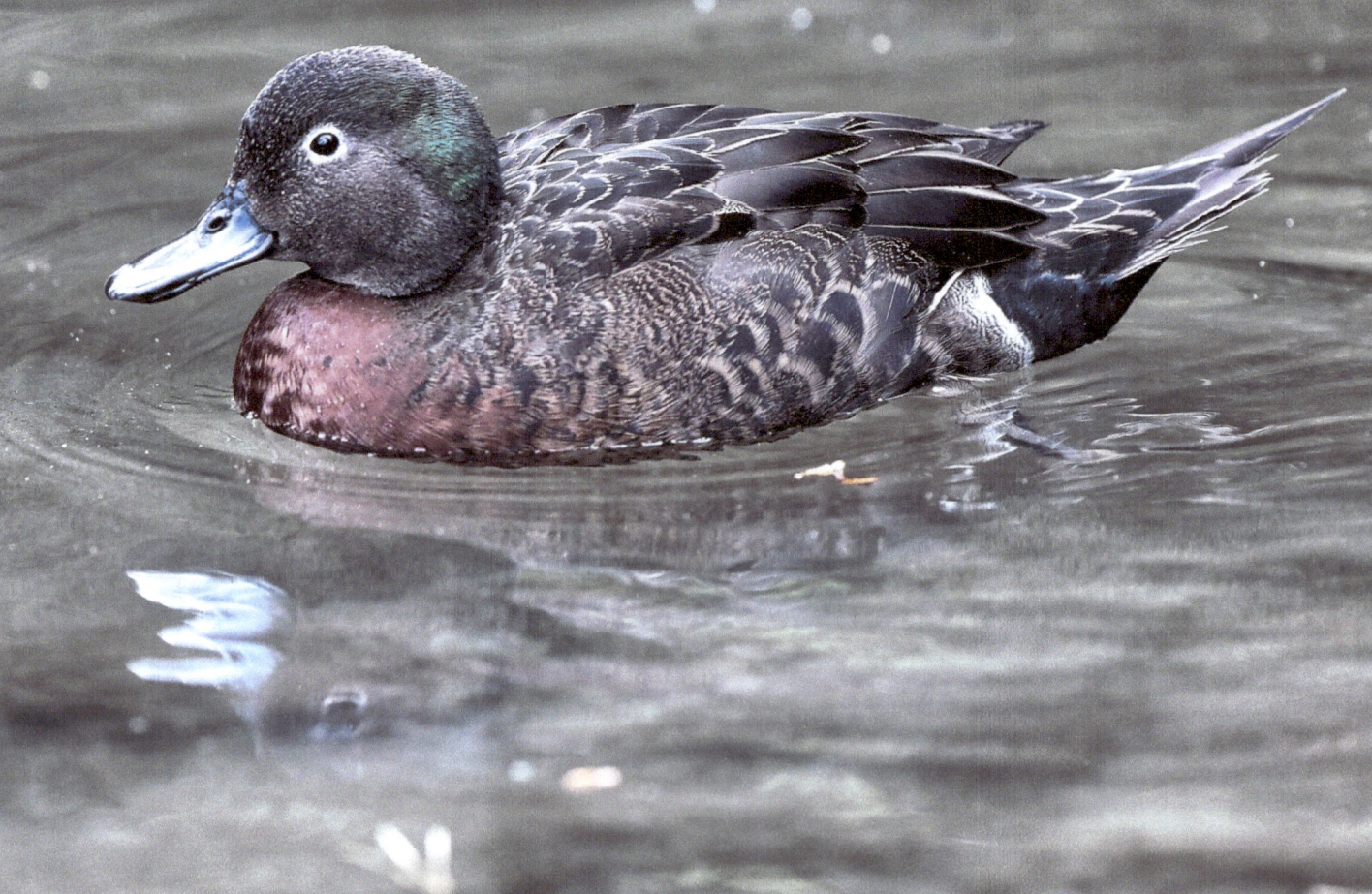

Papango or New Zealand Scaup
Aythya novaeseelandiae

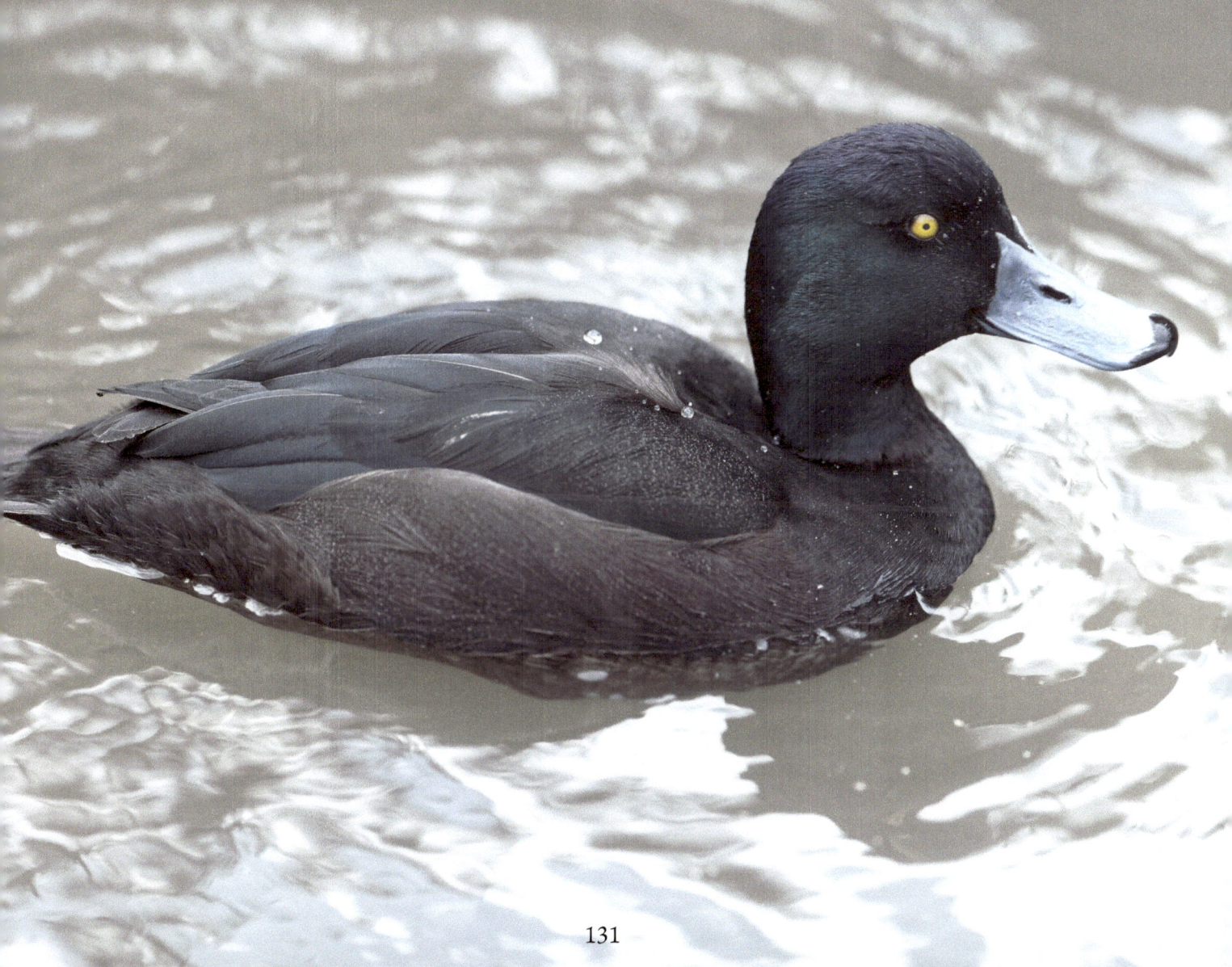

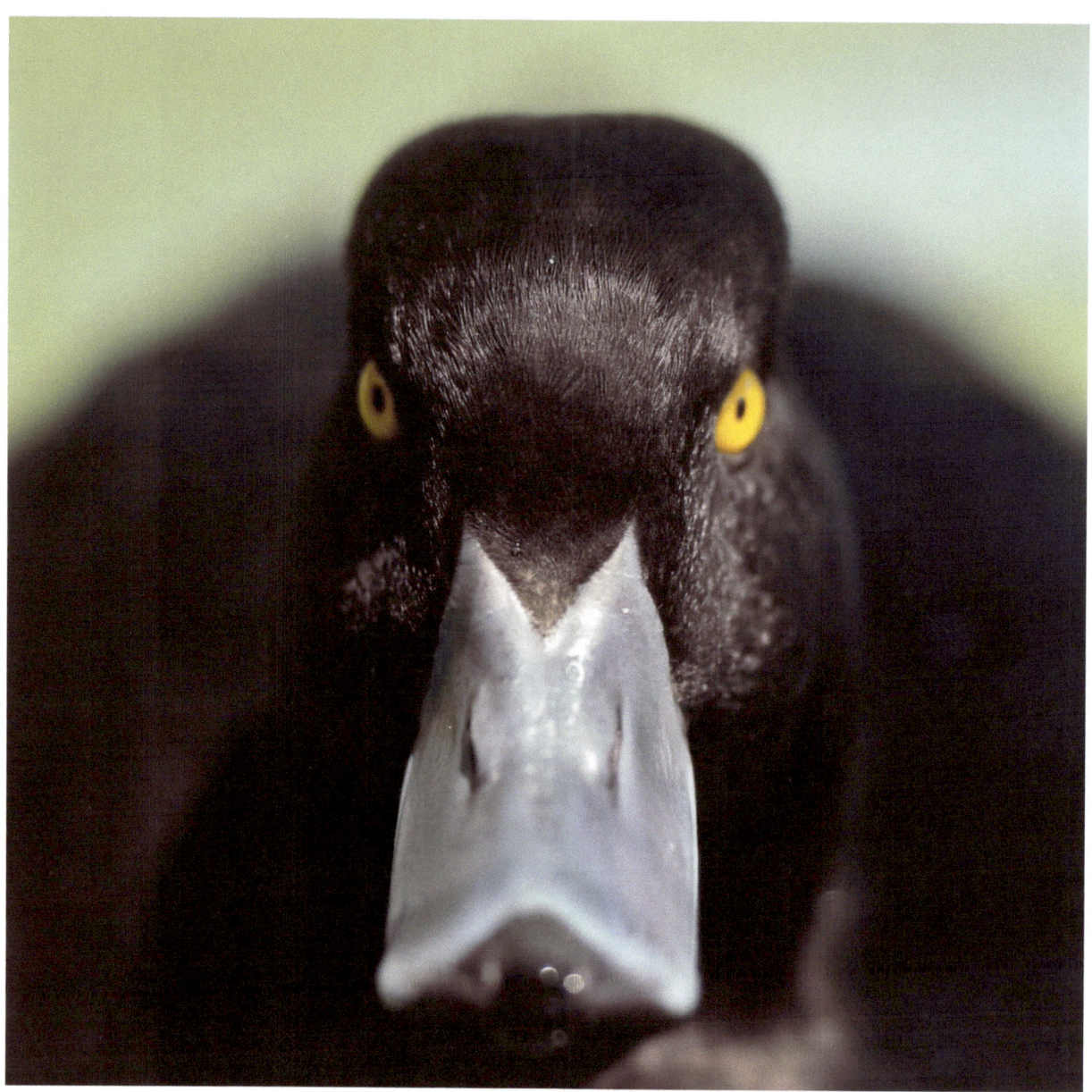

"A few pairs of this sociable little duck inhabit the lakes here every winter. They associate with the mallards and domestic ducks, and when resting leisurely on the water's edge permit visitors to approach them very closely. They are gentle and slow in their habits, and at all times are beautiful objects when seen consorting peacefully with the other ducks inhabiting the lakes."

~W. W. Smith, 1896

Kuruwhengi or New Zealand Shoveler
Anas rhynchotis variegata

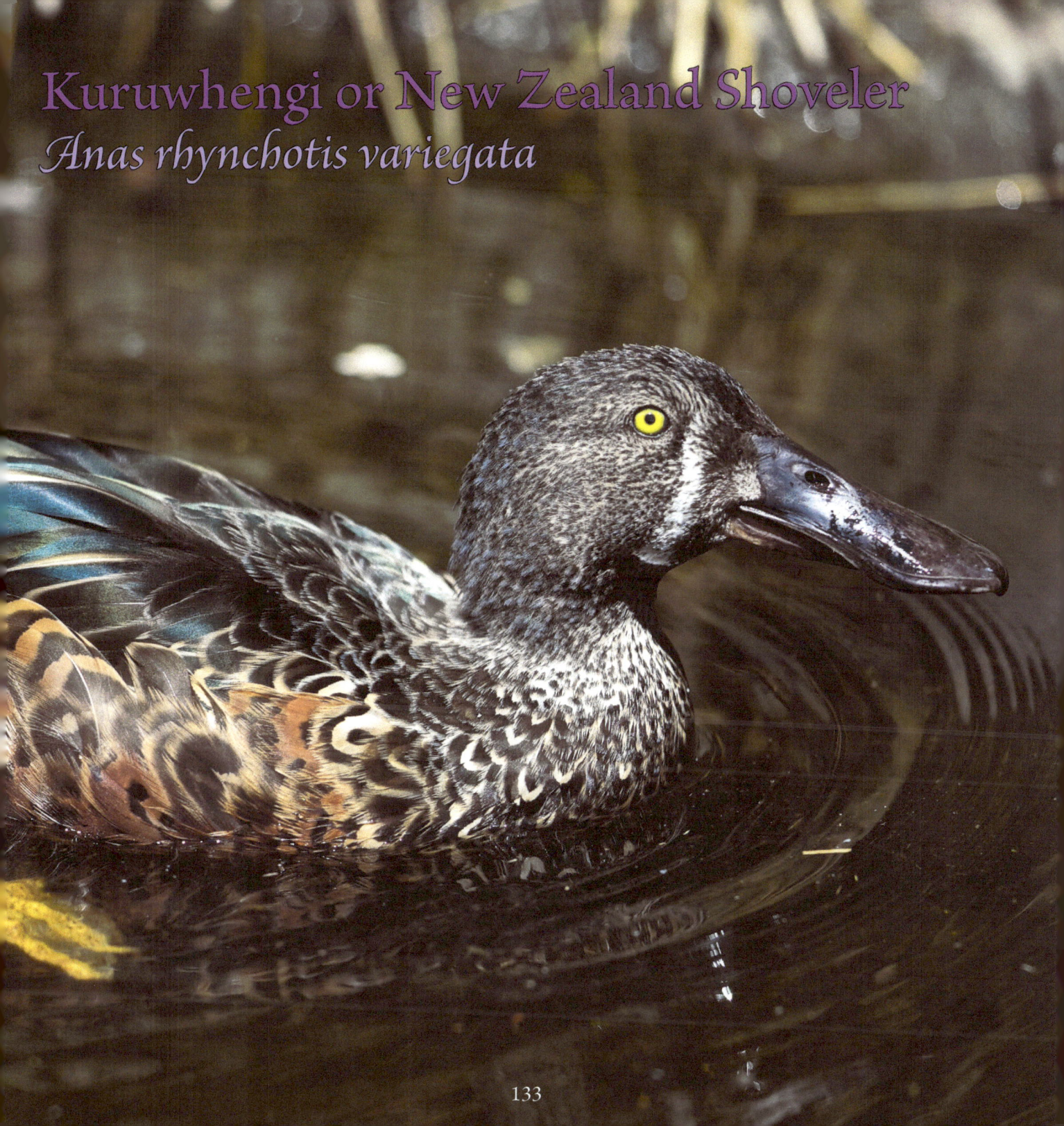

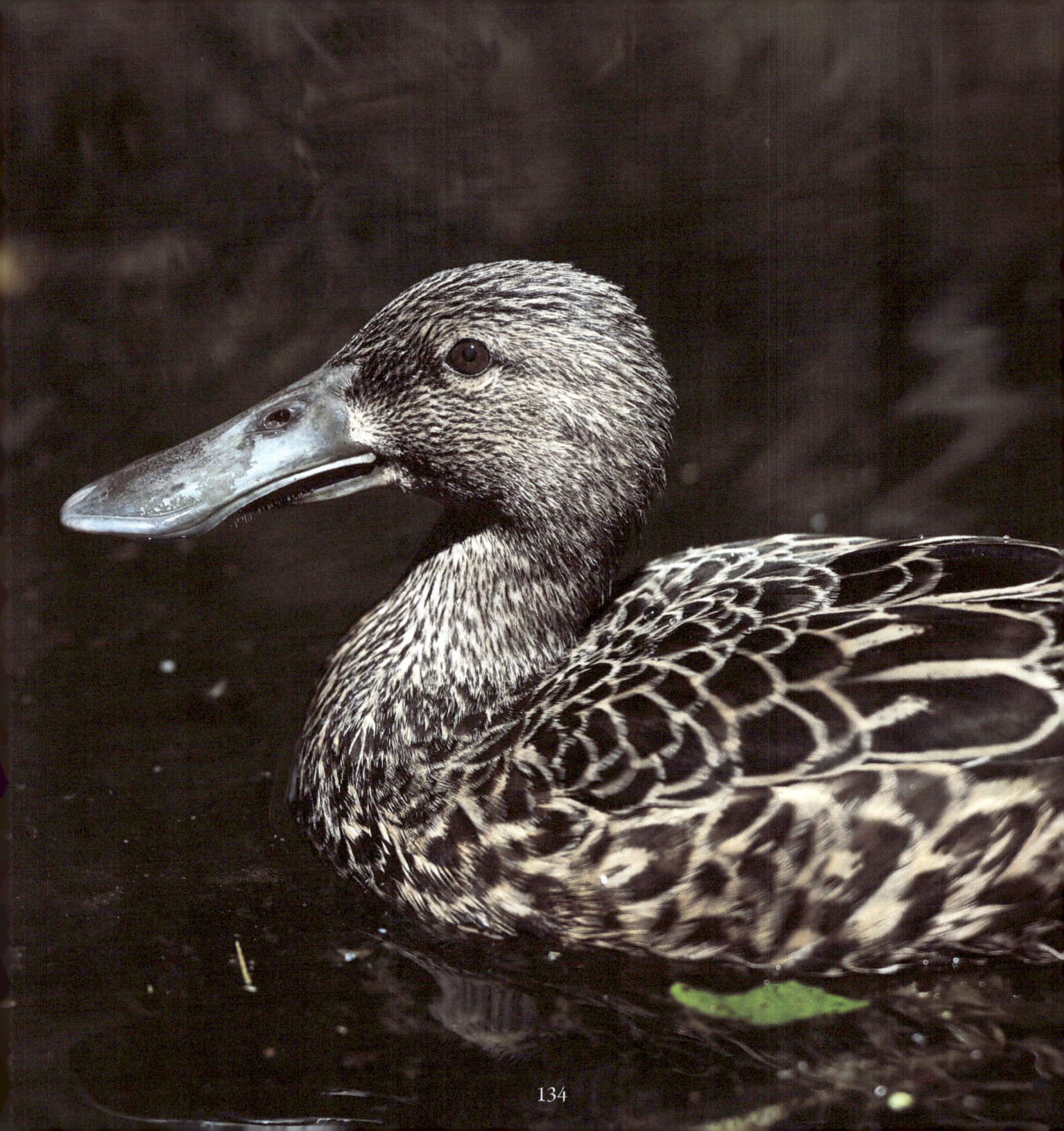

Putangitangi or Paradise Shelduck
Tadorna variegata

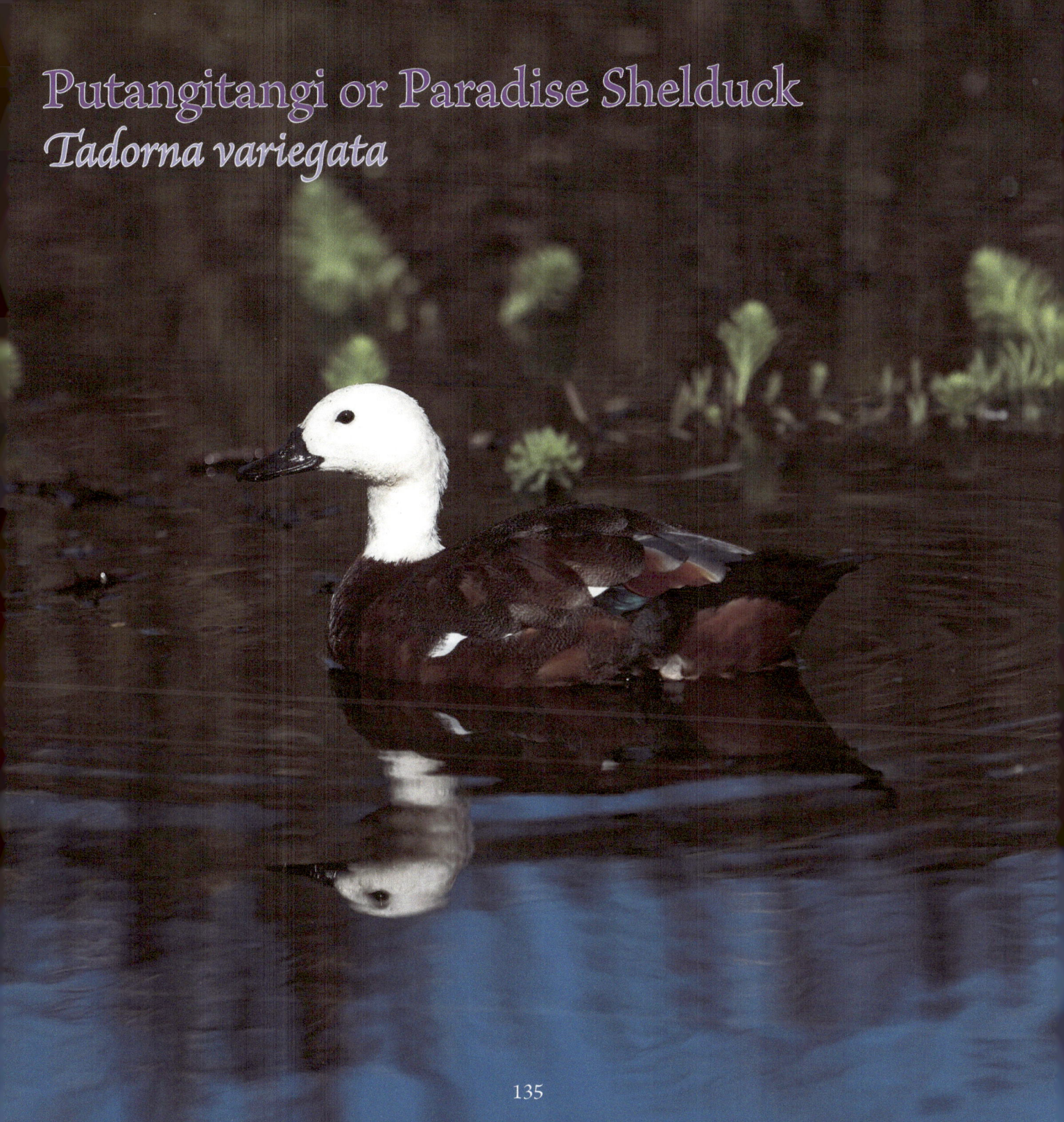

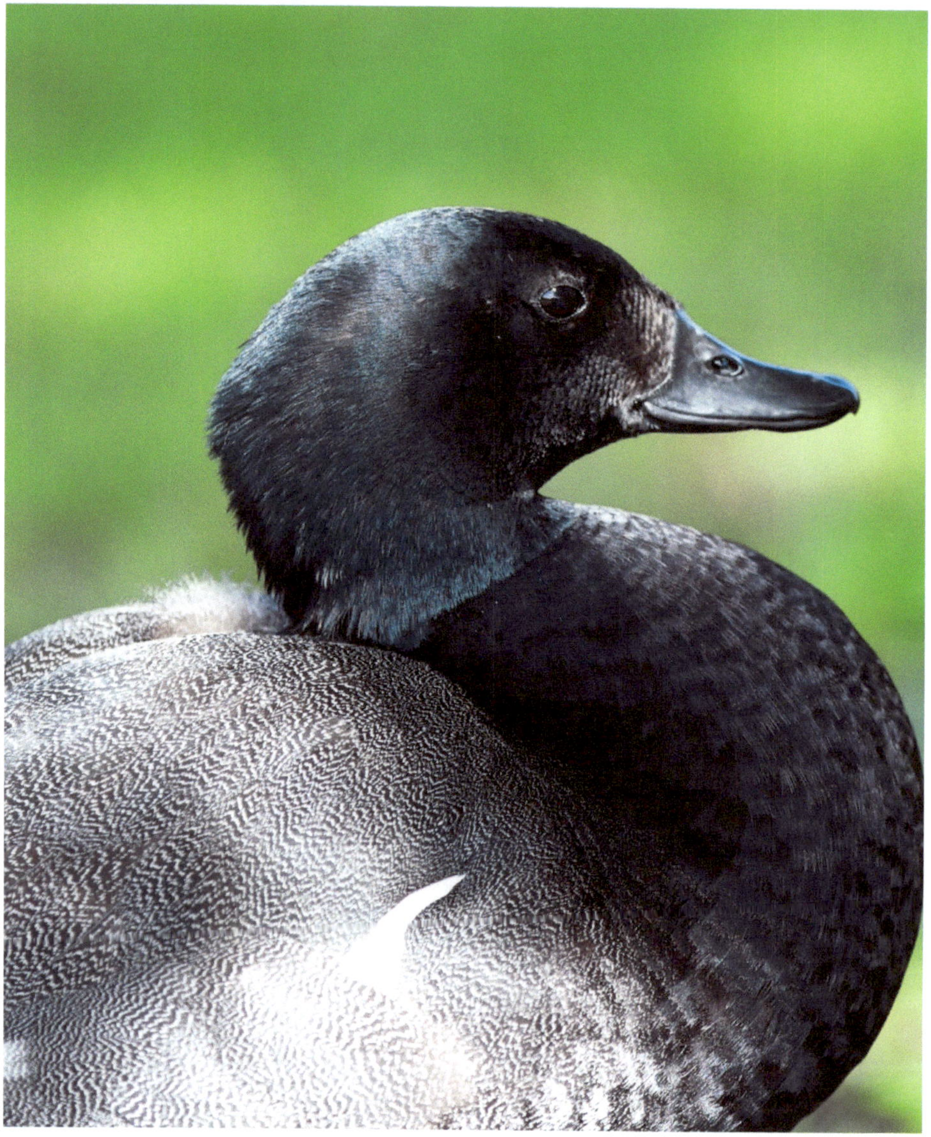

"The Paradise Shelduck is very common on the Jollie and great Tasman River beds, and is never molested. It is a beautiful bird, and I never saw it but in pairs. The cries of the duck and drake are quite distinct… Her note varies exceedingly in pitch, sequence, combination, and duration. The notes are uttered both whilst at rest and on the wing. The sound is not a whistle, but is nearer a clear human cry… The drake's note is very different. The sound differs altogether from that of the duck–it can be very nearly reproduced with a piece of paper and a comb. On the 21st November, 1910, I noted the following variations in the cry of the duck: She uttered the cry whilst walking on the river–bed, changing on taking to the wing, and returning again whilst on the wing. Very often during flight the drake sounded his deep note whilst the duck cried the notes, and one could not help imagining that she was then lamenting a lost brood or desolated home, whilst the old drake, with tears in his voice, was doing his utmost to comfort her… Whilst on the Jollie River bed a duck suddenly appeared before us, fluttering away on the shingle as if wounded and in the last extremity. 'There's a nest somewhere,' said my companion, 'and she is decoying us away from it.' We humoured her maternal instinct, and after preceding us for a dozen yards or so she rose in the air and flew off. Whilst resting after breakfast on the lateral moraine of the Tasman Glacier at the southern end of the Murchison Valley, on the 19th November, 1910, we were much pleased by the actions of a paradise duck and drake. A clear, gentle stream flowed along the foot of the moraine at our flowed along the foot of the moraine at our feet, and the duck waded fearlessly backwards and forwards not more than 15 ft. from us. She approached nearer and nearer each traverse, until she was no more than 8 ft. away. As she moved she constantly emitted a quiet, pleasing sound, the quack (though the term is too hard) of the paradise. After a time she rejoined her mate on the gravel beyond the stream, where they both settled down to sleep in the morning sun. We were delighted with their tameness: it gave us excellent opportunity of noting and admiring the beauty of their plumage. This Murchison Valley was extremely quiet: it has never been entered by stock of any kind, and bird–life was also very scarce at the time of our visit."

~Johannes C. Andersen, 1910

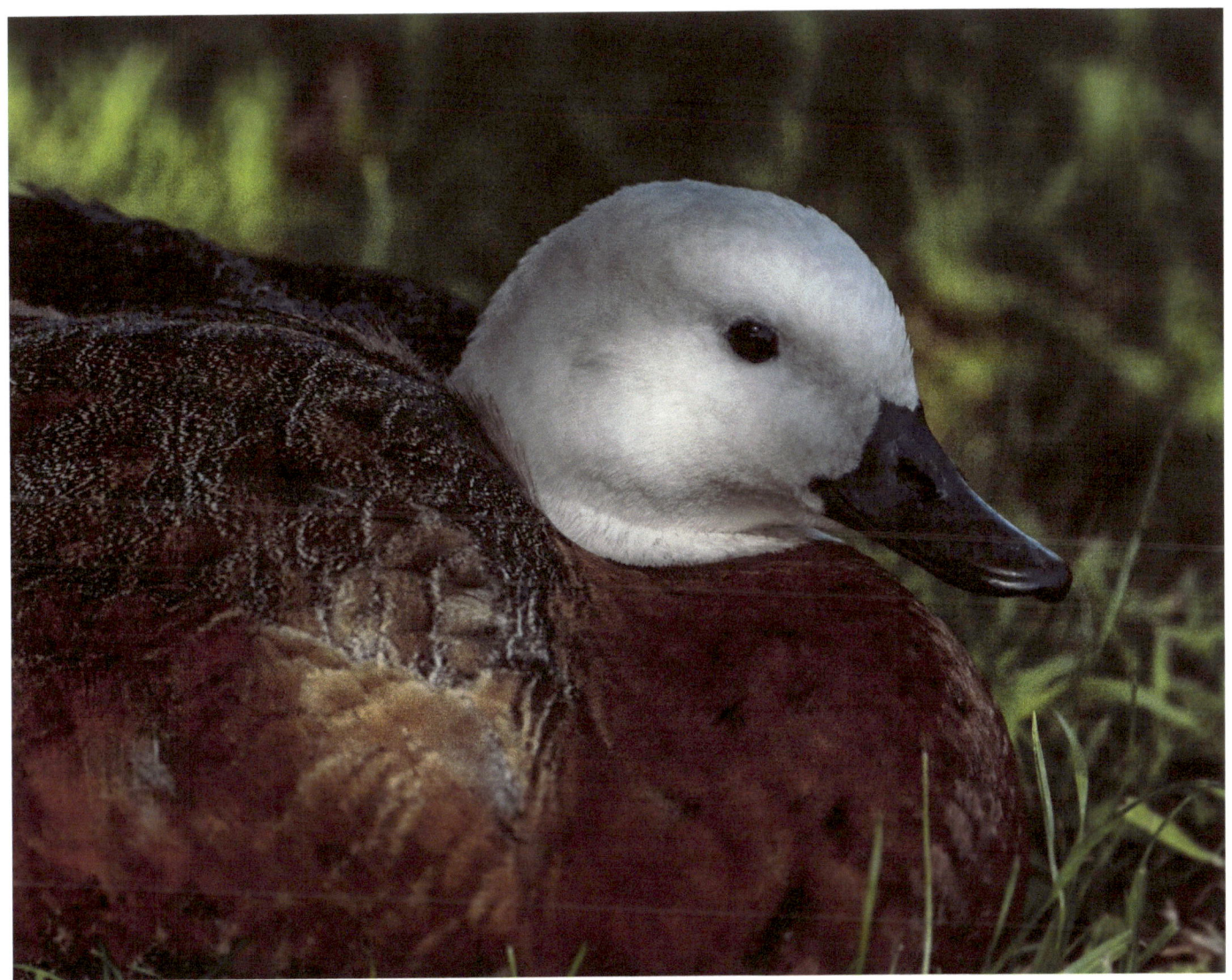

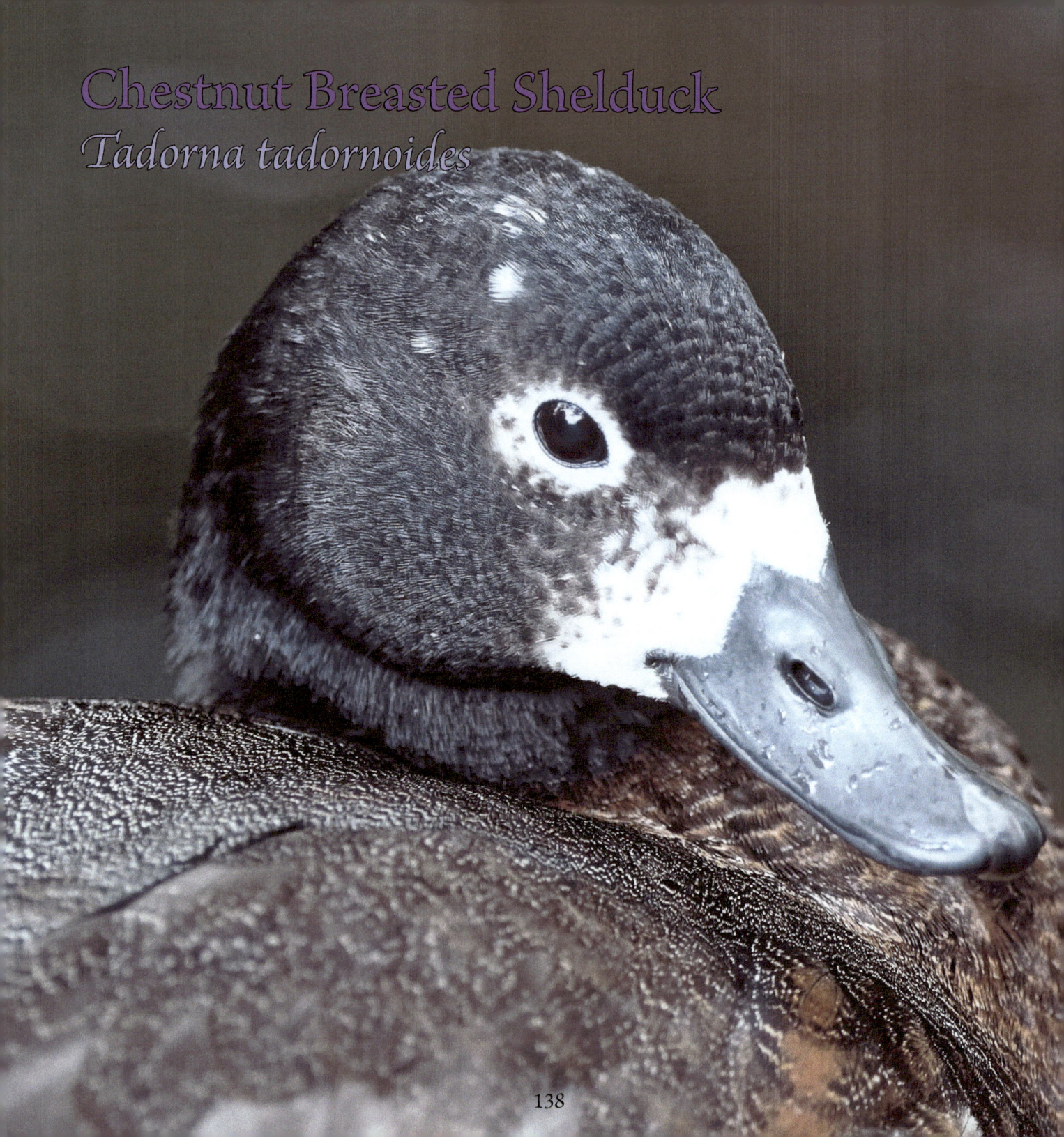

Chestnut Breasted Shelduck
Tadorna tadornoides

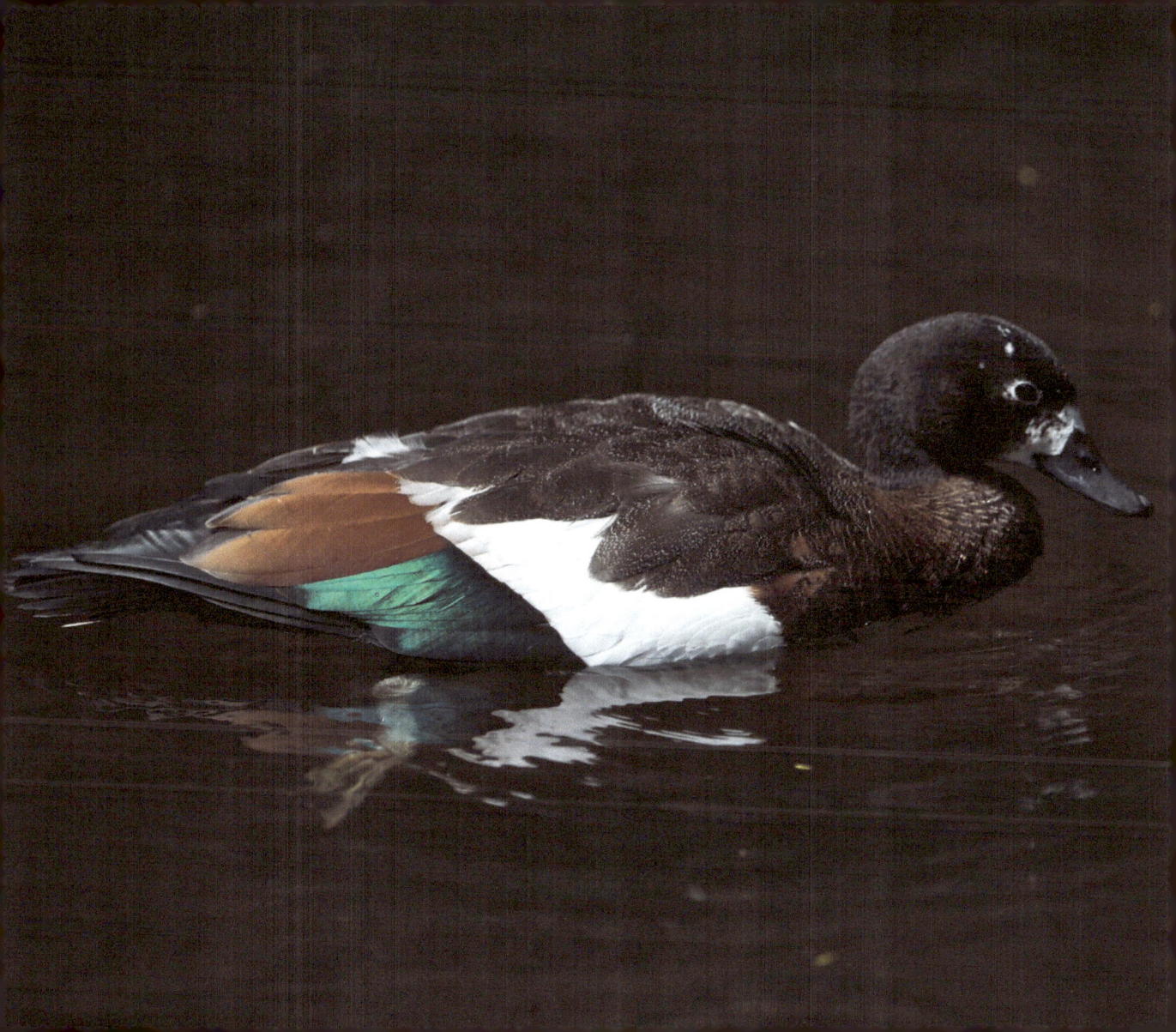

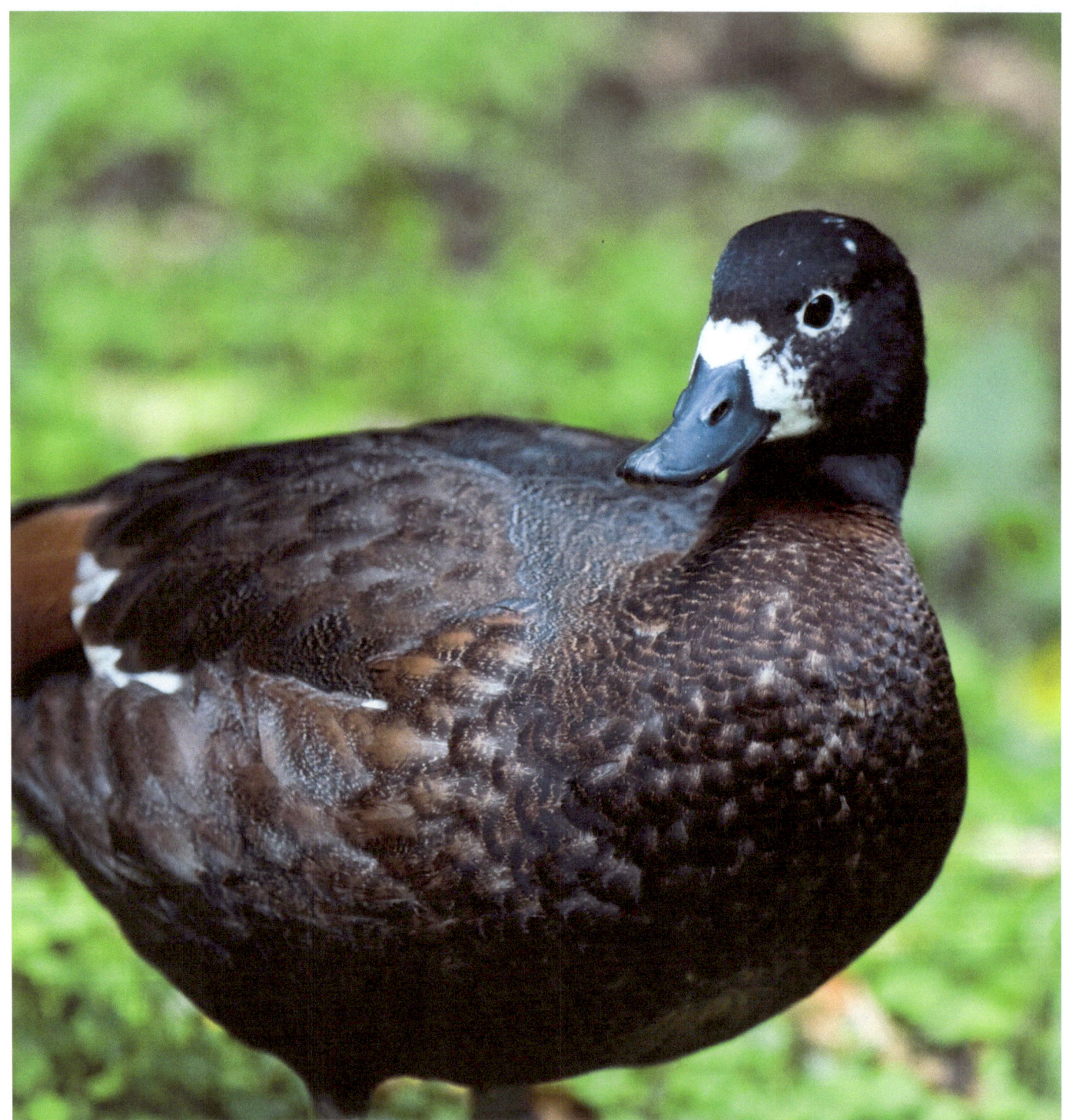

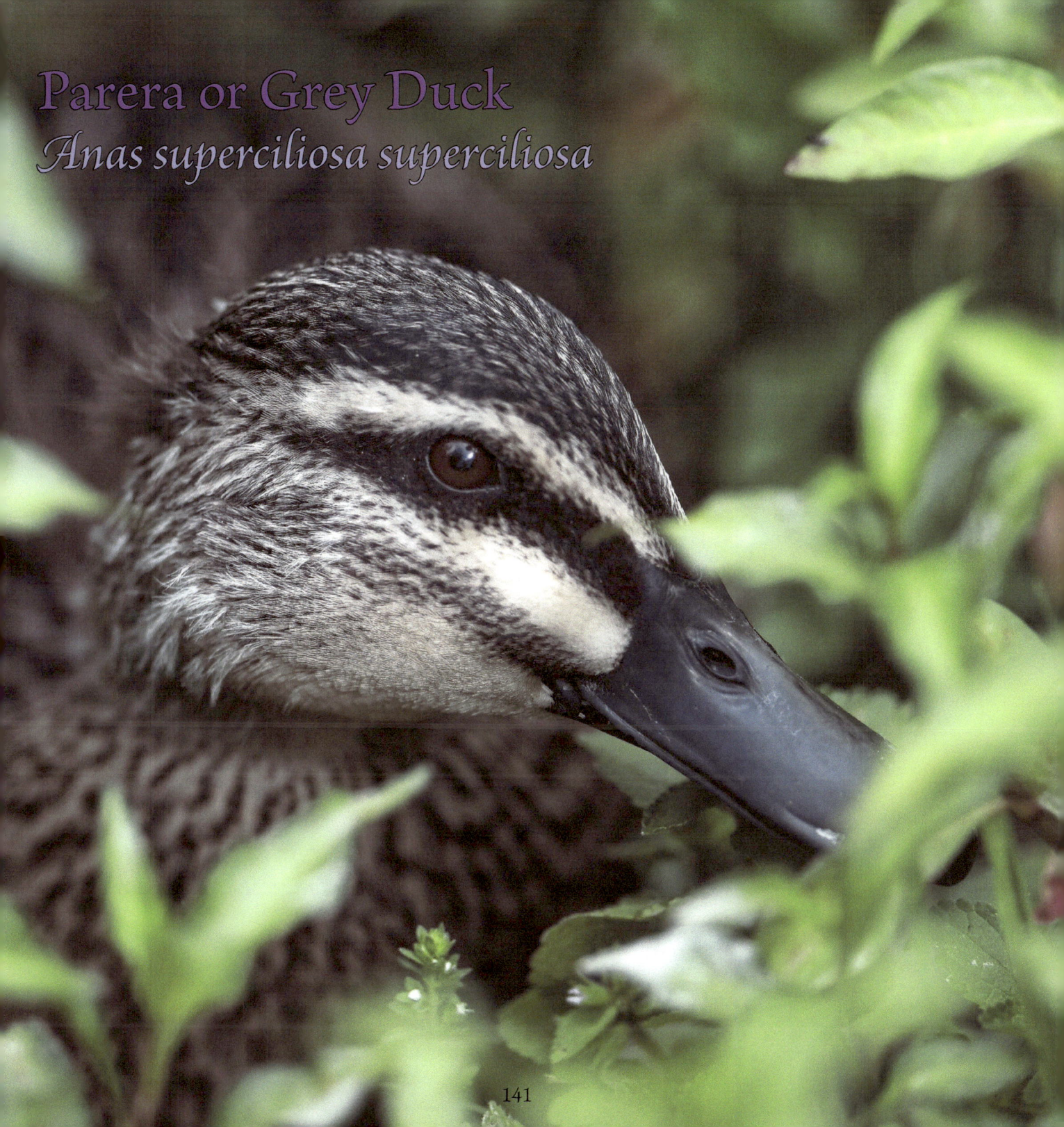

Parera or Grey Duck
Anas superciliosa superciliosa

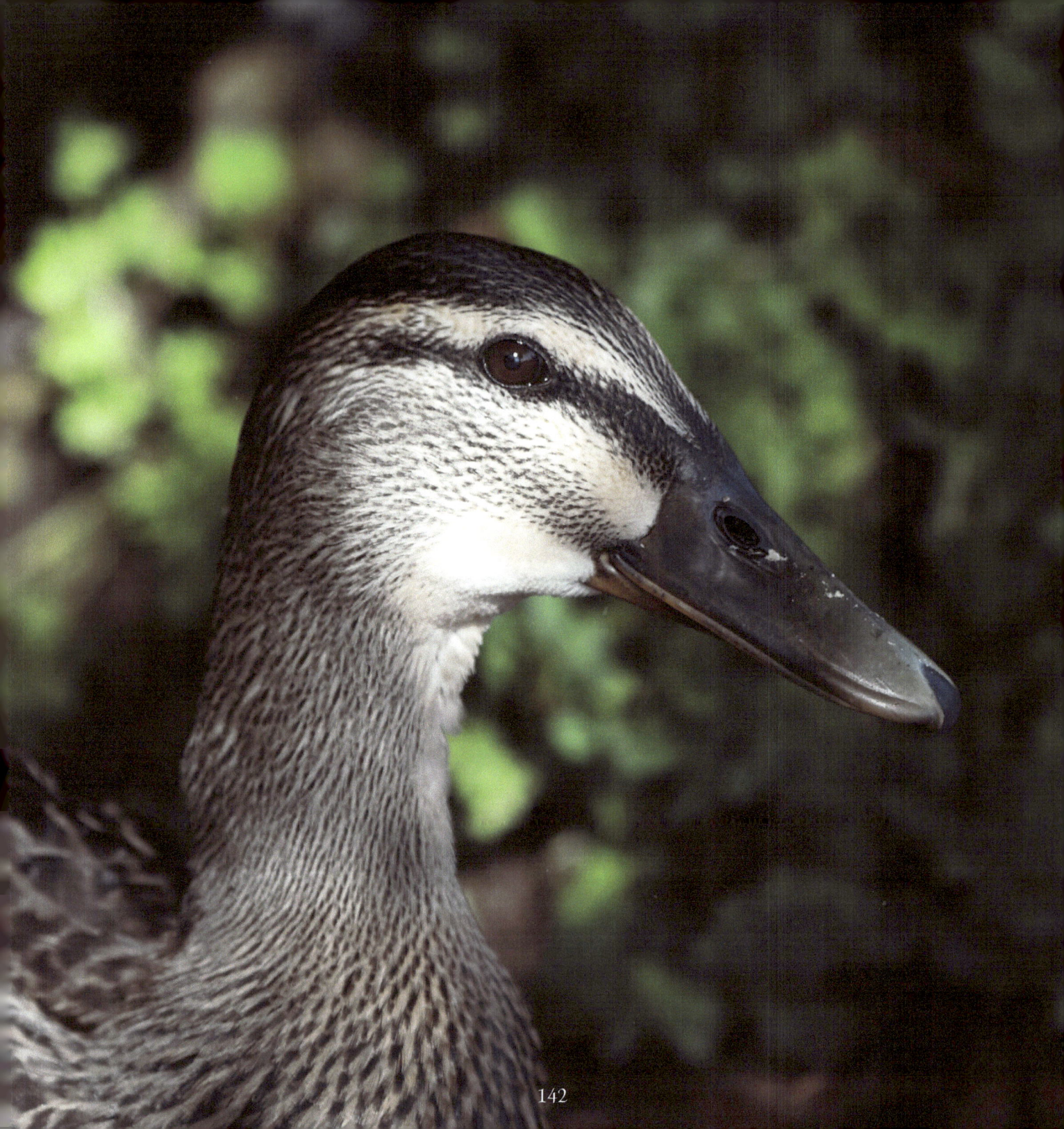

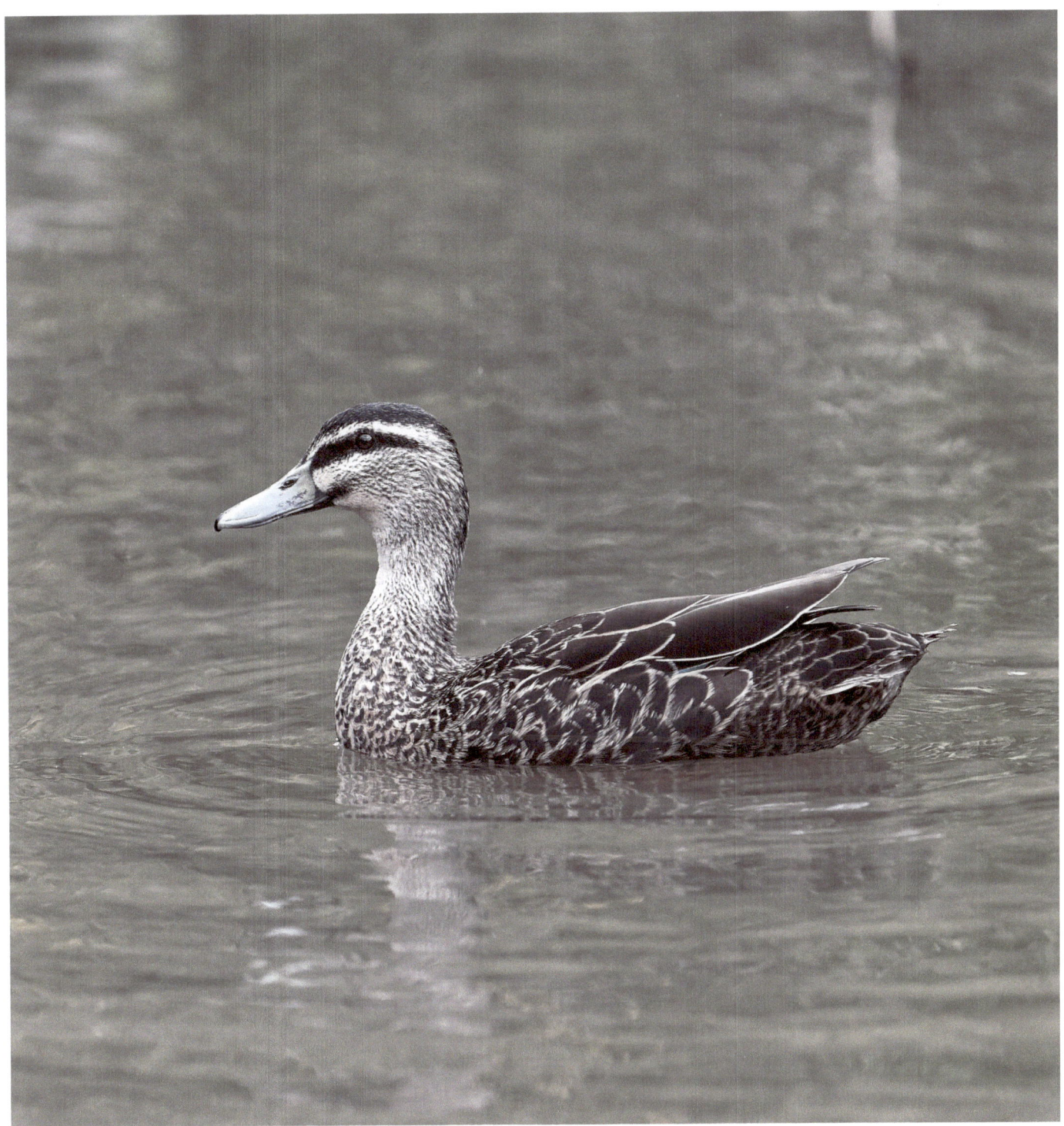

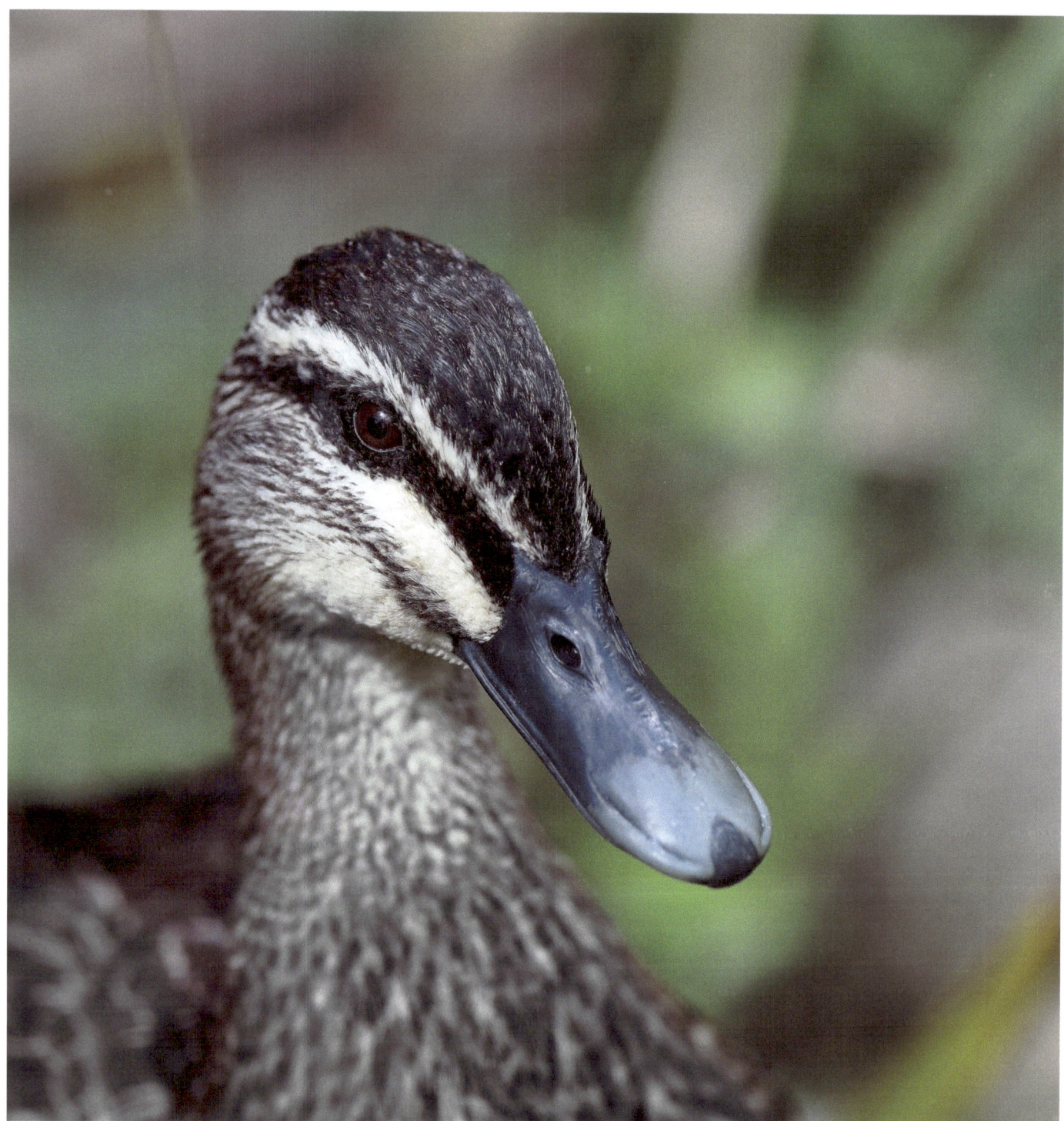

Parera or Australian Coot
Fulica atra

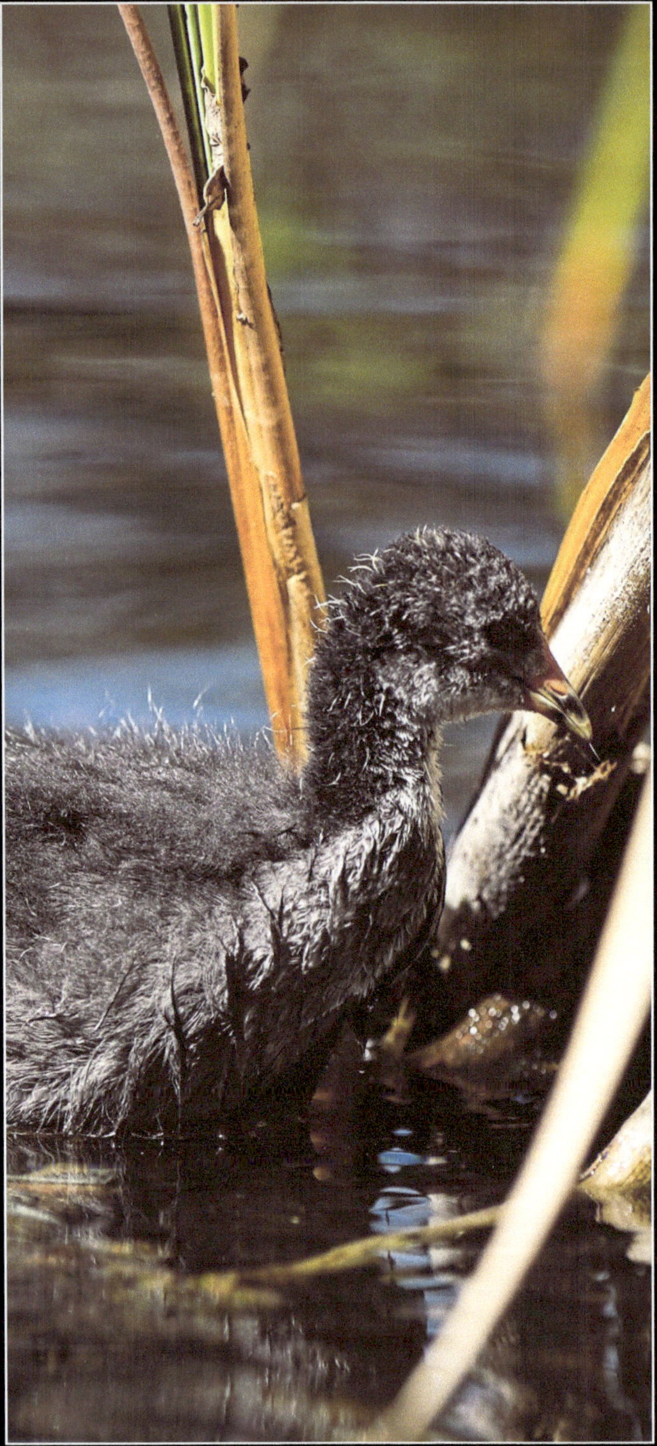

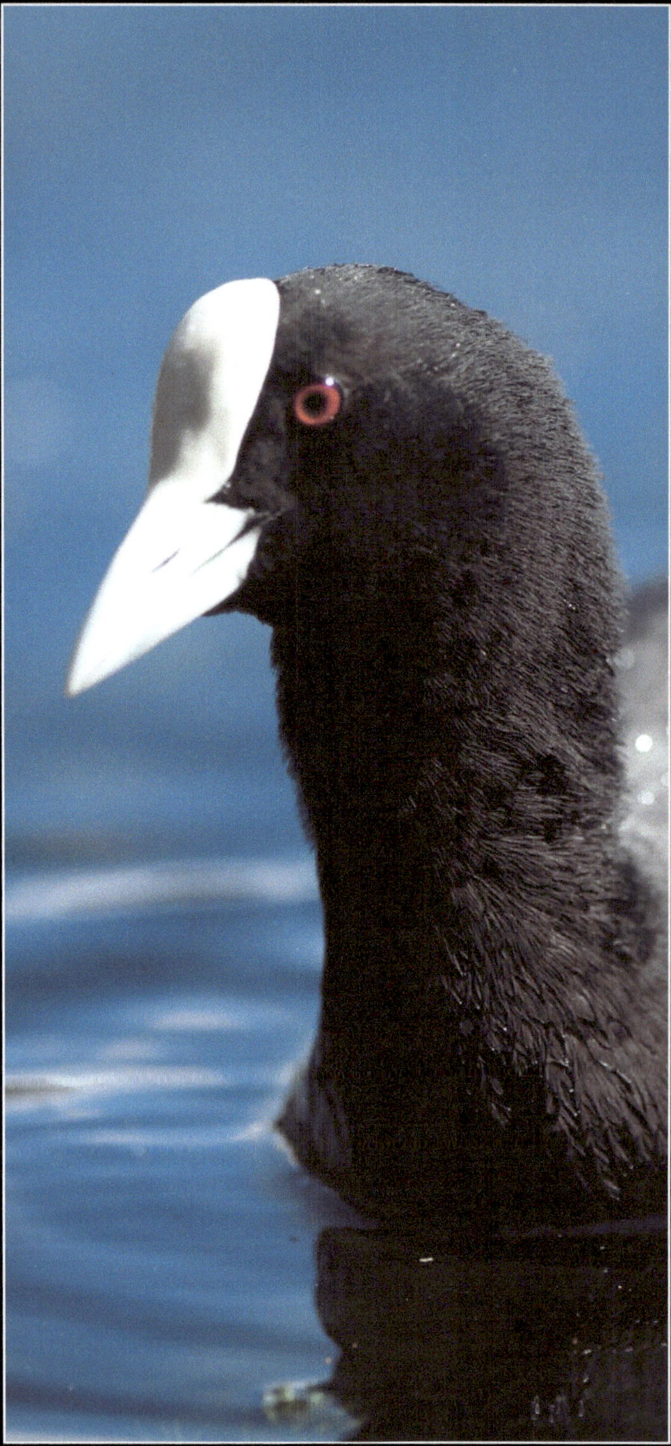

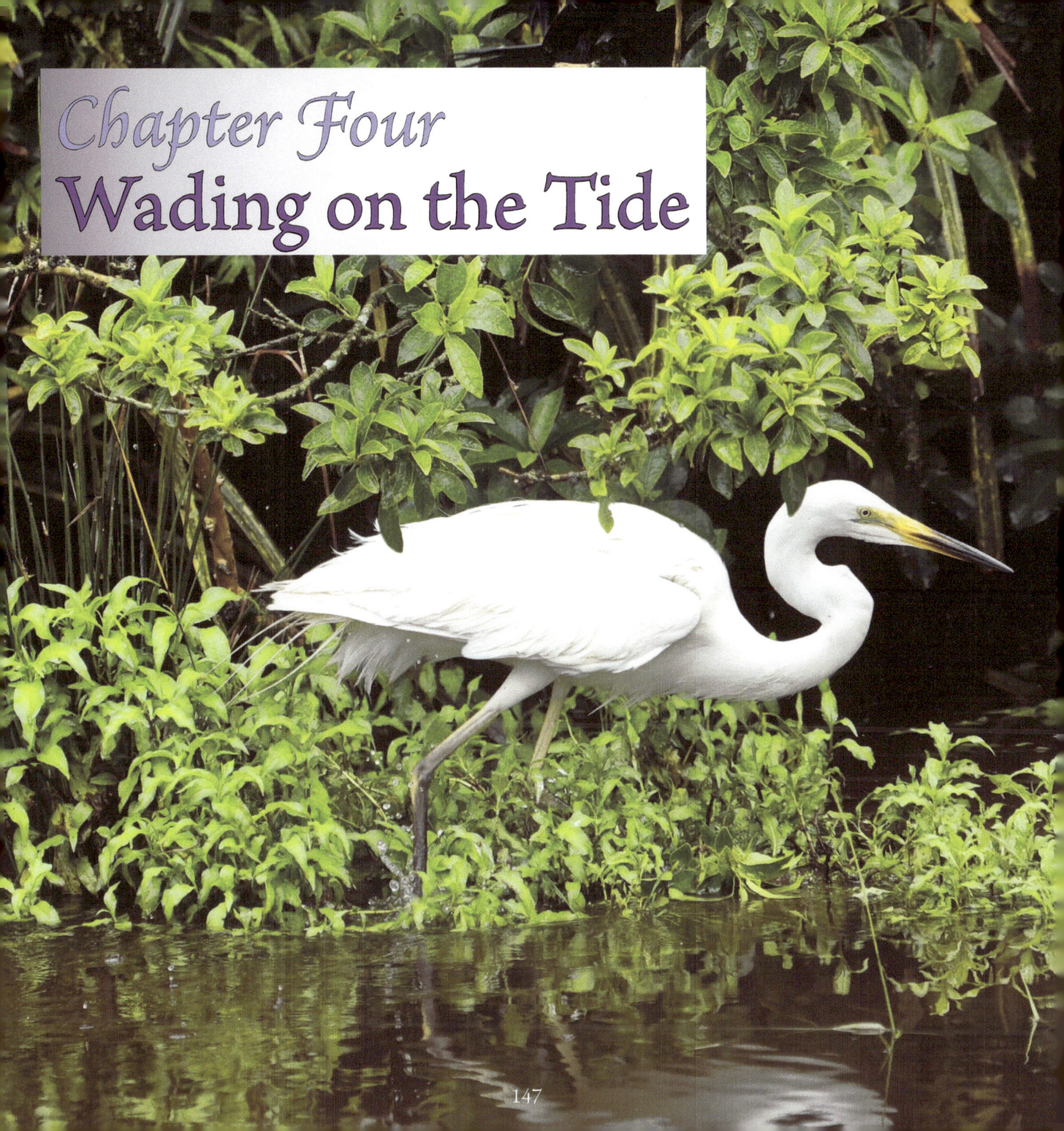
Chapter Four
Wading on the Tide

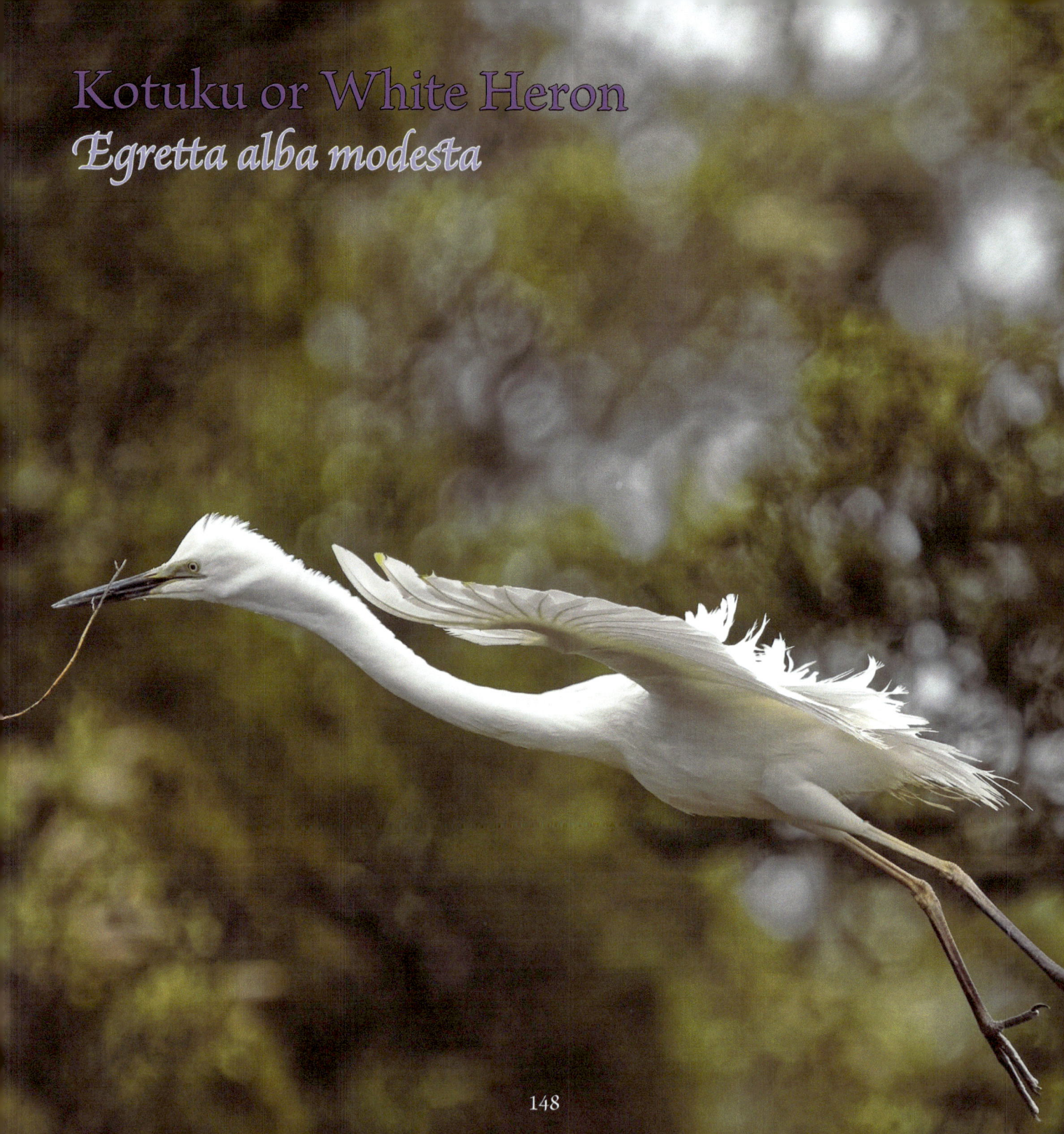

Kotuku or White Heron
Egretta alba modesta

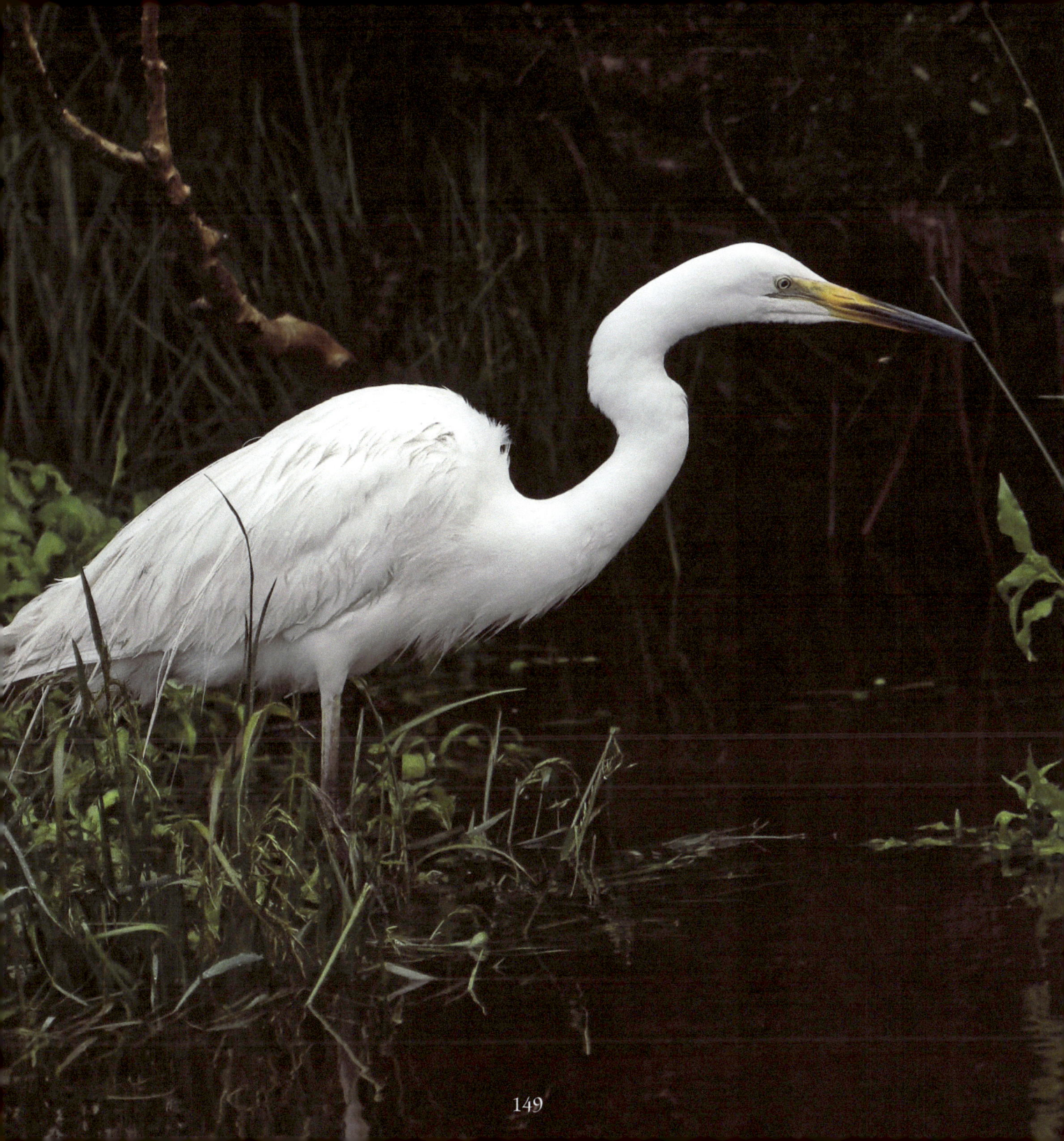

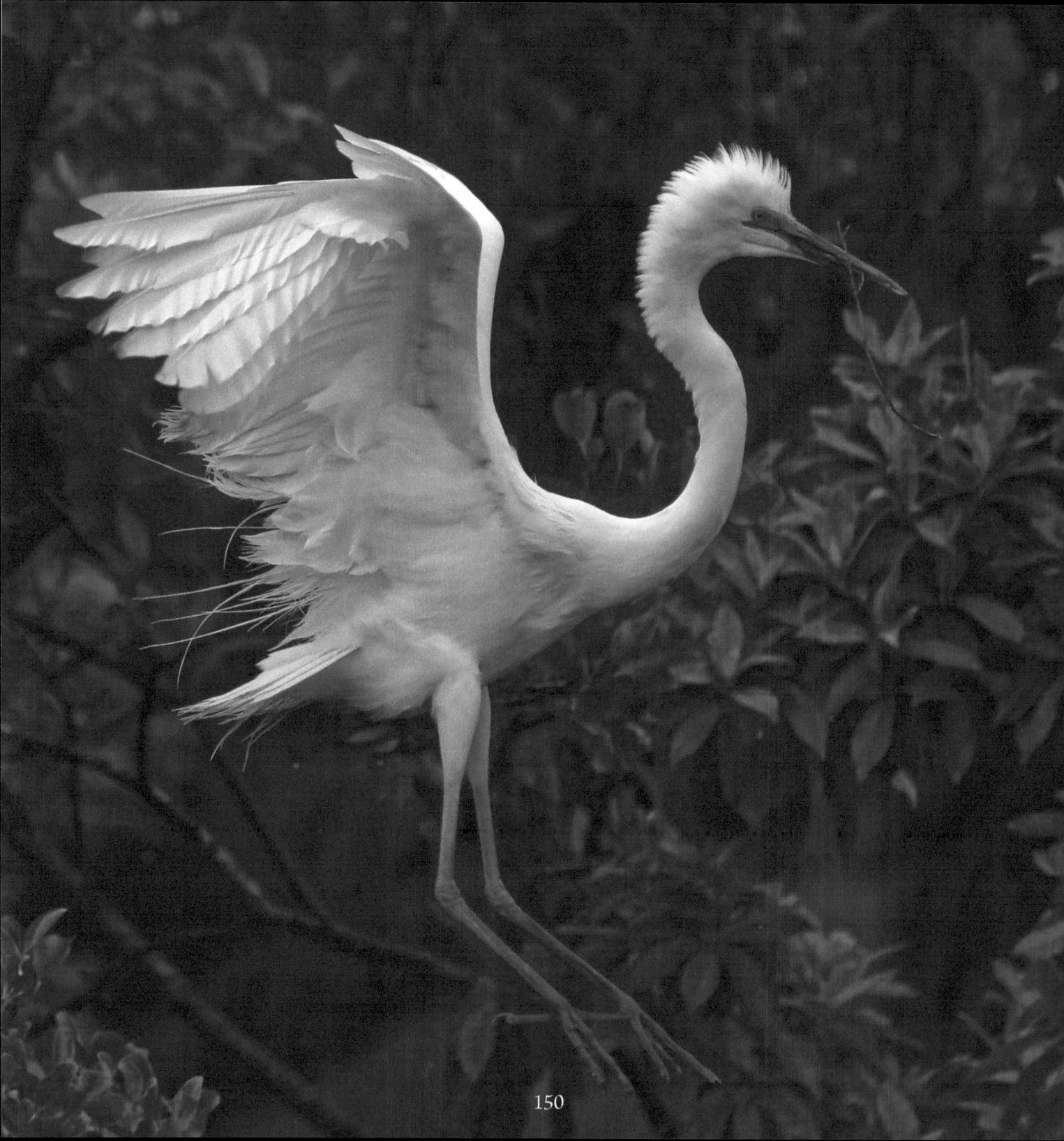

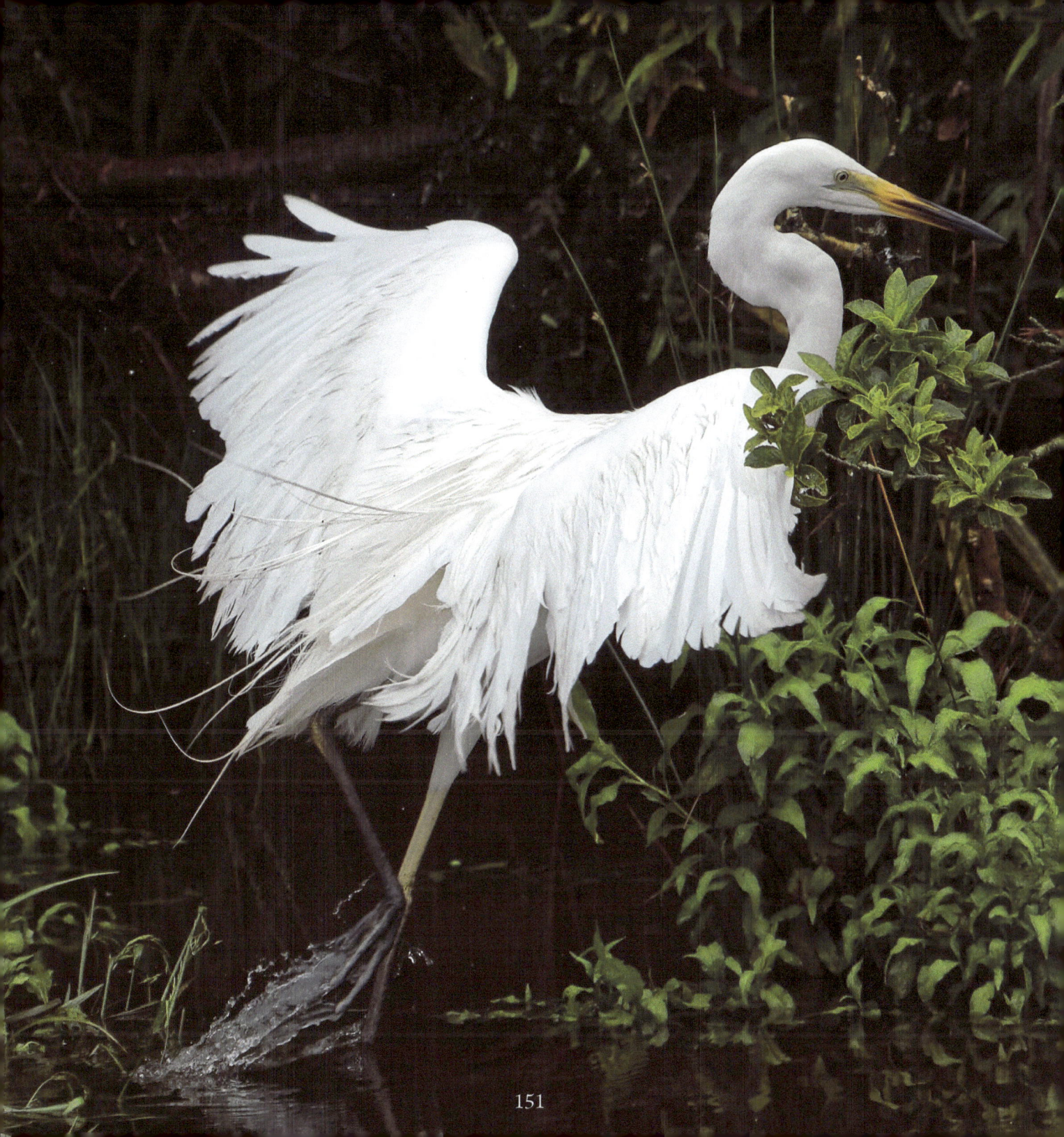

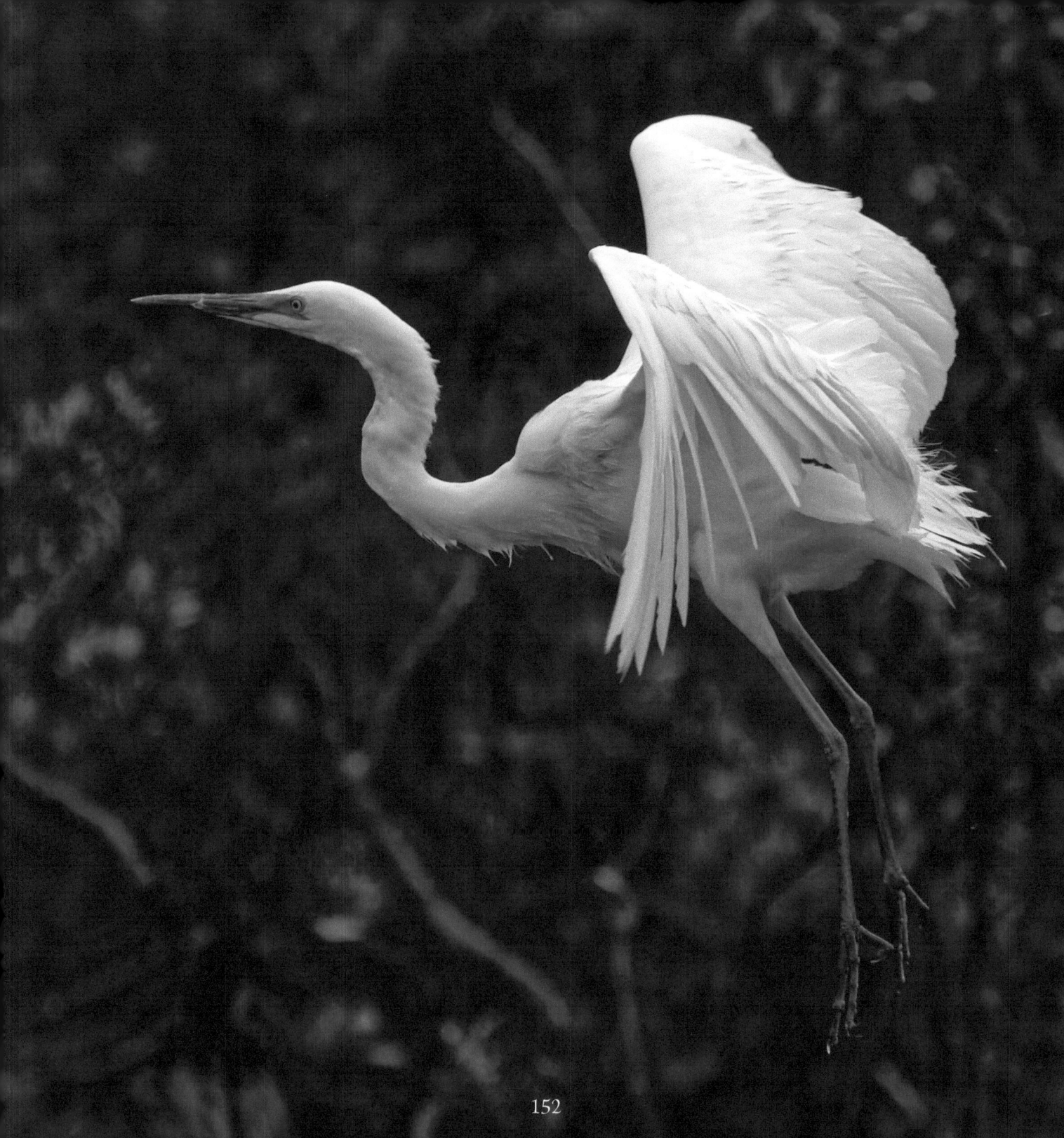

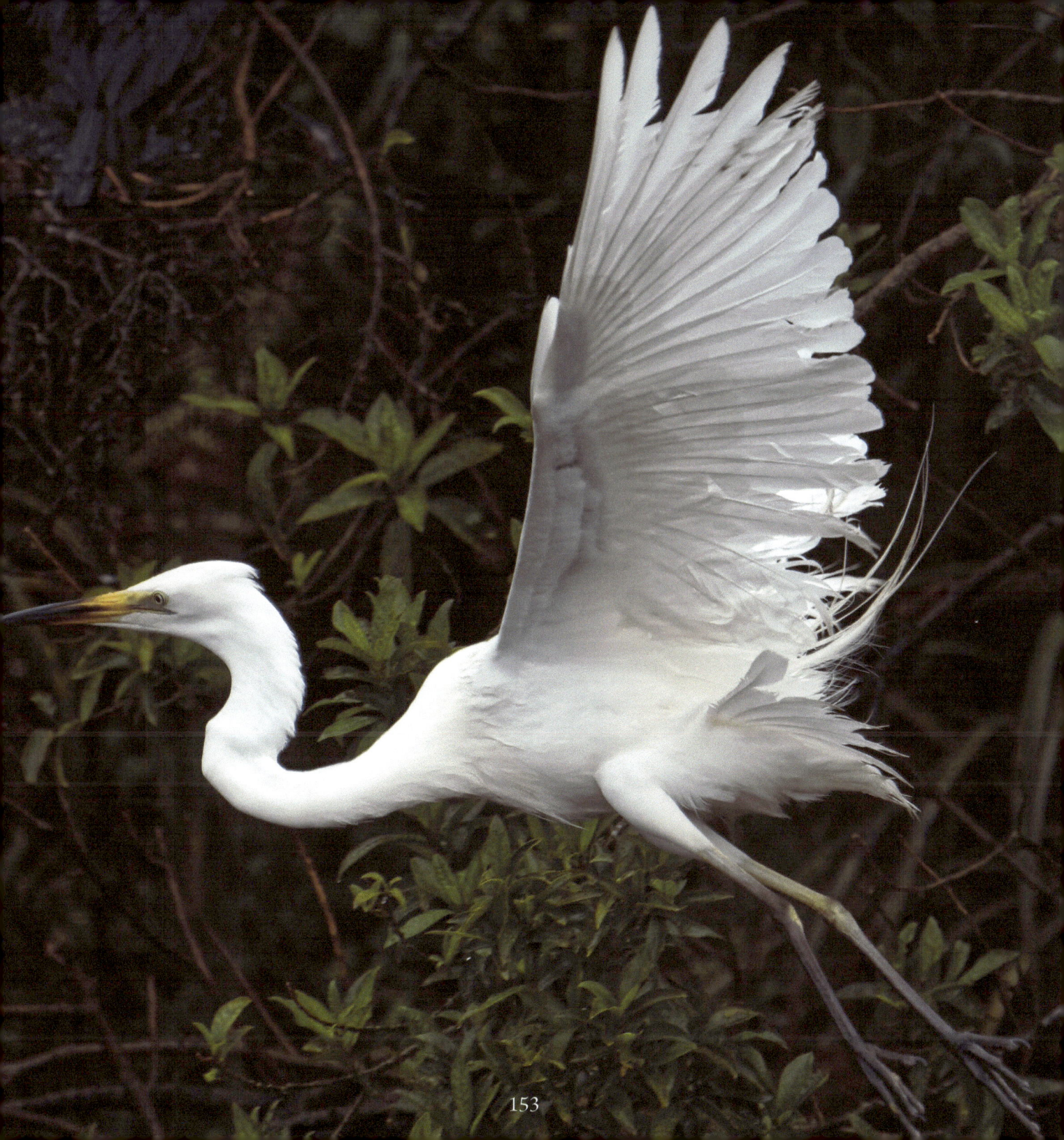

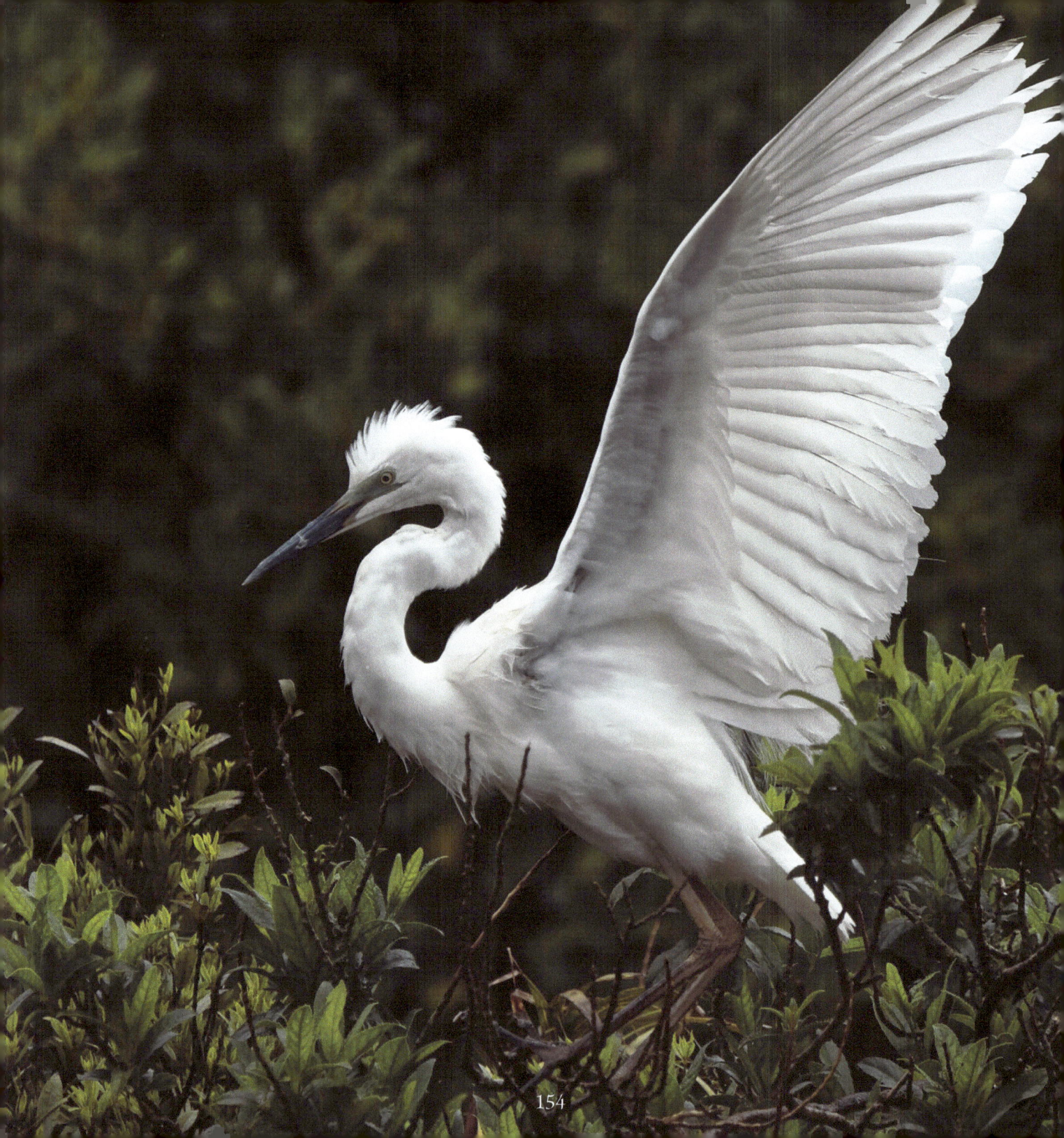

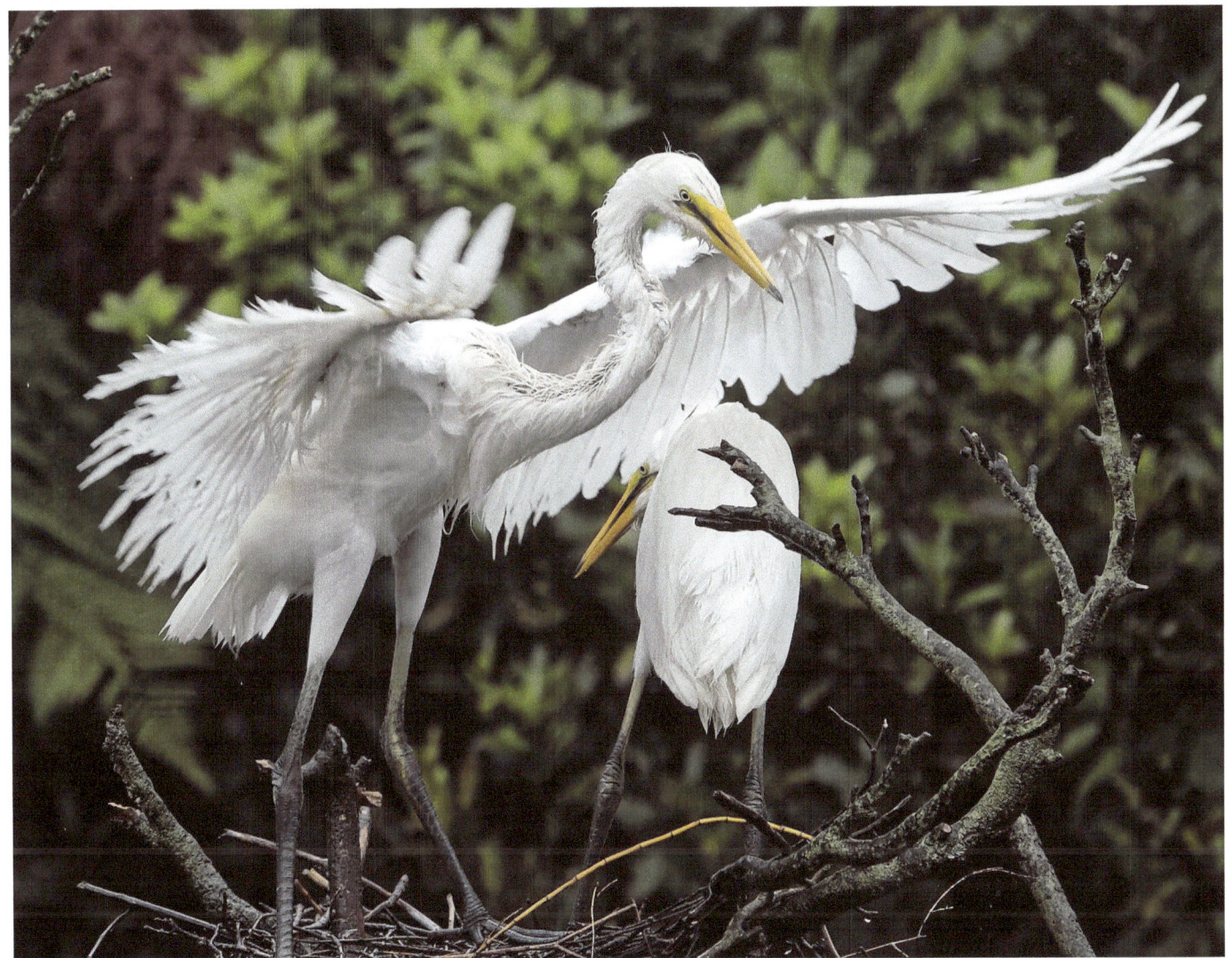

"One of the rarest birds, perhaps, that has ever visited the station is the kotuku, or white heron. Buller describes it as wild and shy; yet upon its first appearance here I rode directly beneath it. It was on the top bough of a large willow, some 50ft. or 60ft. from the ground, and perhaps because I had no gun, or because it was tired after a long flight, I was allowed to admire at leisure… We saw it once again, sailing up the lake, snow–white between the blue of water and sky."

~H. Guthrie-Smith, 1895

"This stately bird appears so rarely in the North Island that the natives distinguish it as 'the bird seen once in a life–time.' In the summer of 1865 a pair visited the Mangrove Swamp at Whangarei, and remained there several weeks."

~Walter L. Buller, 1877

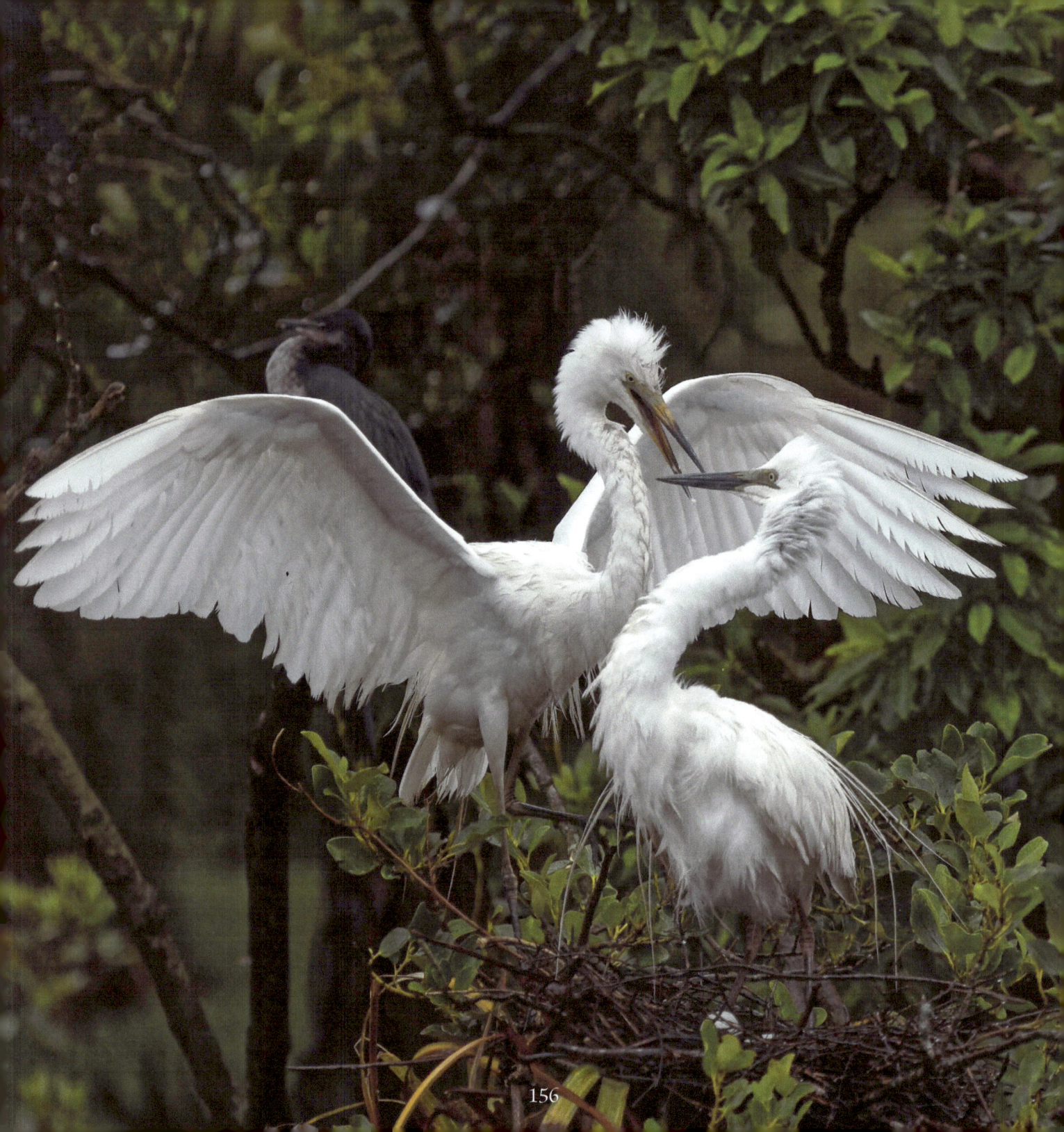

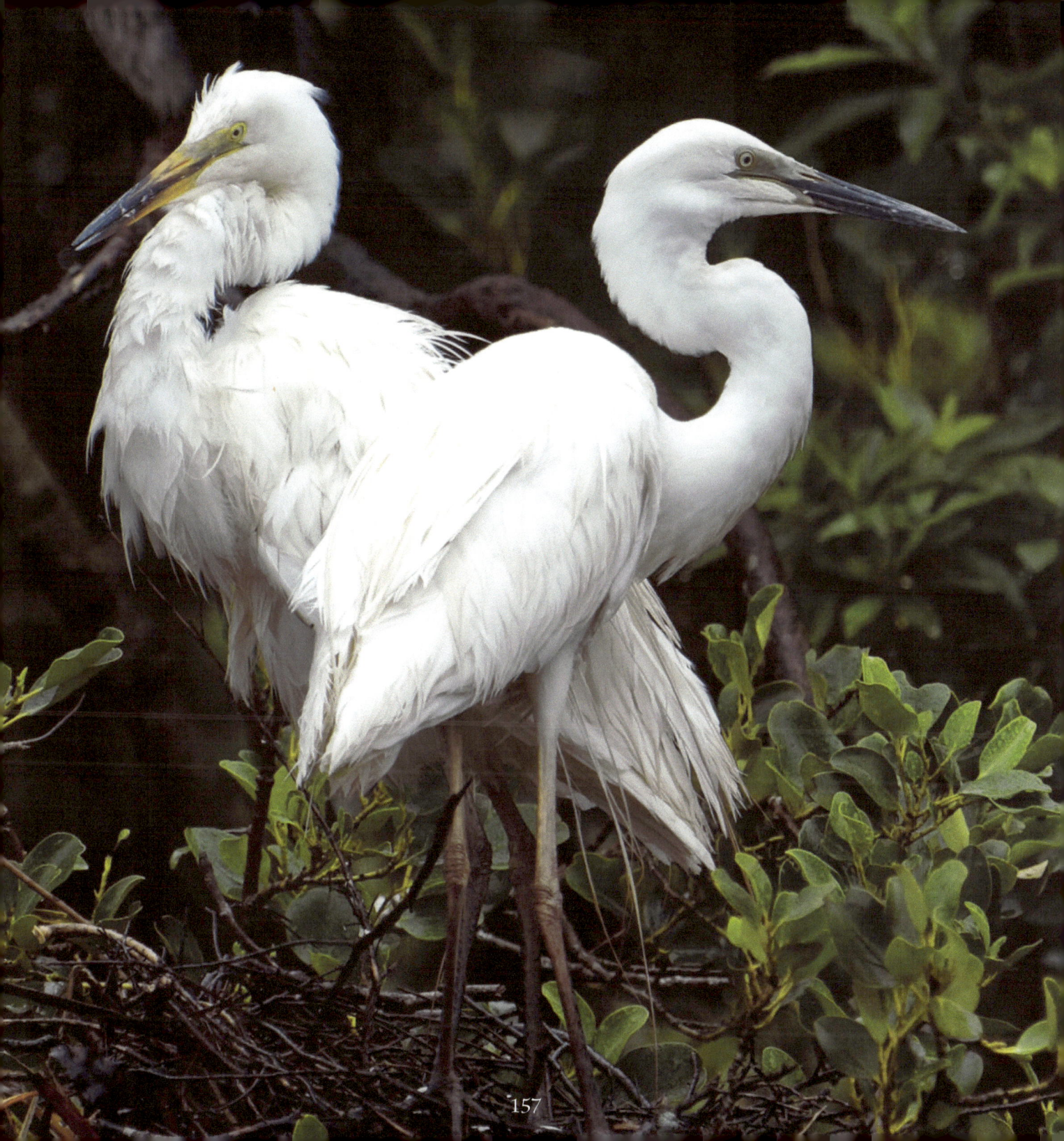

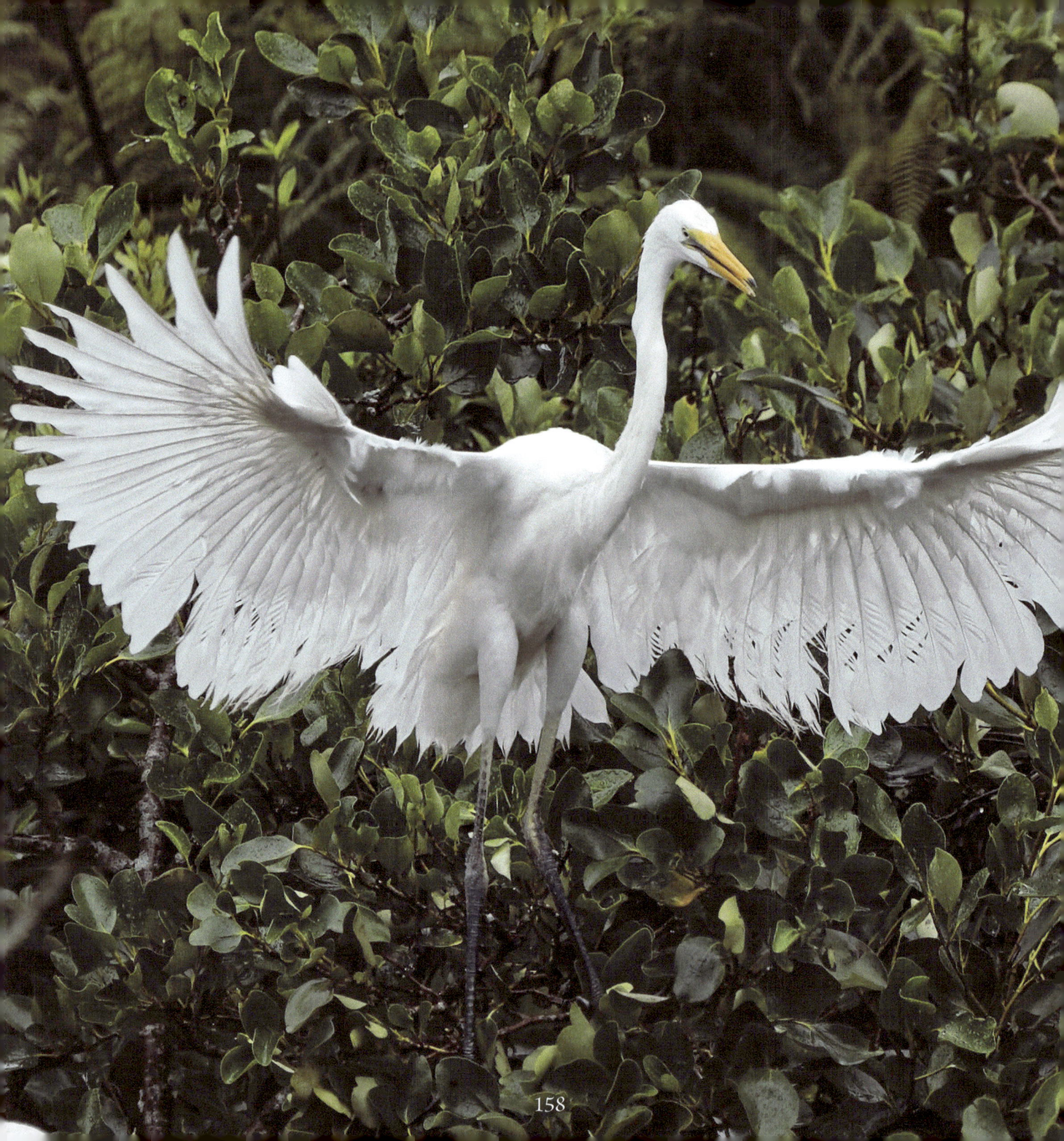

White-faced Heron
Ardea novaehollandiae

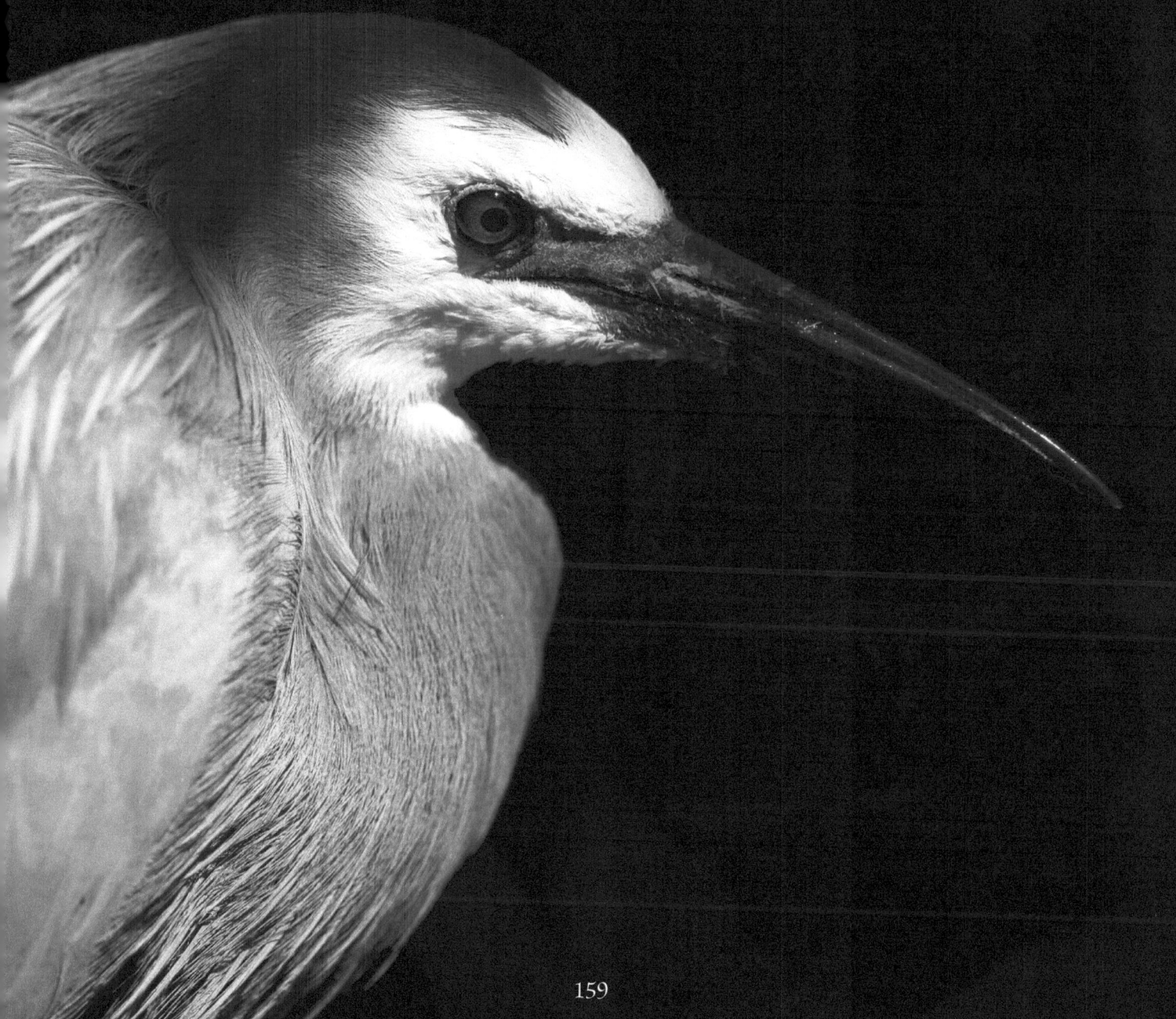

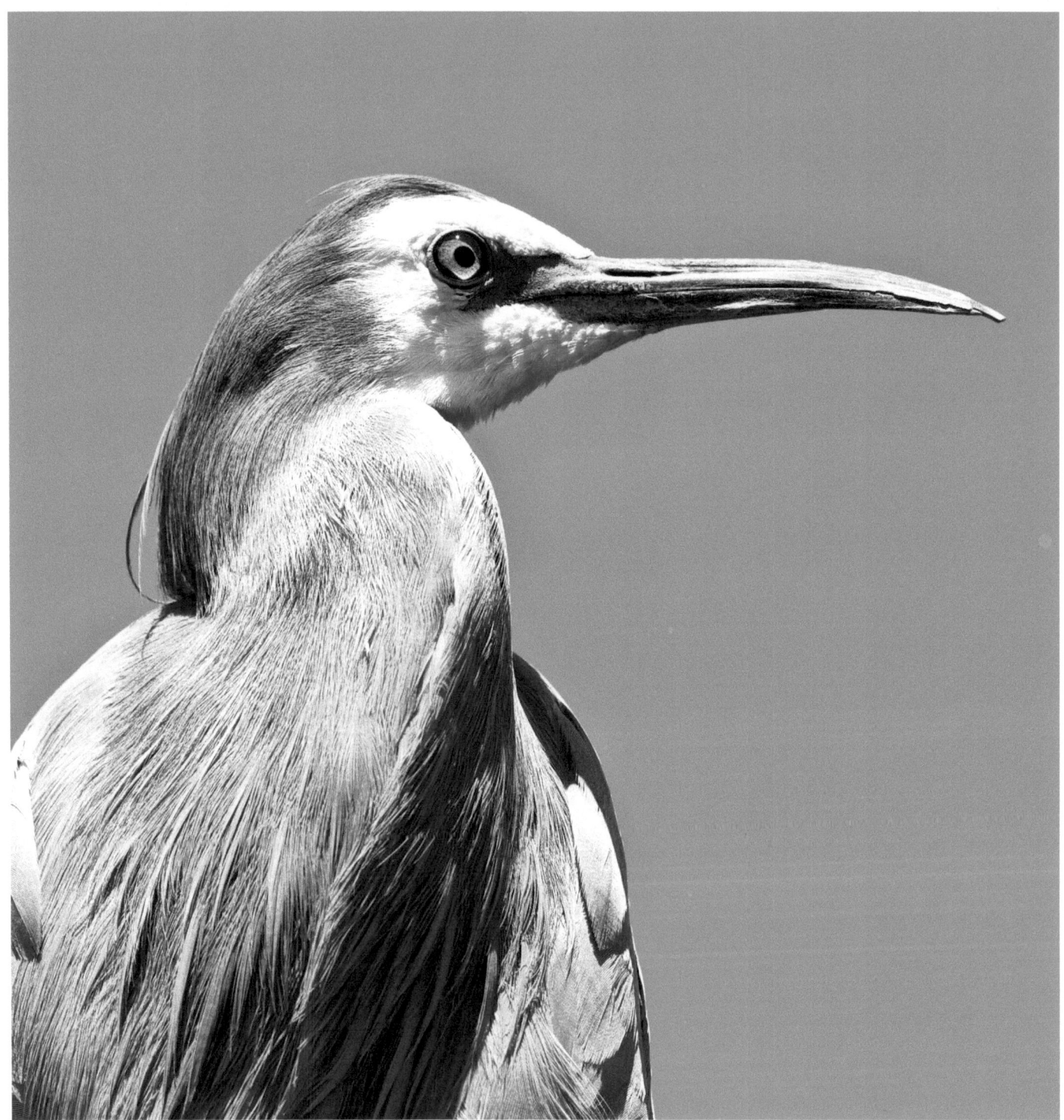

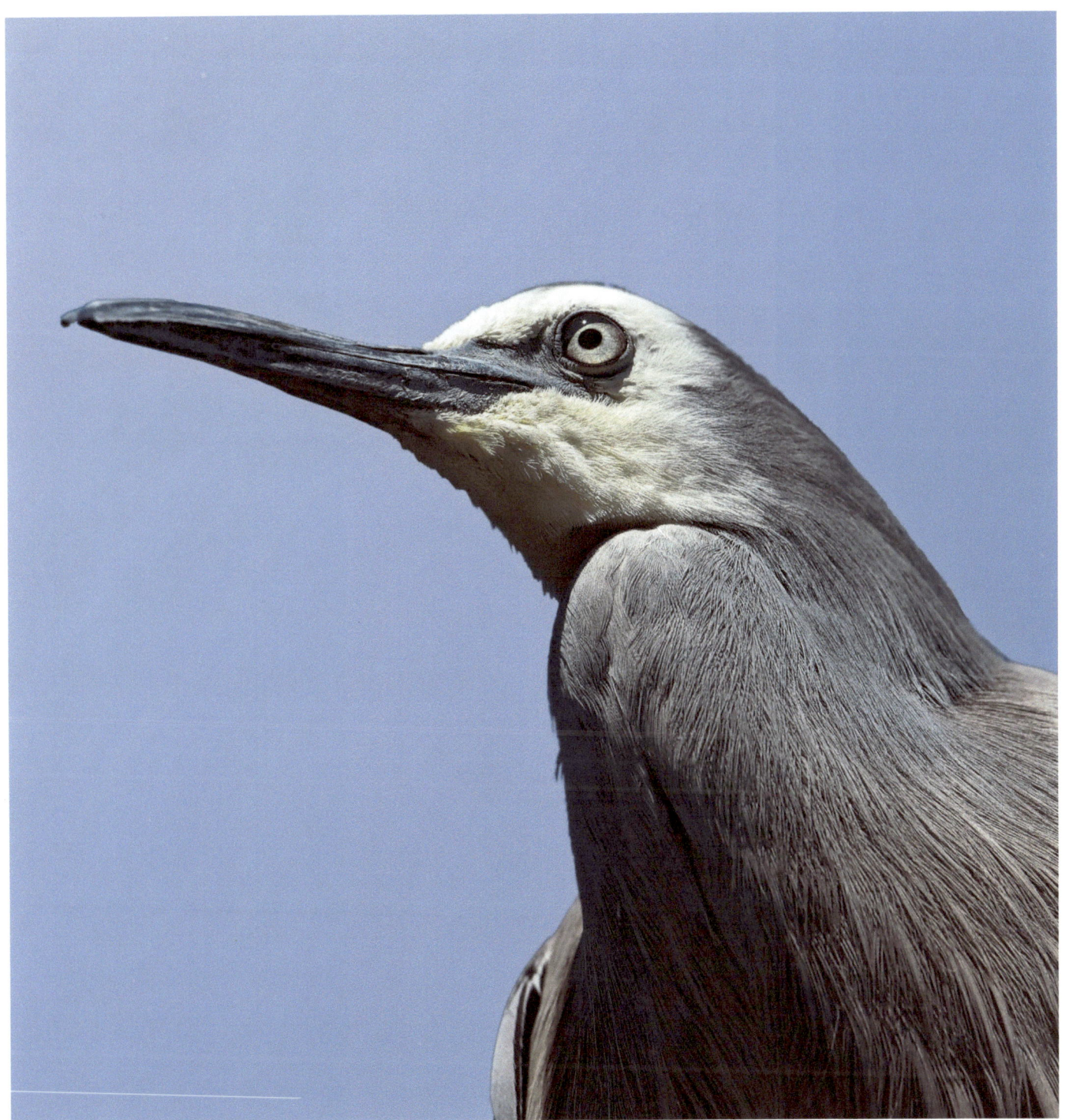

Kotuku–ngutupapa or Royal Spoonbill
Platalea regia

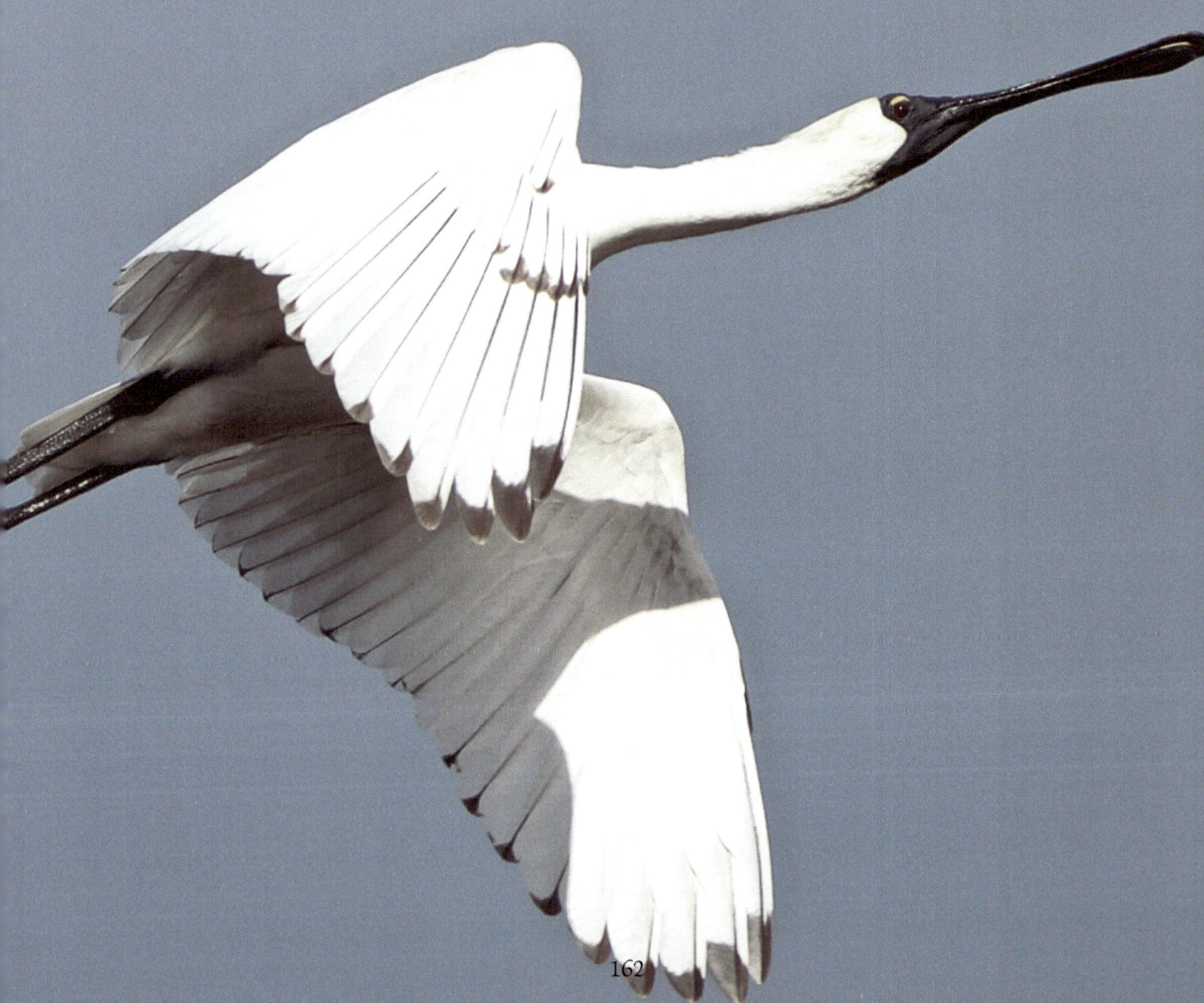

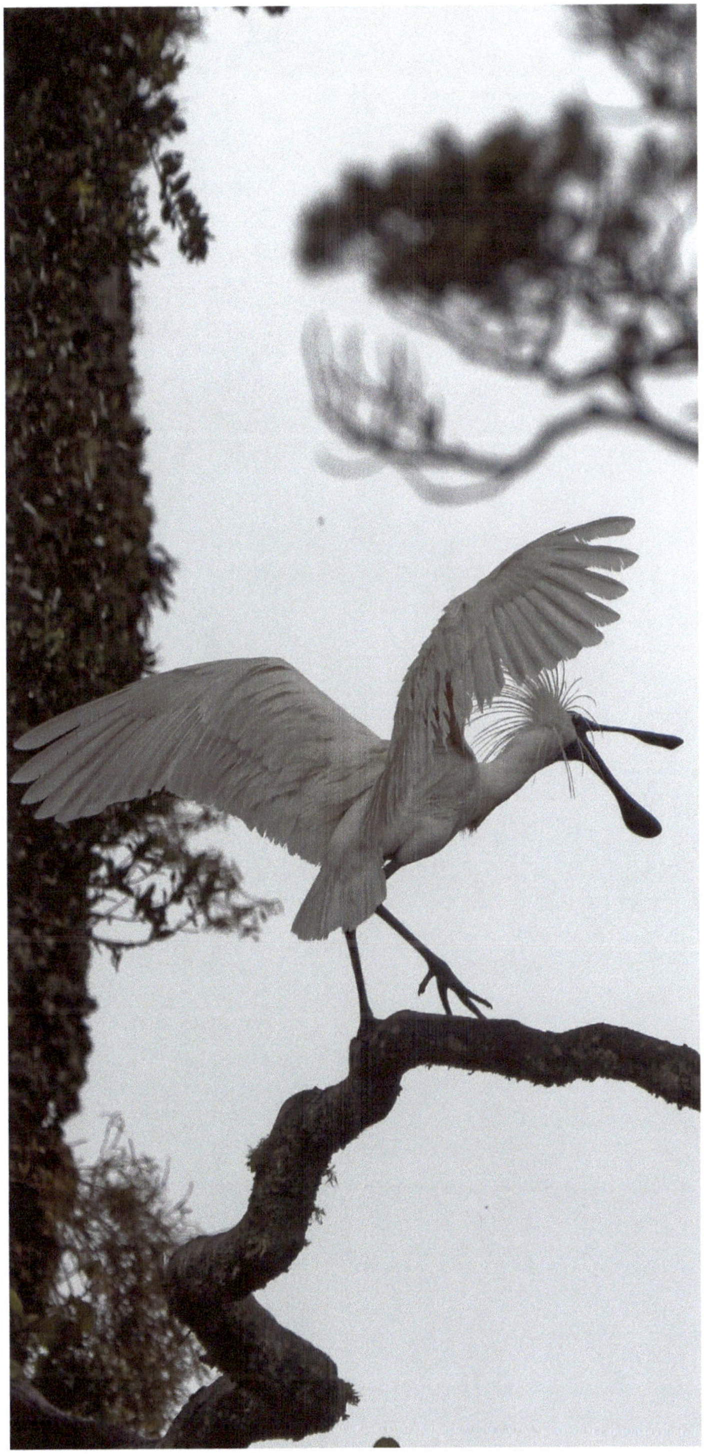

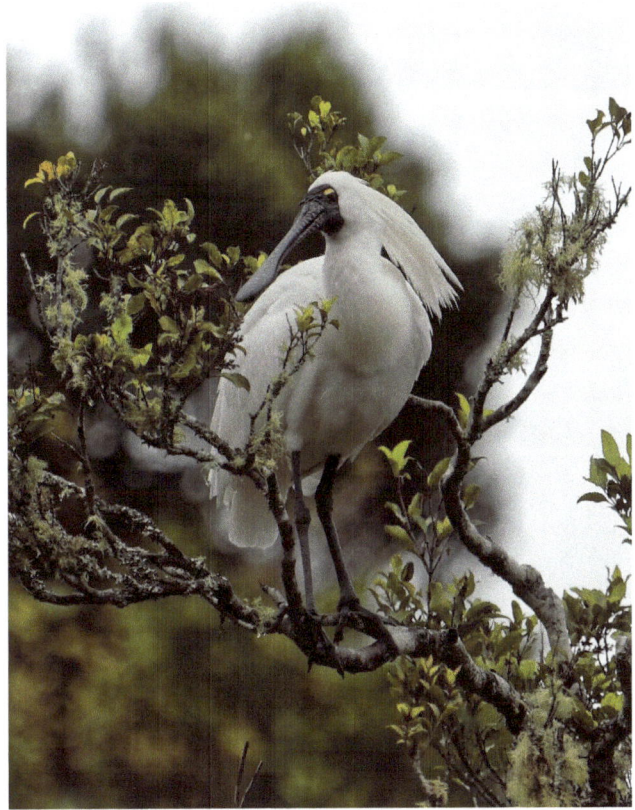

"This fine species may be readily distinguished from the Platalea leucorodia of Europe by the nudity of its face, which, even considerably beyond the eyes, is entirely destitute of feathers, and is of the same black colour as the bill. In other respects, both as to size and plumage, little difference exists between the two species. As with the European Spoonbill also, the fine pairing and breeding season. In its habits and disposition it as closely assimilates to its European prototype as it does in general appearance, for like that bird it takes up its abode on the margin of those marshy inlets of the sea that run for a considerable distance into the interior, and on the banks of rivers and lakes, and feeds upon small–shelled molluscs, frogs, insects, and the fry of fish, which are readily taken by its beautifully organized bill."

~Walter L. Buller, 1876

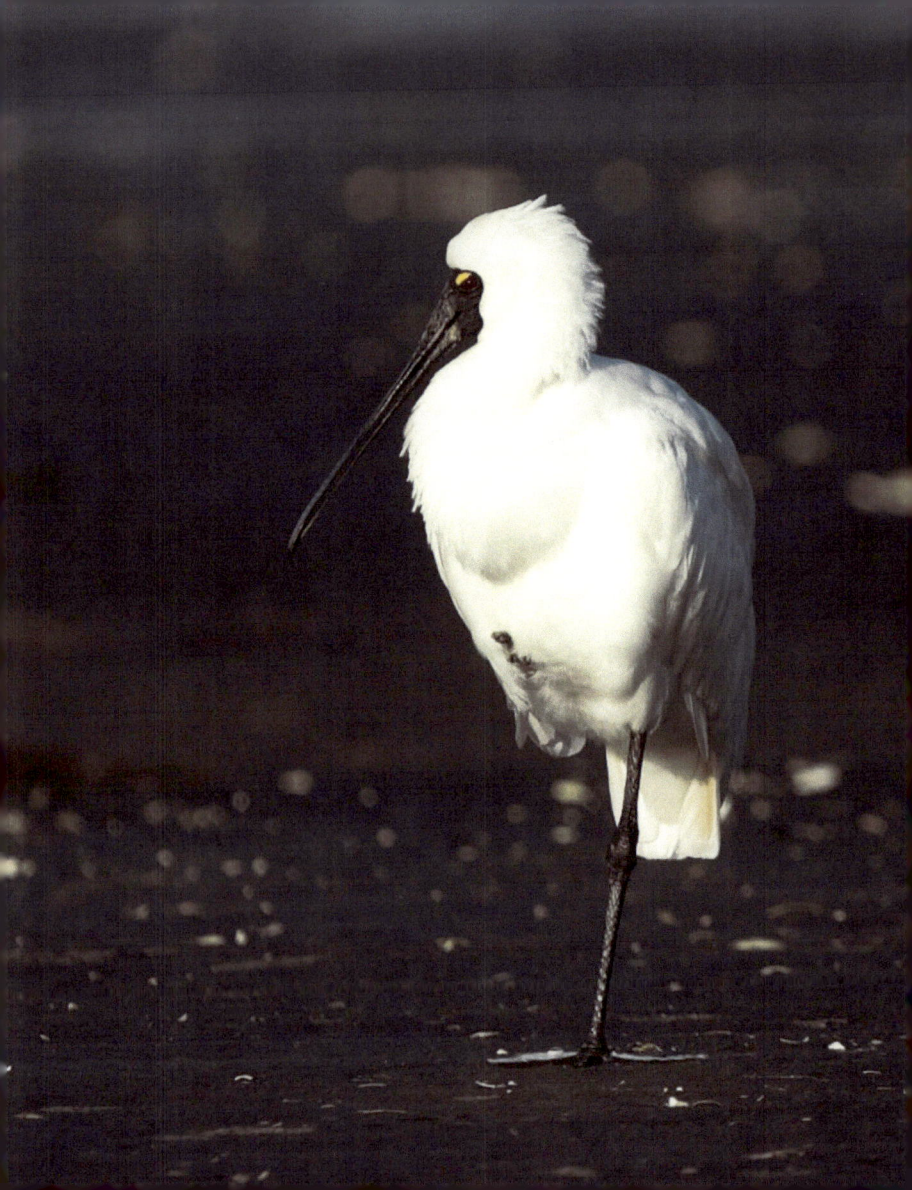

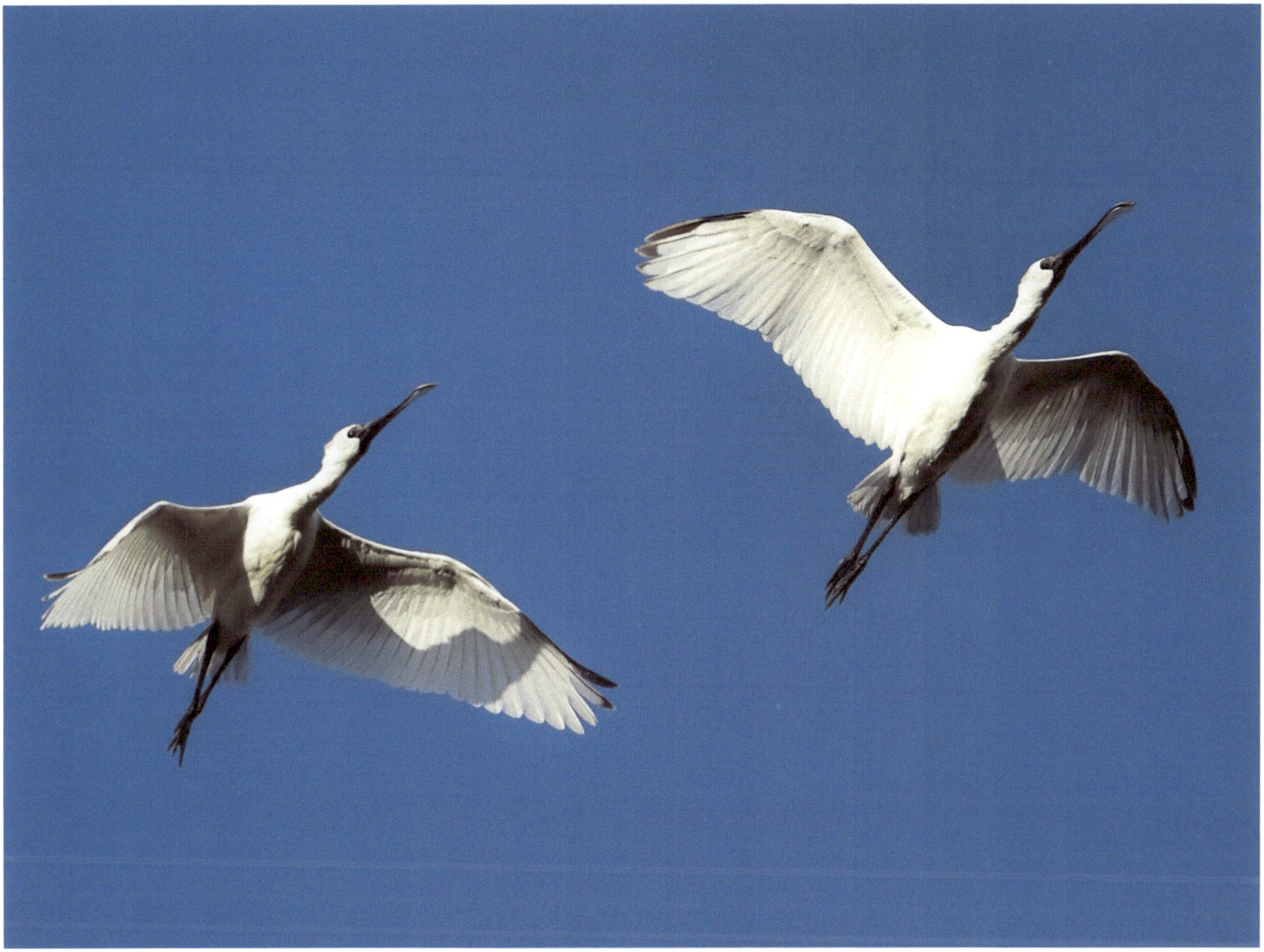

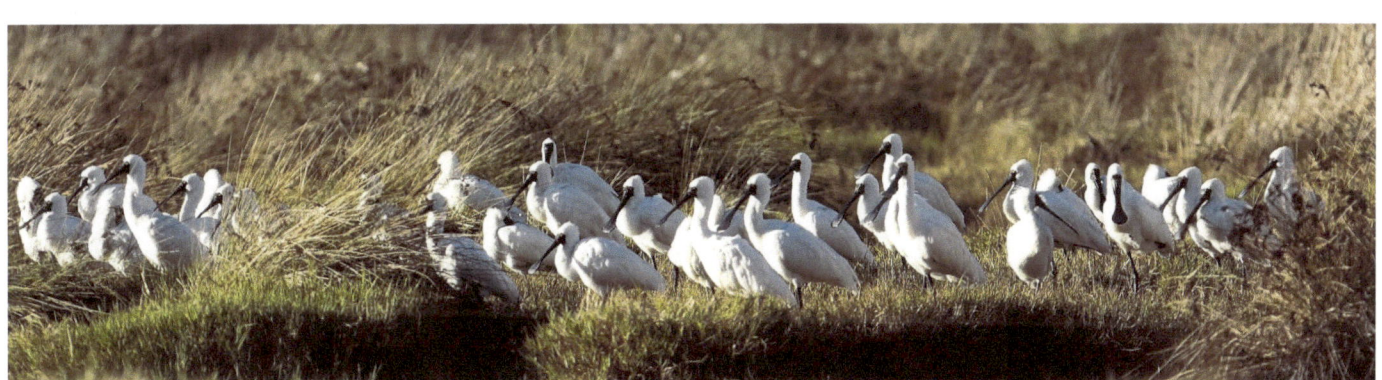

Spur-Winged Plover
Vanellus miles

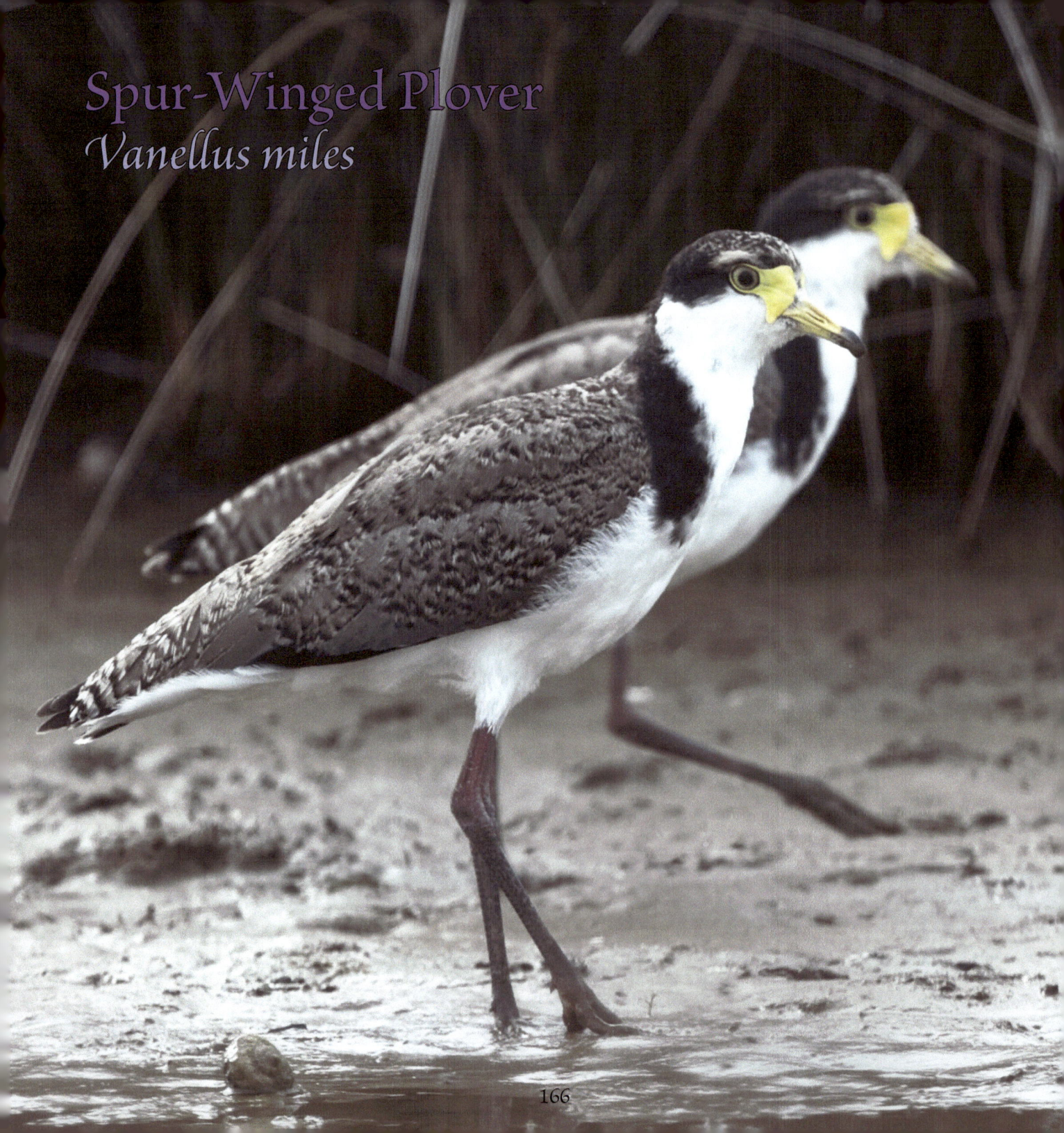

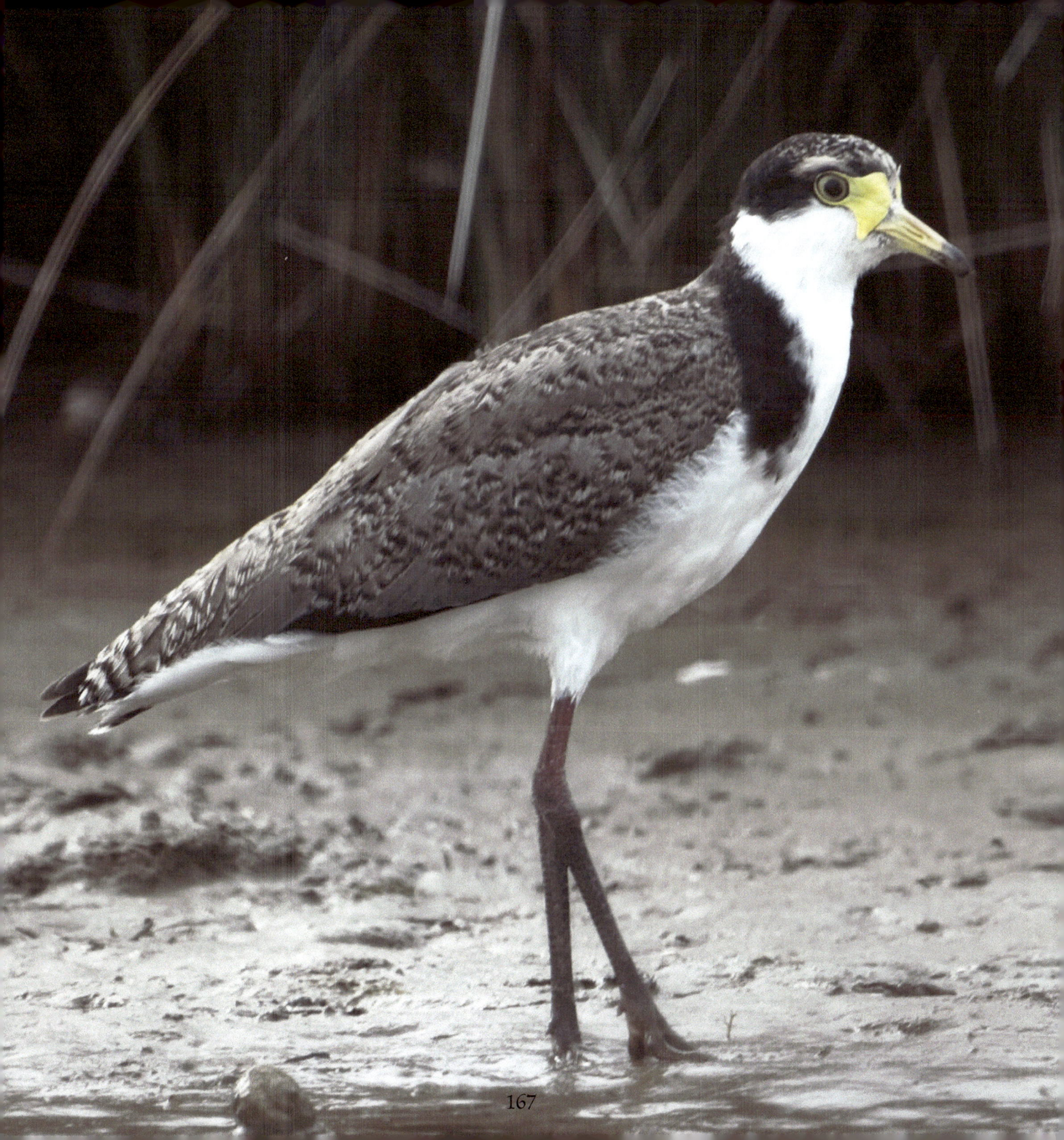

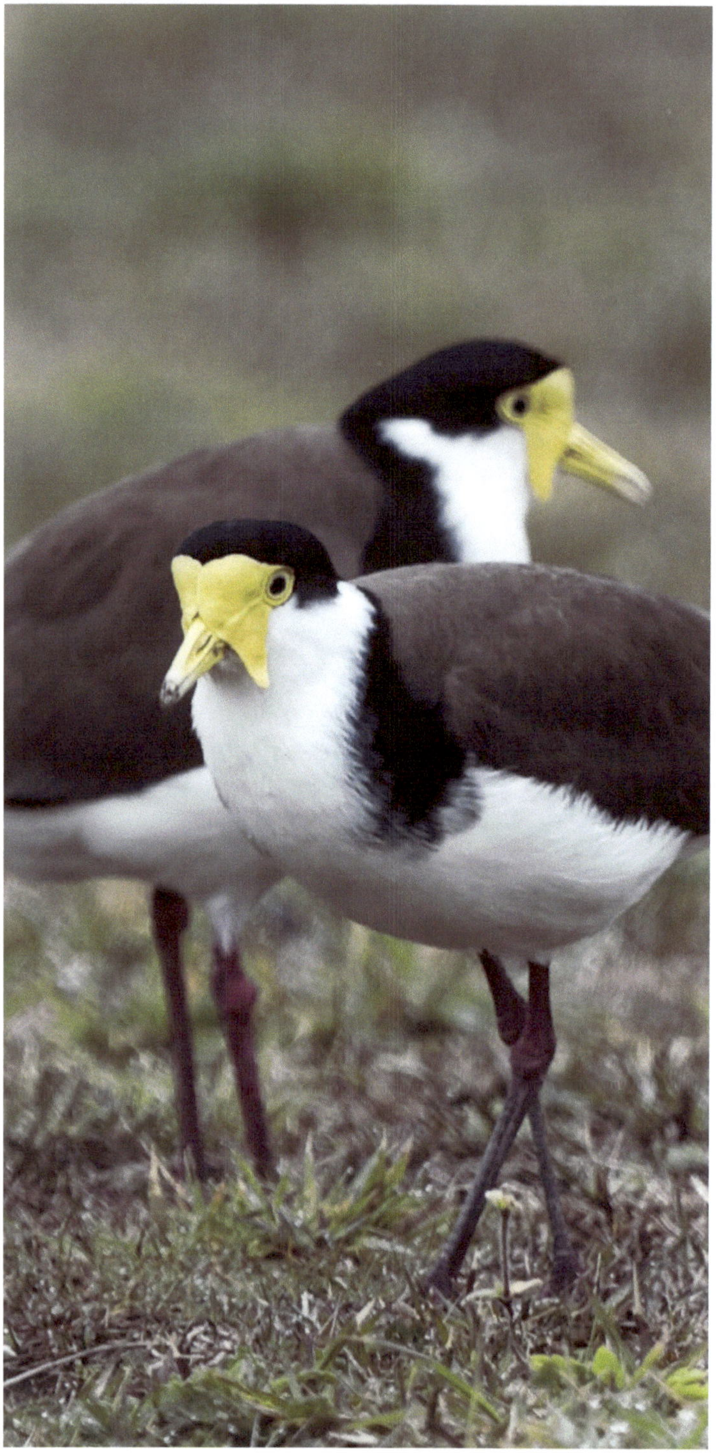

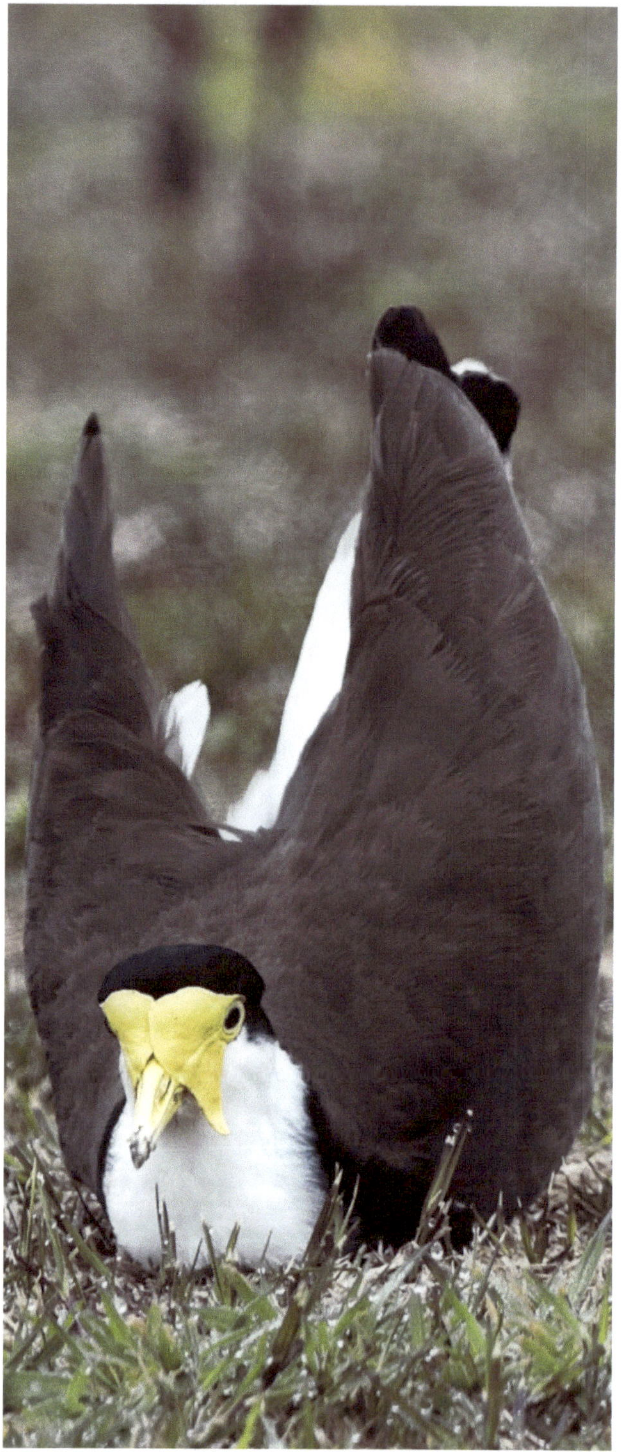

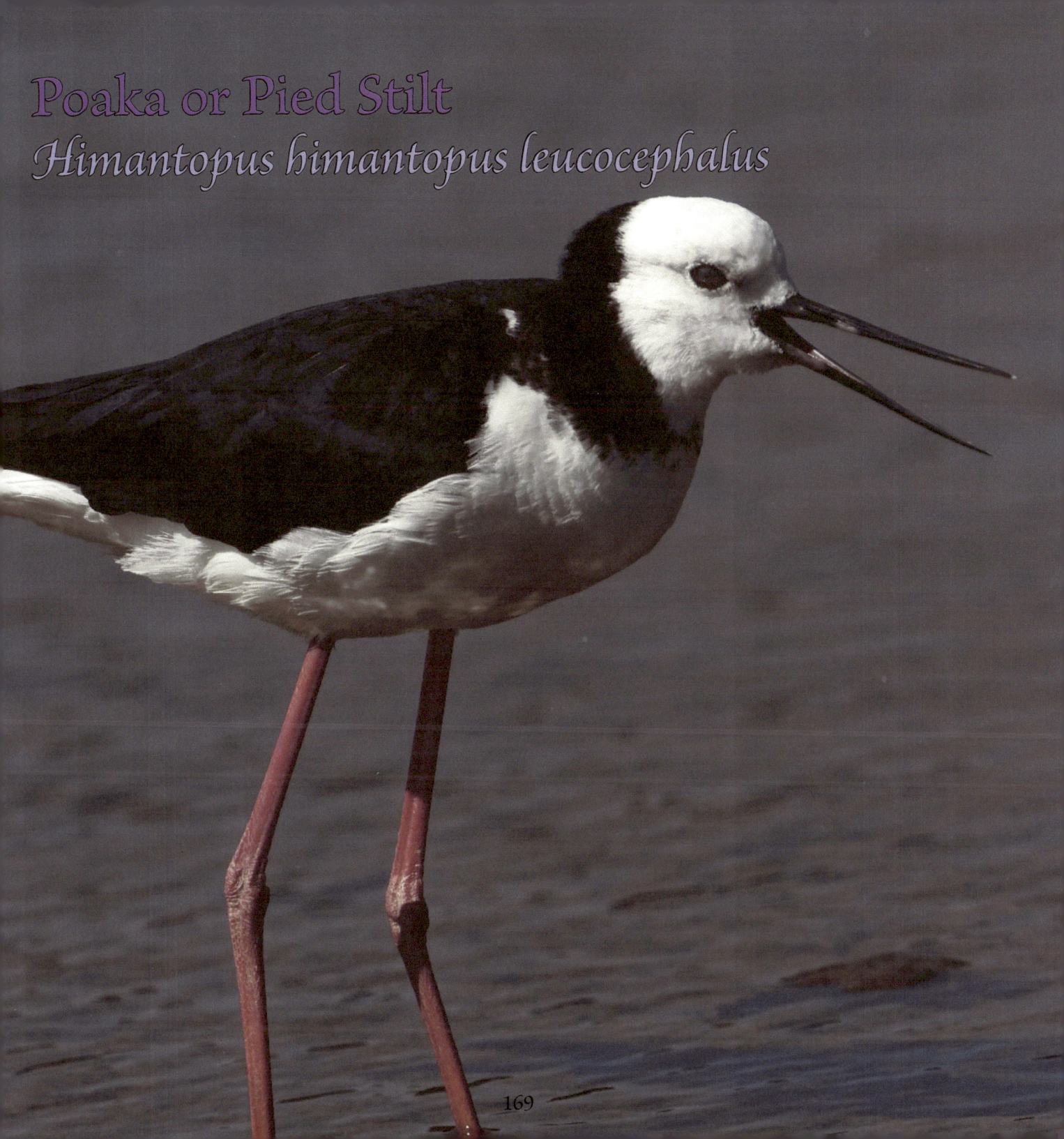

Poaka or Pied Stilt
Himantopus himantopus leucocephalus

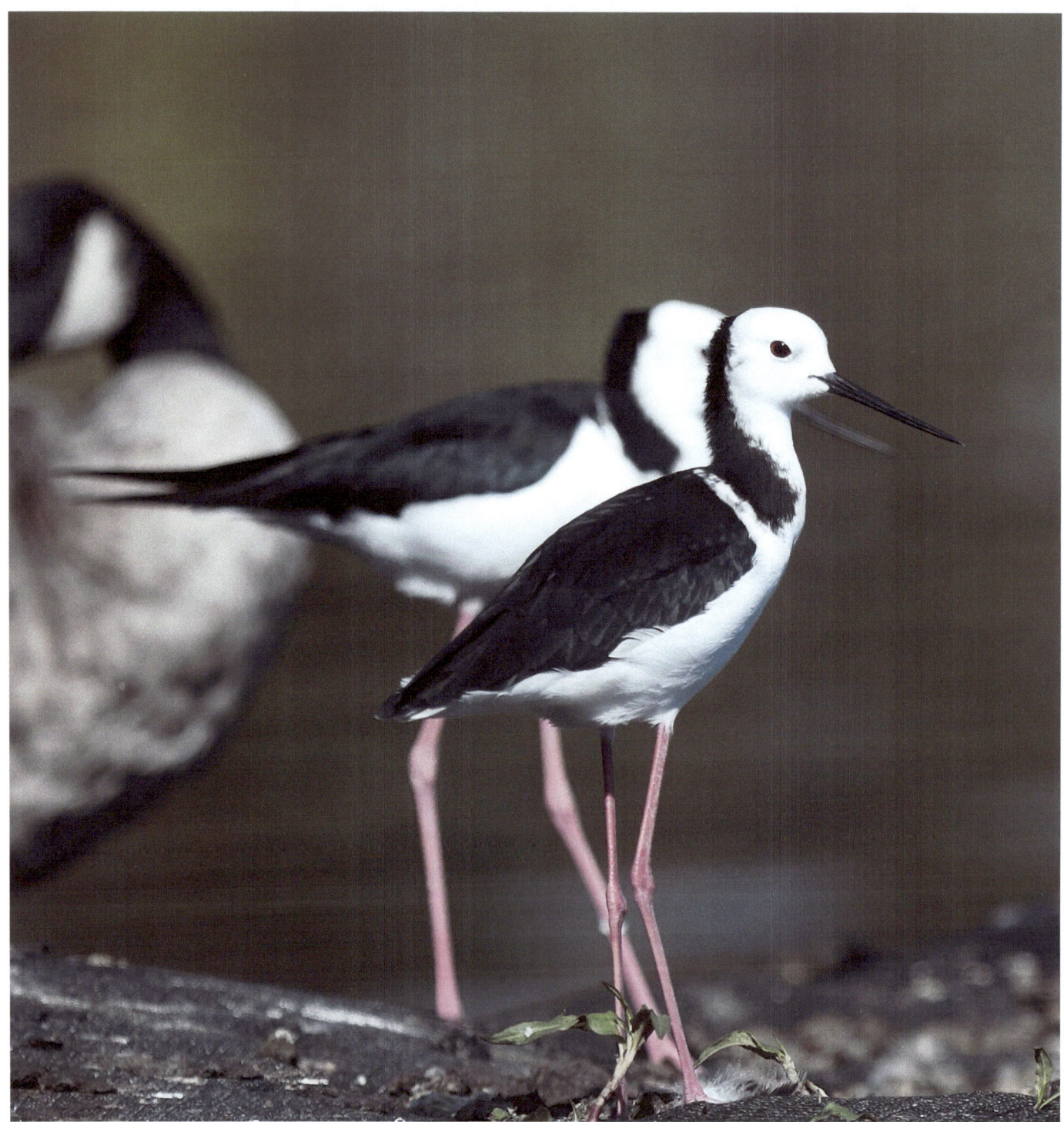

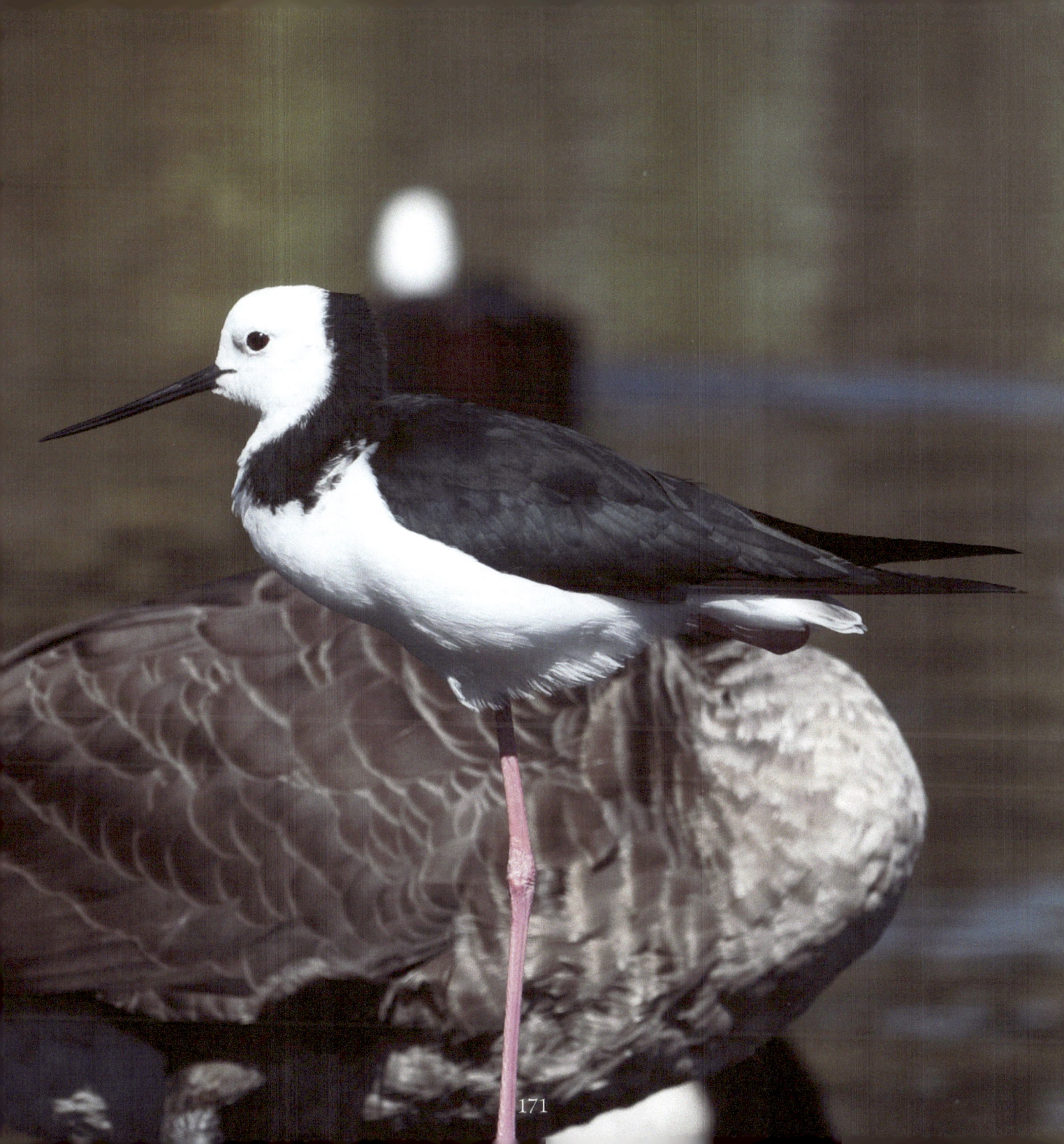

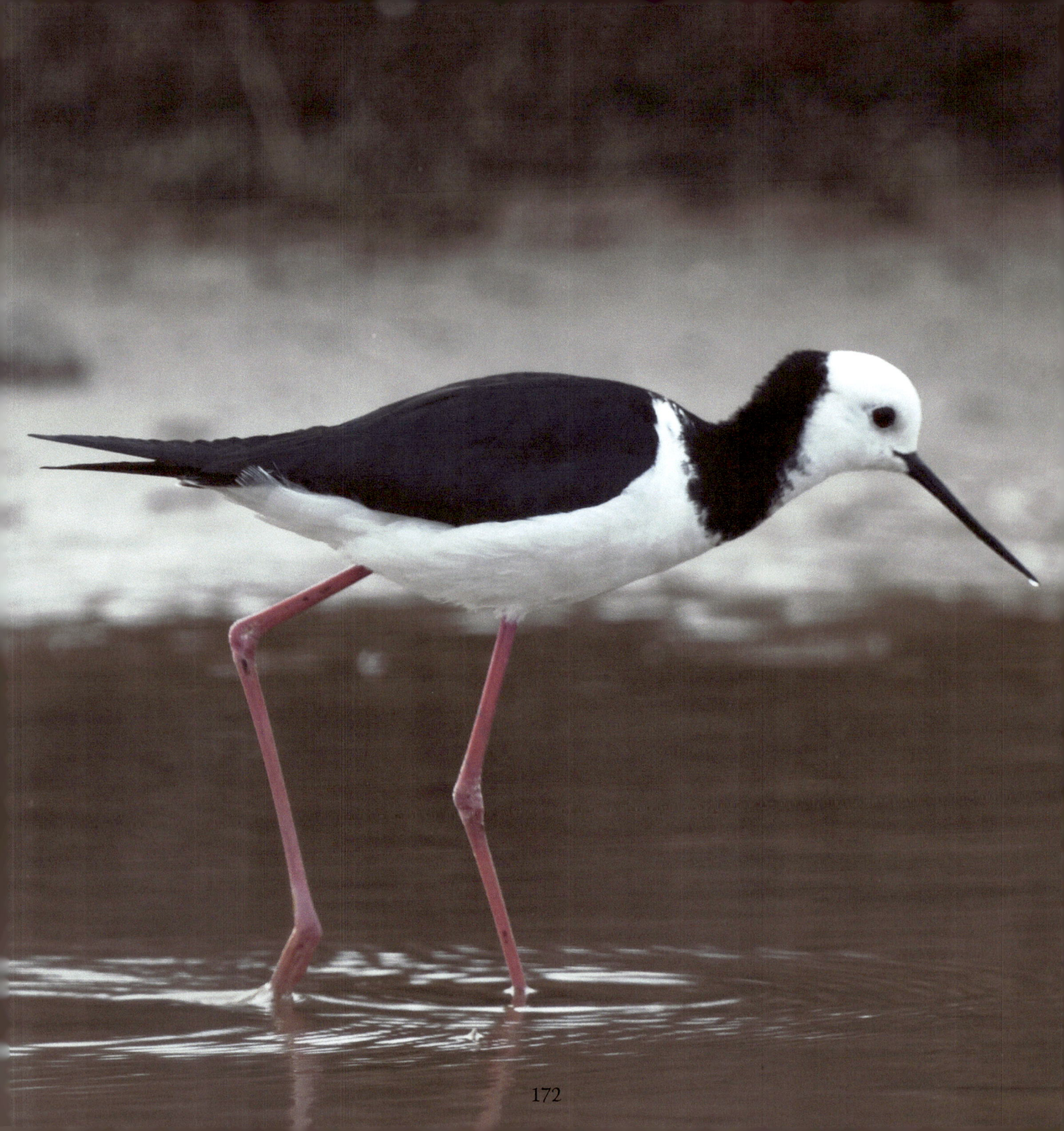

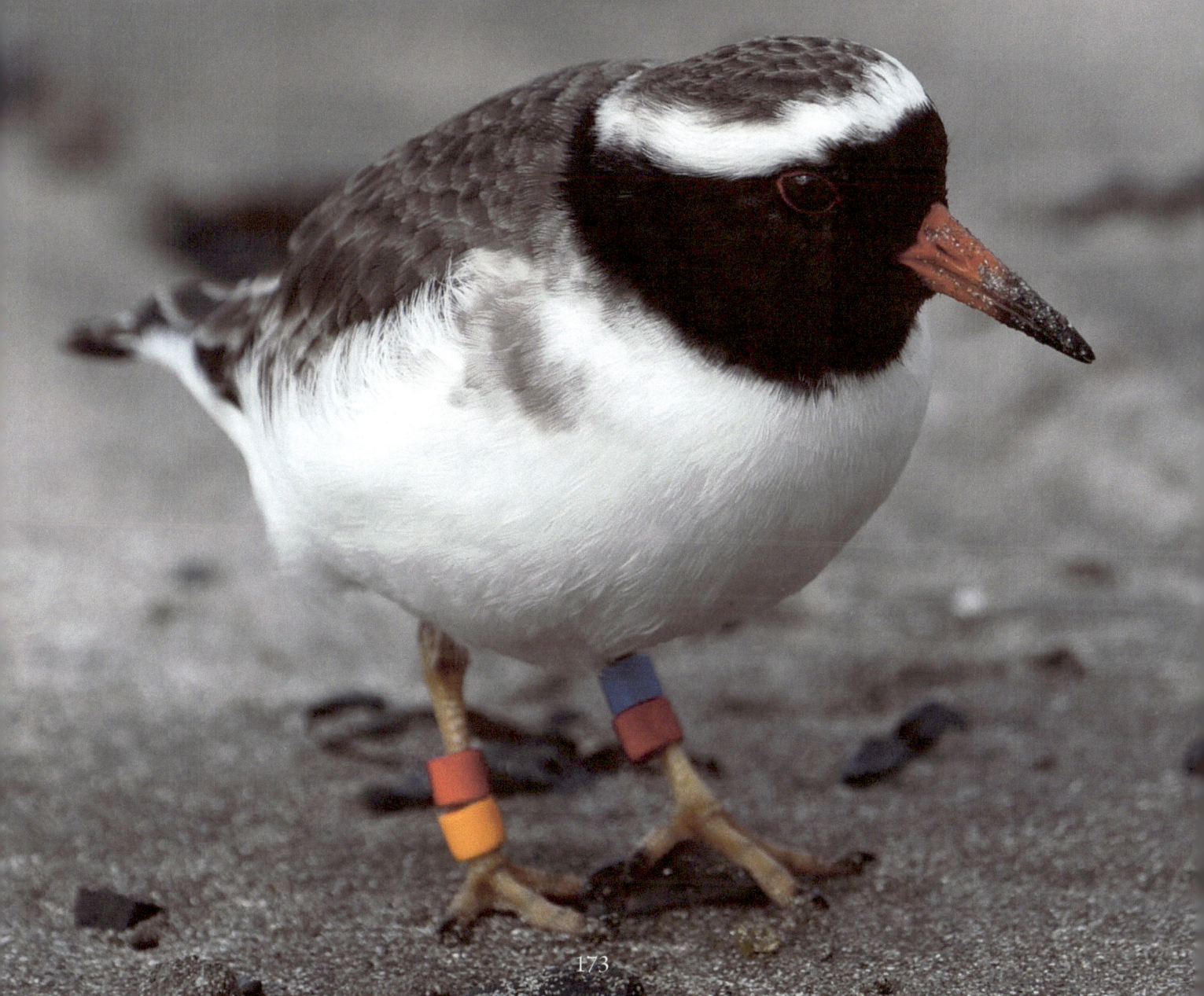

Chapter Five
By the Sea

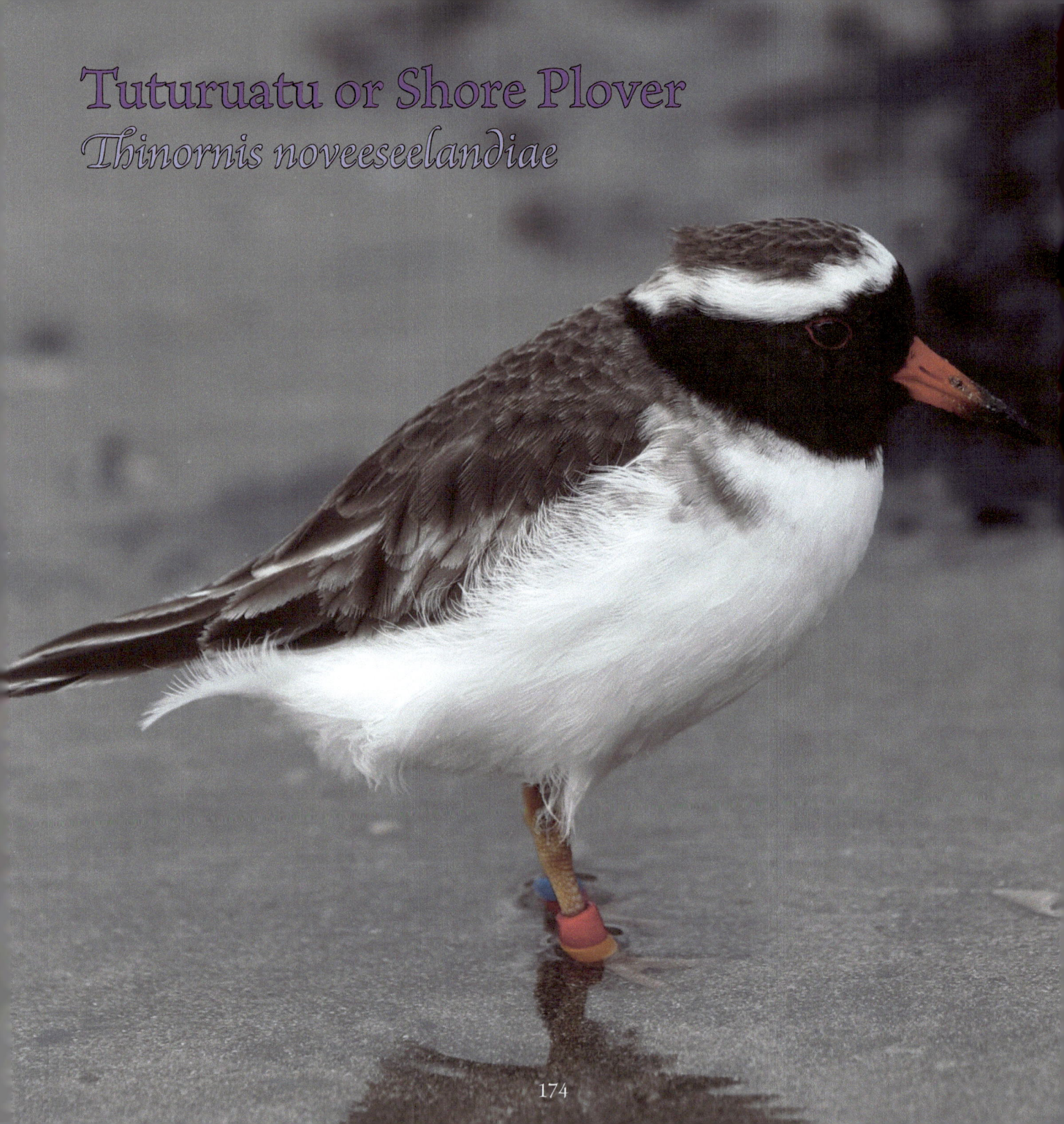

Tuturuatu or Shore Plover
Thinornis noveeseelandiae

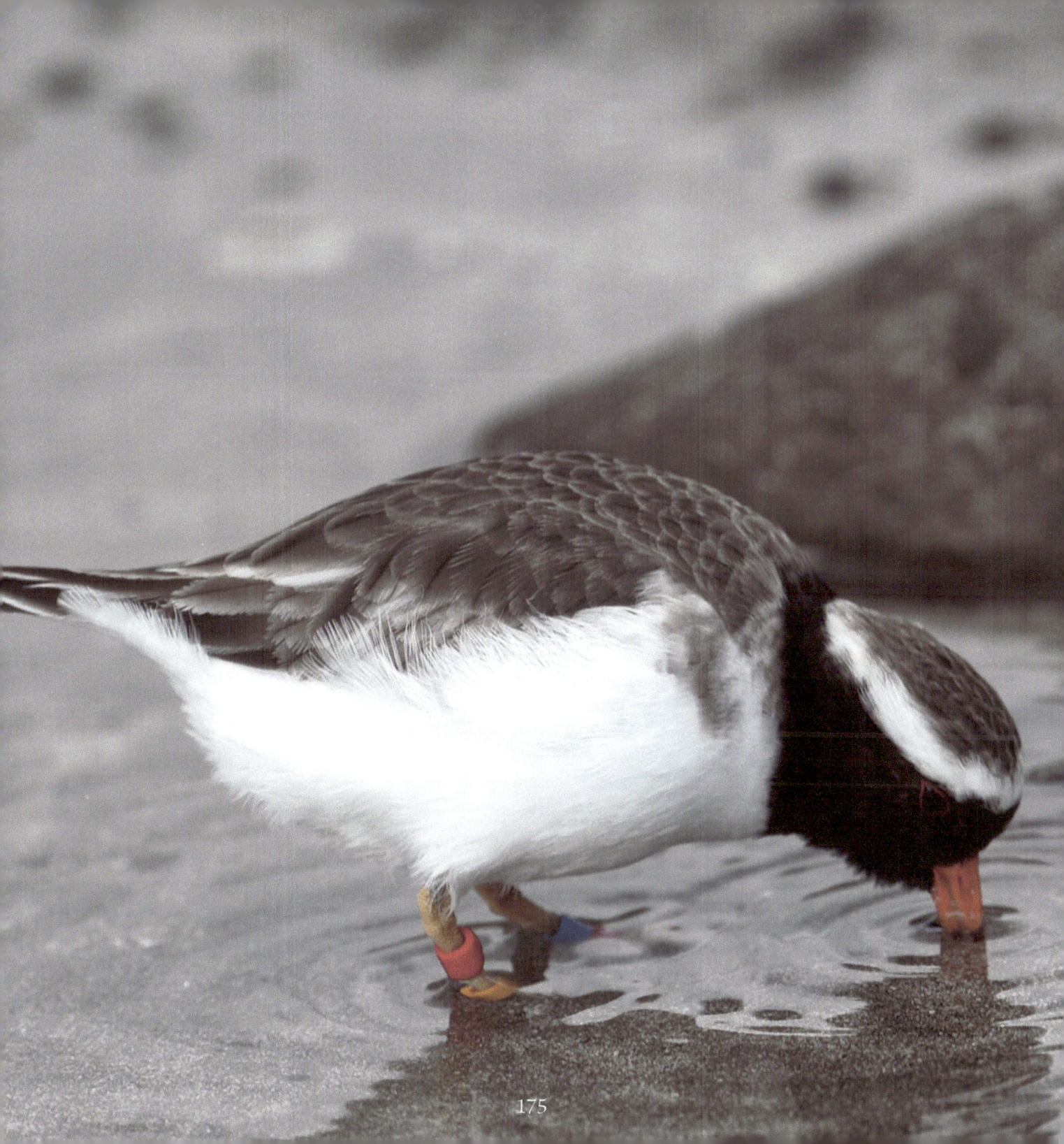

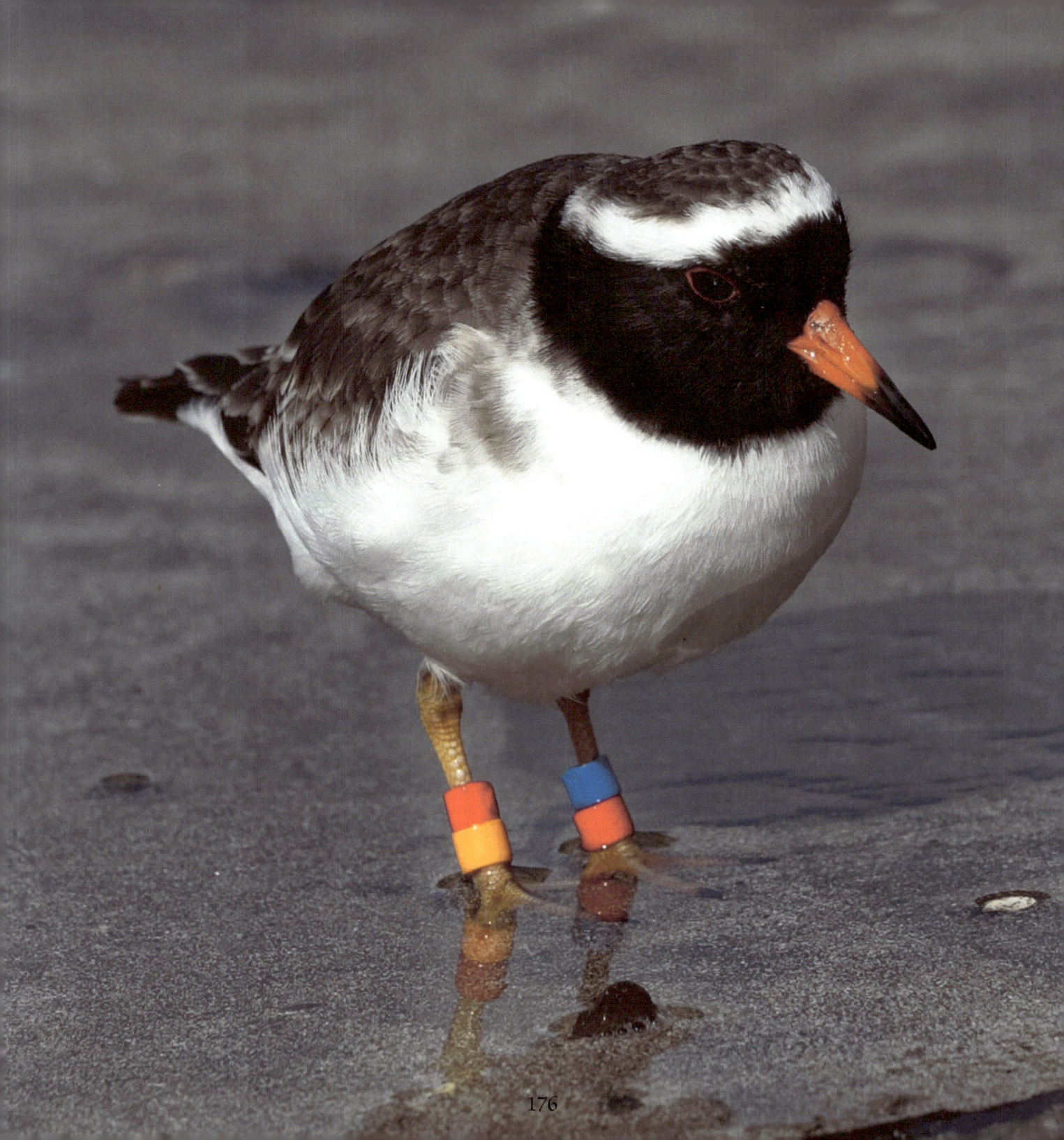

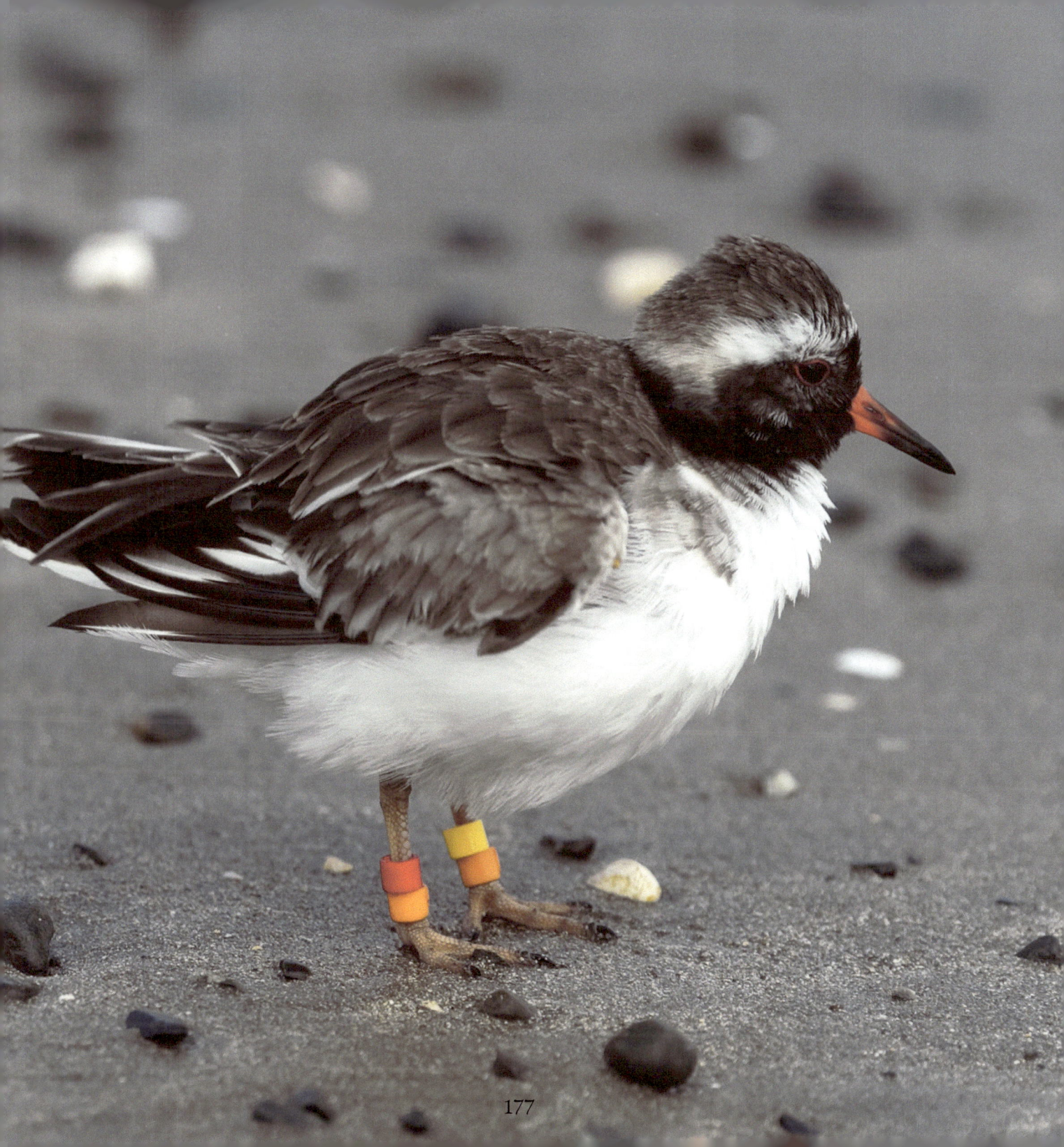

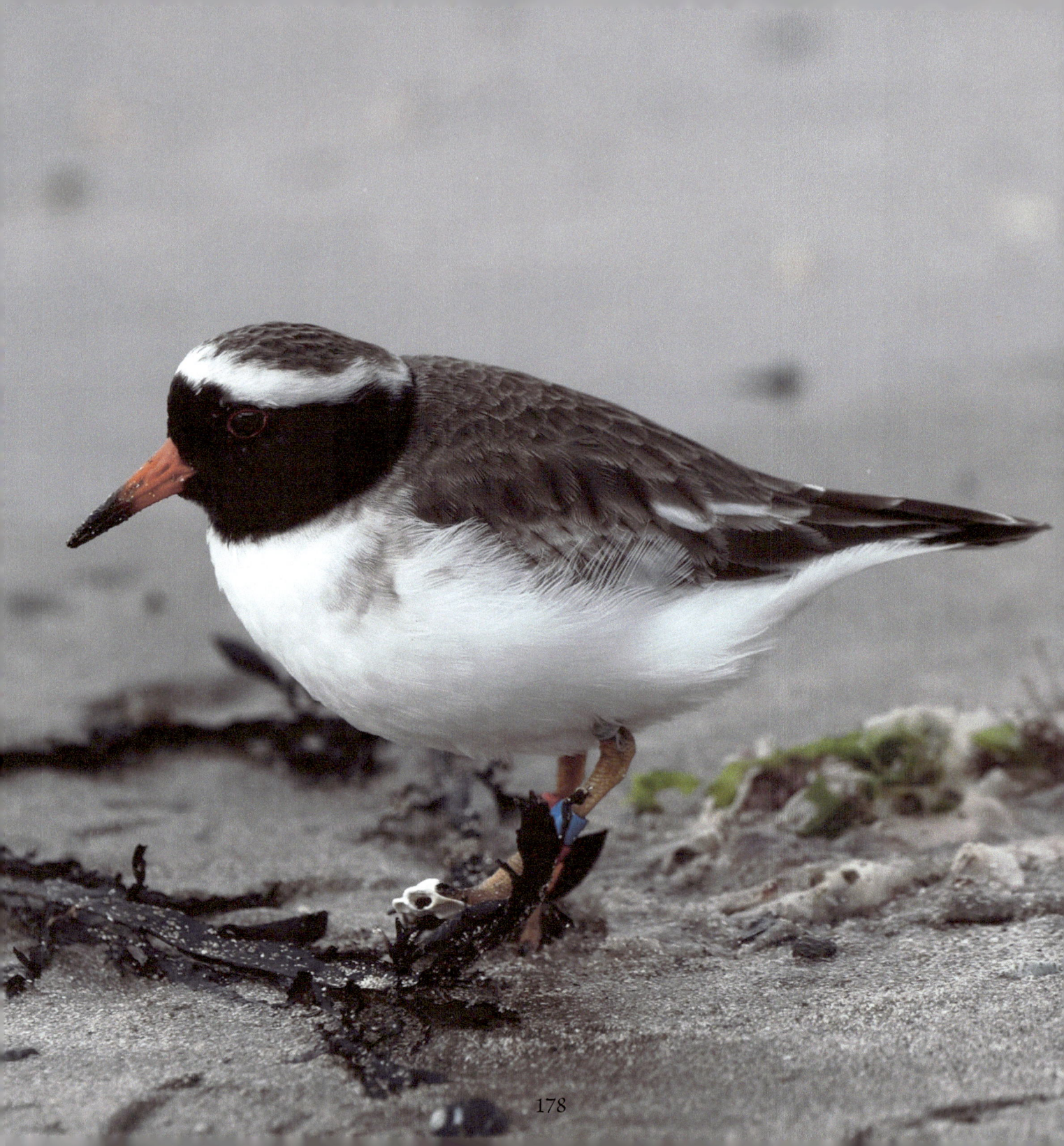

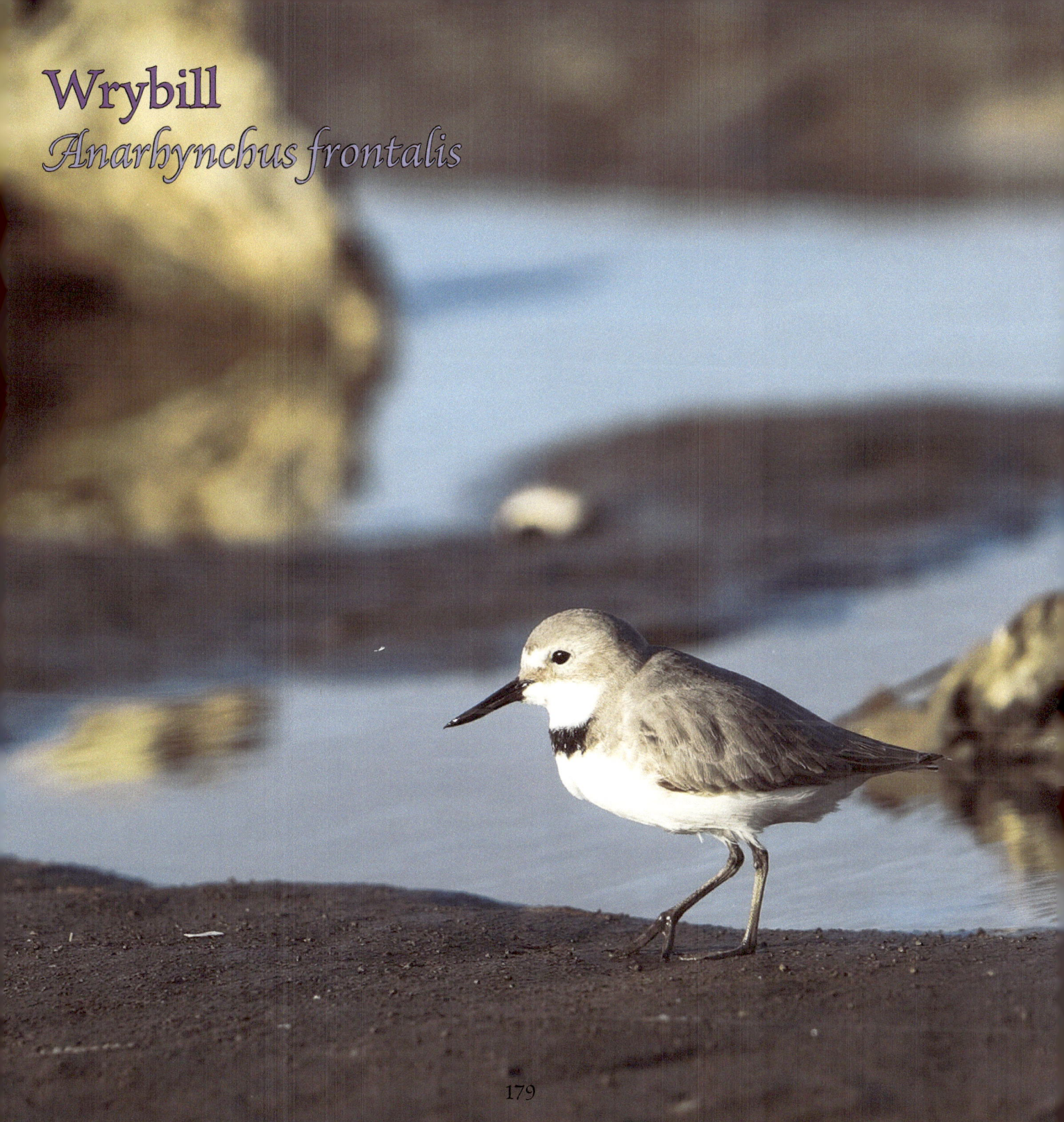

Wrybill
Anarhynchus frontalis

"The Crook-billed Plover, at the breeding season, is less wary than any of its congeners, and its nesting-place would be discovered with very little difficulty, were it not for the wonderful instinct it exhibits in selecting the ground for depositing its eggs. They are simply laid, without any preparation, amongst the pebbles of some river-bed usually, and never far from water, and so well does their grey tint harmonize with the general colour of the shingle around them, that their detection would be almost hopeless if this bird was less confident.

...On approaching the eggs or young, the old bird trots slowly away, assuming a broader and somewhat flatter appearance, by slightly extending the wings, making at the same time a low purring sound.

Breeding season extends from September to December. The young birds are covered with grey down, and appear to have legs long, out of all proportion to the size of the body; at this early stage, the peculiar deflection of the bill, although slight, is perceptible; it is always turned to the right, or off side. Birds of the year, we believe, do not assume the frontlet which distinguishes the old birds, and which is broadest in the male. No satisfactory reason has been given for the peculiar form of the bill of this bird.

~ *T.H. Potts, 1869*

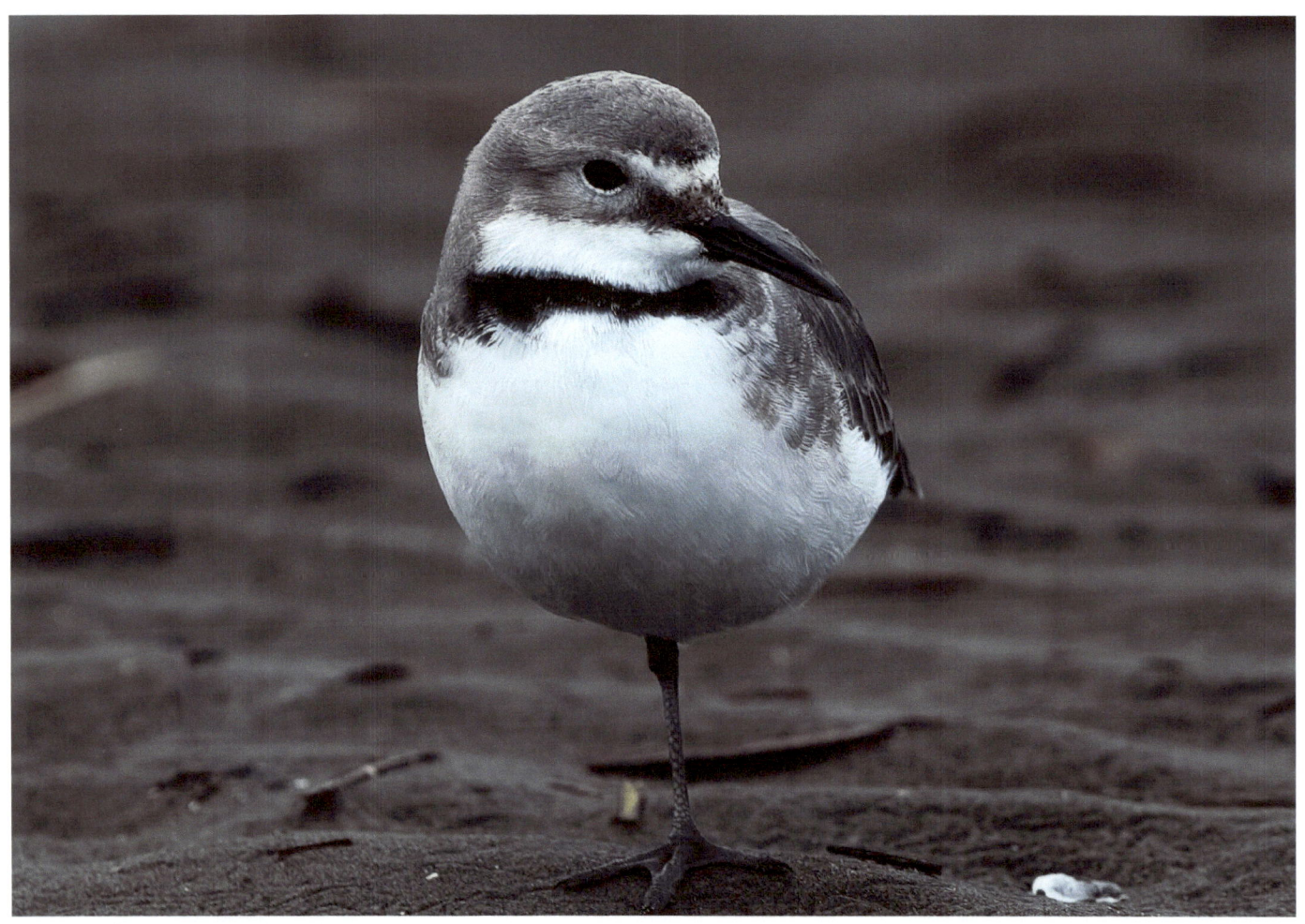

Kuaka or Bar-Tailed Godwit
Limosa lapponica

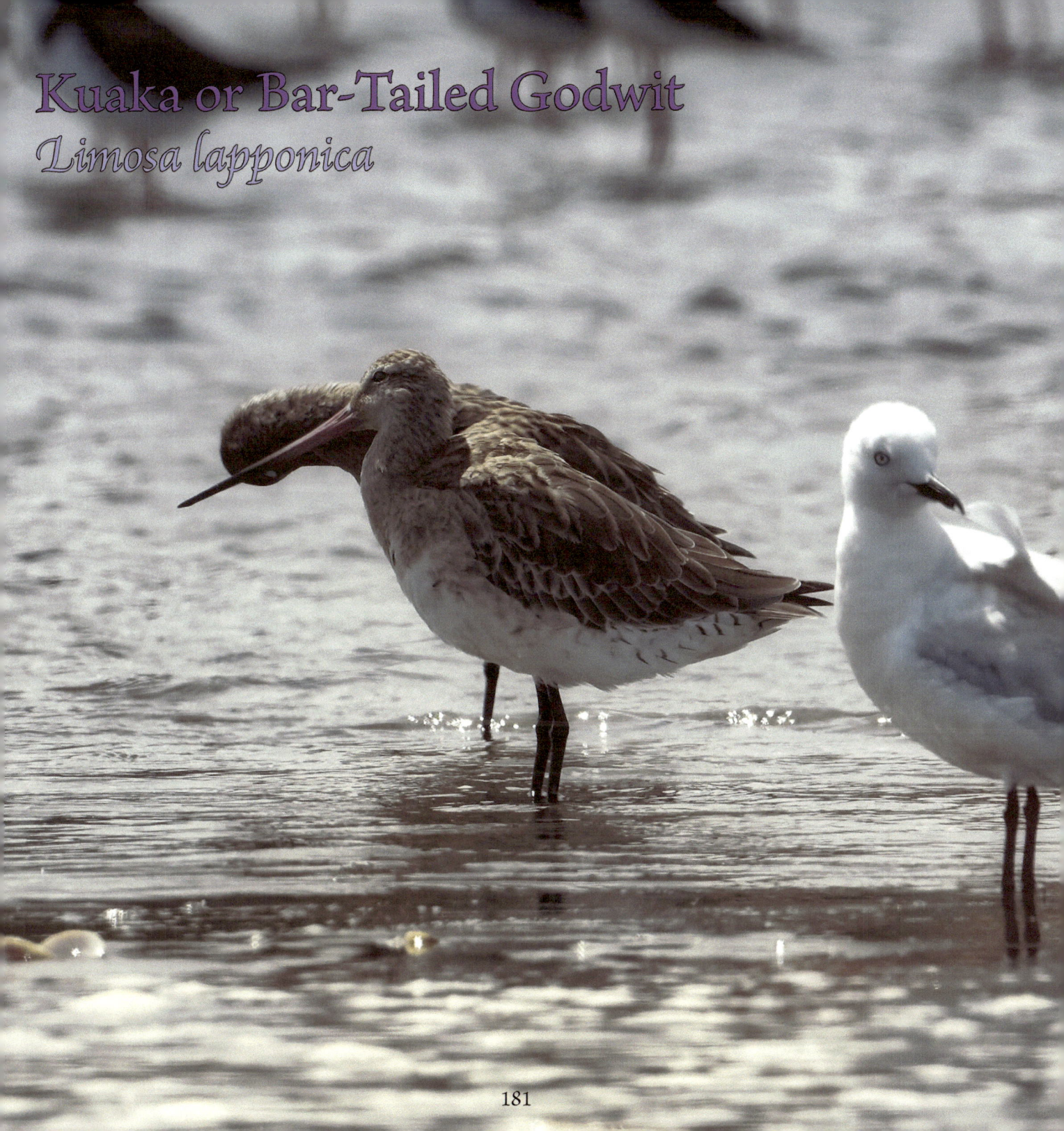

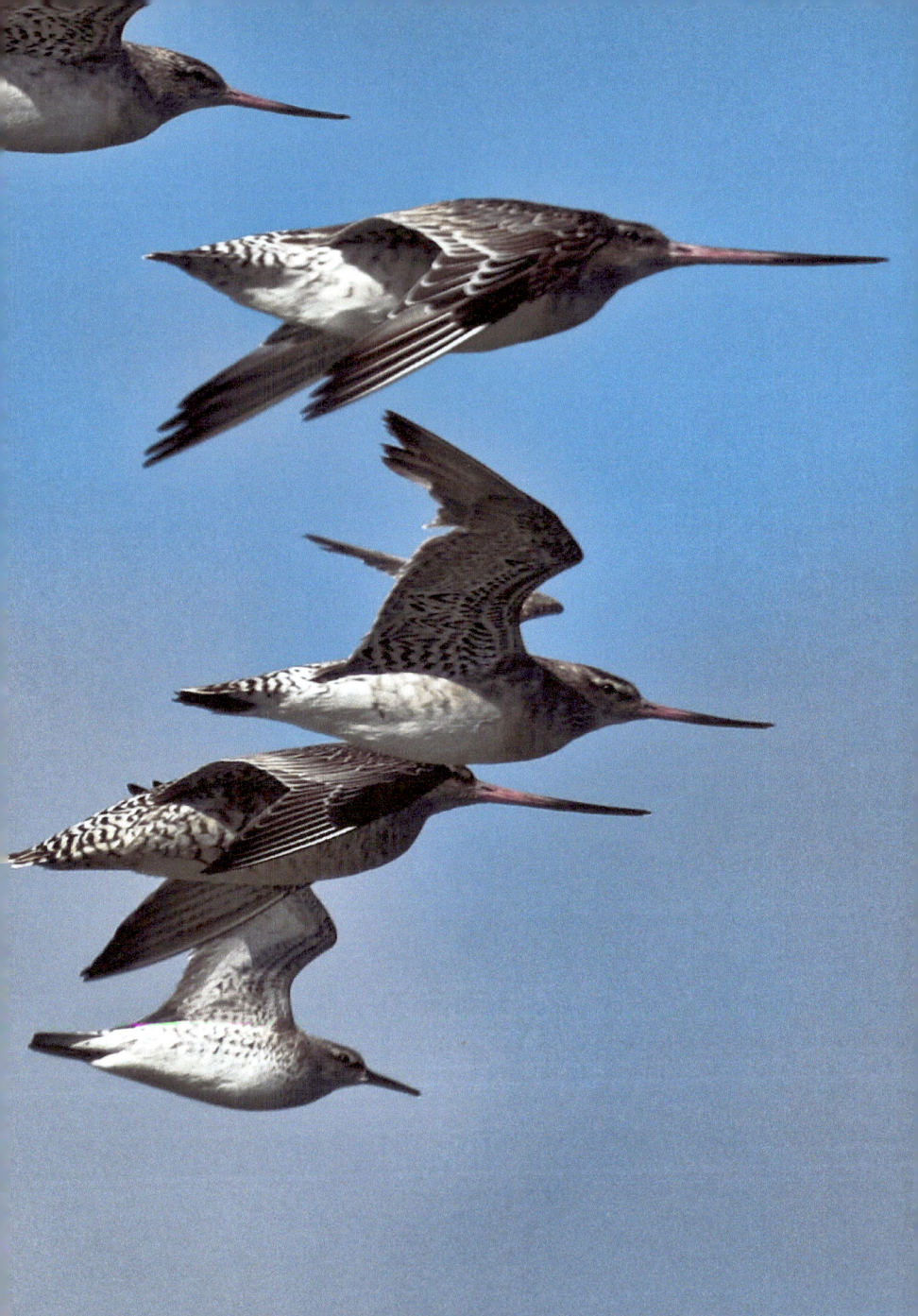

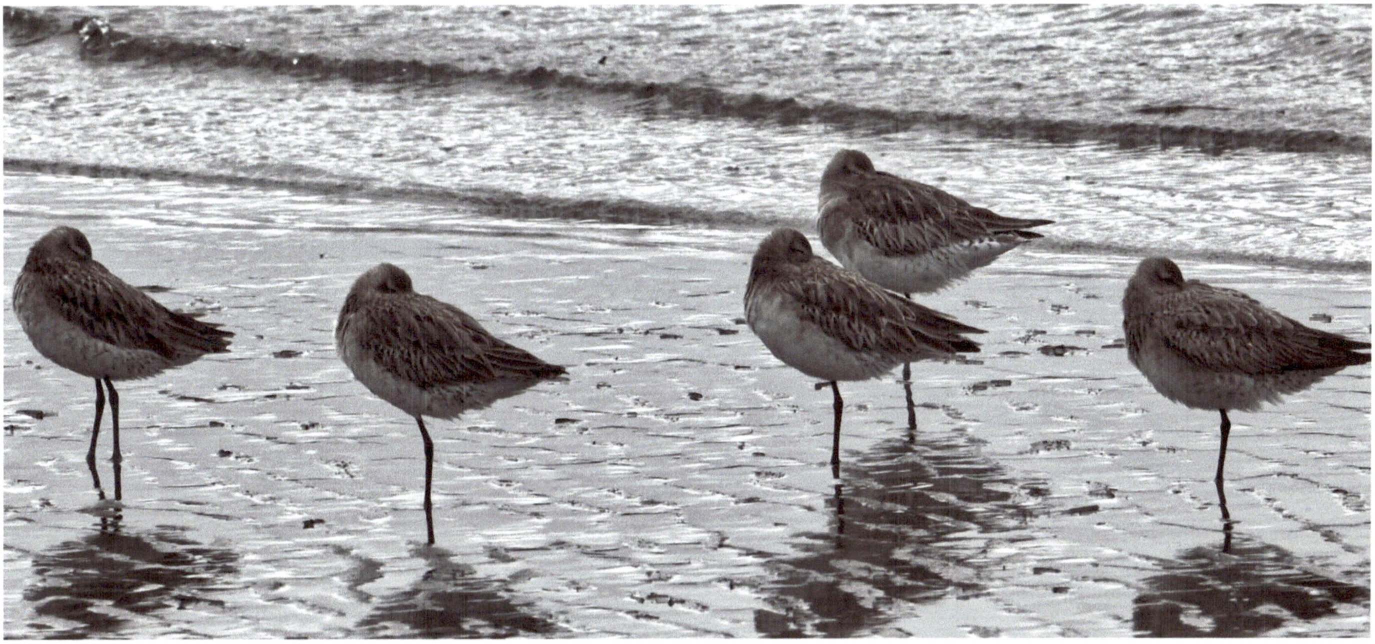

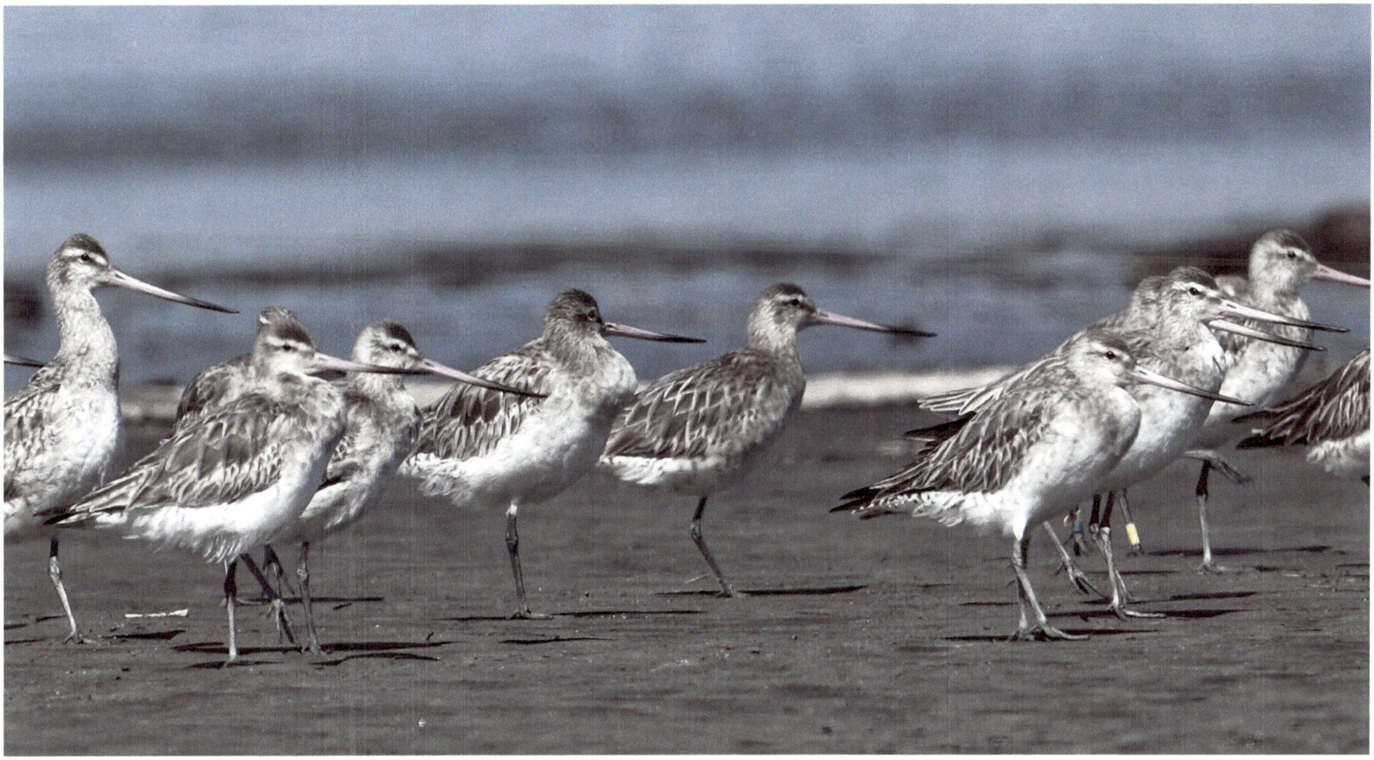

183

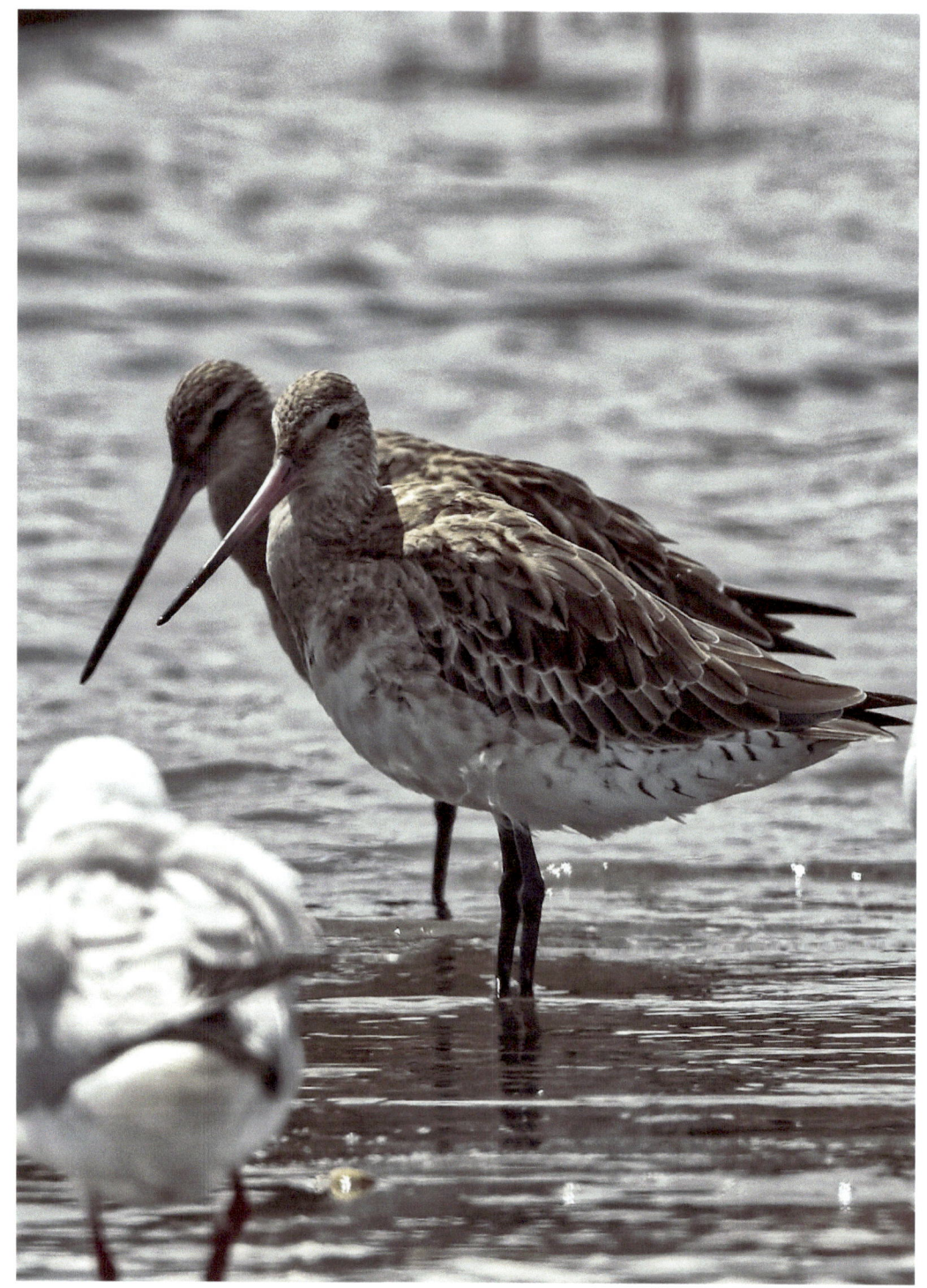

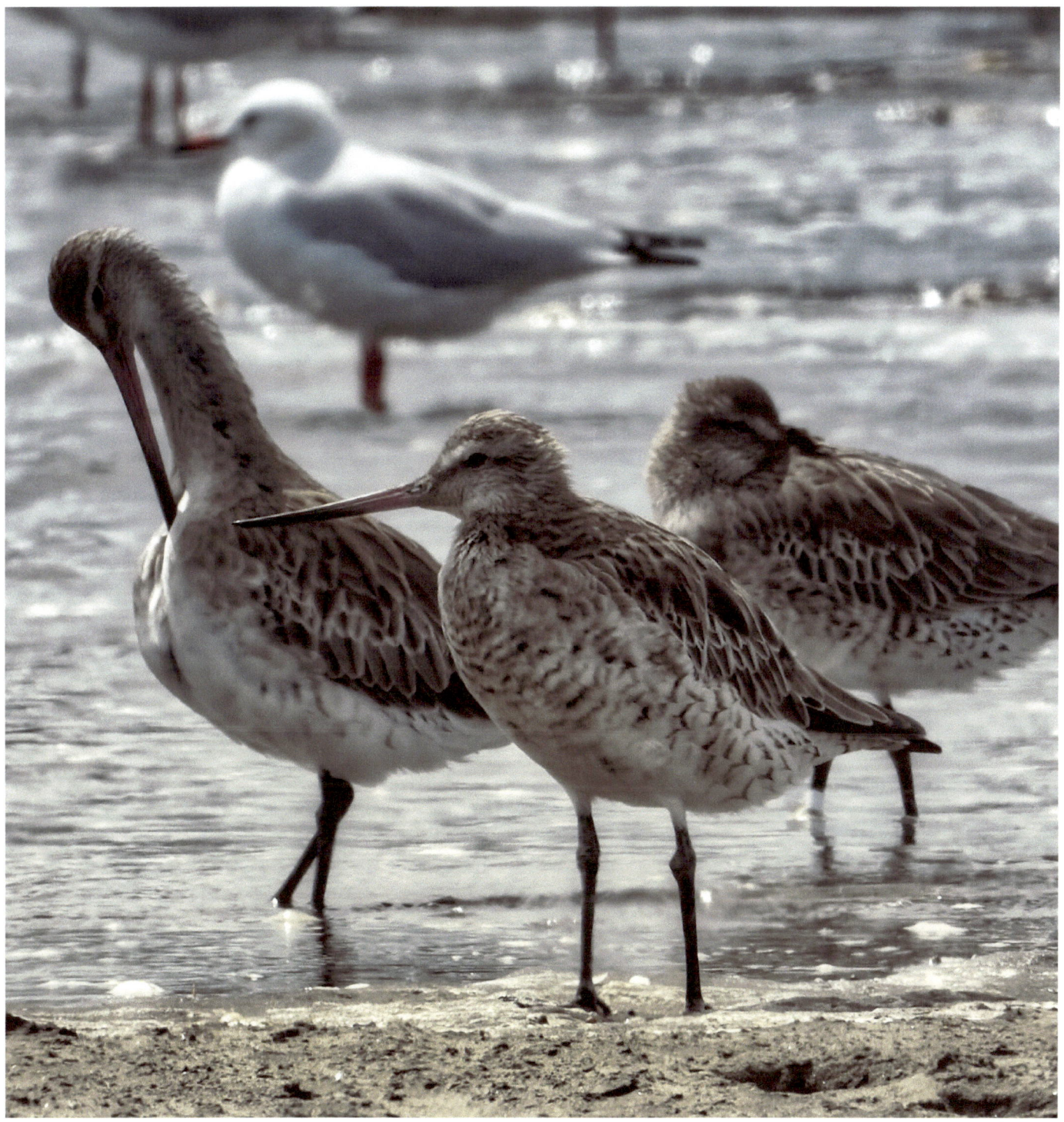

Kotare or Kingfisher
Halcyon sancta

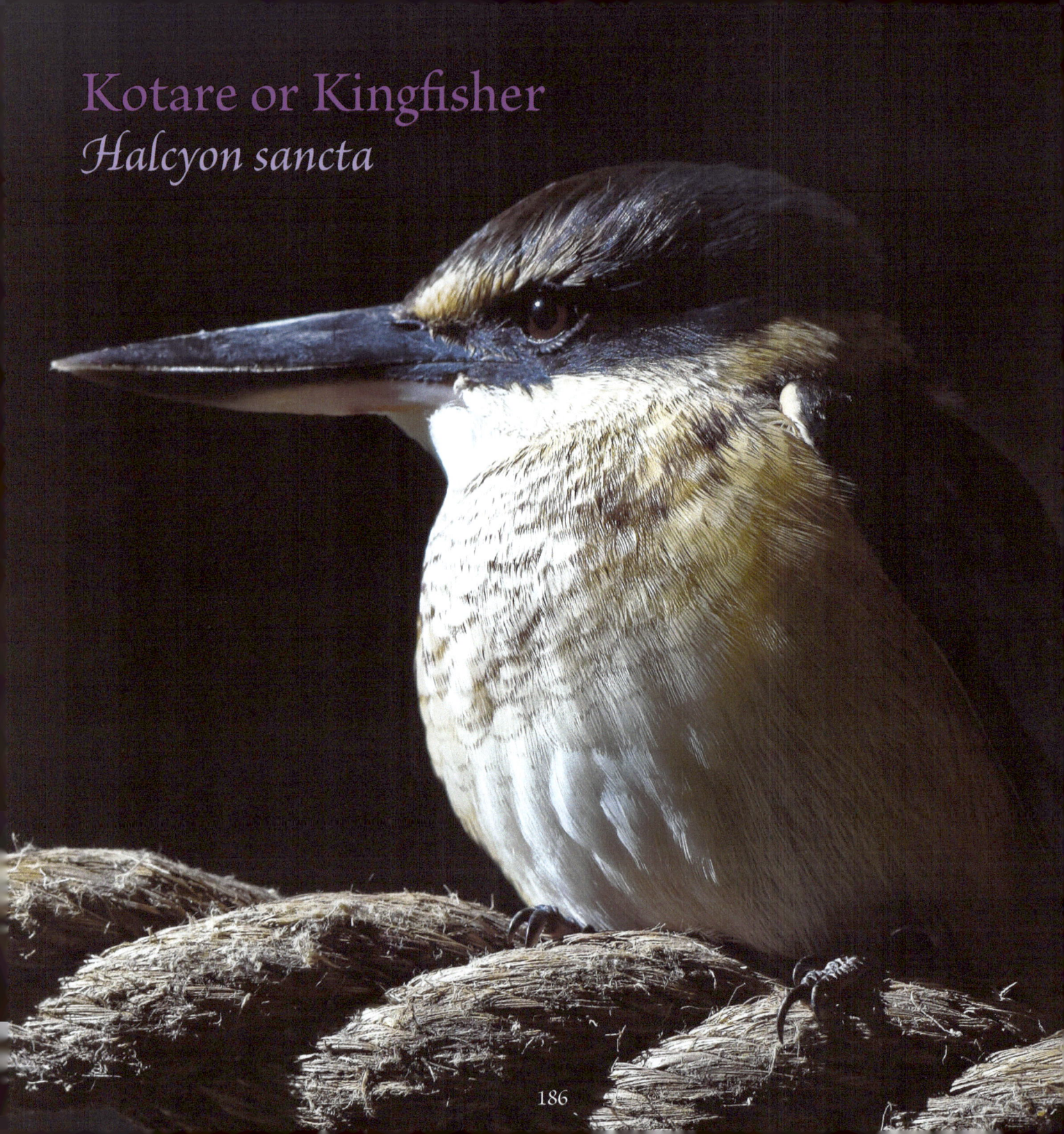

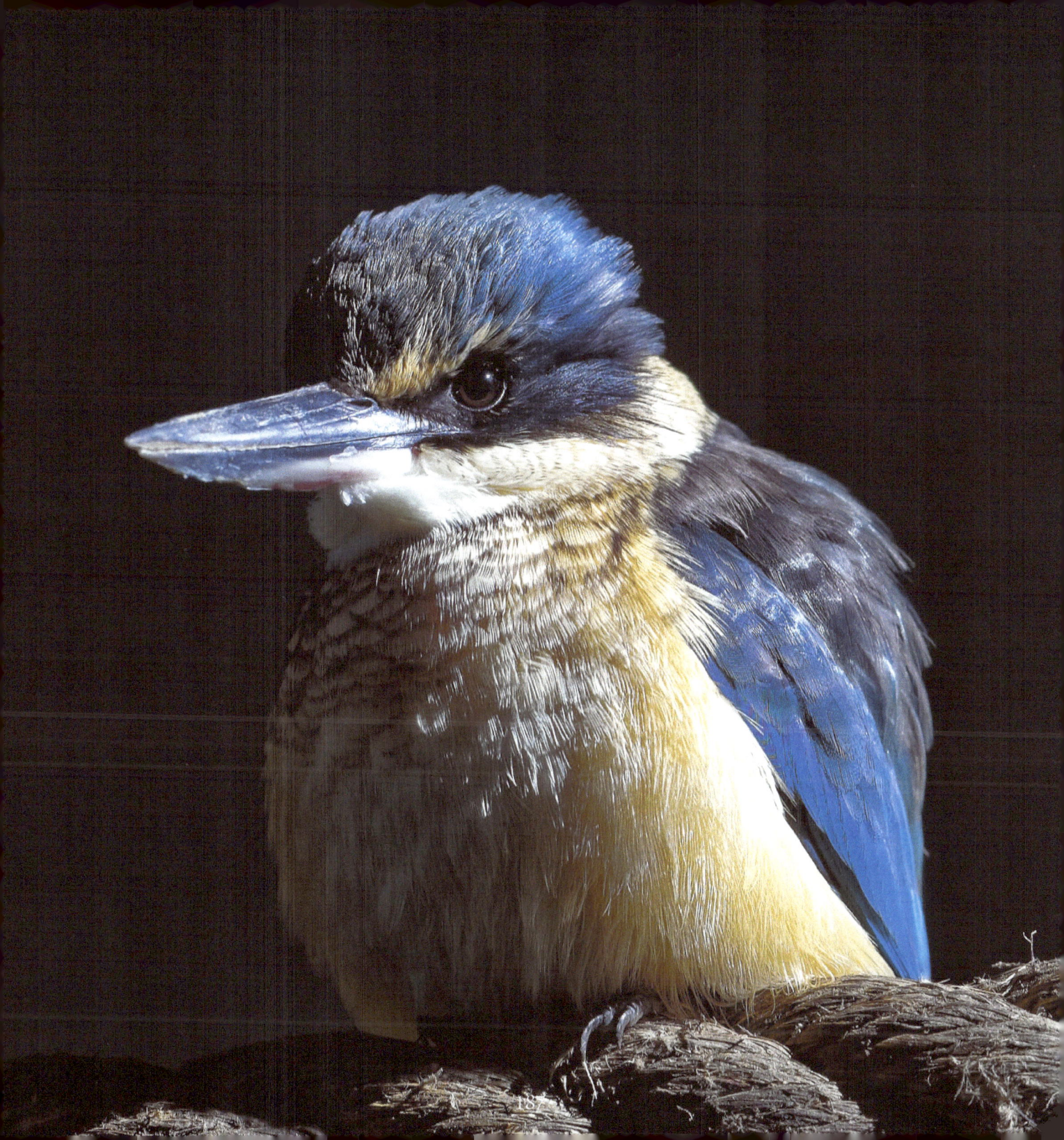

"The Kingfisher, one of our burrowing species. The tunnel-like hole, which forms the approach to its nest, is found sometimes in a bank, and, perhaps, quite as often in a tree. On examining one of these holes, in a bank not far from the sea beach, the floor or bottom was observed to incline slightly upwards from the entrance, the eggs, deposited on the remains of crustaceæ, were not more than one foot back from the outside of the hole. When a tree has been selected for its home, we have been led sometimes to the discovery, by observing the quantity of chips lying beneath; its powerful bill excavates a nesting place in the partially decayed wood... Although this bird may be constantly seen occupying some prominent branch, or stake, when watching for its prey (which, by the way, is of a very miscellaneous character), yet, when approaching or leaving its nest, it always, where possible, seeks the screen of overhanging trees, as it swiftly darts through the gully, permitting but a glimpse of its bright showy feathers. Should any one approach too close to the neighbourhood of its breeding-hole, the parent bird utters a low cry, like cree, cree, cree, frequently repeated... It is rarely to be seen on the ground; after darting down, either in the water, or on land, and securing its booty, it immediately flies with it to some perch, or post of vantage, and prepares it for deglutition, by administering some smart blows with its bill, the sound of which may often be distinctly heard... Fish, crustaceæ, young birds, mice, coleopteræ, bees, and other insects, furnish some portion of the food-supply of the Kingfisher... This bird is one of those fortunate species, whose numbers seem rather to increase than diminish at the approach of civilization."

~T. H. Potts, 1869

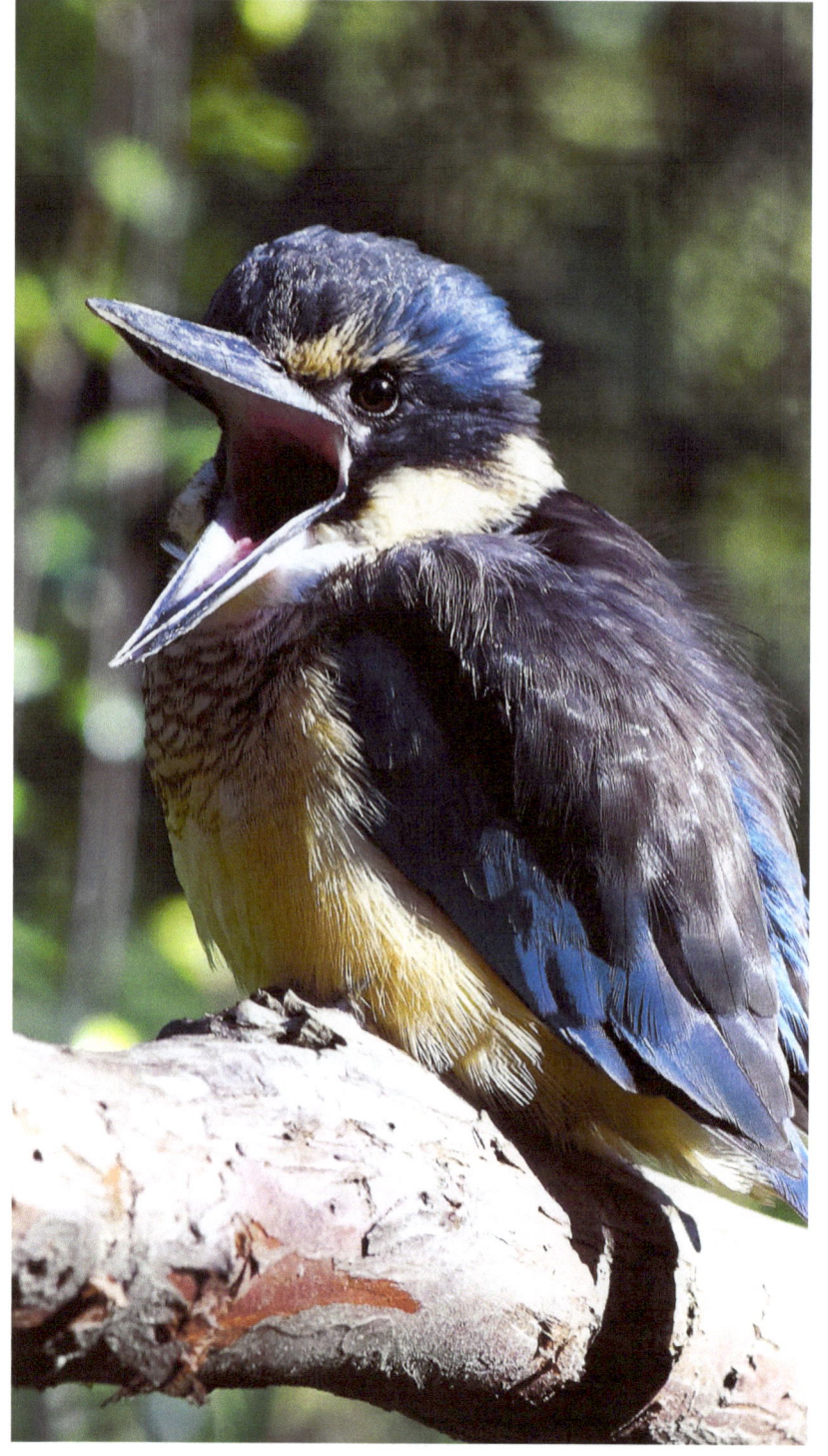

Torea or Variable Oystercatcher (Black Phase)
Haematopus unicolor

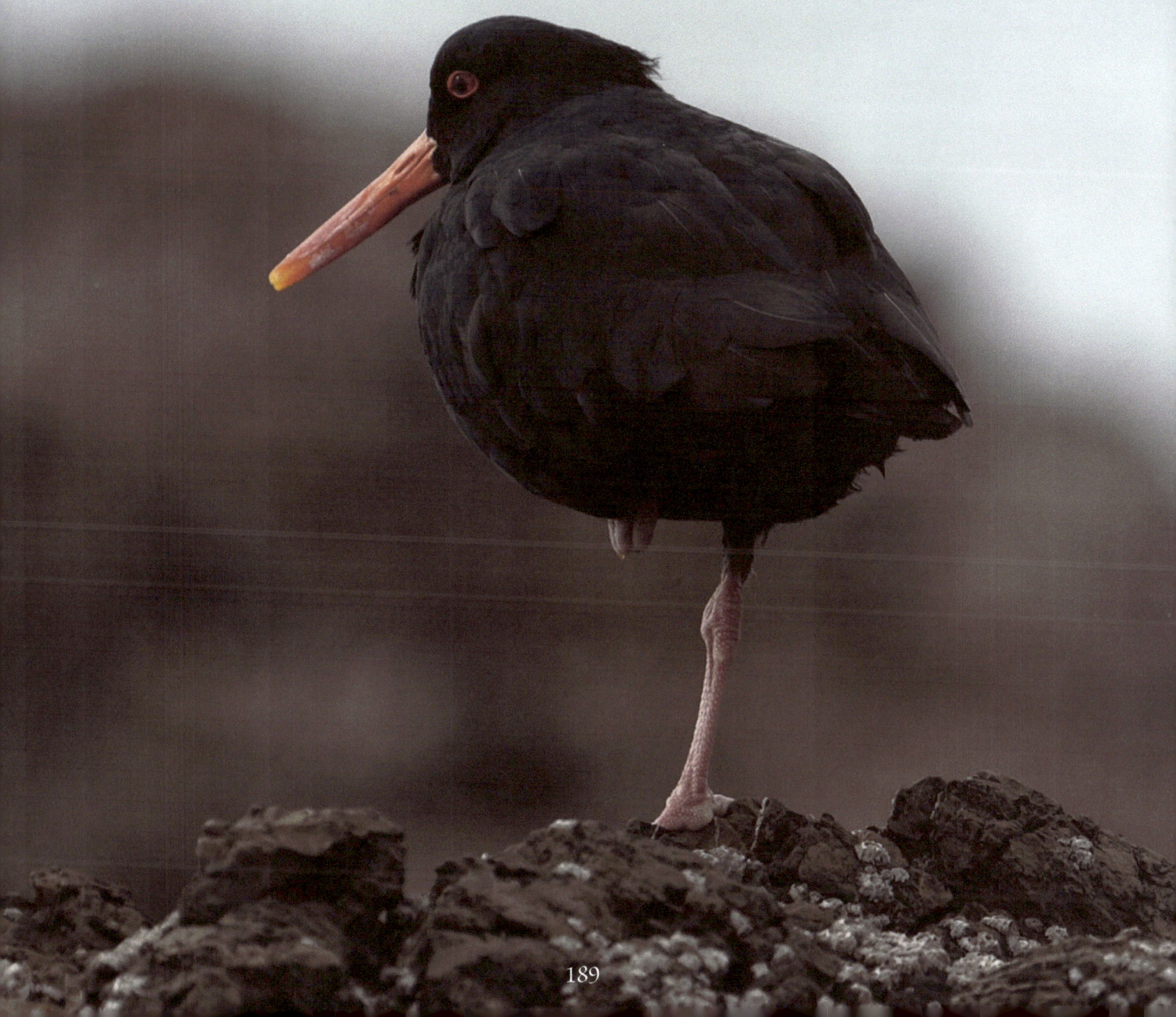

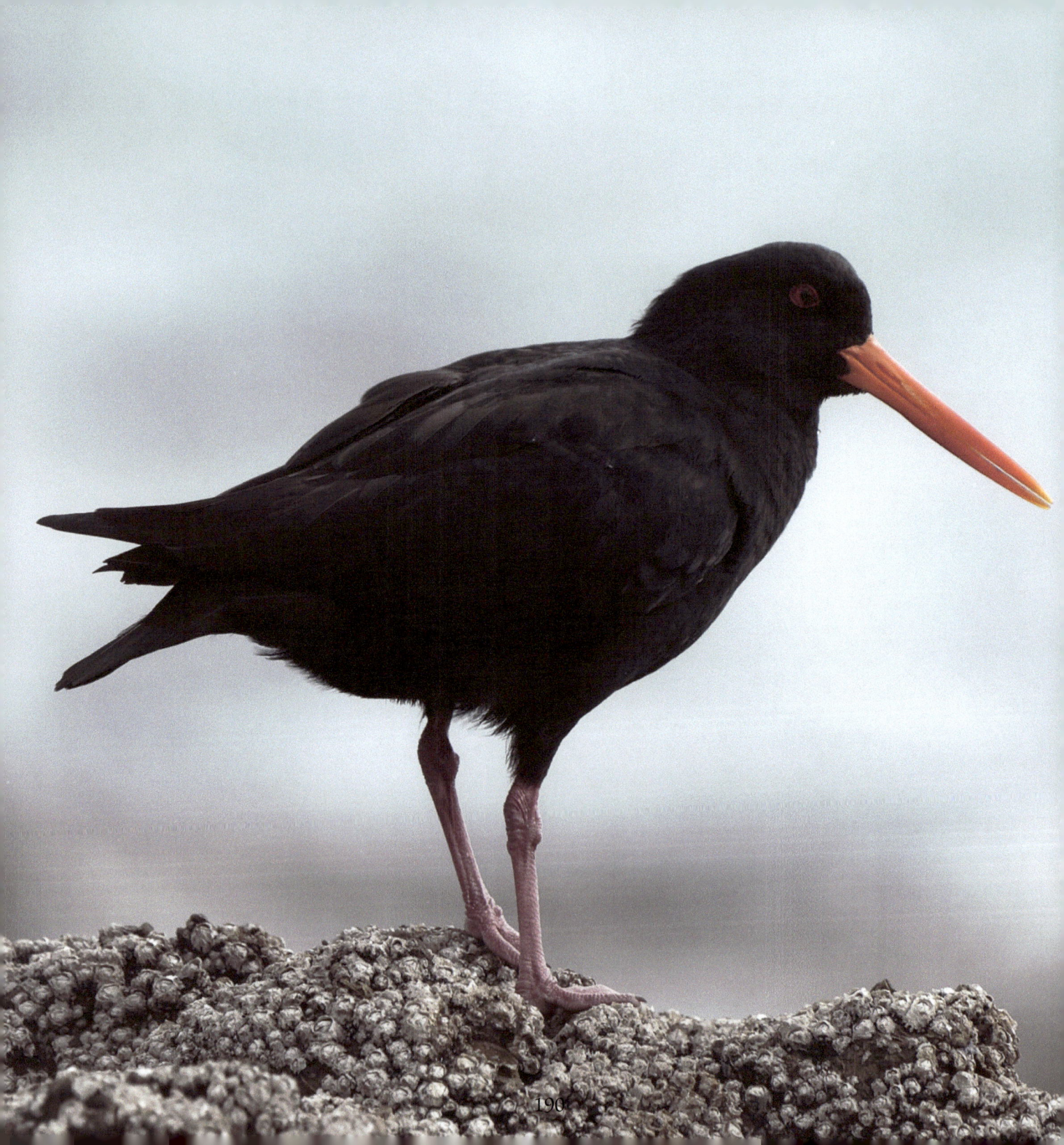

"The Oyster-catcher is one of the wariest and most restless of our birds, ever ready with its clamorous alarm-note, to wake up each echo, and disturb every bird within the sound of its shrill cry; but in the breeding-season it exhibits an intensity of slyness, that is almost supernatural. Usually it breeds in our river-beds, on the sandy spits, without other shelter than what may be afforded by some drift flax, grass, or stick, near which it makes, or discovers, a slight depression, in which to deposit its eggs... A very common frequenter of the coast, as its familiar name imports; in the winter time it assembles in large flocks on the mud flats disclosed by the ebbing tide; though a shore-bird, it is found breeding in solitary couples, often far inland, certainly sixty or seventy miles from the sea, for instance, up the Wilberforce river, nearly as far back as the neighbourhood of Browning's Pass. A pair will boldly attack the Harrier, male and female striking at the Hawk in turn, and driving it to a safe distance from their young. Hæmatopus, that is, literally, the blood-red foot, one of the birds mentioned by Pliny, appears to be universally met with."

~T. H. Potts, 1869

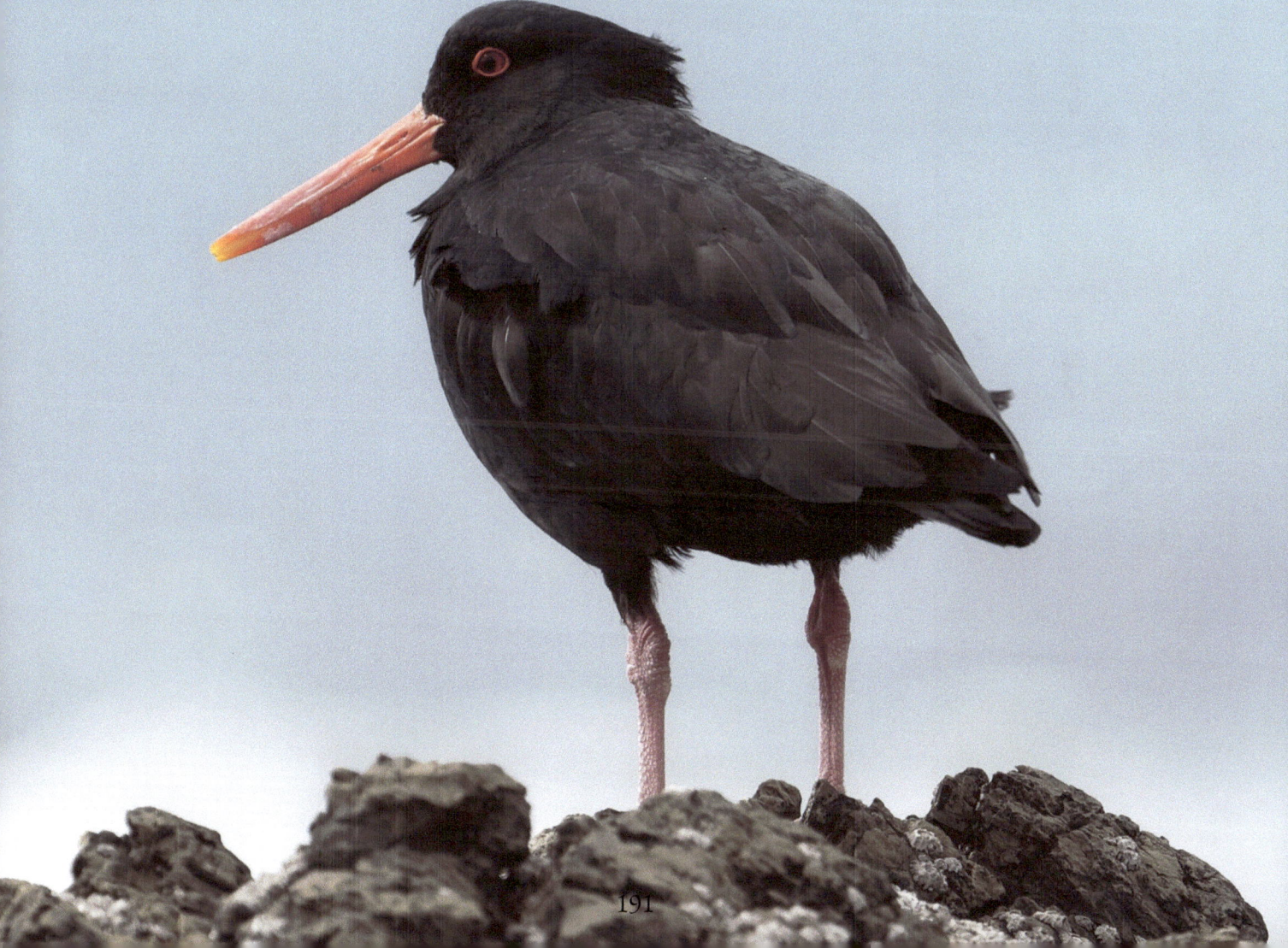

Karoro or Black–backed Gull
Larus dominicanus dominicanus

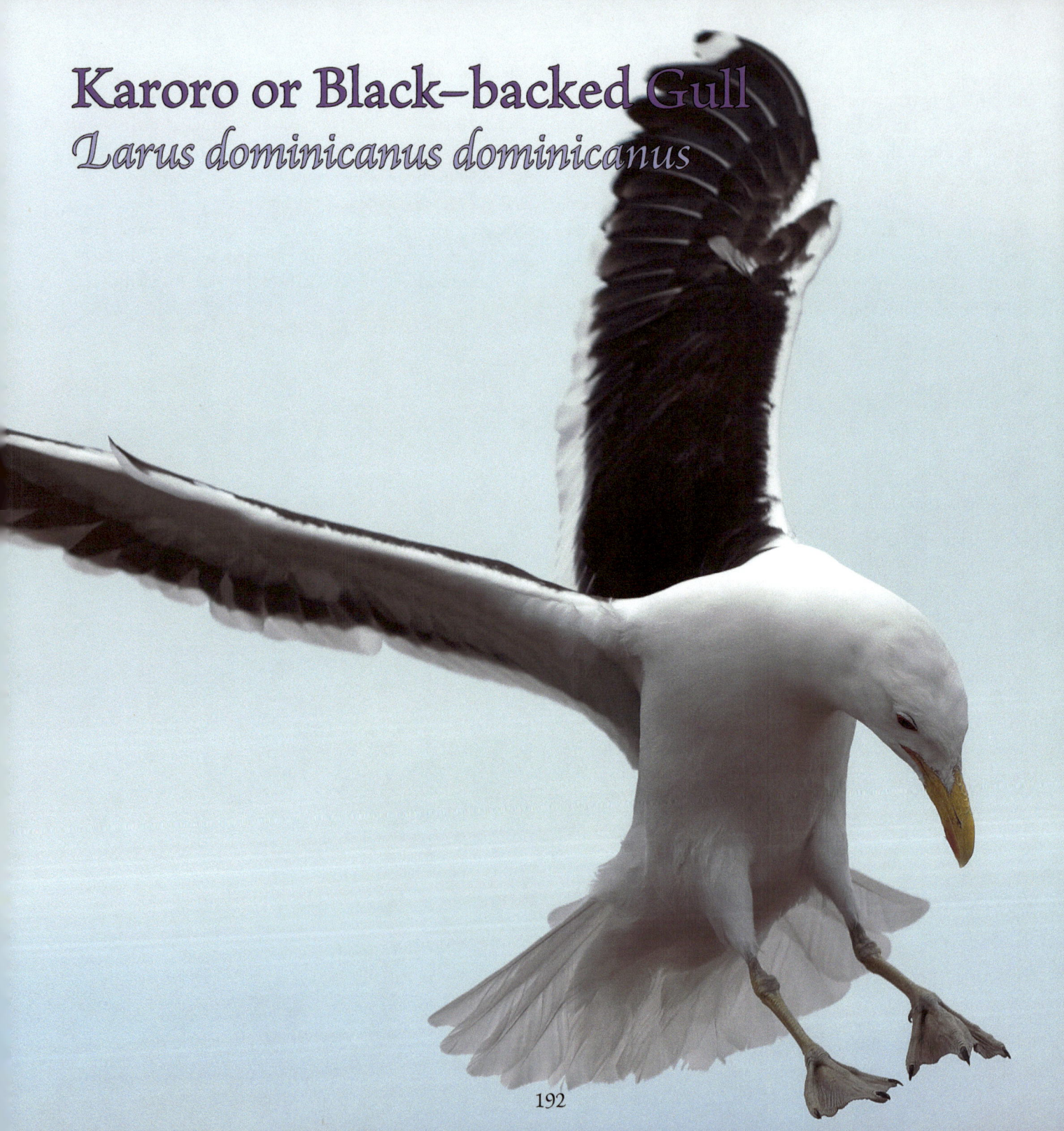

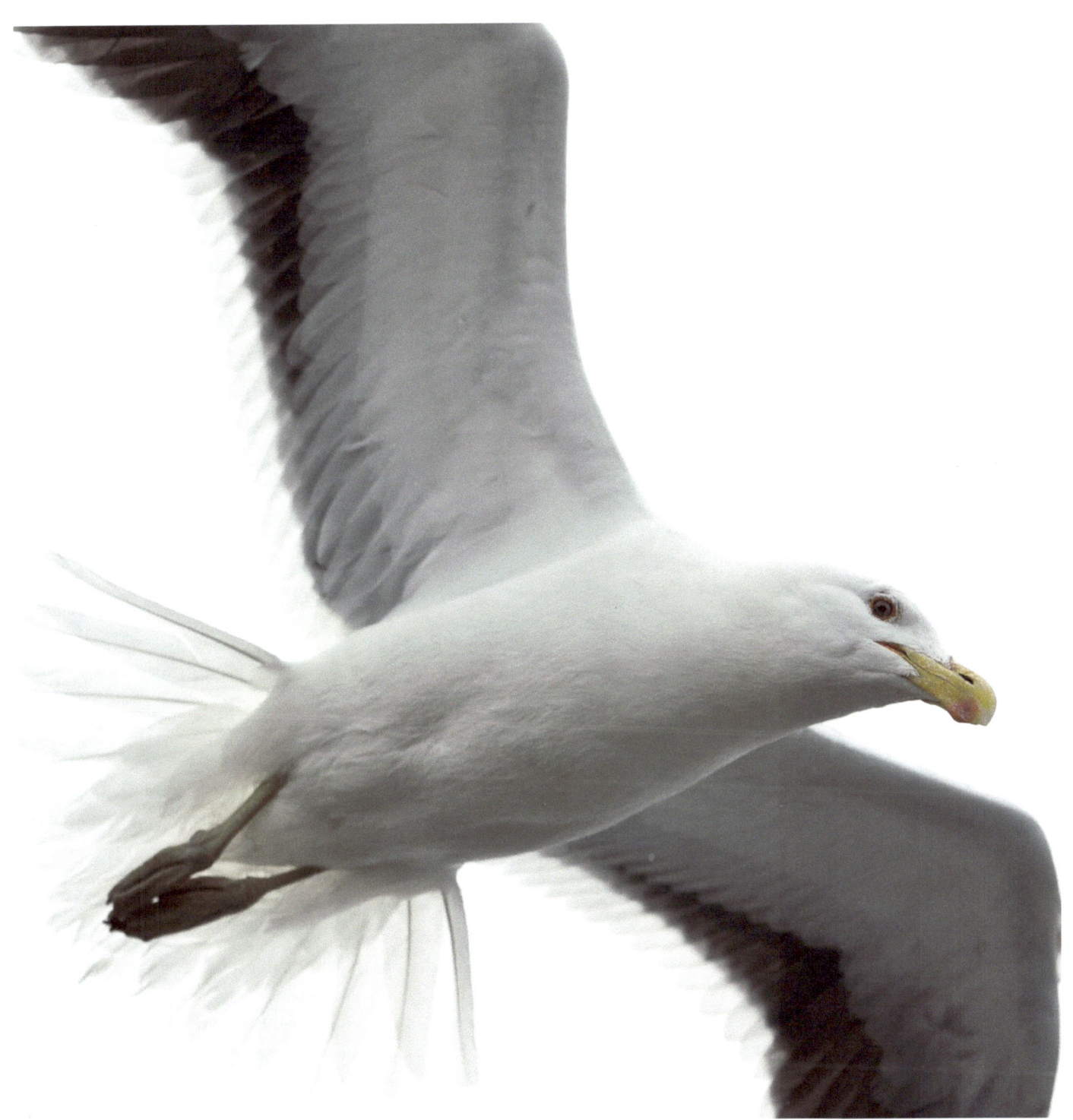

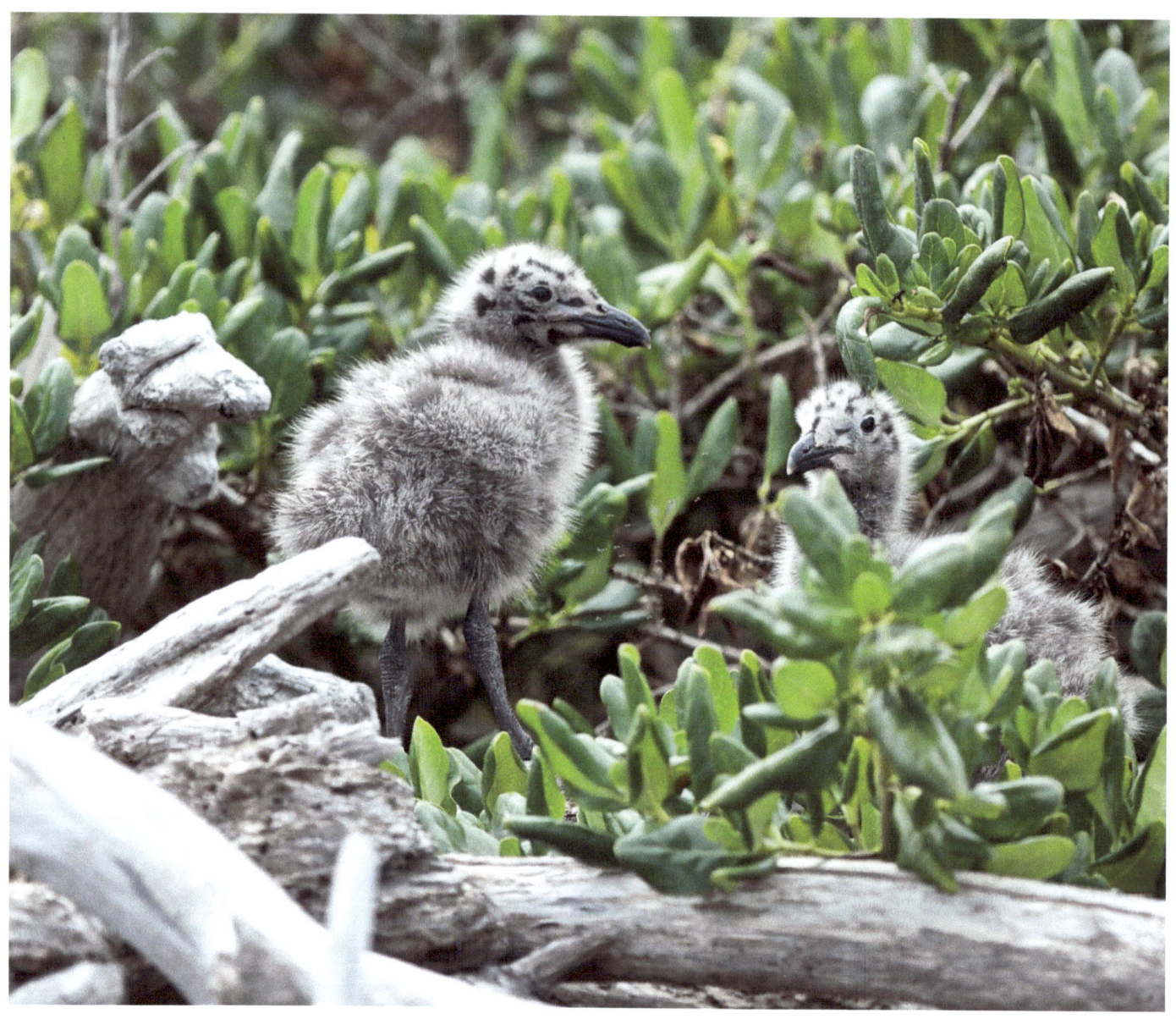

"Simpkins, a publican at Whakatane, obtained a female of this species, when quite young, from White Island, a distance of some thirty-five miles. It became perfectly tame, answering to the name of 'Hinemoa,' and coming into the house at meal-times to be fed. When about two years old it suddenly disappeared, and after a lapse of six months it returned with two young ones, which have since become quite domesticated. By last advices both old bird and young were still inhabitants of the yard, and evinced no desire to leave it."
~Walter L. Buller, 1877

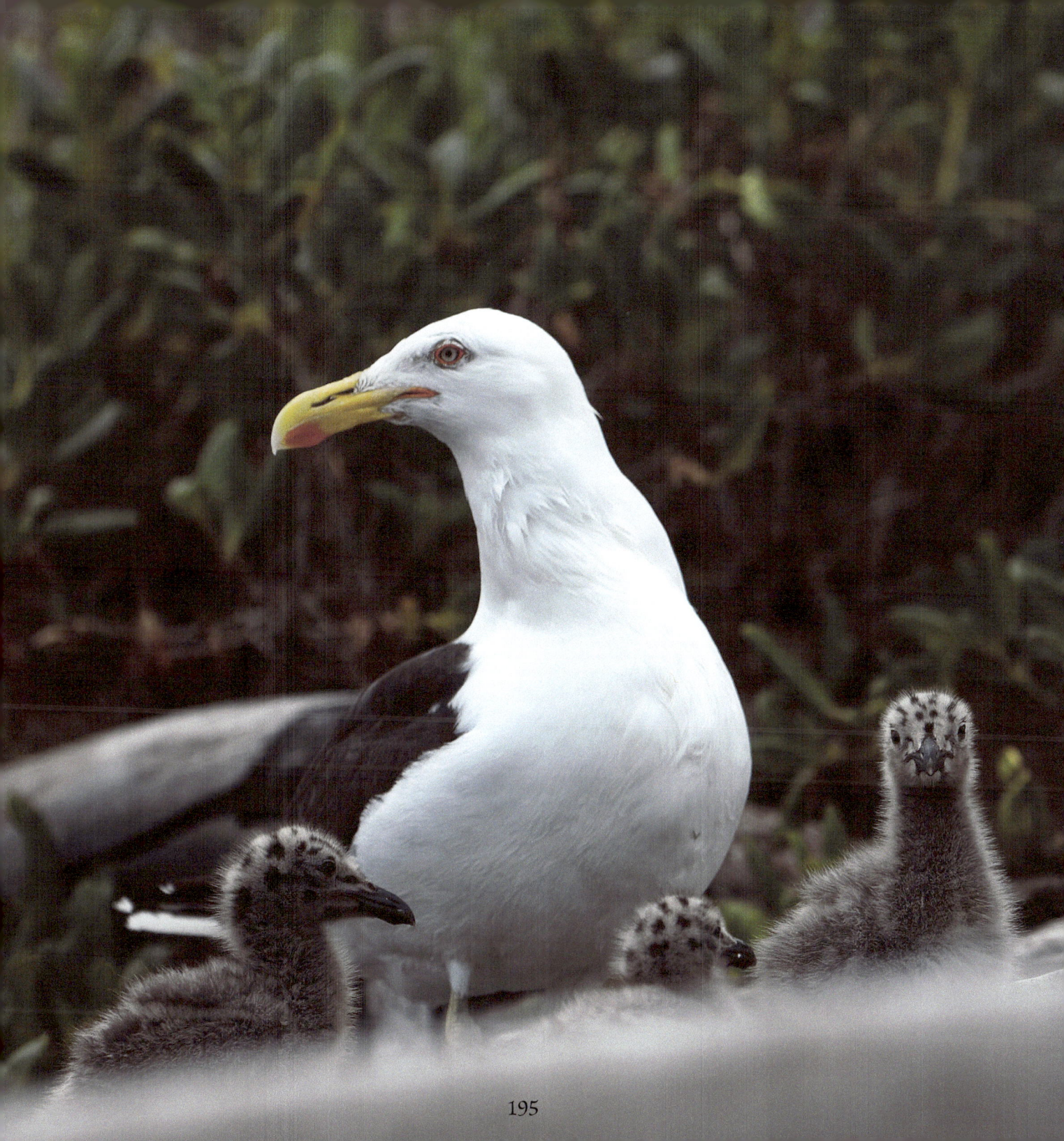

Tarapunga or Red-billed Gull
Larus novaehollandiae

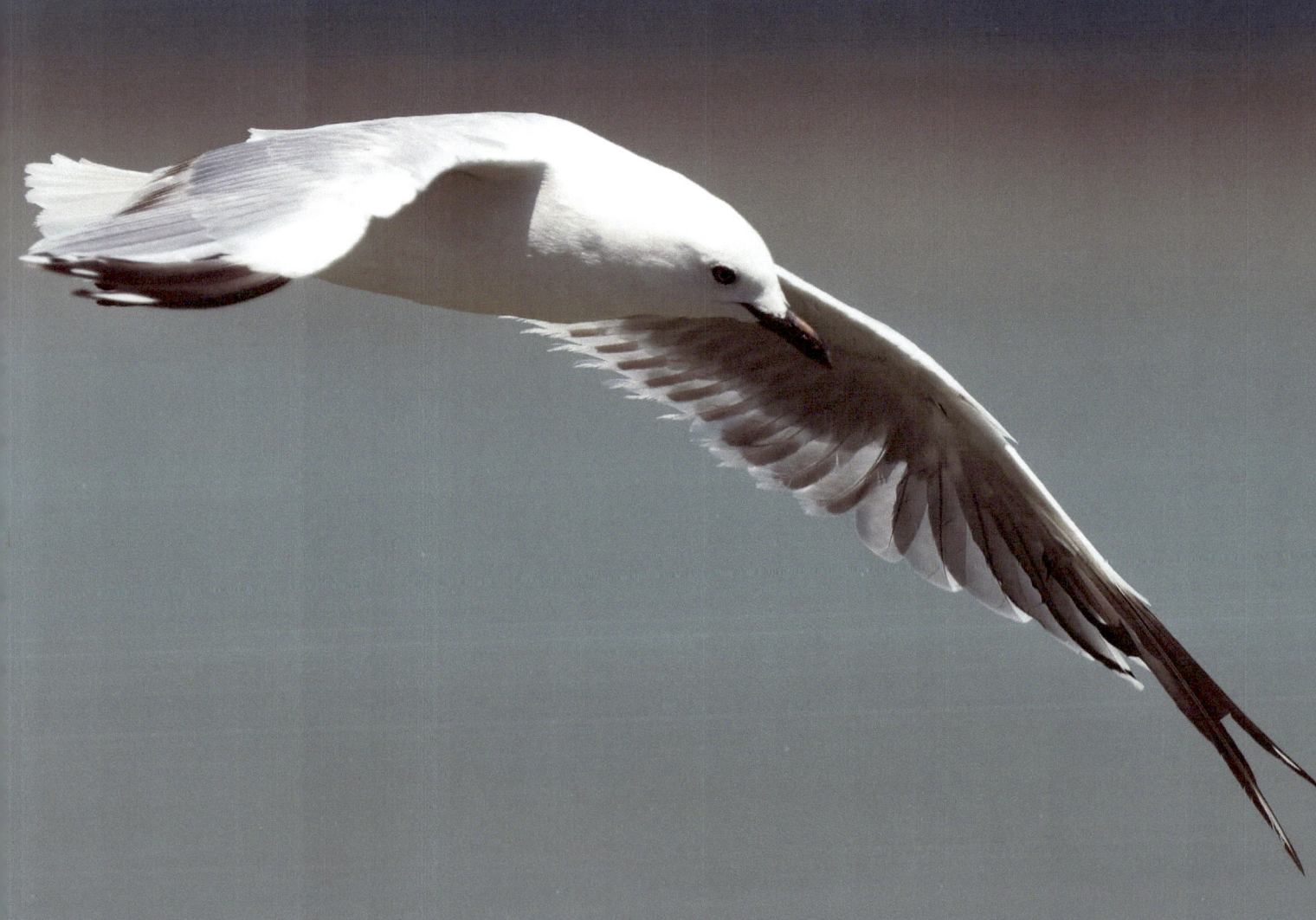

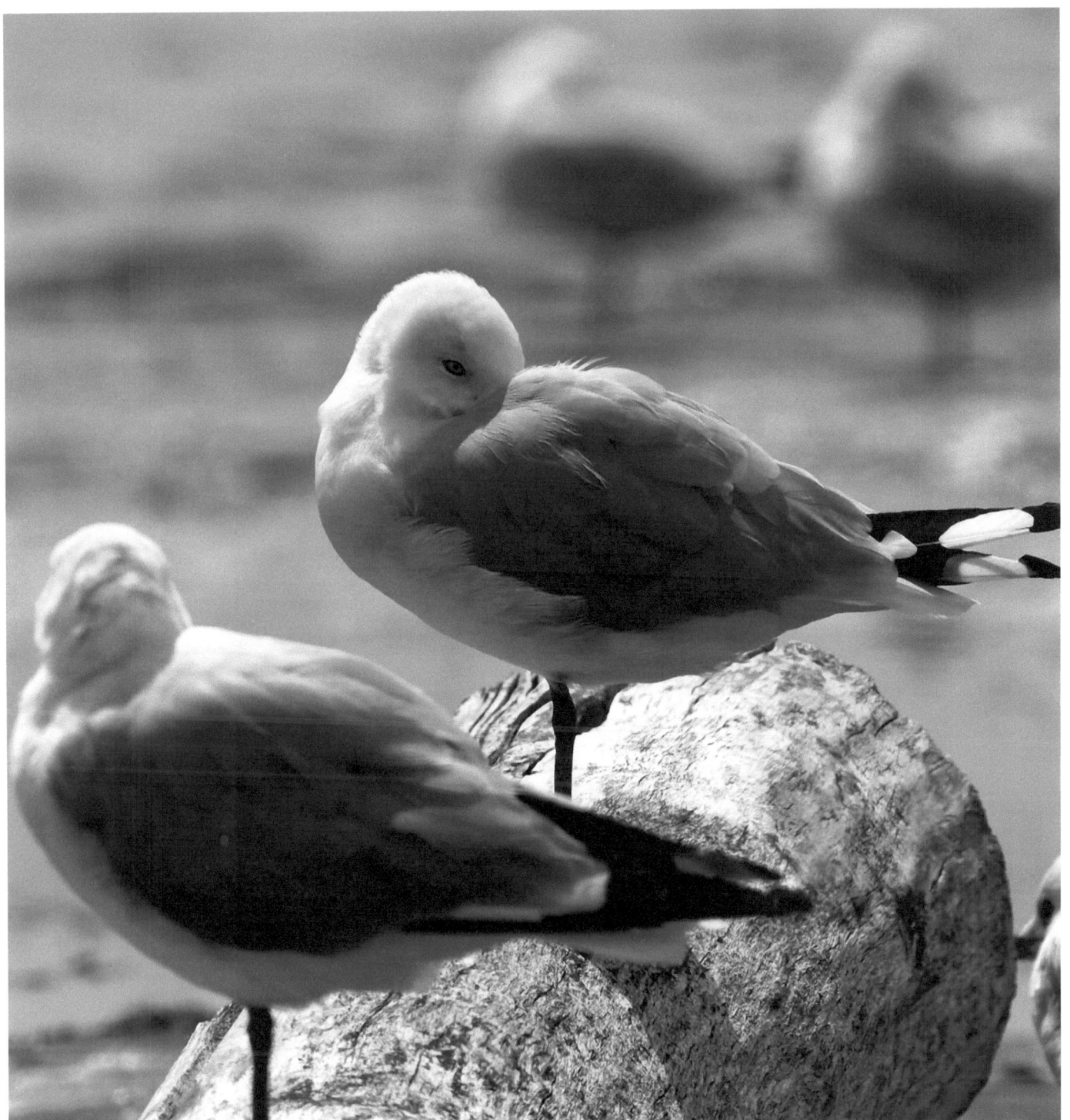

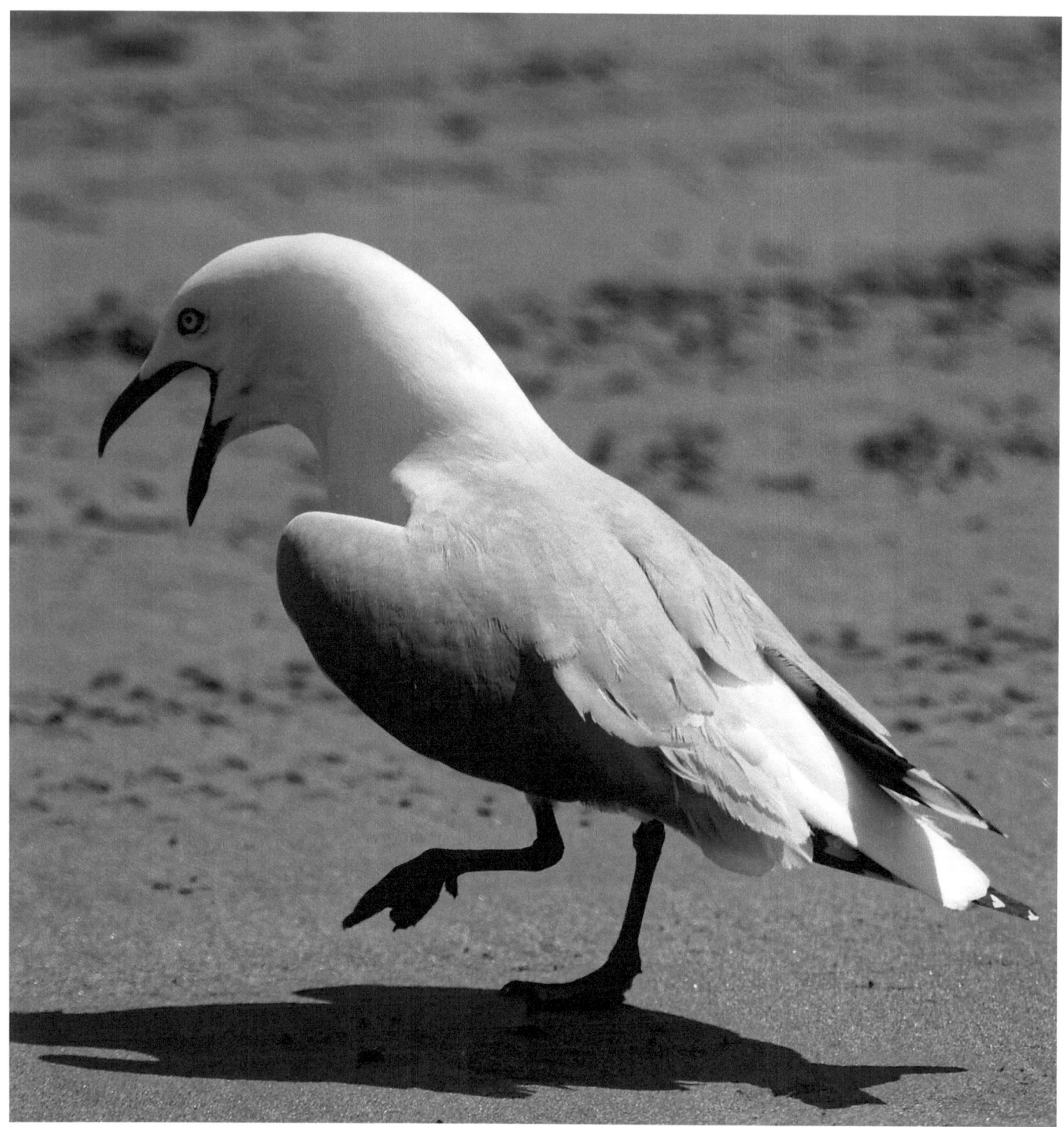

Kawau or Black Shag
Phalacrocorax carbo novaehollandiae

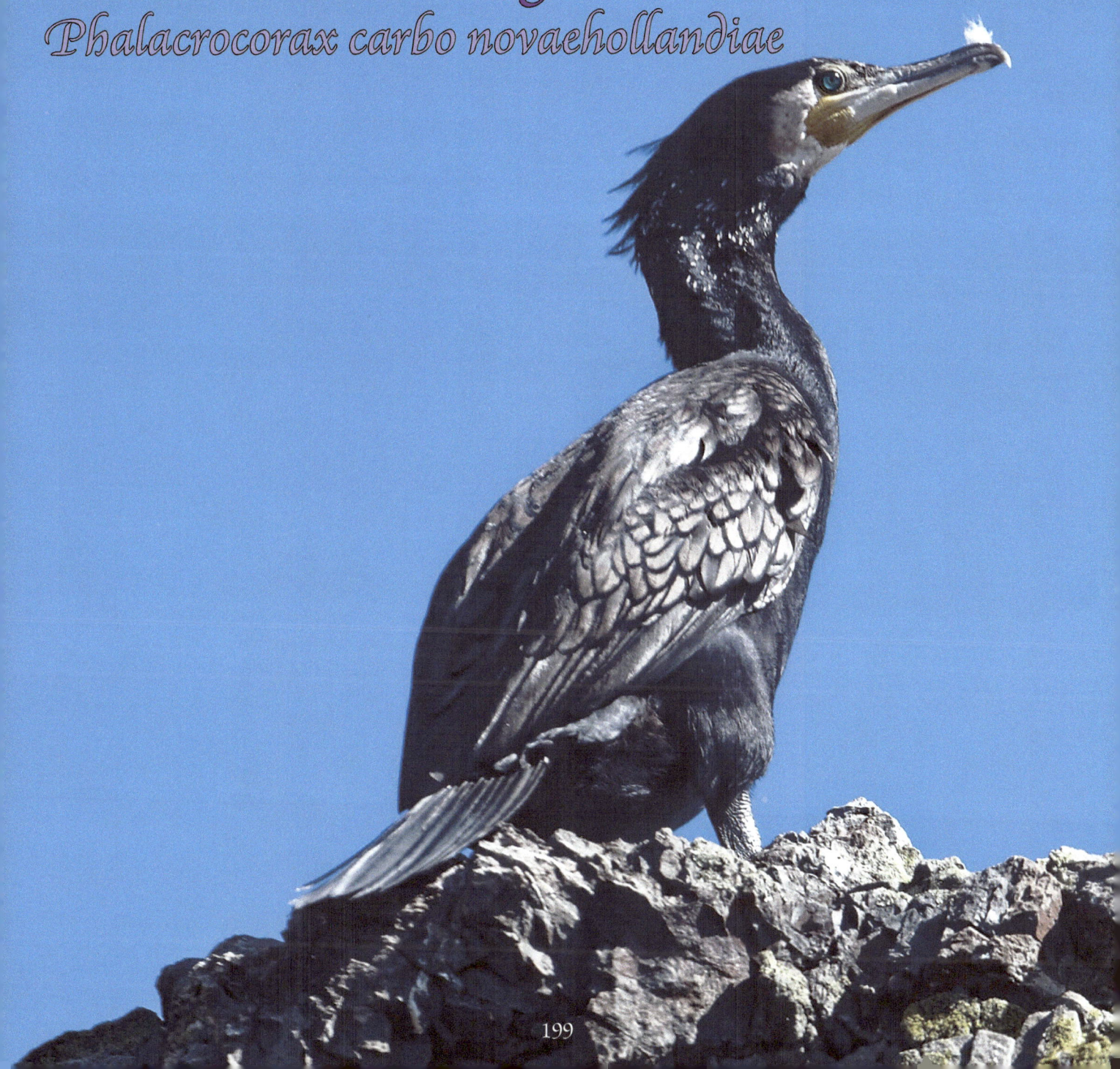

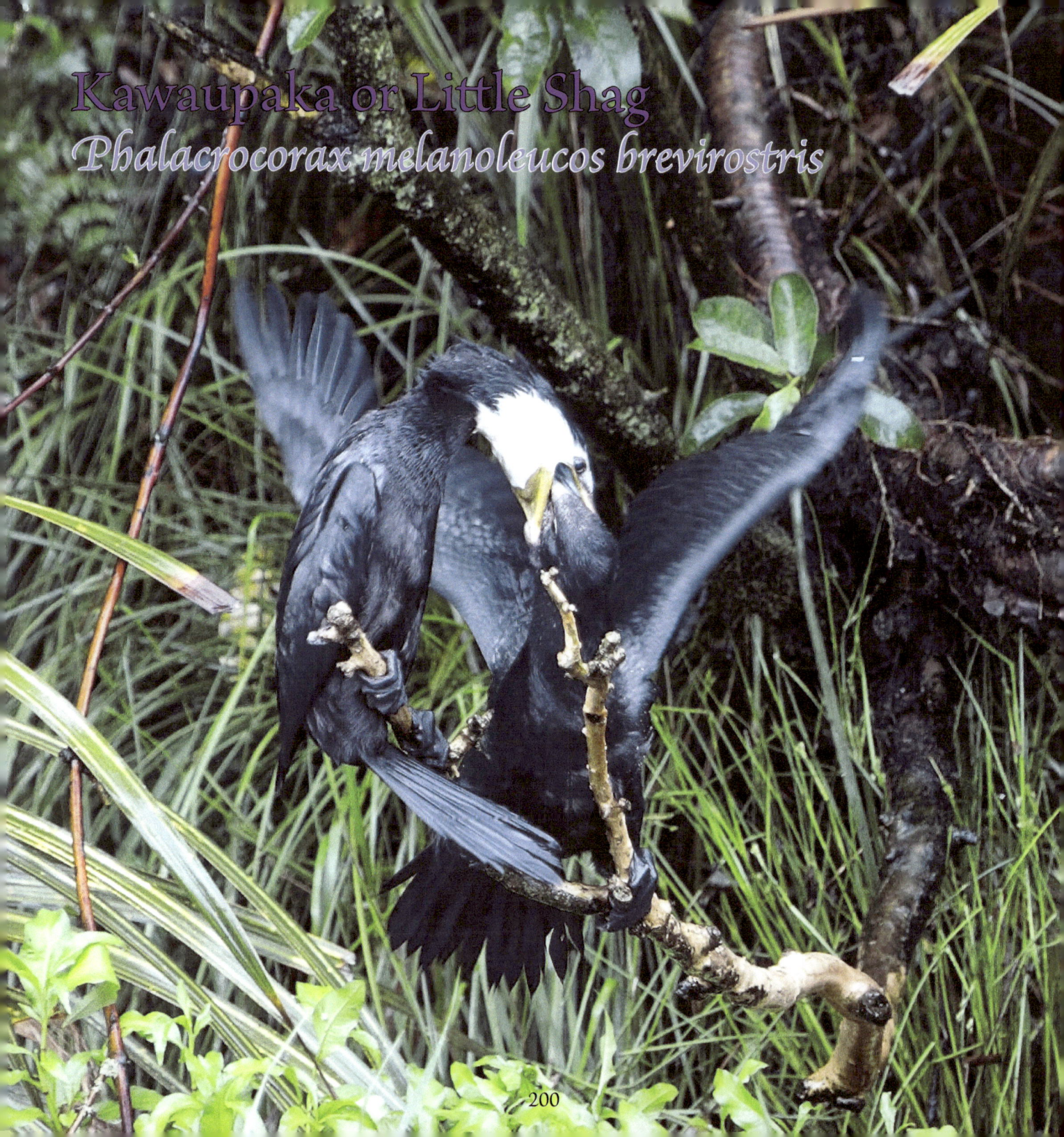

Kawaupaka or Little Shag
Phalacrocorax melanoleucos brevirostris

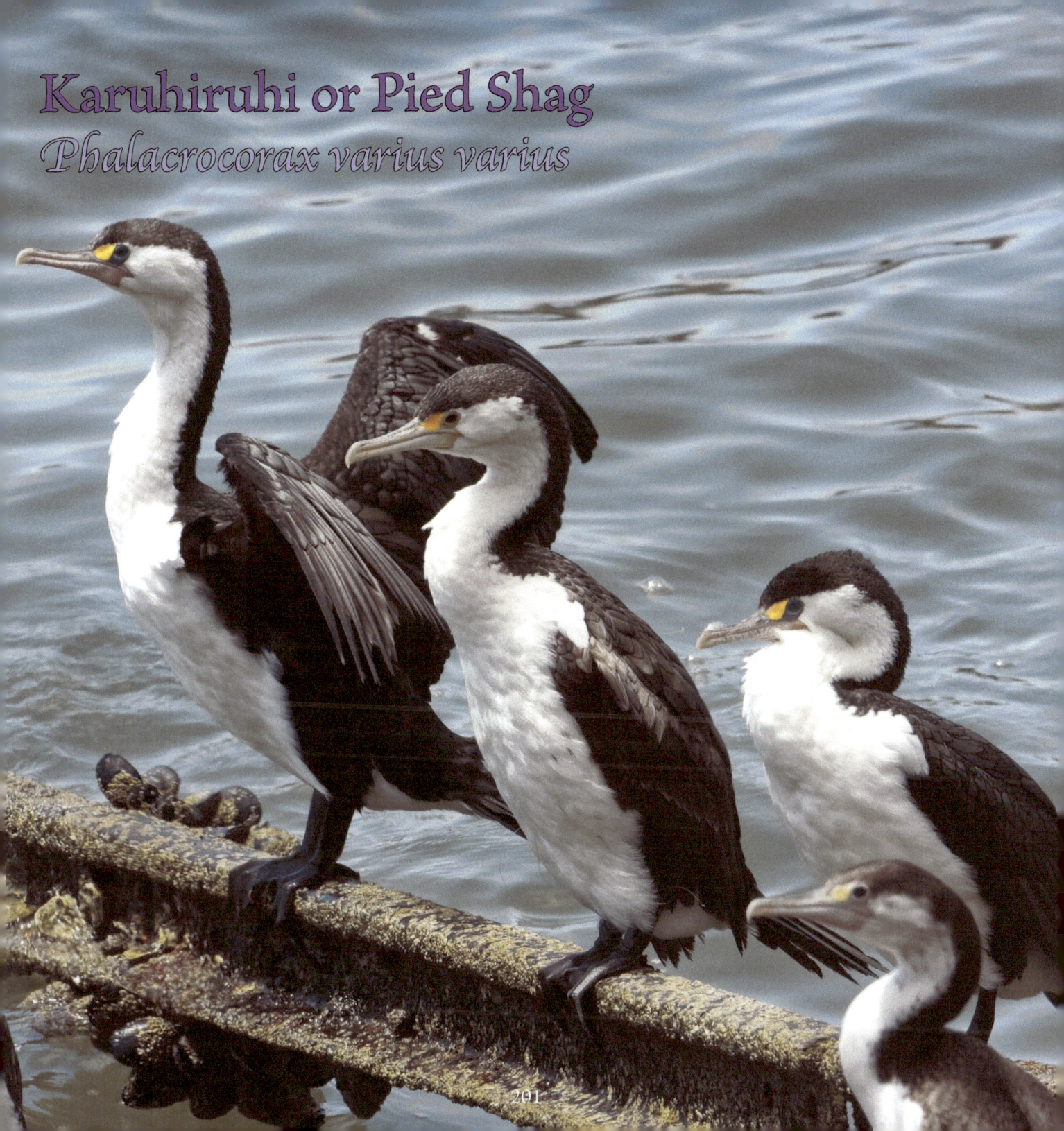

Karuhiruhi or Pied Shag
Phalacrocorax varius varius

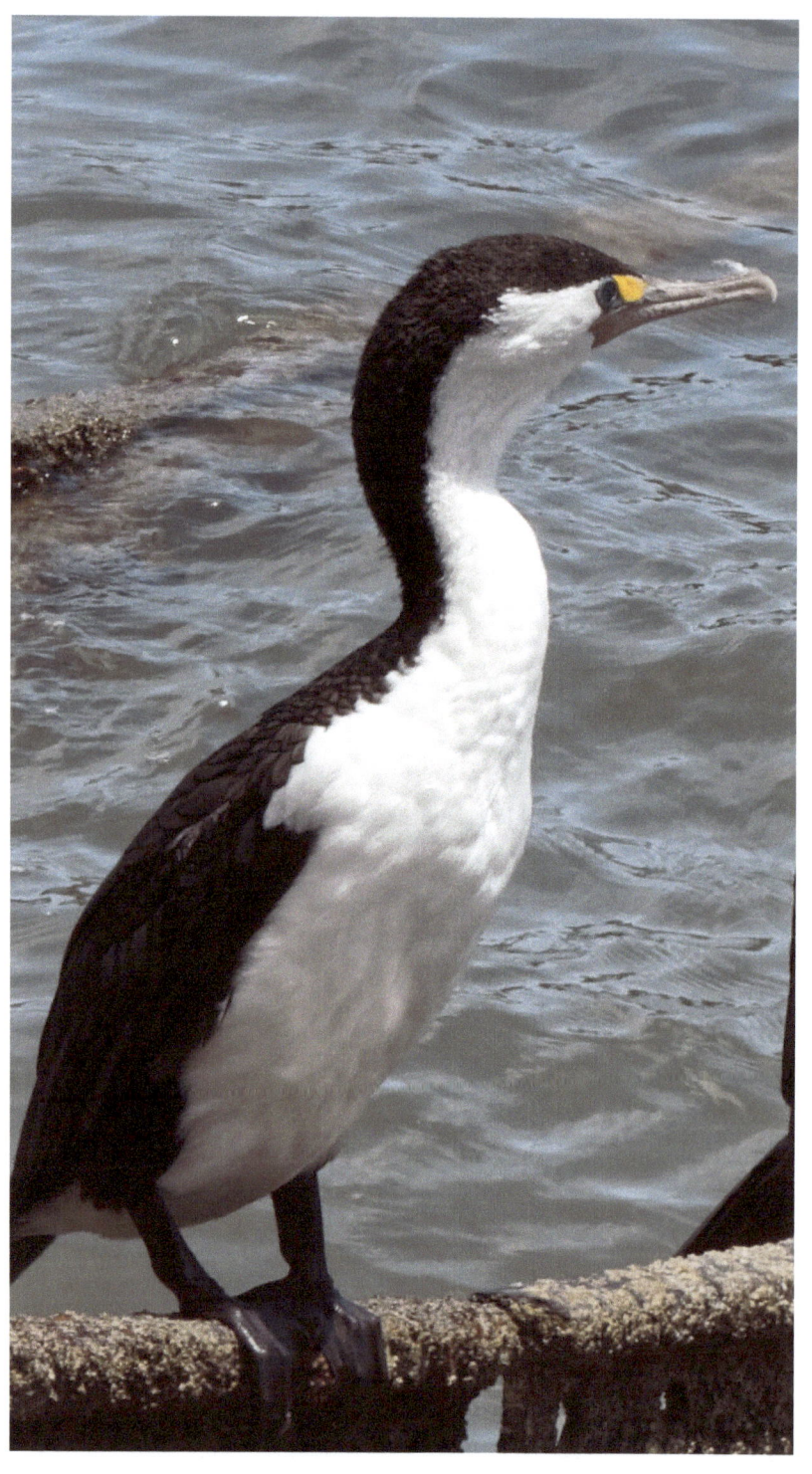

"Captain Mair informs me that at a place called Whakarewha, near Matata on the East Coast, there is a colony of the white–bellied shag where thousands of them breed together. The nests are crowded together on the branches of a clump of pohutukawa trees growing on the cliff; and the old birds may often be seen fighting fiercely for the possession of a dry stick or piece of sea–weed, required for building purposes, or endeavouring to dispossess each other of nests already made. In these fights the young birds are not unfrequently knocked out of the nests, and numbers of dead ones are found lying on the beach at the base of the cliff. The nests are rude structures formed of dry twigs and sticks, bound together by means of a peculiar kind of kelp for which the shags may be observed diving in the sea, sometimes in four fathoms of water. The harrier (Circus gouldi) hovers about this breeding–place and makes an occasional attempt to carry off a young bird from the nest by boldly attacking it; whereupon numbers of the old birds sally forth with loud guttural cries and chase the intruder to a considerable distance. Captain Mair, who has often visited this 'shaggery,' says: 'It is very amusing to watch the old birds feeding the young ones. With a slow flapping of its ample wings the parent bird comes in from her fishing excursion, her capacious throat distended with food. There is much excitement in the nest on her approach. The young birds open wide their mandibles, and thrusting her beak down the throat of her offspring, the careful mother empties the contents of her pouch right into the little one's crop. All this time the delighted recipient is swaying its body to and fro, vibrating its flippers and uttering a perpetual scream of joy.'"

~Walter L. Buller, 1877

Taranui or Caspian Tern
Sterna Caspia

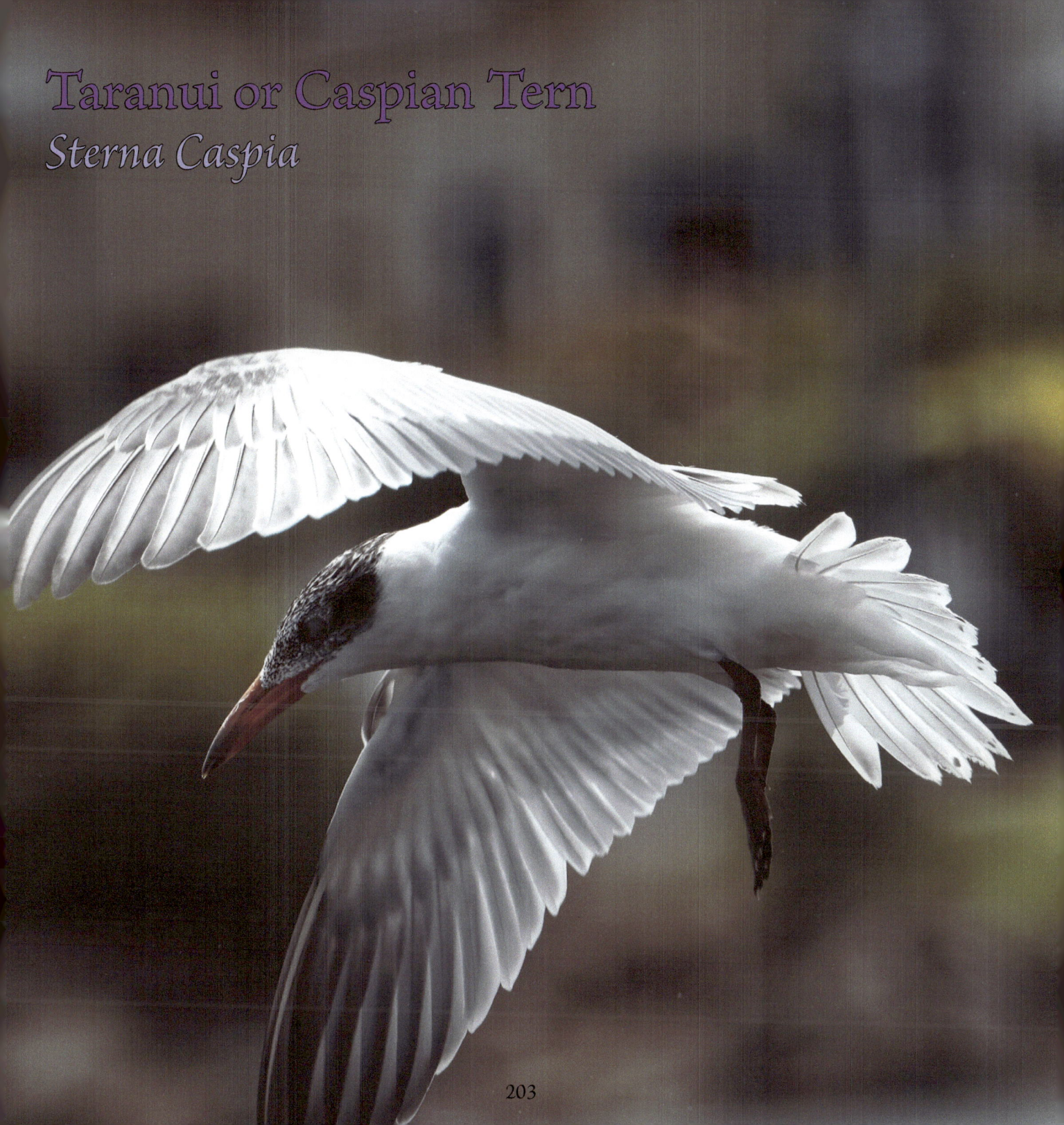

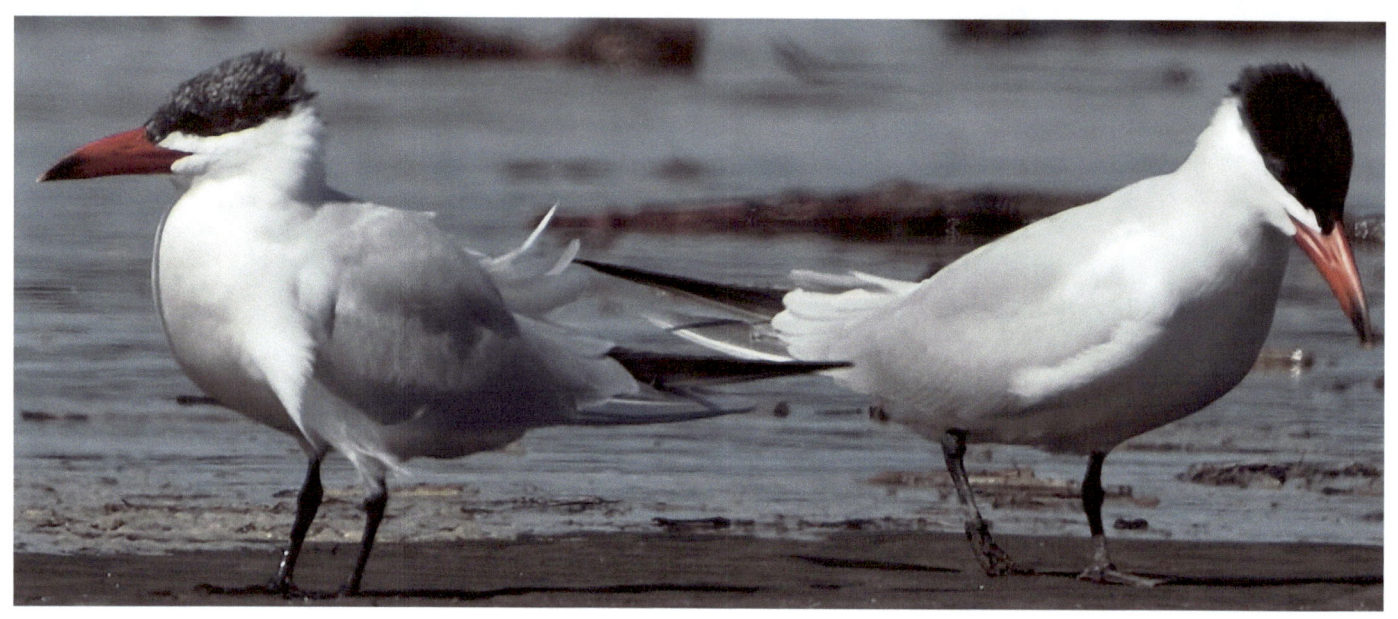

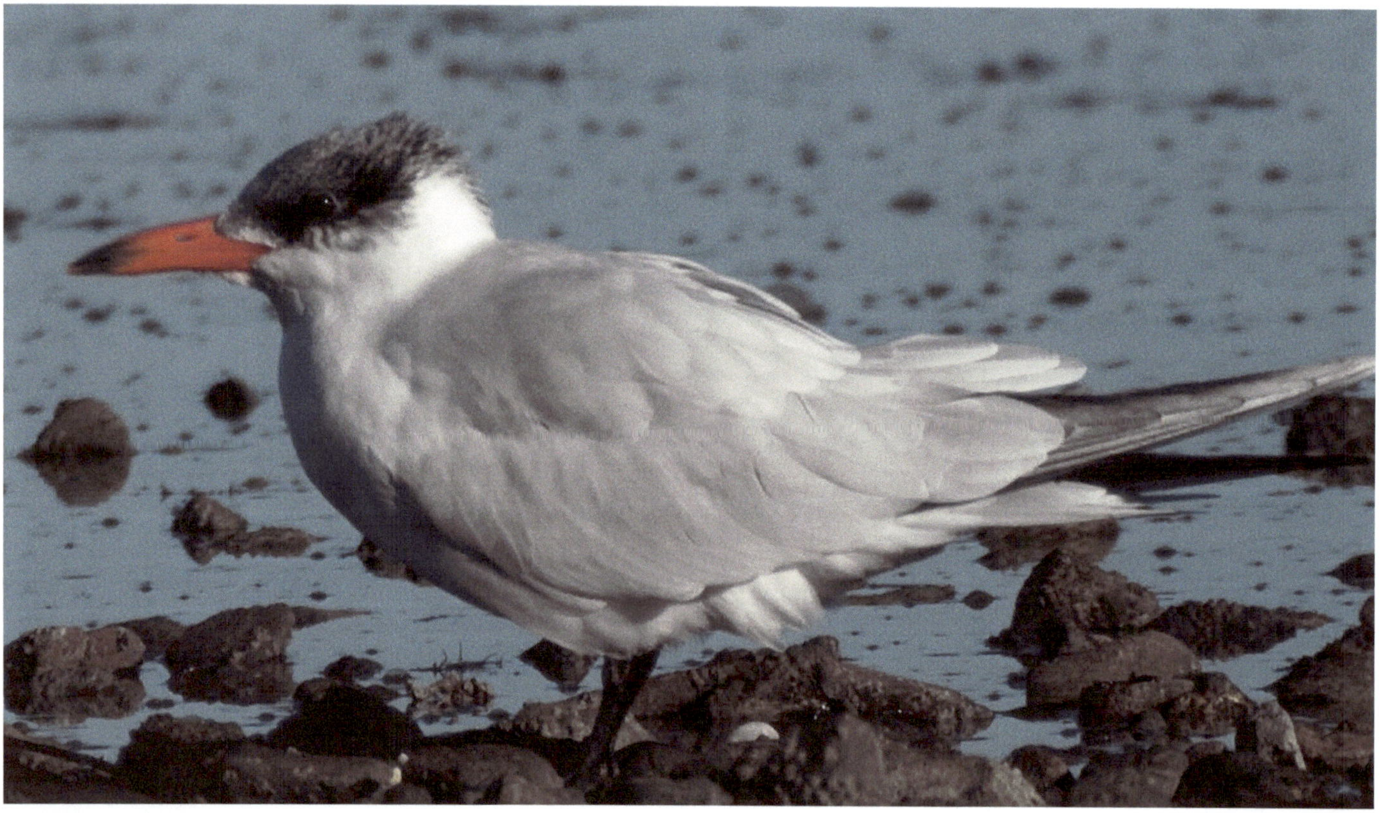

204

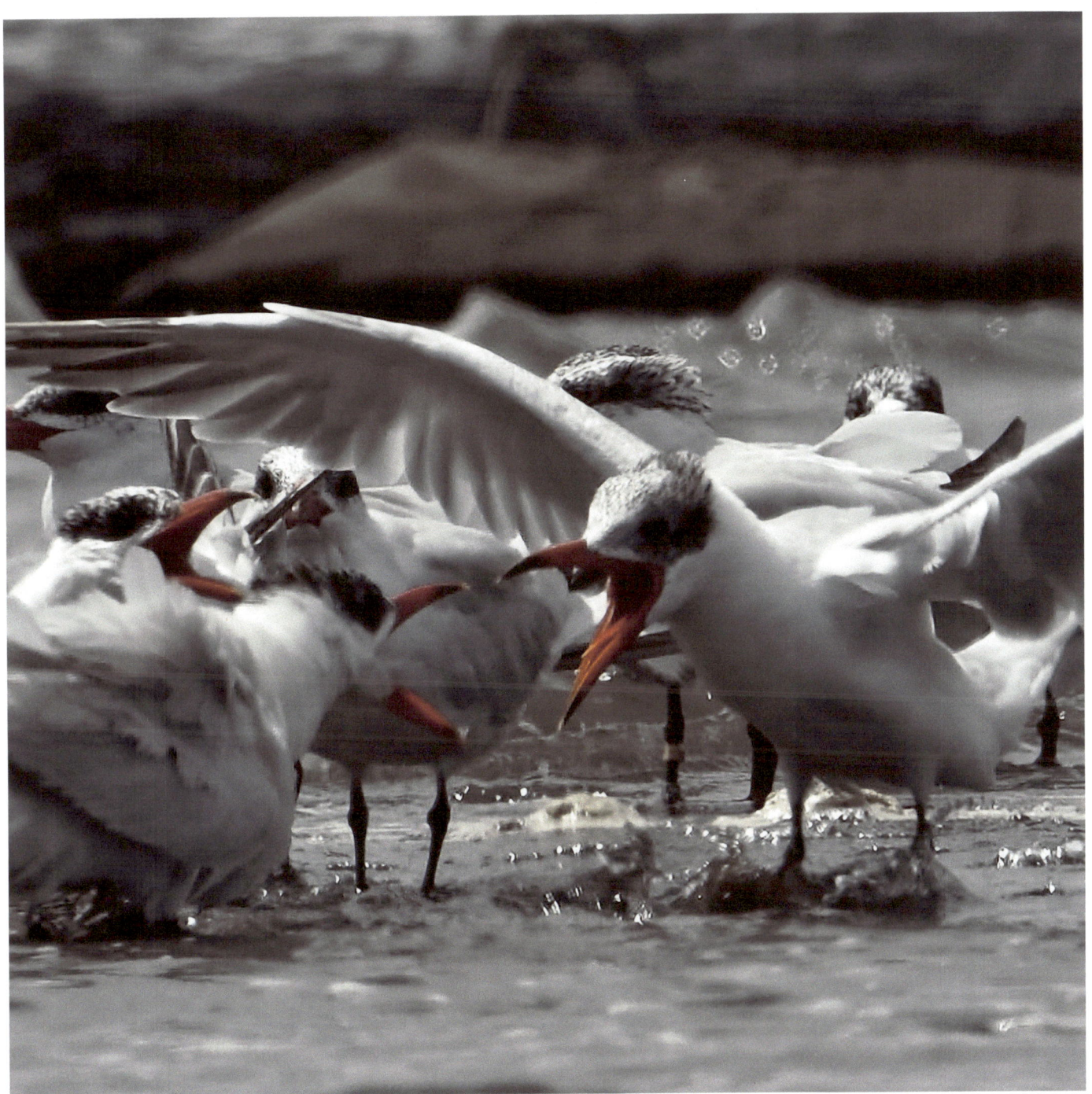

Tara or White-fronted Tern
Sterna striata

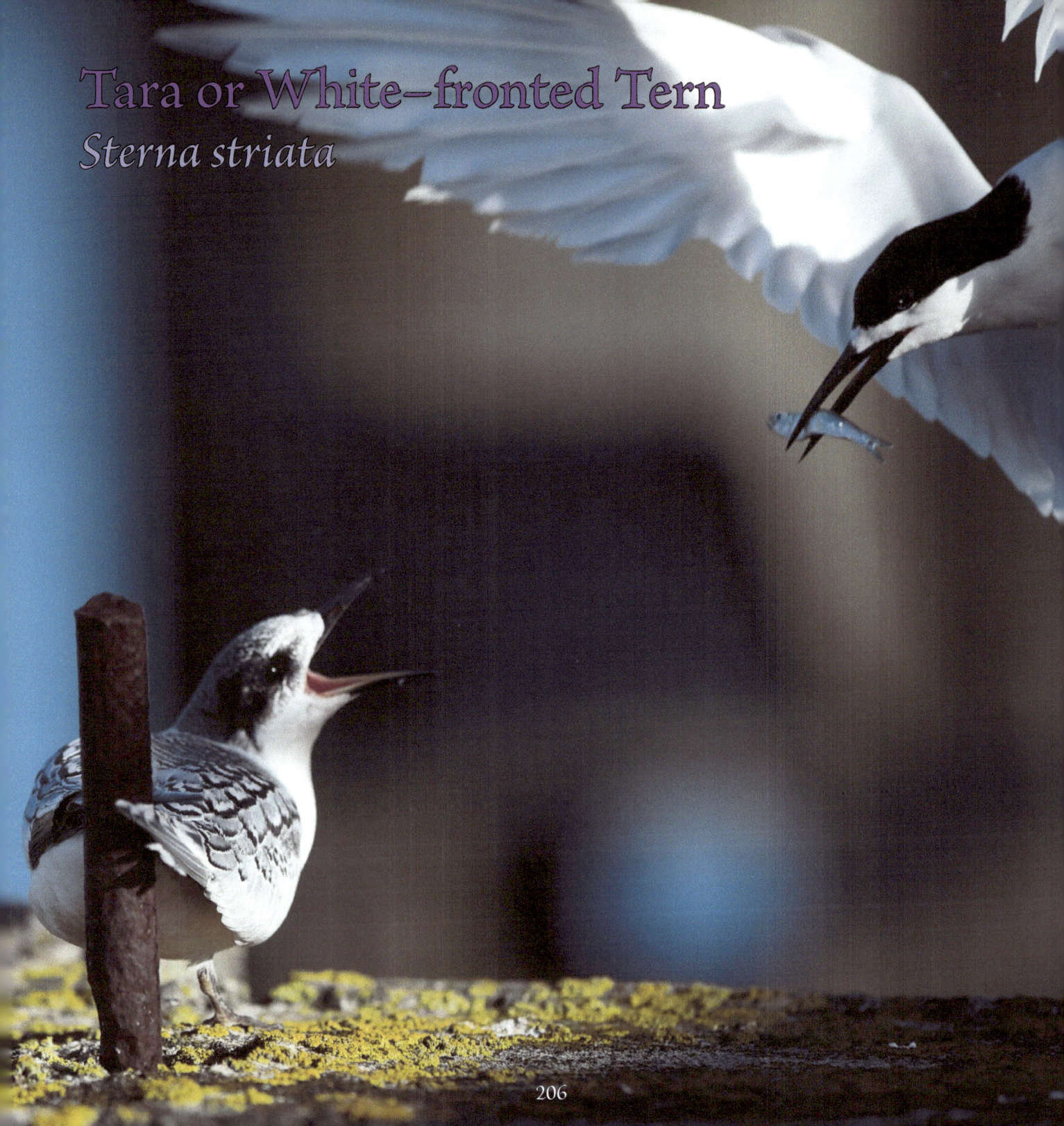

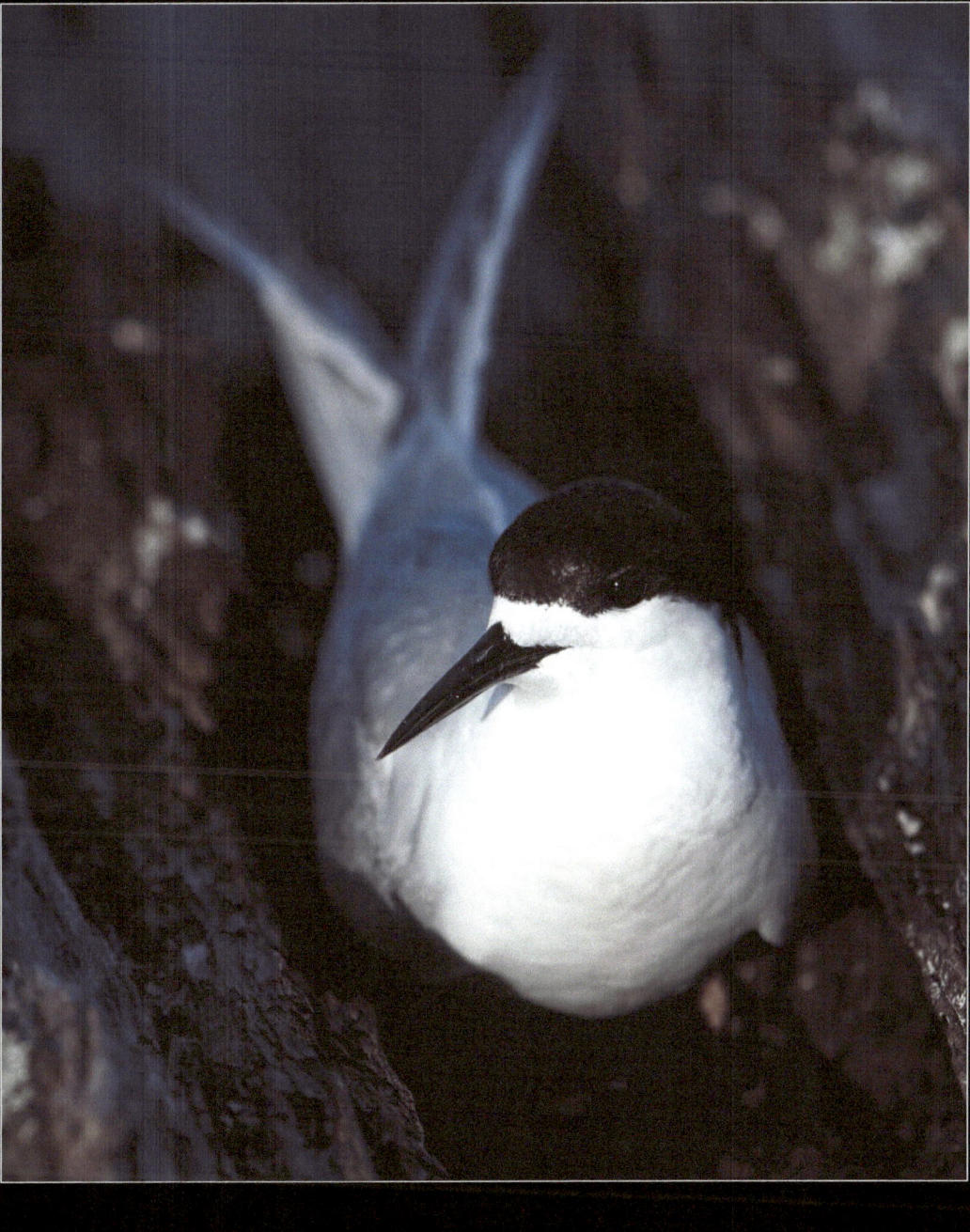

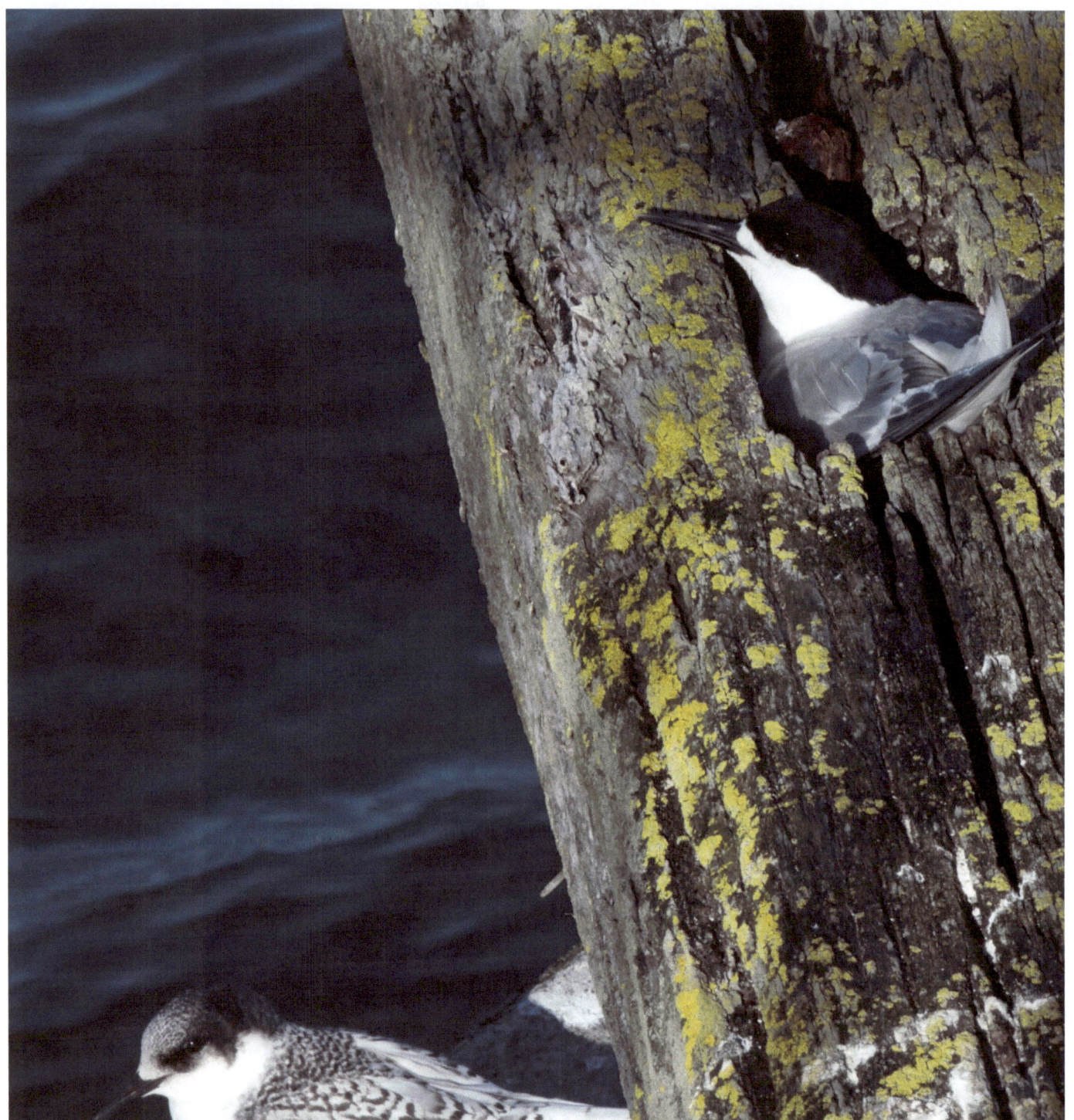

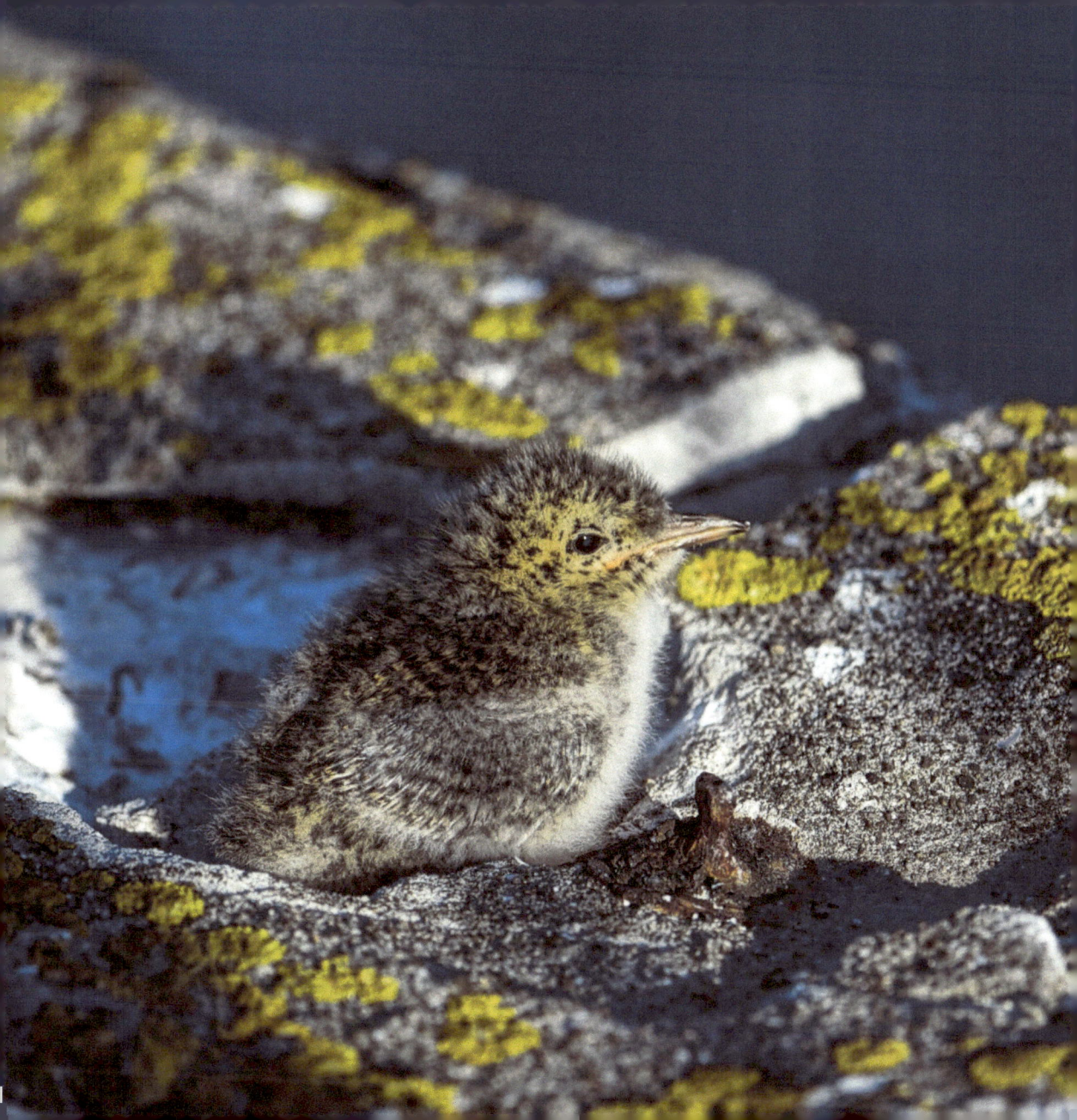

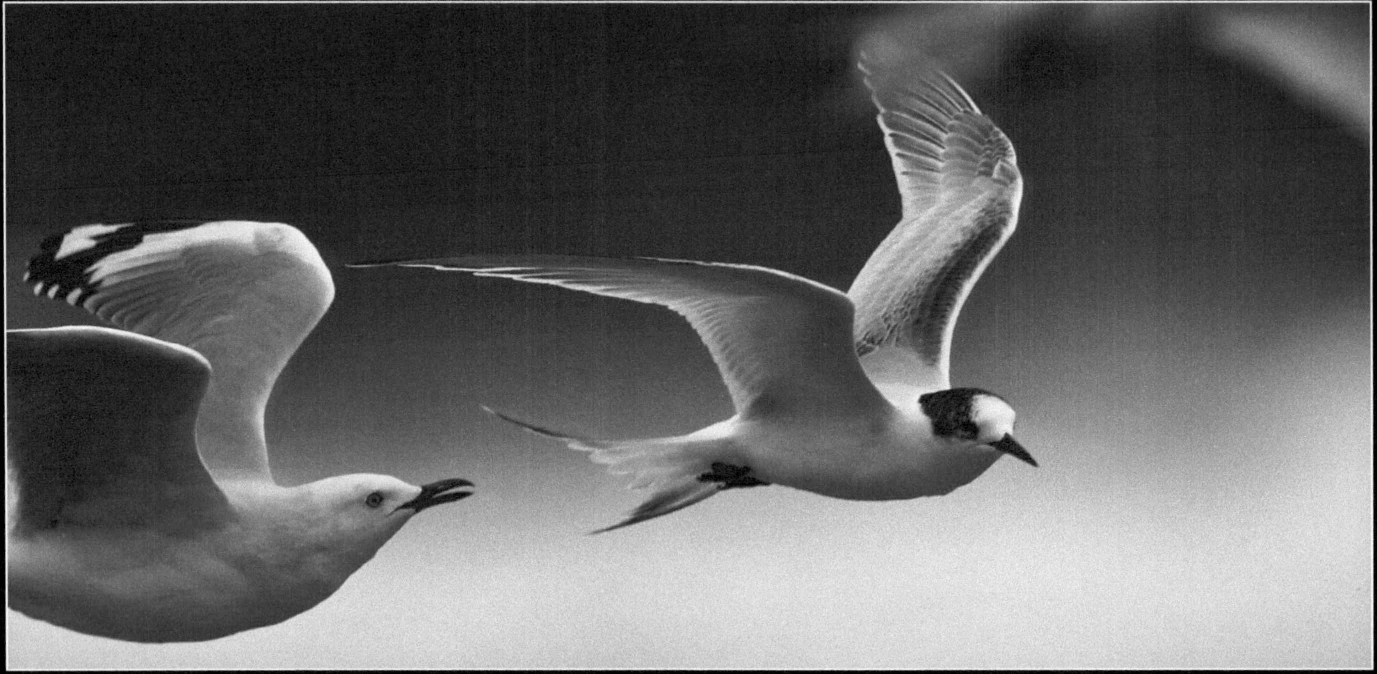

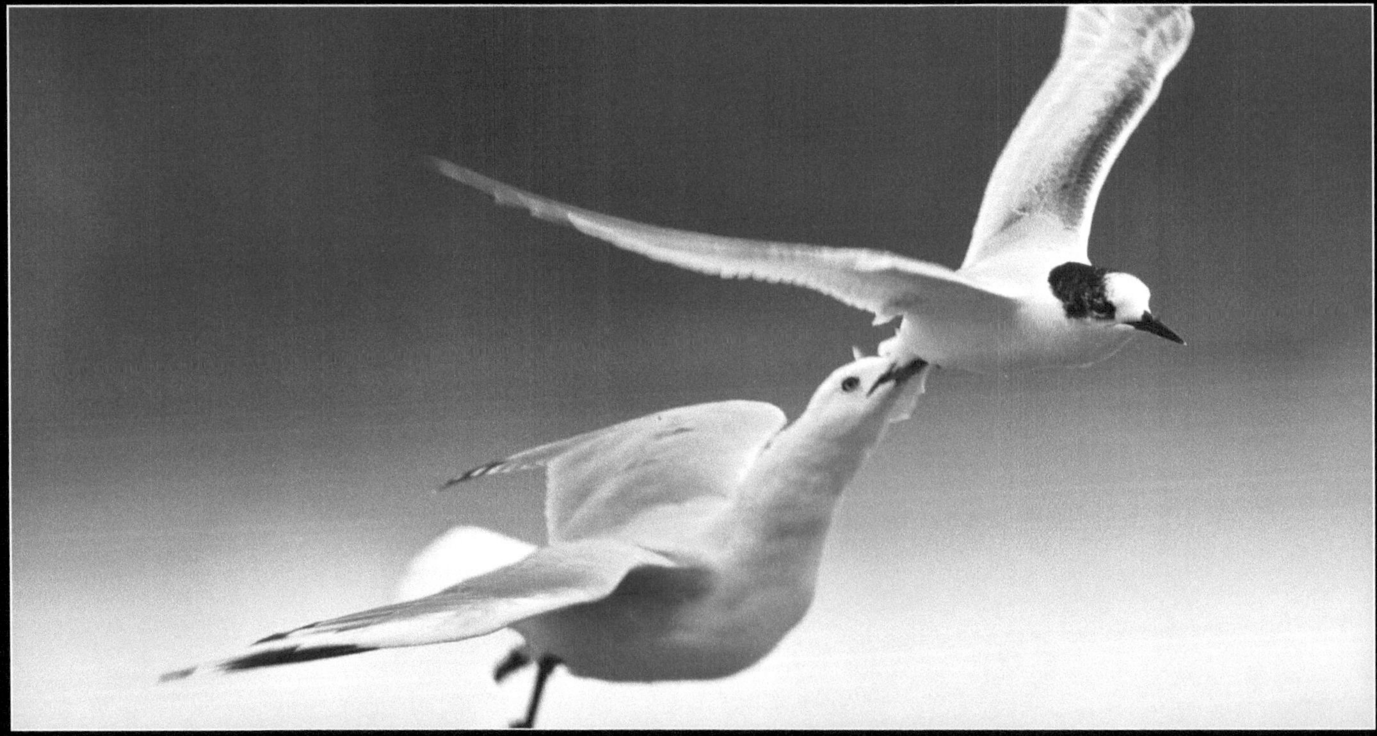

Chapter Six
Out at Sea

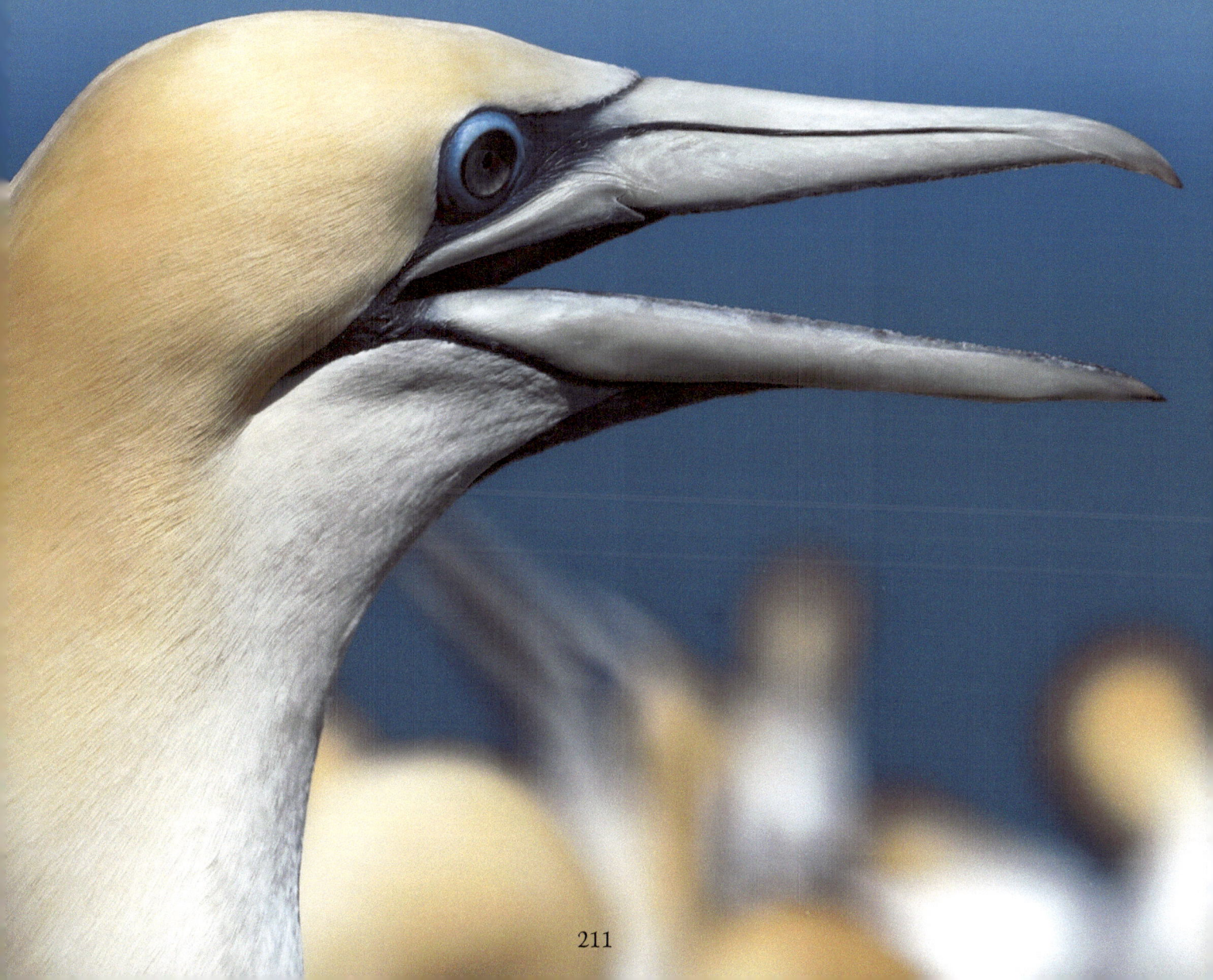

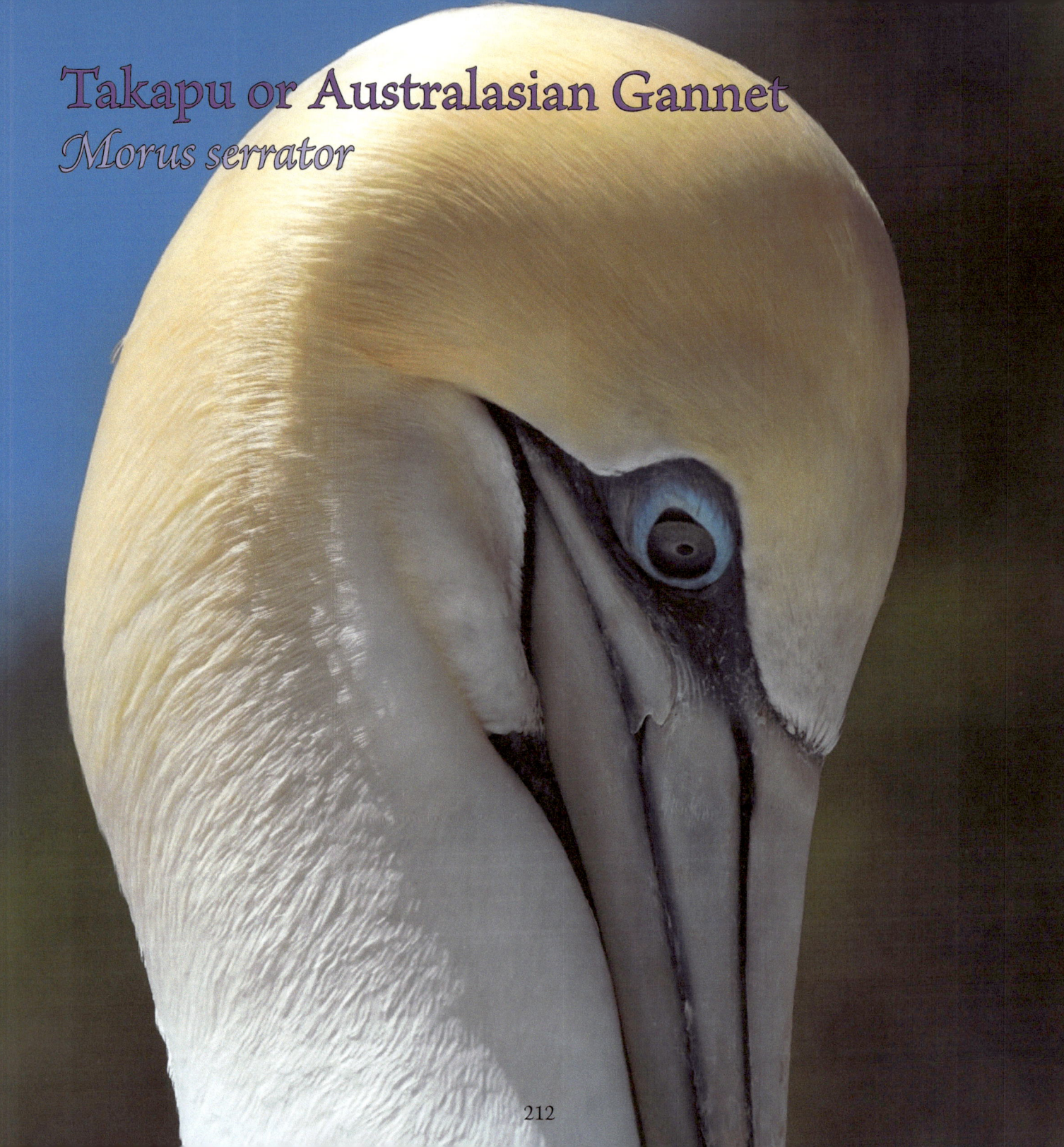

Takapu or Australasian Gannet
Morus serrator

"Fraser Darling has put forward the concept of 'mass stimulation'... He has suggested 'that for birds which nest together in large groups a very important factor in the safety of the colony is the need for most of the eggs to be laid at approximately the same time... In order that this may occur, the majority of the pairs must come to full breeding condition at the same time, and this is accomplished by the sexual excitation produced by the mass of birds in the colonial unit'... Seaweed is, without exception, collected on the surface of the sea and brought by the 'presumed' male bird and presented to the sitting partner. These fresh additions to the nest material are often followed by a complete mutual 'greeting ceremony'... 'Solo-dance.' This is a solitary bowing performance of a bird sitting on the nest: The bird rises on its feet, stretches backwards, shakes its head quickly, and then bows three or four times to the right or to the left; the wings are lowered partly extended and held in this position apart from the body. The whole performance, during which a sharp call is uttered, lasts 5 to 7 seconds. The 'solo–dance' ceremony is frequently started by a bird on a nest without egg. This performance seems to be contagious, and several birds sitting nearby, with or without eggs, may follow suit. It is readily started by any disturbance, i.e., the alighting of a bird in the colony, appearance of a human, or for no apparent reason at all... This usually gregarious performance seems to fall into the category of activities of the gannets leading to the 'Mass Greeting Ceremony.' This mutual display of the Australasian Gannet... actually starts when a mate, on returning to the nesting site, brakes quickly when a few feet away and, frequently calling, lands sharply alongside the nest. Immediately after landing, the birds face

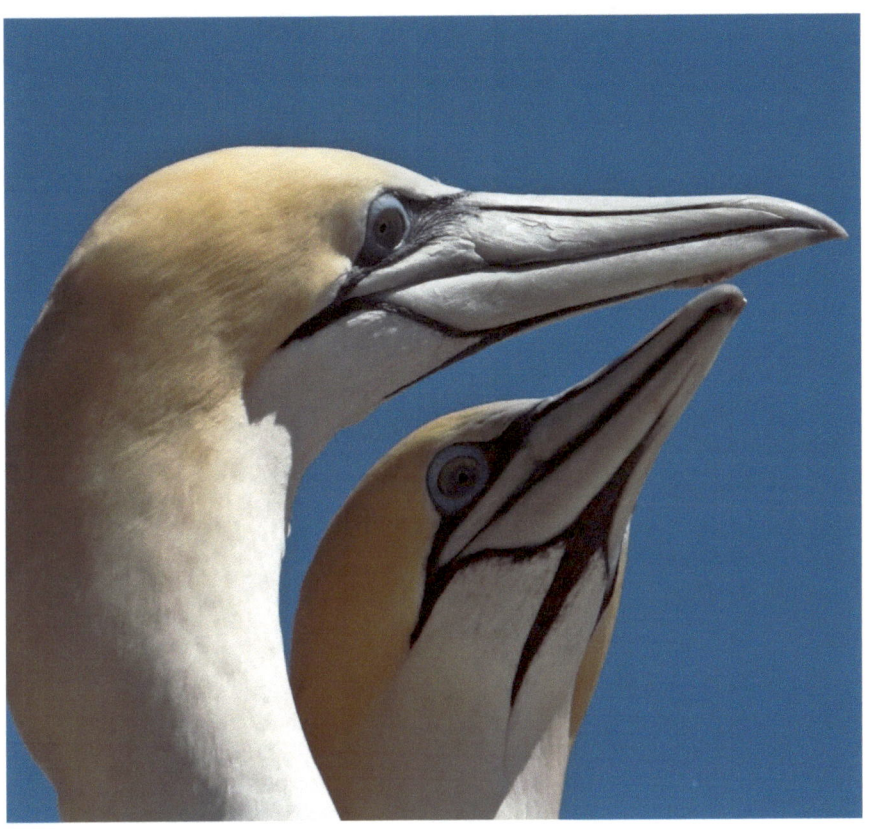

each other, beaks touching, necks stretched, and calling. The beaks are then crossed in a tapping action about six times on alternate sides, the sound being audible at 10–12 ft. in spite of noise made by other birds. It would seem that the demonstrating pair need to express, in an audible manner, the ecstatic emotions which seem to permeate both partners. This is followed by waving and dipping of heads and by stroking of upper half of necks on alternate sides about six times. During the whole of this performance, which lasts up to 10–12 seconds, the birds seem to be completely oblivious of other birds or to nearby man. The tapping of beaks and neck stretching is sometimes repeated. Birds then quieten down, often engaging in an affectionate mutual search for external parasites. At no time does the feeding of a mate occur during this or other displays."

~K. A. Wodzicki and C. P. McMeekan, 1946-47

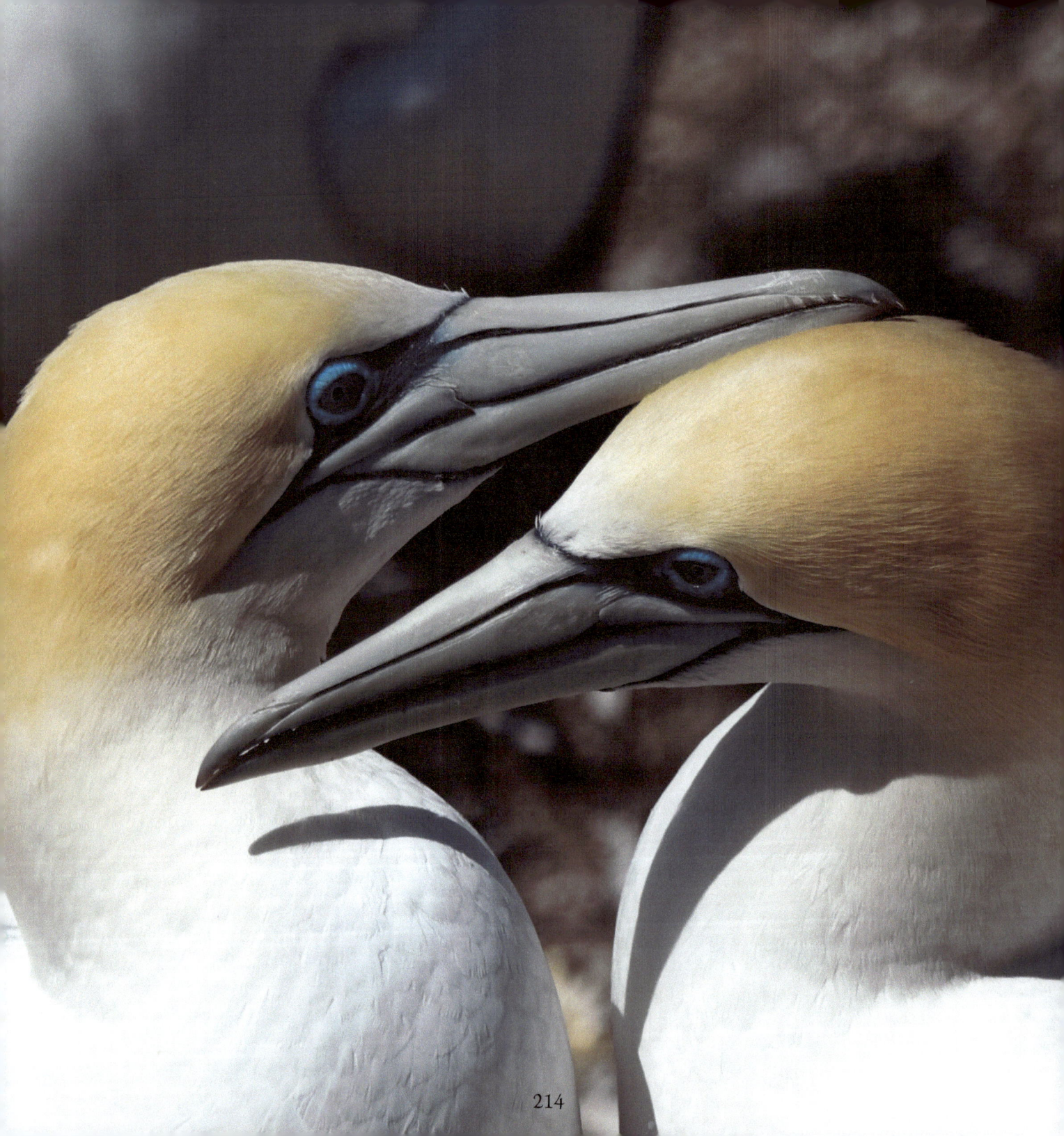

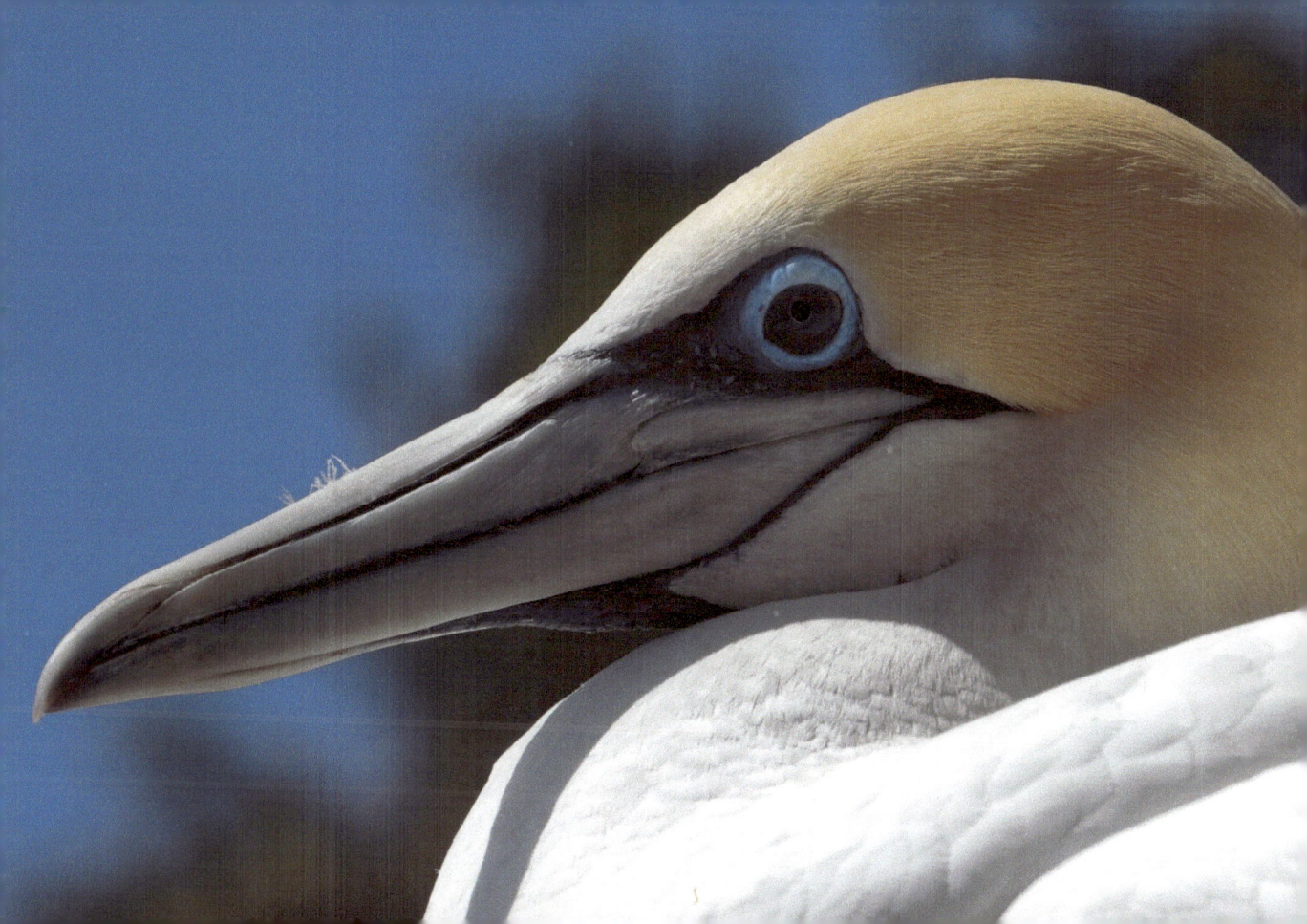

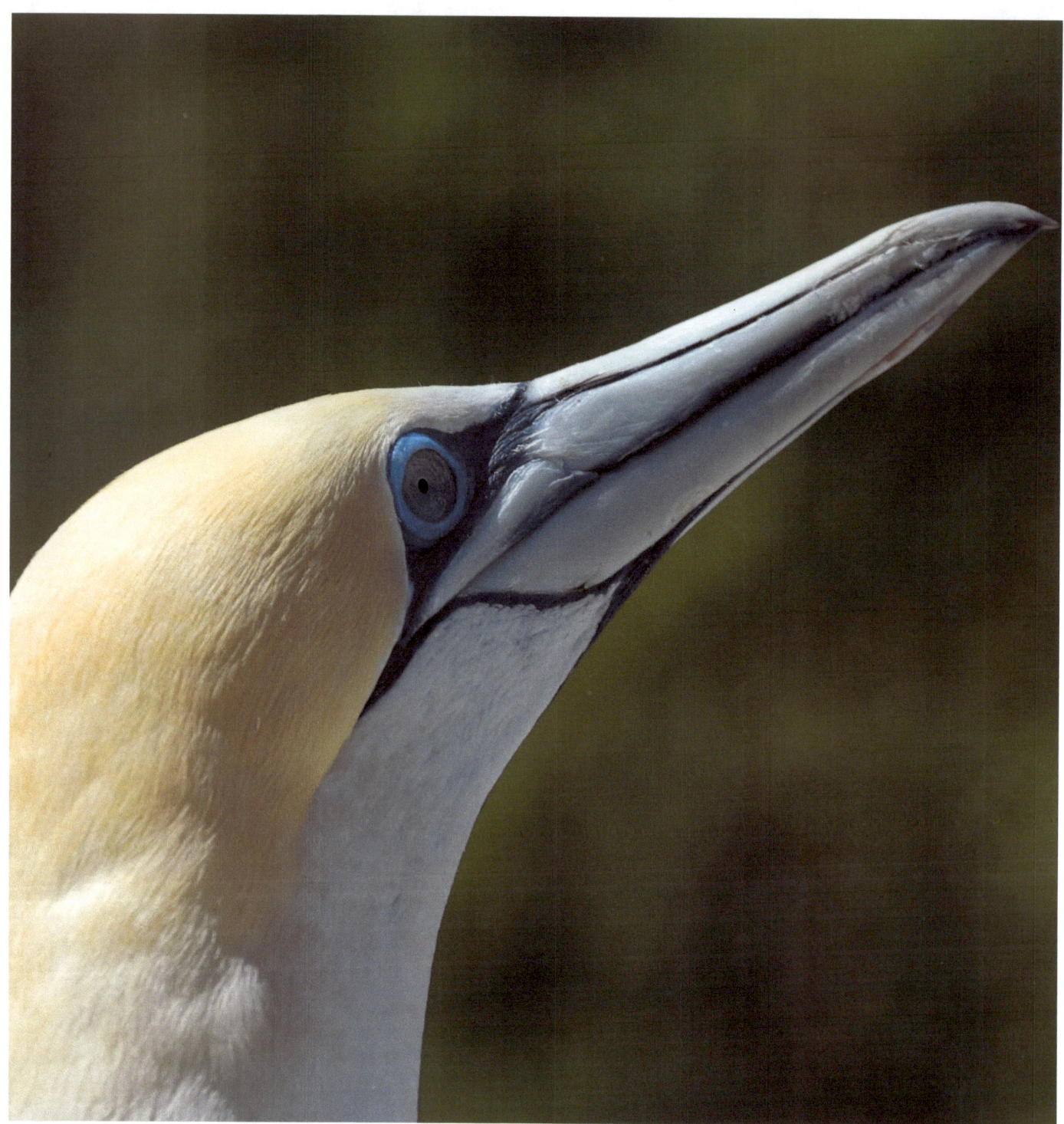

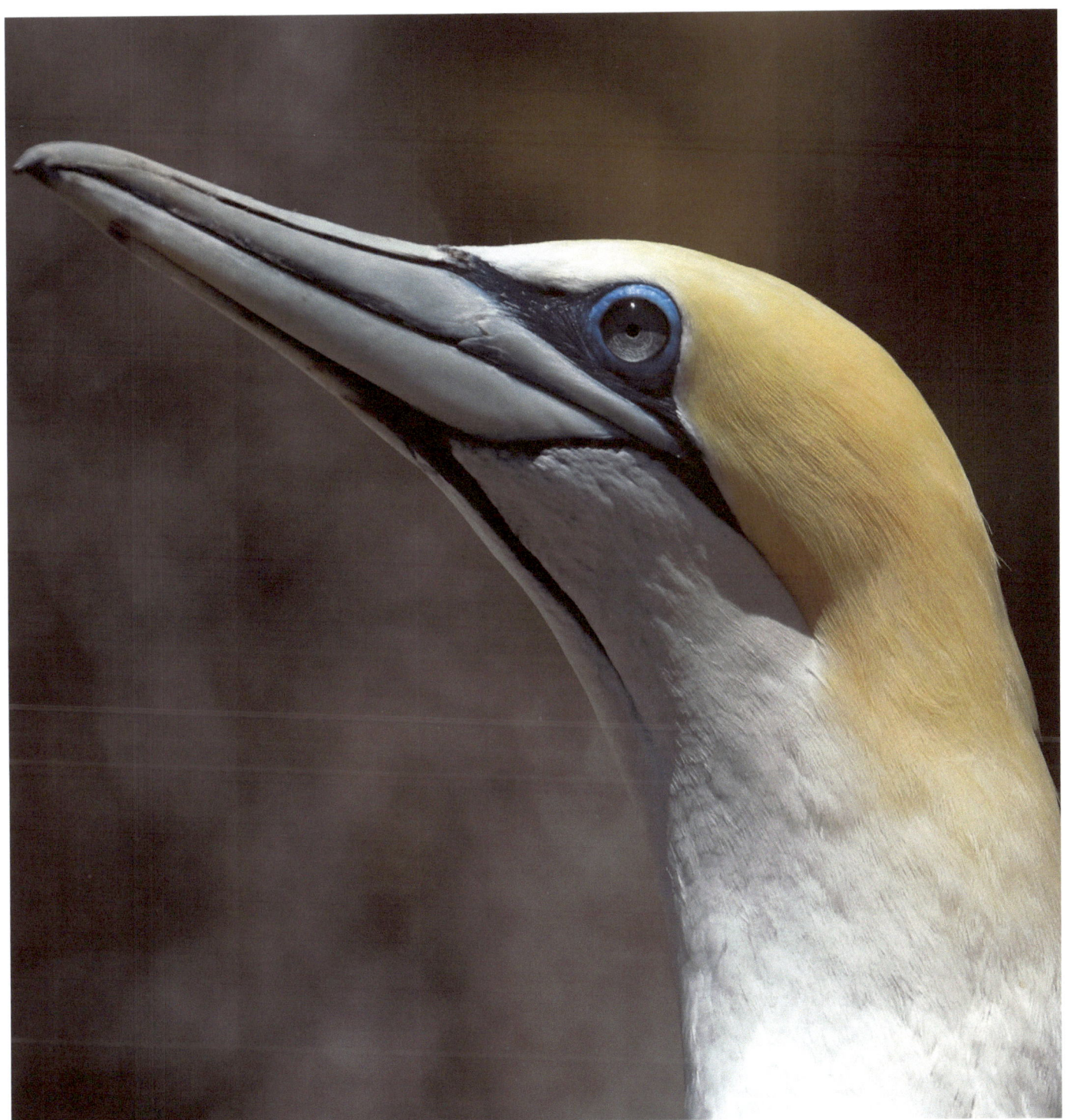

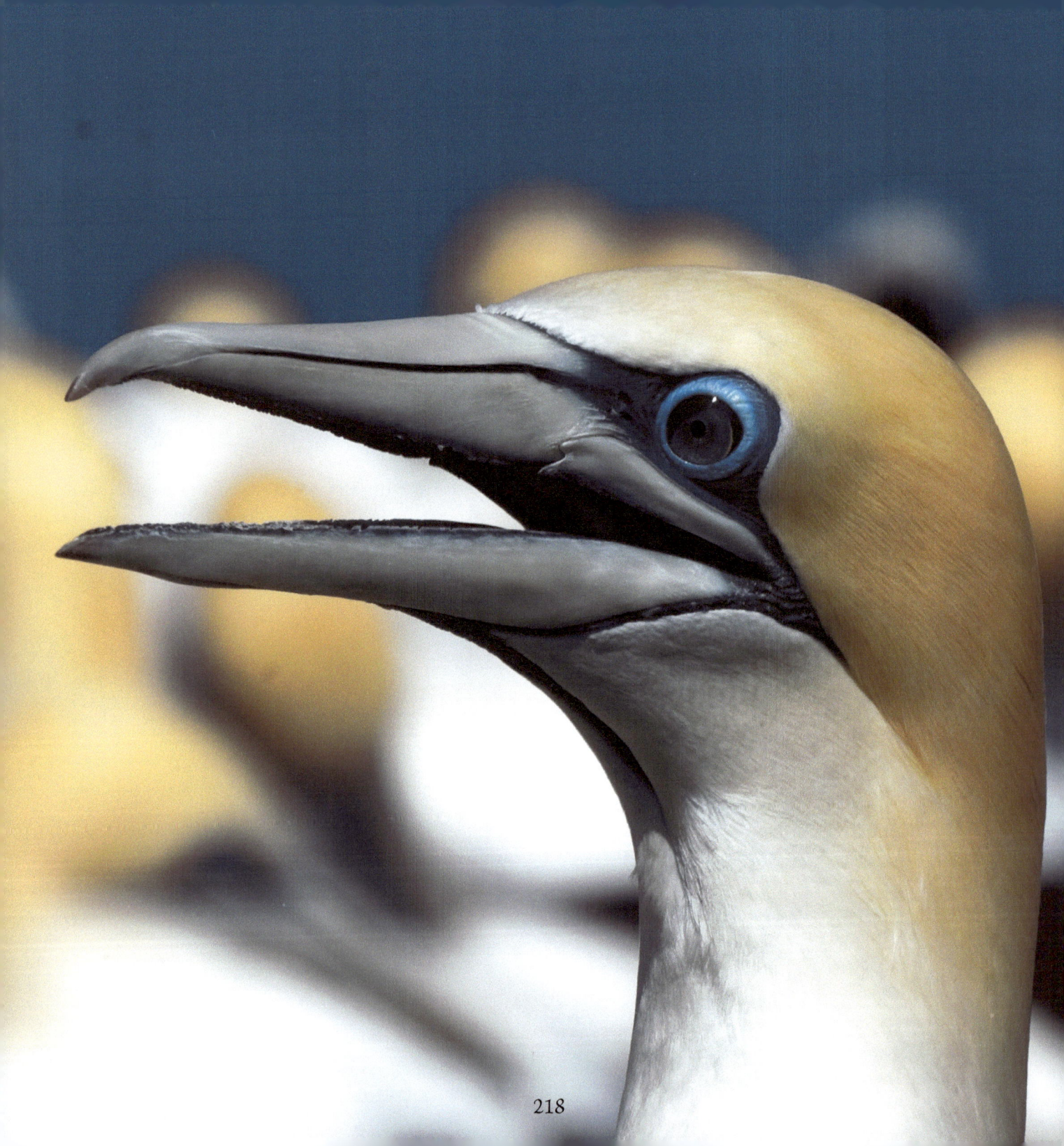

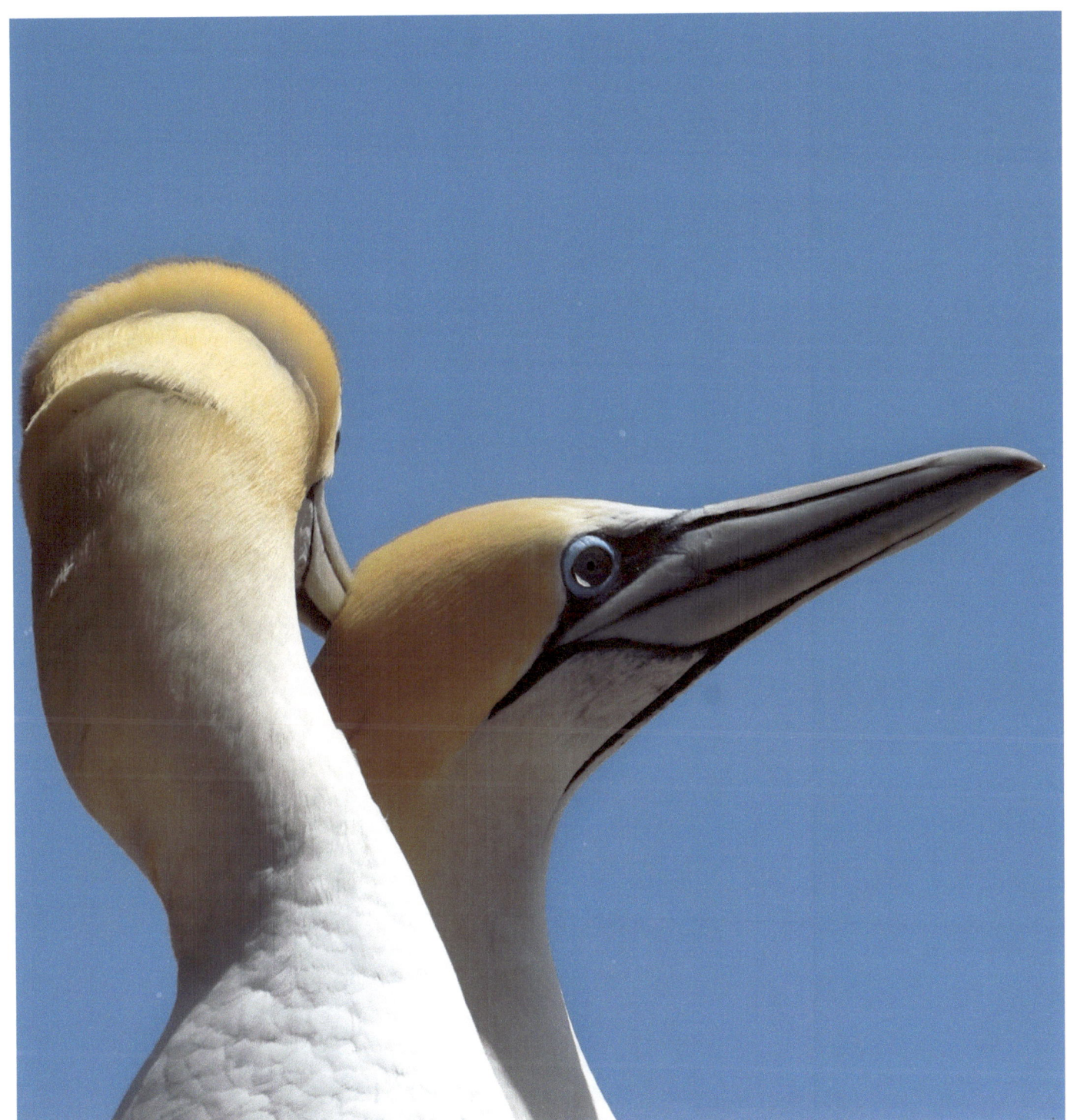

Toroa or Royal Albatross
Diomedea epomophora

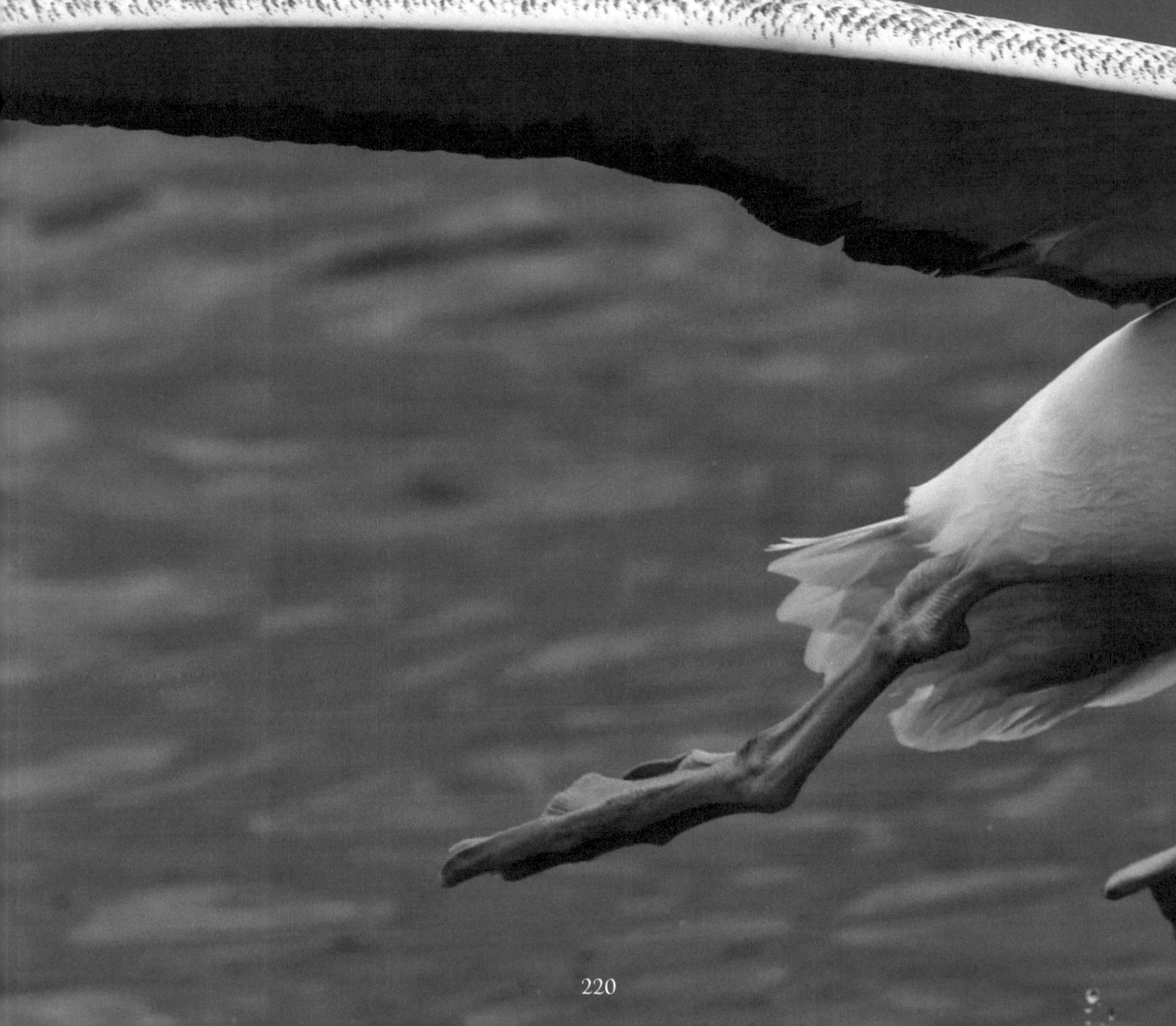

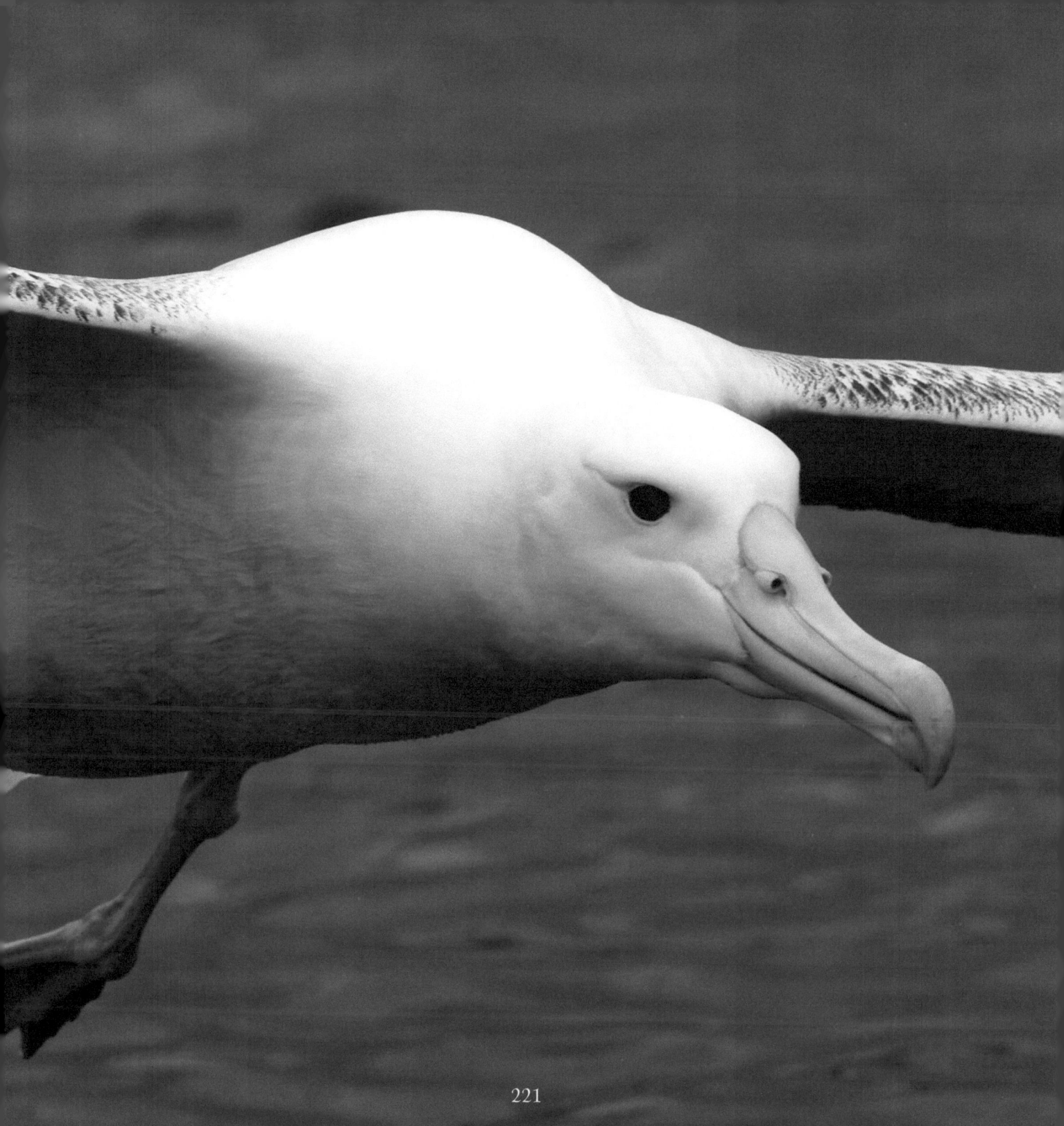

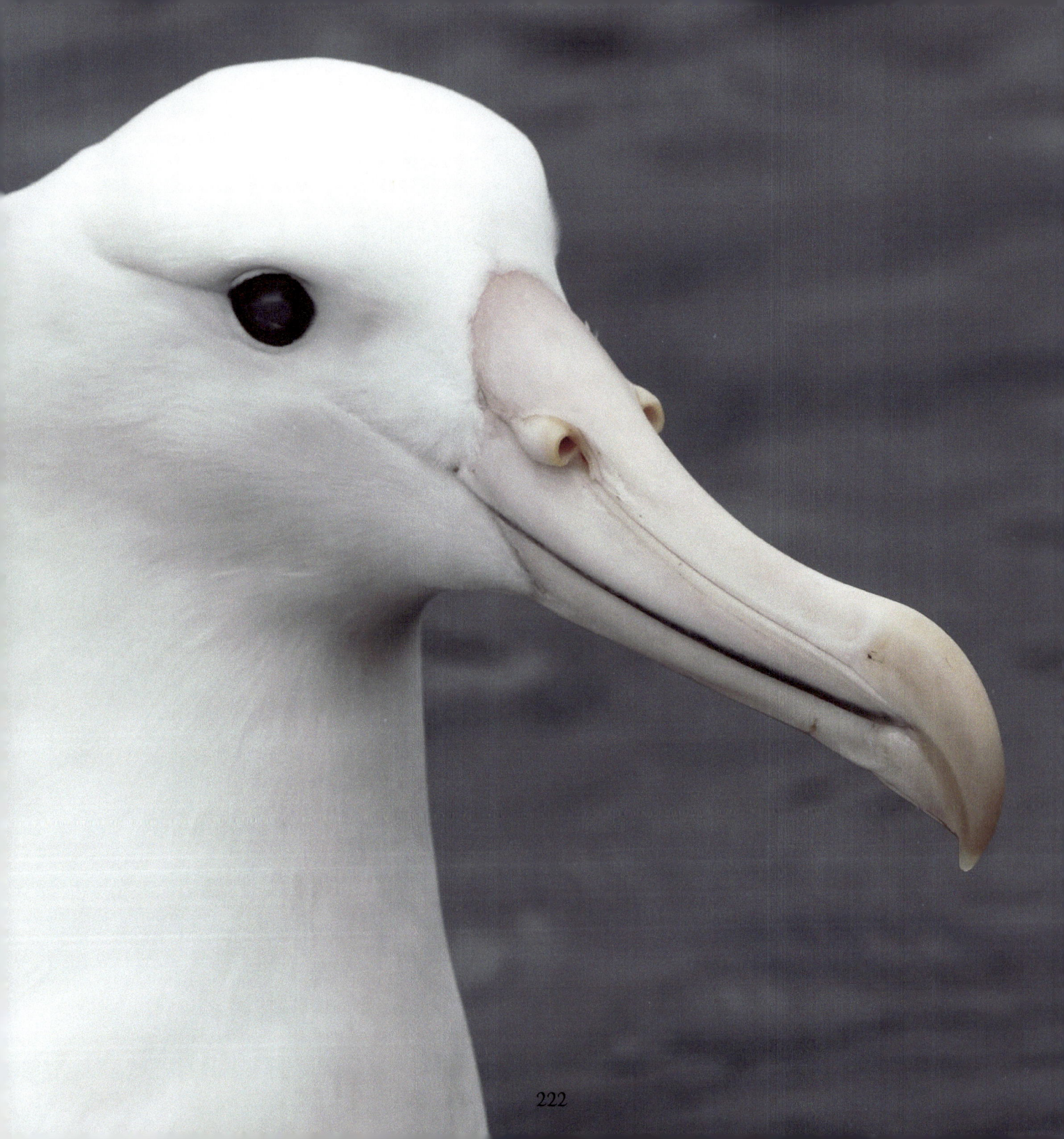

"On the morning of the 5th March a very beautiful Albatros (Diomedea regia) appeared on the scene. It was of enormous size, and wholly white, except the pinions beyond the second flexure of the wing, looking in the distance like a huge Gannet held against the sky, and so conspicuous in its albinism that it could be readily distinguished among a hundred ordinary birds. So near an approach to perfect albinism I have not before met with among the Albatroses... But for the black-tipped wings this magnificent Albatros might have been the one that so narrowly escaped being hooked by the Arawa' passengers. He cruises about amongst the other Albatroses, but always at a distance from the ship. The individuality of this bird is so pronounced that it can be distinguished from the rest at almost any distance, and it will be interesting to note how long it will follow the steamer. It seems to me that we have not yet solved the problem involved in the flight of the Albatros–a rapid, well-sustained motion, ever against the wind, with scarcely any visible movement of the wings... The most remarkable point is that the bird, without any apparent effort–without any visible movement of the limbs themselves–by merely shifting its position so as to alter the angle of incidence, performs an elegant sweep, cutting a great figure 8 in the air, and, as Froude puts it, with the adroitness of an accomplished skater on an untouched field of ice. The one thing that surprises one most, next to this marvellous power of sustained flight, is that the Albatros will soar for hours together without once descending to the surface of the water to feed.... 6th March.–My White Albatros appeared again about 11 a.m. to-day, so that it must have been on the wing during part of the night. There was an easterly gale blowing, and few birds to be seen... 7th March... About 2 p.m. my White Albatros came up to us again, and coursed about in wide circles as before, but disappeared long before nightfall. 8th March. There was a heavy south-easterly gale during the night, lasting four hours. It had abated somewhat in the morning, but I did not expect to see the White Albatros again. However, he overtook us once more about 2 p.m., and, after a circuit fully a mile in extent, he vanished in the wide expanse, returning later on, and remaining with us till the close of the day. 9th March... I watched with much interest for the reappearance of my White Albatros, and, to my delight, true to time, a little after 2 p.m. he came sweeping up in grand style. Since we first made his acquaintance, on the 5th instant, he has performed a voyage, measured in a straight line, of 970 miles; but when the never-ending circles of flight and gyrations in the air are taken into account, probably three times that distance, or, say, 3,000 miles–perhaps even more! This is one of those incidents in the romance of natural history that set the mind thinking; and one is quite prepared to accept Mr. Gould's conclusions as to an Albatros being able to encircle the globe in its unwearied flight. 10th March. When the morning broke the wind had fallen, and there was a haze over the ocean which had not cleared away as the day advanced. I looked out anxiously for my White Albatros at the usual hour, but he did not reappear from behind those misty veils, and we saw him no more."

~Sir Walter L. Buller, 1893

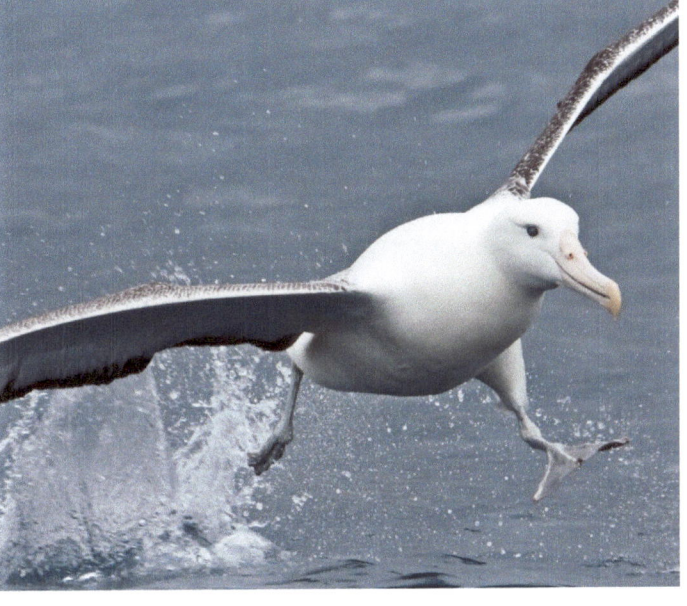

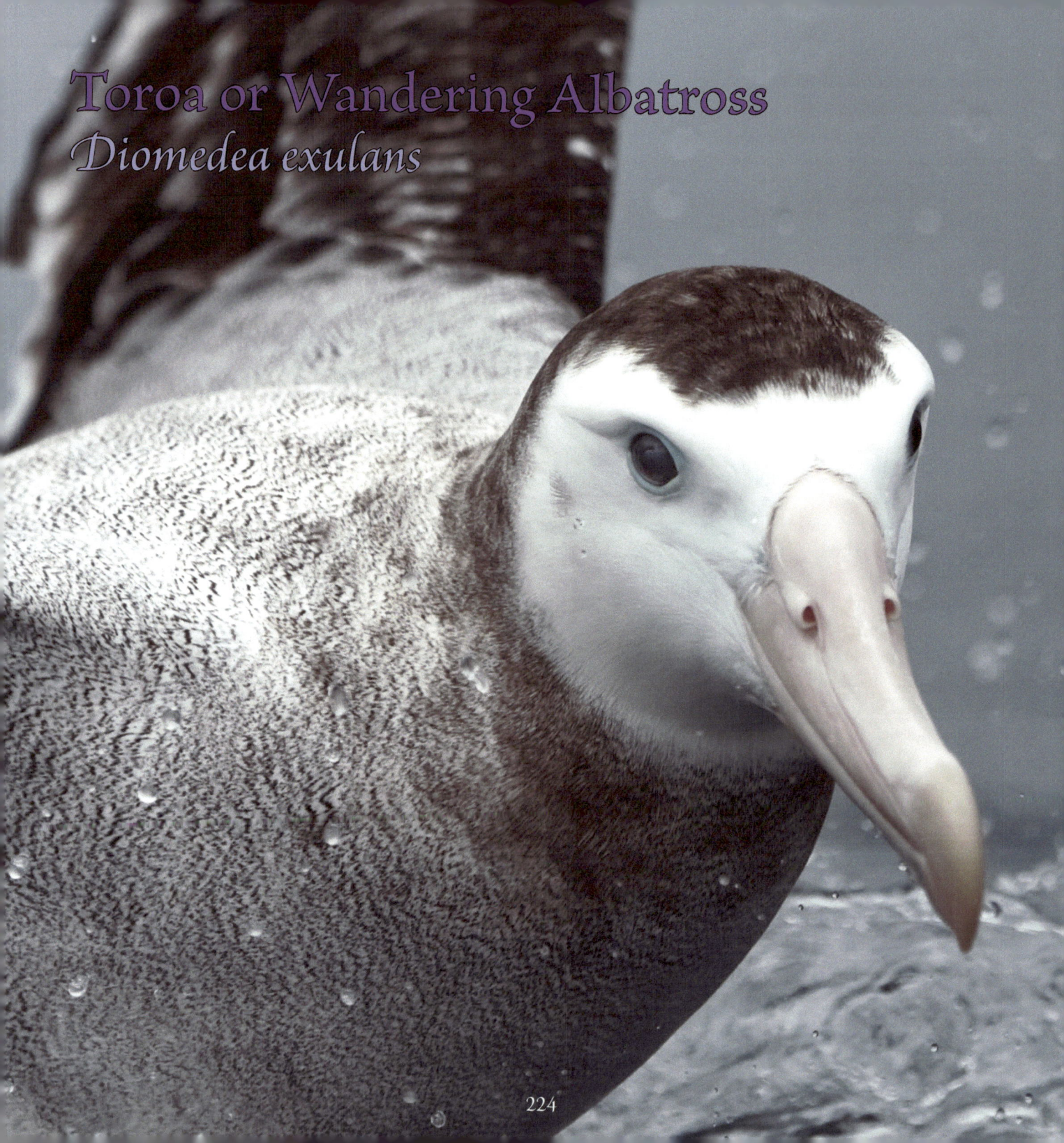

Toroa or Wandering Albatross
Diomedea exulans

"This noble bird may justly be called the king among the sea-birds. Many times during my sea-voyages have I admired its flight and easy sailing over the waves, as it followed our vessel, hundreds of miles from the nearest land. Its power of flight surpasses that of most birds, and is easily accounted for by the unusual development of the muscles of the breast and wings, the latter being equal to, if not stronger than, those of the eagle… When there is little wind and the ocean is calm, albatrosses have great difficulty in rising from the water; when there is a swell they run along the water and rise with a wave. When alighting, on nearing the surface they bend the head back, curve the wings upwards, beating the air with numerous laboured strokes, then, straightening their feet, they let themselves fall. They are fast swimmers, but cannot dive. Their food, which consists chiefly of some of the lower forms of marine life found floating on the surface of the ocean, they scoop up with their bill in the same manner as the ducks… Notwithstanding the ease and grace of the albatross on the ocean, on the land it is a most clumsy and helpless bird. Its walk is slow and waddling, like that of a duck, and it cannot take flight from a level piece of ground. It is for this reason that these birds have been gifted by nature with the instinct of making their nests on the slopes of mountains, for by running down-hill, and labouring hard with their wings, they can at last acquire momentum sufficient to raise themselves in the air. Once there they exhibit their true power, and are seen to the best advantage."

~A. Reischek, 1888

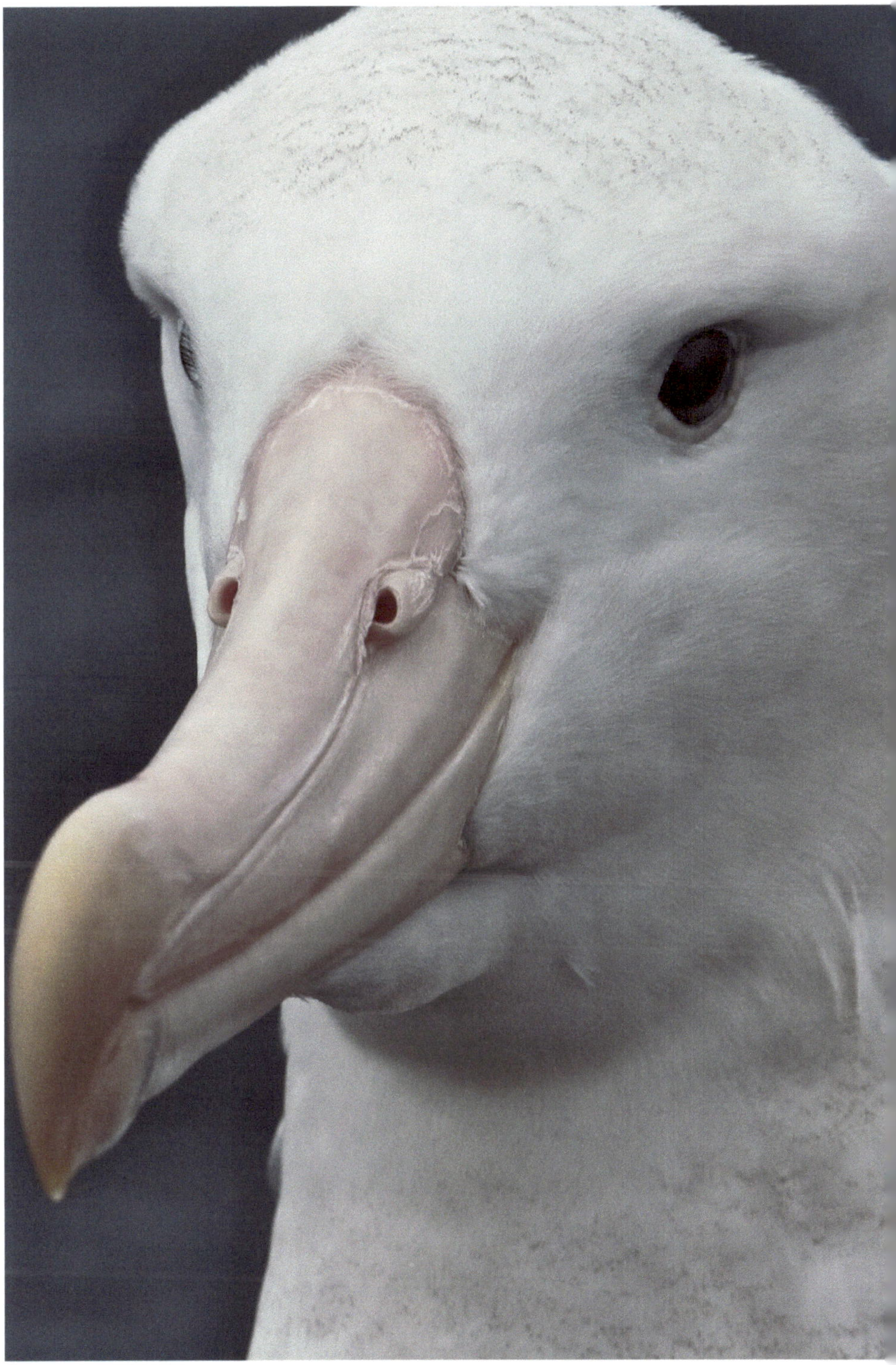

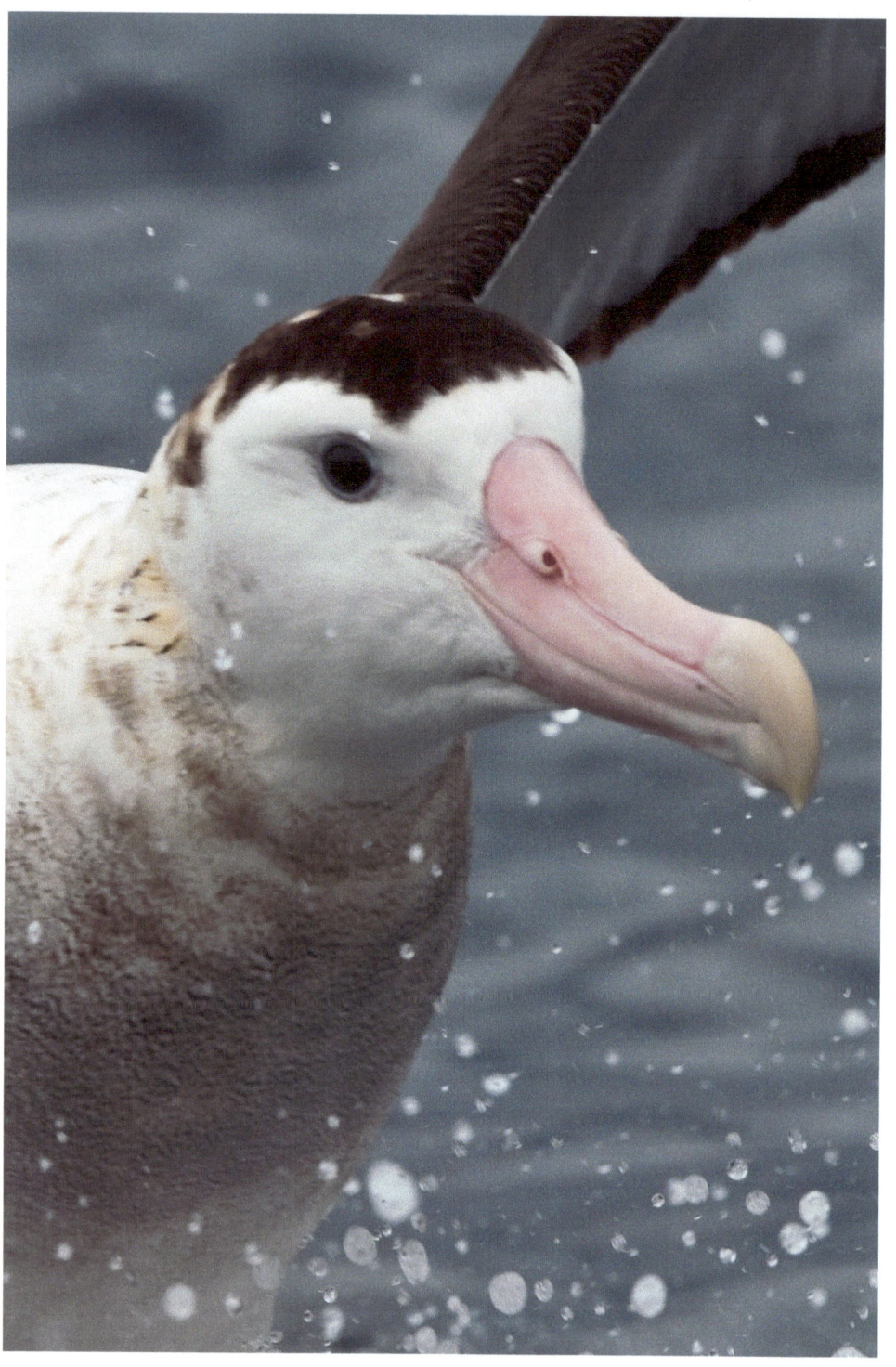

"Captain Fairchild has described to me from personal observation the coming-home of the Wandering Albatros after its long absence from its island sanctuary, and the peremptory manner in which the young bird in possession is ordered to quit the nest, so as to make room for its successor. The ease with which the old birds find their way to their own particular nest among so many is not the least wonderful thing in this marvelous romance of island life. And when I ponder on these strange facts I can only ask, as I have done before, 'What is that divinely-implanted faculty which enables this bird, after wanderings that defy calculation, and perhaps encircle the globe, to find her way back at the right moment, across the pathless deep, to that little speck of rock in mid-ocean where she had cradled her young the season before? Doubtless the same mysterious unerring instinct that guides the swallow in its annual pilgrimage–that leads the pipit, without landmark of any kind, straight to her little nest in the grass, amidst miles of waving tussock–that enables the nesting sea-bird, when she comes back from fishing, to pick out her two painted eggs from amongst the thousands that lie upon the barren rock.'"

~*Sir Walter L. Buller, 1890*

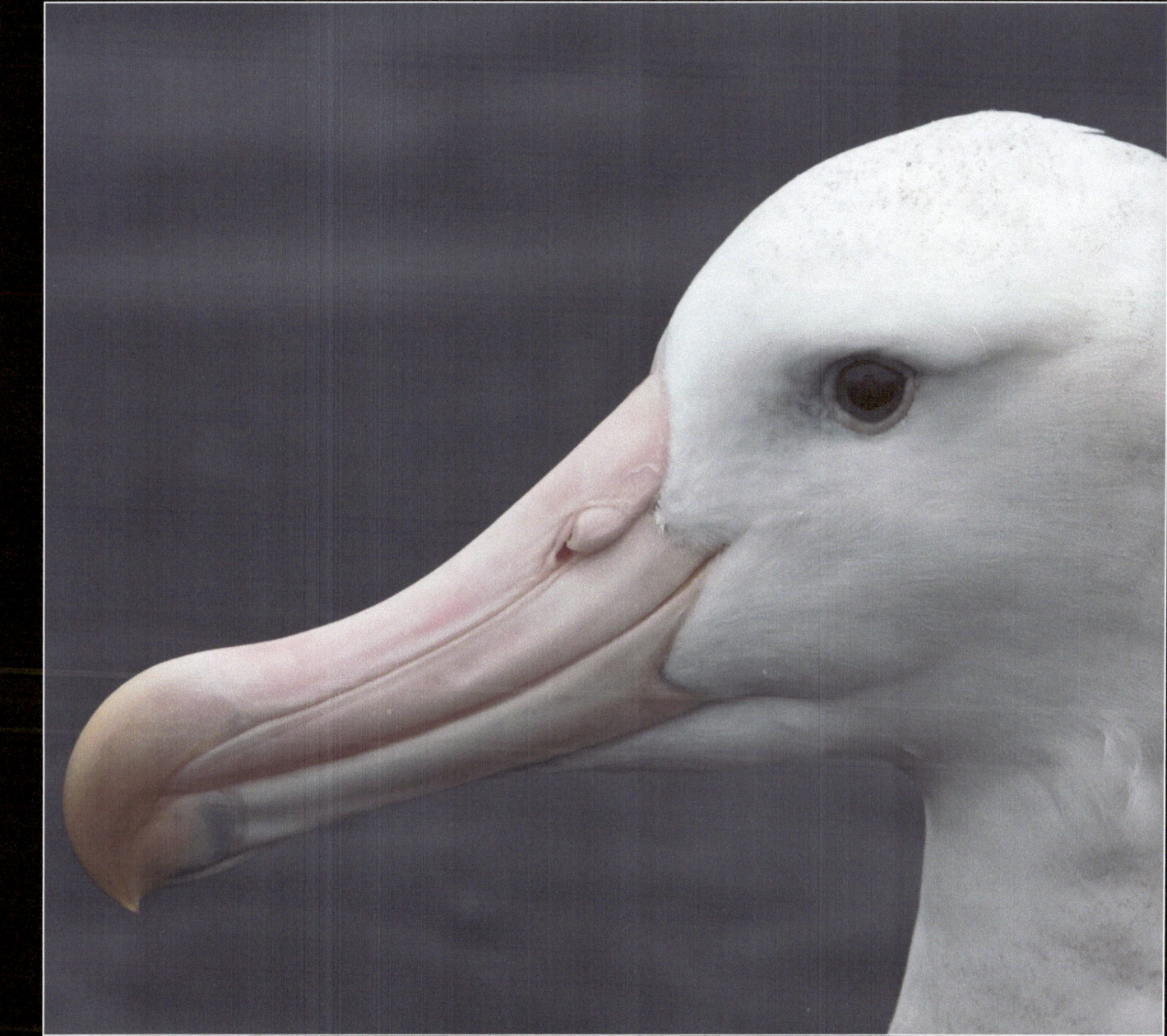

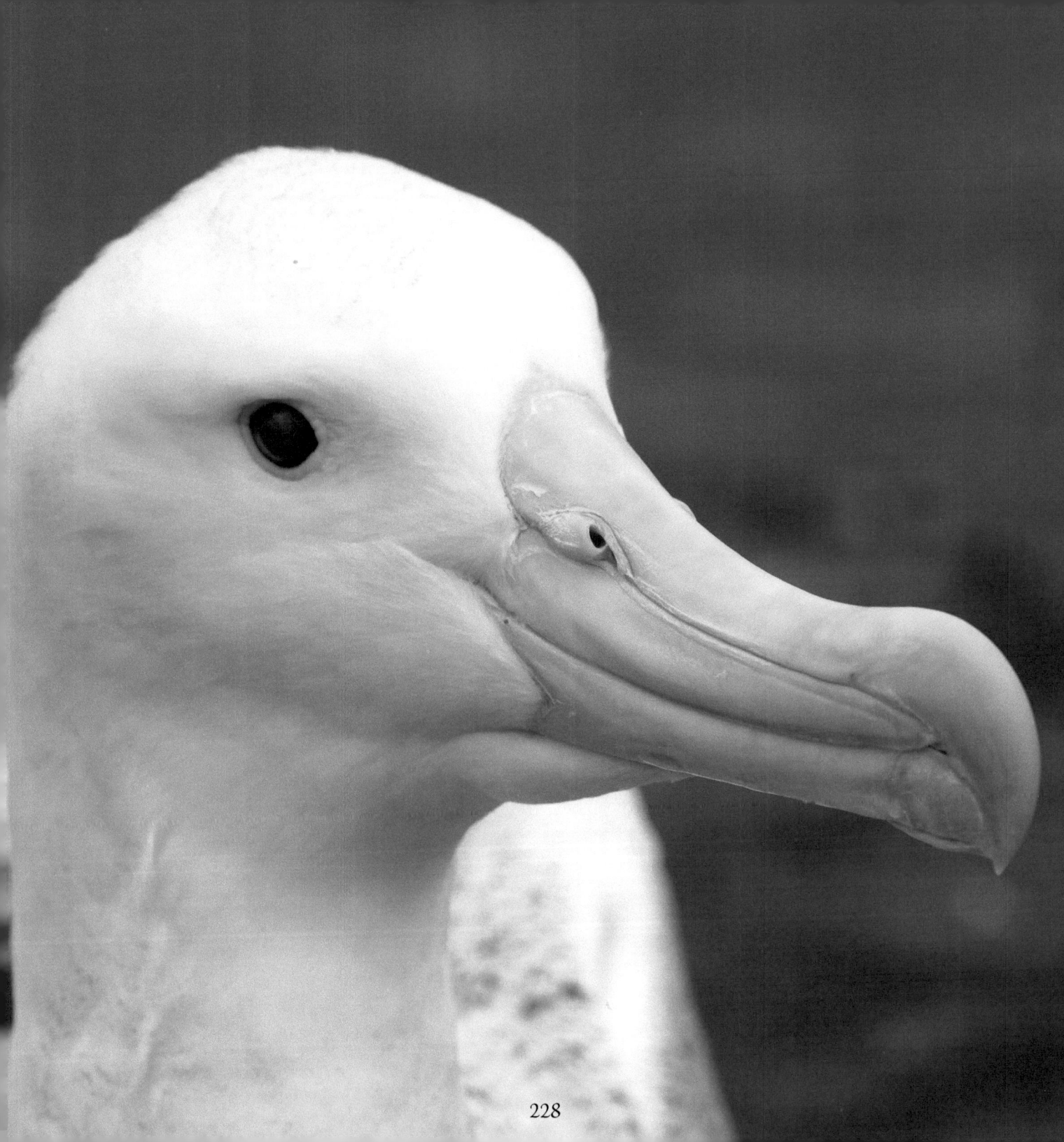

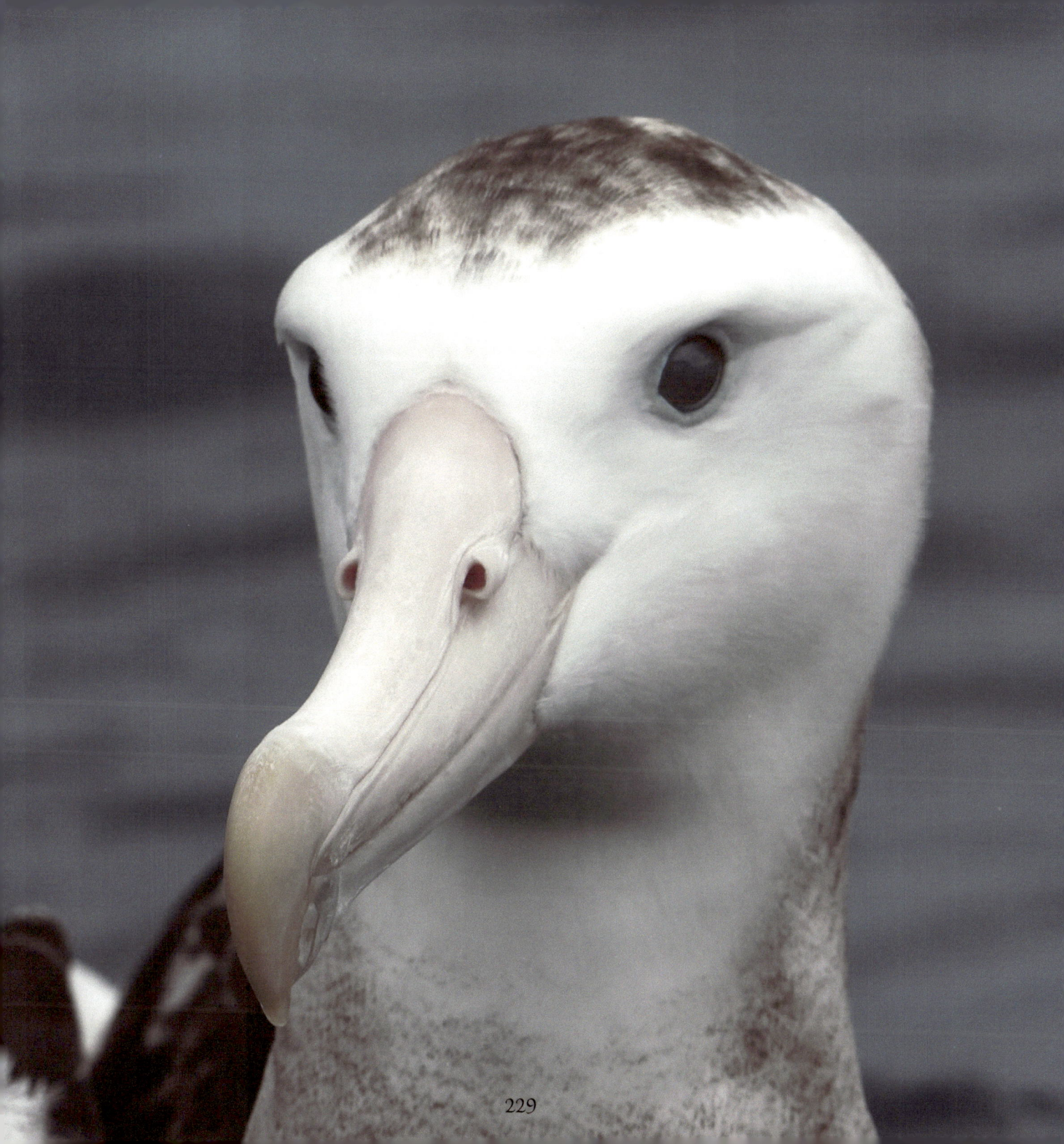

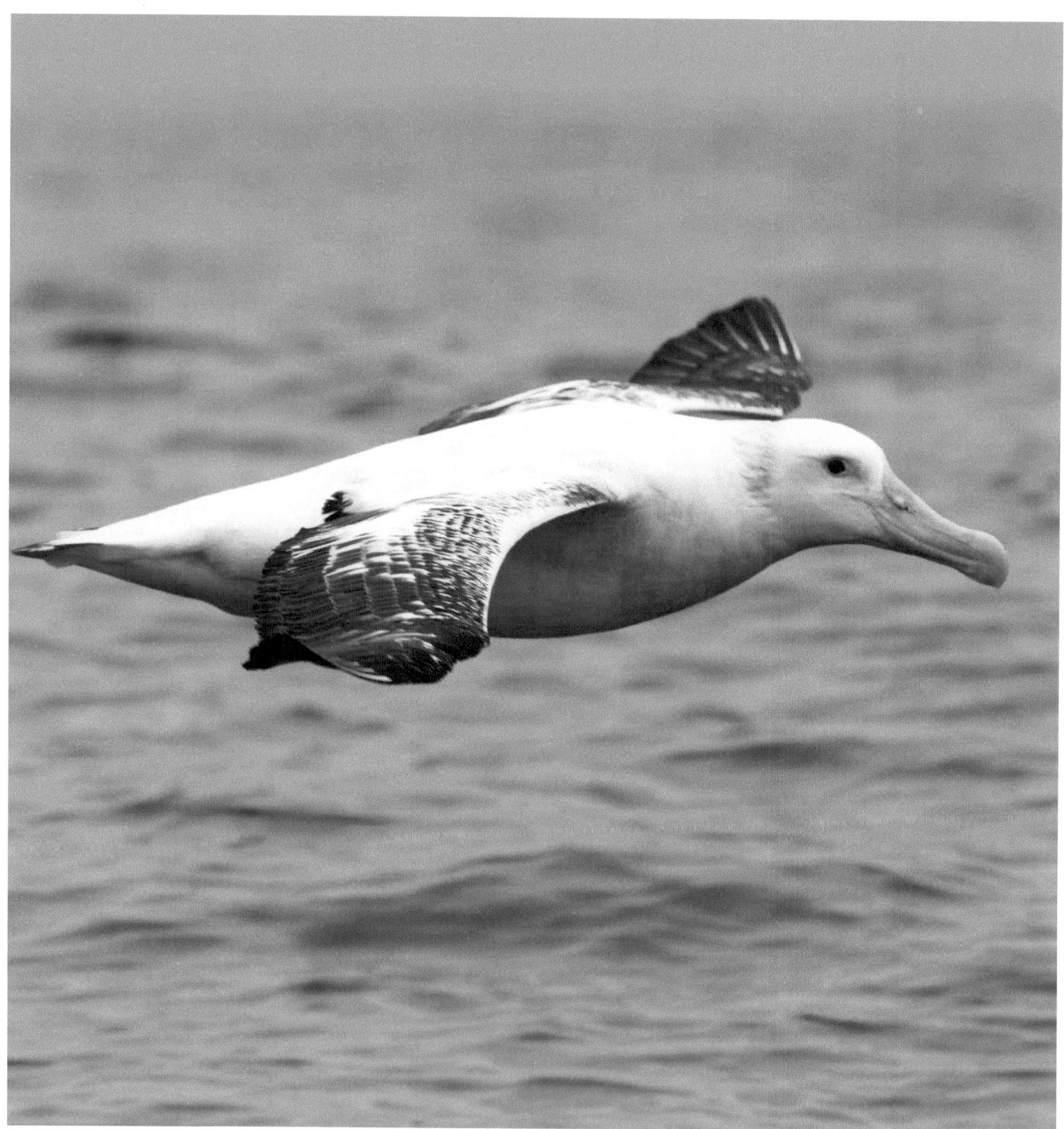

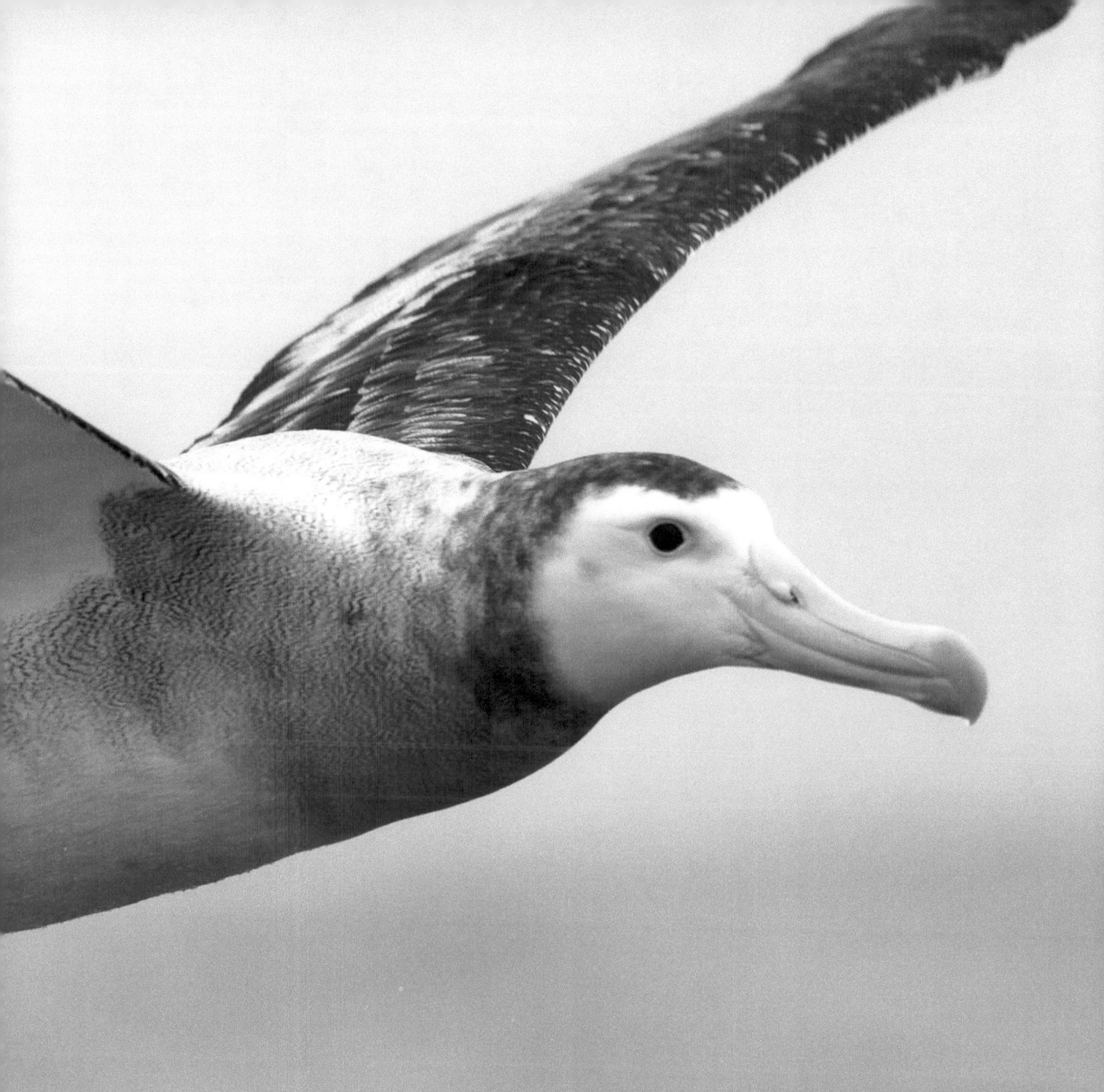

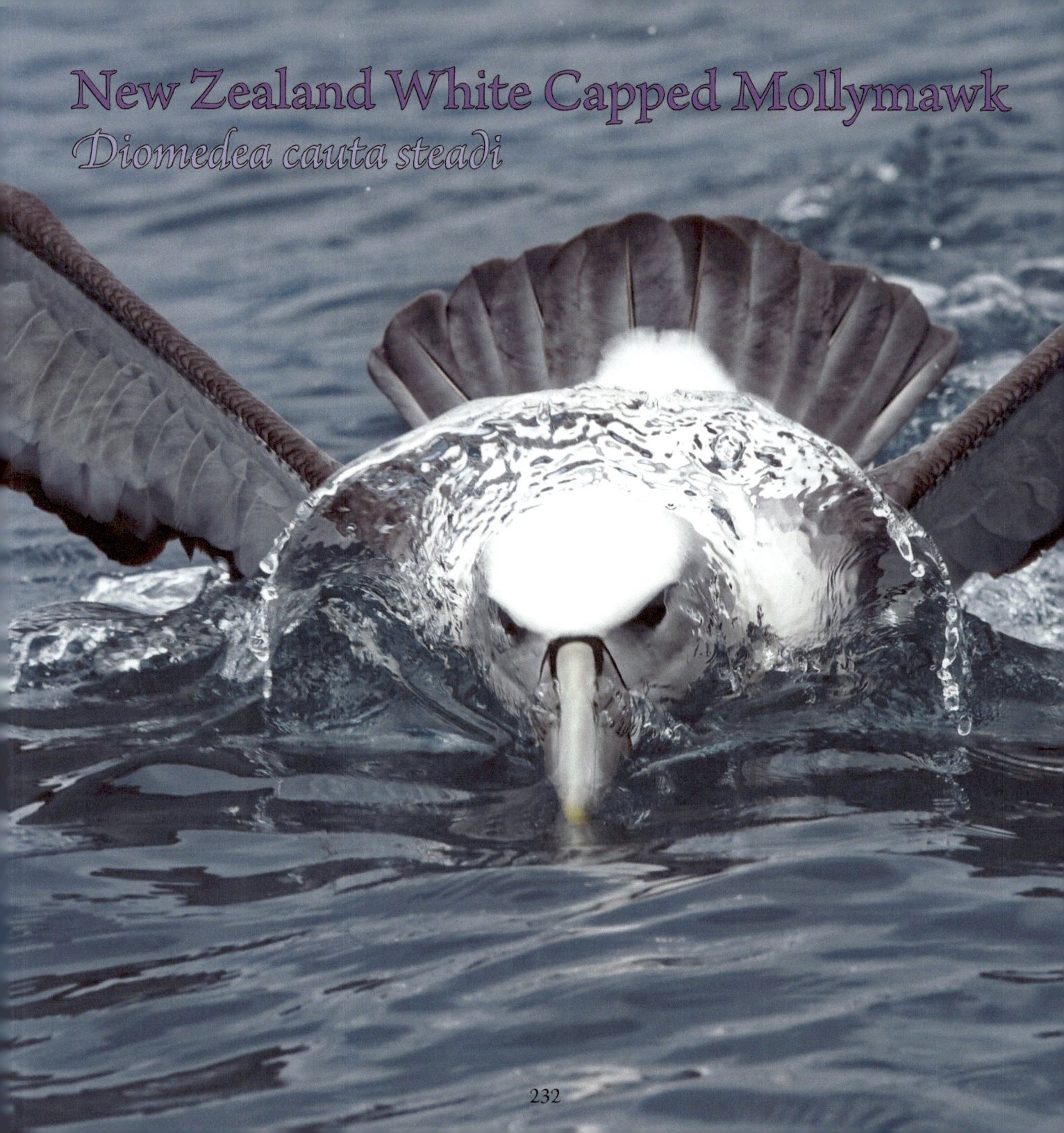

New Zealand White Capped Mollymawk
Diomedea cauta steadi

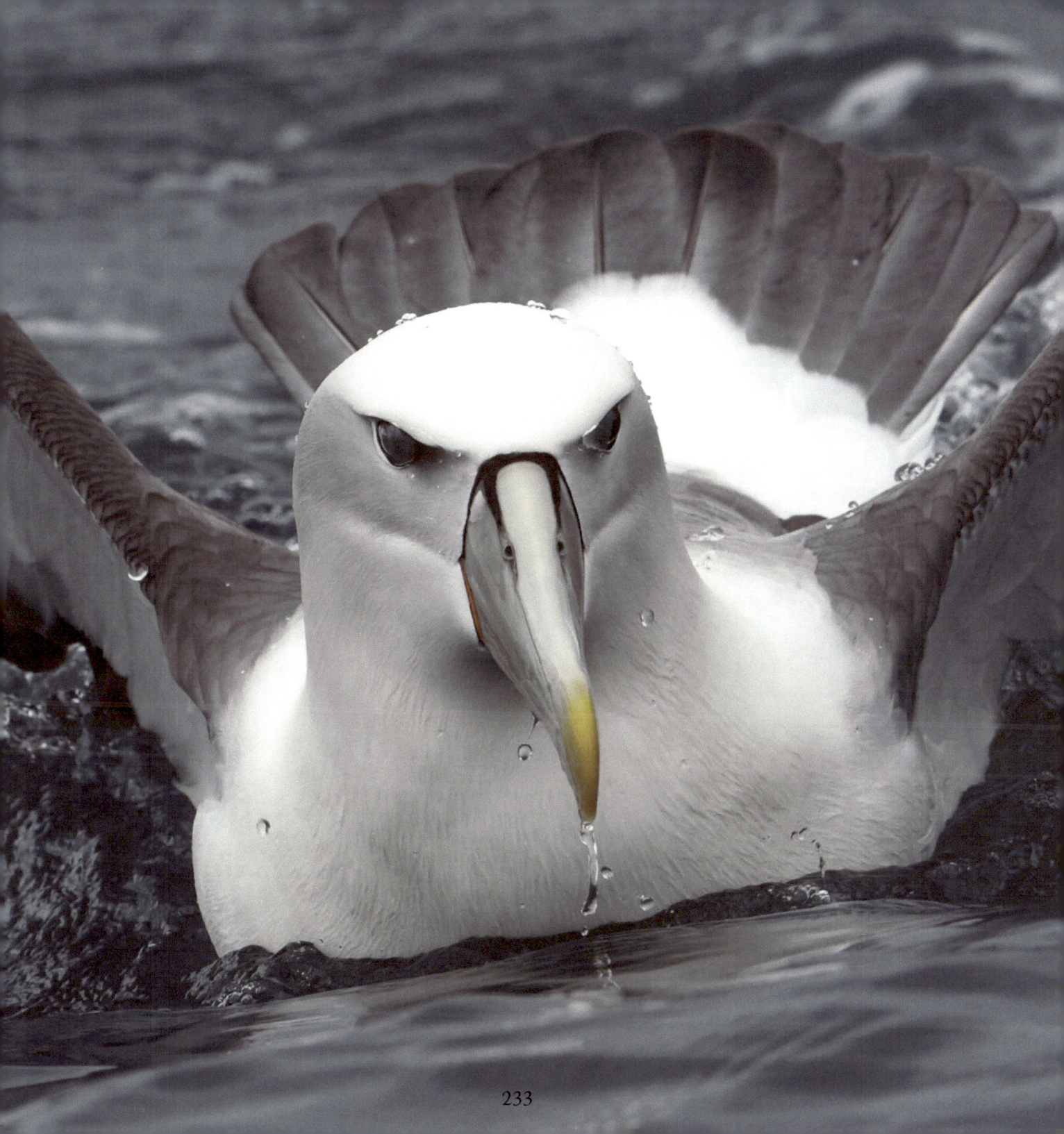

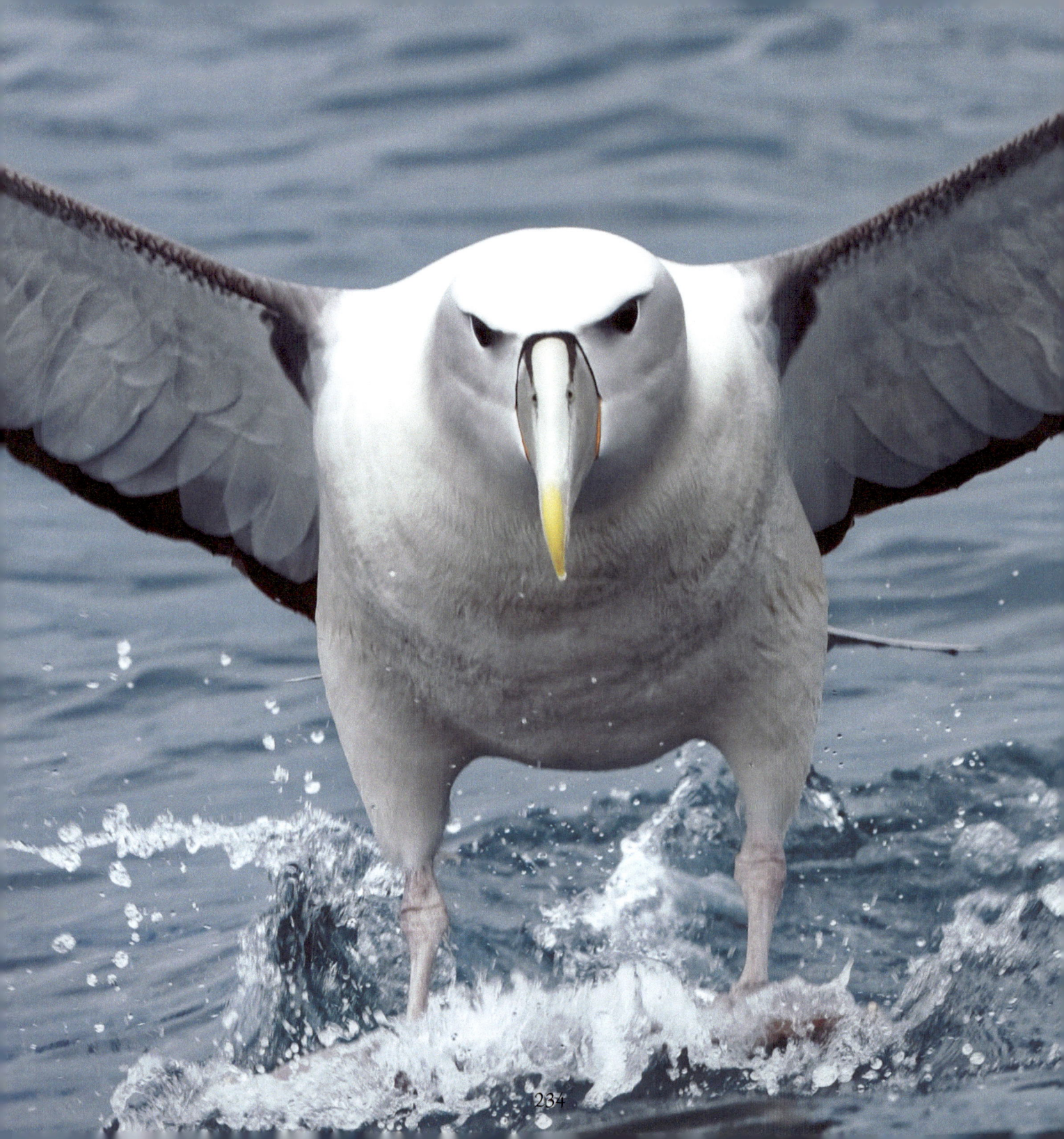

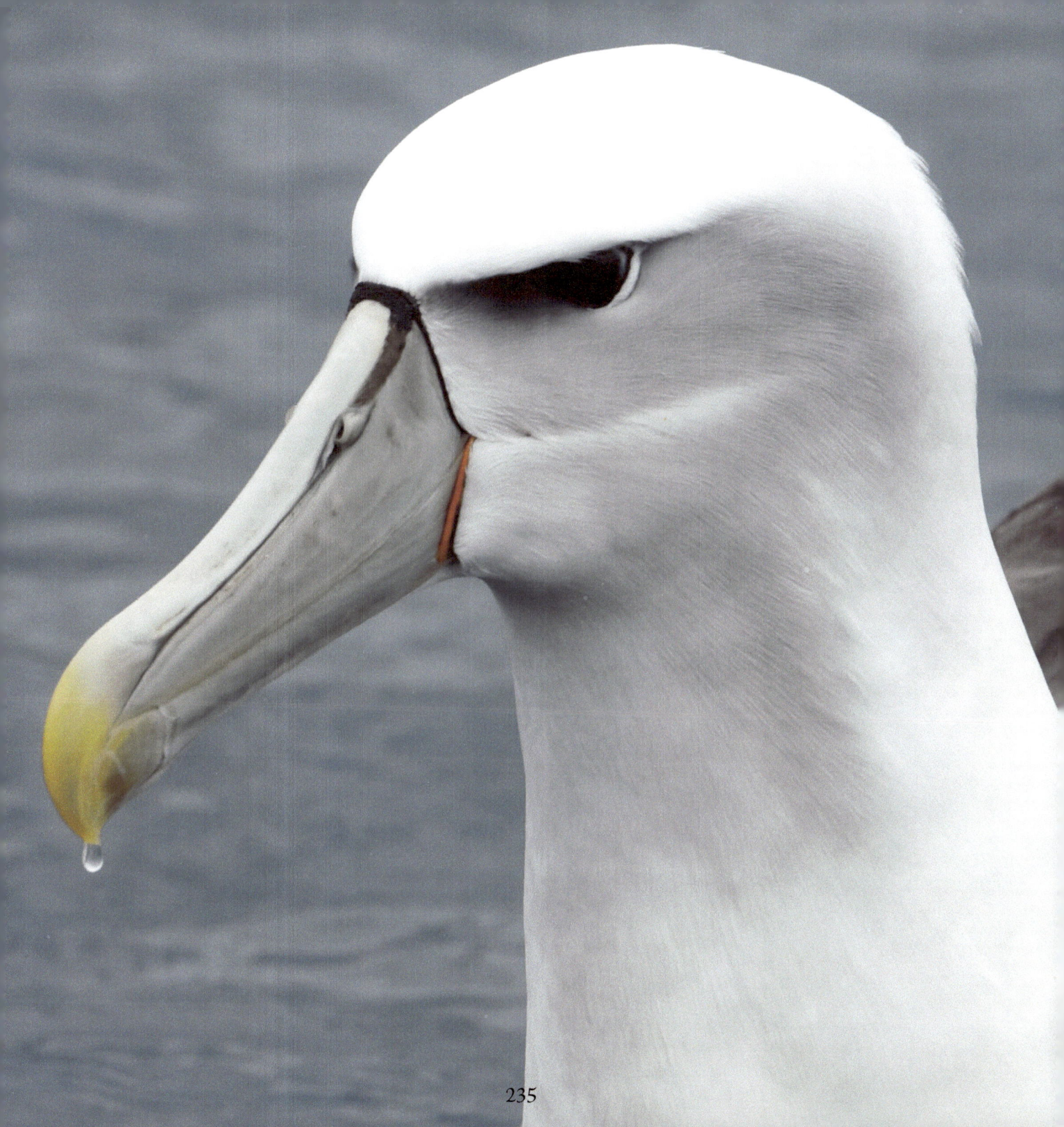

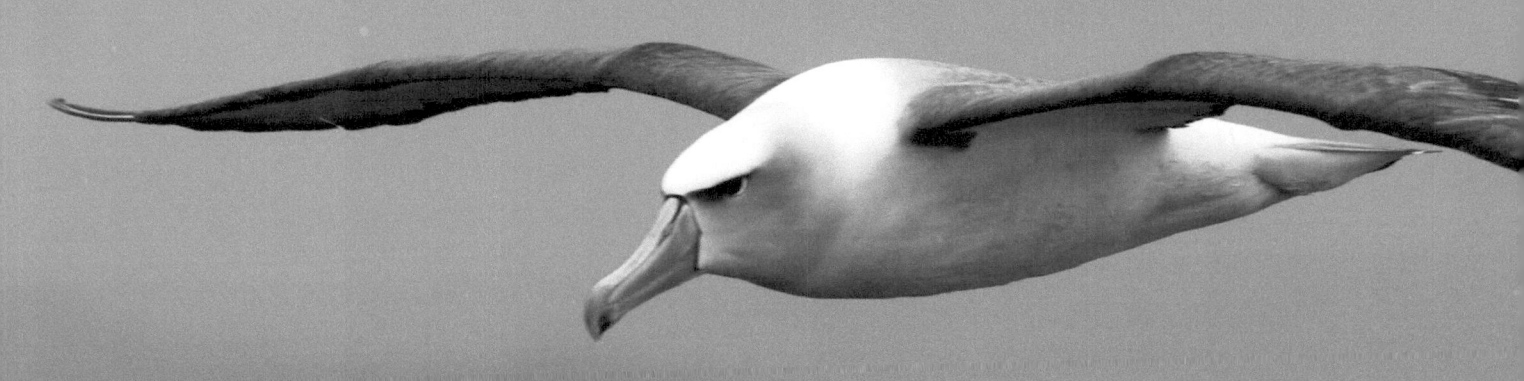

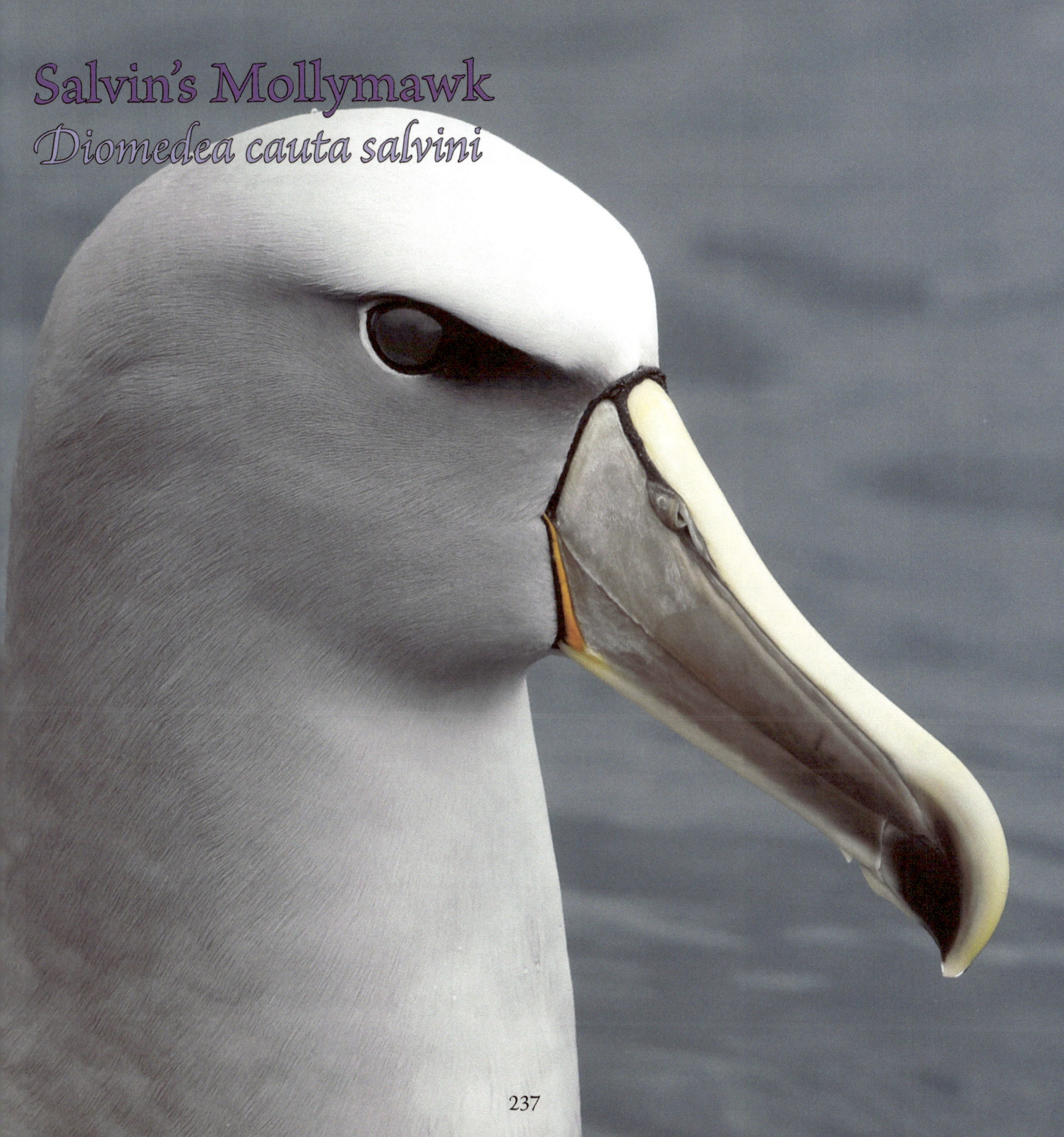

Salvin's Mollymawk
Diomedea cauta salvini

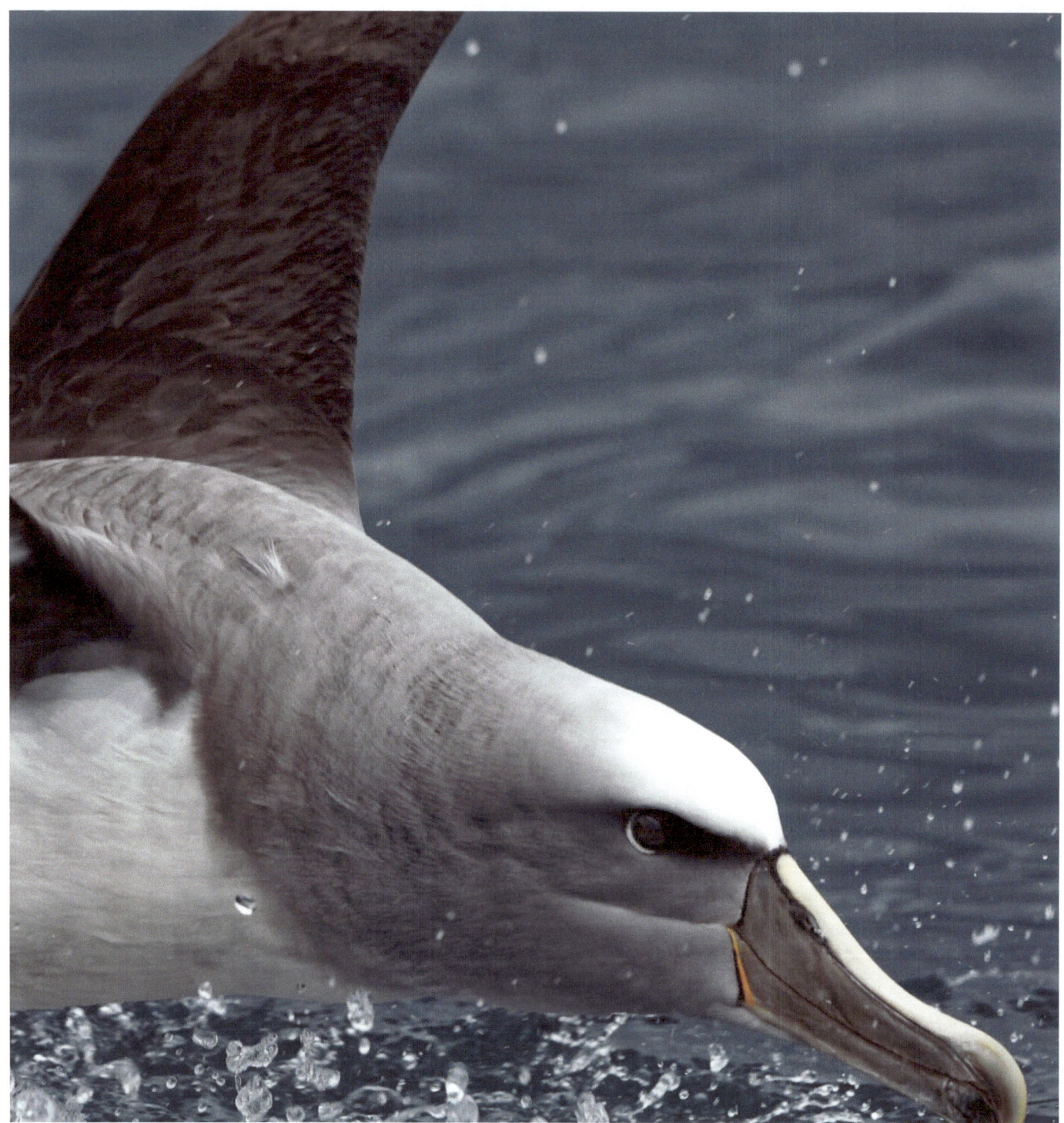

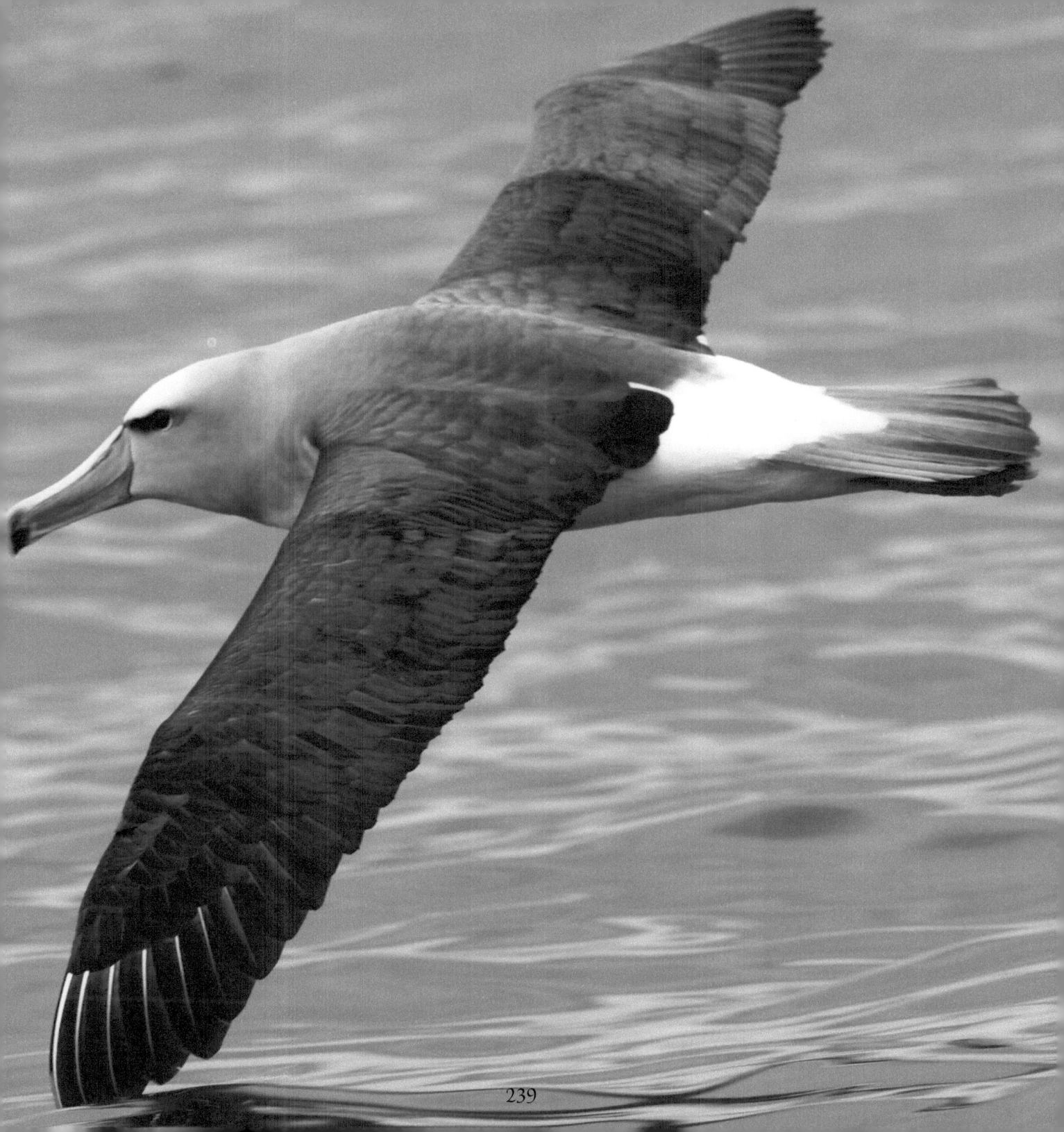

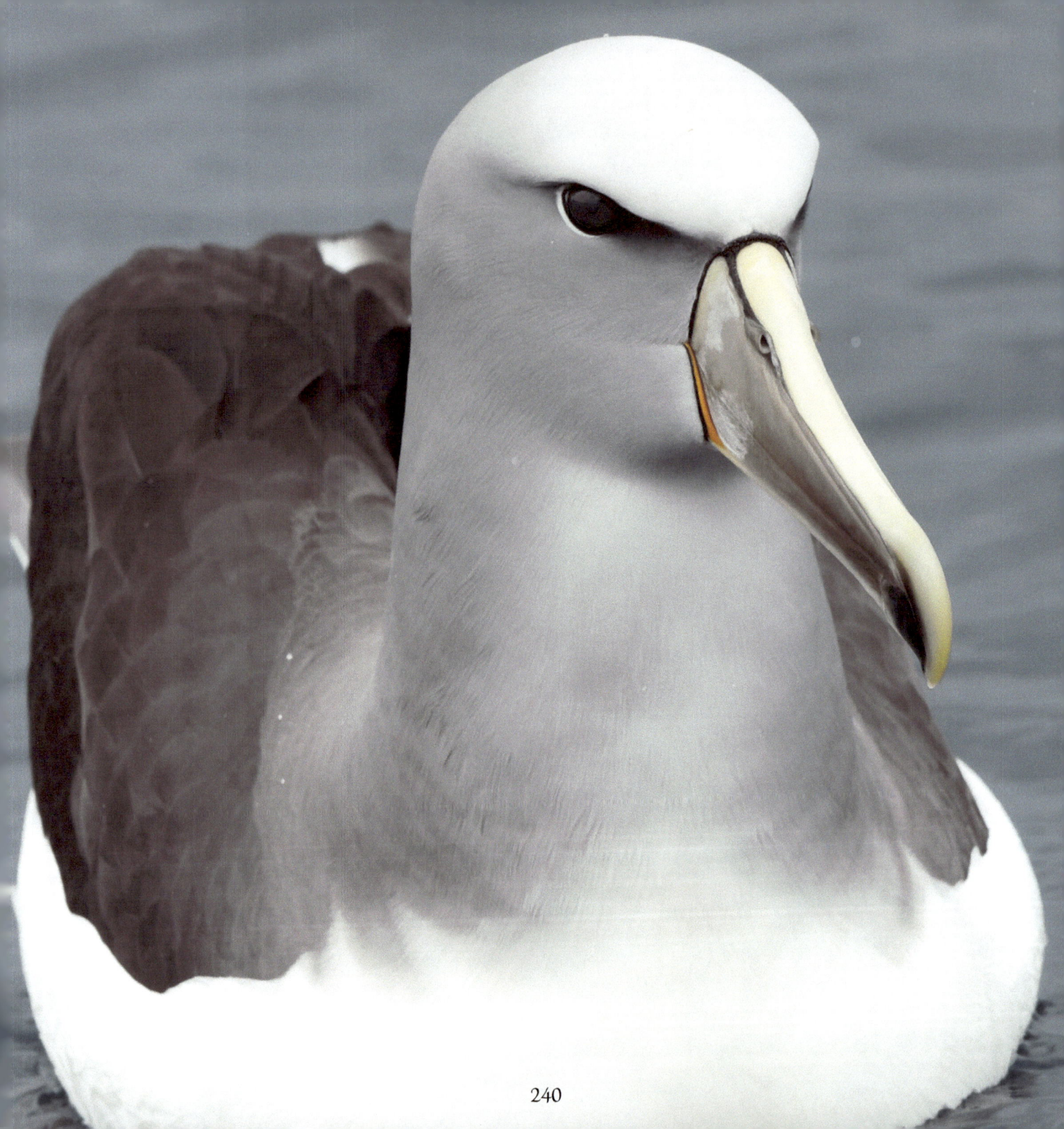

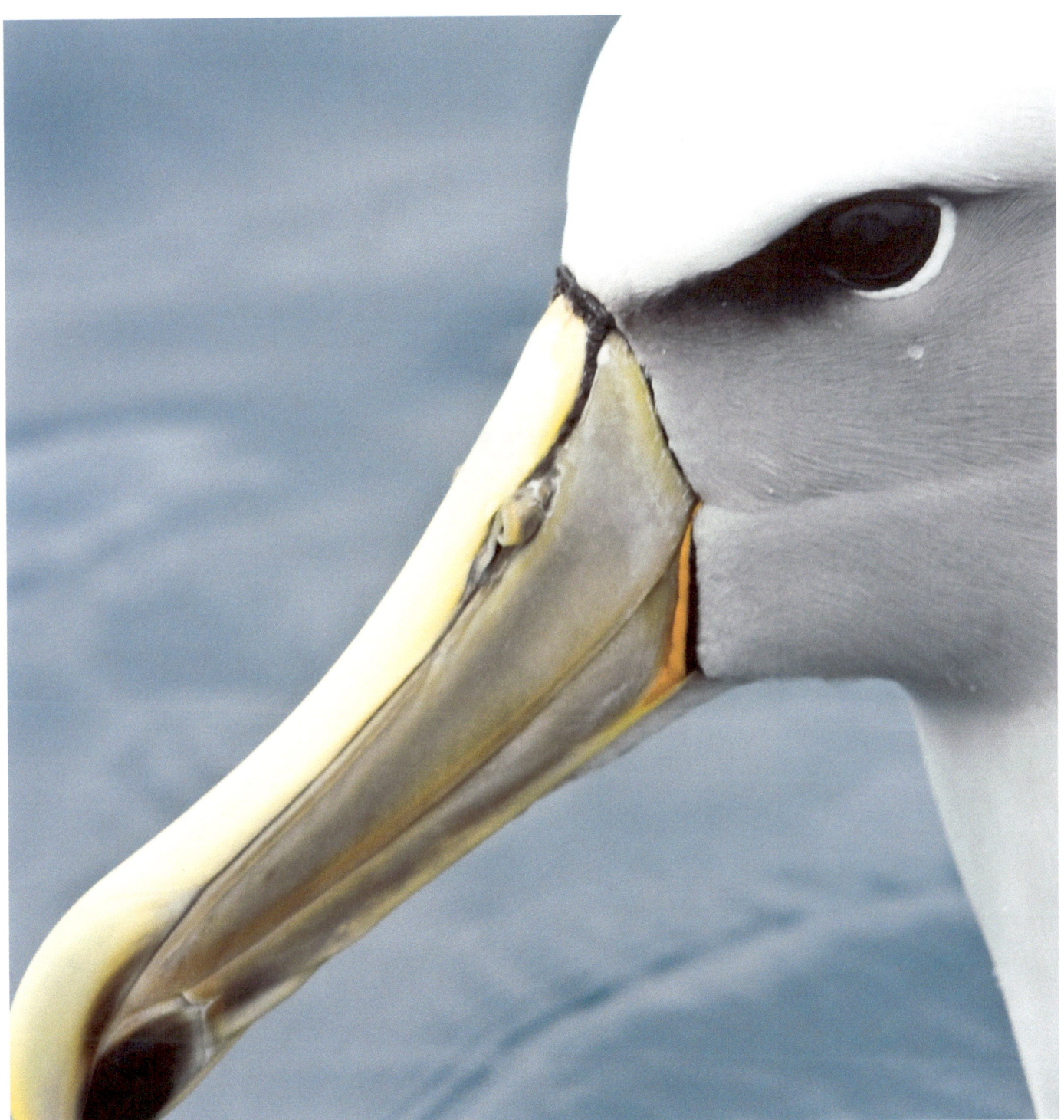

Flesh-Footed Shearwater
Puffinus carneipes

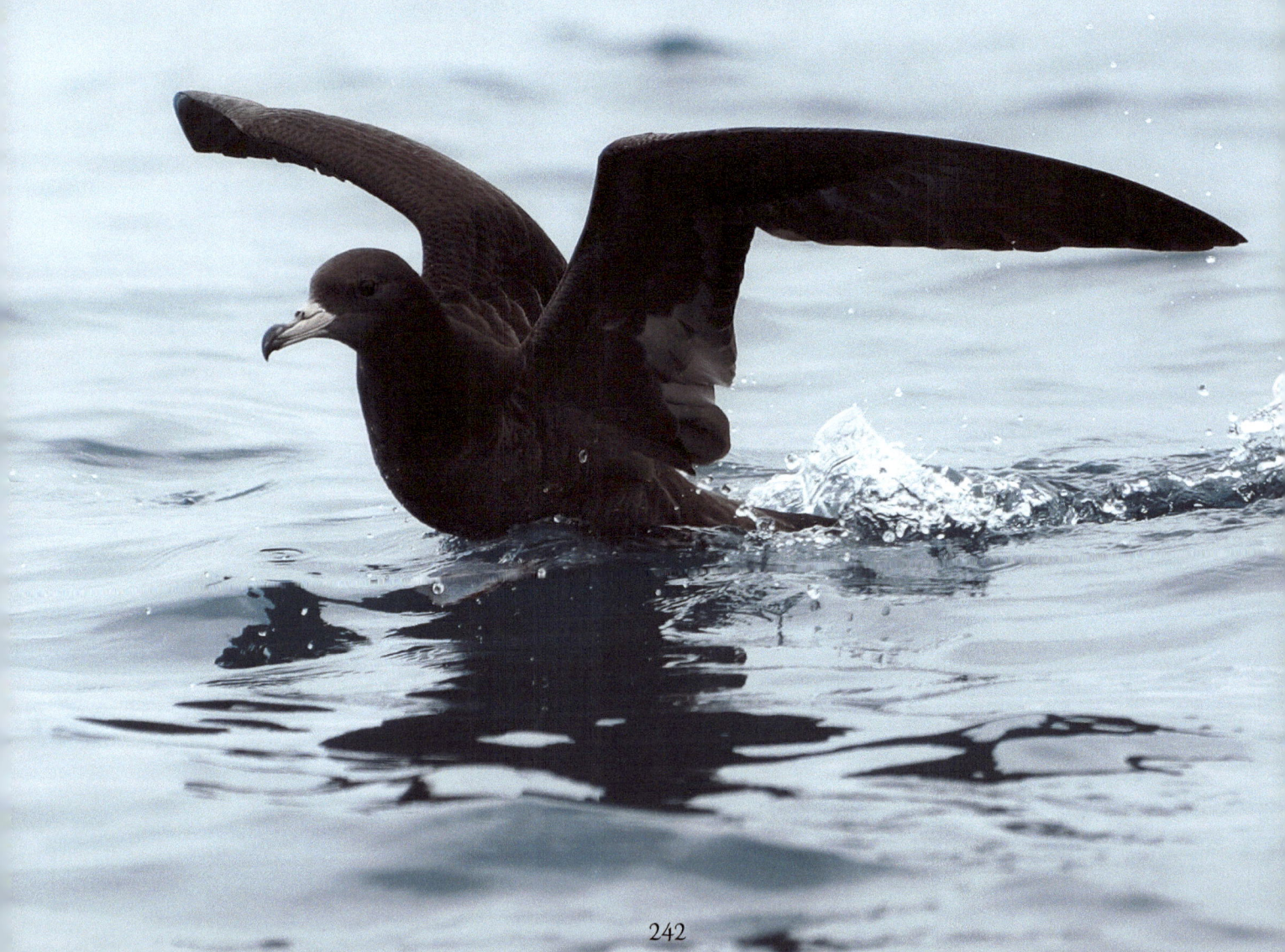

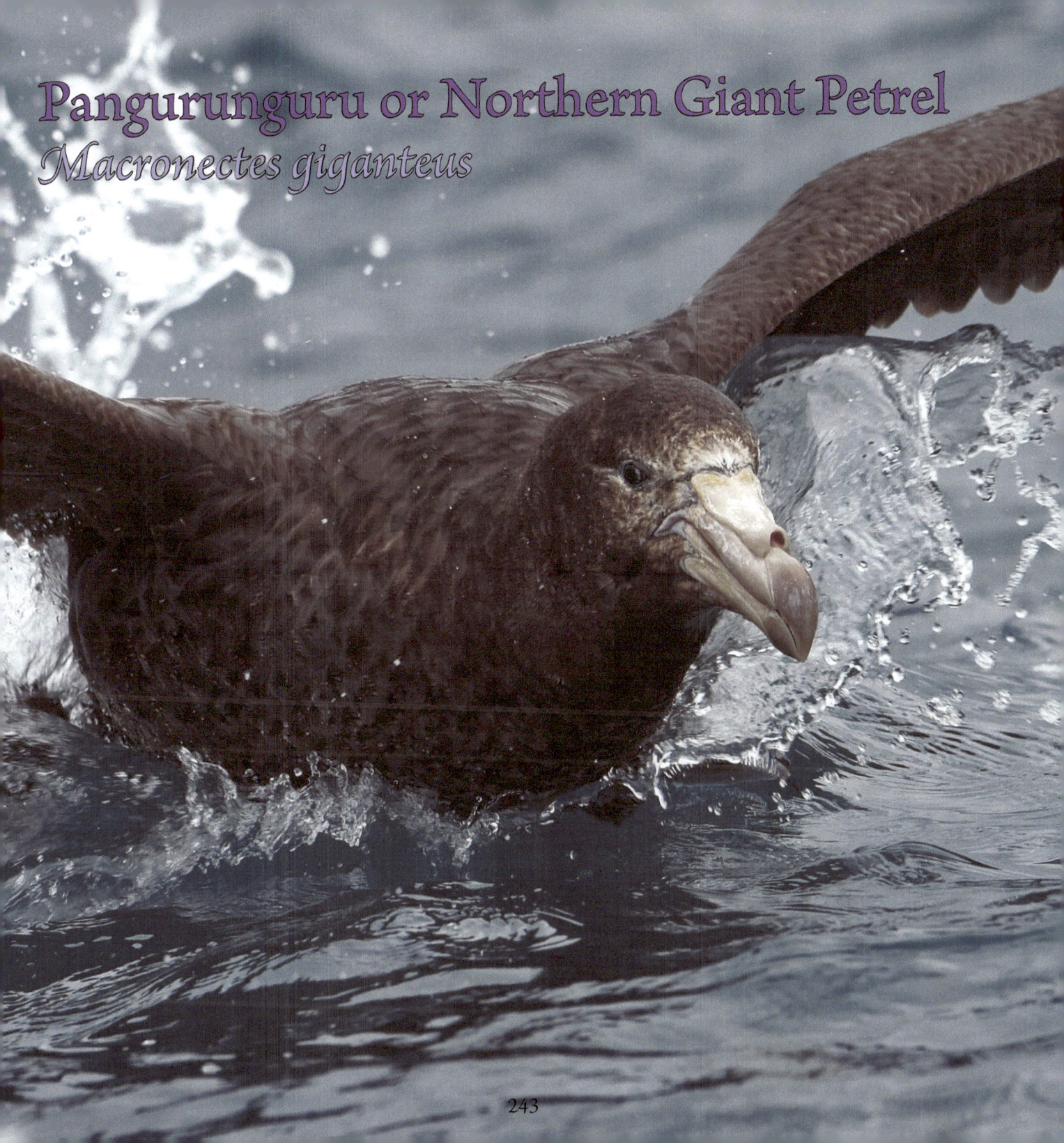

Pangurunguru or Northern Giant Petrel
Macronectes giganteus

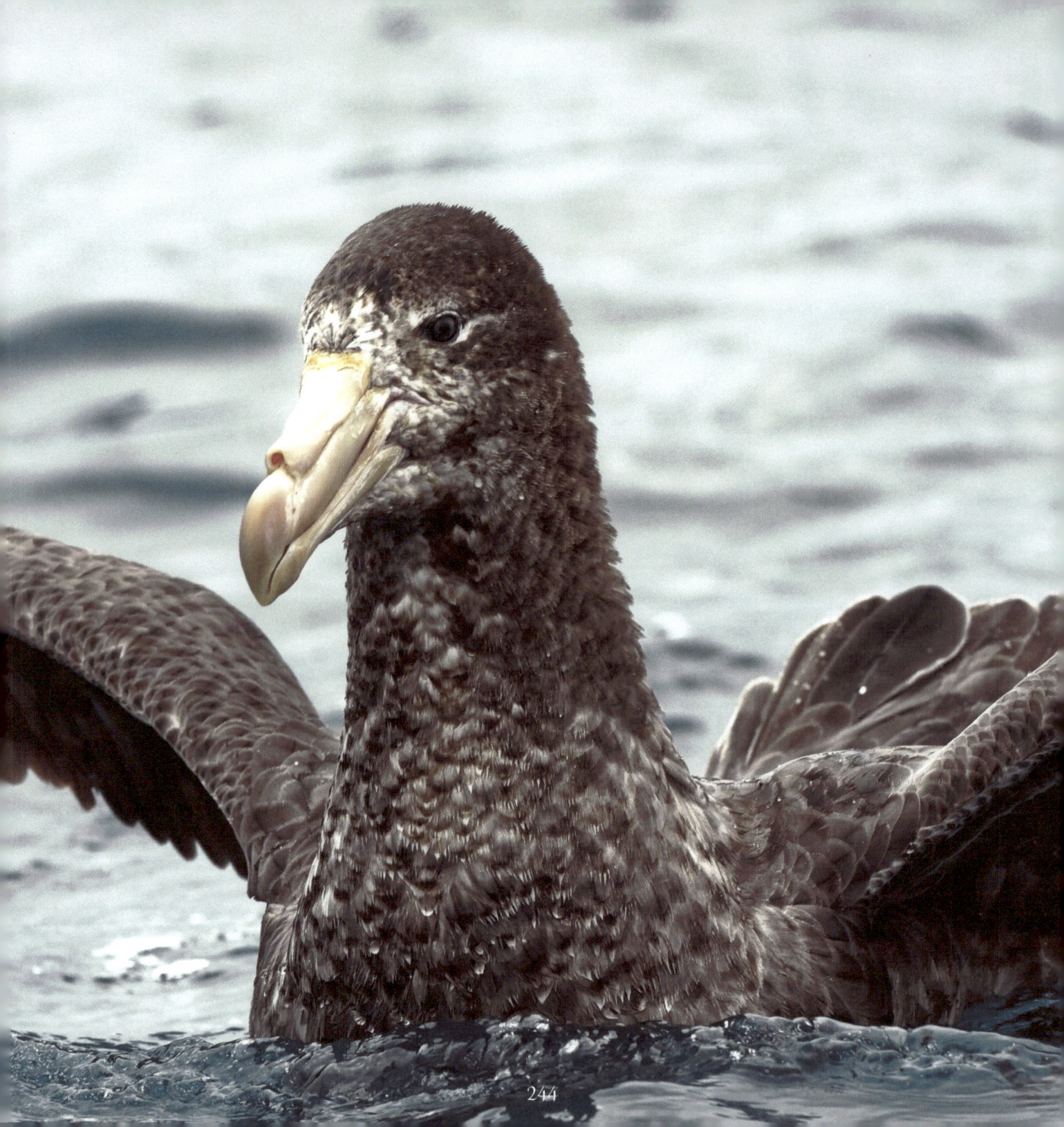

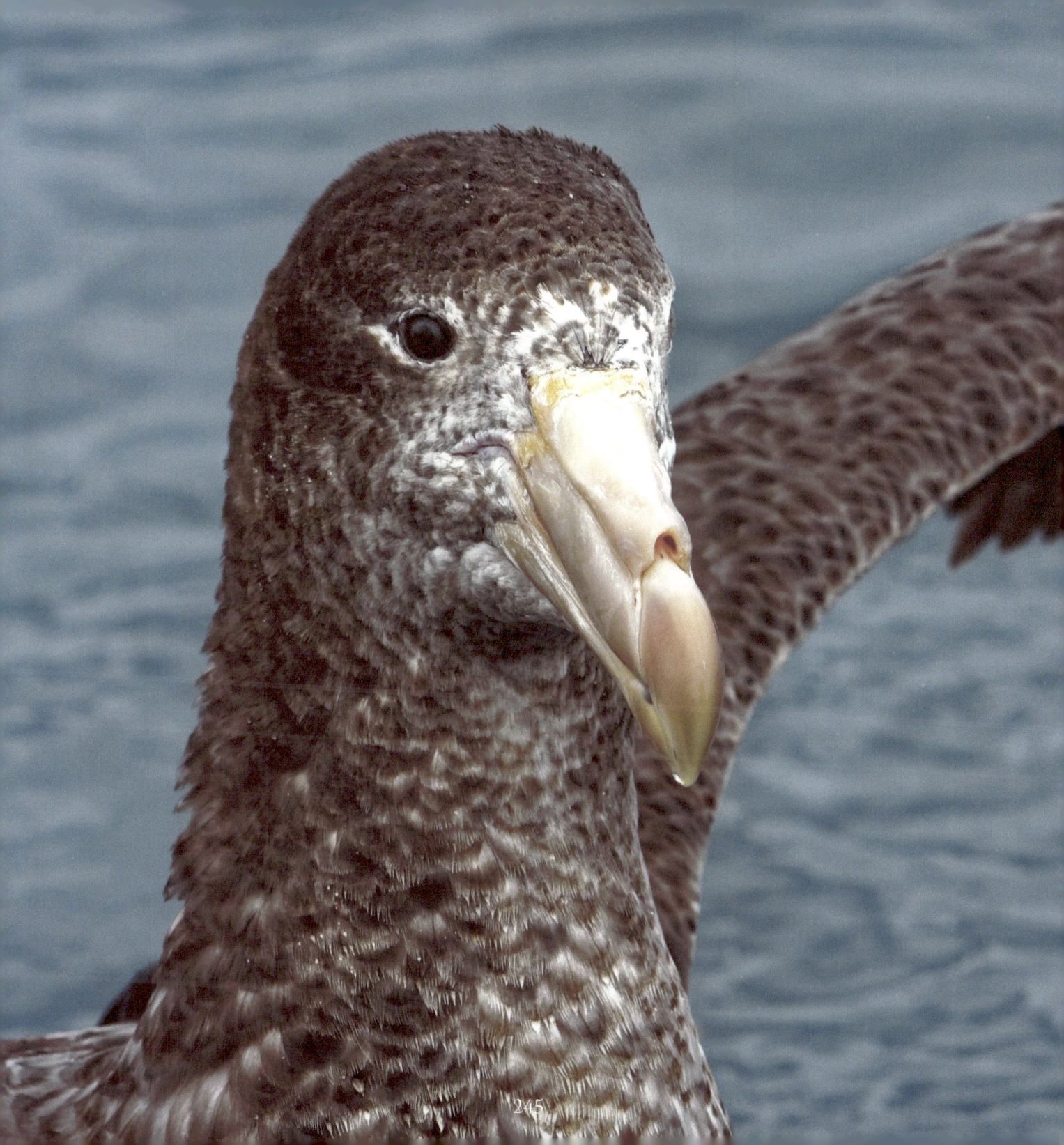

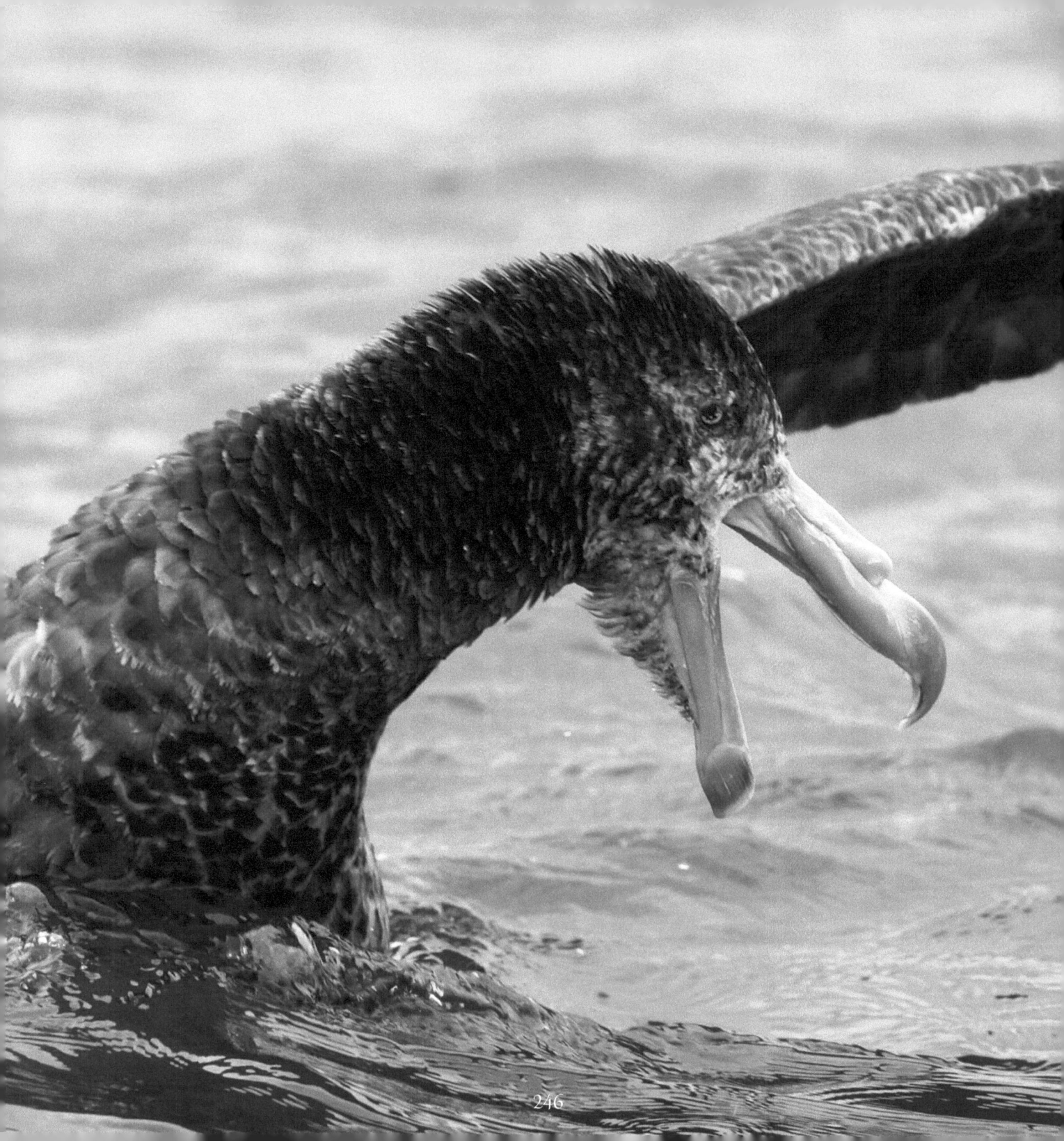

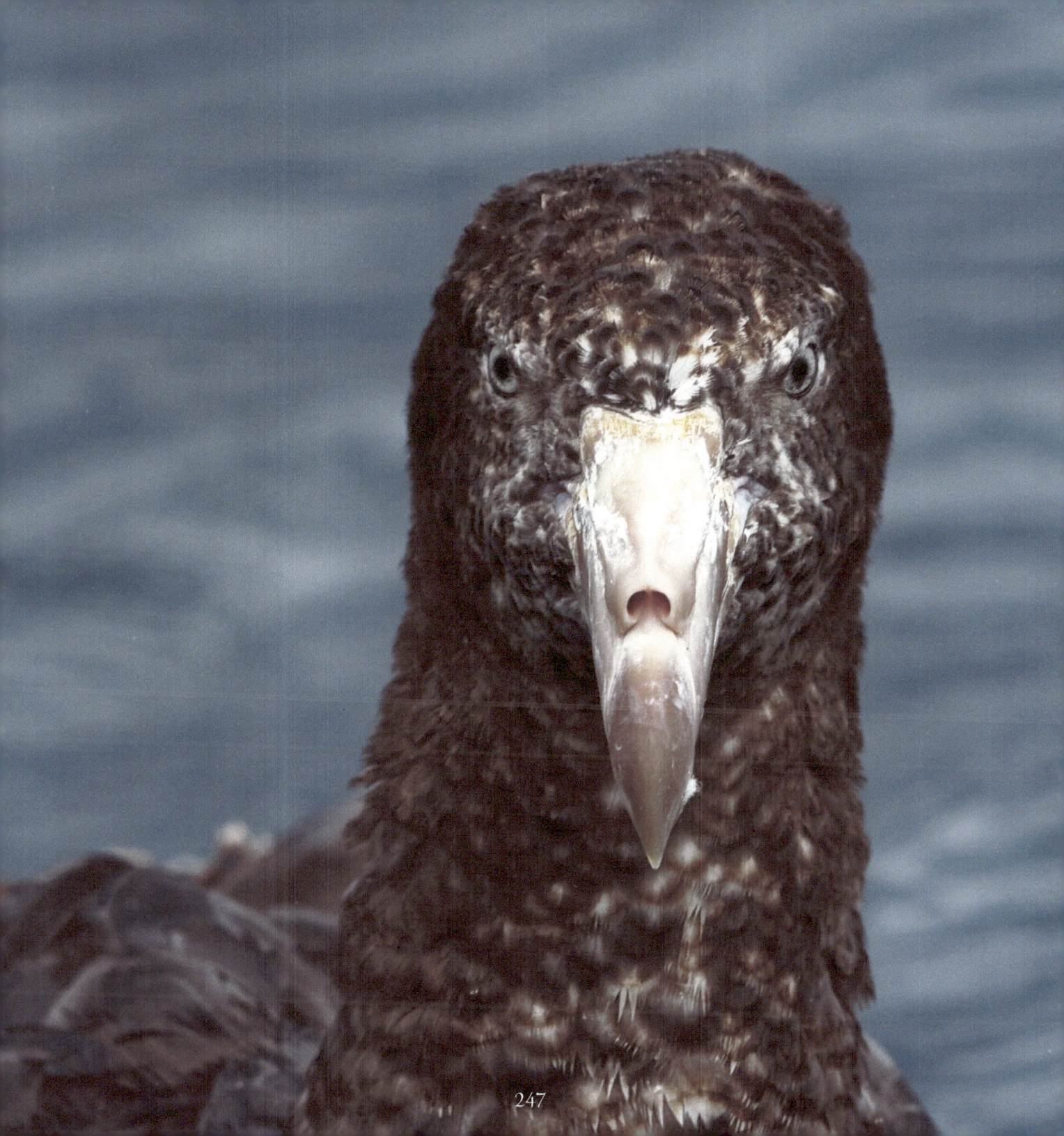

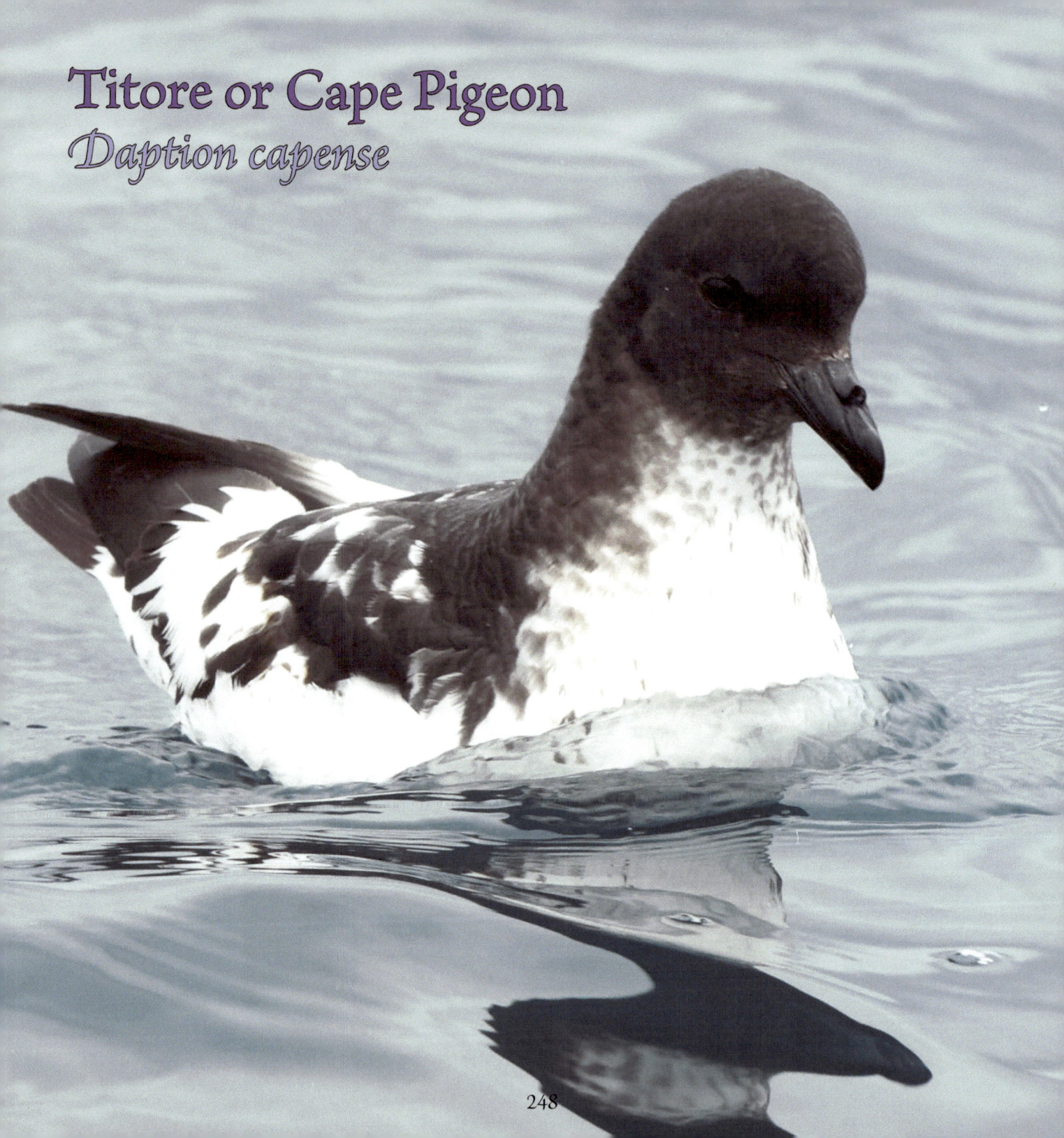
Titore or Cape Pigeon
Daption capense

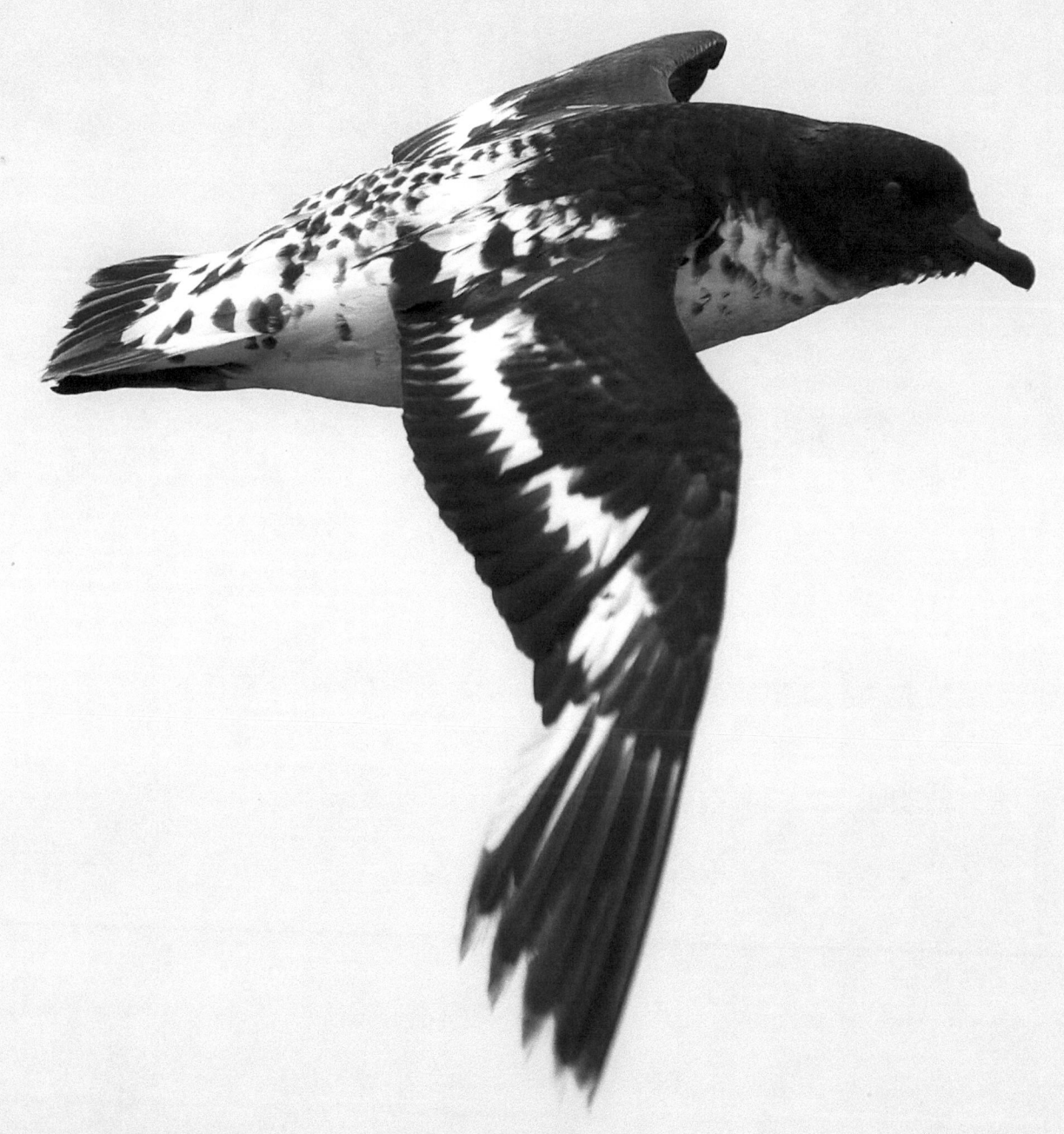

Korora or White-flippered Penguin
Eudyptula minor

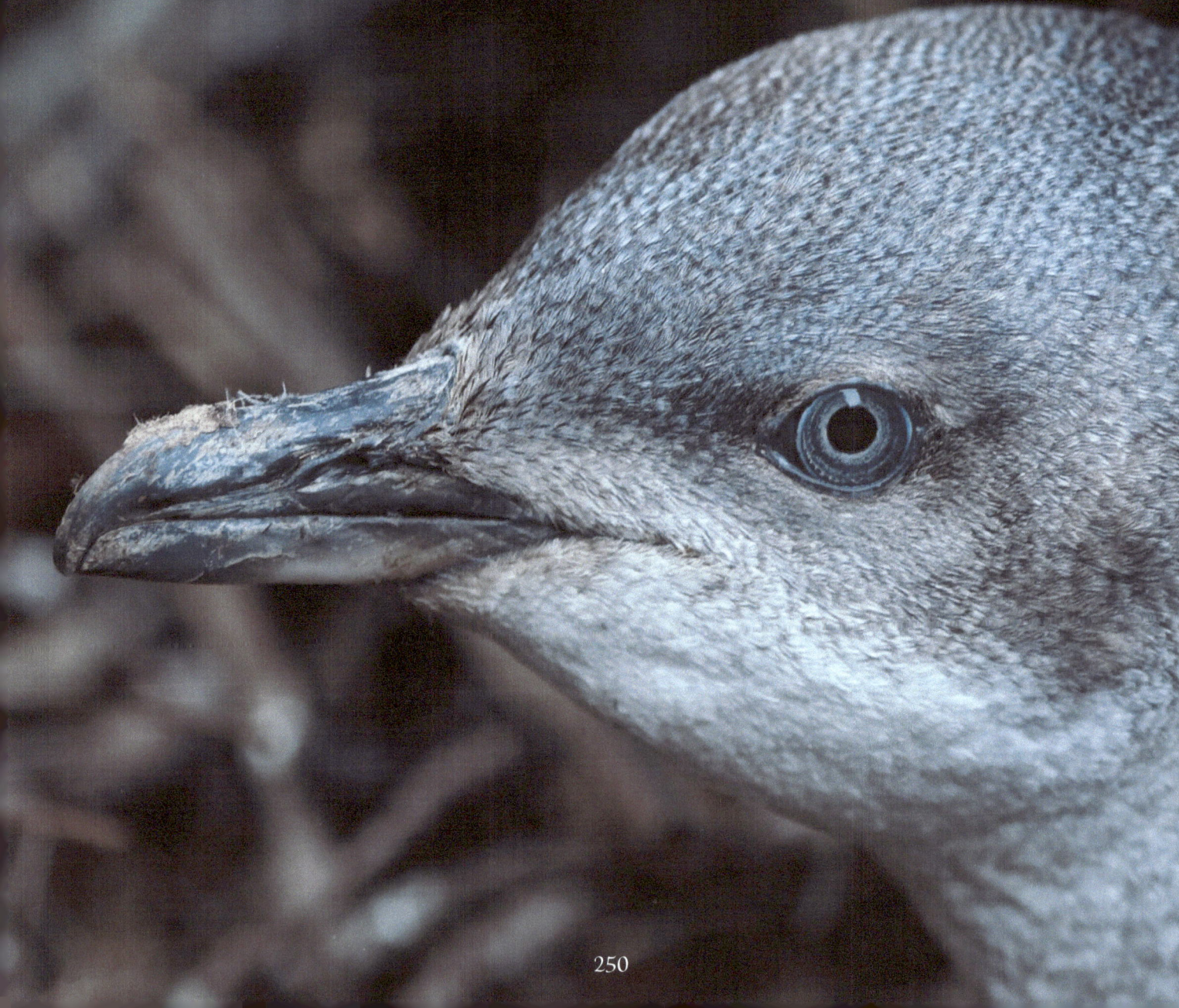

Epilogue

Hokioi (Harpagornis)

"This bird, the Hokioi, was seen by our ancestors. We (of the present day) have not seen it—that bird has disappeared now-a-days. The statement of our ancestor was that it was a powerful bird, a very powerful bird. It was a very large hawk. Its resting place was on the top of the mountains; it did not rest on the plains. On the days in which it was on the wing our ancestors saw it... It was a bird of (black) feathers, tinged with yellow and green; it had a bunch of red feathers on the top of its head. It was a large bird, as large as the Moa. Its rival was the hawk. The hawk said that it could reach the heavens; the hokioi said it could reach the heavens; there was a contention between them. The hokioi said to the hawk, 'what shall be your sign?' The hawk replied, 'kei' (the peculiar cry of the hawk). Then the hawk asked, 'what is to be your sign?' The hokioi replied, 'hokioi-hokioi-hu-u.' These were their words. They then flew and approached the heavens. The winds and the clouds came. The hawk called out 'kei' and descended, it could go no further on account of the winds and the clouds, but the hokioi disappeared into the heavens."

~Dr. Fulton, 1907

Moa

"During the summer 1838 I accompanied the Rev. W. Williams on a visit to the tribes inhabiting the East Coast district. Whilst at Waiapu, a thickly inhabited locality about twenty miles south-west from the East Cape, I heard from the Natives of a certain monstrous animal. Whilst some said it was a bird and others 'a person,' all agreed that it was called 'moa'; that in general appearance it somewhat resembled an immense domestic cock, with the difference, however, of its having a face like a man; that it dwelt in a cavern in a precipitous side of a mountain; that it lived on air; and that it was guarded or attended by two immense tuataras, who, Argus-like, kept incessant watch while the moa slept; also that if any one ventured to approach the dwelling of this wonderful creature he would be invariably trampled on and killed by it.

Colenso... says an old chief of the coast informed him that 'anciently the land was burnt up by the fire of Tamatea. Then it was that the big living things, together with the moas, were all burnt. Two moas, however, survived with difficulty that destruction, but only two; one of these lived at Te Wai-iti Mountains (in the interior) and one at Whakapunake. The feather of this one at Whakapunake has been seen, and was preserved as a plume decoration for the heads of the dead chiefs of note. The name of the feather was Ko-te-rau-o-Piopio (the special plume of Piopio). The forefathers of the Māoris heard of the moa, but they never saw its body, only its bones.' This statement agrees entirely with what I have been able to gather from the Natives in the vicinity of Whakapunake, at the foot of which I have passed in going to and from Poverty Bay during the past thirty-five years. Invariably the same answer is given in reply to inquiries: 'In a cave near the top of Whakapunake the last moa lived, and his feathers were used on great occasions; but this was a long time ago.'

~H. Hill, 1913

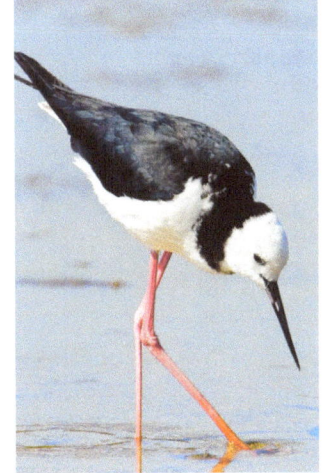

The one that got away

I am in the Pukaha Mount Bruce Reserve climbing a narrow track. On this day, I am driven by the hope of photographing a Kokako. My camera and audio equipment safely in their cases in my backpack, await my destination a kilometre away. The cold wind burns my cheeks as I climb. Its just a half-hour after dawn and no one is around. Korimako call from the canopy and the Tuis are in full song.

The path levels somewhat and I pause to catch my breath. I look up, and there she is. Two and a half metres away. A Pipiwharauroa (Shining cuckoo) in full plumage. My first.

I stare, but dare not move. She looks curiously at me. I look at her. We are frozen in the moment. The light hitting her breast feathers lights her up–she reminds me nothing so much as the cheshire cat in Alice in Wonderland. Beautiful and mysterious at the same time. We stand eye–to–eye; she, appearing unafraid; I, almost shaking with anticipation.

I know I don't have a chance of getting my large bulky camera out in time, but am able to catch a single blurry shot of her with a point and shoot I keep in my pocket. And then she flits from the branch she was resting on, and slips into the bush. I try to follow, but the branches and undergrowth hinder my advance. I see her once at a distance as she moves deeper into the bush and beyond my view. I wait, hoping that she might return, but she fades from sight. I wait a bit more, only now the sun is coming up over the hill.

A mixed flock passes through–Piwakawaka, Popokotea, Tauhou, and a pair of Miromiro. Chatting among themselves as they wend their way through the canopy. I wait a while longer but she doesn't reappear. Lethargic, I sit down, lean back against a ponga, and close my eyes. The birds' calling lulls me…

I sit up with a start, hearing a noise off to the left. Forgetting where I am for moment, I think of the Pipiwharauroa, but it isn't she. Glad that I'm just off the track and hidden from view, I watch as a family, mum and dad, and two young boys pass by. Their voices and footfalls fade into the distance, and then to nothing, finally replaced by a Tui's elaborate vocalisations.

I wait a few moments longer. The Tui becomes silent. The sun is now higher in the sky. I rise, stretch and continue up the track, but no Pipiwharauroa, and on this day, no sightings of Kokako, although I hear one for a time, deep in the bush, beyond my camera's reach. At the end of the day, I head back down the hill, and at the bottom leave the track to cut across a stream, and up a rise to where my van is parked. I know she's out there and I am driven to meet her once again. And so, I return on the morrow. In vain.

It's been seven years ago today. I've not seen a Pipiwharauroa since.

~John Elmer Lee, 2018

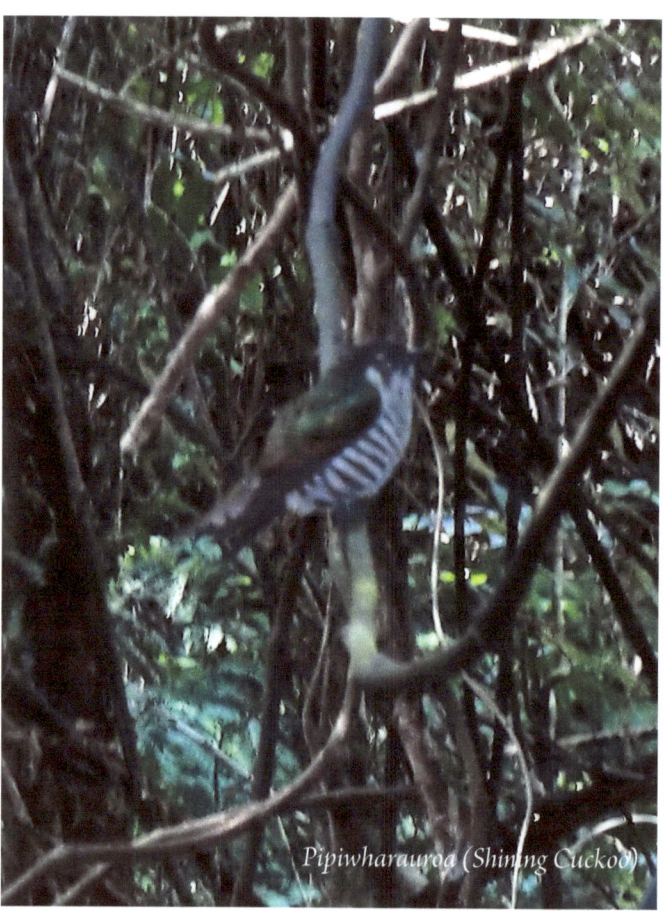
Pipiwharauroa (Shining Cuckoo)

Acknowledgements

As a newcomer to this land, I am appreciative of all those who have gone before me. I am indebted especially to the Royal Society of New Zealand for the rich trove of scientific observations to be found in the Transactions and Proceedings of the Royal Society of New Zealand 1868–1961. This internet searchable database made the job of locating quotes far easier than would have been possible otherwise.

Thanks also, to New Zealand's 19th and early 20th century naturalists. These naturalists' insights and scientific research have left us all an invaluable record of much that no longer exists and much that still remains. In particular, I would like to acknowledge Sir Walter L. Buller, T. H. Potts, H. Guthrie–Smith, Edgar F. Stead, Johannes C. Andersen, W. T. L. Travers, Captain F. W. Hutton, and Richard Henry.

Thanks also to Geoff Moon for his great contribution to bird studies and especially bird photography in New Zealand.

Thanks to the authors of "The Guide to the Birds of New Zealand," Barrie Heather and Hugh Robertson, with illustrator Derek Onley, for showing me the way.

Thanks to the following organisations whose work protecting our native birds has contributed greatly to their continued survival:
New Zealand Department of Conservation
Forest and Bird
Hikurangi Marine Reserve
Hinewai Reserve
Island Bay Marine Reserve
Kapiti Island Nature Reserve
Karori Wildlife Sanctuary
Maungatautari Ecological Island
Nga Manu Nature Reserve
Okuti Reserve
Paraparaumu Scenic Reserve
Pauatahanui Wildlife Reserve
Porirua Scenic Reserve
Pukaha Mount Bruce Wildlife Centre
Rainbow Springs
Wingspan National Bird of Prey Centre

Thanks finally to the magnificent birds that grace this collection of photographs. I am forever in their debt. They have taken me from the Coramandel, to East Cape, and the Bay of Plenty. To Rotorua, Taupo, and Hawkes Bay. To the Manawatu Estuary and on to Taranaki. To Marlborough Sound, Abel Tasmen, and Golden Bay. To the West Coast, to Okarito, to the glaciers and to the Alps. To Banks Peninsula and Kaikoura. To Kapiti Island and Karori and to Mt. Bruce and Maungatautari. The birds have taken me on a journey that has immeasurably enriched my life.

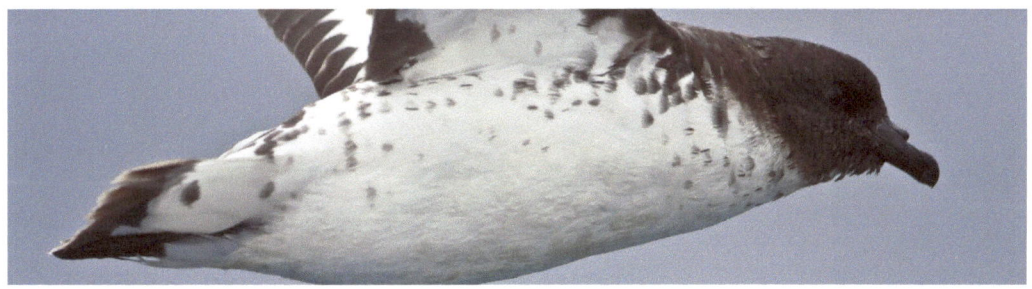

Appendix One
Author's Influences

Vincent Van Gogh

A transformative moment in my childhood occurred when I was ten. I was taken by my mother to see an exhibit of Van Gogh's paintings. Oh, the colour, the subtlety and the intensity. A sunflower seeming to burst forth with sunlight, a field of grain so real and surreal, at the same time, and the mood of clouds playing on some field workers, dark, but movingly evocative. I was astounded. And a door was opened… My photography is an attempt to explore colour and depth with the same awe I felt at that exhibit.

The birds of New Zealand have only added to my astonishment. One bird, the Tui, is to some, a nuisance blackbird, waking you to its raucous calls; to others, a glorious, spectacular rainbow of metallic color, blessed with some of the most varied songs in the avian realm. Another, the Takahe, moves through the edge of the bush like a slowly grazing cow. The light hits, and it becomes blues and greens and cyan, crowned by the biggest, reddest beak imaginable, and oh, those soulful eyes.

New Zealand is blessed with many native birds that have this quality – At first glance, drab and dull, but when examined more closely, spectacular and rewarding. The Tauhou, Korimako, and the Kereru leap to mind – Or the beautiful patterns of feathers, revealed only on close examination as on the Hihi, the Toutouwai, or the Weka. There is colour and form enough for the most jaundice eye, and almost overwhelming to one willing to take it all in.

John James Audubon

My parents owned a copy of Audubon's "Birds in America," and I remember as a child of seven intently staring at the beautiful, and sometimes violent depictions of the paintings. The book endlessly fascinated me. Some days I would go cover-to-cover, studying each page carefully. Other days, I would limit myself to my favourite birds–the Golden Eagle, the Snowy Owl, the Loon or the Kite.

Audubon's paintings are etched in my memory to this day and they've become the inspiration for my photography. The birds, shot and then posed by Audubon, come back to life in his paintings, exuding the very essence and the life of the birds they represent. Although I deal with living subjects, it feels as if Audubon is standing behind me, on every photograph I take, guiding me, asking, "Is the light just so; does it capture the life in the eye? Does the foliage reflect the habitat of the bird? Is there a better angle that might allow the bird's character to be revealed?"

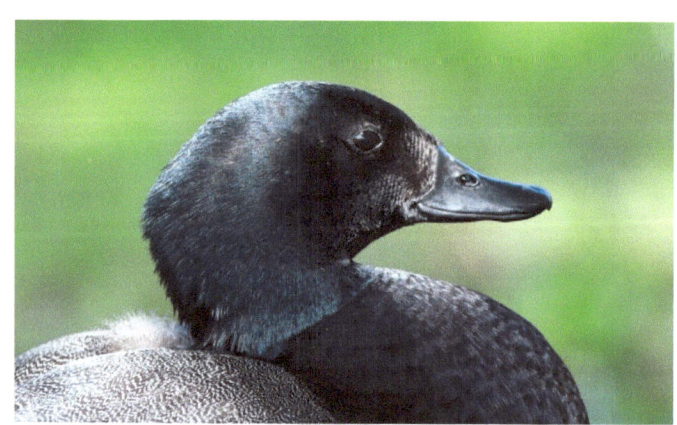

Ansel Adams

Ansel Adams's photographic studies taught me a great lesson. For a photograph to be considered art, interventions by the photographer, at some level, are needed. How the subject is focused is one intervention. Other interventions can be through the camera's placement, the filters used, or the camera's settings. Another manner of expression is to intervene in the darkroom. The darkroom, whether digital or chemical, can assist the photographer to expose what was hidden, or to reveal more closely what the eye saw, rather than what light the film or sensor was able to gather. This was easily seen when, as an amateur, I would receive images back from the lab and be unpleasantly surprised at how flat the colours seemed, how two–dimensional, and most importantly, not at all what my eyes had seen.

Adams did not accept these limitations. Instead, he worked tirelessly in the lab to restore what his eyes had witnessed. Years after he had published an image, he would sometimes take the negative back into the lab and try to reveal still more than his previous efforts had allowed.

His interventions in the darkroom sometimes infuriated critics, who cried foul, that it was somehow cheating. Today the debate rages on about digital photography, just as it did with Adams's darkroom magic, just as it did when acrylics were introduced to painting, and probably when cave painters introduced earthen pigments to the charcoal paradigm. What is important, I believe, is that the artist/photographer must always attempt to express his or her singular vision, and not be limited by the expectations of any given audience. Thus, within the context of photography, one must carefully examine his or her tools, techniques and limitations and how they will affect the finished work. My choices, in my studio, were taken so that I, too, could more closely present what *my* eyes had witnessed.

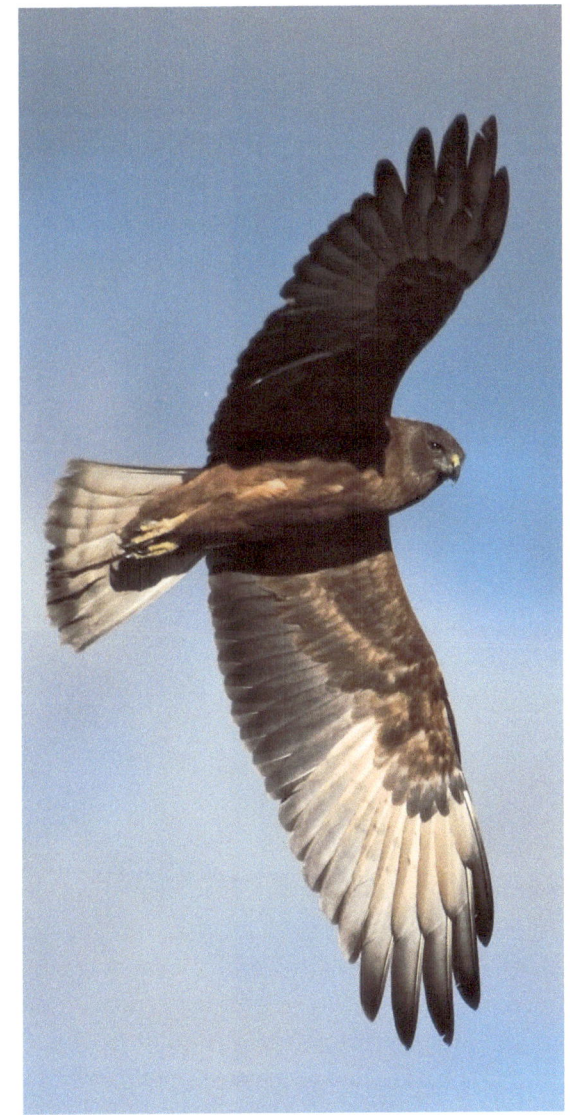

Appendix Two
Field Notes

Birds in the Bush

Photographing birds in the bush, without a hide, is one of the most difficult photographic tasks I have ever undertaken. There is insufficient light. The camera must be hand-held, as a tripod or mono-pod overly restricts movement. Everything happens so quickly, I often have no time to react. At the most inopportune of times the "perfect shot" is marred by a branch or a vine or leaves suddenly getting in the way.

What mediates this are two things. First, I've learned. I've learned to sit still, and to listen. I've learned to take what the birds give me. I've learned to give the birds and their needs my utmost respect. I've learned to put spurious thoughts out of my head as well. And all of this is good.

Second, and more importantly, I've begun to see myself as not the observer of nature, but as a participant in nature. With a place no greater or lesser than the creatures with whom I share it. The birds have taught me to let go of judgement, to no longer see myself as separate, to become, as John Muir advised, "fond of everything that was wild."

On Binoculars

I try to use binoculars as little as possible when I'm out with the birds. Instead, like a one-eyed pirate of yore, I use my one good eye, my lens, to see the world. Why? First, binoculars bring me too close, and can disappoint me when I switch back to my long lens. Oh, I might think, if only my long lens could get me as close to the birds, what shots I'd take. But my one good "eye" is a blessing, because it requires that I be still more patient, more "present," and if I am lucky, handsomely rewarded. Some shots will be missed, but if I had the range binoculars offered, it would be harder still to capture an image, hand held, that was reasonably sharp. So, I count my blessings, accept what is given to me, and almost always leave the "bins" packed away, or back at the studio. Second, it is always preferable for the bird to get closer to me than for me to get closer to the bird. A bird, thus engaged, is seldom as wary as one who sees me as a possible threat.

On Seeing with New Eyes

At times, it is preferable to not research the birds that I seek. Sometimes, I intentionally try to know as little as possible about a bird when heading out into the bush. I might go as far as consulting guide books, or asking local birders where birds may be found in the area, but I often avoid asking about the habits and behaviours of the birds. The reason for this is simple. Often enough, the more I know about a bird, the less I will see. In fact, one of my great birding pleasures is to enter the bird's territory with as blank a mind as possible–to meander up (and down) a track or along a shore, or across a field, letting my mind slowly release its grip on the tasks, schedules, and thoughts of my daily life. When I've managed to quiet my mind, and it is sufficiently empty, without warning the birds will appear, as if on cue.

I can't really describe the process involved, because there is no process. The birds don't really appear. Instead perhaps, I disappear, and I am suddenly attuned to their calls, and to their shapes and forms. I become at ease–ready to be taken by their movements–their shakes and flutters, or the vibrations of a heart beating 400 beats per minute, by their glorious songs, by their intricate dance through the canopy. I am taken by the rustle in the tall grass–the flicker of motion caught in the corner of my eye–their sometimes abrupt appearance as if out of thin air (which, in fact, is exactly right.) They surround me and allow me to witness the most intimate details of their lives, and sometimes, they let me take their picture. It is only later, when I am heading back to my car, that I might question what it was that I saw and heard. It is only then that I will consider reading birding books and asking those who are much better informed as to inner rhythms of the birds' lives. But that is a different kind of adventure.

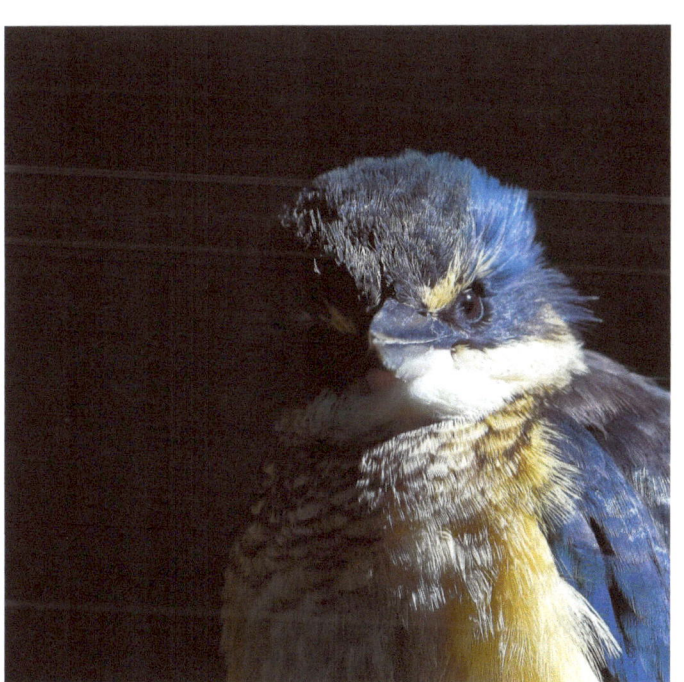

"Bird Eyes"

When I was younger I was an avid collector of wild mushrooms. Of the forty varieties that would frequently find their way to my table, most were found scattered amidst the autumn leaf duff or hidden by spring growth. The method I used to find a variety I sought was to first scan the area for telltale signs, or indications of suitable conditions. And then I would wander through an area, looking everywhere. What allowed me to actually "see" the mushrooms, to separate them from the background, is what my children referred to as "mushroom eyes." Mushroom eyes was a subtle, unconscious shift in perception whereby, after five to thirty minutes, depending on how attuned we were, the mushrooms unexpectedly appeared. And then a call from me or my kids, "Chanterelle!"

I have found that birds in the bush often times require this shift of perception–"bird eyes." To spot a still bird hiding in the canopy or in the tangle of a bush, and in lieu of a telltale call, it has been very useful to learn how to make this shift of focus happen. To shift focus is not something that is easy to explain. It's not staring intently. It's not just unfocusing, to take in more of the surroundings. Perhaps, it is an unconscious shift from the linear mind to the intuitive. Many seasoned birders know how to make the shift. And it is this shift that adds immeasurably to the thrill of birding–being in the moment, all senses working together, for a specific purpose. Yes, it's wonderful to see the birds and their behaviour, but the singular focus of "bird eyes" completes it. For me, this state of being attuned is equal to the actual sighting of a bird.

Standing or Sitting Still

I try to stand or sit still when I'm close to the birds. If a Toutouwai is near I might hold my arm out to see if it will alight or if I'm really lucky it might land on my head, as a Kaka once did – light as a feather. I try to stand still and quiet holding a pose for five minutes, or ten, or more. Holding poses is very beneficial to my bird photography. First, because it puts the birds at ease, and second, because I sometimes must do the same when holding the camera in position waiting for the action to begin, as when waiting for a Tieke to reappear from behind the trunk of the fuchsia tree where she's disappeared a moment before.

The Art of Ambling

Ambling is the preferred mode of walking when I'm with the birds. Usually, the slower the better. Looking around. Pausing at any movement or sound. Quiet as I can be, but occasionally whistling quietly along with the birds. Sometimes I allow thoughts to pass through my mind, but try not to dwell on any.

I stop occasionally and stand very still. Sometimes, I sweep my eyes slowly through the canopy. Sometimes, I gaze with unfixed eyes, trying to detect the least movement. I then move on, step by careful step, or stumbling into things, because I occasionally forget to look where I'm going – up and down hills, around a sand dune, across an unnamed trickle of a creek, a flower here, a smell there, noticing it all.

Taking What is Given

I approach a day in the field seeking birds with one of two camera setups, and it is often necessary to decide, before I set out, which setups to use. I use the first setup if I'm going to a known sight to watch a particular bird's behaviour. For instance, if it is a Kokako that I'm pursuing, I prepare exclusively for that pursuit. My camera and lens are set up to gain the maximum chance of a successful shot – aperture, ISO, lens focal length, extenders or tele-converters attached, etc. I can then devote my time to spotting and am ready for the shot when it comes–often unexpectedly.

The second setup is for shooting without expectation or particular purpose. If I choose this, then I set up my camera for the widest variety of shots possible, without having to resort to lens switches or other time-consuming changes. Aperture is usually set wide open, to provide the fastest shutter speed possible, lens setup without extenders, converters or filters, etc. With this setup there may be shots that I will miss where the bird is too near or far, but I will be able to capture a wider variety of action than if I was set up for a specific situation. Neither technique is better than the other, just more or less appropriate for the purpose intended.

"Life Lists"

There is much to be learned and much satisfaction to be gained in seeking to add to one's life list, the list of birds many an avid birder compiles of the birds he or she has seen and confirmed. For me though, I don't get too excited about tracking my life list. I do want to see Titi on their nests. I do want to see Kiwis on Stewart Island during daylight hours. I do want to see the Rock Wren and a Titipounamu up close, and all the birds I haven't seen as of this writing. I do have my photographs though. I suppose someday, I will go through them and make a count – maybe when I'm too old to lift to my eye the weight of my five kilos of camera and lens.

Short or Tall-approaching birds

When I'm approaching birds in open countryside or on the shore, it is much better to be short than tall. What this means is the lower to the ground I can get, the better. I may find myself crawling across a beach on my belly to get close enough for that perfect shot. For this, I wear clothing than allows free movement, preferably without pockets on the front, so as not to fill up with sand or dirt. Waterproof pants, coat, and boots are also preferred if I expect to encounter damp conditions. When out on the water, sitting in the bottom of a canoe can provide excellent camouflage.

On Hides (Blinds)

A hide can be very useful when observing birds in the wild. The birds do not see me as a threat and much can be gained from this one-sided interaction in understanding birds and their behaviour. This can be both exciting and rewarding. However, when possible, I avoid the use of hides to camouflage my presence, and instead practice the art of cautious approach. When the bird knows of my whereabouts and is comfortable with me, I open the possibility of different behaviours and interactions. This requires great patience, but the rewards are rich.

Nesting Birds

I avoid close-up shooting of birds in nests, because it can place the chicks' safety in jeopardy. Parents will abandon nests at the least provocation. And never, ever, when I come across a nest full of chicks, do I approach or touch birds. Doing so risks scaring the parents away. When approaching a nest, I find that it is better to approach slowly and to keep a distance of at least five or more metres, and better still, to find an advantageous view from afar than to approach too closely.

Learning from Sheep and Cows and Birds

I've noticed, when on a paddock or a station, that birds such as shelducks and magpies are very comfortable in the presence of nearby cows and sheep. This is because cows and sheep are not threatening to the birds. What makes them non-threatening is that cows and sheep are generally not interested in the birds. I use this information to my advantage. First, I stay as low as possible when approaching birds. Second, I never approach directly, but only at an angle. I stop frequently and "graze." Third, I remain silent. Fourth, I make no sudden movements. With sufficient patience, I can approach within five or ten metres of most field birds.

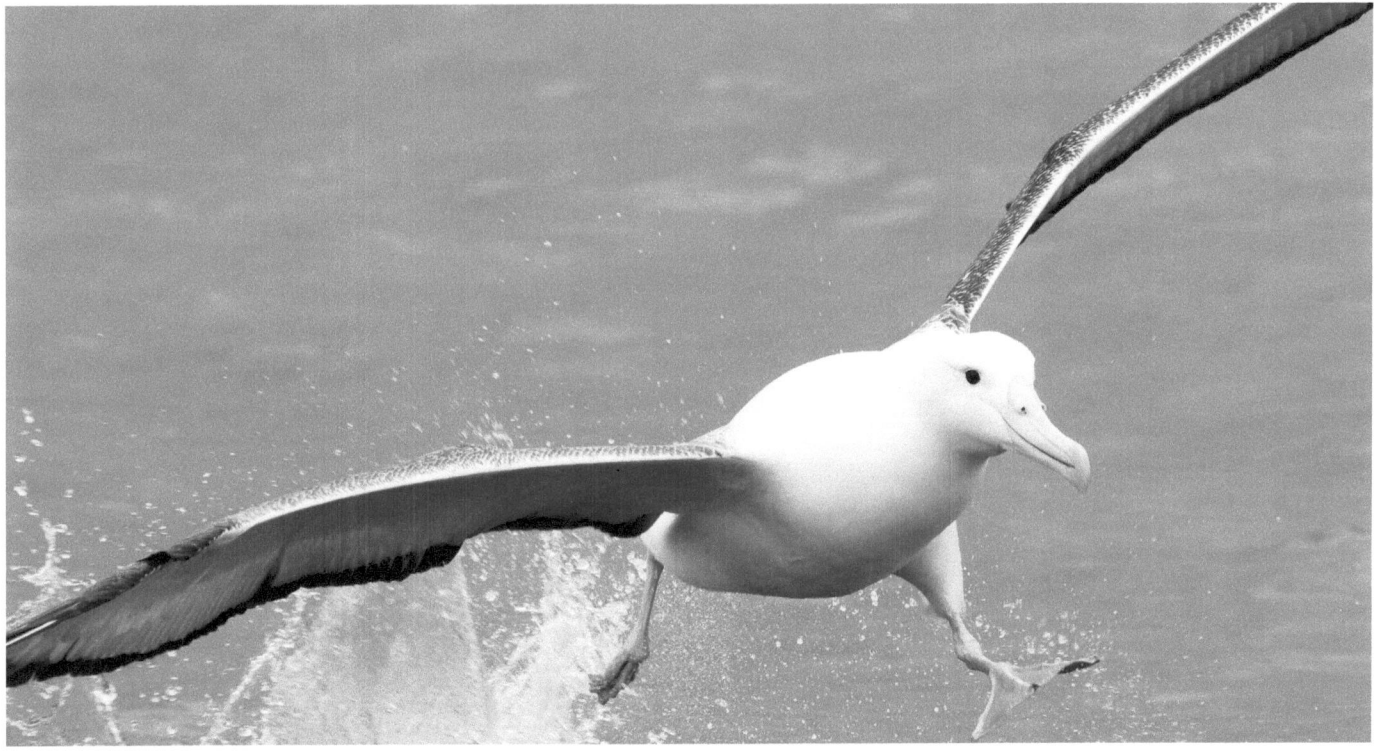

Appendix Three
Camera Settings

Camera Setup–Canopied Bush*

In the bush I am after the fastest possible shutter speed in the low available light. This can be extremely limiting, as birds in the canopied bush are closer and faster relative to their distance from your lens, and with less available light, than any other bird shot I might take.

- Auto Exposure–Aperture Priority.
- Aperture–wide open.
- Narrower Aperture can allow faster shutter speeds, but only close down aperture (f5.6 to f8) if there is sufficient light and only when greater depth of field is required.
- Auto Focus Mode–One Shot (or Equivalent) for birds at rest. AI Focus Auto Focus (or equivalent) for moving birds.
- If possible I select only the center focal point. Any other settings increase the likelihood of the camera not focusing on my subject.
- Exposure Metering–Spot Mode or Partial Mode. Any other settings increase the likelihood of the camera under or over exposing.
- Exposure compensation–None.
- ISO–Up to ISO 1600 (lower is better, but may not allow for bird movement.)
- White Balance–Custom using grey card preferable; otherwise I use Shade setting (or equivalent).
- Image Quality–RAW preferable, Maximum JPEG setting otherwise.
- Flash–I use sparingly to avoid startling birds. I use the fastest possible shutter speed setting allowed by my flash if I do use flash.

Camera Setup–Open Bush and Field

- Open bush allows more available light and potentially faster shutter speeds.
- Auto Exposure–Aperture Priority.
- Aperture–wide open to f8.
- Auto Focus Mode–One Shot (or Equivalent) for birds at rest. I use AI Focus Auto Focus, or AI Servo Auto Focus (or equivalent) for single birds in flight with only center focus point active; I use AI Focus Auto Focus, or AI Servo Auto Focus using all focal points for a flock of birds in flight.
- Exposure Metering– Spot Mode or Partial Mode (or Center-Weighted Average Mode if other modes not available).
- Exposure compensation–minus 1/2 to 2 stops to shoot light coloured birds against the sky or the water.
- Exposure compensation–plus 1/2 to 2 stops to shoot dark coloured birds against the sky or the water.
- To ensure correct exposure I bracket shots when possible.
- ISO–Up to ISO 800 (lower is better for reduced grain, but may not allow for rapid bird movement).
- White Balance–Custom setting using grey card is preferable; Otherwise use Shade, or Cloudy setting (or equivalent) in bush; Use Cloudy or Daylight (or equivalent) in open spaces.
- Image Quality–RAW preferable, Maximum JPEG setting otherwise.
- I close down aperture (f5.6 to f11) if there is sufficient light to gain depth of field. Narrower aperture will force the camera into slower shutter speeds, increasing the likelihood that the shot will be missed due to blur.
- Flash–Not needed unless at dusk or dawn.

Camera Setup–Shore, Open Water

- Shooting shore birds and birds at sea gives me problems the opposite of shooting in the bush–plenty of light, in fact often too much light for the subject of my shot. The risk is blowing out the subject or losing all shadow detail.
- Auto Exposure–Shutter Priority.
- Shutter Speed–1/50 sec. or faster for birds at rest; 1/250 sec. or faster for active birds or birds in flight.
- ISO–Up to ISO 800 (lower is better).
- Auto Focus Mode–One Shot (or Equivalent) for birds at rest. I use AI Focus Auto Focus or AI Servo Auto Focus (or equivalent) for single birds in flight with only center focal point active. I use AI Focus Auto Focus or AI Servo Auto Focus (or equivalent) using all focal points for flock of birds in flight.
- Exposure Metering–Spot Mode, Partial Mode for single birds; Evaluative Mode or Center-Weighted Average Mode for flocks of birds.
- Exposure compensation–minus 1/2 to 2 stops to shoot light coloured birds against the sky or the water.
- Exposure compensation–plus 1/2 to 2 stops to shoot dark coloured birds against the sky or the water.
- To ensure correct exposure I bracket shots whenever possible.
- Image Quality–RAW preferable, Maximum JPEG setting otherwise.
- Flash–Not needed unless at dusk or dawn.

* All settings are for Canon cameras. Please check your owner's manual for your equivalent settings.

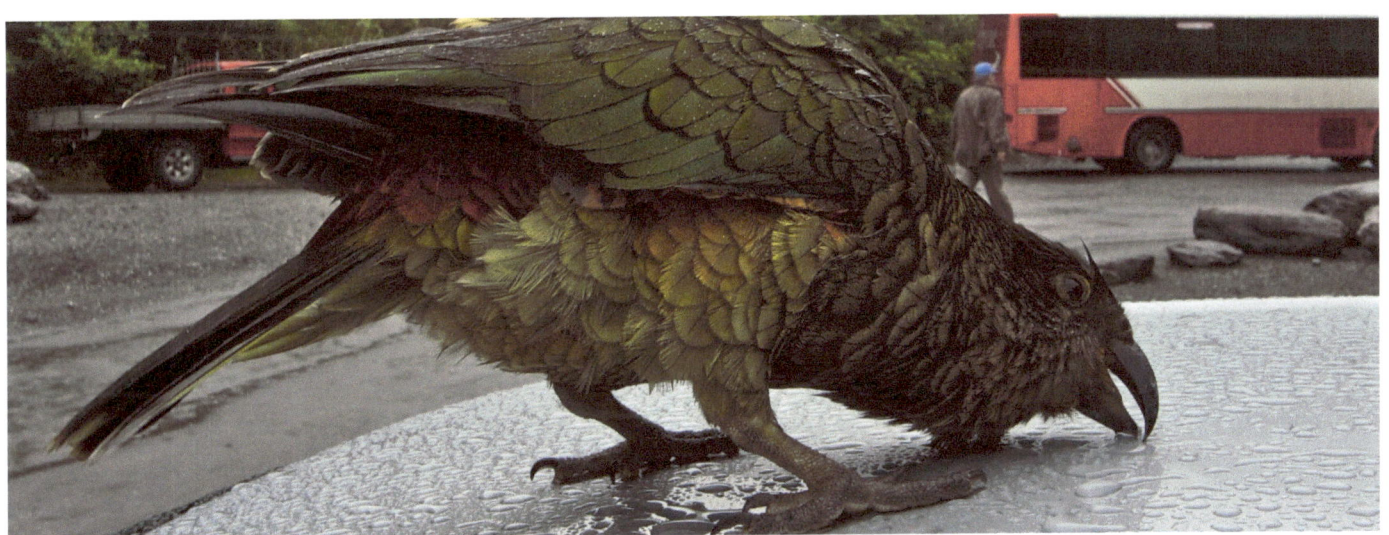

Appendix Four
Meditation in the Bush

When I started taking bird photographs, I didn't know that I would need to learn to meditate, but as most dedicated birders, hunters, and gatherers know, the seeking of any quarry, whether animal, vegetable, or mineral, requires acuity of the senses, and a focused concentration to have the best chance of success. Meditation can be a means to acquire that acuity and focus.

Some people meditate through silent contemplation. Others through esoteric practices, or searching the meaning of koans, or by prayer. For me, there is another form of meditation, what one could call ambling meditation. For those who may wish to practice ambling meditation, here are a few easy ground rules to get you started. First, only wander in areas you know well or where you won't become lost. Second, give yourself plenty of time. Third, being alone may help. Fourth, a mild sunny day can set the mood.

Here's what I do. In an open field, or easily navigable bush, or on a shore, with camera or binoculars ready, or perhaps without accoutrement, I let my eyes, ears and nose be my guides. I follow sounds and fleeting movement in the bush. Smell fragrances on the wind. I do not rush. I stand still for a time, if it pleases me. I wander. I stare. I note everything around me.

I might walk for a time, in no hurry, thinking of nothing in particular, I simply let thoughts pass through my mind, observing the vegetation, the rocks, the sky, the birds, insects buzzing, everything. Continuing my journey, I look to see what is around the next bend. I look under logs. I follow a bird's song in the air. I keep allowing my senses to open up, letting everything in, all that my eyes, ears and nose sense, and filter as little as possible.

In time, there is a shift, where all my senses are not separate inputs but a single experience. All my senses taking in multiple impressions of my surroundings, but feeling them all–at–the–same–time.

When this happens, I may not notice anything new, or I may find myself standing rapt, caught in a moment. I observe this, and then let it pass. I may notice getting tired or feeling energised, notice birds behaving in ways I'd never observed before. Notice feathers on the ground and moss on trees. Notice that I do not feel separate, or that I do. Perhaps, I may even notice the birds and I have much in common, more than that which separates us.

When each of these moments fades, and I am back with my chattering thoughts, I may think it was a waste of time, or perhaps I may think that something has changed within me. I let all these thoughts pass, and my judgements as well. In this meditation, I am seeking not to interpret, but to accept, to be a witness to all that occurs. For ten years, I have maintained this practice when shooting birds, and as I persevered, I began a journey, a journey that changed the way I perceive nature. I no longer walk just to "get there." I occasionally see things that, heretofore, were hidden from me. In the bush, when I let go of my judgements, and opinions, and likes, and dislikes, that which is real remains. For me, that is being "awake."

Over time, ambling meditation has changed more within me than how I see nature. It has allowed me to discover more about my place in nature.

Over time, I have been able to identify many a bird in flight simply by the way they beat their wings, or by their silhouettes. I have learned many new bird songs and how to call birds from hiding. I have begun to see new details of their lives and their hidden behaviours and motivations.

Ambling meditation has inspired me to more than this though. I see myself in a new way, see my relationships in a new way, and see the world with new eyes and with new comprehension.

As I journey through my eighth decade, I find myself more in love with this precious life, and more curious about what's around the next bend in the road. This book, dear reader, is my way to share some of what I've seen and learned.

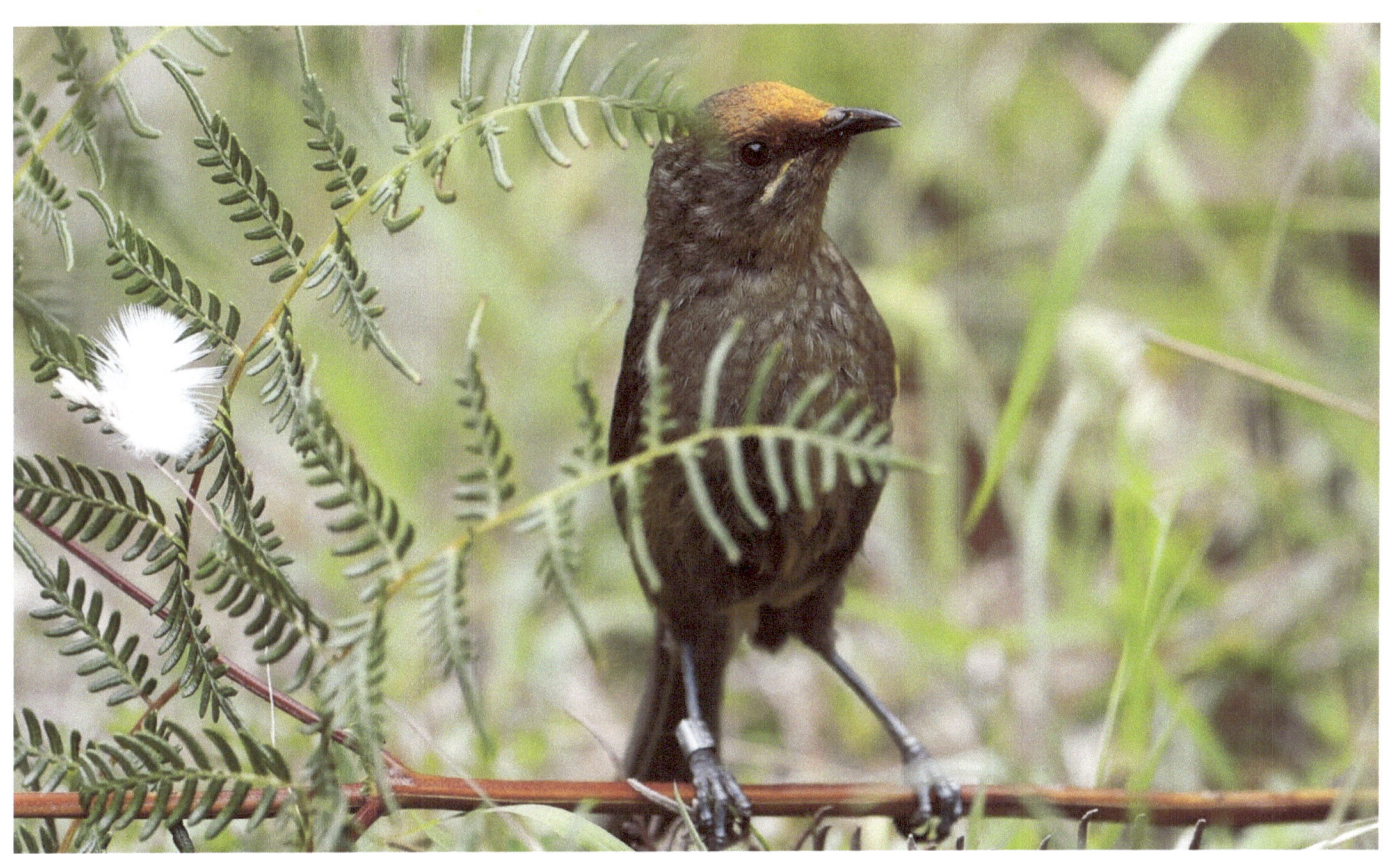

Appendix Five
Quotation Reference

Note: All quotes in the body of this book are excerpted from the Proceedings of the Royal Society of New Zealand 1868–1961
rsnz.natlib.govt.nz

Reference	Page
RSNZ Volume 28, 1895 Art. XXXIV p.372 Bird-life on a Run By H. Guthrie-Smith	12
RSNZ Volume 31, 1898 Art. I p.11 On the Ornithology of New Zealand By Sir Walter L. Buller, K.C.M.G., D.Sc., F.R.S.	13
RSNZ Volume 47, 1914 Art. LVI. p.598–9 New Zealand Bird-song: Further Notes By Johannes C. Andersen	16
RSNZ Volume 40, 1907 Art. XLIV. p.501 The Little Barrier Bird-sanctuary By James Drummond, F.L.S., F.Z.S.	19
RSNZ Volume 2, 1879 Art. III. p.34 By Major Charles Heaphy, V.C.	20
RSNZ Volume 2, 1869 Art. VIII. p.56 On the Birds of New Zealand By T. H. Potts	21
RSNZ Volume 40, 1907 Art. XLIV p.502 The Little Barrier Bird-sanctuary By James Drummond, F.L.S., F.Z.S.	24
RSNZ Volume 4, 1871 Art. XXXIV p.212 Notes on the Habits of Some of the Birds of New Zealand By W. T. L. Travers, F.L.S.	31
RSNZ Volume 10, 1877 Art. XX p. 204 Further Notes on the Ornithology of New Zealand By Walter L. Buller, C.M.G., Sc.D., F.L.S.	37
RSNZ Volume 4, 1871 Art. XXXIV p.212 Notes on the Habits of Some of the Birds of New Zealand By W. T. L. Travers, F.L.S.	41
RSNZ Volume 43, 1910 Art. LVI p.668–9 New Zealand Bird-song By Johannes C. Andersen	54
RSNZ Volume 28, 1895 Art. XXXIV p.373 Bird-life on a Run By H. Guthrie-Smith	55
RSNZ Volume 2, 1869 Art. VIII p.61–2 On the Birds of New Zealand By T. H. Potts	58
RSNZ Volume 33, 1900 Art. XXVII p.254 Our Migratory Birds By Captain F. W. Hutton, F.R.S.	59
RSNZ Volume 4, 1871 Art. XXXIV p.209–11 Notes on the Habits of Some of the Birds of New Zealand By W. T. L. Travers, F.L.S.	61
RSNZ Volume 27, 1894 Art. XXX p. 274–5 The Kea (Nestor notabilis), a Sheep-eating Parrot By Taylor White	70
RSNZ Volume 10, 1877 Art. XX p.202 Further Notes on the Ornithology of New Zealand By Walter L. Buller, C.M.G., Sc.D., F.L.S.	75

RSNZ Volume 28, 1895 Art. XXXI p.344-5 Notes on New Zealand Ornithology, with an Exhibition of Specimens By Sir Walter L. Buller, K.C.M.G., D.Sc., F.R.S.	75
RSNZ Volume 52, 1920 Art. XIII. p. 64 Nature-lore of the Southern Maori By H. Beattie; Communicated by H. D. Skinner	78
RSNZ Volume 18, 1885 Art. XVIII p.97 Observations on the Habits of New Zealand Birds, their Usefulness or Destructiveness to the Country By A. Reischek, F.L.S.	86
RSNZ Volume 88, 1960-61 p.235, 244 The Takahe Notornis mantelli Owen, 1848: 81 A General Survey By G R Williams	91
RSNZ Volume 31, 1898 Art. I. p.2-5 On the Ornithology of New Zealand By Sir Walter L. Buller, K.C.M.G., D.Sc., F.R.S.	92
RSNZ Volume 23, 1890 Art. XV p.112-13 Takahe versus Kakapo By James Park, F.G.S. Lecturer, Thames School of Mines	97
RSNZ Volume 2, 1869 Art. VIII. p.71 On the Birds of New Zealand By T. H. Potts	101
RSNZ Volume 30, 1897 Art. XXX. p.279, 281-3 Notes on Bird-life in the West Coast Sounds By Richard Henry	104
RSNZ Volume 4, 1871 Art. XXXIV. p.211-12 Notes on the Habits of Some of the Birds of New Zealand. By W. T. L. Travers, F.L.S	107
RSNZ Volume 6, 1873 (NZ Falcon) Art. XXX.—On the Birds of New Zealand. By T. H. Potts, F.L.S.	11
RSNZ Volume 28, 1895 Art. XXXI. p.339 Notes on New Zealand Ornithology, with an Exhibition of Specimens By Sir Walter L. Buller, K.C.M.G., D.Sc., F.R.S.	123
RSNZ Volume 29, 1896 Art. XVIII. p. 256 Notes on certain Species of New Zealand Duck By W. W. Smith, F.E.S.	132
RSNZ Volume 43, 1910 Art. LVI. p.657 New Zealand Bird-song. By Johannes C. Andersen	136
RSNZ Volume 28, 1895 Art. XXXIV. p.374 Bird-life on a Run By H. Guthrie-Smith	155
RSNZ Volume 10, 1877 Art. XX.. p.206 Further Notes on the Ornithology of New Zealand By Walter L. Buller, C.M.G., Sc.D., F.L.S	147
RSNZ Volume 9, 1876 Art. XXXIII p.338 On the Occurrence of the Royal Spoonbill (Platalea regia) in New Zealand By Walter L. Buller, C.M.G., Sc.D., President	163

RSNZ Art. VIII.—On the Birds of New Zealand., 1869 Volume 2, 1869 p.68-69x No. B. 65.—Anarhynchus Frontalis, Quoy. and Gaim. Scissor-bill, Crook-billed Plover	180
RSNZ Volume 2, 1869 Art. VIII p.52 On the Birds of New Zealand By T. H. Potts	188
RSNZ Volume 2, 1869 Art. VIII p.69 On the Birds of New Zealand By T. H. Potts	191
RSNZ Volume 10, 1877 Art. XX. p.207 Further Notes on the Ornithology of New Zealand By Walter L. Buller, C.M.G., Sc.D., F.L.S.	194
RSNZ Volume 10, 1877 Art. XX. p.208 Further Notes on the Ornithology of New Zealand By Walter L. Buller, C.M.G., Sc.D., F.L.S.	202
RSNZ Volume 76, 1946–47 p.443–4 The Gannet on Cape Kidnappers By K. A. Wodzicki (Department Scientific and Industrial Research) and C. P. McMeekan (Ruakura Animal Research Station)	213
RSNZ Volume 26, 1893 Art. XIV p.182–6 On the Birds observed during a Voyage from New Zealand to England By Sir Walter L. Buller, K.C.M.G., D.Sc., F.R.S	223
RSNZ Volume 21, 1888 Art. X p.126 The Habits and Home of the Wandering Albatross (Diomedea exulans) By A. Reischek, F.L.S.	225
RSNZ Volume 23, 1890 Art. XXVIII p.234 On, the Wandering Albatros; with an Exhibition of Specimens, and the Determination of a New–Species (Diomedea regia) By Sir Walter L. Buller, K.C.M.G., F.R.S.	226
RSNZ Volume 40, 1907 Art. XLIII p.495 The Disappearance of the New Zealand Birds By Dr. Fulton	251
RSNZ Volume 46, 1913 Art. L p.333, 340 The Moa — Legendary, Historical, and Geological: Why and when the Moa disappeared. By H. Hill, B.A., F.G.S	251

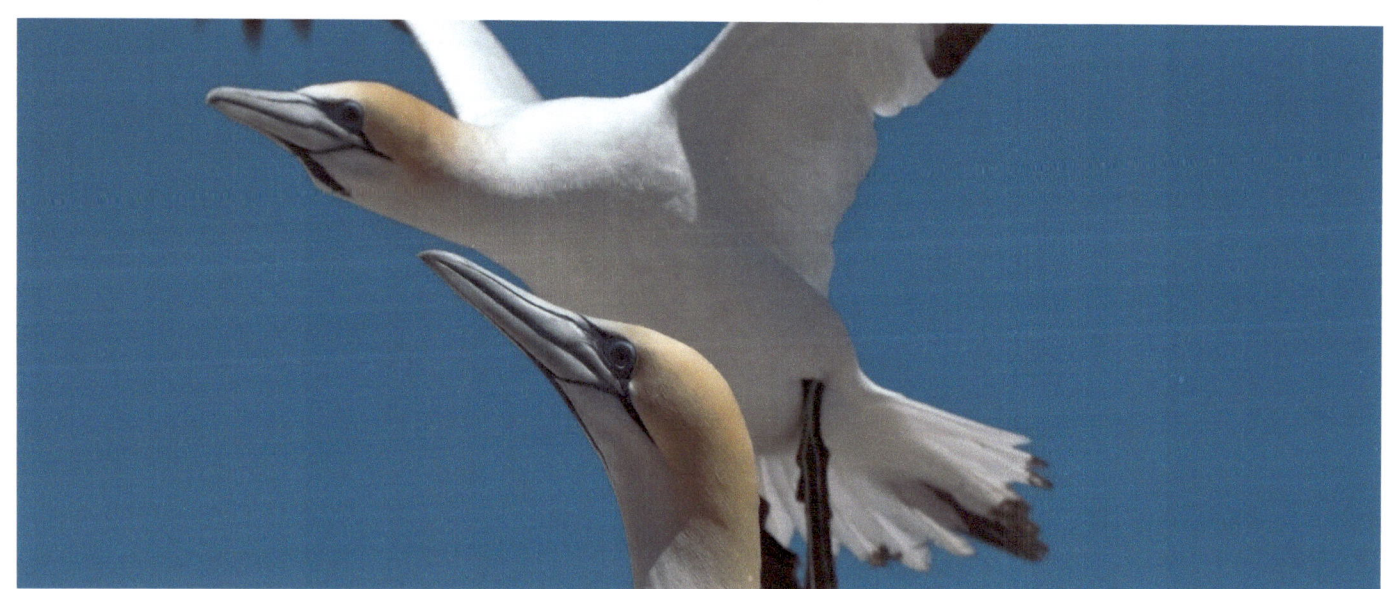

Appendix Six
Further Reading

The decline and uncertain recovery of New Zealand's native birds

For those interested in the views of selected Royal Society members on species survival and extinction, I have included some additional information from the Royal Society's archives from the years 1885 through to 1955.

RSNZ Volume 18, 1885 page 112-117
Art. XXII.—The Protection of Native Birds.
By Hugh Martin

RSNZ Volume 23, 1890 page 201-207
Art. XXIV.—On Rabbits, Weasels, and Sparrows.
By Taylor White

RSNZ Volume 28, 1895 pages 1-27
Art. I.—The Displacement of Species in New Zealand.
By T. Kirk, F.L.S.

RSNZ Volume 40, 1907 page 485-500
Art. XLIII.—The Disappearance of the New Zealand Birds.
By Dr. Fulton

RSNZ Volume 46, 1913 page 330-351
Art. L–The Moa–Legendary, Historical, and Geological: Why and when the Moa disappeared.
By H. Hill, B.A., F.G.S.

RSNZ Volume 81, 1953 page xliv-li
The Royal Society and Conservation
By W. R. B. Oliver, D.Sc. (N.Z.), F.R.S.N.Z.

RSNZ Volume 82, 1954-55 page 827-835
Presidential Address
Changes in the Flora and Fauna of New Zealand
By W R. B. Oliver

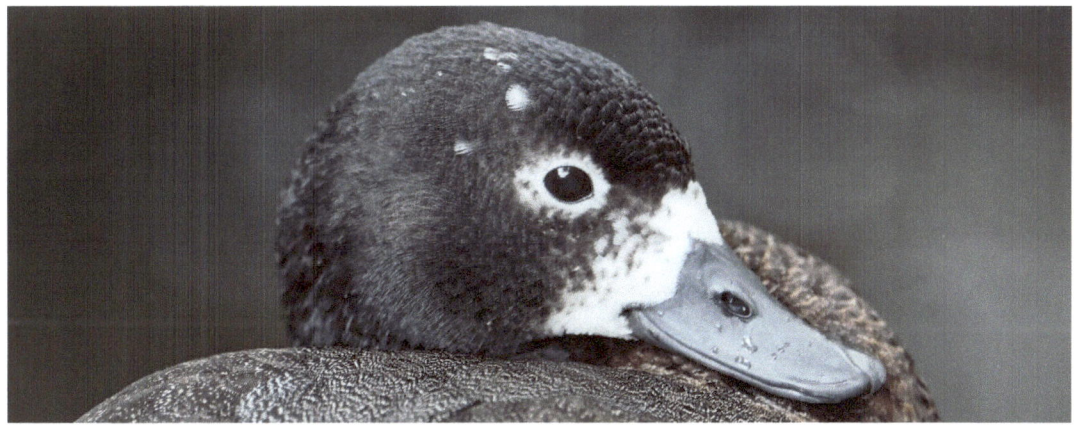

Index

Albatross 220, 224
Anarhynchus frontalis 179
Anas aucklandica 130
Anas gracilis 128
Anas rhynchotis variegata 133
Anas superciliosa superciliosa 145
Anthornis melanura melanura 18
Anthus novaeseelandiae 120
Ardea novaehollandiae 159
Art of Ambling 258
Audubon 254
Australasian Gannet 212
Australasian Harrier 110
Australian Coot 145
Aythya novaeseelandiae 131
Banded Rail 108
Bar-Tailed Godwit 181
Bellbird 18
Binoculars 256
Birds in the Bush 256
Black-backed Gull 192
Black Shag 199
Blinds 258
Brown Teal 130
Bush Parrot 60
Callaeas cinerea wilsoni 29
Camera Settings 260
Cape Pigeon 248
Caspian Tern 203
Chestnut Breasted Shelduck 138
Circus approximans 110
Coot 145
Cyanoramphus novazelandiae 73
Daption capense capense 248
Diomedea cauta steadi 232
Diomedea epomophora 220
Diomedea exulans 224
Duck 141
Egretta alba modesta 148

Eudyptula minor 250
Falco novaeseelandiae 111
Fantail 53
Flesh-Footed Shearwater 242
Fulica atra 145
Gallirallus australis greyi 103
Gannet 212
Gerygone igata 51
Godwit, Bar-Tailed 181
Grey Duck 141
Grey Teal 128
Grey Warbler 51
Gull 192, 196
Haematopus unicolor 189
Halcyon sancta 186
Harpagornis 251
Harrier 110
Hemiphaga novaeseelandiae 77
Heron 148, 159
Hides 258
Hides (Blinds) 258
Hihi 23
Himantopus himantopus leucocephalus 169
Hirundo tahitica neoxena 124
Hokioi 251
John James Audubon 254
Kahu 110
Kakariki 73
Karearea 111
Karoro 192
Karuhiruhi 201
Kawau 199
Kawaupaka 200
Kea 69
Kereru 77
Kingfisher 186
Kokako 29
Korimako 18
Korora 250

Kotare 186
Kotuku 148
Kotuku-ngutupapa 162
Kuaka 181
Kuruwhengi 133
Larus dominicanus dominicanus 192
Larus novaehollandiae 196
Life Lists 258
Limosa lapponica 181
Little Shag 200
Macronectes giganteus 243
Meditation in the Bush 262
Miromiro 46
Moa 251
Moho-pereru 108
Mohoua albicilla 48
Mollymawk 232, 237
Morepork 84
Morus serrator 212
Mountain Parrot 69
Nesting Birds 259
Nestor meridionalis septentrionalis 60
Nestor notabilis 69
New Zealand Falcon 111
New Zealand Pigeon 77
New Zealand Pipit 120
New Zealand Scaup 131
New Zealand Shoveler 133
New Zealand White Capped Mollymawk 232
Ninox novaeseelandiae 84
Northern Giant Petrel 243
North Island Fantail 53
North Island Kokako 29
North Island Robin 40
Notiomystis cinta 23
Notornis 90
On Binoculars 256
On Seeing with New Eyes 256
Oystercatcher 189

Pangurunguru 243
Papango 131
Paradise Shelduck 135
Parera 145
Parrot 60, 69
Parson Bird 10
Pateke 130
Penguin 250
Petrel 243
Petroica australis longipes 40
Petroica macrocephala toitoi 46
Phalacrocorax carbo novaehollandiae 199
Phalacrocorax melanoleucos brevirostris 200
Phalacrocorax varius varius 201
Philesturnus carunculatus refusater 36
Pied Shag 201
Pied Stilt 169
Pihoihoi 120
Piwakawaka 53
Platalea regia 162
Plover 166, 174
Poaka 169
Popokotea 48
Porphyrio mantelli hochstetteri 90
Porphyrio porphyrio melanotus 100
Prosthemadera novaeseelandiae 10
Puffinus carneipes 242
Pukeko 100
Purple Swamphen 100
Putangitangi 135
Quotation Reference 264
Raillus philippensis 108
Red-billed Gull 196
Red-fronted Parakeet 73
Rhipidura fuliginosa placabilis 53
Riroriro 51
Royal Albatross 220
Royal Spoonbill 162
Ruru 84

Saddleback 36
Salvin's Mollymawk 237
Scaup 131
Shag 199, 200, 201
Shearwater, Flesh-footed 242
Shelduck 135, 138
Shore Plover 174, 181
Short or tall - Approaching birds 258
Shoveler 133
Silvereye 57
Spoonbill 162
Spur-Winged Plover 166
Standing or Sitting Still 258
Sterna Caspia 203
Sterna striata 206
Stitchbird 23
Swallow 124
Tadorna tadornoides 138
Tadorna variegata 135
Takahe 90
Takapu 212
Taking What is Given 258
Tara 206
Tarapunga 196
Tauhou 57
Teal 128
Tern 203, 206

Tete 128
Thinornis noveeseelandiae 174
Tieke 36
Titore 248
Tomtit 46
Torea 189
Toroa 220, 224
Toutouwai 40
Tui 10
Tuturuatu 174
Vanellus miles 166
Variable Oystercatcher 189
Vincent Van Gogh 254
Wandering Albatross 224
Warbler, Grey 51
Warou 124
Waxeye 57
Weka 103
Welcome Swallow 124
White eye 57
White-flippered Penguin 250
White-fronted Tern 206
Whitehead 48
White Heron 148
Woodhen 103
Wrybill 179
Zosterops lateralis lateralis 57

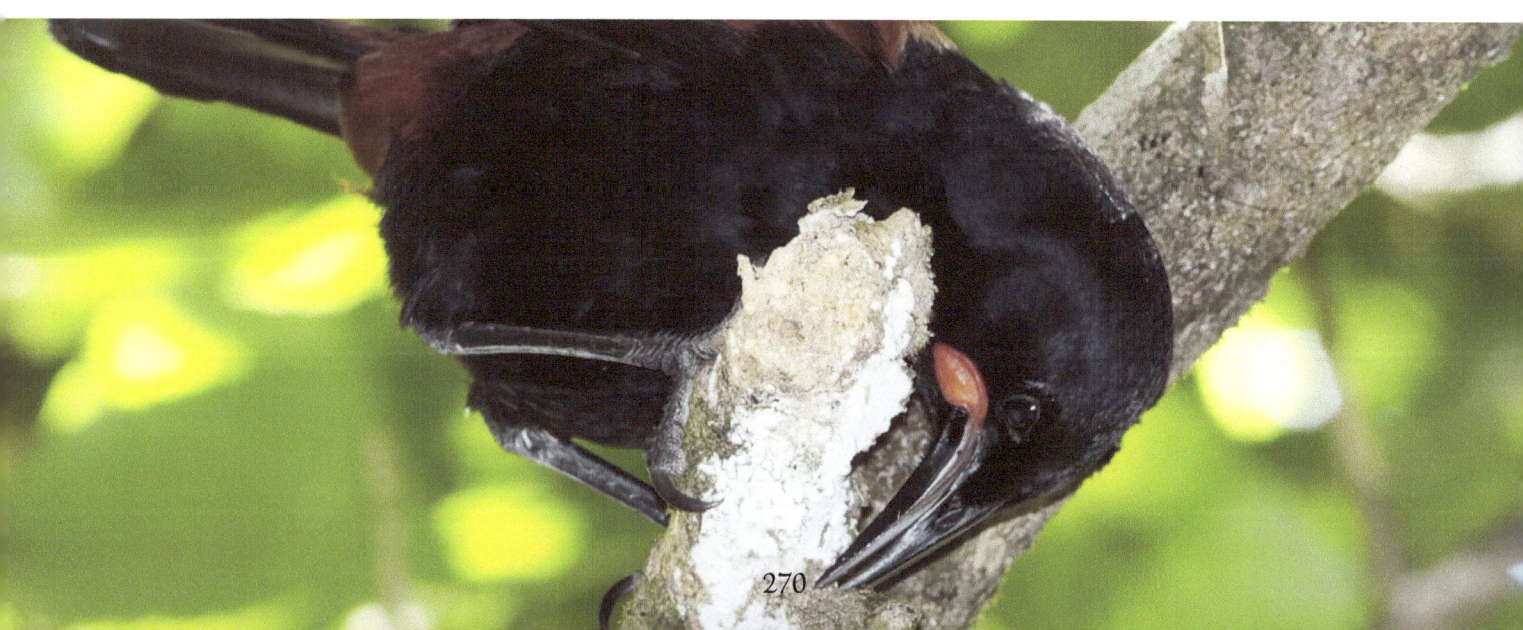